MARICOPA COUNTY CO'
CHANDLER/GILBE[RT]
COLLE[GE]
LEARNING RESO[URCE]
2626 EAST PE[COS]
CHANDLER, AZ 85225

F 392 .L62 M67 1997

Morris, John Miller.

El Llano Estacado

DATE DUE

GAYLORD — PRINTED IN U.S.A

El Llano Estacado

El Llano

Estacado

Exploration and Imagination on the High Plains of Texas and New Mexico, 1536–1860

John Miller Morris

Texas State Historical Association
Austin

DEDICATED TO

Patsy Marie Blair Heflin,
A brave daughter of the High Plains, notable teacher, and good traveler.

Copyright ©1997 Texas State Historical Association
All rights reserved. Printed in the United States of America

Library of Congress Cataloging-in-Publication Data

Morris, John Miller.
    El Llano Estacado : exploration and imagination on the High Plains of Texas and New Mexico, 1536–1860 / by John Miller Morris.

      p.   cm.
    Includes bibliographical references and index.
    ISBN 9-87611-154-1
    1. Llano Estacado—History. 2. Llano Estacado—Geography. 3. Llano Estacado—Discovery and exploration I. Title

F392.L62.M67 1997
976.4'8dc21
                                        96-40185
                                            CIP

Contents

Illustrations and Maps   vii
Preface   ix
Introduction   1

Part One
Lo Llano: Coronado and the Llano Road to Quivira, 1536–1542   9

1. The Cow Nation   11
2. Lo Llano: The Plain beyond Cíbola   23
3. Lost and Found: The Scholar's Quest   31
4. The Llano Road to Quivira   45
5. In Search of Cona   59
6. Deep in the Heart of Teyas   75
7. *Hasta Las Aguas*   95
8. Castañeda's *Genius Loci*   117

Part Two
The Llano Frontier: Geography and Geosophy of Spanish Contact, 1542–1860   133

9. The Plains of Saint Francis   135
10. Land and Logos   149
11. Cibolero Caravans of the Llano Estacado   155
12. Trailblazers Across *Comanchería*   167
13. *La Ceja Y El Llano*: The Hispano Frontier   183

Part Three
The Illimitable Prairie: Anglo-American Imagineers and the Romantic
Discovery of the Llano Estacado, 1803–1844   195

14 *Terra Incognita*   197
15 The Stake Prairie   205
16 Le Grand's Elevated Prairies   213
17 Gregg's Table Land   223
18 The Grand Prairie   229

Part Four
The Great Zahara: National Exploration and Environmental Discovery,
1845–1860   243

19 Prairie Sublime   245
20 Desert Prairie   253
21 Red River Expedition   265
22 Whipple's Ocean Prairie   279
23 Want of Water: A. B. Gray on the Southern Staked Plain   299
24 Pope's Wells   311
25 Language of the Llano: A Conclusion on the Journey of Discovery   325

Bibliography   343
Notes   361
Index   397

Illustrations and Maps

Page	
8	The Llano Estacado. Map
34	Gómara's Buffalo, by unknown artist, ca. 1554. Woodcut
41	Coronado's Eastern Explorations: Conflicting 1541 Route Proposals. Map
52	Coronado's Reunion with Captain Maldonado on the Pequeño Río. Map
63	Pages from the 1596 copy of Pedro de Castañeda's Manuscript
77	Blanco Canyon: Geography and Archeology. Map
101	Arellano's Return Route, following the interior lakes. Map
140	*Mapa del Nuevo México . . .*, by E. Martínez, 1602
152	*Plano Corographico de el Reyno y Provincia de el Nuevo Mexico*, by F. Barreiro, 1727. Map
176	Vial's Second Journey as shown by *Mapa del territorio . . . de Nuevo Mexico . . .*, by unknown artist, 1788. Detail
180	Conjectural Routes of Mares, Vial, and Amangual. Map
185	Comanchero Trails and Toponyms. Map
198	Alyce Hart's English Inscription Stone. Rubbing
201	*Map of the Internal Provinces of New Spain*, by Z. Pike, 1810. Detail
216	Le Grand's Geosophy as shown by *Map of the Republic of Texas and the Adjacent Territories. . . ,* by J. Arrowsmith, 1841. Detail
219	*Map of Texas Shewing the Grants in Possession of the Colorado & Red River Land Company*, by unknown artist, ca. 1835
221	*Map of Texas, 1843,* by J. Arrowsmith. Detail
225	*A Map of the Indian Territory, Northern Texas, and New Mexico . . .*, by J. Gregg, 1844. Detail
240	*Texas and Part of Mexico & the United States showing the route of the First Santa Fé Expedition*, by W. Kemble, 1844. Map
268	*Gypsum Bluffs on North Branch Red River*, by H. Lawrence after unknown artist, 1853. Tinted lithograph
269	*The Mirage*, by unknown artist, ca. 1866. Woodcut
271	*Border of El-Llano Estacado*, by H. Lawrence after unknown artist, 1853. Lithograph

Page

272 *Prairie Dog Town*, by unknown artist, 1866. Woodcut
273 *View Near Head of Red River*, by H. Lawrence after unknown artist, 1853. Lithograph
275 *View Near the Ke-Che-Ah-Que-Ho-No*, by H. Lawrence after unknown artist, 1853. Tinted lithograph
276 *Head of Ke-Che-Ah-Qui-Ho-No*, by unknown artist, 1866. Lithograph
281 *Canadian River Near Camp 38*, by T. Sinclair after H. Möllhausen, 1856. Chromolithograph
283 *Columns of Sandstone, South Bank of the Canadian River*, by H. Möllhausen, 1856. Woodcut
285 *Sandstein-Gebilde in der Prairie nordwestl. von Texas*, by Hanhart after H. Möllhausen, 1858. Chromolithograph
287 *Comanche Camp on Shady Creek*, by T. Sinclair after H. Möllhausen, 1856. Chromolithograph
289 *Bluffs of the Llano Sunrise . . .* , by N. Orr after A. W. Whipple, 1856. Woodcut
292 Rocky Dell Pictographs, by unknown artist after A. W. Whipple, 1856. Woodcut
294 *Remnant of a Stratum of Sandstone near Laguna Colorado*, by N. Orr after A. W. Whipple, 1856. Woodcut
295 *A Conical Hill, 500 Feet High*, by H. Möllhausen after J. Marcou, 1856. Chromolithograph
302 *Castle Mountain Pass, Texas*, by unknown artist, 1857. Woodcut
307 *American Antelope, of the Llano Estacado*, by Middleton, Wallace & Co. after C. Schuchard, 1856. Chromolithograph
308 *Pecos River, Texas*, by Middleton, Wallace & Co. after C. Schuchard, 1856. Chromolithograph
310 [*Pope's Wells*], by H. S. Sindall, c. 1857. Oil painting

Preface

The land of the boundless plain,
Where the prairie dog kneels
As he sits on his heels
And fervently prays for rain.

John A. Robinson

It is pleasant to recall the patience and intelligence that many scholars provided me during the course of this study. Dr. Robin Doughty was a model of practical support, mentoring, philosophy, and personal optimism. I am deeply honored to have been one of his students. Dr. Karl Butzer provided generous help and a steady stream of insights on controversial topics. Dr. William H. Goetzmann and his seminars influenced this work profoundly. I can never repay my debt. Dr. Robert Mugerauer's humanistic teaching and thinking were important sources of inspiration. And to Dr. Terry Kahn, Dr. David Alvirez, Dr. Richard Jones, Dr. Marian Martinello, and Dr. William Doolittle I owe special thanks for their support and assistance.

I am also very grateful to professors Frank Heflin, Fred Rathjen, and Pete Petersen, all scholar-knights from the most urbane and sociable center of intelligent life in the Panhandle—the West Texas A&M history department. Frank Heflin was a key source of accurate and reasoned observations on the Llano, often forcing me to rethink some fast assumption. I should also like to thank JoAnn Byrd and Stanley Marsh 3 for their early encouragement of my regional writing in Amarillo, Texas. Other scholars kindly read and critiqued versions of the manuscript. Dr. Dan Flores provided a significant critique of an earlier version of this work. Dr. Flores's comments and writings considerably enriched my understanding of the Llano and aided my refashioning of the manuscript. A fortunate encounter with Dr. Carroll L. Riley and Brent Riley in Blanco Canyon led to their insightful reading of Part One. Dr. Riley's books and comments grounded my thinking on the archeological context of Coronado. Dr. Don

Blakeslee of Wichita State University likewise was helpful on this important context. Richard Flint and Shirley Flint of Far Cry Plantation in Villanueva, New Mexico, spared me from various errors and provided insight on the conquistador bridge across the Pecos River. Dr. Barbara Simerka of the University of Texas at San Antonio allowed me to test translations on her.

I should also thank Dr. Terry Jordan for early assistance and ongoing commentary. My semester of independent studies with Dr. Jordan was a formative experience. Dr. Paul Schmidt (to whom I owe so much) has been a timeless source of literary inspiration. I will never forget your friendship. A number of people deserve more than mere printed thanks for putting up with me during the writing of this work: David Pittard, Kelly Ignatoff, Anne Kelly, David Rice and Isabelle Rice, Anne Walther, Mary Lenz, Randall Durrett, Belinda Durrett, and Sean Durrett, Bill Norton and Jean Norton, and most of all my talented daughter, Erin Claire Morris. Lastly, this project could not have been completed without the patience and understanding of Patricia McGee. At the University of Texas at San Antonio, Kevin Bryan, Peggy Bynum, and Pat Smith offered office support. Alas, the remaining mistakes and errors are mine, all mine alone.

George Ward, Bill Bishel, and Janice Pinney were wonderful editors and I am proud to have had their distinguished assistance. Dr. Ron Tyler kept my morale from flagging and made the project seem not only possible but also inevitable. Bibliographic assistance was provided by Dorothy Sloan, the late John Jenkins, and Suizanne Chaney. I also benefited from the wonderful assistance of Claire Kuehn, former Librarian, and Lisa Lambert, Archivist of the Panhandle-Plains Historical Museum Research Center. This center has nourished my curiosity for over two decades. In addition, the helpful staffs at the Center for American History in Austin, the Texas State Library, and the Southwest Collection at Texas Tech University in Lubbock provided over the past four years a series of rare documents, maps, illustrations, and books for my Llano studies.

Finally, I wish to thank the many friends and family who live on the Llano. You have all helped me to know and to love the land of our ancestors.

POMPÉE HOUSE
BELL MOUNTAIN
AUSTIN, TEXAS

Introduction

The great plains now, the bare land, the open ranges
The wind's world, sun's empire, plains of the sun
Llano Estacado. And here I think is the heart of it . . .

TOWNSHEND MILLER, *A Letter from Texas*

Suddenly he stopped and remembered that there were certain spots of earth on the wide llano where he had once stood and felt the elation of flying. Yes, the power of the earth surged through him until he felt himself soaring over the landscape.

RUDOLFO ANAYA, *Heart of Aztlan*

To the eccentric who loves old landscapes for their own sakes, now and then the keenest pleasure emerges from one of their least prepossessing manifestations. Such is the Llano Estacado or Southern High Plains of New Mexico and Texas. This greatest of mesas encompasses 50,000 square miles of the American Southwest, from the Canadian River in the north to the Edwards Plateau in the south, from the Pecos River in the west to the fantastic canyonland tributaries of the Red, Pease, Brazos, and Colorado Rivers in the east. The beauty, mystery, and compelling magic of this legendary land still touch the heart and mind. From the dawn of historic contact, a remarkable series of Spanish, French, Mexican, and American explorers have attempted to make sense of its curious environment.

The centuries and cavalcades are gone, but their exploration texts linger on, old landscapes now appearing as textual mirages to the postmoderns of the late twentieth century. Renowned for its flatness and the disorientation it can cause, the historical geography of the Llano Estacado from 1536 to 1860 is the story of human learning: of discovery, exploration, and imagination in one of North America's stranger bioregions. Behind the stirring narratives and brave images of exploration, however, there is another realm, a mysterious and sometimes deceptive story of language and landscape. If it was once easy to get lost on the Llano, it is now easy to get lost in the interpretation of its exploration texts.

Dubbed the "largest level plain of its kind in the United States" and "one of the most perfect plains regions in the world,"[1] in the popular mind this southern extension of the Great Plains is relentlessly boring and monotonous, an ugly giant. Some of its tediousness is due to its sprawling size. The Llano country is huge even by Texas standards—a vast territory that straddles Texas and New Mexico over four degrees of both latitude and longitude. It is perhaps the largest isolated, non-mountainous area in North America, with a single mesa at the center exceeding the combined size of seven of the original thirteen states of the United States.[2] The tableland surface alone is some 30,000 square miles of pure, featureless plain. The semiarid climate restricts the vertical architecture common elsewhere of trees, vines, and shrubs, leaving merely shortgrass plains.

The Llano country can be a lonesome land as well. Cowboys had its melancholic power in mind when they turned an English song on dreadful burial at sea into the western blues hit, "Bury Me Not on the Lone Prairie." On top of the Llano there is a startling horizontal dimension, a merciless flatland formed by ancient sandstorms and regular southwest breezes, by winds that blanketed and smoothed the sky-crowned land with fresh, deep layers of Pleistocene dust. Both the Llano's monotony and size irritate modern travelers on their way somewhere else. I have spoken to many motorists who deplored and decried the lack of scenery. But when you get out of the car and step among the snakes, the landscape changes remarkably. Further beneath the monotony lies a fascinating historical and geographical complexity. It is the fourfold goal of this frontier study to rediscover the historical heart of the mesa, to stake its claim more fully in modern borderland studies, to penetrate the superficial dreariness of this huge and beautiful area, and to examine the production of environmental meaning in a newly discovered region.

For the historical geographer, the Llano Estacado has a long and intriguing time line. It is possible to find here the earliest presence of both Clovis and European peoples in North America. It is a land steeped in legend and lore, with many mysteries of history and geography still not settled. Where did Francisco Vázquez de Coronado cross the plains? Where was Randolph Marcy's true source of the Red River? And where was Pierre Vial on July 4, 1788? Although very good historical research touches upon the region, there is still no comprehensive analysis of the great mesa itself, one in which the landscape itself is the hero, the main protagonist. Frederick Rathjen's 1973 work, *The Texas Panhandle Frontier*, is an outstanding treatment for the approximate area. Dr. Rathjen's approach and treatment reflect the best regional spirit of Walter Prescott Webb. The present work frames itself with different and more generous bioregional boundaries, and it focuses more narrowly on environmental cognition before 1860 in a strange landscape.[3] Its clearest connection to Webb is that I wrote the manuscript in the historian's old undergraduate boardinghouse in Austin, Texas, but then it is precisely the regional patterns of *time with place* that draw the attention of a historical geographer.[4]

In addition to the Llano's rich historical dimension, it also has an intriguing and peculiar geographical context. The legendary horizontality of its plains—averaging a drop of only ten feet to the mile—combines with a magnificent verticality of escarpment "coastline" and canyons to create a landscape of multiple contrasts. As a case study in environmental perception, the dichotomous Llano Estacado is ideal. Rather like examining speech abnormality to discern the process of language acquisition, an examination of perception in and of an "abnormal" region may offer insights into how humans construct environmental meaning.

The emphasis is thus upon the creation of a frontier, the Eurocentric invention of "the Llano" rather than upon the strict ethnography of native peoples, such as the Jumano or Comanche who dominated these plains for so long. This quest for the discursive connection between new people and a new land requires close analysis of explorer accounts from the sixteenth century to shortly after the mid-nineteenth century.[5] The science (and art) of studying old words on a perfect plain is not without pitfalls, but I have tried to follow the best trails. Complementing the semiotics of textual landscapes, a series of regular and happy field trips to the Llano grounded the basic methodology of this study. To envision the historic contacts, I traveled across the Llano for many years while reliving the manuscripts of Coronado, Pedro de Castañeda, Juan Jaramillo, Pierre Vial, Randolph Marcy, A. W. Whipple, Josiah Gregg, J. Frank Dobie, and many others. Whereas the structure of the present work is a blending of geographical descriptions and historical narrations, the focus is not on the explorers' vainglorious lives but rather on their humble perceptions of place.[6]

This study of the geographical and historical consciousness of the Llano Estacado begins with the premise that discoverers sometimes saw what they wanted to believe, rather than believing what they saw. Research in environmental perception underlines the process by which we continually personalize, mythologize, and interpret the world around us.[7] In that process, we sometimes misrepresent, mislead, and misconstrue—perhaps we should call this version the *Mistaken Plains*. We often fool ourselves, deny or exaggerate the existence of area hazards, denigrate the natural world, and ignore the environmental implications of our behavior.[8] Nevertheless, it is important to explore the texts of discovery, because these curious intertwinings of language and landscape help create the "spirit of place," the *genius loci* of our symbolic relationship to this corner of the earth.

This ambiguity in perception—between wanting to know and to control the nature of earth, and wanting to ignore its strictures, dangers, and constraints—has been played out historically and geographically for four and a half centuries on the Southern High Plains of Texas and New Mexico. Most scholars, of course, focus on the "real" or "plain truth," the veritable relations between cultural beliefs and landscape behaviors in this 50,000-square-mile grassland of plains, breaks, playas, and rivers. My intention is not only to sketch the "true" early environment of this flatland but also to explore an anti-world of its perception: ecological disinformation, or *environmental deception*, a process that accompanied the European discovery and exploration of the Southern High Plains. In this sense *El Llano Estacado* is a meditation on the role of human imagination in the discovery—or creation—of environmental meaning.

A major component of this landscape interpretation necessarily involves an examination of the spectacular, mythological, and illusive character of the region.[9] As generations of European adventurers and their descendants journeyed across its endless horizon, they often perceived an irrational landscape, a strange world full of deception. The sheer enormity of the sky and the plain left so many observers feeling insignificant and very much alone. At times, the monotonous lack of perspective left a sojourner virtually *landsick*: disoriented, paranoid, perhaps even perceiving the slight roll and pitch of the surface as a seiche, a slow side-to-side rocking of the deep earth itself. It could easily be a land of illusion and subjectivity.[10]

Indeed, as a domain of mysteries, mirages, and miracles, the Llano Estacado offers an important addition to research in geographical illusions. Early Spanish travelers noted the atmospheric looming and *espejismos* or mirages of the plains. Nineteenth-century settlers were astonished by the Llano's compelling mirages: twenty-five-foot-tall cattle grazing near a fake lake, forty-foot-tall cowboys riding along in the high sky, and sometimes the miraculous appearance of distant towns, floating ethereally above the horizon and visible down to individual windowpanes.[11] Many a morning George Hancock, the hardscrabble 1930s South Plains farmer, enjoyed "a show" as "cities, mountains, and rivers" emerged at sunrise from the landscape. "I once saw a small town with three or four tall grain elevators," he wrote, "with houses and streets as clear cut as if I were standing at the city limits."[12] Even restrained explorers were intrigued by the illusionary nature of the region. But has this illusiveness faded? "Mirages still occur on the Plains," W. C. Holden noted, "but the illusiveness of the land was greater before the sod was broken, and before houses, windmills, and trees detracted from the ocean-like expanses of sky and grass."[13] The retired farmer George Hancock simply thought that modern "pollution has eliminated those sights."

Beyond the atmospheric phenomena, of course, there are the grand historical *fata morgana* of Coronado's "Quivira," LeGrand's "Survey," Marcy's "Great Zahara," Long's "Great American Desert," Pope's "Wells," and so on. These chimera are rightfully in the domain of "geosophy." This study therefore proposes to examine these early cultural aspects of the region's environmental deception. Many of the early visionaries often "saw" the Llano environment in ways that strike us now as delusions. But their attempts to understand the Llano created a rich body of environmental lore. The nature of such beliefs is an important part of the historical geography of the Southern High Plains.[14]

The geographer John K. Wright was an early conceptualist for the regional approach to environmental perception and deception. Wright's important 1947 article, "*Terrae Incognitae:* The Place of the Imagination in Geography," provided a thoughtful background during the organization of this study. Wright posited in his article the idea of "historical geosophy": the history of geographical knowledge whether solid or silly.[15] By referencing historical and cultural conditions and the milieux that produce geographical knowledge as a product, one provides a context for the understanding of time and space.[16] J. K. Wright would certainly have appreciated the Llano Estacado for its status as a sizable *terra incognita*, for its lure as a peculiar frontier land, and for its stimulation of the geographical imagination.

For the investigation of time and space the concept of *terra incognita* is quite useful. This study of the Llano's exploration geosophy therefore covers the sixteenth to the mid-nineteenth centuries, the time when it was an unknown land first to the Spanish and then later to the Anglo-Americans. Wright's three categories of *imagining* are quite suggestive as well. Many of the Llano sojourners fall into one of his categories: "promotional imagining" (Alexander Le Grand and Coronado); "intuitive imagining" (Pierre Vial and Josiah Gregg); and "aesthetic imagining" (Randolph Marcy and George Wilkins Kendall).[17] In the exploration of the Llano Estacado we must be careful to include the imaginings of this greatest Southwest mesa as well. Indeed, imagination is often the bridge from landscape to language.

"Lo Llano," the first of four parts in this saga, examines the earliest Spanish perceptions of the flatland immensity and its escarpment borders. From an initial reconnaissance to the Llano with Cabeza de Vaca's text on the "Cow Nation," we advance into the realm itself on the Lost Coronado Trail. Coronado's travel on the plains is now a classic detective story. The layers of ambiguity and deception surrounding the famous entrada sometimes require lengthy analysis of the surviving accounts. But these narratives in turn document an important and intuitive approach to thinking about the environment. The key to unraveling the four-and-half-centuries-old Southwest mystery—*Where, oh where did the Spanish go, on the plains of Texas and New Mexico?*—is to understand what exactly they saw and how they remembered it in their writings: the simultaneous analysis of landscape and the language used to describe it. Although Coronado's route across the plains and the stay of his army at the mysterious place called "Cona" has been wildly and widely located by numerous investigators, there has never been anything but an embarrassing lack of consensus; "their itinerary seems to be anyone's guess," historian John L. Kessell confessed recently.[18] Indeed, the search for Cona alone involves a score or more of some of the best Trail Detectives, most misleading for the few to be correct. This study attempts to define a smaller and much more likely Coronado Corridor of travel, a trail based on the original semantics and descriptions found in the Spanish chronicles, and the new discovery of possible artifacts. In particular, the narrative account of Pedro de Castañeda reveals a whole new world of pre-scientific understanding for *Lo Llano*. A series of new translations, interpretations, allegories, and recent discoveries provides the basis for hopefully the most comprehensive discussion of the Coronado entrada on the Llano of Texas and New Mexico in almost half a century. The Spanish vision of the Llano proved both complex and elegant.

Three centuries of further exploration and imagination after Coronado unfold in Part Two, "The Llano Frontier." Through the writings of Franciscan missionaries, the reports of conquerors like Juan de Oñate, the accounts of French *voyageurs* Pierre Mallet and Paul Mallet, the travel diaries of trailblazers such as "Pedro" Vial, José Mares, and Francisco Amangual, and then through the songs, place-names, and folklore of the Hispano pioneers, this part continues to build fascination with the shining mesa. There is a distinctive and under-appreciated Hispano interaction with this strange region. Indeed, the Spanish economic and linguistic appropriation of the land suggests a cultural ecology that was often resilient and adaptive in a semiarid context. There are further mysteries to unravel—*Why did the comancheros and ciboleros call this realm "El Llano Estacado"?*—and further musings on ecological meaning. Borderland settlements in New Mexico provided for over two centuries a base of further exploration and exploitation of the Llano Estacado. As guides and informants, the later frontier New Mexicans also provided key insights into this novel borderland environment for wary Anglo-Americans.

An equally revisionist counterpoint to the Hispano geographic inquiry, "The Illimitable Prairie" of Part Three analyzes the invention or "discovery" of the Llano within the Anglo imagination. The vivid aesthetics of a "Prairie Sublime" literary style created an affective relationship to the land, a romantic horizon for the new strangers in a strange land. The prose of the poet Albert Pike, the grand deceits of Alexander Le Grand, the reasoning of Josiah Gregg, and the legendary collapse of the Texan–Santa Fé Expedition as chronicled by George Wilkins Kendall and Thomas Falconer all document an initial American rhetoric of "romantic discovery." The Llano is a deeply romantic horizon, an "illimitable prairie," an extreme spatial environment suitable primarily for the thrilling aesthetic experience of "the infinite."[19] From a socioliterary standpoint, a sense of "space-intoxication" dominated the perception of the new wilderness. Understanding the American romancing of the Llano

Estacado advances our knowledge of how a different culture with different visions perceives the same strange landscape. European and East Coast discourse on the area thus emerged as a "Prairie Sublime" way of seeing, a new rhetoric in the regional discovery process.

The perceptual approaches of classic U.S. explorers James W. Abert, Randolph B. Marcy, A. W. Whipple, Andrew Gray, and John Pope are examined in "The Great Zahara," the last of four parts. First, we rediscover the beauty of the Llano as a "wilderness" area before native removal and massive settlement transformed it almost beyond recognition. Second, the nineteenth-century interplay of romantic and scientific discourse provokes a discussion of environmental deception, the conjoining of the languages of art and science that characterized this period of American romantic imperialism. Third, the documents suggest an emerging, revisionist, and Western school of thought on the "true" nature of the region. In the 1850s, changing root metaphors and the objective speculation by experienced explorers begin to indicate the commercial possibilities of Anglo-American settlement and civilization in a land only recently branded "forever uninhabitable." A significant aspect of this period is the increasing visual and graphic appreciation of the environment. Scores of lithographs, maps, and engravings open the distant eye to discovery and learning.

A final chapter on the semiotics of discovery suggests that environmental meaning was significantly linguistic.[20] For early Spanish and American explorers in particular, there was a need to establish a fitting rhetoric for such a novel landscape. For both groups of European-descent newcomers, perceptions of the immense mesa involved using old forms of discourse to relay new meanings. Narrative styles were essential in the attempt to lay bare its *genius loci*, or "spirit of place." The American explorers, however, with the new industrial techniques and technology at their disposal, vastly increased the empirical content and the graphic visualization about the Llano. Their mesh of narrative styles and increasing visualization in turn created a new Llano, an emotional landscape awaiting the impending arrival of fresh conquerors and settlers.

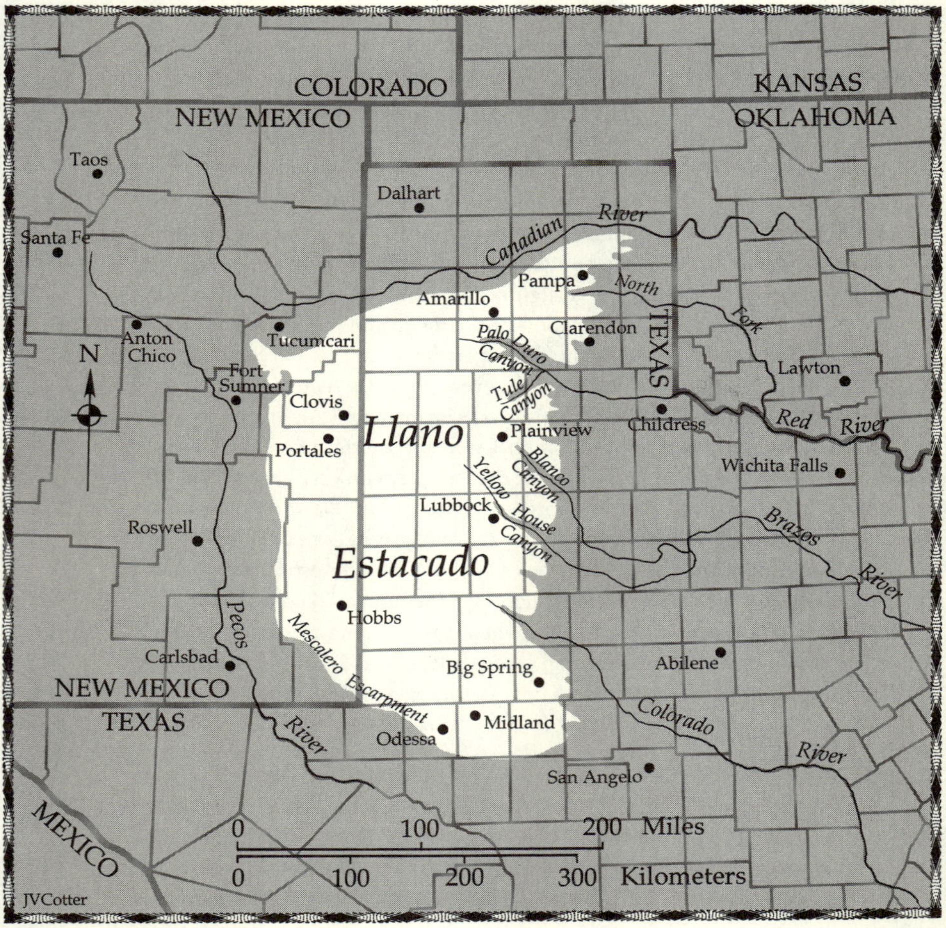
COLORADO
KANSAS
NEW MEXICO
OKLAHOMA
Taos
Dalhart
Santa Fe
Canadian River
Pampa
North Fork
Amarillo
Clarendon
TEXAS
Anton Chico
Tucumcari
N
Palo Duro Canyon
Lawton
Fort Sumner
Tule Canyon
Clovis
Llano
Plainview
Childress
Red River
Portales
Blanco Canyon
Wichita Falls
Yellow House Canyon
Lubbock
Brazos River
Roswell
Estacado
Hobbs
Pecos
Mescalero Escarpment
Carlsbad
Abilene
Big Spring
NEW MEXICO
TEXAS
Midland
Odessa
River
Colorado River
San Angelo
MEXICO
0 100 200 Miles
0 100 200 300 Kilometers
JVCotter

PART ONE

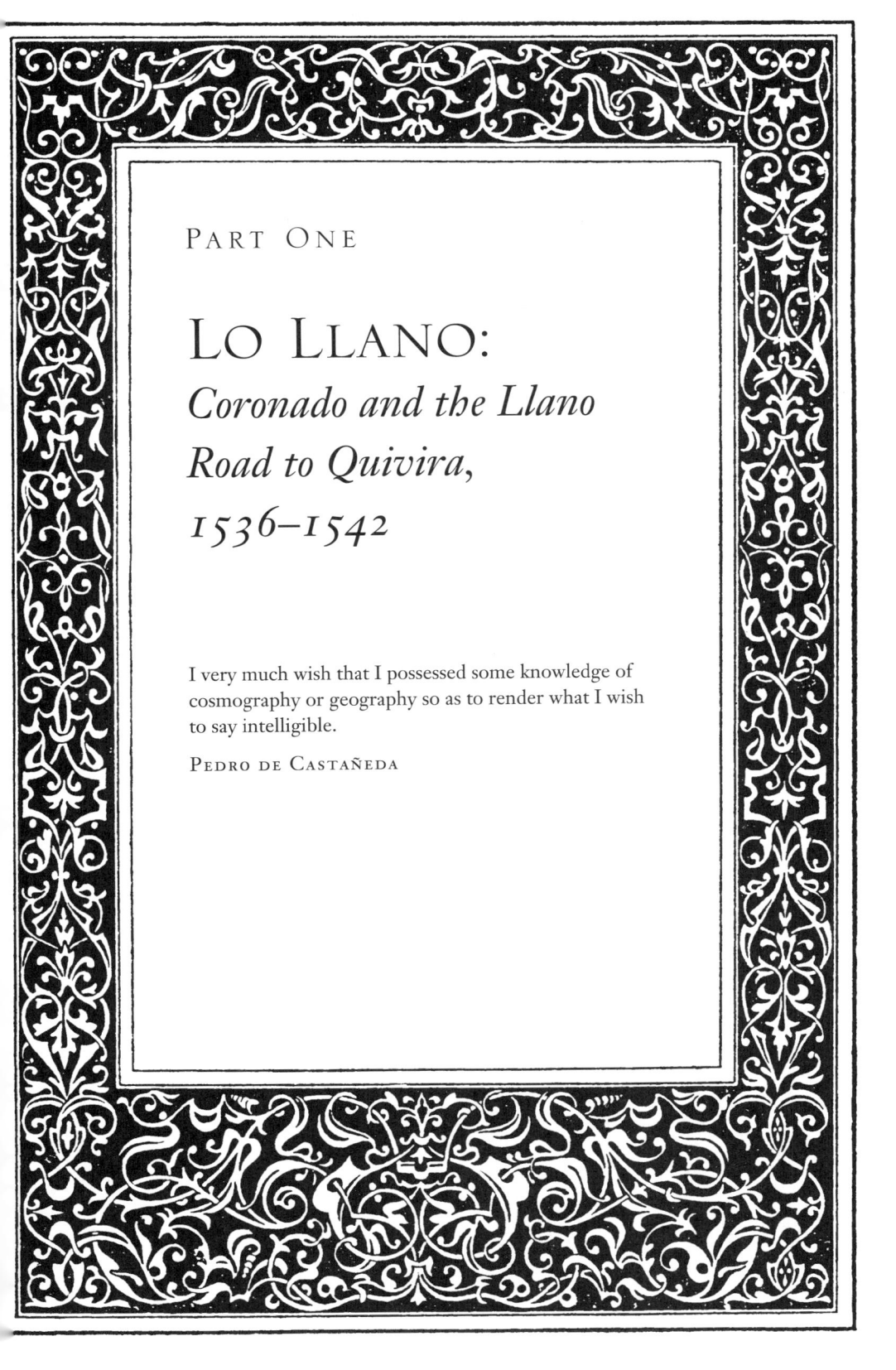

LO LLANO:
Coronado and the Llano Road to Quivira, 1536–1542

I very much wish that I possessed some knowledge of cosmography or geography so as to render what I wish to say intelligible.

PEDRO DE CASTAÑEDA

· 1 ·

The Cow Nation

From this place they began to give us many blankets of skin . . .
Alvar Núñez Cabeza de Vaca, *Los Naufragios*

The first intimation of the Southern Great Plains came early to Europeans in the New World. Only seventeen years separated Hernando Cortés's conquest of Mexico in 1519 from the amazing news in 1536 of populous provinces, including an obscure "Cow Nation," found in the northern *terra incognita*, far beyond New Spain's northern frontier.[1] Contrary to popular imagination, the Spanish crown understood several significant aspects of the plains environment well before the famous expedition of Don Francisco Vázquez de Coronado was formed in 1540. Neither was Coronado the first European to reach the southern plains or talk about them. A Black "Moor" and three Spaniards had preceded him, as even Coronado's own chroniclers sought to acknowledge later.[2] Already by August of 1536, news and dramatic physical evidence of the plains of present Texas had reached the very center, even the very personage of European pomp and prestige.

The most powerful earthly figure in the Old World's penetration of the New World was then a young, vainglorious, and easily bored profligate named Carlos Quinto—Emperor Charles V. To break the tedium of court life, His Holy Casesarian Catholic Majesty enjoyed viewing strange novelties, specially brought from across the Atlantic to entertain him. Cortés had fed this royal penchant for bizarre curiosities with shipments of Aztec treasure and strange animals. Others would follow his lead. When remarkable news surfaced in New Spain, it was natural that both the messenger—seeking reward for meritorious services—and his curiosities should be invited personally to report.[3]

Emperor Charles V was holding court in beautiful Valladolid that summer of 1536, when Alvar Núñez Cabeza de Vaca returned to relate his remarkable story and to display his small stock of wonders. One of four survivors of the ill-fated Narváez expedition of 1527, Alvar Núñez was a man deeply, even spiritually transformed by his encounter with the New World. After disembarking in Lisbon on August 9, 1537, he set out directly for Valladolid to report to the emperor. In his audience before Charles, he told of shipwreck, enslavement, survival, escape, and triumphant procession across the unknown provinces of a northern world. Were there riches in the populous towns about which Cabeza de Vaca heard natives speak? He could not say personally. But as proof of his tale and travels, Cabeza de Vaca produced curiosities for the emperor's perusal.

There was a small group of greenish, crystalline stones, which some fancied bore a resemblance to emeralds. He also presented a collection of sky-blue and greenish blue minerals practically identical to the odd "Turkish" gems—or, as the French said, *turquoise*—minerals that usually passed from Persian mines through Turkish trader routes before reaching the courts of Europe. Lastly, there was his most convincing natural curiosity—the tanned, shaggy pelage of a beast, a new kind of *vaca* or cow. Cabeza de Vaca thus presented his exotic bison robe to Charles V.

A bizarre, monstrous animal from out of the "northern mysteries" was just the sort of thing to amuse the emperor. Cabeza de Vaca's ordinary bison robe, possibly picked up during his sojourn in West Texas, now materially manifested his encounter with a strange environmental realm. This robe presented in the most powerful monarch's court was the first intimation of immense grazing ranges to be found in the unknown interior of North America. It was a zoological symbol of plains, a sign of grasslands running through the rainshadow heart of a vast, new continent. Once this exotic pelage had helped Cabeza de Vaca ward off the cold of night during flight. Now it proved to officials in New Spain and beyond that indeed he had seen marvels, that Alvar Núñez Cabeza de Vaca had seen a new kind of *cabeza de vaca*, whose fatidic skin he wore as a mantle. Already Viceroy Antonio de Mendoza, the dominant representative in New Spain, had interviewed the castaways. He, too, closely examined Cabeza de Vaca's bison robe, and accepted it as evidence of important new lands. The handsome new governor of the raw, frontier province of Nueva Galicia, Francisco Vázquez de Coronado, was one of the first officials to hear Cabeza de Vaca's remarkable story. He also examined the robe. Others knew of its existence, as references to Cabeza de Vaca's marvelous bison robe appear in important documents half a decade later.[4] The robe thus constituted the first evidentiary link between the Spanish imagination and the most magnificent of the southern plains, the immense, isolated mesaland of the Llano.

If Cabeza de Vaca's precious bison robe launched a first impression of the southern plains, it was one magnified as *noticias* or news of the castaways reached print. Captain Gonzalo Fernandez de Oviedo y Valdés published the castaways' *Joint Report* in his rare book, *La Historia General de las Indies*. Cabeza de Vaca himself worked on a lengthy manuscript after his return, a personal narrative of survival and wisdom. Unfortunately, no trace of a possible 1537 edition now exists.[5] But in 1542, while he was merciful governor of distant Rio de la Plata in Paraguay, local publishers in Spain issued the famous Zamora edition of *La Relación Que Dio Alvar Núñez Cabeça de Vaca*. This astounding volume, arguably the greatest of all Southwestern discovery narratives, was a magnificent account of fortuitous survival, harrowing adventures, spiritual rebirth, and triumphant travels and processions across the breadth of the Greater Southwest. One perfect copy of the narrative exists in the New York Public Library. One of its chapters provides the first narrative glimpse into the legendary Llano.

Cabeza de Vaca encountered the periphery, not the core, of the southern plains bioregion in chapter XXX of the Zamora edition. Thoughtful efforts by modern researchers have entirely recast much of the castaways' crossing of Texas. A half century ago, Texas scholars tended to keep their charismatic conquistadors within Texas as long as possible.[6] Why share your regional heritage with another state or country? Although the companions' westward route cannot be identified with certainty, scholars now believe Cabeza de Vaca and his party followed the sinuous arc of the inland coastal prairies southwest across Texas, and rather quickly crossed into present-day Mexico around Falcon Reservoir.[7] After some wandering among the bands of Coahuiltecans, they turned northward and came close or into Texas again near La Junta de los Ríos. Following the Rio Grande from its confluence with Mexico's Rio Conchos, the four survivors were thus exposed to the bison hunting cultures of West Texas, probably the Jumano tribes who frequented the nearby Pecos River and Llano haunts of the buffalo. With no prior European toponyms to guide the mind, the explorer in a plains *terra incognita* is forced to forego landmarks and to describe, as Alvar Núñez did so eloquently, the environmental oddities and curious native lifeways. For Cabeza de Vaca the key environmental perception for this new region was the bison. Each signified the other.

Earlier, in chapter XVIII, Cabeza de Vaca had related his knowledge of the buffalo. As a captive he had once watched his masters set fire to the plains to drive bison onto ranges they preferred. This practice of managing herds by fire likely goes back to the Clovis people eleven thousand years before. "Cattle come as far as here," he said about the southern coastal interior of Texas. "Three times I have seen and eaten of their meat." In 1542 he described for the first time in print the appearance of these distinctive new animals:

> I think they are about the size of those [cattle] in Spain. They have small horns like the cows of Morroco [*sic*]; the hair is very long and flocky like the merino's. Some are tawny, others black. To my judgement the flesh is finer and fatter than that of this country.[8]

Where did the bison come from?

They came as far as the sea-coast of Florida, from a northerly direction, ranging through a tract of more than four hundred leagues; and throughout the whole region over which they run, the people who inhabit near, descend and live upon them, distributing a vast many hides into the interior country.[9]

From his own experience as a trader, he clearly understood the commercial importance of bison robes in the aboriginal trade routes. Cabeza de Vaca and Estevanico also understood, more than any European, that the natives perceived the bison as treasure, a source of wealth. They saw no gold, but there was great wealth indeed in this huge, 400-league nation of cows: a superabundance of the finest animal protein in the New World, a nutritional source that the natives obviously appreciated. These new *vacas* or cows vastly outnumbered cattle on Spanish ranges. Cabeza de Vaca often heard native reports on buffalo, especially from the Jumano bands who made regular forays into the Southern High Plains for bison meat.

A close reading of chapter XXX of the Zamora edition indicates that the four companions likely skirted the far southern margin of the Llano, somewhere in that indeterminate zone where Southern High Plains physiography subtly gives way to the Edwards Plateau and Trans-Pecos. For the historian Cleve Hallenbeck, Cabeza de Vaca's party escaped in October of 1534, wintered with the Avavare natives, then traveled in 1535 as far north as Big Spring, Texas, where strong springs burst from the Llano and watered a pleasant rancheria settlement. From their winter encampment at Big Spring the survivors crossed the Concho watershed and headed for the Pecos River. More recent scholars like Donald E. Chipman do not take Cabeza de Vaca nearly so far north, preferring a southern route among Coahuiltecan tribes.[10] But both sides acknowledge that the four Narváez survivors neared the Cow Nation. To their north, they were told correctly, was a vast plains bison range.[11]

Further perceptual clues of the interior plains to the north emerged even as the castaways walked ever westward. Frustrated by a lack of progress at one point, Cabeza de Vaca told his native escort to take them north instead. However submissive the natives were to these Children of the Sun, they demurred, noting "that except far off there were no people in that direction, and nothing to eat, nor could water be found."[12] Here is, perhaps, a fair description of the Southern High Plains region: it is vast; it is arid; it is low on traditional foods; and it has no permanent settlements. Given the proximate location at this point of Cabeza de Vaca, Estevanico, Andres Dorantes, and Alonso de Castillo Maldonado, perhaps the native reluctance was not only sensible but also in the interests of the Europeans.

The band of four was now stalled in the borderland of northern Coahuila and West Texas. They needed to negotiate their way westward, across an ethnographic divide, from one province to another. Two native women were sent forward as peace emissaries, and they eventually returned with favorable news. They also mentioned the seasonal human use of the southern plains by reporting few people to the west, as "nearly all had gone for cattle [bison], being then in season."[13] Proceeding toward a large river, some say the Pecos River, the adventurers crossed this unknown ethnographic divide and entered a region whose cultural ecology was closely tied to the southern plains bison.

"From this place they began to give us many blankets of skin," Cabeza de Vaca wrote. Possibly it was here that he obtained the famous bison robe displayed to Charles V in Valladolid. He liked these new people—probably one of the various Uto-Aztecan bands now termed "Jumano"—and he relished their kind hospitality. "Because of their seasonal migrations to the north to kill buffalo," writes Chipman, "Cabeza de Vaca referred to the Jumanos as Cow People."[14] They were industrious, intelligent, and much given to generous impulses—not all that dissimilar from modern West Texans. In his narrative this group of "the finest persons" deserved a proper place-name, a name metaphorically linked to his own. "We called them the Cow Nation," he wrote, "because most of the cattle killed are slaughtered in their neighborhood, and along up that river for over fifty leagues they destroy great numbers."[15] Which modern river did he mean for the Cow Nation? Many people believe this is a direct reference to the Pecos River, which ran parallel to some of the best bison range of the Southern High Plains. Others point to the Rio Grande.

This likable Cow Nation was also suffering a drought, perhaps a regional reflection of the global shift in the westerly winds at this time. The natives had planted no maize, they reported, as rains had failed consistently for two years. They therefore begged the strange, new holy men "to tell the sky to rain." Their concern with the climate was so genuine and so touching that the Spanish agreed to pray. And thus, the first Christian prayer for blessed rain for the crops was sent heavenward from the southern plains in 1535. It was the first of many future importunings.

Landscapes were often recalled in terms of food, a primal and gustatory appreciation of the plains environment. Indeed, many of these nomadic native bands may have resorted to agriculture from demographic pressure combined with a deteriorating climate—too many mouths to feed by the old ways. Although the busy natives of the Cow Nation grew some beans and calabashes, and they apparently tried to grow corn, reports of grand maize fields farther to their west, beyond the river, set the party in motion once more. Estevanico, the gifted black servant of Dorantes, was proving especially adept at sign language; he regularly conversed with the natives about the geography and resources of the region around them. The four survivors made arrangements to continue their journey toward the sunset. "We did not wish to follow the path leading to where the cattle are," Cabeza de Vaca recalled, "because it is towards the north and for us very circuitous."[16]

Although Cabeza de Vaca and his companions avoided the main Llano and its bison herds, they understood important aspects of its regional environment from their sojourn in the Cow Nation. Aridity, vastness, seasonal flows of exotic cattle and their human predators, the lack of water, the lack of domesticated foods, and the mobility of the human presence on the shortgrass plains were all reasonable perceptions of a rainshadow landscape, one lurking in the unexplored aboriginal interior to the north. Cabeza de Vaca thought these great plains extended over 400 leagues or a thousand miles. As proof, of course, that the Cow Nation existed, as a symbol of the wonders of the *terra nova*, Cabeza de Vaca could always wrap himself in the mantle of his bison robe.

Traveling toward the sunset for many months, the four companions eventually traversed the Southwest. Swinging south they encountered Spanish civilization once more in the ironic guise of a Spanish slavers' foray in April 1536 along the Pacific Coast, near San Miguel de Culiacán. Hardly recognizable as Europeans, they faced a period of intense re-acculturation as they learned to sleep in beds again, eat with utensils, and the like. Their subsequent tales of survival, their news on the mysterious end of the missing Narváez expedition, and their reports of new lands and peoples roared like a thunderclap over the society of New Spain. Even before their miraculous tour across central Mexico in 1856, desires and demands for exploration of the unknown North were steadily accumulating.

For one thing, much less treasure was recovered after the fall of the Aztec empire than believed possible. Had Montezuma's treasure been spirited northward? Surely there was more gold somewhere. Hernando Cortés prudently bent Spanish energies to the encomienda settlement process of the central provinces. But he also suspected new riches might be found to the north, and he actively conspired to find them first. Other tantalizing rumors of northern treasure enriched the Spanish imagination immensely, but they provided nothing for the royal coffers. In the process of sacking the province of Michoacan, the sadistic Nuño de Guzman managed to obtain a well-traveled captive named Tejo.[17] Tejo's father had taken him as a child from their home at Oxitipar, in the Valles region on the edge of Huastec country, on a long trade venture northward. Father and son traveled to a distant kingdom in the far interior, likely one of the Zuni pueblos at the end of the aboriginal Turquoise Trail. Tejo related his tale of northern treasure and for a brief spell he fired the conquistador thirst for gold. But the tales of Tejo quickly paled when Francisco Pizarro seized Incan gold in Peru. The exploration impulse accordingly shifted far to the south.

Now, with the dramatic reappearance of four Narváez survivors in 1536, envious officials in New Spain had the excuse they needed to investigate rumors of treasure in the north. Although Cabeza de Vaca had reported no wealth on the plains, it was the lure of vast riches that within five years brought the largest and most complex Spanish entrada yet assembled into the heart of the Cow Nation, an expedition whose expectations were as immense as the vast landscape. Instead of great wealth, however, they would find mostly sky and cattle.

Viceroy Antonio de Mendoza, worried about the northern schemes of his arch rival Cortés, proved to be the decisive catalyst in the Spanish exploration impulse that penetrated the southern plains. Mendoza retained the highly intelligent and adaptive Ibero-African servant, Estevanico or "Stephen the Moor," attaching him to his own service. Mendoza also interviewed the other survivors personally. Cabeza de Vaca never claimed to have seen—with his own eyes—treasure and great riches. He heard stories from the natives of distant populous towns with wealth, but his own evidence was meager news to Mendoza. A few green gems, *turquoises*, and the diverting sight and touch of a robe from a new beast were fine, but there was no trace of gold. The situation clearly called for a reconnaissance to find the missing wealth.

After due deliberations, in the spring of 1539 Viceroy Mendoza dispatched northward the bold and charming Estevanico and a French Franciscan from Aquitaine, Fray Marcos de Niza.[18] With their fortitude and zeal the Franciscans were ideal frontier explorers. Many were psychologically prepared—through long prayer and ecstatic trances—precisely for martyrdom in undiscovered parts of the world. But there was also a *visionary* edge to their perceptions and discoveries. Fray Marcos's panicked return later in 1539 produced no physical evidence of wealth either. Estevanico had raced ahead and been murdered, he reported. But the literate Fray Marcos provided linguistic evidence of untold wealth, evidence in a name and a vision. He described a distant panorama of a huge, multistoried, golden city, one resplendent with shining treasure. It lay beyond a fierce *despoblado* or desert of the interior. Beyond this desert Fray Marcos proclaimed that he had seen one of the golden "*Seven Cities of Cíbola*"!

Historians have debated Fray Marcos's account, stopping point, and certainly his motives.[19] For the priest's contemporaries in New Spain, however, his report uncannily tied in with old Portuguese romances about a lost geosophic realm, the *Isla das Sete Cidades*. The musty, old legends said that the Christian Bishop of Oporto and six others fled the conquering Muslims in A.D. 714 by sailing far west into the Atlantic Ocean. They reached new land in a place called Antillia, where each bishop established a resplendent city of lost Christians. The legendary Seven Golden Cities of Antillia now apparently had a New World geographic location. Unfortunately for Fray Marcos, his limited Spanish was dressed up by others, and his vision expanded in the telling from pulpits and plazas. Marcos de Niza's unusual place-name of *Cíbola* was possibly a corruption of the Zuni name for themselves—*Shiwi*—or the name for their homeland—*Shiwana*. Or just as possibly it was a pure reflection of the Zuni word for bison, *Cíbolo*.[20] For many tribes to the south and west the Zuni pueblos were regular sources of bison robes in trade. Whether his intentions were honest or deviously spiritual, Fray Marcos's amazing report touched off a new round of demands for exploration. Bold and foolish alike already had wanted to invade the north; Fray Marcos now gave them a Zuni word of value for their gold disease and a grandiose vision for their low greed.

Spurred by this positive sighting, Viceroy Mendoza agreed to sponsor an official entrada into "the northern mysteries." His choice of command for the expedition fell upon a trusted, young, newly married (and now wealthy with dowry) governor of the western province of Nueva Galicia. Don Francisco Vázquez de Coronado's subsequent expedition from Culiacán to the Zuni pueblo of Hawikuh in 1540 has been ably described and chronicled in many articles and books.[21] For the student of Spanish encounters with the Southern High Plains, however, a novel aspect of Coronado's trek to Hawikuh was the early correspondence about and expectations of *"vacas"* or buffalo to be found in the northeast. Certainly Coronado and possibly some of his captains had seen Cabeza de Vaca's exotic robe; the Spanish already knew the animals existed well before they neared the plains.

The intrepid Captain Melchior Díaz, for example, reported back after his reconnaissance ahead of the Coronado expedition during the bitter winter of 1539–1540. Captain Díaz was a brilliant officer but was unable to reach Cíbola. Nevertheless he gathered excellent ethnographic data about the Zuni natives ahead from local informants along his reconnoiter. "The clothing of the men is a cloak," Díaz reported to Mendoza, "and over this the skin of a cow, *like the one which Cabeza de Vaca and Dorantes brought, which your lord saw.*"[22] Melchor Díaz saw various bison robes among the natives, and with his personal experience of a Southwestern winter, he recognized the appropriateness of the warm, woolly skins in native trade.

Viceroy Mendoza incorporated Díaz's report into his own April 17, 1540, letter to Charles V. No doubt he expected the king to recognize the reference to Cabeza de Vaca's bison robe. The viceroy may well have instructed Captain Díaz to seek information on the strange, hairy beasts reported by the four Narváez survivors. "I have not obtained any information about the cows," Díaz reported back, "except that they are found beyond the province of Cíbola."[23] Beyond Cíbola from the standpoint of Díaz was to the east of the Puebloan settlements, toward the Great Plains.

Although Coronado and his captains knew of the existence of bison well before their conquest of the Zuni pueblo of Hawikuh in 1540, more reliable news on a Cow Nation to their east emerged soon after setting up quarters in the conquered pueblo. Two leaders, fateful emissaries of a Towa trading party, arrived to parley and to exchange gifts. Nicknaming one "Bigotes" for his mustaches and the other "Cacique" for his age and chiefly bearing, the Spanish made the two leaders welcome. They also interrogated the two closely about the eastern geography. Bigotes and Cacique spoke reliably of extensive plains with bison to the east. To give the Spanish a better idea of the animal in question, the chiefs called forth one of their number. As related by Pedro de Castañeda:

> They were made out to be cattle by the picture which one of the Indians had painted on his body, since this could not be determined from the skins, because the hair was so wooly and tangled that one could not tell what the animals were.[24]

They presented Coronado with bison hide gifts, possibly even the robe that Coronado wrote about in his August 3, 1540, letter. "I send you a cowskin," he wrote Mendoza, along with accompanying small gifts of native craftsmanship. Once more a bison robe was laboriously carried across despoblados and mountains, rivers and streams, to reach officials in distant Mexico City.

In late August 1540, the increasingly curious captain-general formally dispatched Fray Juan de Padilla and Captain Hernando Alvarado eastward from Hawikuh with a twenty-man escort. They were to accompany Bigotes and Cacique homeward, and then to explore these buffalo plains as part of a general eastern reconnaissance.[25] Both Alvarado and Padilla were remarkable historical figures, as well as the first expedition leaders to see the great mesa country. Captain Alvarado was a tough veteran of numerous campaigns in the Americas. Every inch a conquistador, his prowess, experience, and instincts could only be clouded by only a glaring weakness—visions of gold. Fray Juan de Padilla was altogether different, a mercurial, ascetic, and brilliant Franciscan from Andalucía in Spain. Arriving in New Spain in 1529, he was serving as guardian of Zapotlán before joining the expedition.[26] Like other great Franciscans from this province in the New World, he was something of a mystic, an ecstatic who dreamed and envisioned himself bringing the word of God to North Africa or other undiscovered lands. Juan de Padilla walked relentlessly and deliberately in search of souls. He had only just returned from an amazing western reconnaissance to the Hopi and beyond before setting out to the east. He may have been driven by an obsession of finding long lost colonies of Christians deep in the northern mysteries, as Southwestern ruins appeared to him as the signposts of old European cities.[27] After weeks of observing and probably writing on the well-stocked pueblos in the Rio Grande Valley,[28] five days of hard travel farther eastward brought Fray Padilla, Captain Alvarado, and their party to the impressive fortress pueblo of *Tzicúic* or Cicúye.

Cicúye was the puebloan gateway to the rich bison plains stretching eastward. Located on a low mesa overlooking the Pecos River near Glorieta Pass, this Towa-speaking population center was the funnel for extensive trade between the people of the eastern plains and the western puebloans. The historian Herbert E. Bolton quoted one eyewitness remarking, "These people neither plant cotton nor raise turkeys, because it is fifteen leagues east of the river [Rio Grande], and close to the plains where the cattle roam."[29] Buffalo robes, dressed skins, headpieces, and rawhide shields were significant plains trade products that circulated all the way to the Pacific Coast. There were also regular exchanges of puebloan shells, blankets, turquoises, and maize in return for deerskins and the nutritious protein of dried buffalo meat.[30]

Accompanied by the popular chief Bigotes, Fray Padilla and Captain Alvarado were warmly welcomed on arrival at Cicúye—or *Tshiquite* in the native tongue. They were greeted with waves of bone-whistle and drum music, escorted by curious townspeople, and treated as honored guests. Here they paused and rested for several pleasant days. Cicúye was indeed a stronghold with thick, defensive, stone walls. With several thousand inhabitants it was also one of the larger permanent towns in the American interior.[31] Alvarado and Padilla were pressed for time though. In early October 1540 they requested Bigotes to join them for the expected trek east to the buffalo plains. He declined to go and recommended instead two of his servants, Ysopete and a fateful man dubbed by the Spanish "El Turco" (The Turk), "because he looked like one." These guides were adoptive captives from the plains, not strictly slaves, and supposedly familiar with the terrain. They were also contrasts in personality and appearance. El Turco was the dominant partner and the better looking of the two. He was also devious, manipulative, and glib in ways that showed great powers of imagination. Ysopete was smaller in stature and rather ill-featured or even ugly. A prominent body tattoo of a bison displayed his connection to the plains. Outshined and outlied by El Turco, this nervous guide found himself in the shadow of his rival, even though he was equal or even more competent to guide the Spanish.

With these reluctant guides, Captain Alvarado's small reconnaissance left Cicúye and traveled east-southeast, probably to the modern Santa Rosa area of New Mexico.[32] They swam across the cold Pecos River and continued eastward. On the horizon in front of them soon loomed an enormous mesaland, one of the world's largest and flattest plains.[33] For Fray Juan de Padilla, this first vision of the Great Plains—a strange steppeland covered with vast herds—must have been a compelling sight. He would return to the plains twice more and achieve martyrdom on their grasslands. On or near the Llano, Alvarado reported a superabundance of buffalo or "cows" as the Spanish continued to call them. Vast herds of these "monstrous beasts" roamed the grassy plains of a peculiar landscape. "I do not know what to compare them with unless it be the fish in the sea," Alvarado wrote.[34] Here indeed were the herds of the Cow Nation spoken of by Cabeza de Vaca. Killing these beasts was troublesome at first. Buffalo bulls gored several of their horses. Spanish swords proved most impractical in hunting these beasts. But the meat from these shaggy animals turned out to be excellent.

On the bison plains—in the very presence of superabundance—the slave El Turco began to use sign language to relate news so incredible that Captain Alvarado, Fray Padilla, and the others soon forgot all about the strange bison. El Turco told of a rich and impressive kingdom nearby. He gave the Spanish linguistic evidence with the sonorous name of *Quivira*, probably after the Kansas Wichita name for themselves, *Kirikurus*. He also regularly maintained that there was in Quivira much gold (or *acochis*, as he called metal). He knew this magnificent realm personally and he told the conquistadors many wonderful stories about the geography of Quivira.[35] El Turco's matter-of-fact comments and deadpan tales of treasure created a major sensation in Alvarado's plains encampment. Here at last was news of a treasure to rival that of Peru. The reconnaissance party quickly turned around and hastened back to

Ysopete, and poor Zabe would serve the Spanish as guides and interpreters.[9]

Coronado needed good guides, as the way ahead was shrouded in mystery, despite the cursory pathbreaking of Captain Alvarado and Fray Padilla the previous autumn. The conquistadors left Cicúye around the first of May and headed south,[10] only roughly paralleling the south bank of the Pecos River. A modern team of researchers, Richard and Shirley Flint of "Far Cry Plantation" near Villanueva, New Mexico, have dedicated time and energy in tracing the Coronado expedition route over the course of the next four days.[11] The expedition advanced south the first day, the Flints argue, past modern Rowe, New Mexico. The Europeans and their allies soon ascended one of the drainages, likely Rowe Rincon (as does today's New Mexico State Highway 34) to reach the tilted passageway of Glorieta Mesa. They camped the first night on this broad strategic mesa, made famous by later travelers and supposed conquerors. Once on the mesa they followed a subtle southern drainage, perhaps Barbero Canyon into the Valle Chimal, which in turn led the conquistadors down into the beautiful Cañon Blanco country on May 3 for a second night's camp. The Flints make a compelling case that the expedition then used a protohistoric trail that led eastward along the Cañon Blanco to its confluence with the Pecos River, perhaps making camp a third night near this Rio de Cicúye.[12]

Although a bit of a detour, following the natural and ancient passage along Cañon Blanco allowed the marchers to avoid the narrow defiles and rough constrictions afflicting the Pecos Valley just below the pueblo. Archeological evidence, especially the presence of petroglyphs, also suggests that Cañon Blanco was a much used corridor of travel for native traders to and from the plains, and presumably for any guides as well. There are numerous other theories on the course and direction of the entrada after leaving the Pecos Pueblo. The historian Herbert E. Bolton took the entrada down the Pecos Valley itself, brushing aside the rough terrain and constrictions. Others take the army far afield, as Albert Schroeder did with his reckless and controversial thesis that Coronado's Bridge must have been built across the Canadian River in distant San Miguel County.[13] Waldo Wedel and John Swanton explored the Pecos River country in 1942, and they thought the evidence pointed to the vicinity of Santa Rosa, a middle-of-the-road locale adopted by others as well. Local New Mexican historians like Fray Angelico Chavez looked even farther south to the scenic, remote, wild Puerto de Luna country.

All of which is to say that there are numerous opportunities to go quickly astray for the entire rest of the route depending on where you site Coronado's Bridge. In looking for our way today to the past, we must turn to modern guides who live on the land and study its history. The general routing suggested by Richard and Shirley Flint is most plausible; indeed, various cavalcades of conquistadors later followed this popular trading trail to the buffalo plains. There is a pedestrian logic—the line of least topographic resistance—to the steady eastward advance from Cañon Blanco to the Pecos River, across the low drainage divide and into the Canadian River tributaries. For the Canadian River was the true aim, the proximate well-watered avenue into the plains—unless led astray.

The army marched ever eastward the fourth day, closer to the southern bank of the Pecos River but still lopping off its northern turns and meanders. At the end of the day they likely neared the ancient Pecos River ford near La Junta. Here, where the Gallinas River emptied into its "junction" with the Pecos River, there was a point of pause. Swollen by snowmelt from the mountains, the combined waters were a torrent. The downstream fords created by the Gallinas River deposition of sediment and debris into the Pecos River were still useless. The geography of the trail was worthy enough: why have to swim two rivers when you need swim only one? By crossing at or below La Junta, the traveler avoided having to swim the swift Gallinas River shortly afterward. But the recharged Pecos River was running very fast and high this time of year from the spring rains and mountain snowmelts. The aboriginal fords may have been judged too risky for advance. Or retreat.

The heavy runoff entailed a substantial delay on May 5 as, for the first time since leaving Compostela, officers and men felt compelled to build a bridge, one capable of crossing all the animals and people. For four days many hundreds of men felled nearby trees, lugged them to the river bank, lashed them together, and labored in cold, rapid waters to build Coronado's Bridge across the Pecos River. Coronado's bridge was likely a *puente flotante* or "floating bridge" of logs, possibly located in the stretch below La Junta, but somewhere between the tiny present New Mexican communities of Tecolotito and Colonias.[14] The general area from modern Anton Chico to Santa Rosa is still a possibility for the bridge crossing, but the downstream La Junta locale is logical. It is still a scenic landscape, one of few residents but oceans of vistas. Once the men and animals wobbled across their floating bridge, on the eighth day out from Cicúye, the Coronado expedition passed from even a debatable landmark into the twilight realm of geographic uncertainty.

Here is a great mystery in North American exploration, one that still engages the romantic and scientific imagination: where precisely did Coronado go after crossing the Pecos River on May 9, 1541? *Quo vadis Coronado?* All agree the expedition crossed the Pecos River, but beyond, on the Plains of Cíbola or elsewhere, the entire entrada seems to disappear.[15] "Beyond that point," a modern Coronado scholar concluded, "until the Spaniards reached the big bend of the Arkansas River, their itinerary seems to be anyone's guess."[16] Were they swallowed up by the vastness of the Great Plains? The road ahead is one of the great mysteries of Spanish exploration in North America, shrouded in controversy, mired in deception. It is our objective to rediscover that road to Quivira, and to rethink the Spanish perception of the plains environment.

After edging across the Pecos River on their makeshift log pontoon bridge in the vicinity of Colonias, New Mexico, the Coronado expedition advanced eastward on May 10, 1541, through the scrub juniper and grassy plains before them. As Jaramillo wrote, they turned to the left after crossing, a direction he remembered as northeast, but east is more correct on the modern map. If they followed up one of the east-bearing Pecos River tributaries like Hurrah Creek near Colonias, New Mexico, they indeed could have marched northeast for several days. The river behind them soon turned almost due south anyway, useless to those headed to Quivira in the northeast level country. The geomorphic reason why the Pecos River abruptly turned south would soon be apparent. Although they could not know it, the eastward aboriginal trail rose gradually before crossing a low divide and reaching the convenient upper drainages of the Canadian River system. Several more days' march would take the entrada past the scrubby Cuervo Mesa area, and soon thereafter they could rest at the springs and waters of the Pajarito Creek branches. Beyond Pajarito were the carmine reds and dark mesa greens of the Laguna Colorada and Plaza Larga country. The trail was not too difficult, as it leaped across level terrain to reach the spring-fed branches of one Canadian tributary after another.

Fairly soon, even the slow-moving Spanish and Mexican allies, averaging sixteen or so miles a day eastward, could spy the dark, low ramparts of the Southern High Plains in the distance. Already as they marched from Pajarito Creek to Tucumcari Creek, they could see more of the curious mesa outliers or mounts shed off by a great mesaland to their south. Possibly they passed near Pinco Mesa or Redonda Mesa or south of one of the Tucumcari Peaks near modern Interstate 40. Stretching out to their right, the huge Llano mesaland appeared as an elevated horizontal expanse of unknown proportions. As the expedition lumbered on, however, the unknown mesaland to their south suddenly curved outward in a great eastern arc to stand before them. Beyond Barranca Creek, Monte Revuelto, and San Jon Creek, the great mesa now increasingly blocked their way. They could turn north, as Bolton takes them, to hug the Canadian River—a very sensible course—or simply climb the low, juniper-cloaked ramparts before them. So far they had avoided the difficult ramparts of the Llano's northwest corner by sliding along its Canadian and Pecos tributaries, a path of least topographic resistance that natives and pedestrian Franciscans alike appreciated. For similar reasons, the wagons and stock of later gold-crazed Europeans—-the forty-niners racing *west*—used a similar stretch from Tucumcari to Cañon Blanco.[17]

But around the middle of May El Turco must have recognized and seized his opportunity as chief guide: the entrada would now enter the mesa to the east and south, turning away from the strong spring-fed tributaries of the Canadian River system. The treasure was deep in this level country ahead. Spanish outriders sought an easy ascent, possibly the historic Arroyo del Puerto favored by recent scholars.[18] It was a briefly laborious but otherwise unremarkable ascent. No chronicler bothered to mention it, much less to record trouble with the wheeled artillery carts or animals. But shortly after climbing onto the Llano at the behest of El Turco in mid-May of 1541—between present Ragland and San Jon—the Europeans found themselves soon entering an utterly fantastic environment.

"*Y caminando para salir a lo llano,*" wrote the best chronicler, Pedro de Castañeda de Náxera of their advent into the Great Plains: "And marching in order to cross the Plain, which is beyond the whole mountain range."[19] This immense heaven's tableland east of Cicúye—a country called "*lo llano*" by Pedro de Castañeda in his classic narrative of the Coronado expedition—was a region of unbelievable flatness. Now there were no forests, no towns, no rivers worthy of mention, no background mountains, and no landmarks. An anonymous *Relación* stated that here the expedition "came to land as level as the sea, in which plains there are innumerable cattle. . . . The land is so flat that men get lost if they draw apart by half a league."[20] "My silence was not without mystery and dissimulation when I spoke of the plains," Pedro de Castañeda wrote later, "for there things were remarkable and something not seen in other parts."[21] Castañeda's ellipsis in his "*lo llano*" place-name implied a perceptual generality about the flat landscape, one foreshadowing the linguistic emergence of the *Llano Estacado* in a later age. Its "plain-ness" was singular. Thus, "*lo llano*" expressed well the initial perceptions of unity in the vastness of this novel rain-shadow environment.

The Llano was so level and so featureless that the Spanish gradually grew disoriented by the monotony of it all. Castañeda was perplexed by the phenomenon of illimitable earth and sky. While some of his geographical concepts were erroneous, he, more than any of his contemporaries, has conveyed to posterity the European encounter and perception of the buffalo plains. He described "Lo Llano" by reference to its intrinsic elusiveness and deception, and he gave us the earliest real sense of place for the Southern High Plains. "It was impossible to find tracks in this country," Castañeda complained, "because the grass straightened up as soon as it was trodden down."[22] This new landscape almost seemed to reject man's presence. Coronado himself wrote to the king of Spain saying that there was "not a stone, not a bit of rising ground, not a tree, not a shrub, nor anything to go by."[23]

Around May 18, 1541, the Coronado entrada encountered "the domain of the cows," the early summer grazing grounds for millions of buffalo. The climate was cooler and damper then; good spring rains on the Llano provided luxuriant short grasses and recharged thousands of freshwater ponds later called playas. Coronado wrote of the great buffalo herds that "there was not a single day until my return that I lost sight of them."[24] Pedro de Castañeda described these novel beasts by referring to both well-known and exotic animals. They have "very long beards like goats," woolly hair "like a sheep's," carry their tails "like a scorpion," have a great hump "larger than a camel's," and shed their hair around the middle "which makes perfect lions of them."[25] At first the Spanish horses shied as they encountered buffalo bulls. This was, after all, the first real contact on the plains between the two species for 9,000 years or so. The mounted conquistadors who first hunted the bison also made various tactical mistakes. Inevitably there were gorings of horses by *los toros*, or the bulls. But the conquistadors learned from their mistakes, and buffalo meat soon proved to be a tasty trail staple.

Scouting through a heavy morning ground fog two days later on May 20, 1541, several of the advance guard observed strange, continuous markings on the ground, as if someone was deliberately dragging lances along the ground. Following these curious markings brought the conquistadors to a small and most curious encampment of bison-hunting natives. Wearing tanned skins and living in tipi-like tents, these "Querechos" were the first denizens of the buffalo plains that Coronado's party encountered. They were nomads, *los naturales* of Lo Llano, who traveled, said Castañeda, "like the Arabs, with their tents and troops of dogs loaded with poles."[26] Today the term "Querecho" is taken to refer to the ancestral eastern Apaches, the Athapaskan-speaking tribes that diffused southward onto the Great Plains after A.D. 1250, perhaps dislodged and swept south by aspects of cold climatic change and tribal war. Although relative newcomers to the Southern Plains, eastern Apaches were an adaptive, highly skilled hunting people. They had traded the flat expanses of the north for those of the south, and their skills in roaming the plains were second to none.

They dominated the northern Llano country of the mid-sixteenth century, and they actively traded—and perhaps warred—with the pueblos to the west. Indeed, their provisioning of the puebloans with warm robes, rawhide shields, and bison protein helped maintain an old symbiotic set of relationships between agrarian pueblo and nomadic ranchería. Some confusion over the exact nature of the Spanish term "Querecho" still exists.[27] But if the bison had reminded Cabeza de Vaca of the North African environment, it was the nomadic Querecho way of life that led Castañeda to draw a similar inference. The Spanish quickly understood that the strange markings had been made by the large native dogs lugging tent poles and equipment from one campsite to another.

As the main army trudged up to the nameless Querecho camp, in the vicinity of Tierra Blanca or Frio Draw, the impassive Indians emerged to greet the Spanish and ask who they were. The Querechos used sign language so well that the Spanish were greatly impressed. Although these nomadic eastern Apache bands ate flesh raw, drank blood, and had peculiar habits, the Spanish thought they were "a kind people and not cruel." They could scarcely imagine that the descendants of these kind people would become feared precisely for their Apachean guile and cruelty. The Querechos lived by seasonally roaming the Llano and fighting its periodic thirst with ingenuity. "They empty a large gut," Castañeda wrote, "and fill it with blood, and carry this around the neck to drink when they are thirsty."[28] Coronado immediately interrogated the Querechos regarding the gold of Quivira. The natives sensibly professed various degrees of ignorance, but they did mention a great river—the Mississippi River perhaps—with many settlements to be found in the east. The great mound cultures of the Mississippi Valley may have been familiar to El Turco as well. The next day the uneasy Querechos packed everything up on dog travois and moved away from the strange crowd of interlopers. Two days later on May 22 the expedition encountered a second group of *Querechos rancheados*.

Coronado's sprawling entrada was now entering the heart of the great plateau in the last week of May. Although hard evidence of the route is completely lacking, circumstantial evidence points to the Blackwater Draw area, a mid-crossing of this gigantic mesaland.[29] The Spanish drifted southeast from their escarpment ascent, most likely into and down the northern side of the ancient Portales Valley corridor, moving from one shallow drainage or waterhole to the next. Castañeda later accused El Turco of leading the Spanish too far in the direction of Florida, that is, to the south, and perhaps he did so with great deliberation. This middle zone had few landmarks, but with its pastures and freshwater lakes it was nevertheless an important corridor. The anthropologist Carroll L. Riley traces a major prehistoric trade route across the Llano between Cicúye and the upper Red River in this approximate area. Natives hunted and traveled across this expanse long before the Spanish arrived.[30] As Coronado and the others drifted along, bewildered and confused, they saw "other roaming Querechos and such great numbers of cows that it already seemed something incredible."[31]

But was there an end to this strange and apparently boundless flatland? How close was Quivira? Already one hunter simply disappeared in late May, swallowed up by this strange immensity of grassland. Conquistadors rode out to the far margins of the procession, shouting and blowing trumpets, but the noise and clamor were to no avail. They also lit smoky prairie fires to attract his attention, but the lost hunter never came back. Once a man strayed too far, perhaps thirst, fatigue, and fear combined to cause him to strike about wildly, crazed with panic, until he dropped and died in some god-forsaken spot on the lone plain. There were other risks to hunters, including goring bulls and very dangerous snakes, although the narratives pay them little attention.

There was no choice, of course, but for the others to continue ahead, abandoning the lost man to his unhappy fate. Still the loss may have pleased El Turco, just as others saw it as an omen. Extremely level prairies were now all around them, in all directions a flat nothingness. Day after day of marching without visual orientation had challenged virtually everyone's sense of direction. Swerving to avoid the dark clouds of bison were troublesome and confusing as well. The advance guard began marking the way by using piles of buffalo dung, bones, and whatever few stones they could find.[32] Like the lone hunter, they were lost as well.

· 3 ·

Lost and Found: The Scholar's Quest

It is impossible to ignore the question of the route taken by Coronado across the great plains, although the details chiefly concern local historians.

George Parker Winship

Coronado's children still have the precious ability to wonder. And you who are so sophisticated, unless you can feel at home in the camps of Coronado's children, never imagine that you understand bold Drake or eager Raleigh or stout Cortez or any of the other flaming figures of the spacious, zestful, and wondering times of great Elizabeth and splendid Philip. They are of imagination all compact.

J. Frank Dobie, *Coronado's Children*

A few years ago I informally set out with a car, a compass, and a child to retrace Coronado's march to and across the Llano. From the lonely New Mexico state historic marker near Bernalillo, New Mexico, we drove past a lost Coofor Pueblo, heading northeast as the chronicles note, to the low mounded ruins of the Pecos Pueblo, the humble remnants of once mighty Cicúye. Keeping to the south bank of the "Rio de Cicúye" where possible, we motored southeast along Glorieta Mesa. At Anton

Chico the delightful mountains of the Santa Fé National Forest began to give way to scrubby plateaus and plains. The picturesque old community of Anton Chico still had a Mexican American presence of vigor and pride. The Pecos River was quite brisk though shallow. There was certainly plenty of timber, enough for laborers working under Spanish supervision to build a crude wooden bridge.

But the timber fringed the river downstream as well. And by traveling a little farther east I could avoid having to cross the Gallinas River just beyond. In going eastward the rough *cordillera*, or mountain range of the Sangre de Cristos, mentioned in the old chronicles, fades from the western horizon. Not far from Santa Rosa Lake State Park, I thought it likely the expedition had already crossed the Pecos. Here the river increasingly turns southward, continuing its 100,000-year-old history of stream piracy. Quivira was to our east, not south, "in the level country" (*en tierra llana*), El Turco had told the captains back at Tiguex. They were prepared to follow him into the level country. My daughter was prepared to follow me there as well.

At Santa Rosa we crossed the Pecos River, aware that the Spanish had availed themselves of better upstream timber for their crossing than we found.[1] To the east now stretched shortgrass plains, occasional arroyos, curious mesa outliers, and the dark green scrub junipers of the colorful Santa Rosa country. Motoring east on an obscure back road, Route 156, my old Boy Scout compass showed a bearing a little north of true east. Even though the modern road was based on an east-west survey, I knew the magnetic declination in these parts could throw a compass off true north. Like an outrider I also explored the roads north and south as well, to the consternation of my passenger.

The best course seemed to head toward the natural drainages along a divide between the northeast Canadian tributaries of Cuervo Creek and Pajarito Creek with the southwesterly Pecos tributaries of old Arroyo San Juan de Dios and Arroyo Alamogordo. Pajarito Creek especially tugged the sojourner to the northeast, a bearing the chronicles refer to several times. Most likely Captain Alvarado had been this far and could still advise the expedition. Entering the upper Plaza Larga territory was an easy transition. To the north squatted the distant Cuervo Mesa. To the east lay other mesa outliers like Tucumcari Peak. The escarpment of the Llano soon loomed closer as an obvious obstacle. Was it time to ascend and cross this low obstacle?

Near the forlorn town of Ragland, New Mexico, we entered into the Llano, briefly climbing up the unimpressive escarpment. From here we struck out eastward for Quivira along a geometric latticework of farm-to-market roads north of Clovis, New Mexico. Not far across the state line near Friona, Texas, in Parmer County, the legendary flatness of the landscape was especially noticeable, a flatness characterized by the miraculous appearance of round small lakes or playas. "For five days I went wherever they led me," Coronado had written

Charles V of his guides, "until we reached some plains as bare of landmarks as if we were surrounded by the sea." It was true. There were no natural features whatsoever.

The mountains of the *cordillera* were well behind us; now the designer colors of arroyos, "breaks," canyons, and mesas of the Santa Rosa and Plaza Larga country were gone as well. Stopping for a soda in Friona, I pondered the next move. I, too, noticed a strong perceptual difference in these plains. "There are many excellent pastures with fine grass," Coronado had noted in his October 20, 1541, letter. I, too, saw good land and many farms with fine, irrigated crops. These plains were different from the Santa Rosa breaks with the latter's scrubby vegetation and tough bunch grasses. "Here the guides lost their bearings," Coronado explained. I, too, had lost my bearings on the expedition route beyond this point. Where to go now? Before us lay an elaborate and gridded maze of rural Texas roads.

It was not a personal question of being lost, of course, since we carried good maps. Rather it was a question of not knowing where to point my car after the first tactical encounter with the flatness and loss of landmarks. What could the many Coronado scholars and researchers tell me now? Unfortunately there were horrible controversies on the road ahead for the largest and grandest entrada to open the Southwest and Texas. The lack of consensus was truly shocking. There were some forty theories and suppositions by famed researchers and writers that needed to be explored. But the further I dug into the existing scholarship, the more lost I became. It was all so disorienting. Which scholar's route was correct, making all the other researchers into modern El Turcos—false guides, feigning to take me where I wanted to go, but instead leading me far astray? Like Coronado in the middle of May 1541, I realized that my learned guides to the route ahead were quarreling and arguing for this way or that. It was time to find a bearing.

Coronado's lack of orientation on the plains was a problem for both the expedition and its literary rediscoverers. Shortly after his straggly, harassed, and disorderly army returned to New Spain with no gold, the expedition sank from sight as a costly mistake. Many of the leaders, including a disabled Coronado, were forced into court to answer serious charges of misconduct and abuse. Some others hung their heads as well. Viceroy Mendoza protected Coronado, but by the close of the sixteenth century, the Spanish had little incentive to recall either the man or his costly blunder into the northern mysteries. Although important documents did survive in this age of scribblers, many others, including an official chronicle and Captain Tovar's papers, doubtless did not.

A dozen years separates the return of the failed expedition from its published notice in Spain, so great was the shame. In the small town of Anvera in 1554 Francisco López de Gómara released his second edition of *La Historia General de las Indias*, including a brief account of the Coronado entrada as one of

Untitled, by unknown artist, from Francisco López de Gómara, *Historia General de las Indias (Primera y segunda parte de la historia general de las Indias con todo el descubrimiento y cosas notables . . .)*, 1554. Woodcut, 2¼ × 2½ inches (image). The primal European image of the American Southwest, with the distinctive (if small-headed) bison. Although the woodcut was produced in Spain, it reflected eyewitness testimony and contemporary accounts. *Courtesy the New York Public Library, New York.*

the updated features. What has endeared Gómara's book to generations of rare-book dealers, however, is that he illustrated the story with a 2¼-by-2½-inch woodcut featuring a recognizable buffalo (see page 34).

The Anvera artist who made the woodcut had never seen such a monstrous creature himself, but he had access to the testimony of Coronado's veterans. Of interest is the sly smile on the buffalo's face, which makes the animal appear almost friendly. A variant of the woodcut adds a stark landscape, a nothingness with a few stones and plants in the foreground. Gómara's smiling buffalo was only an individual exemplar of the vast herds mentioned in his text. Some of the author's remarks on the plains seem to be based particularly on the conquistadors' experience with the Llano. In a telling detail on its featureless nature, Gómara remarked it was so easy to get lost east of Cicúye that the Spanish were forced to pile up heaps of dry dung to serve as markers "in the absence of stones and trees, so as not to get lost on their return."[2]

A rival group of imperialists first showed a keen interest in publishing Coronado's adventures. Italians were sensitive and competitive in geographic knowledge about *terrae incognitae*. The Venetian author Giovanni Battista Ramusio accordingly compiled various Italian translations of significant Spanish documents for his *Terzo volume delle navigationi et viaggi* (1556). Ramusio's book diffused Coronado's letters thereby to other lands. Thus, the piratical Richard Hakluyt published the Cíbola narratives by lifting them from Ramusio's work and translating them into English in his third volume of 1600. For several centuries thereafter the Coronado expedition was of antiquarian interest. To be sure, mapmakers, new editions, a few new compilations, and translations kept the name and memory of Quivira quite alive, but otherwise Coronado and the expedition were facing historical obscurity. Even Coronado's burial in the old church of Santo Domingo in Mexico City was soon lost from memory.

The rediscovery of Coronado and the ascent of the Gilded One into popular imagination began with new rivals to the Spanish, especially the early-nineteenth-century Americans who migrated westward. After the Louisiana Purchase in 1803, Spain disputed a vast border with these upstart inheritors of Hakluyt's "Dark Spanish" legends. To scholars in Europe, and then increasingly in the United States, the questions of Coronado's route began to be a point of historical interest.[3] The great breakthrough came in Paris, in the 1830s. A French scholar, Henri Ternaux-Compans, while compiling and translating Coronado documents for his "Cibola" volume nine, made an important discovery in the vast Uguina Collection. While combing through old documents, he found a rare 1596 Seville copy of a lost manuscript by a regular member of the expedition. His 1838 volume, *Relation du Voyage de Cibola*, thus covered the Coronado expedition in some detail by including a hasty French translation of the critical, hitherto missing narrative by Pedro de Castañeda.[4] As the English borrowed from the Italians with Ramusio's volume three, so now the Americans borrowed from the French with Ternaux-Compans's volume nine.

The rediscovery process was hastened after the annexation of Texas and the resultant Mexican-American War ended the border dispute for all practical purposes. The inheritors of the American Southwest—once the northern half of Mexico—had won both a new land and a new history. Both literary and military explorers fanned out in the late 1840s and 1850s to explore this land and to discover its legendary background. The versatile Lt. James H. Simpson did both in his intelligent reports and surveys, even projecting in 1869 a plausible route for Coronado up to and beyond Cíbola.[5] The indefatigable Henry Rowe Schoolcraft also published a Coronado map. Other less cautious but more popular writers joined in the growing speculation of the 1850s and 1860s on the Coronado expedition. Initially they followed Lt. Simpson's lead and focused on the identification of legendary Cíbola with the pueblos of New Mexico and Arizona Territory. But Coronado also entered New Mexico's Rio Grande Valley and traveled eastward into the plains, as Ternaux-Compans's 1838 Castañeda narrative made quite clear. And where was the "Gran Quivira" that showed up on the ancient globes and in the rare early maps now gathered by antiquarians?

The rediscovery of Coronado in the 1850s owed a great deal to the American popular fascination with sensational legends of treasure in a new land. The fabulous "Seven Cities of Cíbola" was good copy and the popular press was quick to print discourses, much as the Italians had printed "Sette Cita de Civola" on their early maps. H. M. Brackenridge's *Early Discoveries by Spaniards in New Mexico, Containing an Account of the Castles of Cibola* appeared in 1857 to a receptive American audience, eager for authentic word on the exotic "Castles of Cibola."[6] But Brackenridge had only the foggiest notion of Cicúye's actual location, and after that his route wandered aimlessly. Much more influential was attorney W. W. H. Davis's *El Gringo: New Mexico and Her People*.

Davis's work was notable for its literary qualities, but his enlightened research was the lasting legacy. As U.S. attorney for the New Mexico Territory, Davis took pains in *El Gringo* to provide a proper historical and ethnographic background for the new possessions. At a time when many Americans honestly thought the Spanish had simply rounded up wild Indians and grouped them into pueblo towns (savages not thought capable of organizing village life for themselves), Davis sought historical evidence to tear these degrading notions apart. He based his conclusions on "the earliest and most positive testimony we have upon this subject . . . in the journal of Castañeda de Nagera, the chronicler of the expedition of Coronado of 1540."[7]

El Gringo quoted a fair amount from Castañeda's account, using it as eyewitness testimony to confront wildly racist American attitudes about the inhabitants. The book was also one of the first American works on the Coronado route beyond the Rio Grande River. Unfortunately, the attorney's geographical understanding of "Gran Quivira" was avoidably but horribly confused with New Mexican ruins, "*Gran Quivira*," explored and named on a geosophical fancy by Major Carleton from the U.S. Army. Indeed, from a modern standpoint the Davis route to Quivira is pretty hopeless, but his reading of Castañeda did point him toward the eastern plains:

> It will be recollected that when Coronado left the main army to search for the Gran Quivira they were some considerable distance out upon the plains east of the Rio del Norte, and that in his march he took a southwest [sic] direction until he arrived in that country. He mentions passing some salt lakes, which are yet to be found in that region.[8]

How did this court circuit rider explain the present bone-dry landscape of Carleton's ruins with Castañeda's verdant perception of Quivira? Davis pointed to three centuries of rapid environmental change and consequent depopulation, claiming that the springs and streams have dried up and ceased to flow since these villages were deserted. It was an early use of the Coronado narrative to discuss environmental change and damage.

Other Eastern scholars and their urbane Mexico City counterparts rediscovered the legendary road to Quivira at about the same time. Buckingham Smith's *Florida* compilation of Spanish documents from 1857 gathered important new information for research. In Mexico rare documents were also gathered in private collections, particularly the collection of the incomparable Don Joaquín García Icazbalceta from the 1860s. The well-stocked Mexico City library of this noted bibliophile contained many rare manuscripts. A surviving 1742 manuscript on the conquest of New Galicia by Matías de la Mota Padilla added interesting details on the expedition route. Don Icazbalceta also brought the Castañeda manuscript from Paris to Mexico. With the original long lost, this version completed by a routine copyist in Seville on October 26, 1596, was the unique *logos* or word of Castañeda.

A second East Coast wave of interest in Coronado began to build with the further settlement of frontier New Mexico and Arizona in the 1880s. A new U.S. Bureau of Ethnology was becoming active in the region. From Santa Fé in October 1889, Adolph Francis Bandelier mailed his "Quivira" article to New York publishers. He speculated on Coronado's route across the plains, correctly taking him to Kansas for his destiny with Quivira.[9] Bandelier's solid ethnographic reasoning was a significant contribution, one heightened with the appearance of his book on Coronado, *The Gilded Man*.[10] From the West Coast, H. H. Bancroft's sprawling volumes on the Southwest added a fresh compilation of detail. But the most important new source of Coronado research appeared at Harvard University in 1891 in the unlikely guise of a twenty-one-year-old undergraduate, George Parker Winship.

Winship's interest in Coronado began with the casual recommendation of Professor Edward Channing on a topic suitable for the Harvard undergraduate's "Seminary of American History." Channing suggested the young man examine a recent acquisition by the trustees of the Lennox Library of New York

City. There Winship found the Icazbalceta manuscript of Castañeda's narrative. Over the next five years he transcribed, translated, and vigorously researched the entire Coronado expedition. By 1896 he was the finest Coronado scholar of the day. That same year he published his magnum opus, "The Coronado Expedition, 1540-1542," in the Smithsonian *Fourteenth Annual Report of the Untied States Bureau of Ethnology, Part I*.

In addition to stirring considerable interest on the expedition route across the plains of Texas,[11] Winship's stunning English translation of the Lennox Manuscript turned the unique copy of Castañeda's narrative into an American classic of exploration literature. In 1904 he reprinted his translation as a popular Trails title, *The Journey of Coronado*. With only minor editing, his remarkable literary translation has seen new printings down to the present day.[12] But most of Winship's work was done in the realm of serious East Coast "armchair geography"; he never did extensive fieldwork, such as riding the plains of Texas and New Mexico. Instead, he turned his excellent bibliographic skills to good use as librarian of Brown University. What matter that he knew little of the Southern High Plains personally? He certainly wrote convincingly enough of them for an East Coast establishment audience.[13]

For decades after Winship's gifted popularization of the expedition, "Coronado Fever" ran high across the Southwest United States. Like El Turco, American promotional genius saw the value in a good exotic name.[14] On restaurants, tourist courts, schools, highways, streets, and chamber of commerce brochures the name of Coronado was splashed across the cultural landscapes of Kansas, Texas, Oklahoma, New Mexico, and Arizona. Why was the name Coronado chosen over Vargas, Oñate, Espejo, and the others? He was *first*, of course, but there is a further identification factor between the American newcomers and the first conquistadors. Like Coronado's multicultural army, many of the more recent arrivals were young newcomers after quick riches. In Coronado they had a man like themselves, willing to cross great stretches of rough geography to find one's personal Quivira. In the boosterism of the 1920s, dozens of towns and communities sought to associate themselves with the expedition route, partly to enhance tourism and partly to perk up local pride.

Indeed, by now the fusion of East Coast scholarship with local boosterism had created a distinct romantic horizon for Coronado. Artwork and illustrations celebrated the romantic pulse. The very name now conjured up something deep within the subconscious of the Southwestern mind: the search for wealth. Like the conquistadors of old, these residents were drawn to the same region, only this time by the lure of fortunes to be wrested from the land in agriculture, ranching, trade, minerals, and real estate. Like Coronado, the Americans were get-rich dreamers. The pursuit of myth and the lure of treasure still motivate the mind in this land of promise.

Coronado Fever crested as a romantic horizon with the 1540–1940 Cuarto Centennial festivities. The idea to mark the expedition's 400th anniversary first arose in Peter Hurd's Roswell in 1930. Nothing much was or could be funded during the worst of the Depression, but in 1935 the New Mexico legislature launched a thinly financed "Coronado Cuarto Centennial Commission," aimed at celebrating the entrada and attracting paying tourists throughout 1940. A raucous U.S. Congress approved a regional pork-barrel grant of $200,000 for celebrations in 1937, and New Mexico's politicking Senator Clinton Anderson obtained further federal largesse in 1939.[15] The money would buy goodwill south of the border (the bill passed shortly after Franklin Roosevelt announced the U.S. "Good Neighbor" foreign policy for the Americas), and it would fund an elaborate program of celebration for Southwestern voters.

The official United States Coronado Exposition Commission proved especially energetic in funding a massive outdoor pageant, *The Entrada of Coronado*, an eighteen-part historical dramatization of Coronado's travels in the Southwest. The international "pageant writer" Thomas Ward Stevens dashed off the heroic script, subtitled in case of doubters, *A Spectacular Historic Drama*.[16] Author Paul Horgan signed on as consultant. Miss Lucy Barton of New York's Traphagen School of Design directed WPA workers in the assembly of 1,000 authentic period costumes. Les Marzolf of Chicago assembled a sixteenth-century army of props and designed a portable sound stage over 300 feet long and up to 40 feet high. The New York producer Jerome Cargill managed the entire entrada. Finally, cast, costumes, properties, and stage design rushed into action on May 29, 1940, in Albuquerque.[17] The outdoor minidrama met with rousing ovations.

The Entrada of Coronado toured over eighteen towns in Arizona, New Mexico, and Texas from May to October, 1940. Six of the towns were on the Llano, where Little Texans of New Mexico and West Texans watched with interest as the Turk, "false guide," led the Spanish "far into the high plains of Texas and Oklahoma."[18] Although the pageant was the most spectacular form of commemoration, there were also busy artists and illustrators, special journals and articles, social groups, and numerous local celebrations undertaken in the Southwest to mark the occasion. The University of New Mexico published Hammond and Rey's new translations of pertinent Coronado documents in volume two of the Coronado Cuarto series. Historian Herbert Eugene Bolton agreed in 1939 to write a scholarly volume (but it took him almost a decade to finish the narrative, and then he fought to have it published elsewhere for more money). For the general public the U.S. Post Office released on September 7, 1940, a violet Coronado Expedition commemorative stamp to mark the national exposure. As subject matter, the Post Office chose a suitable vignette from the highly romanticized painting of "Coronado and His Captains" by the regional painter Gerald Cassidy.

Gerald Cassidy was a tubercular Easterner who moved to the dry climate of Albuquerque in 1912. He fell in love with the Southwest and quickly appreciated its rich heritage. A few years later he moved to a modest studio in Santa

Fé. An early member of the local Santa Fé art colony, his large paintings and murals portrayed the romantic qualities of the landscape and its history. Cassidy's evocative and symbolic "Coronado and His Captains" epitomized the arrival of bearded Spanish horsemen into a new land. In the left foreground a priest reads calmly and silently in the Bible. Horses, people of European descent, Christianity, and the arrival of literacy would indeed separate prehistory from recorded history, especially for the Querecho plains and Teyas canyons of Texas and New Mexico.

A stubborn research problem persisted, though, one emerging in the publications of the 1930s and 1940s. A new generation of scholars had to grope their way beyond Pecos Pueblo or Cicúye. Already there were three proposed Coronado trails from Corazones to Cíbola. Now there were competing and multiplying theories and divergent routes proposed for the expedition's crossing of the plains. Each route had its local proponents, in part as competing businessmen and city officials wanted the bragging rights to an association with Coronado. A. Grove Day's commemorative book from 1940 provided a thrilling narrative for the expedition and kindled new interest in the route as well. In his *Coronado's Quest*, this Stanford professor of English takes the reader far south on the Llano, with conquistadors riding through fogs into lost Querecho camps.[19] Bolton's masterly *Coronado, Knight of Pueblos and Plains* (1949) pulls the reader far northward, down the Canadian River, thence suddenly reversing course to drift south onto the Llano, then twisting eastward.[20]

One maverick student of the expedition, the geologist David Donoghue, boldly argued in the 1930s that there was no need to share Coronado with Kansas and Oklahoma, as Coronado's Quivira was simply the big northeast bend of the Canadian River in the Texas Panhandle, not the distant Arkansas River.[21] For Texans, Donoghue's 1541 route had the obvious virtue of keeping Coronado and Quivira mostly to the Lone Star State. This strange theory was wildly popular before and during the official 1940 celebrations.[22] It would take old and new scholars alike, such as Paul Jones, John Swanton, and Waldo R. Wedel of Kansas, to stamp out these chauvinistic Texas regional heresies.[23] The best existing knowledge of the Llano road to Quivira was summarized in the WPA Writers' guidebook to New Mexico (1940), which noted the bridge, "supposedly at Puerto de Luna," and the route on the Eastern Plains beyond, "led towards the northeast for a short distance, then turned in a general southeasterly direction to a point presumably near the headwaters of the Brazos River on the plains of Texas."[24]

The question of where the Spanish went—on the plains of Texas or New Mexico—has yet to be answered satisfactorily. Like Coronado, we postmoderns are the inheritors of many rival routes and competing uncertainties (see map, page 41). After lumping and sorting, there are essentially four broad corridors for Coronado's crossing of the Eastern Plains. First, there is a trans-Canadian school of thought associated with Albert Schroeder and William Brandon. These scholars interpret the chronicle accounts of northeast bearings literally

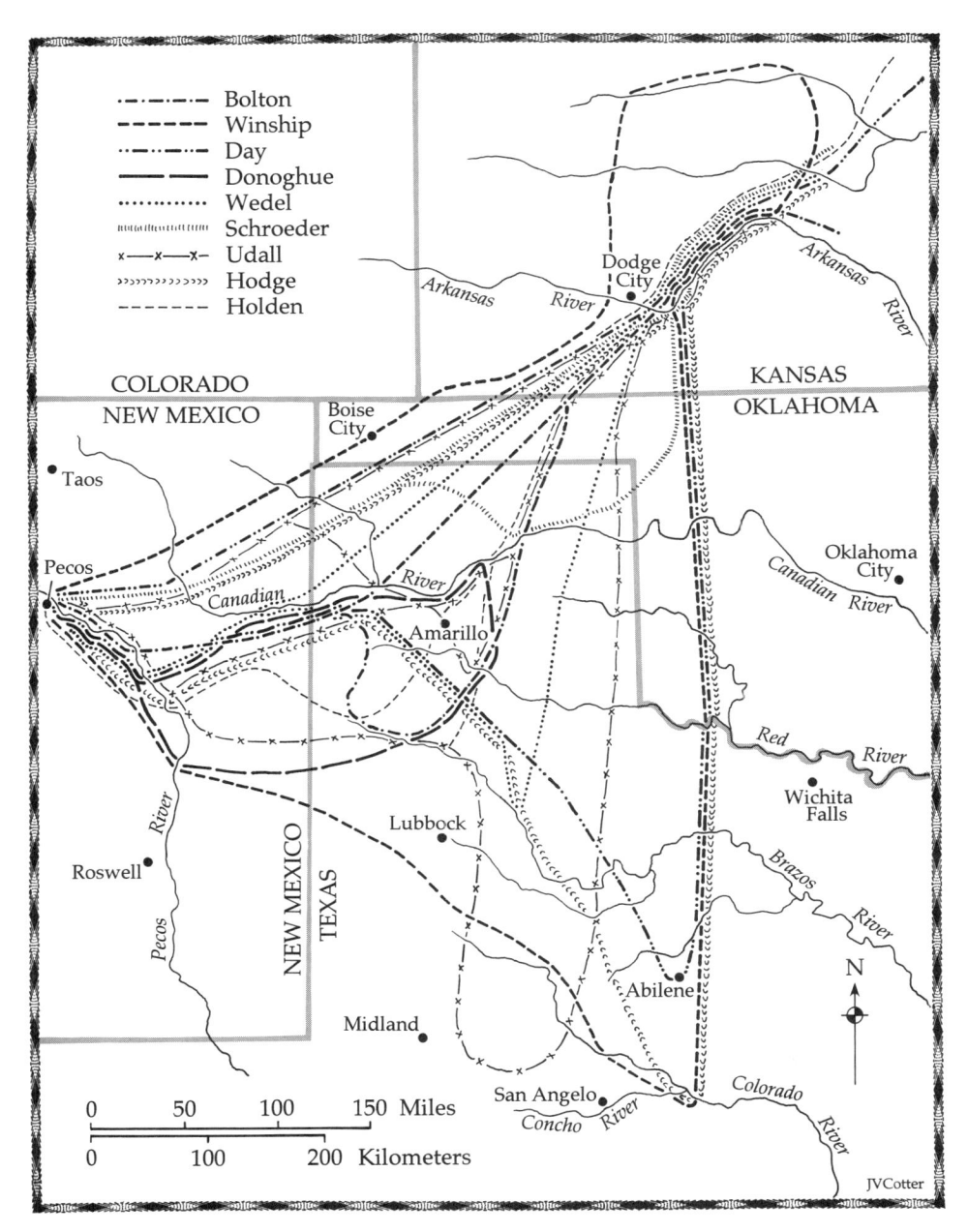

The historic confusion and uncertainty of Coronado's route in Texas is reflected in widely contradictory trails proposed for the expedition route. Conflicting interpretations of expedition texts and geography have led many Trail Detectives far afield. *Map by John V. Cotter.*

and at length. Coronado avoided the Southern High Plains altogether, they argue, building a bridge over the Canadian River instead, and following a northeast route over the high plains, a course similar to the later Santa Fé Trail across the Great Plains.[25] Second, the most dominant school of thought arose in the scholarly aftermath of the Cuarto Centennial in the 1940s. This line follows Bolton's lead on a northern, tortuous crossing of the Llano, where the Spanish emerge into the scenic depths of Tule Canyon (*Barranca Grande*) and enter into Palo Duro Canyon (*Cona*) just east of Canyon, Texas. Already the material culture of Canyon's new museum was projecting Coronado onto the nearby Palo Duro Canyon State Park, and Bolton confirmed their desires after a visit.[26]

As the finest West Coast expert on the expedition in his day, Bolton took the unusual step of visiting the Llano plains and canyons to examine the landscape himself. Good citizens in Canyon and Amarillo surrounded and fêted the famous visiting scholar, and they roamed the canyonlands with him to everyone's satisfaction. Bolton's first vision of the deep northern canyonlands was an epiphany. He was impressed and gave much comfort to tourism in Canyon, Texas, by nominating Palo Duro Canyon as the "second barranca." Already the horse trail into the new Palo Duro State Park was known to local boosters as the "Coronado Trail." Local artists continued to paint romanticized versions of Coronado, his captains, priests, and guides, all stopping to admire the marvelous scenery of Palo Duro Canyon. This vision was just what the bureaus who printed and diffused the subliminal artistic illustrations wanted the average tourist to do: stop and take a rest; take some time to admire the view.

This northern Llano route of Bolton's was largely adopted by another West Coast savant on the Coronado expedition, the famous geographer Carl Ortwin Sauer. Like Bolton, Sauer was a highly regarded researcher on the Spanish Southwest. His brilliant monograph *The Road to Cíbola* (1932) was an instant classic in historical geography.[27] Sauer's closely reasoned discourse on the Turquoise Trail from Culiacán to Hawikuh presented a credible statement on the route as far as Cíbola. Beyond Tiguex and beyond Cicúye, though, Sauer's footing was less sure. As late as 1971 Sauer followed Bolton's Palo Duro Canyon arguments for the site of the mysterious second barranca—the region Castañeda called "Cona."[28] Sauer's keen sensitivity to botanical evidence (in the chronicles and landscape) was an important variable. His own brief account directed attention to the High Plains environment and especially the ethnographic context of the Querecho and Teyas natives.

A third school for Coronado's crossing of the Llano is best termed the middle-crossing approach. Lubbock historian William Curry Holden spent many days puzzling over Coronado's plains route.[29] Already by Holden's time the landscape was succumbing to incessant fencing and other obstacles to the free flow of movement, so it was becoming more difficult to wander around as Coronado might have done. But W. C. Holden was a determined seeker. Although both land and climate had likely changed, Holden definitely saw a middle-crossing pattern. As a local historian who knew the Llano more intimately than either East Coast scholars or West Coast scholars, Holden's reasoning on the route should be examined closely.

A fourth and older avenue of inquiry focuses on a radical advance into the far Southeast. In 1896 Winship carried Coronado all the way off the Llano and well down to the central Colorado River bottoms east of San Angelo. The Concho River is another favored location for Cona, as Stewart Udall's well illustrated *To the Inland Empire* attests. Frederick Hodge, who updated Winship's work, favored the southeast advance, as did A. Grove Day in his work, *Coronado's Quest* (1940). And then there is J. W. Williams's quaint *Old Texas Trails* with its elaborate, lengthy, and intense ecological reasoning for the far southern route. At the far end of a booster's hope, an Austin newspaper clipping from the 1930s claimed that old Spanish signs on a rock just west of the city, near springs gushing into the Colorado River, had likely been left behind by the Coronado expedition. At the rate of his rapid advance southeast, it was clear he would soon be in the outer Houston suburbs.

To help clear some of the geographical confusion, various congressional interests in the 1980s requested the U.S. National Park Service to designate officially a "Coronado National Trail" as part of the esteemed U.S. National Trails System. As ordered by Congress, the National Park Service studied the request diligently, but reached an obvious conclusion in its assessment of a trail potential:

> Although the route does not meet the criteria for national trail designation and administration, other options for commemorating the expedition should be considered that transcend current limitations brought about by the need to determine the actual expedition route.[30]

No more than the scholars, the government was unable to reach a consensus on the route of the Gilded Age adventurers. *Quién sabe?* The National Park Service map of the official study area graphically expressed the spatial problem. Where the route in the modern United States was deemed uncertain, the Park Service staff shaded in an appropriate "Zone of Uncertainty."

By far the largest of the three Zones of Uncertainty, an enormous area, stretched eastward from Cicúye pueblo, ranging from Kansas in the north to middle Texas in the south (see map, page 41). The spatial logic of all this uncertainty certainly lends itself to alternative visions of commemoration and designation. One likely alternative is a Coronado "Heritage Corridor" whereby a broad swath of land is cited for its possibilities. This corridor has political appeal since a number of communities could benefit from tourism and related development. (Better to share in uncertainty than to risk being in the small number of towns singled out on the basis of sketchy, conjectural evidence.) But even finding a reasonable, agreeable corridor, in an otherwise immense zone of uncertainty, filled with quarreling scholar-guides, is a daunting challenge.

Indeed, Coronado's route across the plains of Texas is both an old mystery and a new problem. Like the expedition itself in June of 1541, we are still lost.

But we, like they, are not without further recourse. Can we not return to expedition texts and the landscapes themselves, to their semantics, vistas, and captured memories to search for a new way? Perhaps now is the moment to find an agreeable corridor. We need a way out of the official Zone of Uncertainty. Like others before me, I wanted to find that corridor. It was especially important to find the canyonland paradise Castañeda called "Cona," a popular landscape of the Teyas natives. Into Cona the expedition eventually traveled for food, and there they stayed to rest and recuperate. Finding Cona was clearly a key to the whole corridor-route problem.

Each of the four basic corridors proposed over the last hundred years needed reevaluation for perceptual and spatial bias. Somehow, amazingly, the Coronado expedition always seemed to be tugged toward the researcher. The revisionist Santa Fé Trail school, for example, downplayed the significance of the Llano and favored a literal northeast bearings approach. This direction pulls the expedition to the High Plains north of the Llano, with their comparable levelness. But how literal were the remembered bearings and distances, many recalled after the passage of decades? A bearing can be mistaken, but the vision of a deep Llano barranca lingers in the memory. The northern or Palo Duro Canyon school favored a bias toward landscape and spectacular canyon scenery. This direction tends to pull the expedition into the present boundaries of Palo Duro State Park, at least in the popular mind of the Texas Panhandle. The Portales Valley, or middle-crossing, school favored a logical *dis*orientation approach: Coronado could best get lost—as we know he did—in the fat middle of the Llano, not around its scenic edges. And finally, the southern Colorado River/Concho River school favored a perceptual bias toward the present-day ecology. Where can we presently find the abundance of fruits, trees, and especially the nuts spoken of in the texts?

The search for a realistic corridor, a greatly slimmed down "zone of uncertainty," must of necessity begin with the small group of surviving expedition accounts: Castañeda's *Relación* or Narrative, Jaramillo's *Relación*; the two surviving letters of Coronado; the report of Hernando de Alvarado; the intriguing manuscript *Relación del Suceso* (anonymous); another *Relación* (the *Traslado de la Nuevas*, perhaps by Don García Lopéz de Cárdenas); and the manuscript *Postrera de Sívola* (probably by Fray Torobio de Benavente [called Father Motolinía]; it was copied out by hand for Winship by the great Mexican bibliophile, Don Joaquín García Icazbalceta).

These texts provide a suitable interpretive challenge to the adventurer and fool alike. Although all these documents have been translated into English, these translations need close examination to disclose any perceptual bias. What was the original Spanish perception of the environment on the road to Quivira? Indeed, the search is not so much for Quivira's mythic gold and jewels as it is for Cona's prosaic nuts, fruits, and *frisoles*.

· 4 ·

THE LLANO ROAD TO QUIVIRA

And while we were lost in these plains. . . .
CORONADO TO CHARLES V, October 20, 1541

Mas allá—Farther on.
EL TURCO TO CORONADO

If all the scholars and all the evidence still deny the Llano a Coronado trail, then we must look for another way: a Coronado Corridor. Any such heritage corridor for the stretch east of Pecos Pueblo must begin with a consensus that the expedition did encounter and cross the Southern High Plains. Arguments for a trans-Canadian trail, a route much farther north that bypasses the Llano altogether, simply misinterpret the abundant environmental commentary to the contrary. There is a wholeness to the expedition narratives that points directly to the Llano. Indeed, the accounts of Coronado, Jaramillo, Castañeda, and the related manuscripts are in remarkable general agreement as to the course, the events, and the proximate geography of the Llano Road to Quivira. Discrepancies in time and distance of course exist, but one can set priorities. Coronado's October 20, 1541, letter to Charles V was written so shortly after the Llano encounter that its reportage of time is widely respected. Let us do so as well. Likewise, the *Traslado de las Nuevas*, the *Relación Postrera de Sívola*, and the *Relación del Suceso* all appear to be contemporaneous if terse accounts.

In addition to these bibliographic works, the greatest level of detail and narrative focus clearly belongs to the 1560s account by that *vecino* of Culiacán, Pedro de Castañeda de Náxera.[1] Writing or dictating his anecdotal account in 1563, some twenty or more years after the events, Castañeda's recollected dates, distances, and bearings are more general signifiers than precise recordings. Perhaps he had access to important documents now lost to us, such as Pedro de Sotomayor's reputed official account of the entrada.[2] Although Castañeda's account is told from the perspective of a humble soldier, his penchant for close environmental observation and narrative detail sets this work above all others. Especially with respect to the Llano environment, the Lennox Manuscript copy of his narrative must weigh heavily in the rediscovery of a Coronado Corridor. This 1596 copy now in the New York Public Library provides the *logos* itself, the longest, most detailed, and most unfiltered text on the initial European exploration of the Llano bioregion.[3]

Perhaps a logical beginning to the geographic dilemma of Coronado's Llano Road is with the recognition that the expedition was indeed lost toward the middle of May. Juan de Jaramillo said their misdirection was a calculated effort by El Turco to confuse them. They were supposed to be lost. Since they had always followed "the guidance of the Turk," Jaramillo reported, he "led us off more *to the east*, until we came to be in extreme need from lack of food."[4] "We had been led astray," asserted the writer of the *Relación del Suceso*, adding that they had been pulled to the southeast, that is, toward the Llano.[5]

Coronado eventually subscribed to the conspiracy theory as well and allowed El Turco to be garroted in Kansas for his double treachery. Given Spanish behavior at Cicúye and the sacking of Tiguex, there was an undeniable motive for the puebloans to urge El Turco in April to lose the Spanish on the Llano that summer, to take the aliens where their horses and soldiers would collapse from hunger. The angry Towans at Cicúye knew the plains fairly well. Perhaps at Bigotes's instigation, they suggested the Llano as the closest and best landscape to enervate the Spanish army.[6]

All the accounts agree that a week or so beyond the Pecos bridge they encountered bison, then Querechos, then they got lost. "*Es la tierra tan llana que se pierdan los hombres apartandose media legua*"—It is a land so level," the author of the *Relación Postrera de Sívola* said, "that men lost themselves after drawing off half a league."[7] Beyond the Querecho camps they entered a state of complete disorientation. With no landmarks in sight, the other guides showed less confidence and even argued with El Turco. Already one of the Spanish hunters had disappeared, swallowed up by the landscape. At some point the Spanish must have felt that queasy sensation of being truly lost.

Where is the best place to lose an army of trail-hardened horsemen? The question is not as fatuous as it sounds. Although the Southern High Plains is an enormous region, its configuration is such in the north (where Bolton places the expedition) that a mounted rider is rarely more than a three-day ride from some kind of orienting, featureful topography. Consider the many tributary draws of the Canadian River Valley; the great gorges of Palo Duro and Tule, and the orienting Tierra Blanca Creek. The terrain is remarkably flat in the playa stretches, but is there enough room in the north for conquistadors—no simple fools in crossing a *despoblado*—to get lost and confused? Perhaps the best place to get lost on the Llano is in the middle-crossing corridor. Between the Pecos-Canadian drainage divide in New Mexico all the way southeast to the Brazos and Pease headwater canyons in Texas, there is a truly immense, flat stretch. The ground covers well over three degrees of longitude (almost one hundredth of the earth's circumference at this latitude). If a treacherous guide wished to confuse the conquistadors, the best choice was the middle or southern portion of the Llano, not the northern realm.

The accounts also agree that after the nomadic Querecho camps, the Spanish entered more sinister plains, extremely level, where the guides blamed the landscape itself for a lack of progress. The *Relación del Suceso* suggested they went 100 leagues to the east and 50 leagues to the south or southeast.[8] If this is not a literal statement, it suggests a combined vector drift around 15° to 25° to the southeast, thus pulling the expedition toward a middle crossing as well. Castañeda thought they traveled to the northeast after the Querecho camp, but later he corrected himself by noting "the great detour" they made on the plains "toward Florida," that is, well to the southeast.[9] Jaramillo's narrative provides, perhaps, the best locational clue to their subsequent direction. "We traveled in the said direction some eight or ten days," he wrote, *"along the waters found in the cattle country."*[10] This is a key piece of environmental perception. Jaramillo turns our attention properly to the drainage patterns of the Llano, this "cattle country" or Cow Nation.

As it were, the dominant surface drainages of the Southern High Plains flow southeast, "toward Florida." With the important exceptions of stretches of Tierra Blanca and Frio Draw in the far north, all the other principal streams—Running Water, Blackwater Draw, Yellow House, Sulphur, Seminole, and so on—meander southeast, usually along a general vector of 20° to 30°. Jaramillo's account is convincing because it is a practical response to the lack of conventional water. By approximating the southeast drift of the middle-crossing drainages of, say, Blackwater Draw and Running Water, the Spanish could often camp close to a traditional water feature. This area is along the northern edge of the so-called Portales Valley.

Circumstantial evidence thus pulls our attention toward the northern Portales Valley area. From the Plaza Larga and Tucumcari country, a desperate El Turco could have steered the group quickly onto the Llano, perhaps indeed at Arroyo del Puerto. Jaramillo noted that after crossing the Pecos, "we turned more to the left [that is, east], which must be more to the northeast, and we began to enter the plains where the cattle roam."[11] They then drifted southeast over the upper Frio drainage to reach the lengthy southeastward streams of Running Water and Blackwater Draw. The immense scale is appropriate. It is certainly a large enough area in which to get thoroughly lost. The general drift to the southeast seems correct. Jaramillo's "waters found in the cattle country" are there. There is a vector drift averaging 25° to the southeast. And the landscape does become more level, more featureless, more deceptive, more frightening. It is difficult, of course, to get lost in the modern landscape of the Texas Panhandle. All the roads, fences, houses, windmills, elevators, signs, and poles have added a vertical orientation that has domesticated and denatured the earlier possibility of getting hopelessly lost.

Coronado's men were seasoned explorers not easily confused. Finding where it is possible for them to get lost—at least a week's ride from the eastern edge of the Llano—points again to the middle Running Water/Blackwater Draw area, roughly by mid-May 1541, in the area of present Lamb and Hale Counties. The area is east enough for better rains and finer soils or the "good pastures" Coronado spoke of, which also meant bison on the summer grazing ranges. The Hale County area is not only productive, flat, and featureless land but it is also still many days ride from the eastern edge. In short, Hale County is a good place to start with the realization that one is lost.

These *llanos* or plains were perceptually different from the earlier *despoblados* or deserts crossed by the expedition members. The lack of reference points and landmarks caused profound disorientation. "*Era tan peligroso caminar ni apartarse del campo*," said one of the chroniclers, "*que en perdièndole de vista se quedaba perdido*" ("It was so dangerous to draw away from the camp, because to lose sight of it was to find yourself lost").[12] Noisy herds of bison, first the younger *toros* or bulls, then vast mixed herds farther inland, often blocked their progress and slowed their pace. They were forced to wait or make detours, adding to the general expedition confusion. Sometimes they saw other roving Querechos in the distance, but the nomads were reluctant to approach the long train of newcomers. El Turco projected a dogged confidence, but the daily monotonous nothing of the middle-crossing—the thickest portion of the Llano—gnawed at the confidence of others.

Gradually a sense of illimitability may have settled upon them, a feeling of dread associated with the thought that these plains were endless. "I did not find their limit," Coronado admitted. "*Los llanos proceden adelante, ni se sabe qué tanto*" ("The plains stretch away ahead nobody knows how far"), said the author of *Relación Postrera de Sívola*.[13] In our own age the thought of earthly illimitability is remote. The world seems much smaller with few, if any, empty spots. But for conquistadors penetrating a *terra incognita*, an unknown, unending expanse was an environmental hazard to be reckoned with. Were they walking farther into a void, as a knight might wander in the infernal wilderness of an evil wizard?[14] Their world was becoming larger, not smaller, as Spanish cosmography grew by leaps and bounds.

The environmental metaphor that summed up the Llano's monotony, immensity, and amazing levelness was its paradoxical analogy to the ocean, *El*

Mar. "The Spanish came to some land as level as the sea" (*Relación Postrera de Sívola*); it was "as if we had been swallowed up in the sea" (Coronado); "*En estos llanos, que son como quien anda por el mar*," (anonymous chronicle); there were so many bison that "I do not know what to compare them with, unless it be with the fish in the sea" (*Relación del Suceso*).[15] The ocean metaphor was even more appropriate when freshwater supplies became a concern, as with mariners adrift at sea. Accustomed to drainage environments with regular flowing streams and rivers, the Southern High Plains environment was peculiar to say the least. "I was in great need of water," Coronado reported. Instead of the usual dendritic networks of creeks and rivers, they mostly saw curious *lagunas redondas*, the playas "as round as plates" in Castañeda's words.

The ocean metaphor also enabled the Spanish to take stock of their situation and to formulate a subsequent plan of action. The problem with El Turco's efforts to lead them astray was that his efforts worked only too well. He had guided them to the land of levelness and accomplished his first designated task. But the landscape quickly frustrated the Spanish. Their food dwindled with each day in the heart of the great mesa. Coronado's desire for results was growing. Camp skeptics may have wondered if the road to Quivira was going to be a repeat of the road to Cíbola: a tired army arriving to find no gold, but anxious to get mere food.

At this juncture the Spanish decided to act. Was it because of Ysopete's anger with El Turco? Juan de Jaramillo reported that after wandering for days on the Llano, Ysopete suddenly threw himself to the ground one morning, saying by signs that it were better the Spanish cut off his head than that they should proceed farther in the wrong direction, as El Turco was certainly taking them. Castañeda agreed that Ysopete had felt slighted by the Spanish; his advice was ignored, his guidance unwanted. Troubled by his guides' open quarreling, Coronado questioned El Turco intently. Early on, the Querecho camps had supposedly signed information about settlements, including a "Haxa," located to the east. But Ysopete's open recalcitrance now reinforced other feelings. Uncertainty gnawed at them as to their course, engendered perhaps by too many days on the plains. El Turco countered with the assertion that Haxa, a lavish settlement, "was one or two days away."

The nature of deception is such that both observer and deceiver are linked by trust. Despite daily evidence to the contrary, Coronado still wanted to believe in El Turco. The captain-general quickly became convinced that there was a rich kingdom somewhere; El Turco was living proof that his vision was true. The question was finding it. Maize supplies were dwindling to nothing. There were doubts in the camp. Were they lost? It was clearly time to send out a reconnaissance. The captain-general turned to the veteran Captain Diego López, a personal friend, for assistance at this crucial point.

The López reconnaissance marked a literal turning point on the Llano Road to Quivira. Coronado instructed his captain to take ten outriders and a guide, to proceed for two days on a course, then return to report news of settlements or any signs of them. At this point the ocean metaphor of the Llano enabled the Spanish to take stock of their situation and to formulate a plan. They needed a course as sailors at sea often need a course when out of sight of land. Their background familiarity with celestial navigation was now an important cosmographic asset. If they were astray on these plains, as at sea, they must return to celestial navigation, rather than invisible landmarks and arguing guides.

But what course could they take? The answer depends largely on the interpretation of Castañeda's Spanish. The old narrator was fond of ellipsis in his dictation or writing, or perhaps his hasty grammar left ambiguities behind. In any case, translating his prosaic text can be something of an art as well as a science. Consider the following translations and underscoring of a key passage:

Winship: The general sent Captain Diego Lopez with ten companions lightly equipped, and a guide to go toward the sunrise for two days . . . [and discover Haxa, and then return to meet the army, which set out in the same direction next day.]

Hammond and Rey: The general sent Captain Diego López ahead with ten companions, lightly equipped. He traced his direction toward the rising sun by means of a sea-compass, for he instructed him to travel with all speed for two days.[16]

The perceptual nature of what happened is vastly different from Winship to Hammond and Rey. Consider what Castañeda actually wrote in Spanish as it appears in the manuscript transcription in the Lennox collection of the New York Public Library along with a slightly revised English translation:

Castañeda: *el general embio adelante a el captian diego lopes a la ligera con diez compañeros dandole rumbo por una guia de mar hacia adonde salia el sol que caminase dos dias a toda prisesa . . .*

Revised: The general sent forward Captain Diego López lightly equipped with ten companions, striking a course by means of a sea-compass whither rises the sun, that they for two days at all speed . . .[17]

As correctly noted by Hammond and Rey, Castañeda's simple Spanish wording may point to an important perceptual nuance. Winship's "toward the sunrise" translation is easily interpreted as a euphemism for a general easterly course, a vague direction that constitutes another "zone of uncertainty." But perhaps what Castañeda, simple soldier that he was, wanted to say was that López literally followed a *"rumbo,"* a rhumb-line course familiar to sailors of the day. If Castañeda's semantics are to be believed, López's men had a sixteenth-century nautical compass of some kind for their orientation. Thus, the instrumentation of European science had arrived on the plains.

Like mariners lost in a calm, featureless sea of grassland, López and the main camp under Coronado were likely using *"salia el sol,"* or sunrise solar bearings to navigate their way out of this flatland wilderness. Guides in both camps could observe dawn and mark the course. A nautical compass would have been most useful, of course, in holding to the sunrise bearing throughout the day as the sun angles change rapidly. That both groups were using sunrise azimuth orientations is implied also by the necessity of reuniting. How else could López and Coronado meet again on the oceanic plains if their bearings were not identical? For López and his outriders the problem was complicated by the reverse leg of the reconnaissance. Proceeding toward a *salida del sol* bearing seems easier than following a reverse course away from it, especially if one has to reunite with the main camp proceeding toward you. Hence López's need for a nautical compass, *"una guia de mar"* said the text, to follow throughout the day a reverse course across a body of land as featureless as the Atlantic Ocean.

If, as has been proposed, the expedition was now in the northern middle-crossing of the Llano—somewhere in lower Hale County, Texas—then we can establish an approximate solar bearing followed by the expedition across this last stretch. Coronado's chronology indicates an approximate lapse of three and one half to four weeks after leaving Pecos Pueblo, putting López's reconnaissance near the last week of May.[18] Computer software is such these days that it is no trouble to calculate an accurate four-and-one-half centuries-old sunrise azimuth. For June 1, 1541, the McDonald Observatory suggests an azimuth of 61° 36' at sunrise for the coordinates of Hale County. This bearing means that the sun peeked above the horizon about 28° 24' north of due east at that time and place. A nautical compass or compasses would enable each group to roughly hold this approximate *rumbo* or rhumb-line during the day. In other words, both López and Coronado may well have traveled an agreed east-northeast course of about 61°, that is, well to the north of due east assumptions.

The day after López's departure the main camp followed his 61½° east-northeast course as well. Castañeda said they went *"por el mesmo rumbo"* ("by the same rhumb").[19] His use of the word *rumbo* suggests familiarity with the new nautical discourse common on Atlantic Ocean crossings. As such, his term may signify that a reasonably precise course was followed, one keyed to the instrumentation of the day. López's men, on their journey out, inadvertently mixed with and then stampeded a large bison herd. Once moving, the fleeing mass of buffalo could not stop when they encountered an arroyo. The bison quickly tumbled into this drainage feature (was there a small river nearby?), along with three Spanish horses swept up by the stampede. The arroyo soon filled with a churning mass of dying animals as the rest of the herd crossed over on the backs

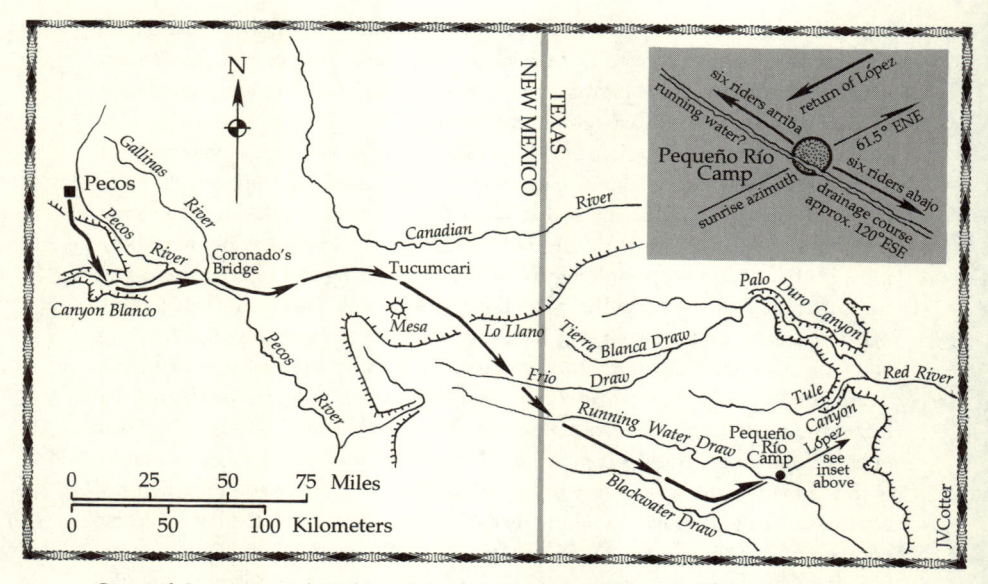

Coronado's reunion with Maldonado's reconnaissance force on the Llano depended heavily on a sea compass augmented by the riverine mud flats of the *Pequeño Río*. Map by John V. Cotter.

of the unfortunate beasts below. This incident of plains life was part of the marvelous nature of the region they were traversing.

On the third day after López's departure, the captain-general began to anticipate the return of his captain. Although the main camp advanced much more slowly than the light outriders, López was now on his reverse leg. That is, both groups were advancing toward each other; logically they could be expected to meet that day. But reuniting depended upon the care and accuracy of their mutual bearings and markers. Normally, the Spanish could dispatch flanking outriders from the main camp to "cut for sign" of López's returning men. But the tough, resilient, spring grasses of the Llano resisted their efforts at tracking. There were also a lot of bison trails leading hither and yon, like paths in a maze, but these were of little use as well.

Coronado's opportunity came that day with the appearance of an environmental landmark, one that gives a topographic clue to their approximate position on the Llano. Heading around 61° east-northeast the main camp reached and camped along the banks of a welcome *Pequeño Río*, Castañeda's "Small River."[20] Here they could get running water for themselves and their stock, rather than the bison-stirred, stagnant, hot waters of the upland playa terrain. Castañeda's word choice in describing this feature is significant. This was not an ordinary *río* in the sense of the "Rio de Tiguex" (Rio Grande) or the "Rio de

Cicúye" (Pecos River). The base flow of the Pequeño Río was much too small for that kind of identification. But still, in the context of the Llano drainage this feature presented definite riverine characteristics. For Castañeda, the linkage of language and landscape was an important struggle in his perception of the Southern High Plains. New lands demanded a new language.

In addition to a refreshing stopover at running water, the Pequeño Rio also provided a means to cut for sign of López. The Spanish dispatched six men upstream and six more went downstream. The logic was impeccable and adapted to the peculiar landscape. These search parties were to search "*por el rástro de los cauallos en las entradas o las salidas del rio*"—"for the tracks of the horses in the entrances or the exits of the river." They were to find López by scouring the muddy banks of the Pequeño Río looking for horsetracks at the crossings. This stratagem was necessary, as Castañeda noted, because the tough prairie grasses otherwise obscured their tracks. The Pequeño Río was ideal for cutting for sign as it constituted a rare riverine corridor on the plains. López's horsetracks would stand out conveniently in its muddy crossings like signposts of European presence in a bison world. Moreover, this small river likely crossed their east-northeast bearing at a very convenient angle, as the Llano drainages flow east-southeast around 120° (see page 52).

This intersecting watercourse is not, of course, an insignificant, nameless, ephemeral arroyo or draw, now lost to time. Castañeda's recognition and word choice imply a notable riverine environment in the fastness of the Llano, one undoubtedly still present in the modern landscape, however strangled or buried by modern civilization. Most of the surrounding Southern High Plains is so flat that ordinary rainfall has nowhere to drain off. So the late spring and early summer moisture mostly gathers in the mesa's 34,000 shallow surface depressions called *playas*. There are only a few developed drainage systems of any consequence in a land where even small rivers are rare. At which one of these drainages did Coronado camp? Along which watercourse did he dispatch search parties to look for López?

There are two principal candidates for the title of Pequeño Río, given a sunrise azimuth bearing of 61½° east-northeast. The northerly possibility is the Tule drainage of Swisher County, composed of the North, Middle, and South Tule Draws. Conceivably, Coronado could have encountered Middle Tule Draw, the largest of the three. The Middle Tule was formerly a lush, spring-fed, stream drainage system. Good springs issued from the Ogallala sands and Dockum sandstones, nourishing a winding ribbon of trees, vines, and shrubs along its course. Game of all types—bison, bear, antelope, deer, fish, turtles, prairie chickens, wild turkeys, and predators like wildcats, coyotes, and wolves—frequented the running waters and pools. Now withered and dry from heavy groundwater pumping, the Tule drainage is a pale shadow of its former hydrological glory.

The second and more likely possibility as Castañeda's Pequeño Rio is

Running Water Draw, the "Agua Corriente" of eighteenth-century New Mexican lore. This lengthy drainage rises in distant Curry County, New Mexico, and receives stochastic charges of surface runoff. But near the conjunction of Hale, Lamb, Castro, and Swisher Counties, a remarkable group of bluff springs once provided a strong, year-round baseflow for downstream Running Water Draw.[21] Flowing and bubbling from the southeast-dipping Ogallala sands and gravels, these springs in the vicinity of Edmondson, Texas, supported abundant habitat and wildlife. Southeast of this springland area, the flow of Running Water was indeed an *agua corriente* resembling in its brisk course a "small river." Indeed, the very briskness of the flow downstream of this *ojo de agua* source region was perceived and wedded into a later Hispano toponym: *Agua Corriente*, the stream of "running water." This linkage of language to landscape was a key piece of environmental perception by the comancheros and ciboleros of the late eighteenth century, but Castañeda's expression is no less a signifier.

Perhaps there is a natural progression of language and landscape, from Castañeda's "*pequeño río*" to a bison-lancer's "*Agua Corriente*" to a homesteader's "Running Water Draw." The stretch of Running Water Draw between Edmonson and the vicinity of Plainview, Texas, merits special attention for a Coronado Corridor. Following a *salida del sol* azimuth to the east-northeast, the main army would have almost certainly encountered this drainage feature in some form. Moreover, at this particular riverine location a mounted horseman is still many days' ride from the eastern edge of the Llano, or any native settlements remotely resembling El Turco's reputed city of Haxa. This location also implies that Captain Diego López's reconnaissance would have found only more of the same flatland beyond this stretch of small river.

The upstream search party of six men apparently rode past López's returning men that day. Nor did López see any traces of the others wandering up and down the Pequeño Rio as well. Two camp natives, "*en busca de fruta*" as Castañeda said, were scouting for the occasional, vitamin-C–rich plum thickets to be found in the draw.[22] These sharp-eyed *indios* discovered horsetracks crossing the Pequeño Río about three miles upstream from the main camp. The warriors followed the tracks quickly, found the missing captain, and guided a grateful López and his outriders downstream to the expedition camp on the Pequeño Río. Captain López delivered his scouting report personally to the captain-general. Castañeda later summarized the bad news, saying, "*que en ueinte leguas que auian andado no auian visto otra cosa sino vacas y cielo*" ("that in the twenty leagues they had traveled, they had not seen another thing except cows and sky").

Vacas y cielo! Only cows and sky. Was this not the very soul of the Cow Nation spoken of by Cabeza de Vaca, Bigotes, and Alvarado? After traveling over fifty miles, López had seen no evidence of any settlements. Remarkably, on the reverse leg of the scout he missed the main camp by only a league, a testimony to the crude accuracy of the nautical compass and the mutual faithfulness of both groups to the sunrise azimuth. López's disappointing news served only to discredit El Turco in the eyes of the skeptics. Castañeda related that at this point Ysopete's star began to rise. This bison-tattooed Wichita native of the Kansas plains had always said that El Turco lied. Ysopete knew Quivira was far to the north, but the Spanish had preferred the blandishments of his despised rival.

A concerned captain-general now dispatched one of his best friends for a further reconnaissance. Captain Rodrigo Maldonado and his company left the cool running waters of the Pequeño Río behind, and set out "*el cual camino,*" "on that same road," presumably the same 61½° east-northeast azimuth bearing as taken by López. Coronado trusted Maldonado to lead the advance guard, while the encumbered main army followed. Given the characteristic featurelessness of the plains east-northeast of the Plainview area, Maldonado's men attempted to mark their course by piling up mounds of dirt, bison dung, and whatever meager stones they could find at hand. Likely the nautical compass that served López accompanied them as well. Both groups would stay the "salia el sol" course for lack of an alternative.

From the area around Plainview, Texas, in the vicinity of Running Water Draw, a bearing of 61½° east-northeast crosses the playa-strewn terrain of northeast Hale County, cuts across the southeast corner of Swisher County, and then advances into the heart of Briscoe County. This azimuth effectively points Captain Maldonado's riders toward the steep escarpment country of the Briscoe County canyonlands, while outflanking the much lower relief escarpment to their due east. Castañeda relates that Maldonado took four days to reach the edge of the great mesa. In four days, the outriders could indeed reach these canyonlands. Delayed by animals, the necessity of hunting, and the slower pace of unmounted expedition members, the main body—the *real* or *campo*—probably averaged only seven leagues or eighteen miles a day. Both Coronado's letter and Fray Motolinia's later account suggest that Maldonado's men encountered a new tribe of bison hunters while on their course. These new nomads with tattooed eyes willingly led the advance guard back toward their modest rancheria settlement. In this manner, Captain Maldonado and his men at last encountered an edge to the Llano.

No one knows precisely which of the eastern canyons Maldonado suddenly rode upon. Castañeda's chronicle mentioned only a *barranca grande*, or large canyon, "*como las de colima*" ("like those of Colima") in Mexico.[23] In the headwaters of the Red River the flatland Llano suddenly and dramatically gives way to deep canyonlands along most of its northeastern edge, especially in Briscoe County. In parts of the north the Llano escarpment is a dizzy thousand feet higher than the flats far below. The incredible flatness of the plains above conceals the Briscoe canyons; only at the last moment do riders realize they are on the edge of an abyss.

Stopping at the caprock edge with their new hunter-guides, Maldonado and his escort surveyed colorful canyons that descended hundreds of feet to rough, scrubby flats and timbered headwater creeks far below. These eastern canyons had been patiently eroded by the headwaters of ancient Texas rivers like the Colorado, the Brazos, and especially the Red River. Along the northeast-facing escarpment in Briscoe County there were many cool and surprisingly verdant canyons. Powerful discharge springs poured through these fantastic canyonlands, their tumbling cascades ringing in the canyons. These waters nourished excellent habitat for bear, deer, buffalo, antelope, and numerous birds. Besides an abundant wildlife, Captain Maldonado found something even more important to Coronado: camps of a new tribe of native people.

Following Maldonado's scouts, Coronado rode ahead and the main army, allies, and porters trudged after him across the apparently endless Llano. They encountered the great edge in the same order as they marched, in tired variable groups and weary processions. They descended into the Barranca Grande in early June of 1541, somehow managing the artillery carts, and using their human porters to shift other loads. Which canyon they entered is still a great mystery. Was it part of Palo Duro, Cañoncito, Tule, or Quitaque? Or, increasingly less likely, was it Las Lenguas, Blanco, Yellow House, or even one of the canyons much farther south? A prestigious researcher can be cited for almost any of these canyons.[24] But the semiotic evidence points to the headwater canyons of the Red River drainage in Briscoe County. The general area around Tule Canyon, not far from present Silverton or Quitaque, Texas, would be a good choice for entering into Barranca Grande country.

Led by native guides, Maldonado's *abanguardia* followed an old bison trail down the steep-sided canyon. The scenery was spectacular during the long descent and the going was rough. But the sense of reaching some kind of human destination would have spurred them on. Once on the bottom the expectant conquistadors followed the tattooed native hunters back to the smoky fires and noisy camps of a large nearby rancheria. Favored camp locations were along or near brisk streams, many headed by springs gushing from the foot of the great escarpment. Where these streams poured into larger drainages, such as the Prairie Dog Town Fork of the Red River, the combination of wood, water, and food were particularly pleasant. These fringing woods were cool and shady in the increasingly hot afternoons. The native hunters almost certainly had sent a runner ahead warning of the arrival of alien guests, and the camp dogs— inflamed by the new scents—would have announced their immediate presence.

Later chronicles give the impression that news of Europeans had preceded Maldonado's arrival in the Red River canyonlands. It is likely that Cabeza de Vaca's miraculous procession only six years earlier to the south was known to some if not many. The strange appearance of the Europeans—the bearded countenances, the bizarre clothing—created interest and awe of course. But for sheer excitement there was now a novelty missing from the earlier accounts of the Children of the Sun: huge, powerful, four-limbed animals with immense angular heads. The sight of Spanish horses was something to stir the mind of these plains hunters. Like the other roaming nomads, the new natives were quite adept at sign language, although the Spanish quickly discovered that these natives were enemies to the Querecho. After Captain Maldonado and his men dismounted and rested, the *naturales* or natives gathered at a spot in the encampment where elders ceremoniously presented Captain Maldonado with a large pile of soft, tanned, bison robes. Despite careful Spanish scrutiny, no gold, silver, or jewels were seen. Indeed, the pile of bison robes seemed to be the only sign of wealth.

After four days of riding, Maldonado's men looked forward to eating and resting in the friendly rancheria. Unlike the standoffish Querechos, these newcomers were good hosts. A few unfortunate soldiers were dispatched back to report to Coronado. These riders retraced their ascent of the great mesaland and located their crude markers of stones and dried bison dung. Piled up into mounds during their outbound course, they could follow this rude course in reverse even as the main camp lumbered toward them, eyes straining to discern the small piles of rocks and manure marking the way. As auguries, however, the markers were most inauspicious. A few stones and plenty of dry manure—were these the signs of a road to wealth?

The reunion of Maldonado's messengers with the main expedition brought welcome news of a sizable native encampment, one close to firewood and good running water. As the news made its way through the procession there was the inevitable speculation. For the three Franciscan priests there was the possibility of proselytizing new natives. For the captains there was the hope that reliable news of Quivira and its supposed wealth could be obtained finally. For many others the thought of running water and trees was enough to quicken their steps. Renewed with purpose, the army followed the crude trail markers and guides, at last to arrive at the great *bordo* or edge of the plains. They could see they were on the edge of an immense escarpment. Below them stretched a panorama of canyonland country.

· 5 ·

IN SEARCH OF CONA

To fit the all-but-ancient story of Francisco Vasquez de Coronado to the modern map of Texas involves a type of detective work almost without a parallel. If one unravels the case, there is no criminal to break down and confess. If one touches basic truth toward a correct solution, there is no ancient jurist who can come back across four centuries and lend a knowing nod.

J. W. WILLIAMS, *Old Texas Trails* (1979)

I shall undertake to show that the routes proposed by previous historians are clearly impossible . . .

DAVID DONOGHUE, "The Route of the Coronado Expedition in Texas" (1929)

"*Yllego a una barranca grande como las de colima*" (and so the camp came to a great barranca like those of Colima), wrote Pedro de Castañeda. The chronicler's choice of geographic comparison is of special interest. Geologically, the Colima state district of western Mexico is quite different from the Llano. There the terrain is marked by volcanism, deep subterranean fires that shaped the regional high plateaus and fertile soils. Vegetation is much more lush, but the traveler coming suddenly to the edge of the Colima high plateaus shares with a traveler at the edge of the Llano the prospect of perilous descents into steep-sided *barrancas* or ravines. The earth seems to open up in a new dimension—beneath your feet—as you survey the dizzying panoramas beyond and below.

The chronicles are silent on Coronado's actions at the eastern *bordo* or edge. There is not the slightest word to indicate an aesthetic appreciation of the view. Despite this lack of evidence, the most enduring twentieth-century image of the expedition in Texas is precisely a romantic, mythical vision of Coronado, his Spanish captains, a priest, and El Turco (sometimes already in chains), all pausing at the eastern edge to admire spectacular canyon scenery. Regional artists have long seized on this hypothetical landscape as a suitable subject for paintings and illustrations. Indeed, the artistic apotheosis of Coronado's discovery of the Barranca Grande presents a problem for the trail detective. Artists naturally lean toward spectacular backdrops, and thus the traditional chosen locale for Coronado's discovery of canyonlands has been a romanticized perspective of the local—and beautiful—Palo Duro State Park.

One wants to believe in such a mythic moment because of its linkage of past to present. Numerous illustrations suggest that Coronado and his followers were not that dissimilar from the tourists of today. The message is that the designated scenic landscape of the twentieth century must have also attracted the admiration of the sixteenth-century Europeans. From a local booster perspective this vision is indeed reassuring, and so several generations of brochures, paintings, magazine illustrations, and the like have all but convinced most residents of the Panhandle and elsewhere that Coronado stopped at a picturesque Palo Duro State Park overlook to admire the scenery.[1]

It is a nice romantic vision to see the view that apparently entranced the first Europeans in this part of Texas. We pause to view the painting of Coronado pausing to admire the view. But there is no evidence as to whether this epiphany ever happened. He could equally have been irritable, bored, or nervous about the necessity of descent. "To the sensibilities of most sixteenth-century Europeans," a historian writes on Coronado's patrol at the Grand Canyon, "unbridled wilderness holds little aesthetic appeal."[2] Analysis of the narratives leads me to believe that Coronado was *not* within the boundaries of Palo Duro State Park. Most likely he was many miles away, at the escarpment edge around Tule Canyon or even farther east in Briscoe County. The modern regional preoccupation with placing Coronado's entrada within the present state park sometimes assumes ridiculous proportions. A women's club in Canyon, Texas, once sought the advice of historians at West Texas State University on Coronado's route. The women had heard the expedition passed through Canyon on its way to the nearby state park, but they needed to know *the exact street* downtown in order to place a commemorative marker along the main highway. They wanted to be honest in their geography while still enticing the traveler into a detour.

A number of mythic geographies have attached themselves to the expedition.[3] European cosmographers, sensitive to exotic words, adopted the Wichita *Quivira* as an important signifier for their maps in the 1560s, about the time Castañeda was writing his narrative at Culiacán. Actual place-names like Quivira, Cicúye, Tiguex, Rio de las Palmas, Rio de Tiguex, and a few others also began appearing on European maps. The relationship of these words to their actual geographic location was completely fluid. Quivira quickly drifted to the West Coast of North America, and Cicúye—the gateway to the Llano—followed. For better or worse, it was the Dutch geographers of the sixteenth century who vaguely sketched the land between Cicúye and Quivira. In Ortelius's great 1564 map, "Orbis Terrarum," the proximate location of the Llano was on the coast of California near modern Los Angeles. The actual relationship of words and their illustrative colored towns to the physical reality of North America strikes us as completely erroneous. But for the great cosmographers of the late sixteenth century, language was part of the display of visual information. They charted toponyms as well as coastlines, with gradually improving results for both.

Local myths of the Coronado expedition show a similar fluid basis between language and reality. The linkage of Coronado's name to Palo Duro State Park began in earnest with the early park improvements of the 1930s. Depression-era Civilian Conservation Corps crews built "El [sic] Coronado Lodge" in 1934 on the scenic north rim of Timbercreek Canyon. Later in the 1930s a "Coronado Trail" was popular as a bridle path. Like the first Europeans, locals and tourists rode weary horses down a scenic trail into Timbercreek Canyon, along the bottom to Sunday Canyon, and from there to the strangely compelling phallic formation known as the Lighthouse. Later a "Coronado Visitor Center" deepened the guilt-by-association between the expedition and the displayed state park landscape. In regional art and place-names the presence of Coronado lives on in Palo Duro State Park whether he was there or not. This gentle geosophy reminds us that language creates the cultural landscape. Just as the global Dutch filled their blank spaces with legendary names, so does the local booster. Language is the stuff of legends, old and modern.

The actual arrival of Coronado's *campo* into the canyon flat rancheria was remembered less for its romantic grandeur than for its gratuitous greed. Pedro de Castañeda recalled an ignoble scene after the captain-general inspected the large pile of bison robes. Conquistadors gradually began to claim shares of this meager wealth, exciting the possessive wrath of others. Soon a wild scramble developed as soldiers ignored decorum and looters grabbed what they could take. Bearded toughs seizing Amerindian property is not a romantic concept for a post office mural, but it is accurate historically. This behavior was in stark contrast to the ministrations and selflessness of Cabeza de Vaca's party. "We coveted nothing but gave whatever we were given," Cabeza de Vaca had written. Castañeda captured the surprise and concern of the native women that their prized robes were unceremoniously seized by the newcomers:

> The women and some others were left crying because they believed the strangers were not going to take anything, but instead would bless them as Cabeza de Vaca and Dorantes had done when they passed by there.[4]

This statement has the ring of truth in several respects. Quite likely this new tribe of natives had anticipated that the Europeans would merely bless these precious articles, and then benignly redistribute them back to their owners. If so their disappointment would have been keen and sudden as the common expeditioners snatched and scrambled over the skins like wolves. That the Spanish would covet property and keep the offering was an unexpected affront. But their awesome horses, numbers, and weapons kept the natives' anger in check.

Down on the lower canyon flats of the Barranca Grande the Europeans and their horde made camp near the rancheria. The two groups intermingled, using their hands to communicate. Their quest for the gold of Quivira led officers to gently interrogate *los naturales* by means of their guides' ubiquitous sign language. These people clearly differed from the neighboring Apachean Querechos of the flat plains. Their language was Teya, a Uto-Aztecan derived tongue with important associations to the Tompiro of the Salinas Pueblos. They were likely the results of ancient Tanoans pushing southeast into the Rio Abajo country below Albuquerque. Some of these ancestors, a group known as the Piro, diffused eastward from the Rio Grande to the Pecos River frontier, becoming the Tompiro. And some of these Pecos frontiersmen continued eastward, became avid bison-hunters, moved onto the Llano, exploited the herds, traded widely and freely, and eventually settled in the transcultural lush eastern canyons where they became the protohistoric Teya. A half-century after Coronado they became the well-known Jumanos of later history.[5] Like the Querechos, these friendly people hunted buffalo on foot. Distinctive tattoos from cuts filled with charcoal decorated their eyes and chins. They also gathered wild plants and fruits, and they likely retained some ancestral agricultural traits, cultivating small garden plots of beans for instance, although Castañeda remembered no maize fields. They were called "*Teyas,*" the first recognizable appearance, some say, of the word "Texas."[6]

Castañeda intrigues us with the ambiguity of the very name for Texas. He says these people used the name of Teyas as something of a warning about their valiant nature. They were called Teyas, "*por gentes valiéntes como diçen los mexicanos chichimecas o teules porque los teyas que el campo topo puesto que eran valientes*" (as a sign of a valiant people, as the Mexicans say Chichimecs or *Teules* [fierce gods], because the Teyas that the camp met in that place were brave). Rather than suggesting the traditional "friends" or "allies" of the agrarian East Texas Caddoans, this chronicler suggests it was a warning of power—"Tough Guys" or "Don't Mess With Teyas."[7]

Mingling with this tribe, the Spanish were intrigued by two encounters. An older Teya women in the camp was an albino. Her pale white skin attracted their curious and perhaps unwanted attention. She bore a fanciful resemblance to a Castilian lady, Castañeda thought, even as her facial tattoos marked her clearly as something other than a "lost Christian." Also of interest, there was a Teya elder who signed that he had once seen other Europeans. The old native was blind now, but he claimed to see in his memory the four "Children of the Sun." The Spanish following his account interpreted his signs to refer to

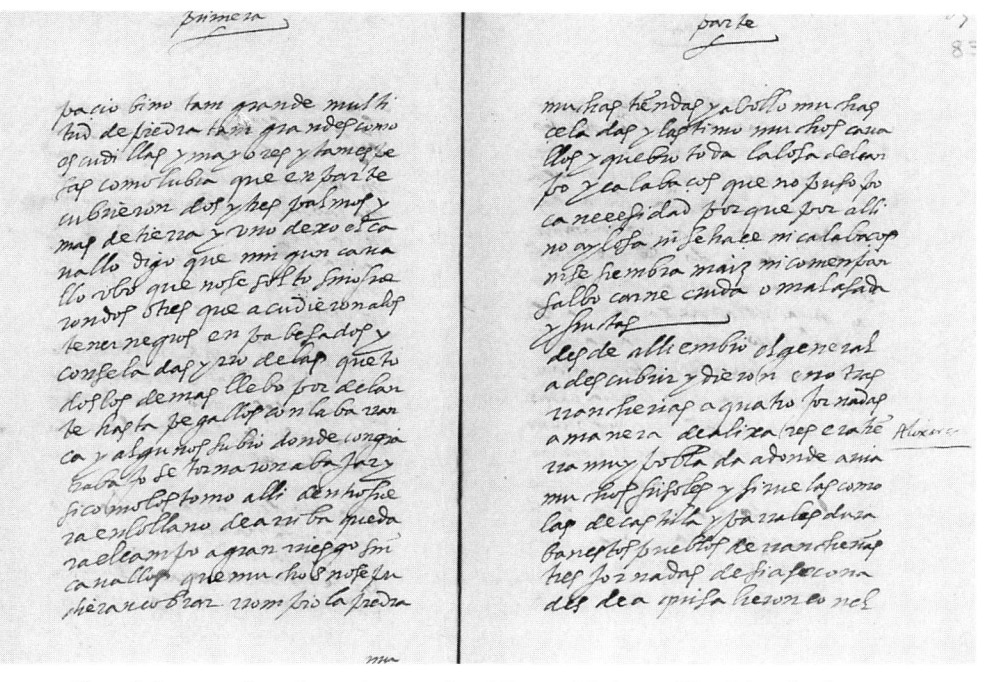

These facing pages from the 1596 manuscript of Castañeda's ch. 20 of Part I describe the West Texas hailstorm that smashed Coronado's barranca camp. Grateful that their horses were not scattered on "lo llano," the narrator goes on to mention news of a populous land called "cona." Note the copyist's marginal "Alexeres." *Courtesy Rich Collection (#63), Rare Books and Manuscripts Division, New York Public Library, Astor, Lenox and Tilden Foundations.*

Cabeza de Vaca and his three companions. Jaramillo claimed reasonably that this elder had seen the castaways further to the south, an observation in remarkable accordance with the geography.[8]

After their exertions and anxieties in crossing the immense plain above, the expedition was ready for a good rest. There were bellies to fill with native foodstuffs, horses to graze, and trail-sore muscles to relax. But late spring can be a tempestuous time in the Texas Panhandle. The collision of weak cold fronts with a jet stream migrating northward on its annual pilgrimage often occurs in this region in late May and June. At the dry-line boundary, cool dense air flowing across and pouring off the Llano sweeps underneath advancing, warm, moisture-laden air. As the warm moist air is forced aloft, massive quantities of water vapor condense into living processions of thunderclouds. The sight of a late-spring storm forming in the troposphere above these canyonlands is magnificent, to say the least. "Canyons, escarpment, and prevailing winds make the Llano Estacado edge the great tornado-spawning ground of the Southern

Plains," writes the historian Dan Flores.[9] Violent storm-cell formation builds towering masses of cumulonimbus clouds, many reaching ethereal heights. Within hours one of these supercells can build itself almost twice the height of Mount Everest, providing a startling extension of the vertical dimension to the sky above the canyons, in contrast to the monotony of horizontal plains.

Out on the plain vision is so unrestricted that it is possible to watch four or five separate remote cells, storming off in the distance. Inside these thunderstorms violent updrafts gather water droplets, take them repeatedly to freezing heights, and layer by layer, build up a load of hail. The entrada had only been resting a few days in the Barranca Grande when just such a massive June thunderstorm blew up. The eighteenth-century scholar Mota Padilla says the storm struck the conquistador camp at three o'clock in the afternoon.[10] This *torbellino* or tempest sent everyone scurrying for cover as high winds initially tore through the camp. Reverberations of thunder echoed off canyon walls and thick sheets of rain lashed the hundreds of men, women, and children. Suddenly a hard and violent hailstreak struck the camp.

The memory of a West Texas hailstorm lingers in the mind because it is so elemental. Castañeda wrote of the experience as an ordeal, even beginning Chapter XX with his account of how *piedras grandes*, great stones, struck the army. His eyewitness testimony is again a credit to keen environmental perception. The storm began in the afternoon as a *grandissimo ayre* (terrific wind) followed by heavy rain. Hailstones "as big as bowls and larger" soon fell on them. The torrents of hail proved "as thick as raindrops." A severe hail-streak does indeed contain sizable quantities of hail, and individual hailstones may be enormous and dangerous—up to six inches thick. The bouncing hailstones piled up on the ground until the barranca flats were cloaked with their icy whiteness. In places the hail piled up "two and three and even more spans," remembered Castañeda.[11] Tents were smashed, Spanish armor and headpieces battered, and much of the entrada's everyday crockery hopelessly shattered.

Maddened by the onslaught, most of the expedition horses bolted for better cover, stampeding toward the steep canyon walls of the barranca in an effort to escape the incessant blows. Servants attempted to protect and restrain some of the horses by holding shields over their heads. As the fearful storm finally passed, the Europeans emerged from cover to survey the damage. A number of the army tents were torn. The loss of the earthenware pots, bowls, and cups was an important irritation, as these and the better majolica utensils could not be replaced. By great fortune most of the panicked horses were confined by the steep-sided barranca walls and could therefore be recovered. A few had scrambled onto such remote heights that the trembling animals were turned around and led down only with difficulty. Castañeda thought it had been a close call. If the army had been caught by the hail-streak "*fuera en lo llano*" (out on the llano), their horses would have bolted and scattered to the four corners, possibly never to be seen again.[12]

Amazed that they had survived such a fearful storm with no loss of life, the captain-general requested the Franciscan priests to hold a special mass. The next day, around June 4, 1541, the army gathered before Fray Padilla and Fray Antonio de Castilblanco to offer their Thanksgiving prayers to God. Thus it passed that eighty years before the misrouted Pilgrims of Massachusetts gave thanks in the fall of 1621, the misrouted Spanish had given their own special Thanksgiving to God for his protection from the violent weather of West Texas. Shortly after this mass, many historians believe, Coronado called a council of war to determine their future course. Meeting on the Feast day of the Ascension of Our Lord (June 5, 1541), the council agreed that Coronado and a small chosen group would reconnoiter Quivira. The vast bulk of the army would gather provisions and return to the Rio Grande pueblos.[13]

Even while resting in this *primera barranca*, said Mota Padilla, Coronado sought out adjacent populous settlements. Undoubtedly he questioned Teya leaders closely, hoping against hope to hear word that the rich kingdom of Quivira was nearby. There was also El Turco's supposed kingdom of "Haxa" or "Harahe," also said to be close. Coronado also may have hoped to find *Cristianos perdidos* (lost Christians), possibly even survivors of the Narváez expedition still held in captivity. The Spanish historian Antonio de Herrera suggested that rumors of lost Christians impelled Coronado to draft letters of arrival and greetings, which were dispatched with the outriders exploring the surrounding country.[14]

No one knows where these outriders ranged. They may have explored the four compass points, or they may have followed the gestures of the Teyas. To their west stretched the extensive Palo Duro Canyon system, with its steep-sided, colorful canyons, screaming eagles, and dense breaks. A rider could follow the winding course of the Prairie Dog Town Fork of the Red River for many leagues. To their north was more escarpment country, not only the other side of the Palo Duro system but also the broken terrain of Mulberry Creek. Beyond lay another flatland spur of lo llano before one encountered new ravines and canyons sloping down to a large river. To their east lay a succession of scrubby plains, less flat and dissected with numerous erosional tributaries feeding the Red River. And to their south?

Once more the crucial passage is in Castañeda's narrative:

> *desde alli embio el general a descubrir y dieron en otras rancherias a quatro jornadas a manera de alijares era tierra muy poblada adonde auia muchos frisoles y siruelas como las de castilla y parrales duraban estos pueblos de rancherias tres jornadas desiase cona.*

From here [first barranca] the captain-general sent out [riders] to reconnoitre, and they reported on other rancherias. At four days journey by way of the badlands was a very populous land whither were many beans and plums like those of Castile and wild vineyards. These settlements of rancherias stretched for three days journey. It was called Cona.[15]

This terse entry is the first mention of Cona, the most important geographical place-name in Texas connected to the expedition. Clearly the location of this mysterious Cona is also central to an understanding of a Coronado Corridor. Unfortunately, Castañeda's remarks are elliptical and subject to interpretation. Winship and his later editors had particular trouble with the key phrase *"a quatro jornadas a manera de alixares,"* an issue of environmental semantics that we will turn to later. For now, the question is: whither Cona? In which direction lay this populous land of beans, plums, and grapes?

The search for Cona has preoccupied a fine assortment of talented citizens and scholars. Texas millionaires, distinguished regional historians, kindly scientists, and peaceable retirees alike have all read the evidence, reached a verdict, and quarreled ever after. They are the trail detectives of the Llano Estacado. The solution perhaps was easier for some because they knew in advance where they expected Coronado to go. In his finely researched book, *Coronado, Knight of Pueblos and Plains* (1949), the historian Herbert E. Bolton simply advanced the army from Tule Canyon to the west-northwest, deeper into the cloistral sixty-mile-long Palo Duro Canyon system, until the abutments gradually soar nearly a thousand feet high within the contemporary state park boundaries. Referring to a chronicle account of this second barranca or *barranca de los llanos*,[16] Bolton commented that Palo Duro Canyon, "now a State Park, was and is *par excellence*, the 'Barranca of the Plains.'"[17] The eminent geographer Carl O. Sauer followed Bolton's lead in this crucial matter.[18]

But Bolton's estimation of Castañeda's environmental semantics is most debatable.[19] Indeed, one wonders why so many people assume that the Coronado expedition used the same picnic spots as present day-trippers do. What is known—and the accounts all agree on the result—is that the entire entrada packed up and left the Barranca Grande or "first barranca" as it is often called. After some four days of travel they reached another ravine, *"una postrera barranca"* or *barranca de los llanos*, where they settled in for several weeks of recuperation. From here Coronado and thirty men set out on a long march to Quivira itself, while the rest of the army prepared for a grueling return back across *lo llano*. But which direction did they take to Cona?

Most of the present and past trail detectives turn the entrada south, but north, east, and west courses also have their supporters. The texts are silent on this fundamental geographic point except for the *Relación del Suceso* which notes the army "proceeded 150 leagues, 100 to the east and 50 to the south [or 'southeast' in the Munoz copy]"[20] Usually this remark is taken as a general southeasterly drift, but a literalist could argue the point. Bolton thought they strategically moved to the northwest, deeper into the fastness of Palo Duro Canyon.

Perhaps this would lessen the distance between them and Quivira. Why should the Spanish go south when their suspicions and interrogations said Quivira was to the north?

The most compelling circumstance was the absolute necessity of feeding some 1,800 people—hundreds of conquistadors and servants, the thousand or so Mexican allies, and the hundreds of new captives taken from the upper Rio Grande pueblos. As noted earlier, the expedition spatially concentrated their hunger, unlike the bands of roving Querechos who dispersed their food gathering activities. Coronado and his captains had to provide some three or more *tons* of food every day for the many mouths of the army. Feeding all the soldiers, priests, African servants, native allies, herders, women, and children was a staggering logistical problem, not to mention the needs of the horses, mules, dogs, and diminishing livestock. Maize for the horses was in extremely short supply as the Barranca Grande Teyas planted no corn. In this light, Castañeda's coda to the announcement of Cona is relevant: "where there were many beans and plums . . . and wild vineyards." That is, Cona was memorable not for its sheer, towering, picturesque canyon vistas but rather for its abundance of seasonal foodstuffs. Perhaps the search for Cona involves not grand scenery but simple comestibles.[21]

The conjunction of memory, experience, and food, I believe, is the key to Cona's location. After their weeks on *lo llano* the Spanish army was now marching on its stomach. Castañeda dwells, lingers even, on the food resources of this special place. Considering that a steady diet of bison meat might be proving monotonous, there is a sense that Cona is remembered through the palate as much as anything. Like Marcel Proust's *Remembrance of Things Past*, our narrator's memory is stimulated by the fond recollection of exotic smells and tastes encountered in this land.[22] There is both a strategic and a mnemonic connection between Cona, Coronado, and food in the Texas Panhandle. The strategic question is not where does a huge expedition *wish* to go after crossing the dreaded plains, but where do they *have* to go to survive? Like locusts, their very numbers could quickly eat a regular Teya rancheria out of tent and home. They could disperse into small, foraging bands like the roaming nomads, but this would disintegrate all their power and purpose. It was best to keep together and find the largest and closest supply of food while the leaders thought things over.

The mnemonic connection of Cona to food is made by Castañeda's memory. In writing his narrative twenty years later, he drew heavily on reconstructive memory, which in turn draws on personal experiences. The most important associative factors of Cona for Pedro de Castañeda were its nutritional resources. In his long, introductory paragraph on Cona, over 40 percent of the text is directly related to food, its quality, and its procurement. Indeed, in Cona the Europeans came closest to dwelling in the land of Teyas. If food was a critical concern, then so too was the growing season. As the sun's warmth sweeps northward in early summer, an advancing front of seasonal ripening occurs. By advancing to the south the entrada stood a better chance of gaining on the seasonal maturation of vitamin-rich fruits in particular. A journey of *quatro jornadas*, or four days, at an average of seven leagues a day, is a gain on the growing season of about seventy miles—a small but strategic advantage to hungry men and their dependents.

At this point we are properly within the province of the many "trail detectives" who have sought and found Coronado's Cona over the past 150 years. Like finding gold from the Lost Dutchman's Mine, both professionals and amateurs have struck it lucky at locating Cona—in about a dozen places in two states over three hundred miles of plains, canyons, and river bottoms. Sites from the North Canadian River all the way down to the Concho River have serious supporters, elaborate computations of trail distances, and plenty of legalistic logic.[23] Winship favored distant Colorado River drainages. David Donoghue, sure that Coronado never left the Llano Estacado, put Quivira in the Canadian River breaks much farther south. The famous geologist-millionaire-collector Everett Lee DeGolyer of Dallas saw Cona in the drainages east of Yellow House Draw. The distinguished historian Herbert E. Bolton was convinced, of course, that Cona was the upper chasm of Palo Duro Canyon. Abilene attorney R. M. Wagstaff naturally found Cona just south of Abilene, on the pleasant banks of Elm Fork of the Brazos River. Some trail detectives have more scholarly credentials than others, but it is still basically a frontier, where the measure of a theory is the measure of a person's close relationship to the land.

One of the most dogged of the trail detectives in the search for Cona was a modest high school mathematics teacher named J. W. Williams. Williams taught at Wichita Falls Senior High School from the 1920s to the 1950s, but his consuming interest was tracing old, lost Southwestern trails across present-day Texas. His articles on Coronado, Moscoso, and many other trailblazers were later collected and published as *Old Texas Trails*.[24] Although many of Williams's suppositions on the Coronado expedition are controversial, there is no doubt of the passionate interest he took in correlating Castañeda's ecological description of Cona with the twentieth-century biogeography of the Southern Plains. Over many years he corresponded with pioneers and other local residents in the ceaseless search for detailed information on the extent and range of fruits—and especially pecan trees—in the plains region. Williams's environmental perspective was ahead of its time for amateur historians. As his evidence grew, so also did his convictions.

By 1959 Williams was sure that Cona was on a verdant stretch of the North Concho River, nestled among the shady pecan bottoms northwest of San Angelo, Texas. His reasoning was intently ecological and keyed to his interpretation of Castañeda's additional reference to *nueses* or nuts in the second barranca. For Williams these "nueses" could only refer to pecan trees, and he asked "What is the evidence?"

Simply it is this: Coronado reached the pecan country—and native pecans do not grow in Palo Duro Canyon, or Tule, or Quitaque, or in any of the canyons to the south or, with one minor exception, in any of the counties that border these canyons on the east. Coronado had to journey beyond the High Plains to reach the pecan country.[25]

Many of Williams's observations on the environmental parameters of Cona—the presence of grapes, ripening cycles, and nuts—do bear strong consideration, even though he takes Coronado on an exceedingly long, needless, and improbable journey far to the south. But his biogeographical arguments, or "elegant horticultural insights," were critical in persuading another perspicacious trail detective, former U.S. Secretary of the Interior Stewart L. Udall, that Cona was perhaps best located in Sterling County on the banks of the North Concho River.

Udall's sensitive, original, and beautiful book, *To The Inland Empire: Coronado and Our Spanish Legacy* (1987), gives a flattering presentation of Williams's thesis on the geographic location of Cona.[26] Udall can claim his expertise in Coronadoan studies honestly, as a true and great son of the Greater Southwest. Yet even Udall has problems in reconciling the obvious incompatibilities among what he called "The Texas Route Mysteries." Despite qualms he finally came down on the side of Williams's Coronado Trail to the North Concho River:

> ...no one has disputed the conclusions [Williams] developed while he was sleuthing in the bushes, although his site on the North Concho tributary of the Colorado River is more comparable to an arroyo or a valle than a barranca. Yet if Williams' evidence is irrefutable, it is obvious that he knocked Herbert Bolton's Texas trail thesis into a ten-gallon hat: he disqualified Tule and Palo Duro canyons as the two historic barrancas; he established that the Spaniards were not only led off the Llano but actually entered the valley of the North Concho River (a tributary of Cabeza de Vaca's "river of nuts") and intersected the path followed by De Vaca six years earlier.[27]

For Udall, the "obvious mistake" made by Williams was at the conclusion of his article when he asserted that the first barranca was at Quitaque Canyon, some two hundred miles north of the San Angelo area. The correct solution should be, therefore, to move the first barranca south, toward the North Concho.

It would be easier of course to move Cona north out of the Concho Valley, toward the Briscoe County canyonlands between Tule and Quitaque, because that is where the expedition now was. Williams's biogeography was interesting but based on the early-twentieth-century record and not the mid-sixteenth-century record, with its different climate and successional vegetation. Who is to say that Yellow House Canyon did not have pecan trees in the 1540s? Williams's model assumes ecological stability over almost 400 years—an unlikely assumption. Even worse, the 200-mile distance between his first barranca and Cona is simply too long. It is the equivalent of a great trek, not a strategic move to nearby food resources. Could an outrider ride 200 miles to find Williams's Cona, explore its opportunity, and then return to the main camp in the Barranca Grande within the short time frame allowed before the army moved? These and other objections limit the utility of Williams's thesis, just as they do that of Bolton and most of the other researchers.

By now most people find themselves increasingly confused as to the First Barranca or *barranca grande*, and the Second Barranca or *barranca postrera*—"the last ravine." Bolton also referred to the second barranca as the *barranca de los llanos*, but it is usually known by its *Cona* toponym. Sometimes only the word *barranca* appears in the texts, and context alone determines which one of the two is being referenced. It may help to understand the confusion by plotting the various contending hypotheses. A practical field guide to the Coronado trail detectives and their geographic choices is presented in Table 1.[28]

TABLE 1
TRAIL DETECTIVES OF THE CORONADO ENTRADA

Advocate	*Profession*	*First Barranca*	*Second Barranca/Cona*
Herbert E. Bolton	Historian	Tule Canyon	Palo Duro State Park
A. Grove Day	English Professor	East Escarpment	Elm Creek /Brazos River
E. DeGolyer	Geologist/Collector	Yellow House Canyon	Rolling Plains East
David Donoghue	Geologist	Palo Duro Canyon	Tule Canyon
Frederick W. Hodge	Ethnographer	Blanco Canyon	Colorado River
W. C. Holden	Historian	Lake /Yellow House Canyon	Blanco Canyon
Carl O. Sauer	Geographer	Tule Canyon	Palo Duro Canyon
Albert H. Schroeder	Historian	Canadian River (Kansas)	Canadian River (Kansas)
J. H. Simpson	Army Officer		
Stewart Udall	Politician	Colorado River uplands	North Concho
Waldo R. Wedel	Archeologist	Yellow House Canyon	Blanco Canyon
J. W. Williams	Math Teacher	Quitaque Canyon	N. Concho/Sterling Co.
G. P. Winship	Librarian	Colorado River	Colorado River/ Coleman Co.

With so many suitors and rivals to correct, it is probably easier just to find the right path out of this maze than to find and note all the errors in the list of Cona candidates. Indeed, most of the hypotheses must be wrong for the few to be correct. Again it behooves us to turn to the environmental semantics of the texts themselves for answers. It is likely no accident that Pedro de Castañeda dwells on the tastes of Cona. His personal experience of the land of the Teyas was about the search for food. His casual remarks strongly imply that Cona was a favored environment, one rich in plant and animal foods. Cona must also be a logical place, like Sonora's settlement of Corazones, to take some 1,800 hearty appetites to survive for more than the next few days.

Coronado had similar logistical problems after the inglorious conquest of Cíbola. There he quickly dispatched scouts to reconnoiter the territory. In this manner Captain Alvarado found the pueblos of Tiguex, with their quantities of food and stores, a magnet for the possessive Spanish army. Supporting themselves on the stored protein of the dispossessed puebloans enabled the Spanish to conquer the fertile valley of the upper Rio Grande. Now in the canyons of the northeastern Llano they must seize a parallel opportunity: to quickly find a nutritional environment of wild and domesticated plant and animal foods, one capable of supporting a large concentration of people. Like Tiguex it would be a populous realm because the natives would also gather and concentrate to exploit the resources. Quivira could be located and investigated later, once an adequate and close base of operations had been located. The strategic requirements are clear: Cona needs to be close, about four days away (thirty to thirty-five leagues, or sixty-five to seventy-five miles), well-watered, with good timber, populous, rich in wild foods, and likely raising a few domesticated plants. It would be best if found to the south in order to intersect the earlier ripening cycles of fruits.

The question is, starting from the Briscoe County canyonlands, where do some 1,800 or more people first go if they are to live off the land and native food procurements? For Coronado, word of Cona must have sounded like word of Tiguex, a further base of operations in the quest for gold and wealth. His outriders may have carried messages for "lost Christians," but they assessed native food stores in their travels with an eye to the "live Christians" left behind. The key to locating Cona lies in correlating the hermeneutics of the Spanish accounts with the present landscape. Perhaps the best approach is to re-experience the expedition narrative, to rediscover the fullest meaning of Castañeda's environmental semantics. The journey begins with a scout's discovery of populous rancherias *"a quatro jornadas a manera de alixares."*

There has never been a satisfactory interpretation of the Lennox manuscript phrase *a manera de alixares* despite its obvious and crucial significance. George Parker Winship spelled it *alijares* and dodged the problem in a rare moment of translation ellipsis—"and they found another settlement four days from there . . . "—the ellipsis followed by his explanatory footnote: *"A manera de alijares*. The margin reads Alexeres, which I cannot find in the atlases. The word means threshing floor, whence Ternaux-Compans: 'autres cabanes semblables a des bruyeres (alixares).'"[29] Hammond and Rey's translation is little better: "After four days they came to other rancherias resembling *alixares*," with a footnote noting "Alexeres, in the margin."[30]

The place-name Winship sought in the atlases was likely "Alijares," a royal pleasure resort in the ancient Moorish kingdom of Granada. The name itself is redolent of a strong Moorish or North African etymology: Alijar, Alhambra, Algeciras, Almeria, and the like. An old meaning of *alijar* is "Bedouin camp or settlement."[31] But in the context of Castañeda's phrase a reference to a royal resort seems quite out of place. Hammond and Rey suggested the rancherias themselves resembled *alixares*, but they fail to mention what an *alixar* is or is not. Bolton suggested that, "when viewed from a distance they reminded one Spaniard of Alixares. Did he mean the settlement looked like a sycamore grove—*alisales*—or like the suburb of Granada on the mountainside above the Alhambra?"[32] Probably both of Bolton's suppositions are incorrect.

A more suitable interpretation is that *a manera de alixares* is a descriptive and locational qualifier for the four-day journey, not a qualifier for the rancherias. Consider that a sixteenth-century *alijar* (or *alixar*) was a wasteland or stony piece of ground. As the Spanish gradually pushed the Moors southward down the Iberian peninsula, they encroached upon semiarid landscapes linked to Moorish signifiers. *Alijar* may have been one of these linguistic borrowings, a signifier applied to overgrazed, marginal, stone-strewn, or wasteland pastures in the south of Spain. Particular stone-slabbed pieces of ground or *alijares* probably did make good threshing floors, a point picked up by the French scholar Henri Ternaux-Compans in his *Cibola* volume. As demographic pressure increased in Spain, the verb *alijarar* became important: "to divide waste lands for cultivation."[33] When one took up these rough, stony, marginal lands, he naturally became an *alijarero* and she an *alijarera*.

It is really a question of environmental perception. If today I ask a resident on the eastern Llano escarpment to give me a local equivalent for "wastelands" or *alijares*, most would not hesitate to refer to the local "breaks" and "badlands": those rough, barren, stony, eroded stretches that characterize many portions of the eastern Llano escarpment and its gnawing tributaries. A later copyist's marginal note of "Alexeres" provides an elegant red-herring. Castañeda's *"a quatro jornadas a manera de alijares era tierra muy poblada"* is more easily translated "At four days journey in the form of wastelands was a land very populous." The key perception is, therefore, the geomorphological intention in Castañeda's humble words. How better to describe the way than with an appropriate Moorish signifier?

This linguistic link with the ancient Mediterranean landscape also made a lot of geographic sense. From a Barranca Grande in or very near Briscoe

County, Coronado's key scouting party traveled south about four days across a landscape often marked by wastes or badlands. But then they found a landscape rich in wild foods, with encampments of a new and friendly tribe stretching for days along a principal watercourse—Cona! Perhaps it is no coincidence that one can travel *south* from Briscoe County for days, encountering memorable badlands like the fantastic wastes in Caprock Canyons State Park.

In setting out from their first barranca shelter, the conquistadors likely followed one of the traditional Teyas trails to the south. That this route was *a manera de alijares* suggests the geomorphic presence of badlands along the way. The most sensible route was likely a trace following the frontal range of the Llano to the south. By approximating the eastern escarpment, the traveler never felt especially lost. The ramparts to the west provided good orientation. Timbered drainages along the way provided the quantities of fuel needed for campfires, a most welcome relief from having to burn bison *bonigas* on the flat plains above.

The headwater creeks of the Red River are even nicely spaced as one parallels the southern drift: the North Prong, the South Prong, the North Pease, the Middle Pease, and the South Pease provided refreshing draughts of water after crossing the badland landscape. To be sure, reliable Teyas were on hand for the course and general direction to Cona. One of these new guides greatly impressed the Spanish with a powerful arrow shot clean through the shoulders of a buffalo. After some four days or sixty to seventy miles of travel they crossed a major drainage divide. It was time for the promised land of Cona. Led by Teyas guides, they likely turned southwestward for a brief spell to access the *boca* or mouth of a spacious but shallow barranca, a canyon that penetrated the eastern flank of the Llano. This last barranca was of much more modest dimensions than the Barranca Grande, but still it commanded attention.

"*Y ansi llego el campo a la prostera barranca*" (And so the camp came to the last barranca), wrote Castañeda.[34] His fuller description should be quoted at length for its wealth of insight into the geography of Cona:

> . . . que era una legua de bordo a bordo y un pequeño rio en lo bajo y un llano lleno de arboleda con mucha uba morales y rosales que es fruta que la ay en françia y sirue[las] de agraz en esta barranca la auiã madura abia nueses y galinas de la calidad de las de la nueba españa y siruelas como las de castilla y en cantidad . . .

> [And so the camp came to the last barranca] that was a league from side to side. A small river ran in the bottom. And there was a flat full of woods with a lot of grapes, mulberries, rosebushes with a fruit like that in France, and plums. For verjuice in this barranca they used ripening grapes. It provided nuts and fowl of the quality of those from New Spain and plums like those of Castille and in quantity . . .[35]

Castañeda's memory of Cona is clearly keyed to food. Yet his description is so clear, so observant, that one wonders how there could be so many competitors—the majority great pretenders—for the crown of Cona. Like the Spanish led by Teya guides, I found Castañeda's semantics took me straight to the only place that made sense: the Garza-Complex rancherias of Blanco Canyon.

· 6 ·

Deep in the Heart of Teyas

> There are places, in Yellow House, in Blanco particularly, where I have stood on the rim, or a mesa top, and in my mind raced golden autumnal light bareback across and into country so rounded and feminine and smooth that I experienced profound sensual arousal.
>
> Dan Flores, *Caprock Canyonlands* (1990)

For many summers I have returned to Blanco Canyon to enjoy the skyscapes, the wind, and the natural history. It is easy to underestimate the canyon's potential for a Coronado Corridor, since it lacks the scenic grandeur of Palo Duro Canyon or the lush vegetation of an overgrown North Concho River. Yet it is in Blanco Canyon that armchair research and field observations collide strongly for the trail detective seeking the true trace of Coronado. You grow to appreciate the subtlety of the canyon: the cold fire of the starfields at night, the tart, pulpy taste of squawbush, the feathers of hawk and turkey vulture. Blanco Canyon suffers piteously now from the desiccating influence of civilization. Some of the heaviest groundwater pumping occurred upstream. In late June the bed is dry for most of its length. The remaining trees look stressed in the intense heat of July, as if the water table was weak and unreliable. Old photos suggest that the tree cover was once denser and more extensive than today. But the hands of humans and the quirks of hydrogeology have spared some important stretches of the older, damper ecosystem. It is still possible in a few places to enjoy cool, fringing woodlands, to splash in water year round, and to taste grapes and plums. At these spots one can recognize the Cona of old narratives.

Blanco Canyon is not especially deep. By the standards of past and present it is a more modest rent in the earth than a Barranca Grande to the north. But it cuts fairly far into the eastern escarpment, with large promontories of the Llano sweeping majestically out on either side to embrace it. From a broad mouth, about seven miles wide south of Silver Falls, the canyon winds north-northwest for over ten leagues or some twenty-six miles. For half of this length it averages about a Spanish league or some 2.6 miles in width. Along the escarpment crest one notices expansive outcroppings of a bleached, bone-white caliche, a soil horizon that gives the shallow barranca a distinctive white-rimmed appearance.[1] Two centuries after Coronado, Hispano frontiersmen in the region chose distinctive environmental signifiers to convey geographic meaning. The toponym "Blanco" was thus born in deference to the extent and exposure of these brilliant white caprock soils. Naturally the small river draining this soil became the "White River" with Anglo settlement, although farther upstream the course name changes to "Agua Corriente" or "Running Water Draw."

There is no clearly defined line where the canyon begins, but the modern English Ranch south of U.S. Highway 82 contains the best vistas of the broad canyon mouth. Two enormous, irregular arms of the Llano veer apart with the barranca flat expanding east into a drainage landscape of grasslands, mesquite scrub, and half-timbered sandy creeks debouching into the river (see map, page 77). Public access to the White River is limited at present. There is an important stop at the modest Silver Falls state roadside park off U.S. 82, the broad highway between Crosbyton and Floydada, Texas. Silver Falls is a tiny patch of public land but an excellent place to dream of Cona and Coronado. Several large historical markers in the area commemorate the mop-up U.S. military conquest and ambitious pioneer settlement of the canyon. But the cold metal markers are silent on its more remote European past, including the possibility that in the summer of 1541 the Coronado expedition spent its longest time in camp in Texas near here. Cona was where they dwelled in Texas.

For millennia the White River provided a natural corridor for man and beast. The convenient topography of Blanco Canyon made it a natural gateway to the interior of the Llano. Like nearby Yellow House Canyon to the south, its archeological treasures of bone and stone must be tremendous. After the Brazos River forks into the Double Mountain and Salt Fork branches, a journey up the Salt Fork—past the awful gypsum belt—brings the sojourner to numerous freshwater tributaries of the northern Brazos watershed. Here the Brazos River begins to strain in its reach for the distant High Plains of New Mexico. In wet years scores of escarpment tributaries in Knox, Garza, and Crosby Counties feed dozens of creeks pouring into the White River. Even today a good June downpour can provide hundreds of brief, noisy waterfalls splashing off the Llano toward the black willow–cottonwood creeks below. As a dominant drainage, the White River provided an important corridor for the annual summer buffalo hunting of the Teyas.

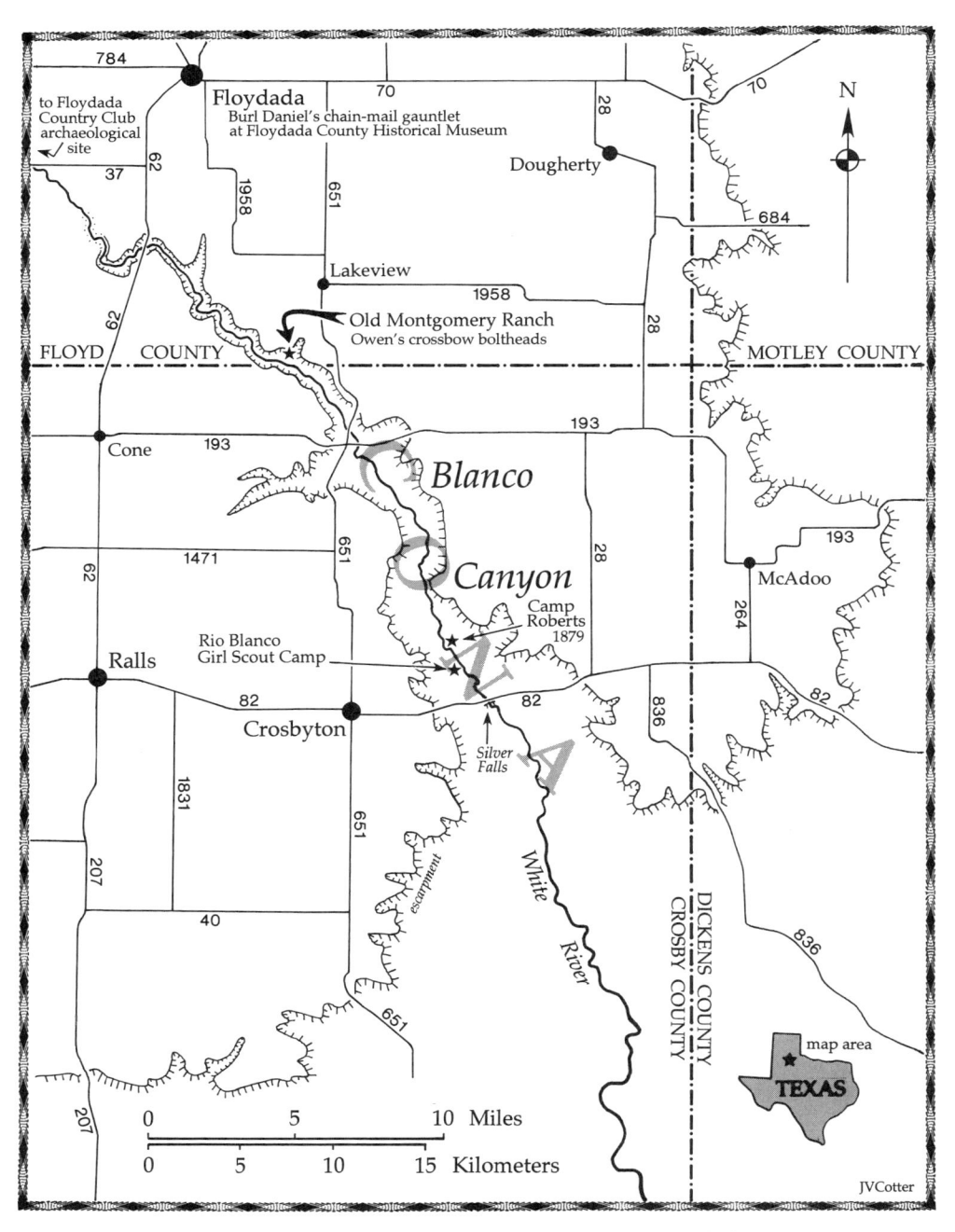

The scenic geography of Blanco Canyon invites the closer attention of scholars as a possible site for the Coronado expedition. Was the Spanish sojourn with the "fierce" (not "friendly") *Teyas* of Cona somewhere in Blanco Canyon? *Map by John V. Cotter.*

The possibility of small-scale agriculture in the area was raised by the distinguished geographer Carl Sauer. Commenting on Castañeda's reference to *frisoles*, Sauer noted, "Frisol has been construed as meaning mesquite, but *frisol* or *frijol* was the Spanish name for the cultivated *Phaseolus* beans."[2] Sauer's suggestion about the cultivation of *Phaseolus vulgaris* (or "kidney beans" in Winship's translation) was controversial at the time. The usual interpretation by Bolton and others that the Teyas were mobile hunters without agriculture was therefore "unsatisfactory." Sauer was an expert on the domestication of plants, and his views bear strong consideration. Efforts to link Castañeda's *frisoles* to mesquite beans clearly miss the demographic point of Cona: food procurement for numerous people.

One of the secrets to Cona's success as a demographic center may have been its geographic suitability for hunting, gathering, and domestic bean cultivation. Blanco Canyon was a good candidate for a Teya or Garza-Complex center of summer agriculture. It had running water from upstream runoff and springs for limited irrigation. The growing season was also coincident with summer hunting on the nearby plains. Nature here can be surprisingly generous with rain in the summer growing season. There were also the fertile, loose, and friable soils of the canyon flats. These sandy, alluvial soils were much more easily planted and worked with simple digging sticks than the tough sods of the adjacent plains, where even the heavy treads of the passing Spanish and their herds made little impression.

Castañeda's casual reference opens up the possibility that Cona was a semi-domesticated landscape, one in which wild food production was supplemented by the hand of simple agrarians. The Teya or Garza-Complex people were themselves possible relatives of the eastering Tompiro puebloans from New Mexico. Some agriculture was in their blood, as the ancestral past at Gran Quivira and the Salinas pueblos indicated, so why not in the fertile eastern canyons? The Teyas certainly had important contacts with other cultivators, especially the Caddoans of Kansas and East Texas. Were the first farmers of Blanco Canyon typically women? One suspects that many of the menial duties of cultivation were born by rancheria women, children, and servants. Casting about for a stronger nutritional base of operations, the Spanish would have preferred a land with as many domesticates as possible, an area rich in wild foods, and a populous nation with plenty of natives to procure fresh or yield stored foods. The Garza-Complex centers of the upper Brazos watershed were likely the best new base available to the Europeans. That Blanco Canyon could once have supported a large population of Teyas, thus drawing the attention of the nearby Spanish to its nutritional promise, must be reconciled to the desiccated appearance of this barranca today.

The climate was cooler and wetter in the mid-sixteenth century, a result of the global "Little Ice Age" in which the Thames of London and the Rio Grande of Tiguex both froze over.[3] Charged by late spring thunderstorms and fed by perennial springs, the flow of the White River was more regular and ample then. Beaver hydraulics may have played an important role in water retention and marshland development, slowing the runoff, altering the formation of gallery woodlands, and shifting moisture outward to nourish trees, bean patches perhaps, and other dense and favorite browse.[4]

The most important modern alterations of the Blanco Canyon riverine ecosystem began with the overgrazing herds of the late-nineteenth-century ranchers. These herds trampled banks and grazed out stabilizing vegetation, contributing to sedimentation, rapid runoff, gullying, and erosion. Increasing investment in farm irrigation wells after 1900 marked the first mechanized assaults on the famous Ogallala Aquifer, tucked underneath the plains on either side of the canyon. As heavy drafts on the upstream Ogallala groundwater increased in the 1930s, 1940s, and 1950s, aquifer levels sank correspondingly.[5] Most of the old White River discharge springs, which heretofore provided a year-round baseflow for the river, gradually dried up—as inevitably did the small river and its pools. Yet it was the cool water from these springs that had nourished the haunts of frogs, catfish, turtles, snakes, minnows, and their predators along its length. The role of any climatic change in the big dry-out is difficult to say.

As the longest northern drainage of the Brazos River, the White River could accommodate the extensive and dispersed camps of large Teya rancherias. The Spanish accounts suggest that the native rancherias of Cona stretched for *tres jornadas* or three days, perhaps up to fifty miles. This figure, however, may have included other Brazos headwater encampments, such as the nearby Yellow House Canyon area with its Garza sites. Like an arrow shot into the Llano's eastern flank, the White River ecologically penetrated the immense grasslands to the west. For the Teyas this shallow barranca provided a convenient and comfortable summer headquarters during the annual harvest of buffalo meat. In gathering supplies for the coming winter, Blanco's strategic location, good springs, wild game, workable soils, wood fuel, and native plant foods commanded due respect from the Garza people.

Blanco Canyon also provided hunters with convenient access to the bison herds grazing on surrounding pastures. From their sprawling camps along the river with its short tributaries, hunters could easily walk—half a league or so in either direction—to reach the low escarpment walls. The climb to the top is neither fatiguing nor perilous and can be made quickly in innumerable places. From these overlooks they could survey the surrounding flat grasslands, seeing for long distances, watching for the moving herds and other opportunities. Much as I admire Bolton's history, I often question his geography of Cona. Blanco Canyon's accessibility to the plains is so much greater than the deep, steep walls of Palo Duro Canyon.[6] Anyone choosing to walk out of a barranca, hunt on adjacent plains, butcher a large animal, and return laden with meat and trophies will appreciate the geographic advantages of the former canyon. It takes a lot of time and effort (and some risk-taking) to regularly climb out of the rugged Palo Duro for hunting, much less to stagger down from the heights with heavy loads of meat or with dog travois. With its abundant plant foods and wild game Palo Duro certainly had a strong native presence of some kind, but Blanco Canyon must be recognized for its summertime convenience to hunters on foot.

Castañeda's gustatory appreciation of Cona fortunately provides an impressive list of biogeographical details. The matching of old language to modern landscape is not without risks, as the conflicting testimony of the trail detectives illustrates. One also assumes—from all the impacts of man and nature in this barranca over the last four and a half centuries—that appearance and conditions could have changed notably between Castañeda and ourselves. With these necessary cautions aside, however, preserved parts of Blanco Canyon correlate remarkably with the natural history of Cona as related by Pedro de Castañeda.

What drew the Teyas to Blanco Canyon, in turn drawing the Spanish, was the providence of nature in endowing this excellent *barranca de los llanos* with springs and running water, with timber for campfires and tent poles, and especially with its hundreds of acres of vitamin-rich fruitlands. The deep alluvial soils of canyon flats and the surrounding drainage watershed were ideal for nourishing innumerable thickets and coppices of fruit-bearing plants. Cona was a garden of edible delights in the memory of both Castañeda and Jaramillo. Consider Castañeda's basic inventory of Cona's plant resources:

PLANT RESOURCE	SPECIES ATTRIBUTION	COMMENTARY
frisoles [frijoles]	*Phaselous vulgaris* bean cultigen	Sauer suggested presence of domesticated beans marked agricultural activity and stored food surplus from prior harvests.
siruelas; siruelas como las de Castilla	*Prunus angustifolia* Chickasaw sand plums	Plums found in abundance; large thickets to be expected. Plums resemble those of Spanish province of Castile.
parrales	*Vitis* species; cf. *Vitis acerifolia* "wild vineyards"	A *parral* is a wild vineyard; unkempt vines that need trimming and pruning to the Spanish eye. Suggests overgrown mound of grapevines on slopes and stream trees.

Plant Resource	Species Attribution	Commentary
uba [uva]/[aba]	*Vitis* or grape species; "pulse" in Sauer's account. Locally called "Possum Grapes."	Mistranscription in Lennox manuscript; Sauer suggests "aba" for copyist "uba," whence his attribution of "pulse," or the edible seeds of pod plants like beans and peas. More likely attribution though is "uva" for grape.
morales	*Morus microphylla*, "mulberries"	Mountain mulberry; scrubby tree up to 20 feet high in canyons and on slopes. Edible sweet fruits in abundance in wet years.
rosales . . . que es fruta ing bush of good la que ay en francia	Bison berries.	Unknown, possibly Fruit-bearing bush of good taste and size; *Rosales* could refer to any of several edible berries found in Blanco Canyon, such as squawbush or bison currants.
de agraz . . . madura	*Vitis* or *prunus* species	They made verjuice from Cona's fruit, a tart drink or mild liquor made by expressing the juice of sour or unripe fruit.
nueses	Probable *Carya illinoinensis* species; possible Hickory or *Juglans* species. Wild pecans or river walnuts.	J. W. Williams argues strongly that this is a reference to pecan trees, but the River Walnut or Little Walnut (Juglans microcarpa) is a candidate. Edible Hackberry seeds may have been gathered.

The recollection of Cona's fruits and berries underlines its importance as a summer nutritional center for the peoples of the High Plains. Whereas men processed the adjacent protein of bison herds, women processed the abundance and variety of wild plant foods, providing fiber and vitamins for the diet. The presence of well-watered alluvial soils in Blanco Canyon favored the development of extensive fruitland areas. Along the active tributaries and the White

River itself, woodlands of cottonwood, hackberry, juniper, sandbar or black willow, soapberry, mulberry, little walnut, and possibly pecan shadowed the watercourses. These woods interfingered with the surrounding grasslands providing a sinuous series of understory and fringing habitats. Grapevines sprawled over many trees competing for sunlight, looking so overgrown that the Spanish were reminded of *parrales* or wild vineyards.

Several stretches of Blanco Canyon today retain the sight and the flavor of Cona. Silver Falls is a modest set of waterfalls dropping the White River into a small ravine just off U.S. 82. Now a state roadside park, Silver Falls has quaint CCC improvements: stone steps leading to the streamside, markers and picnic sites, and a masonry pool and outlet for an old spring still weeping a little. Not far away from the park a pioneer stone house hugs an overlook. Grapevines trail up trees, maidenhair ferns mark wet spots, and the suggestion of cool shade is a welcome relief from the heat. The flow of the White River is embarrassingly low now in the summer, usually only a small rivulet unless there has been a cloudburst upstream. Former springs are now damp seeps, at best. Nevertheless, Silver Falls still has an aura of lushness, an air of repast and repose that gladdens the heart. A stretch of the White River below, on Mr. Otis English's ranch, has an exceptional waterhole with "Twenty Foot Falls" (actually twenty-one feet high according to a local). Heavy shade, a fenced-off colony of rare orchids, cool springs, abundant grapevines, and other food plants provide a refuge from the dry plains above.

A second preserved piece of pre-settlement ecology is found at the Rio Blanco Girl Scout Camp, a regional campground for the Caprock Girl Scout Council. This important area benefits from good woodlands and the rare year-round presence of water in bends and pools of the White River. Various buildings, a concrete swimming pool, and many picturesque improvements currently support an active summertime population of seasonal campers. Of course, it used to be Garza-Complex tents instead of Girl Scout wood bunk-buildings, but the allegoric principle is the same: this is a nice place for summertime living. Cool air gathers in the barranca at night. The night noises are friendly, although the large paw prints of a puma have been seen.

Under the careful stewardship of George and Pam Moore, the Rio Blanco Girl Scout Camp retains several primitive and hiking areas of great charm and instruction. The Moores have made their home in Blanco Canyon for many years. Camp Ranger George Moore is a bright, friendly native of Louisiana who settled into Rio Blanco in the 1970s. One suspects his roots in the place now run about as deep as the big camp cottonwoods. His wife Pam is a fountain of knowledge about the plant resources of the campground, a patient and kind person willing to share her knowledge. While there are a few other primitive areas on the adjacent private ranches, the Rio Blanco primitive area along Big Sandy Creek and the camp nature trail along the river provide a convenient window into the past landscape.

The most perfect of all Cona plant foods was the wild plum. Wonderful thickets of wild plums are still common in the lower Blanco Canyon area, even while they are becoming infrequent in the wild elsewhere. The Canadian River had plenty of plum thickets of course, but no entrada. In his classic biogeographical survey of the Coronado expedition, J. W. Williams noted that the area "across the headwaters of the Brazos was a land of wild grapes and wild plums."[7] Based on the reminiscences of John Duncan Young, J. Frank Dobie preferred a plum range just north of Blanco Canyon. "All old range men know," he wrote in a 1929 classic, "that the finest plum thickets in the whole cattle country were on the Pease and Red Rivers."[8] On the sandy outwashes of the myriad escarpment streams, particularly at important junctions with the White River, dense thickets bear the tart, reddish yellow fruits of the Chickasaw Sand Plum in profusion.

For the plum lover or plain pomologist Blanco Canyon is a better choice than Palo Duro State Park. Plum thickets in Blanco abound with the sand, sunlight, drainage and moisture. "Two varieties of plums are noticeable," *The Hesperian* of Floyd County noted on the abundance, "namely, a small red plum and a large sort. The latter is called the wild goose plum."[9] The small red plums are Chickasaw plums, while the wild-goose plums are most likely from the related and thickety *Prunus* species, *Prunus Munsoniana*. Of the Chickasaws, Camp Ranger George Moore speaks of "tons of wild plums" and "immense stands" in the Blanco Canyon area. The primitive area of Rio Blanco Girl Scout Camp indeed has superb mature colonies of *Prunus angustifolia*, suggesting a superabundance of this good fruit from even small acreages. If the current profusion of Rio Blanco's primitive area were projected onto the simplified landscape upstream and down, Blanco Canyon could have sustained large rancherias. Plum thickets have even colonized the sandy swales along the edge of the plains above. It is possible to see them by following the maze of dirt roads above leading to neat farmhouses overlooking the canyon.

These sinuous plum thickets of the Brazos headwaters region bear vast quantities of fruit in the heat of June and July. Further downstream on the White River other immense thickets occur, especially at junctions with significant tributaries. A mature Chickasaw plum thicket is excellent habitat, of course, similar to the old thick gorses of England. Hundreds of reddish gray, spinescent, twiggy shrubs interlace their branches to form a dense labyrinth up to twelve feet high or more at the center. Innumerable birds, rabbits, mice, possums, porcupines, snakes, skinks, lizards, and their predators avail themselves of cover, shelter, chase, and food in the big thickets. The three-quarter-inch fruits ripen from May to July, coincident with Coronado's arrival. As for the taste of these sand plums, I have watched local farmers deliberately stop their pickups next to stands, get out, and contentedly sample the wares at the end of a workday. They enjoy munching on the fruit and watching the sunset, moving with gestures and comments that seem unspeakably ancient. Wives once made a delicious sand plum jelly, but store-bought goods and jobs leave more fruit for the other mammals now.

Castañeda's reference to *rosales* or shrubs "with a fruit like that in France" could refer to any of the other fruit-bearing bushes still common in the preserved areas of Blanco Canyon.[10] The name suggests the *Rosaceae* or Rose family of plants, a large family of herbs, shrubs, and small trees with a number of known genera found in the region. The Rose family is known for its nutritional value. Texas botanists Donovan S. Correll and Marshall C. Johnston explain the rose's ancient "production of miscellaneous fruits edible to man is not surpassed by any other family of plants; among these are the apple, peach, pear, cherry, apricot, plum, almond, strawberry, raspberry and blackberry."[11]

While impossible to make an exact attribution, just enumerating the Rosaceae possibilities underscores a point that modern Blanco Canyon and prehistoric Cona were both well endowed with fruit and berry plants. Wild hawthorns (*Craetageus* species), dewberries (*Rubus oklahomus*), wild plums (*Prunus angustifolia*, and possibly *Prunus Munsoniana* or *Prunus mexicana*), prairie roses (*Rosa arkansana*), silver mountain mahogany (*Cercocarpus montanus* var. *argenteus*), and brook cinquefoil (*Potentilla paradoxa*) represent important Rose genera found in the extended area of the White River. Many other native species found in the vegetation zones between plains and river were also utilized by the Teyas for food, seasonings, herbal remedies, ceremonies, and dyes.[12]

Two other Blanco Canyon plants with fruits significant to a hungry stomach are "squawbush" and "buffalo currants." The local squawbush or skunkbush sumac (*Rhus aromatica*) is a tall shrub bearing in June a number of acidic, reddish orange berries. The fruits are mostly seeds with a coating of tart, lemony pulp. As snacks straight from the fetid-scented bush they are primitive to the modern palate. However, a mass of gathered fruits make a refreshing version of country lemonade when pulped and steeped in cool water. Squawbush thickets up to ten feet tall are also excellent habitats for wild game. An older vernacular name for this smelly sumac is the Quail-bush, a reference to the partiality shown it by "gallinaceous birds" like quail, prairie chickens, and turkeys (Castañeda's *gallinas*).

Much more praiseworthy in taste are the understory stands of buffalo or golden currants (*Ribes odoratum*). This interesting shrub in the Saxifrage family blooms in March with fragrant, showy, yellow flowers. By the time the Spanish arrived, the tall bushes would be laden with clusters of ripening, delicious, sweet black currants. Buffalo currants are so tasty—if the migrant birds have left any—that even the jaded modern palate wants to continue sampling the June bushes. Could Castañeda have had these delicious currants in mind when he wrote of "fruit like that in France"? *Ribes odoratum* are found farther north and east on the Great Plains, so it is likely the plains tribes in general were familiar with them as a seasonal food resource. The native appreciation of all edibles may have been quickly imparted to members of the Coronado expedition during their sojourn. Curiously, some of the first Anglo pioneer accounts of Blanco Canyon mention the same sacred trilogy of fruits: grapes, plums, and currants. Under a White River grape arbor in the summer of 1886, settlers enjoyed the perfect landscape for repose, as "red plums, blue currants and purple grapes, in their luscious ripeness filled the air with their pungent sweetness, while birds sang their merry songs against a sky of blue."[13]

In the mind's eye Cona was a busy place in 1541. Strung out along the shallow barranca—and downstream for many miles—the Teya rancherias were a loose coalescence of matrilineal clan tipis, brush arbors, fires, small garden plots of beans (and perhaps some squash or tobacco), meat and hide processing stations, bathing and fishing spots, ceremonial centers, and playgrounds. Some of their adaptive cultural ecology had likely passed to them from their days as plains village farmers centuries before.[14] Known to archeologists as the Garza Complex, the Teya camps were distinguished by a local micaceous pottery type called Tierra Blanca Plain. Shards of these thinner, smaller pots are frequent in Blanco Canyon and the upper Brazos watershed. Some of the Tierra Blanca pots have loop handles for ease in transport. "They carried on a vigorous trade," writes Carroll Riley, "especially with the Galisteo towns and Tunque Pueblo but also with Pecos, obtaining glazed wares, obsidian, turquoise, and Gulf of California olive shells."[15] Teya modifications had shaped the land for generations, particularly through their use of fire. The landscape of Cona was animated by the talk, laughter, shouts, sport, arrivals, and departures of hundreds of men, women, children, babies, and dogs in the course of a day. As a social and ceremonial place for the Teyas the place was sacred.

For most of the Europeans Cona would also be their home for the next few weeks while they gathered provisions and rested for the long haul back to Tiguex. Based on new geographic information from knowledgeable informants in the rancheria, Coronado was now aware that the province of Quivira was well to their north. For whatever reason it seemed likely that El Turco had grievously misled the expedition. Castañeda, Jaramillo, and Coronado all mention the lack of provisions, making a further long advance by the entire army a risky proposition. At a meeting of the captains and ensigns at their camp in Cona, Coronado secured permission to send a reconnaissance in force to Quivira with himself at its head. Don Tristán de Arellano would take charge of the army, gather provisions, and then recross the plains for the Rio Grande valley to await Coronado's return.

To the camp's great disappointment and anxiety, the captain-general, thirty soldiers, some servants and allies, Fray Juan de Padilla, several nervous Teya guides, a pleased Ysopete and a disgraced El Turco all rode or walked northward out of Blanco Canyon. They traveled, it was said, "by the needle" of a compass for the province of Quivira. After earlier displays undermining El Turco's authority, a confident Ysopete was now in front, looking forward to freedom in his old Pawnee homeland. El Turco traveled with the party heading north, but strong chains restricted his movements. He was no longer a guide but a prisoner under guard. Castañeda related that the scared Teya guides of this reconnaissance force soon ran away. Coronado was forced to send back a messenger for replacement guides while he camped and waited. Anxious about the future, many conquistadors left behind at Cona supplicated to join the captain-general, come what may. But Coronado was deaf to their appeals. They must gather food for the journey back; he was continuing north out of sight and contact for the foreseeable future.

Under Captain Arellano's leadership the Spanish and other Europeans made the best of the situation. For fifteen days, Castañeda related, they dutifully gathered daily rations and laid in provisions for the return trek. We can reconstruct some of the daily camp rhythms, and even match language to landscape from a study of Castañeda's narrative and contemporary Blanco Canyon. Above all a spatial sense emerges, one that says Cona could be quickly lost to sight, swallowed up by surrounding and featureless plains.

In the morning smoky fires kept mosquitoes at bay while the army roused itself for another day. Breakfasts featured less traditional staples and more game and wild fruit. African servants and other aides soon attended to the routine chores of Captains Arellano, Tovar, Cárdenas, and others. Spanish women were few in number, but María Maldonado, Francisca de Hozes, and the native wife of Lope de Caballero accompanied their husbands and performed wifely duties. The reduced Franciscan contingent of priests under Fray Antonio de Castilblanco said morning prayers. They would minister, read, and rest, and some doubtless visit the nearby Teyas to proselytize. The thousand or so camp natives (attached to the expedition back in New Spain for military purposes) were kept busy as well, some foraging, grooming, cooking, cleaning, scouting, watching the remaining livestock, and laying in provisions. In their rest they may have played *patolli*, the Aztec game resembling Parcheesi. A good deal of the chores attendant to the horses probably fell to their lot.

Almost a quarter of the soldiers were recent *hidalgo* arrivals to the New World from the Spanish province of New Castile.[16] These were mostly young men with great aspirations but little plainscraft. Almost a tenth of the camp soldiers were not Spanish at all, but Portuguese, Italians, Frenchmen, at least one German bugler, and a roving Scotsman named Tomas Blaque or Thomas Blake. Old and young, experienced and inexperienced alike, small parties of conquistadors set off in the morning to kill bison on the nearby plains. These small parties and lone hunters left their camps along the White River for a short trek over the grasslands of the flats. At convenient points they climbed bison trails up the 200- to 250-foot scarp woodland slopes found on either side of the White River. At the top they found themselves once more high on the Llano. They soon learned that beyond the *bordo* or edge of the canyon, they entered the vast, flat plains on either side at the risk of profound disorientation. Routinely, many of the young and more inexperienced hunters got lost after wandering out into the plains. Intent on the chase, they failed to note course and direction.

"They wandered from place to place without knowing how to find their way back," Castañeda wrote, "even though they could hardly miss the lower or upper ends of the barranca in which the camp was located."[17] The old narrator's reference to the linearity of this barranca—"*aquella barranca que arriba o abaxo auian de atinar*"—is an important clue. It suggests computing a canyon length in accordance with the known width of one league, or a barranca 2.6 miles wide by some twenty-six miles in length at a one-to-ten ratio of width to length. The adverb *arriba* or "above" refers to the barranca headwaters, and the adverb *abaxo* or "below" suggests the broad mouth of the ravine. The topography of Blanco Canyon agrees very well with these semantics; indeed, its straightforward linearity is a geographic asset compared to the bewildering, sprawling wilderness of Palo Duro Canyon, where returning to any *bordo* or edge is no guarantee of reaching camp shortly.

That these hunters could—with a brisk walk or ride—find themselves lost on the Llano cannot be doubted, despite the many trail detectives that locate Cona and the Spanish far, far away from the High Plains: distantly downstream the Colorado River, the North Concho River, the Clear Fork of the Brazos River, the Rolling Plains, the Canadian River, or elsewhere. The environmental semantics of the chronicles make clear that the camp hunters were not unusually clumsy or stupid, but that the plains surrounding them were sinister, deceptive, so unusually flat and devoid of orientation as to defeat usual perception, and to invite special comment. These plains within walking distance of Cona were the same plains that had already swallowed up one mounted hunter and several equipped horses on the outbound journey.

"Thus, we lost one man, and others, while out hunting, were lost three or four days," noted the *Relación del Suceso*.[18] "*Es la tierra tan llana, que se pierden los hombres apartandose media legua*" (It is the land so flat that men lose themselves in drawing off half a league), warned Father Motolinía in the *Relación Postrera de Sívola*. Castañeda as usual provides the details:

> *perdiose en este comedio mucha gente de los que salian a caza y en dos ni tres dias no tornaban a bolber a el campo andando desatinados a una parte y a otra . . .*
>
> (Many people of those who left [the barranca] to hunt got lost in this time, and they did not come back in two or three days. Trying to return to the camp they wandered like madmen to one place and to another . . .) [19]

The danger is real enough at Blanco Canyon because the plains *on either side* are treacherously monotonous and level. Within a short distance of the edge, one enters a featureless terrain of grassland. Large herds of buffalo bulls grazed out on these plains, separate from the herds of cows and calves. Spanish hunting parties killed at least 500 of these bulls, thought Castañeda. Inexperienced, excited, and young hunters might find themselves at a bull kill-site with only a hazy notion afterward as to how to get back to Blanco Canyon. In the heat of the chase, with the wild animal darting here and there, they lost sense of their proximate geography. After the kill, they were startled to find no landmarks of any kind for reference.

There was a labyrinth of occasional bison paths but these could lead anywhere. Trying what they thought was a sensible course, these inexperienced hunters advanced until time itself became their enemy. Failing to reach the *bordo* when they should have, young hunters panicked and struck out on another course, only to lose hope and seek another way, until at last they simply wandered about, becoming *desatinados*—foolish, mad, wild, crazy men. Thirst, heat, and the endless sense of being swallowed by a geographic immensity affected their judgment. There is a psychology of place to these plains, to these *llanos* that drove men crazy, that can be met best by the great Llano itself. Cona was in a barranca with the Llano on either side.

They learned and shared remedies for the profound disorientation they suffered. Castañeda remembered one stratagem in which the hunter marched from the kill site in one direction to scan for the barranca, then retraced his way back to the slaughtered animal to take another course to scan for the edge, continuing to return and depart from the kill until at last he perceived the correct course or encountered others coming and going who could provide guidance. This course of action was not without its risks, nor did it let the Europeans venture very far into the plains, since they would naturally try to keep within reasonable distance of the escarpment coastline.

More sophisticated camp hunters used a second stratagem, a form of celestial reckoning. After the confusing tumult of a bison bull kill, they paused and waited quite a while, resting and watching the sun. Gradually, when they were sure on the western declension of the afternoon sun, they could perceive a course back to the canyon. Knowing which way was west helped these hunters plot mental map courses back toward the barranca. They did not have to hit a mark with their courses. They merely had to reach any edge of Blanco Canyon to return at a glance to a landscape of orientation. Blanco Canyon was well suited to such a technique. The northern thrust of the barranca made reckoning easier: if west of the canyon, go opposite the afternoon sun; if east of the canyon, go toward the afternoon sun. Castañeda thought this solar reckoning could only be done by *hombres entendidos*, or wise, experienced men. Many young hunters embarking into the flat grasslands above learned to follow these more successful and prudent hunters.

"*Es cosa de notar que como la tierra es tan llana*" (It is a remarkable thing how the land is so flat), recollected Castañeda about these old hunting forays on the plains above Cona. Castañeda inserted this exclamatory comment on the infernal plains between his discourse on the two stratagems used by hunters. This language, attention, and unusual behavior does not suggest the rolling plains of the south or east, the lush breaks of the North Concho, the pecan-lined banks of the distant Colorado uplands, or other remote resorts where so many whisk the expedition—and Cona with it.[20] These landscapes have plenty of general orientation features in their topography. What is needed is a featureless landscape, one in which an individual could not fail to get lost.

The chronicler's phrase and its justifying position are strong arguments that the land in which they hunted for provisions was the same immensity they dreaded having to cross again. Both were so flat as to be worth noting. Hunters were forced into defensive measures by this unusual disorientation that turned an ordinary man into a *desatinado*. The renowned old Texas physical geographer Robert T. Hill understood this notable flatness, which caused him to comment in 1900:

> The Llano Estacado is a vast region so nearly level that it has no relief perceptible to the eye. . . . The general flatness, which continues up to the very brink of its surrounding escarpments, is marked only by long swales, like the faintest troughs of the gentler swells of the ocean, and their depressions are so slight that their shallowness has been appropriately described by Castañeda, the historian of the Coronado expedition, as being "like a bowl, so that when a man sits down the horizon surrounds him on all sides at the distance of a musket shot."[21]

These lost soldiers provided another important ritual to a day in Cona—the evening muster and count of the missing. At dusk various officials conducted a head count and often enough there were hunters thought to be missing, some for several days. The peril of these men drove the Spanish to adopt regular tactics to provide orientation. They prepared great fires at night, but these flames were poor beacons to men out of sight of the barranca itself. Noise carried far across the land, and so various noisy efforts were made to attract a lost man's attention. Soldiers sometimes fired off one of the *carros de artilleria*, a mounted cannon artillery piece, that let loose a resounding boom echoing confusedly in the canyon. The German bugler and other men sent out mighty blasts from the *trompetas*, while others beat army drums. The regularity of these activities helped many of the near-confused, but others were so lost, wrote Castañeda, that all the fuss was of little use. Although no account mentions it, Teya hunting parties probably encountered the occasional lost soul and provided guidance back to the shelter of Blanco Canyon.

After some fifteen days of these risks and rewards, Don Tristán de Arellano judged the provisions sufficient for the return journey. All outlying hunters were called in, or found if missing. Arellano's orders transformed the sprawling camp, as men gathered their kit and prepared to break camp for good. From now on the fruits of Cona would have to be carried with them. After his fall from a horse, Captain Diego Lopez's arm was still mending poorly. The servants loaded up the equipage, the soldiers shouldered their packs and weapons, the priests arranged their clerical baggage, and the camp natives gathered their food and tattered belongings.

All suspected that the return trek across the immense flat plains would be a trying one. Many had hoped that sudden countermanding orders from Coronado would arrive, turning their course to the north, to the wealth of Quivira. When no such orders appeared and the provisions were judged adequate, there was nothing left of their dreams but to face the disappointing return to the hostile pueblos of the Rio Grande Valley. One late June morning the army broke camp and some 1,700 people marched off to the west, climbing the scarped woodland of Blanco Canyon, and then plunging back into *lo llano*.

What is not known is whether the Europeans left anything favorable for the Teyas to remember them by. Compelling historical research in epidemiology suggests that close proximity to European intrusion in the sixteenth century was a death warrant for many indigenous New World populations. The collapse of native populations did not even require the infectious presence of the Spanish, since their diseases diffused along aboriginal routes as well. In contrast to Coronado's destruction at Tiguex—the Black Legend or *la leyenda negra* of Spanish cruelty and wanton waste of lives (popular with nineteenth-century Englishmen and Americans)[22]—Arellano's army fought no battles and killed no known Native Americans on the Llano or at Cona.

But what diseases, viral infections, influenzas, or other dangerous portmanteau microbes were left behind with the Garza people cannot be ascertained at this time.[23] It is likely that the warm summer weeks of direct and indirect contacts between the large rancheria and the large Spanish camp, both linked by the waters, provided potential lines of disease transmission. Whether then or later, there is "growing acknowledgement that Native American populations a century or so after European intrusion were roughly one-tenth or less their contact size."[24] If an epidemic had broken out and swept the Teya and Querecho rancherias in the post-contact period, the loss of life would have been enormous. Certainly by a century later Pecos and the other pueblos had suffered grievous demographic losses.[25]

What else the European and Mexican allies left behind is the stuff of archeological dreams in the latter 1990s. There is good reason to believe that bits and pieces of expedition debris accumulated in the conquistador camps and surrounding area during their extended stay at Cona. Finding that debris, especially the metal artifacts, and accurately linking this material to the Coronado expedition will go a long way in settling the Texas route mysteries. Increasingly, the backwaters of Blanco Canyon have been the focus for such a search. Sixteenth-century Spanish artifacts are genuinely rare in the Texas Panhandle. Nevertheless, in the past few years a small treasure of just such possible artifacts has surfaced, a cornucopia that is drawing the much-needed attention of skilled and professional archeologists from New Mexico, Texas, and Kansas. "Everyone likes to believe that the Coronado expedition of 1540-41 camped in their canyon," noted anthropologist Donald Blakeslee. "Up until now there has been little or no proof, but the evidence turning up in Blanco Canyon looks very good."[26]

It was South Plains farmer Burl Daniel who found the first possible expedition artifact near Blanco Canyon in the early 1960s. Daniel was plowing near a playa lake when his discs turned up a three-fingered chain-mail gauntlet of antiquarian interest. Daniel retrieved the curious item and kept it in his house for years. It is now on display in the Floyd County Historical Museum. Perhaps a conquistador lost a gauntlet in the excitement of a bison kill. In 1963 another Floydadan, J. S. Hale Jr., found a fairly large piece of antique chain-mail vest in the same general area, eroding from a gully draining to the White River. The vest was later stolen during a move, but a discussion of both artifacts appeared in a 1966 local newspaper story.

Not quite thirty years later another local, Jimmy Owen of Floydada, was sweeping a stretch of the Q. D. Williams Ranch south of Floydada when his metal-detector led to an important find. In the mesquite terrain adjacent to the White River, Owen found an unusual iron crossbow point, and then a copper crossbow bolthead. The Coronado expedition is known to have carried crossbows, weapons rarely or never seen on the plains afterward. Owen's crossbow points and Burl Daniel's chain-mail glove strongly suggest the early period of Spanish penetration of the plains. Jimmy Owen is a local collector—another of J. Frank Dobie's "Coronado's Children"—who started out sweeping for old coins, iron arrowheads, and such, but graduated to searching passionately for Coronado's expedition. By now he has unearthed a number of metal artifacts from Blanco Canyon, including many more crossbow boltheads from one locale alone, an old Spanish-style horseshoe, nails, and other possibilities. There are parts of the canyon where you have to be careful not to step into one of his holes.

Owen's discoveries helped fuel a growing archeological interest in the canyon as a contact site. Jim Word, a veteran Texas archeologist living in the area, pointed to the possibilities of the known Garza-Complex sites at the Floydada Country Club in the upper canyon. Jack Hughes and Waldo R. Wedel were other well-known archeologists with an interest in Coronado's Trail. Joining with Donald Blakeslee of Wichita State University and Wedel's son, the quartet even used an airplane to survey for Coronado's route across the Texas plains. News of their aerial search in turn reached Nancy Marble of Floydada, a gifted museum curator and researcher. Marble remembered the old newspaper story of Burl Daniel's gauntlet. Putting two and two together, she located Daniel in a nursing home in New Mexico, obtained the chain-mail gauntlet from a shoebox for museum display, and brought news of the old artifacts to the attention of the archeologists. From there the excitement continues to build. I was fortunate to join in the Coronado Project 1995 "shovel survey" on the Q. D. Williams Ranch, an opportunity for an amateur to learn from some of the best. Here in the middle portion of the canyon not far from the old Montgomery ranch-house, archeologists focused their attention. Searching with Jimmy Owen at a known site, Ray Macha found another copper crossbow bolthead. Over the fall and winter of 1995 even more crossbow boltheads were found, an unusual trove that caused intense speculation.

Attention currently focuses on the Floyd County section of Blanco Canyon—from the puebloan pottery shards at the Floydada Country Club site to the boltheads and antique hand-forged horseshoes coming off the Q. D. Williams Ranch sites. There are still important cautions to observe. Local news accounts and optimism in late summer of 1995 suggested that the recent evidence was all but incontrovertible, that Coronado has been certified absolutely to have been at these sites. "Historical finds prove presence of Coronado," trumpeted the front-page headline in Floydada's newspaper on September 7, 1995.[27] But, in fact, no comprehensive proof of European occupation in 1541 has yet been found *in situ*. It may even be very difficult to find absolute evidence for a camp residency that lasted only weeks, and occurred over four and a half centuries ago. It is the areal quantity of early Spanish-era artifacts that point to the canyon, even though some, like Burl Daniel's gauntlet, were not discovered there at all.

Furthermore, many investigators, if not most of the 1990s "Coronado's Children," regard Blanco Canyon as the *first* barranca—the Barranca Grande—and not the second ravine or Cona, which they locate to the north. Jim Word and Richard Flint point to the plentiful Rio Grande Glazeware shards at the Floydada Country Club site as evidence that Blanco was the first barranca. "Apparently he spent the night and was hailed out down in the canyon," Jim Word suggests, "That's why we find all the broken pottery and stuff."[28] The venerable Jack T. Hughes also considers Blanco Canyon as the likely first barranca. Hughes is extremely knowledgeable of the Texas Panhandle, having examined its old secrets for decades as an archeological explorer. A scientist who resembles a veteran comanchero or contrabandista, Hughes also thinks the expedition went north, perhaps to Quitaque, after a brief stay and hail-out in Blanco Canyon.

The growing abundance of discovered metal artifacts may suggest a longer stay by the Spanish in the area, more suggestive of the weeks of Cona than the four or so days spent in the Barranca Grande. It is possible, however, that the known hailstorm scattered horses and men who shed a volume of cultural debris around the canyon, an abundance now coming to light. A lingering question is whether the Spanish would have called Blanco Canyon a "Great Ravine," when after all at the Montgomery Ranch sites it is not so deep, nor its breadth so intimidating. The copper crossbow boltheads are quite suggestive of expedition members in the general area, but Spanish hunters wandered far and wide, likely shooting at bison up in the canyon and out onto the plains. Since they hunted all along their Llano trail, it is conceivable that boltheads might be found in a wide general area. Those used and lost in hunting could even be expected to be found a distance away from the newcomers' camps.

Further studies and tests on the artifacts are also needed. Hand-forged Spanish horseshoes from Blanco Canyon may be touted as mid-sixteenth century Coronado artifacts, when in fact they closely resemble the hand-forged Spanish horseshoes produced in San Antonio and elsewhere as late as the nineteenth century. Mexican hand-forged horseshoes from stolen or traded stock likely entered the canyon over several centuries. In the eagerness to find evidence there is always the risk of indiscriminate looking as well. Many artifacts are only known outside of their stratigraphic context. Fortunately, the Coronado Project, led by Donald Blakeslee of Wichita State University, is looking closely and methodically at the archeological context. The support and unstinting hospitality of ranch owners and local citizens alike make this project practical and significant.

My own dreams of the expedition in Cona wander to the remaining verdant stretches of the White River, even beyond the Floyd County line and deeper into Crosby County's Blanco Canyon. Nearer the *boca* or mouth of Blanco Canyon the canyon is less congested. There is more room for a populous expedition to spread out, and indeed the width of the canyon opens up to the full league or 2.6 big miles remembered by Castañeda. This lower area was an important part of Cona as well. Fed by more generous tributaries, it offered excellent possibilities for domesticated crops and rancheria camps. Not far above FM 2591 in Crosby County is a beautiful landscape of White River canyon valley, an expanse with large natural campgrounds. This special place has attracted newcomers for many centuries. The first Texas Rangers in the Panhandle settled here, when Capt. G. W. Arrington and his company rode into Blanco Canyon in the fall of 1879. They established Camp Roberts on an excellent terrace site in this valley and dug a well. Not so far away was the lonely gravesite of Gregg, a soldier killed in the final Indian wars and buried on a nearby knoll. Visiting the ranger site one day with George and Pam Moore, it was easy to understand the attractions the same area might have had for the Coronado expedition. It also was a place to dream of conquistadors and allies, gathered around a constellation of campfires along the White River after sunset. Large Garza-Complex sites, with acres of pottery shards and untested soils, are just up the river. Blanco Canyon still retains many archeological possibilities. Perhaps the shaman El Turco was right, and we need to look *mas allá*.

·7·

Hasta Las Aguas

> My emphasis on the production of America as something "new"—that is, semiotically created—challenges the view of the New World as a natural entity, discovered, revealed, or imperfectly understood. Consequently, I am less interested in issues regarding a distortion or misrepresentation of the New World than in how a new region of the world was invented, and how fiction (literary or otherwise) and history constitute complementary forms of understanding the "West" and "the Americas."
>
> José Rabasa

The struggle to express *lo llano* in words was a particular challenge for the Spanish. They were called upon to describe a landscape possessing little apparent signification. This land was large and flat, something of a nothing. The only identifiers of this expanse were the roving hunters, the strange animals, and the curious waters. Putting the return journey into words was difficult as there were few if any fixed points of reference. Not surprisingly, a sense of failure dogged the main army, and there was even less incentive to record their return course. With the important exception of Castañeda, most expedition texts thus provide few details about the journey back to Tiguex. The accounts of Coronado and Jaramillo suggest a nameless, featureless background to the more important questions of personalities and arrival in Quivira. We have only the slimmest of textual evidence on their journey to and from Quivira itself.

The language of the *Relación del Suceso* and Coronado's October 20, 1541, letter to Carlos V suggest the return of the main army was a struggle for nutrition. The specter of famine hovered over the landscape, expressed as the absence of corn. Coronado wrote of men now having only meat to eat, "because we had reached the end of the corn" taken from the province of Tiguex.[1] Having been led astray by El Turco, the Spanish had exhausted their own supplies of maize without finding suitable replacements. It was said that Quivira had "corn and houses of straw," but Teya informants convinced the conquistadors that Quivira's corn was in "small supply" and far away, some forty days journey to the north. There would be no maize until then. "Considering this, and the small supply of food that was left," Fray Motolinía wrote, Coronado and thirty men could conceivably reach Quivira, but not the many hundreds of other hungry mouths. If the hope of gold in Quivira pushed Coronado forward, it was the certainty of corn in Tiguex that forced his army back. Their return journey was hard, the *cronica* author suggested, with people and animals suffering nutritional distress, "because there was nothing to eat except meat."[2] The lack of maize for their horses was a particular concern.

As far as the Spanish knew, the puebloan settlements in the upper Rio Grande Valley were the closest sources of cereal cultivation and storage. In that direction the main group must direct their steps. Around July 2, 1541, Capt. Tristán de Arellano judged the army preparations as adequate for a good start back across the plains toward the maize fields and granaries of Tiguex. The next morning the Europeans, the Afro-Iberian servants, and the native Tlaxcalans, Mexicas, and Tarascans broke their summer camp in Cona. Filing along Blanco Canyon in a long and impressive procession, the hundreds of riders, foot soldiers, priests, servants, wives, herders, and allies began a strategic retreat dictated solely by hunger. El Turco's plan had worked well in this regard. There had been no defeat at arms, nor was there any stored wealth worth fighting over in this strange land. The first intense smell of Old World gunpowder in Texas was for the animals, not the rustic Querechos and Teyas.

Capt. Tristán de Arellano had taken great care to keep the peace and to secure experienced Teya guides to lead the way back. These guides were charged to take the army on the shortest return way possible to Tiguex. As Pedro de Castañeda noted:

> . . . el campo salio de la barranca la buelta de los teyas a donde tomaron guias que los bolbiesen por mas derecho camino[.] ellos las dieron de boluntad porque como es gente que no para por aquellas tierras en pos de ganado todo lo saben.

> (The army marched out of the barranca the return way of the Teyas, whither they took guides that might take them back by a more direct road. They gave them willingly because, as a people that did not settle on these lands, in the pursuit of game they know it all.)[3]

This statement underlines the point that their return trail would be along the shortest feasible route, as known by knowledgeable natives. Some time that day the procession left the confines of Cona behind and climbed the low ramparts to advance into the forbidding plains themselves.[4]

Knowing the power of *lo llano* to disorient newcomers, Captain Arellano had little choice than to entrust their safe and speedy return to these Teya guides. Doubtless they could have wandered back to Tiguex on their own, but time was of the essence if their nutritional distress was not to become deadly. The Teyas guides were experienced in travel across the Llano from their pursuit of the bison; they also had traveled to Cicúye itself from time to time to trade and visit. The Teyas, too, had their troubles holding a steady course on the Llano, but they had learned a clever stratagem to maintain a regular course in the flatland, as Castañeda reported.

Each morning on the plains they carefully reoriented themselves by observing the direction of the rising sun. After projecting the course for the days journey ahead, they set out in the desired direction. To avoid the confusion caused by the gradual climbing of the sun, they shot an arrow in the desired direction and then advanced toward this marker. Before reaching this signpost they fired another arrow over the first shaft to extend the straight-line solar reckoning course. Firing consecutive arrow over arrow and making small intuitive adjustments enabled the Teyas to avoid the drifting and noonday meandering that afflicted the Europeans in this oceanic prairie.

There is only one slender clue to the general nature of this course or *el rumbo* that they followed. Castañeda stated that they followed their arrow-shooting guides "*todo el dia hasta las aguas adonde se auia de hacer jornada*" (all day long *toward the waters* whither they were to make camp).[5] This course of action has an absolute ring of truth about it. Indeed, it is the most sensible way of crossing the plains in the summer. In the morning one sets out a straight-line course toward a distant waterhole, arriving to its welcome waters at the end of the day to avoid a "dry camp." On the morrow one repeats the process.

In this manner the main camp would have adequate water for two of three daily meals, plus convenient water for bathing, watering the horses, and filling the water skins both in the morning and at night. *Hasta las aguas* provides then the most useful metaphor for a return route. Between Blanco Canyon and the distant Pecos River we must seek a corridor, a route among the waters of the Llano. Fortunately, the limited drainages and lakes of the interior of the plain considerably simplify the reconstruction of such a road. Moreover, this return course must be logical, an ordinary corridor of travel for the Teyas themselves, or, as Castañeda's words suggest, the Spanish were following "*la vuelta de los teyas*" (the return way of the Teyas).

The competency of the guides cannot be questioned as the chronicles tell us that the total return journey to Tiguex took only twenty-five days.[6] This figure allows for less than two weeks to cross the Llano and reach the Pecos River, with a further twelve days to reach Cicúye and Tiguex beyond.[7] Historians who take the expedition and Cona much farther to the south of Blanco Canyon often fail at this point to explain adequately how nutritionally impaired men and women managed to march from the vicinity of Abilene or San Angelo all the way to the upper Pecos River in New Mexico—a distance of some 350 miles as a crow flies—in only thirteen days.

The contrary case holds for Bolton's historiography; if Cona is at Palo Duro Canyon, the Spanish did not need thirteen days to reach the Pecos River by a more direct course. To be sure, there were frequent delays on the return journey caused by the necessity of hunting and butchering meat for the camp. Some sixty to seventy bison were often brought to camp as daily provisioning. Nevertheless the time frame favors their more or less direct transversal of the Llano from an eastern barranca to the Pecos River in about two weeks. Blanco Canyon fits this bill nicely. In this light a return corridor of travel would advance westward from Blanco Canyon to reach the subtle waterholes and waters of the ancient Portales Valley.

From near Portales, New Mexico, to just west of Lubbock, Texas, the Portales Valley stretches for over 100 miles across the Llano. It is not a "valley" so much as it is an extremely low-relief, ancient drainage basin now pocked with the pitiful remnants of once magnificent Ice Age lakes. During the last glaciation of North America the Portales River was an active drainage network with outlets in either or both Blanco Canyon and Yellow House Draw. Large Pleistocene lakes once watered a superabundance of game comparable only to the savannas of historic Africa. The waters and adjacent beach-like dunes around them attracted both wildlife and Paleo-Indian predators alike. Indeed, the earliest cultural presence of mankind in North America is found in the Clovis projectile points still turned up in this type-locality region.

A climatic and possible anthropogenic extinction process around 11,000 B.P. rended the ancient Pleistocene savanna.[8] The herds of camels and horses, the mammoths and ground sloths, the giant armadillos and sabertooth tigers, and the many other species all faded into the bone and stone records buried beneath the wind-blown soils. The global warming period called the Holocene epoch subsequently dried out the big pluvial lakes of the Portales Valley, leaving behind a series of stepping-stone, shallow, spring-fed, often salinized lakes dotting the shallow basin. Huge cyclogenic dust storms (whose ferocity we can only guess at) desiccated and mantled the region periodically, leaving behind the present series of remnant lake features.

These remnants of a wetter, more active drainage pattern still provided a natural corridor of travel, however, one likely in use for twelve millennia or so. Like connecting the dots, the experienced Teyas could advance *"hasta las aguas"* across the Llano here. Even as the playas shrank from the summer sun and their waters turned flavorful in the seasonal cycle of bloom and growth, the hidden waters of the Portales Valley remained faithful to the sojourner. They were large enough to be found and permanent enough to be relied upon.

As the return journey is poorly documented by all, even Castañeda, we can only trace a reasonable return route, aware that informed speculation and cautious conjecture suggest a possible path, not a known certainty.[9] The conjecture lies basically in determining a logical and direct route for the Teyas to reach the Pecos River, assuming Cona was on an upper Brazos watershed such as Blanco Canyon. Thinking as a Teya is not a surefire approach, but the results may help in visualizing such a practical and timely return course. Fortunately, such a course can also be tied to Castañeda's narrative in several important instances. There are saline lakes south of Blackwater Draw, for example, but none north of it.

The first of *las aguas* encountered west of Cona were the cool running waters of Blackwater Draw. Advancing west along a course approximated by the present Highway 82 from Crosbyton to Idalou, Texas, likely brought the Europeans to the northern vicinity of modern Lubbock. As the first major drainage west of Blanco Canyon, Blackwater Draw offered an excellent, well-watered, and desirable campsite, especially if one had some 1,750 people in tow. To get to Blackwater Draw from Blanco Canyon as a Teya would, it is merely necessary to hold a westward course. At sunrise you note the position of the sun, of course, but a more useful tool in going west were the telling, long, early morning shadows cast across the plains. Using the human body as a gnomon, these shadows must be correlated to the seasonal path of the sun.

By the end of June 1541, the sun was rising and setting over 26 degrees north of due west. But by taking bearings from morning shadows (bearing to the left, right, or even following the shadow), one can negotiate a reasonably direct course to the west, a course that can be held as the sun climbs by resorting to the consecutive arrow stratagem. Of course the declension of the late-afternoon sun offers a renewed and confirmatory sense of direction. Between Lubbock and Abernathy, Texas, Blackwater Draw runs south, offering a direct, flanking target to a westward course from Blanco. Somewhere on this stretch the expedition probably camped and paused briefly. Hunters fanned out into the adjacent herds to replenish messes with fresh if monotonous meat supplies.[10]

From Blackwater Draw the Way of the Teyas led farther west, arriving at the refreshing waters of Yellow House Draw only a convenient day's journey away. Running through Lubbock and Hockley Counties, Yellow House Draw winds west in a brief beeline for the Pecos River. Passing over to the Yellow House branch of the Double Mountain Fork of the Brazos River allowed the guides to reach the lower Portales Valley paleodrainage system.[11] Perhaps for several days or more the expedition paralleled the westerly meandering of Yellow House Draw, stopping for a night's camp at favored locations along its spring-fed waters. The Teyas were now taking the Europeans along the ancient network of trails that advanced west-northwest along the upper Yellow House watershed. Holding a bearing allowed one to cut off the meanders while ensuring the arroyo could be accessed at the end of a day.

Yellow House Draw is not very conspicuous compared to the eastern canyonlands. Indeed, its shallow course peters out fairly quickly in northern Hockley County. Adjacent to its course, however, one formerly encountered a memorable experience: enormous, sprawling, noisy colonies of curious, subterranean rodents. Extirpation campaigns in the early twentieth century killed off the massive prairie dog colonies of the middle Llano. Pioneers thought the hordes of rodents ate grass destined for cattle or crops, and the troublesome prairie dog holes crippled horses and sometimes a stumble killed a good citizen. For years the citizens of Lubbock have maintained a small captive colony in Mackenzie Park solely for the amusement of locals and tourists. But the real sense of millions of prairie dogs along Yellow House Draw is gone from the text of the modern landscape. Not surprisingly, however, Pedro de Castañeda did not fail to remember their presence. *"Auia por aquellos llanos unos animales como hardillas en gran numero y mucha suma de cueuas de ellas"* (There were some animals like squirrels over these plains in great number and a great sum of holes of these [creatures]).[12]

Yellow House Draw and the other *aguas* on the return trip also offered important plant resources to the hungry traveler. In their preoccupation with maize the conquistadors may have overlooked the array of local vegetation that broadened the diet of the nomads. Squeamish about adopting Teyas customs of drinking blood or relishing the stomach juices of freshly killed bison or foraging for wild plants, the all-meat, high-fat menu of the Europeans was probably vitamin-poor and low in carbohydrates. The hundreds of native allies from New Spain who accompanied the expedition were perhaps less fastidious in foraging along the trail among *las aguas*. The all-meat diet created nutritional distress and a strong craving for the amino acids of maize. "There are food plants in abundance," the historian Dan Flores wrote of Yellow House's natural history in *Caprock Canyonlands*, but the soldiers may have failed to recognize many of the new plants as food.[13] "On this journey they had a very hard time," said the *Relación del Suceso*, "because almost all of them had nothing to eat except meat, and many suffered on this account."[14]

Nearing the head of Yellow House, the Portales Valley opens into a remarkable series of curious lake basins hidden in the semiarid flatland around and ahead. Yellow Lake, Illusion Lake, Silver Lake, Bull Lake, Coyote Lake, Great Salt Lake, and other stepping-stone lakes are among the legendary "Lost Lakes" of the 1870s, an appealing Victorian vision of secret oases in the heart of a great desert.[15] Many of these lakes are salty from high evaporation rates, but geologists also wonder about the discharge of deep-brine seepage to the surface. Many of the Lost Lakes were nourished by freshwater springs, however, providing a welcome and convenient camp for people. Nomads and game may have used the precipitates, although better quality salt was traded by the Caddo tribes to their east.

Hasta Las Aguas • 101

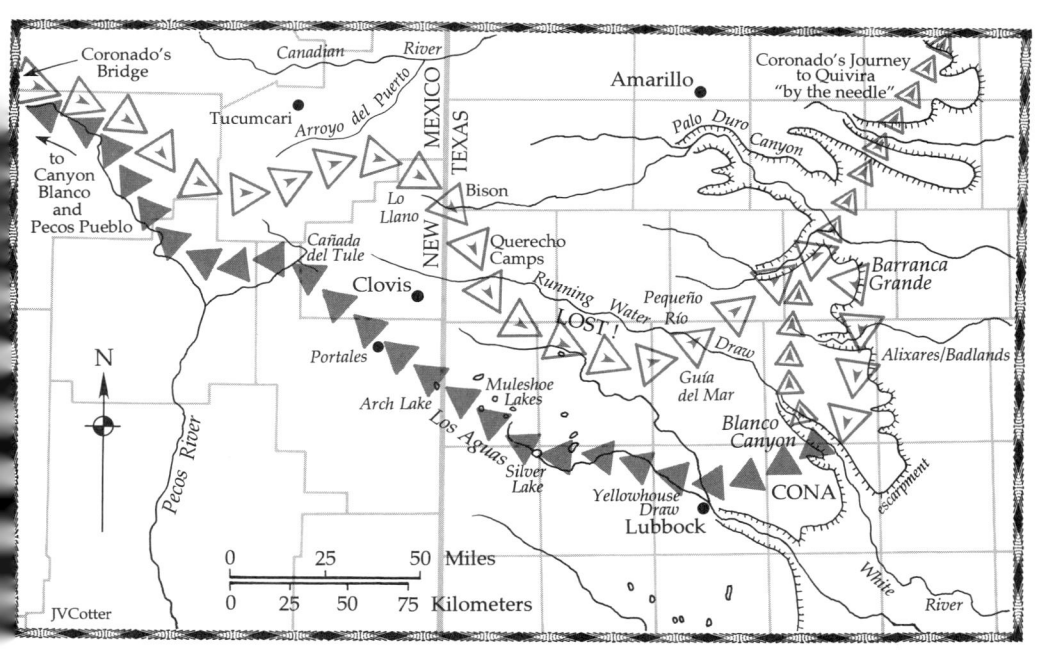

Teya guides led Coronado's main camp back across the Llano in the summer of 1541, following an efficient corridor among the interior lakes. *Map by John V. Cotter.*

Some forty of these saline lakes can be found in the interior of the Llano, stretching from Bailey and Lamb Counties in the north to Gaines County in the south.[16] It seems highly likely that Arellano's force availed themselves of this summertime opportunity to follow a chain of reliable lakes across the remaining half of the Llano. Both saline and freshwater lakes there formed a wet camp-corridor of travel to the west-northwest. Following this hydrological *rumbo* or course along the buried ancient drainage of the Portales River would bring natives and Spanish alike to the western or Mescalero Escarpment. From this edge obvious drainages led to the green ribbon of the distant Pecos River.

That Coronado's army camped among the Lost Lakes of the Llano seems certain. Castañeda's account of great salt lakes on their return convinces all but the most foolish trail detective that their course was among the salt lakes of the Llano only. The question lies rather with figuring out which of the forty-odd lakes they could have visited. The presence of many salt lakes in the drought-prone south of the Llano caught the attention of Winship, Hodge, Williams, and Udall. If Cona was in the Colorado drainage below, then the salt lakes of the ancient Simanola Valley could have been reached on the return journey. Three other researchers, Holden, Bolton, and Wedel, turned to the northern or Portales line of salt and freshwater lakes.

It is the latter or northern line of stepping-stone lakes in Bailey, Lamb, and Hockley Counties, that I find geographically compelling. This line has obvious advantages in starting from Blanco Canyon, as one is moving west-northwest from an ancient outlet of the Portales River to its desiccated headwater lakes. It is a natural route for experienced guides to take from the Brazos drainage. Taking only thirteen days to convey their horde of guests across the Llano, the Teya guides indeed used a *mas derecho camino*, a more direct road. That these lakes form a diagonal course intersecting the Pecos River road to Cicúye provides this important element of directness (see map, page 101).

The first of the stepping stones was possibly Yellow House Lake or Illusion Lake to its north. These lakes are conveniently accessed from Yellow House Draw below. Castañeda wrote that they found "*en este camino muchas lagunas de sal*" (on this road many salt lakes).[17] A further day's journey could have taken them to nearby Silver Lake. At least one researcher thinks the expedition definitely passed by Silver Lake in the summer of 1541. Edwin L. Kiser argued in 1978 that Castañeda's account of a fantastic bison bone bed on the margins of a salt lake could be correlated with a known palaeontological site known as the Silver Lake Bison Site.[18] Castañeda's Chapter 8 of Part III notes various marvels or *cosas admirables* encountered on the plains. In this chapter he devotes a precious paragraph to their encounter with a gigantic heap of bones, a Golgothic sign of something, but of what they were not sure. "Another thing one found, at the shore of a salt lake on the south side," he wrote, "was a great pile of cow bones as long as a crossbow shot or very little less. It was two spans high in places and three fathoms wide or more in places where there is no people to place them like that."[19] This gigantic pile of bones was a silent signifier of the mystery of the plains environment.

Striving to explain this unusual phenomenon, the Europeans rejected the idea of human agency. Something about the sight and location led them to believe that no people had created this *vaca* necropolis. In a prescient foretaste of the scientific impulse of the Western mind in the New World, veteran soldiers and young adventurers alike gathered round the enormous drift of bones on the south shore and theorized. Whereas the medieval mind conjectured on monsters, allegories, and the supernatural, these children of the Renaissance resorted to a new discourse with the landscape: they examined this buffalo graveyard as an admirable thing subject to practical environmental explanation.

They concluded that strong and seasonal northern winds periodically stirred the lake waters into wave action. Huge waves picked up the bones of the old and weak bison who had previously died in the lake margins, and deposited these remains into the present drift pile. Castañeda thought the number of bison needed to make this funerary pile was enormous. While this explanation does not satisfy modern criteria, it does underscore the mental impulse provided by the American Southwest in the ratiocination of physical geography. The Renaissance spirit of inquiry into natural causes—what later minds called "natural history"—already provides a lambent edge of critical Spanish thinking about the plains environment, one that has been poorly appreciated. It would be nice to see more regional artwork that portrays Castañeda studying the Texas environment, rather than a histrionic Coronado and cast, admiring scenery they may not have seen with feelings they may not have felt.

Silver Lake Bison Site is a large, mineralized bone bed about 100 feet south of Silver Lake, a saline basin on the county line between northwest Hockley County and northeast Cochran County. Fed by underground springs and seepages on its sides, Silver Lake was named centuries later for its illusive suggestion of silver when seen at a distance. At three-quarters of a mile long (north-south) and a quarter of a mile wide (east-west), it is only a dried-up puddle of its lacustrine glory during the Late Wisconsin glaciation. Arguments that the expedition returned via Silver Lake are suggestive rather than positive, as no definite proof exists, "nor will it ever be definitely proven," notes Kiser.[20] Nevertheless, the point is well taken that direct physical evidence of bone beds on the south side of salt lakes can be found in the Portales Valley—that is, among the northern line of salt lakes. Calling Castañeda's account "the first palaeontological site report, and perhaps also anthropological site report recorded in the American Southwest," Kiser concluded that Silver Lake was the most likely candidate matching the Spanish description.

A further day's journey away to the northwest lay the pleasant alkaline lakes and wetlands of present-day Muleshoe National Wildlife Area. The three Muleshoe lakes and their marshes were also a likely camping site for those traveling *hasta las aguas*. Fed solely by surrounding surface runoff, these precious wetlands filled with the spring and fall rains. The waters were often too alkaline for fish but frogs and many other species of pond life were part of the food chain. As a stopover for migrating wildfowl on the Central Flyway, this interior drainage south of Muleshoe, Texas, attracted many hundreds of thousands of seasonal residents. Sandhill cranes, ducks, geese, and magnificent whooping cranes paused here to rest and jostle one another. After the heat and dust of a summer march, the waters and game of this sanctuary in wet years were an oasis for people as well. Nearby prairie dog colonies provided the curious barking that broke the silence of these plains, and herds of buffalo supplied more meat for the hunters. "They killed a world of bulls and cows, for there were days when they brought 60 to 70 head into camp, and it was necessary to go hunting every day," said a chronicler.[21]

From the vicinity of Muleshoe the ancient lakes lead northwestward into modern Roosevelt County of New Mexico. An especially large saline basin lies ahead. Once known as "Laguna Salada" or "Great Salt Lake," this basin is now commonly referred to as Arch Lake. Located just west of the Texas–New

Mexico state line, Arch Lake is a flat, shallow expanse of evaporating water with a bitter taste. A remnant surrounded by sticky mudflats, one has to imagine its great ancestor laying down deposits of Tahoka clay for over fifty square miles.[22] Like other saline basins in the area, Arch Lake has a pronounced north-south axis, probably linked to geological processes of the deep-brine aquifer below. Castañeda's memory of a bone pile on the south shore is suggestive of the north-south geological axis of the Portales salt lakes as well.

Perhaps he had Arch Lake in mind when he mentioned that they encountered and tasted salt lakes with big, table-sized slabs of salt floating on the surface. These floating slabs were four or five fingers thick, but the salt from them was too bitter. Better tasting brine salt, he thought, was found below the waters where it crystallized.[23] Once more we see the curious and observing spirit in Castañeda that explores and remembers the plains environment through the taste buds. Modern dunefields or lunettes on the south and eastern sides reflect the presence of strong north winds scouring the basin and piling up lots of sand if not bones. Although the alkaline waters of Arch Lake were too bitter to drink, small water-table springs feeding it may have provided fresh water for horses and people.

A harsh march lay ahead, on the same west-northwest course as before, before reaching a true oasis in the plains at old Los Portales.[24] The cool, clear, freshwater discharge of Portales Springs has drawn thirsty travelers for many centuries. These important springs gush from a group of small caves with overhanging drip formations south of Portales, New Mexico. These hanging formations over the caves resembled *portales* or porches to the Hispanos returning to this land two and a half centuries later. Stopping at these convenient springs, one sipped the water and enjoyed the porch-like views. Teyas guides likely frequented these springs on routine trading trips to Cicúye. Los Portales may have been a regular stop on the aboriginal trade route to East Texas as well as for those Teya groups who often wintered outside Pecos Pueblo.[25] They were certainly utilized by later Hispanos crossing the plains to hunt and trade.

From Portales Springs the road likely advanced again northwest to the head of modern Taiban or Alamosa Canyon. Springs south of Melrose, New Mexico, and below the railroad station at Taiban, New Mexico, were good native camp sites. Mid-nineteenth-century U.S. military maps recorded an important *camino* in this area with a regular "Cañada del Tule" campsite.[26] Headwater springs in the canyon provided draughts of good, cold water to slake the thirst. More importantly, Captain Arellano and the others had reached the western edge of the great plain now. Taiban Creek flowed west, not east, a clear indication that the Pecos River lay downstream. Descending the canyon, perhaps pausing at Stinking Springs along the way, they were only a good day's march from the distant green cottonwoods at the juncture of Alamosa Creek with the Pecos.

Plotting their crossing along the above general corridor can be summarized as leaving Blanco Canyon (day 1), travel on the plain (day 2), Blackwater Draw (day 3), Yellow House Draw (days 4 and 5), Yellow Lake (day 6), Silver Lake (day 7), Muleshoe Lakes (day 8), Arch Lake (day 9), Los Portales (day 10), Cañada del Tule (day 11), Stinking Springs (day 12), and finally reaching the east bank of the Pecos River (day 13). Such a sequence of *hasta las aguas* just allows for crossing the Llano within the general thirteen-day time frame mentioned by Castañeda.

The Pecos River was profoundly orienting to Arellano's men. Their guides correctly noted that the Pecos River (or Rio de Cicúye, as the chronicles called it) joined the Rio Grande (Rio de Tiguex) about twenty days' journey to the south, from where the combined river turned east.[27] This solid geographic perspective is further evidence that the Teyas knew exactly where they were and where they were going. The conquistadors could find their way back to Tiguex from here, and perhaps they now allowed their faithful Teya guides to return to their families in the eastern canyonlands. Pedro de Castañeda remarked that they reached the Pecos River some thirty leagues or seventy-five miles below the wooden bridge constructed on their outbound journey. This note suggests that their juncture with the river was in the vicinity of old Bosque Redondo or Fort Sumner, New Mexico.

Bosque Redondo lies at the junction of Alamosa Creek with the main Pecos River. The famous site still has a calm, fresh, shady atmosphere after crossing the hot plains. For some travelers, like Billy the Kid, it is an eternal resting place. Giant cottonwoods rustle their leaves in the summer breezes. The appearance of so many cottonwoods at this juncture inspired the later Spanish place-name of *Bosque Redondo*. Here wood was in abundance for campfires, and the fresh, living water of the Rio de Cicúye slaked all thirsts. Now choked off by Lake Sumner and other dams upstream, the Pecos was a much brisker river in 1541. Arellano followed up the eastern banks of the Pecos for three or four days before seeing the reassuring sight of their intact floating bridge. Nowadays there is little need to wait for a bridge to cross since the flow of the river has been greatly reduced. One can wade across mostly at will except at the impoundments.

The all-meat diet of the plains apparently sent these vitamin-starved travelers to browsing among the fresh plant foods of the eastern river banks. "We marched upstream along its bank," Castañeda wrote, "almost everywhere it contained bushes with fruit which tasted like muscatel grapes. They grow on light branches an estado high and have leaves resembling parsley. There were unripe grapes, much wine, and marjoram."[28] Treating the Pecos banks as a salad bar, the conquistadors munched bison berries and grapes on their journey upstream. The second day brought them into a beautiful valley stretch of the Pecos River, an area still serene and sere. The Spanish-American pioneers of the 1860s called the place "Door of the Moon" and settled their plaza of Puerto de Luna within a hard day's journey of the Llano to the east. In the late 1930s and 1940s New Mexican researchers commonly located Coronado's Bridge at the small town of Puerto de Luna; state maps of New Mexico still show a marked "Site of Coronado's Bridge" at the end of State Road 91 south of Santa Rosa. The actual floating bridge was probably another thirty miles or more upstream, nearer the confluence of the Gallinas River with the Pecos. After a few more days of travel along the rapid river, the main army reached and recrossed their wooden bridge in the vicinity of Colonias, New Mexico. Now began the uphill four day trek via Cañon Blanco and Glorieta Mesa to the fortress pueblo of Cicúye. They were finally on a recognizable road, a major trading route from the eastern plains along which bison robes, headpieces, shields, bois d'arc, flint, and dried meat flowed toward the nearby Pecos Valley.[29]

Bigotes, Cacique, and the other Towans in Cicúye cannot have been happy to hear of the returning Spaniards. Fortunately for them, Tristán de Arellano had no notice of any confession from a doomed El Turco, one which implicated the elders of Pecos Pueblo in a plot to lead the foreigners to their destruction. No treachery was yet proven. But the Towans did not know this either. Perhaps El Turco had talked and told all? They decided to close their pueblo to the outsiders and they refused to honor Spanish entreaties for precious corn. "*El cual se hallo de guerra*" (they found it at war), penned Castañeda of Pecos Pueblo.

Arellano chose wisely to continue their advance to Tiguex rather than stop now to punish the unfriendly inhabitants. But the hostility concerned him for the sake of the missing Coronado and the other thirty soldiers who were also to return via Cicúye with news of Quivira. As the conquistadors approached the pueblos of the Rio Grande, the inhabitants who had moved back towards their former homes and fields fled once more to the surrounding hills. They had not forgotten the cruel Tiguex War of the past winter. The army settled once more in Coofor or "Parched Corn" Pueblo and began to requisition supplies of corn. Tired and disappointed, the bulk of the expedition settled down to await for word, any word, of their captain-general's fate. They had seen and heard nothing from him for many weeks.

Coronado, Fray Juan de Padilla, servants, and the chosen thirty soldiers had left the rancheria encampments at Cona determined to reach the province of Quivira.[30] From the Teyas or Jumanos the captain-general obtained reluctant guides for the trip north. Ysopete was now in favor while El Turco wore chains and was in disgrace. "Although I realized the hardships and dangers I should encounter on the journey due to the lack of water and maize," Coronado wrote the king, "I considered it best to go, in order to serve your majesty."[31] A few days after leaving Cona, however, the native guides ran away. Coronado was obliged to halt and wait until new ones could be secured. Again he ordered a reluctant main army to return to Tiguex from Cona.

There is little doubt that Coronado's reconnaissance to Quivira set out *north* from the second barranca, but beyond agreement as to this general cardinal point, no recent study has appeared on his route from Cona to the banks of the distant Arkansas River. This void is not the fault of scholars. There are only fragments of text from otherwise reliable sources with which to work. Coronado's own letter to the Charles V on October 20, 1541, contains merely one long sentence on this major leg of the journey:

> And with only the 30 horsemen whom I took for my escort, I traveled forty-two days after I left the force, living all this while solely on the flesh of the bulls and cows which we killed, at the cost of several of our horses which they killed, because, as I wrote Your Majesty, they are very brave and fierce animals; and going many days without water, and cooking the food with cow dung, because there is not any kind of wood in all these plains, away from the gullies and rivers, which are very few.[32]

There is also one long sentence in another eyewitness source, the *Relación* of Capt. Juan Jaramillo:

> And when everything was ready for us to set out and for the others to remain, we pursued our way, the direction all the time after this being toward the north, for more than thirty days' march, although not long marches, not having to go without water on any one of them, and among cows all the time, some days in larger numbers than others, according to the water which we came across, so that on Saint Peter and Paul's Day we reached a river which we found to be there below Quibira.[33]

Finally, much has been made of a further statement in Fray Motolinía's *Postrera de Sívola*:

> Francisco Vazquez set out across these plains in search of Quivira, more on account of the story which had been told us at the river than from the confidence which was placed in the guide here, and after proceeding many days by the needle [i.e., to the north] it pleased God that after thirty days' march we found the river Quivira, which is 30 leagues below the settlement.[34]

All this testimony is useful but much too brief to draw any meaningful conclusions on a specific route. What is needed is someone like the aging *vecino* of Culiacán, Pedro de Castañeda, penning memoirs of the sights, tastes, and curiosities of the landscape through which they were traveling. Instead, he gave a terse, nine-word, hearsay account, "*el general siguio sus guias hasta llegar a quiuira*" (the general followed his guides until coming to Quivira). Failing the discovery of new documentation, the trail detective can only speculate on the probable road Coronado's reconnaissance took out of Texas.

There are some clues. Taken together the texts suggest a slow reconnaissance northward through a typical Great Plains environment. The marches were neither long nor stressing, as Jaramillo noted. Indeed, the pace may have been set by those walking, like Fray Juan de Padilla. Coronado's use of dried buffalo chips for cooking-fuel invites sympathy from a king over the hardships of a nobleman on the trail. It is also one of the most telling clues that they spent much time on the treeless High Plains. The lack of wood on the High Plains was a major annoyance to someone accustomed to the verdant forests of Nueva Galicia. Coronado did qualify his remark that there was not any wood by noting this condition applied "away from the gullies and rivers, which are very few." The implication is that topographic breaks were infrequent, but useful sources of wood and water when found. This observation holds particularly true for a line of travel to the north, that is, a course which *intersects* the dominant east-west flowing drainages of the High Plains between Cona and the Arkansas River.

Formerly, Texas patriot-scholars claimed that Coronado never left the confines of Texas. Beginning in 1929 David Donoghue argued that the captain-general's reconnaissance merely reached the Canadian River, which has a Great Bend somewhat similar to that of the Arkansas River. This shrewd piece of revisionist reasoning, which appeared in the state's leading history journal and soared to popularity in the 1930s, kept Quivira safely in the Texas Panhandle and away from those fools in Kansas.[35] The eminent Catholic historian Carlos E. Castañeda found this argument so persuasive that he adopted it and later martyred Fray Juan de Padilla in the Texas Panhandle, a grievous miscarriage of geography. Unfortunately, a Canadian River Quivira also requires Coronado to travel at a snail's pace of only a few miles per day from a Cona at Blanco Canyon. A healthy child could have walked from Blanco Canyon or its vicinity to the Canadian River well ahead of Coronado's forty-two-day journey. No, it is much more certain that Coronado did cross the Canadian River, as well as the North Canadian, Cimarron, and other tributaries on his way to Quivira. There was a general lack of wood except for the infrequent east-west riverine corridors they crossed marching north, where wood and water were suddenly found in local abundance.

Archeological evidence strongly suggests that the Quivira of the Spanish accounts is in accord with the Wichita claims of Kansas. There is little reason not to honor fully the Kansas claims to Coronado; indeed, it is beyond the scope of this Southwest regional study to revise them. Most researchers accept the correlation that the reconnaissance force reached the Arkansas River at Ford, Kansas, just east of Dodge City, on the Feast Day of Saint Peter and Paul, or July 8, 1541. The historian H. E. Bolton did useful deductive thinking by starting at this accepted point—the natural ford crossing of the Arkansas River, just as the great river turns dramatically northeastward—and then worked backward to reach Palo Duro Canyon, his positive location for Cona. The line between these two points represented a probable line of daily march. A Blanco

Canyon version of Cona shares many similarities with a Palo Duro one, with a few important differences. Map lines drawn from Ford, Kansas, back to these respective locations indicate that a trail to Blanco Canyon would take longer and involve a more northerly course than a trail to Palo Duro. The timing difference may be significant for the apparent slowness of the group. They likely rested at good campsites for whole days or more, further slowing their progress.

Bolton and others have been equally taken with the comment in Motolinía's *Relación Postrera de Sívola* that Coronado traveled "many days by the needle." The phrase is an interesting question of semiotics, and demonstrates the power of ambiguity to enliven the past. There are literalists—a sin that afflicts all trail detectives at some point—who apply this statement unmercifully to the event and the trail. In this sense, a medieval Coronado literally dangles a magnetized needle from a piece of string and follows the needle's northern course over plain and arroyo, magnetic declination and all. It is more likely the group used a regular sea-compass, an instrument available and of great utility to their mission. They also made estimates of latitude in some manner. Bolton argued persuasively that they did in fact follow a literal magnetic bearing to the north, and there is a lot to admire in his detailed approach. But there were others whose opinions on the course may have counted, and these were the Teya guides and a triumphant Ysopete.

These guides may have had considerable responsibility for getting the Spanish to Quivira. Coronado himself never mentioned a compass, only that the guides directed him there. The Teyas undoubtedly had regular experience with several aboriginal trade routes from the Southern High Plains north to the Wichita grass lodges and cornfields of Quivira. Other trails linked them to the Pawnee or Harahey people. Castañeda reported earlier that the Teyas told them there was no *buena derrota* or good course to Quivira, but this statement did not preclude the presence of regular foot trails for these active traders. Coronado scholar Carroll L. Riley, for instance, finds important trade routes from the Garza-Complex settlements of the caprock, through the Wheeler-phase natives of western Oklahoma, all the way to the Arkansas River.[36]

It indeed may not have been the best of roads, but it is likely that a regular trading network did exist, and furthermore, that Coronado's party used extensive parts of it to their advantage. The Teya guides may also have known the best waters for these trails. Checking their guides' course with a compass would show the Spanish that, on average, they were indeed traveling "by the needle," that is, on a course slightly east of true north. Bolton's estimate of the magnetic declination was "ten or twelve degrees east of true north."[37] This declination gives their trek a gentle drift to the east to arrive at the Arkansas River ford, or that was the way the guides were going anyway, and the direction showed up on the compass as due north.

There is no certain evidence of their camps along such an aboriginal route. The following trail sketch is only a possibility. From Blanco Canyon or Cona,

Coronado and the replacement Teya guides may have advanced north across plains and along the eastern escarpment. Wood and water periodically appeared along the major drainages intersecting their path, offering opportunities to rest ("not long marches"—[Jaramillo]), and to fill their water containers ("not having to go without water on any one of them"—[Jaramillo]). The first river of consequence was the Prairie Dog Fork of the Red River. Crossing this shallow, vermilion river they moved northward and soon advanced onto the High Plains proper, perhaps around Clarendon, Texas. Once on the High Plains their course would be smoother across the immense grassland, but not too far from the watered drainages flowing along and off the mesa to the east.

The Llano stretches eastward in a series of great spurs here, and it makes sense to cut across them. Thus, camps along the Salt Fork of the Red River, the North Fork of the Red River, and the Washita are viable candidates. In between these camps, of course, were the intervening stretches of huge prairies. Here only dried chips were available for fuel, and vast herds of buffalo grazed. These plains are equally part of the magnificent levelness characterizing the Llano to the west. The size of these herds was, as Jaramillo noted, "according to the water which we came across." The fact that not a day passed without sizable herds indicated perhaps that the native course optimized the availability of water.

The Canadian River lay ahead. It is sad that it receives no mention in the accounts, for it too has a strong spirit of place. Near Canadian, Texas, they possibly camped and rested for a spell. This broad valley had the huge bison herds linked to the good water below and the fine pastures above. It was a familiar point for the Teyas. At some point messengers dispatched from the army at Cona caught up with Coronado and urged him to send for them. He dashed all hopes, declined to do so, and sent the messengers back, forcing Arellano's compliance in returning to Tiguex. From the cool cottonwoods of the Canadian Valley, Coronado continued a northern course, crossing Wolf Creek, and thereby soon passing out of modern Texas. The trail may have crossed a drainage divide here, thus joining a northeasterly tributary of the nearby North Canadian River (Beaver River to the west). Again, there were plenty of vast, lonesome High Plains between these infrequent *arroyos* and *rios*. The sky-crowned impression of the Great Plains environment would have dominated their daily experience. There was abundant meat on these level plains, even though several of their horses were gored to death in the process. The days of June were lengthening as summer approached. Beyond the North Canadian was the low Cimarron River, another divide, and then finally they saw the mighty Arkansas River, which Ysopete joyously recognized.

In early July of 1541 Coronado and the chosen thirty were on the north bank and advancing northeast along the great bend of the river. Although they were going downstream, their accounts mention that they were thirty leagues "below"—in latitude—the province of Quivira. Within a few more days they encountered a party of Wichita bison hunters. Using Ysopete as an interpreter as well as a guide, Coronado learned that Quiviran settlements were farther downstream. The Spanish were keenly disappointed after reaching the Wichita villages. Instead of rich towns of stone they saw only rude villages of thatched grass lodges. The tattooed natives had no gold or silver whatsoever. Despite the greatest care in searching, the conquistadors saw only a single copper ornament worn by the so-called Lord Tatarrax. For Ysopete these villages were home, and as promised he was granted his freedom for conducting them there. For Coronado these rustic encampments were the end of a very expensive dream.

For the better part of another month, Coronado and his companions ventured farther into the province of Quivira. They "discovered" more settlements and made further inquiries about the surrounding region. But there was no quick wealth as Europeans saw the matter. The Spanish were gratified, however, with the verdant landscape and the pleasant summer climate of Kansas. Juan Jaramillo noted the fertility of the soil and the flowing creeks. For Juan de Padilla these undiscovered lands were the perfect geography for the Franciscan mission. There were also herds of innumerable buffalo, lots of plums, and grapes in abundance. The Wichitas not only hunted the nearby buffalo but also farmed large plots of maize, beans, and squashes near their villages. From hearsay Castañeda gathered the impression that the land and climate were similar to that of Spain.[38]

Although the inhabitants of Quivira received Coronado and his men peacefully, by the end of July the Spanish were not inclined to linger anymore. There was no gold and their force was small. At the village of Tabas, near modern-day Lindsborg, Kansas, the captain-general called a council of war. All agreed that it was time to recross the plains and rejoin the main army before winter caught them. There was also the vexation of El Turco's presence as unfinished business. Kept under Captain Alvarado's guard, the chained captive lived as one without hope. Under severe torture by his captors he now broke down and confessed. He said he had lied and misguided them. He claimed that the people of Cicúye—angry at the Spanish treatment of Bigotes and Cacique—had used him in a plot of revenge.

The hope of the Towa puebloans was that El Turco would tell tales and set the conquistadors to wandering on the empty plains of the Llano. There the Europeans would perish from lack of food, or wander until they were too weak to cause more trouble. Angered at this huge deceit and further inflamed by El Turco's desperate cries that there was gold, only *mas allá*, farther on, Coronado let his captains settle the issue. The matter was probably arranged under Captain Alvarado's supervision. At night the camp butcher slipped a rope around the Pawnee's neck and garroted him quickly. *Mundus non vult descipi*—the world does not like being deceived.

Coronado's men now hastened in August to return to Tiguex. Early fall rains were already lashing the land. After obtaining a supply of maize from the Wichitas, Padilla erected and blessed a formal cross to claim the land, souls, and any wealth. They departed with all haste. Accounts suggest that new guides helped them in their return, and these guides were charged with saving them precious time. There was no need to return to Cona when they wished to reach Tiguex instead. The gateway from the plains to the pueblos was Cicúye or Pecos Pueblo, of course, and so that den of treachery was the intervening destination. The chosen thirty and their retinue probably recrossed the convenient Arkansas River ford thirty leagues upstream and set out on a general southwest course across the High Plains of Kansas, Oklahoma, Texas, and New Mexico.

These plains were the familiar blank levelness where dried cow dung was the only fuel, where muddy playa water might be the only water, and where other exotic animals roamed among the bison: elk, deer, antelope, and wolves. Cursory testimony from everyone except Jaramillo on this stretch of the trail defies close analysis, but it is probable that they returned along or near another native trade route running in almost a direct line from the angle of the Great Bend toward the Canadian River and Cicúye beyond. This route advanced across the upper watersheds of Arkansas River tributaries like the Cimarron, Beaver, and Canadian Rivers. As such it shares some similarities with the later Santa Fé Trail. After crossing the Arkansas ford, said Jaramillo, their guides led them on a new course, a different trail from the one to Cona: "taking the right hand [road], they led us along by watering places and among cows and by a good road, although there are none either one way or the other except those of the cows, as I have said."[39] Curiously, there is a well-maintained "Coronado Inscription" on a stone from Cimarron County near Goodwell, Oklahoma. The rustic, incised, ancient-looking message "Coronado 1541" has impressed few scholars, but the locals like the idea, and in general the Beaver River country of the Oklahoma Panhandle is quite plausible for a return route. The Colonial Dames of America thought so in 1936, when they erected a nearby rock marker proudly stating: "In This Vicinity Coronado Passed 1541."[40]

The tactical conception is to cut across the headwaters. This semi-direct route again intersperses easygoing flat plains with periodic topographic breaks for wood and water. A corridor of travel that spatially maximized easy plains with convenient watered and wooded camps was likely the *camino* in the chronicles. For people without horses, the flatness of the High Plains was a topographic asset. The flat stretches made it easier and faster to move around with dog travois, for example. Jaramillo reported further in his narrative that they had encountered their outbound trail after many days of travel.[41] Recognizing their trail across the Llano is less likely than their recognition of a landscape with features, such as the upper Canadian River watershed. Captain Alvarado and Fray Padilla could have recognized the Canadian Valley as well from their first trip into the plains. Ascending if necessary and then crossing the Canadian River, they turned west-southwest to head the divide and reach the Pecos River. They knew this *Rio de Cicúye* well. They now backtracked with ease on the road to Pecos Pueblo.

The Towa natives there might have killed him, but they had just been fought and humiliated by a timely Spanish force under Capt. Tristán de Arellano. Other captains were roaming the distant pueblos of the Rio Grande taking grain and seizing supplies for the coming winter, but it was a loyal Captain Arellano who set out to find news of the missing captain-general. He was therefore already at a sullen and subdued Pecos Pueblo when Coronado and the others rode in wearily. There was great rejoicing at their reunion. By the middle of September 1541 both groups had returned to army headquarters at Tiguex. Like the fabulous Seven Cities of Gold, Quivira had been a major disappointment. But the army was intact and the Spanish still had their leader.

All that changed with a string of disasters and setbacks over the winter. During a December horse race, Coronado fell from his mount and received a severe injury when another horse kicked him in the head. As he slowly recuperated over the winter he gave up his half-hearted plans for further exploration onto and beyond the buffalo plains. Perhaps there was an element of superstition as well. It was reported that long ago in Spain a friend had declared "that he would become a powerful lord in distant lands, and that he would have a fall from which he would never be able to recover."[42] Through various ruses Coronado built a consensus to abandon the search, even though many conquistadors wished to stay and look further. A fierce native revolt at Corazones, a revolt against a subordinate's excesses that cut his lines of communication, finally settled the issue.

Around the first of April 1542, the disillusioned mass set out on the long trail back to Spanish settlements in New Spain. Coronado was often carried on a cowhide litter slung between two plodding mules. He looked less like a leader than an invalid, and camp discipline slackened noticeably as they neared Culiacán. At this settlement the official expedition began breaking up. Many soldiers drifted away. Some, like Pedro de Castañeda, settled into the exciting frontier life of Culiacán itself. Coronado slowly continued on to Mexico City to make his sad official report to Viceroy Mendoza. Within a few years he was forced to stand trial before the Royal Audiencia on serious charges of expedition mismanagement. Others were in disgrace or before courts as well. Mendoza protected Coronado from the worst charges, and even restored him to activity in governmental affairs, but virtually all his contemporaries considered that his health—and perhaps his mind—had been irreparably damaged in the riding accident. On a Saturday night, September 22, 1554, a broken Francisco Vázquez de Coronado died at his home in Mexico City at the age of forty-four.

For three centuries following his death, the achievements of this great explorer went little noticed by the world at large. The official attitude was that an expensive, two-year, speculative venture led by a thirty-year-old protégé had turned out to be an economic bust. Many of the participants were obliged to defend themselves before a ponderous and capricious bureaucracy, but when the litigation ceased so did much of the attention. Documents and maps were soon lost to time. Even Coronado's tomb in the old church of Santo Domingo, three blocks north of the better-known cathedral in Mexico City, was lost from memory for many decades.[43]

Why is it, then, that we find ourselves so stirred by the Coronado expedition some four and a half centuries later? In part our remembrance is keyed to the sheer geographical exuberance of these conquistadors' travels. In only two years Coronado's men ranged from California to Texas. Organized Europeans were at last penetrating the unknown interior of the continent. Their conclusions on the breadth of the new land slowly diffused back to European mapmakers and attracted further interest. The expedition proved that the Spanish could enter the new land by following the aboriginal trade routes. For students and scholars the narratives also provide a priceless account of the existing environments, including of course the first lengthy discussion of the Llano of Texas and New Mexico. This written documentation constitutes a direct link between Southwestern prehistory and history.

The Coronado entrada further compels our remembrance because it provides a cultural context for the contemporary landscape. Dozens of towns and places celebrate the fact—or the geosophical fancy—that Coronado's men, women, and allies once passed through their locales. Scores of years before the English landed, died freely, and eventually settled the east coast of America, the Spanish had been active in the Southwest, a fact of considerable pride now for many communities in Arizona, New Mexico, Texas, Oklahoma, and Kansas. Hispano roots in the Southwest appeared to deepen with the Anglo-American scholarship, appreciation, and romantic cult of the expedition. Yet the surname Vázquez (the name by which Francisco's contemporaries knew him) is ignored in favor of the English preference for "Coronado," a little-used name then that now emblazons restaurants, hotels, motels, schools, highways, streets, gift shops, societies, and pageants across half a dozen states as a sign of the land. The Coronado name is our Quivira, our mirage of the mind.

Indeed, the very name of Coronado now conjures something deep within the subconscious of the Southwestern mind: the search for riches. Like the conquistador of old, many of the present residents of the Southwest are drawn to the legendary realm by the lure of fortunes to be wrung from the environment. There is treasure to be wrestled from the Southwest in the form of minerals, agriculture, timber, trade, and of course its generous and captivating real estate. Like Coronado, we also are dreamers. For a humble scholar like myself, the Grail is simpler: somewhere in the canyonlands of the northeast Llano is a site for Coronado's encampment in the barrancas. The West Texas spring hailstorm that struck their first barranca camp in 1541 not only pounded the people and animals but it also smashed equipment, supplies, and especially the crockery. This storm likely pounded enough of these sixteenth-century cultural artifacts into the ground to render the site detectable.

The smashed gourds are long gone of course, but somewhere on a ranch in the eastern Llano—and I think I know where to look—there may be a site, a rich site, with a scattered treasure of broken majolica and crockery shards, glass trade beads, crossbow boltheads, and other bits of sixteenth-century European metal debris. Here in the legendary Barranca Grande are the dreams of modern archeologists. Supposedly, a man named Nystel once came across a site in the 1870s characterized by hundreds of broken shards of fine glazed pottery, but it is an old vague tale by now, almost lost to time. In a sense perhaps it is best that the Barranca Grande majolica shards and casual artifacts remain undiscovered for awhile. As long as we have mysteries, we have motivation to explore the world. The Coronado mysteries are too grand and too sublime to dispel all at once.

The pursuit of treasure—in all its forms—still motivates the mind in this land of beauty and frustration. There is one comparable and perhaps equally glorious Southwestern pursuit: the search for truth. It is this final search that compels us to establish and fix the spirit of place for that portion of the "northern mysteries" that Pedro de Castañeda casually called *lo llano*. Not content with a narrative discussion alone of the plains, Castañeda wrote further chapters to elaborate on these unusual flatlands. These words open new windows into the early Spanish perception of the mesaland. They also constitute a human statement on the role of insight in discovery and learning.

·8·

CASTAÑEDA'S GENIUS LOCI

Agora diremos de los llanos que es una tierra llana y espaciosa . . .
PEDRO DE CASTAÑEDA

A comparison of Ternaux's translations with some of the Spanish texts which he had rendered into French . . . showed me that Ternaux had not only rendered the language of the original accounts with great freedom, but that in several cases he had entirely failed to understand what the original writer endeavored to relate.

GEORGE PARKER WINSHIP

George Parker Winship never cared for Henri Ternaux-Compans's French translation of Pedro de Castañeda's narrative. He thought the Ternaux version was "much more characteristic of the French translator than of the Spanish conquistadors."[1] Winship's own translation was exceedingly literary and often beautiful. Unfortunately, it also reflected a distorted East Coast perception of the Great Plains, one characteristic of the 1890s eastern establishment. Nowhere is this more clear than in Winship's flawed translation of Castañeda's "los llanos." Like Winship, one needs to separate from a distant translation, however beautiful, and reread the humble Spanish text of Pedro de Castañeda for a closer understanding of the region. He was there, after all, and Winship was not. Can we recover a land seen through the eyes of a Golden Age adventurer instead of through the lenses of a Harvard bibliographer who never lived on these plains?

Pedro de Castañeda's family came to the New World from the obscure Spanish town of Najera on the Bay of Biscay. The son of a conquistador, Pedro de Castañeda was only a common soldier accompanying the main army. When he sat down around 1563 to record a truthful account of the Coronado entrada, however, he proved to be an uncommonly strong narrator. He reported with spontaneous objectivity and unusual clarity. Although he sought to preserve the memory of all their many curious discoveries, one region of the new lands obviously dominated his memory—the Great Plains. Although he spent only a season on the plains, he devoted almost a quarter of his written narrative to the "truthful discoveries" between Cicúye and Quivira, that is, to the Great Plains environment and peoples. This region was obviously a point of renewed interest in the 1560s. Perhaps Castañeda's audience wished to know if the wild rumors about Quivira were accurate. In any case, he wrote at length on the plains and its societies, devoting entire chapters in Part Two and Part Three to the *cosas admirables*—the excellent things—of this strange part of the world.

Surprisingly, Castañeda's personal experience of the Great Plains was limited solely to the Llano and its margins. He did not travel north to Quivira, like Jaramillo or Padilla, as one of Coronado's chosen thirty men. Instead he humbly returned across the plains with Arellano's main army. In the latter two parts of his narrative, however, he expanded his vision to encompass "*los llanos*," the Great Plains proper. His general comments were lucid and presented a reasonable geography of this vast region. But his personal experience of the Southern High Plains dominated his perception of the other plains beyond. More than anything, his lengthy discussion of the plains environment sprang from the memory of his encounter with the Llano portion of it. In the process of preserving an account of the Road to Quivira, he more properly captures the peculiar *genius loci*, the Llano spirit of place that first struck the European imagination.

If Castañeda's memory conveys the ordinary conquistador's perspective, then the High Plains, or *los llanos* now, was perceived as a vast desert. "*Lo que de estos llanos,*" he wrote, "*se bio todo era despoblado*" (The thing about these plains is one saw it was all a desert).[2] The key word is *despoblado*, a highly descriptive Spanish word for a desert or uninhabited region.[3] Winship's popular translation completely fastens on the issue of depopulation: "No settlements were seen anywhere on these plains," he translated. What Winship meant, of course, is that there were no permanent town settlements there. After all, Castañeda left a good account of the rancheria tents of the Querechos who dwelled seasonally in this cosmic domain. But does not Castañeda's *despoblado* refer also to the landscape and environment rather than to people? In this sense his word choice conveys a warning to others about this land. It implies a difficult or challenging environment, one not very suitable for colonial settlement or traditional cultivation. The short-grass plains of the Llano masked their agricultural treasure well, even as they profligately displayed its largess of stock.

This initial European perception of the plains as an uninhabited desert—a flat and spacious *despoblado*—conjured up images of sparse vegetation, scant human presence, a lack of wood, possible water shortages, salt lakes, drought, and the like. Even more daunting were the perceived parallels between the Llano and North Africa. Tales of Moorish nomads and harsh deserts could be directly compared to the Querechos of the plains. "*Andan como alarabes*"— "They travel like the Arabs," he wrote of the nomads.[4] And they used "Moorish packsaddles" on their dogs. Earlier the expedition had crossed two stretches of *despoblado*, one near the Sonora Valley and the other beyond Chichiticale in southern Arizona, so Castañeda had the prior experience of the Sonoran Desert as a reference. His perception of the Llano as a *despoblado* thus adds the important element of aridity into the sense of place.

A second environmental metaphor of the plains was the nearness of *el çielo*: the sky. The light of the Llano has the full weight of the sky behind it. There is little to filter, block, or screen the sky-crowned view. To wander on the mesa, as Georgia O'Keeffe later did from her home in Canyon City, is to experience the fullness of the earth's atmosphere. The experience is not for the agoraphobic. The sky has an oceanic quality, a sharpness and clarity as if this gaseous window on the universe were less scratched and dirty. Unfortunately, George Parker Winship's East Coast translations (which are still circulating widely) missed the whole point of Castañeda's perception of this sky realm.

"The country is like a bowl," Winship translated, "so that when a man sits down, the horizon surrounds him all around at the distance of a musket shot."[5] It is difficult to make sense of this remark. What Castañeda actually said was, "*es la tierra de hechura de bola que donde quiera que un hombre se pone lo cerca el çielo a tiro de ballesta*" (It is the land with the shape of a globe, so that wherever a man places himself, the sky is about him unto a great distance).[6] Note that the key word *bola* is best translated as "ball" or "globe," that is, an inverted bowl or *bolus* shape. The sensation of shape should be *convex* in nature, but Winship's translation conveys the opposite or a *concave* sensation. Furthermore, *a tiro de ballesta* is an idiomatic expression or slang for "at a great distance," not Winship's foreshortened measure of a "musket shot." Perceptions of distance were distorted. Even the improved 1940 Hammond and Rey translation of Castañeda has problems with this perception of this environment.[7]

The problem before us is that what Castañeda perceived, remembered, and recorded of the Llano is not always rendered accurately. Winship's translations were very influential; thus, his English renderings fully persuaded historians of the concavity thesis and worse. Consider a related Winship passage on the Llano from Castañeda's Chapter 8 of Part III "The reason for all this was that the country seemed as round as if a man should imagine himself in a three-pint measure, and could see the sky at the edge of it, about a crossbow shot from him, and even if a man only lay down on his back he lost sight of the ground."[8] Naturally we try to imagine this bizarre vision, seeing ourselves lying down in the concavity of a three-pint measure with a cocked crossbow, inside Winship's earlier "bowl." Other historians quickly followed this lead. "It is a fact observed by all the travelers on the High Plains," Walter Prescott Webb noted in *The Great Plains* about this passage in Winship, "that because of the extremely level surface one gets the impression of being in a concavity; it is uphill every way one looks."[9]

Webb's "fact" of concavity and "uphillness" is quite interesting even if it is not exactly what Castañeda meant. Perhaps our modern illusion is that the levelness looks uphill rather than downhill in all directions. The ambiguity was somewhat noticeable as even Webb went on to confess: "Just what Castañeda means by saying one lost sight of the ground when he lay down on his back is not clear."[10] Turning to the Spanish presents quite a surprise: *"causaba todo esto ser la tierra tam redonda que do quiera que un hombre se ponia pareçia que estaba en la cumbre y uia el çielo a el rededor de si a tiro de ballesta y por poca cosa que se le ponia delante le quitaba la uista de la tierra* (Causing all this is the land, which is so round that in whatever part a man places himself it seems that he stands on the summit, and he sees the sky round about him to a great distance, and so very near a thing [the sky is], it suggests that the view separated him from the land).[11]

What Castañeda wanted to say about the High Plains was that here one felt the great *convex* curvature of the earth, a subtle illusion of the horizon perhaps, but one that expanded the very presence of the sky. Instead of Winship and Webb's prone observer in a concave slough of despair, the actual text suggests a more exalted perception: the fortunate observer at the top of the world, a Petrarch of the Plains who feels the cosmic "standing out" or *ex stasis* of a landscape view that removes the mind from the earth. No matter where you stood the land seemed to slope away gradually from the observer in all directions. It is a keen deception, conducive to ecstasy or, as later travelers called it, the presence of the sublime. On parts of the plains today, ranchers, hunters, and farmers can still experience the curious sensation of the abstract sublime. It rises from the dimensional disorientation caused by the extremely level gradients, averaging about ten feet per mile, combined with the rolling microtopography of subtle deflations and playa drainages. Distances and scales become uncertain in these plains.

Winship's "horizon" does not do justice to the fullness of Castañeda's *el çielo*. There was a cosmic quality to this land. First, you could see far, you could perceive remote objects at a great distance. Second, there were the distorted or illusive appearances, as when a solitary buffalo (with the sky showing beneath his torso) resembled four distant pine trees.[12] Something about this sky created uncertain appearances. Sound carried over great distances as well, providing an enhanced acoustic dimension to the ether. The land and sky together promoted deception and illusion as Castañeda reminded the reader in his account of lost hunters and mirages.

Second, there was the overwhelming presence, the absolute nearness of the sky : *lo cerca el çielo*. Sky surrounded you as a dominant medium. The northwest Llano near Tucumcari rises to 5,000 feet above sea level. The average elevation of 3,500 feet brings the lowland observer closer to magnificent turquoise heavens. On moonless nights there are brilliant stars and planets all around, a panoply stretching right down to the full 360° horizon, as at sea. But unlike the sea there is no vessel between you and the flat wilderness of water. The vision of the sky is here unobstructed and all-encompassing. One feels more exposed to the atmosphere here. It can be terrifying when there is no protection from the elements. During a severe electrical storm thousands of lightning bolts pound the ground. People and horses alike must roll on the ground in abject fear. The raging blizzards of winter, these freezing typhoons of snow and ice called "Northers" after their Arctic air-mass sources, are still dreaded and feared. Yet there are many beautiful skyscapes: brilliant sunrises; shimmering mirages; fanciful cumulus clouds; distant slanting *virgas* or rainshafts; towering cumulonimbus thunderstorms; rainbows; the rare borealis, sun dogs, and dusty Western sunsets. As the jet stream winds its sinuous way northward in late spring and early summer, the Llano's *el çielo* becomes the active and elemental playground of the sky gods.

Castañeda's sensitivity to the environment of the Southern High Plains was especially acute in Chapter Seven of Part Two, "which treats of the plains that were crossed, of the cows, and of the people who inhabit them." Long cloaked by eastern establishment perceptions, editions, and translations, his terse comments reveal a wealth of insight into the *genius loci* of these plains. Castañeda's memory here recorded an essential core of regional understanding, one often keyed to perception itself. In Chapter Seven he gives a distinct sense of place for the Llano, one that later American explorers could recognize and join with him in agreement. Many of the chronicler's intuitive remarks point to certain idiosyncratic features that, taken together, constitute a regional sense of identity, a chorology of place. In particular, Castañeda's rudimentary discussions of the hydrology and the geomorphology of the Llano deserve recognition. To some degree we are still engaged in solving the same mysteries that he first pondered.

"Some round ponds were discovered," he wrote, "like plates, of a stone's throw in width or larger. Some were fresh and some salt." These *lagunas redondas*, "round ponds," were the famous playas of the Llano Estacado. Castañeda recalled these curious wetland features of the dry featureless plains, but only with the aid of modern airplanes can ordinary people and great artists like Georgia O'Keeffe really see the sea of shining "Silver Dollars"—the hundreds and hundreds of sun-glinting round playas, filled by seasonal rains and dotting the landscape of farms and corridors. Migrating wildfowl have the best view of the playa country, but after heavy rains the quiet, low glidepath into Amarillo's airport offers a stunning vision of their abundance and wetland raiment. The genesis of playas on the Southern High Plains is still debated by the scientific community. The mystery lingers. We wonder, as did the first Europeans, why are these lakes so very round? Was it wind or water that shaped these pleasant curiosities?

Nineteenth-century pioneers speculated that wallowing buffalo broke through the sod surface and started the process. They even called these shallow basins buffalo wallows. In the twentieth century a cosmic few wondered if meteorites played a role in pockmarking the land with these tiny oases. Some important geological studies pointed to gradual water infiltration, dissolution, land subsidence, and solutional piping,[13] while others stressed erosion and wind deflation processes.[14] In the latter view, scientists such as Thomas Gustavson, C. M. Woodruff Jr., and Vance Holliday argue that both surface winds and waters shaped these peculiar landscape features.[15] Over many millennia ancient southwest winds generally deflated soil from the young Pecos Valley, and the millions of tons of dust and dirt blanketed, smoothed, and polished the surface of the new mesa with the Blackwater Draw Formation. The finest silts and clays of this formation were carried the farthest, to the northeast, while the coarser, sandy material settled out more quickly in the southwest. Despite the level, depositional nature of the Llano surface, various deflating winds also formed and developed localized depressions within the flatland, especially in the deeper, more wind-erodible soils of the Blackwater Draw Formation.

These small depressions gradually began to gather adjacent rainfall and erosive surface runoff. In the north-central Llano, where the clay loam soils were often thick, fine-textured, and less permeable to water, these depressions often grew deeper from wind erosion and rounder from increased rainfall and greater centripetal erosion. Heavy rains washed in erodible sediment from all sides, keeping the aspect of the lakes fairly nicely rounded. Deflating winds during dry, dusty spells whisked away much of the material eroded into the basins and then some. The fluvial and the aeolian—the water and the wind—in the Gustavson model thus created thousands of round lakes "a stone's throw in width or larger." Perhaps Castañeda's use of the modifier *redondas* for these ponds does correlate with a Coronado Corridor in the north-central Llano, an area where better rainfall, finer clay loams, active centripetal erosion, and strong deflating winds all had created an abundance of small lakes that were memorably rounded.[16] Playa depth and width in general depended on important variables of soil texture and erodibility, thicknesses of the Blackwater Draw Formation, permeability, and water tables. At the bottom of each playa new soils are mixed and formed with plant debris and lake sediments and then subjected to periodic blowouts. Gradually the basin expands over many centuries until it develops into a mature playa.

Other geologists study the subtle underground processes, the complex and mysterious interactions of plants, permeable soils, dissolution, and natural recharge in explaining playa development. On the Southern High Plains they point to the role of water infiltration in developing "recharge playas," catchment basins that gather and slowly percolate their precious waters downward through the filtering earth to recharge the vast Ogallala Aquifer below the surface. This process is thought to be aided greatly by organic acids from pond plants that promote carbonate dissolution, piping, and voiding beneath the playa.[17] A good observer, Castañeda remembered the luxuriance of the vegetation around the playas. "In these ponds there is some large weed," he wrote, "Away from them everything is very short, a span or less." Actually, he used the term *yerba crecida*, usually translated as "tall grass," perhaps wild buckwheat, but any number of tall pond plants could be referred to, especially the bulrushes.[18]

Approximately 25,000 playas currently dot the Llano.[19] Most are only one to ten acres in size and very shallow, but a few old-timers reach upwards of a mile in width and a decent depth. Additionally, there are about forty ancient lakes which intersect the zone of saturation, giving them more permanence but increased salinity—Castañeda's *lagunas de sal* that figured so prominently in their recrossing of the Southern High Plains. Playas are fascinating ecosystems that fill with water, then bloom for months in waves of plant growth as the water evaporates. Most playas "flower" during the cyclic summer growth season. The open-water zone gradually dries up and gives way to emergent aquatics, in turn receding to the weed zone. Few people realize how ancient and important the playas really are. Some of their soils are radiocarbon-dated to 10,000 years, with a few large basins going back 35,000 years ago.

Unfortunately, bonanza farming in the twentieth century has taken a heavy toll on the poorly appreciated playa basins. Waves of farm-extension agents and maximalist bankers have combined with bulldozer thinking to encourage farmers to mutilate, fill in, drain, and destroy many natural playas. By concentrating the former shallow waters in deep pits at the center, for instance, the fertile playa soils could be put to the plow. Today feedlots often locate near a large playa in order to use its natural drainage to collect and store the substantial animal wastes generated by their industrial operations. Some nuclear waste at Pantex has apparently contaminated the playas of the weapons base. Clearly the renewed appreciation and preservation of these distinctive features is in order at this point, although this view is not always a popular one with hard-pressed residents trying to increase agricultural production.

A further distinctive attribute of these curious basins is the presence of lunettes, crescent-shaped mounds of dunes that are often found around the east and southeast sides of the deeper and larger playas. Lunettes are present in Africa and were named by their observers in Australia. There are a thousand or more of them on the Southern High Plains alone. Some of their sandy ridges reach forty feet in height. Stabilizing vegetation helps to anchor the dunes in many places. Castañeda surely observed them, especially the lunettes in the saline basins. Scouring the lake sediments and Blackwater Draw soils, the deflating winds of the Llano episodically piled up these dune ridges, although not all large playas have them.[20] Some of the ridges have been slowly building for 20,000 to 30,000 years. Lunettes also contain important archeological material, from the first appearance of the Clovis People in North America to XIT campsites.

Playa grasses, sedges, forbs, and indicator plants like spikerushes made up a lush, sizable extent of the round pond area, as Castañeda notes.[21] Healthy playas have a complex wetland ecology that supports dozens of species of insects and microinvertebrates as well as the usual frogs, turtles, snakes, raccoons, and other predators. Each spring and fall great flocks of migrating wildfowl use the recharged playas for habitat stopovers. The Llano playas are therefore an important part of the Central American Flyway. Dense colonies of arrowhead or "duck potato plants" provide food, and good stands of *Scirpus* species or bulrushes (there are seven species alone found in Llano playas) offer adequate cover.

Although Castañeda could not have suspected it, the role of all the vegetation in and around these distinctive wetlands may be an important one. Playas concentrate plant organic debris, which oxidizes and forms carbonic acids. At the margins of the pond, these natural acids could infiltrate, leach, and dissolve the underlying caliche. Thus, a playa might slowly expand as the organic acids promote a gentle subsidence radiating outward. Annular expansion of the playa continues until a threshold size is reached relative to the catchment area and precipitation patterns. This infiltration theory is controversial, however, as new studies return the focus to the strong role of the wind in playa genesis and development.[22]

This system of interior drainage is remarkable, something to be remembered, a *cosa admirable*. The playa country thus constitutes an effective alternative to what would be the wasteful runoff behavior of affluent stream networks. That is, instead of rains pouring off rapidly, as in the integrated stream networks of the Sierra Madre or Mississippi Valley, this amazingly flat landscape gathers and confines the scarcer moisture into thousands of ephemeral round oases. There is a minimum of erosion really, and the low gradients and high soil porosities conserve the precious rains and snows. Gathered in the playas some of the moisture slowly percolates and filters below. The Llano of first contact with Europeans was thus an extraordinary landscape of conserved moisture. Castañeda's comments remind us that *los llanos* can be recognized, can be perceptually understood, as the region where the land becomes so flat that traditional drainage patterns turn upon themselves, leaving behind circular ponds ringed with the dominant shortgrass plains. One could sense the difference.

What Castañeda could not have recognized is that some of the playa waters percolated deep below. There they had merged over 10,000 years to form a vast, freshwater aquifer in buried Pleistocene sands and gravels. Although 90 percent of the surface moisture is lost to summer evaporation, a good recharge playa may filter about 10 percent of its annual runoff downward. This moisture reaches a saturation zone and mixes with the ancient rains of earlier times in the huge Ogallala Aquifer. From here the groundwater flows slowly, mostly eastward, until it reaches strong discharge springs, further hydrologic features that Castañeda did recognize and comment upon.

A second critical distinction was that these plains had no woodlands, no trees. "*No tiene arboleda*" (It has no woodland), Castañeda observed, but then he qualified this sweeping generalization by adding, "*sino en los rios que ay en algunas barrancas*" (except along the rivers that are in some ravines). Again there was a good deal of geography behind the simple observations. The lack of trees on the plains owes much to the regional climate and fire ecology. Fire often swept the Llano, whether natural or man-made. The Spanish themselves ignited the prairie grasses of the Llano, hoping the soaring smoke plumes would attract their lost hunters. Fed by winds scouring the level plateau, these burnings were less often the dangerous man-killers than the popular imagination supposes. But combined with drought, blizzard winds, and other climatological constraints, fires actively suppressed woodland formation.

This truism does not hold, however, as Castañeda noted correctly, on the margins of the great mesa. On the edges of the mesa, fire-adapted trees like Mohr's and Rocky Mountain Juniper clung to upper canyon rims. These xerophytic remnants of the ancient Rocky Mountain forest still crop out on a few north-facing slopes. Further down in these cool *barrancas* were groves of good timber along the watercourses. Dominated by Plains cottonwoods, these drainages also nourished stands of hackberry, willow, mulberry, plum, oak, and Rocky Mountain juniper. In the wetter reaches, tall cottonwoods and understory trees laced together to form a lush gallery woodland or *arborleda*. On the nearby flats were mesquites and redberry junipers. In short, despite the terseness of his comment, Castañeda makes the crucial distinction: no trees on the flat plains above; good timber in the watered canyons and margins below.

A third distinctive characteristic of the Llano were *algunas barrancas* (some canyons), geomorphological features that Castañeda mentioned several times. Undoubtedly, he is referring to the entrenchment canyons of the eastern Llano escarpment. But what is he trying to tell us about these barrancas? Winship relates the key passage as follows:

> These are no groves of trees except at the rivers, which flow at the bottom of some ravines where the trees grow so thick that they were not noticed until one was right on the edge of them.

Therefore, the thick tree growth in the canyons hid the rivers from view until one practically stood on their banks. The historians Hammond and Rey concurred:

> There are no trees except along the rivers which there are in some barrancas. These rivers are so concealed that one does not see them until he is at their edge.

As one who always had trouble understanding what the devil Castañeda was talking about on the plains in English, the Spanish comes as a great relief:

> No tiene arboleda sino en los rios que ay en *algunas barrancas que son tam encubiertas* que hasta que estan a el bordo de ellas no son vista.[23]
>
> It has no woods except in rivers that are in some barrancas that are so concealed that until you are standing at the edge of them, they are not seen.

That is, the point is not that thick tree growth hid the headwater rivers; rather, it was the *barrancas* or canyons that were concealed from sight. Ranchers and other residents know intuitively that fringing riparian timber does not hide a watercourse so much as it reveals the very existence of a watercourse to the thirsty. From a vantage point one can trace easily the course of a headwater by noting the fringing gallery woodland.

Castañeda's key perception of the barrancas country was precisely that one *suddenly* encountered the hidden abysses. "[These barrancas] are so concealed that until you are standing at the edge of them, they are not seen." Slogging along across the Llano, only at the last minute does one feel and see the earth give way to the steep, vertical-sided barranca. It can be an eerie experience, the vertiginous sensation of which lingers deep in the memory. After walking across an apparently endless horizontal expanse, a veritable rent in the earth opens up with little forewarning. The venerable Mota Padilla captured this distinctive topography in his 1742 account of Coronado's expedition: "*pasaron una barranca profundo, que fue la primera quiebra que vieron de la tierra desole Tigúes*" (they came to a deep barranca which was the first gash they had seen in the earth since Tiguex). Mota Padilla's *quiebra* (fracture, gash, fissure) has an important geological background, one that needs explanation.

A geomorphic process known as "solution and collapse"—linked with a restless deep-brine aquifer and active surface erosion by wind and water—has steadily carved away at the eastern escarpment. This fascinating entrenchment process gives the eastern barranca country of the Llano a special, complicated, and beautiful fractal "coastline." Furthermore, groundwater erosion or sapping by the Ogallala Aquifer below contributes significantly to the entrenchment by giving the barrancas steep sides *"como las de Colima"* (like those of Colima). Areas with heavy groundwater erosion can be expected to have deep, vertically-sided ravines, or, as Mota Padilla called them, *barrancas profundas*. One part of the plains has this distinctive geomorphology to perfection: the northeastern escarpment in Armstrong and Briscoe Counties, Texas, stretching their cape and bay coastline southward. There the canyons were deep and the groundwater springs ran strong.

When Castañeda thus refers to some barrancas, hidden from sight until one reaches the very edge of them, he is likely describing the northeastern escarpment. The western or Mescalero escarpment has an entirely different feel about it. The Pecos River, or the *Rio de Cicúye* as Castañeda called it, is a relatively new stream-piracy system. This river first isolated the mesaland to the east about 100,000 years ago, leaving the Llano as a high, stable, fairly dry, remnant plateau. Climate, wind, plant, and complex soil processes then combined over millennia to form an extensive "pedogenic carbonate horizon," that is a level caliche layer that capped the top, hence the famous white "Caprock." The fact that the conquistadors were forced to build a bridge indicated that the Pecos River was still actively carving its way southward. But it had not had enough time to carve *deeply* into the western rim of the remnant plateau. Consequently, the western escarpment is a low rampart, noticeable but not very impressive. Neither Castañeda, nor Jaramillo, nor Coronado, nor any other early recorder felt the western edge worthy of any particular comment. But the northeastern barrancas of the Texas Panhandle were different, and they were commented upon in all the accounts.

Groundwater erosion is low in the west as well, so the Mescalero escarpment runs in a fairly straight north-south line with little entrenchment coastline. But the exquisite difference and extent of groundwater erosion in the east and northeast is obvious. Greater average rainfall eastward, greater frequency of recharge playas, and the greater discharge seeps and springs of the Ogallala Aquifer all combine to form lusher, steeper, more vertical canyon walls that quickly drop hundreds of feet to the distant bottoms. As the groundwater saps the rocks below along ancient lines of permeability, the entrenchments advance toward the headwaters and surreptitiously eat into the flat plains above. Thus, the northeastern barranca coastline of "capes and bays" is both extensive and intensive. Walking along on the Llano above, one suddenly encounters a deep abyss, one of the many rents whose existence is mostly hidden from sight (*que son tam encubiertas*) until standing at the edge (*a el bordo*). Only at the edge does one really see the fissure and experience the distortion of perceived distance.

Captain Cárdenas and some of his men were likely reminded of the summer before, when they confronted the illusive nature of the Grand Canyon in

Arizona. There, what they thought was an ordinary small stream far below, their native guides assured them was a deep and mighty river. Modest rocks seen from above by the Spanish turned into immense formations as tall as cathedrals when brave soldiers climbed down the canyon flanks and drew closer. Scale and perspective were likely distorted in the Texas canyonlands as well, for the horizontal and vertical dimensions also collided chaotically. After the openness of the surrounding horizon, this sudden vertical dimension opened a new aspect of spatial experience. Although tourists enjoy these aesthetic shivers, there is no evidence that the Spanish gave up gold-hunting for pretty vistas.[24]

Castañeda's recognition of deep, concealed, timbered canyons strongly suggests his routine familiarity with the barranca country of the northeastern escarpment. Placing the main expedition much farther north, or deeper into the Rolling Plains, or south as far as the Concho River, takes the geography away from the semiotics and removes the landscape from the language. Castañeda's casual mention of a visual concealment factor is potentially a significant match with the entrenchment canyons of the Red River headwaters and tributaries.

The next clue is no less precious. "*Son de tierra muerta*" (They are of dead earth), he writes of the barrancas (not the rivers). Castañeda's vocabulary is simple, but again the perception behind the words is complex. What exactly is *tierra muerta*? Does it add something important to the sense of place, or should we forget it like everyone else has done? Many farmers and ranchers of the eastern escarpment, the enduring soil conquistadors of the present, would probably regard this as an oblique reference to the "breaks," the erosional badland stretches centering around Quitaque and Caprock Canyons. Traveling from Brice, Texas, to Post and from Wayside, Texas, to Roscoe, one sees a great deal of rough, barren, stony, "dead" soils, soils that could be described simply as *tierra muerta*.

But *muerta* has other nuances keyed to other perceptions. When used with color, for example, it means faded or washed out. Were these canyons of washed-out earth? Surely one imagines that the first Europeans in these magnificent canyonlands would notice all the bright colors of the ancient soils. Sculpted by rainfall and runoff, blasted by wind and ice, and eaten away at their bases by groundwater erosion, the eastern barrancas provide a vivid and colorful spectacle of "dead soils" from the Quartermaster, Dockum, Triassic, and especially from the blood-red, very "dead" soil of the Permian formations. Indeed, the entrenchment process opens a rent into the earth so that one can see ancient earths. Old "dead soils" like the "Spanish Skirts" in Palo Duro State Park were once buried but now appear in a dazzling procession. Again the deeper canyons of the northeast Llano are especially characterized by exposed, colorful, barren soil formations of former dead epochs.

The question of access into these barrancas is equally significant.

Castañeda once more provides the essential clue, noting the canyons *"tienen entradas que hacen las vacas para entrar a el agua que esta honda"* ([The barrancas] have entrances that the cows make to go to the water that is far below).[25] Winship mistranslated this key passage, giving "There are paths down into these [rivers], made by the cows when they go to the water *which is essential throughout these plains.*"[26] What does Winship's augmentation mean? For Winship and the eastern imaginers of the Spanish contact with the Llano, *que es honda* meant that the Great Plains were dry and water was essential, a good point perhaps but not what Pedro de Castañeda saw and said. Even the trusty Hammond and Rey translation fails: "They [the rivers] are of dead earth, with approaches made by the cattle in order to reach the water which flows quite deep."[27] Winship says that water was essential and Hammond and Rey say the river currents were deep, both pointing to a misunderstanding of the word *honda*: "profound, deep, far below the surface, low with respect to neighboring places."[28]

What Castañeda wanted to say is that the steep-sided barrancas of the northeast Llano could be very troublesome to access were it not for the regular bison trails. These natural entradas led to the cool, refreshing springs and streams, waters found *far below* the dry surface of the adjacent plains. In this sense *el agua que esta honda* is a prescient observation on the elemental nature of the Llano's hydrology. What Castañeda's comment suggests is that regular water was geologically *honda*, far below the adjacent plains surface and caprock. This observation makes sense and is a key perception of the Ogallala springlands of the eastern escarpment coastline. Thousands of playas recharge the aquifer, until this concealed freshwater sea eventually discharges briskly and *honda*—"low with respect to neighboring places"—as a thousand springs and seeps in the eastern entrenchment canyons. Roaring Springs, near Matador, Texas, was once a good example of these powerful springs.

Before they were mostly sucked dry by irrigators short-circuiting the ancient process, these deep Ogallala discharge springs provided a dependable baseflow for the headwater tributaries of the Red River, Brazos, and Colorado Rivers. These deep springs also sapped away at the cliffs above to create the sudden, steep-sided canyons like Tule and Quitaque that amazed the regular expedition members. Most likely the descending natural bison trails or barranca *entradas* were regularly exploited by the expedition. Their horses would have negotiated the twisting paths as did the buffalo. Because of steep slopes in the northeast, access onto or off of the Caprock can be a problem. That the expedition accounts report no grumbling about entering or leaving suggests the Spanish availed themselves of these natural doorways.

To complete the depiction, Castañeda described in Chapter 8 of Part III the "unusual things that were seen on the plains, with a description of the bulls."[29] This chapter focused on the wildlife, or more particularly on the unusual *vacas* or bison that characterized these plains. Castañeda's description of buffalo was highly imaginative, drawing numerous analogies with the characteristics of other animals: the beard of a goat, the woolly hair of a sheep, the mane of a lion, the tail erect like a scorpion, and the hump of a camel. The size of the bison herds often astounded the Spanish, as did the separate herds of young bulls. "There was no one who could count them." Perception in this flatland sometimes played tricks on the mind. Castañeda thought that buffalo at a distance "looked like cleared pine trunks with the crowns joining at the top."[30] This curious and anecdotal deception points directly to the refractive atmosphere and its capacities for mirages and fata morganas.[31] Forests appeared on the horizon, only to disappear as one drew near.

Considered together, Castañeda's observations on the environment, the sky, the bison, the round playas, the steep barrancas, the dead soils, the mirages, and the waters all suggest a sophisticated familiarity with the Llano, especially its middle and northern half. Although he amplified his familiarity to encompass "los llanos," the Great Plains as a whole, much of his recollected sense of place derived from his personal sojourn on the Southern High Plains. If he devoted a good deal of his narrative to the memory of these plains, it was because they fascinated him. There one saw "outstanding things not seen anywhere else."[32]

Once uncloaked, Castañeda's environmental semantics provide critical insight into the historic *genius loci*. He provides the baseline "spirit of place" for the Spanish encounter with the Llano. His account also reflects a Renaissance spirit of inquiry, a spontaneous interest or *curioso* into natural causes and phenomena, one that associates discovery with learning. This *lo llano* made one think. For anyone attempting to retrace the way to Quivira, the old chronicler left a number of important perceptual clues. East of Pecos Pueblo there was a distinctive region, quite unlike anything hitherto encountered. Spectacular levelness characterized *lo llano*. Look for the narrated presences of plains, sky, bulls, fruits, playas, edges, natives, and barrancas. And look for the reported absences of hills, trees, rivers, town settlements, and other crops.

It was a flat and spacious realm where the soul was directed—like the waters, the fissures, the mind, and the mysteries—inward. It was an introspective landscape. In this sense it was fitting for reflection and contemplation, as the next round of Spanish explorers discovered at once. Although the Coronado entrada was a dismal commercial failure and a personal embarrassment for Viceroy Mendoza, at least the entrada priests found no wanting of what they desired: souls. Indeed, it was the lure of lost souls that launched a new discovery impulse barely four decades after the failed expedition.

This theographic impulse was stronger, purer, and more persistent than the road to quick wealth. Perhaps its only fault was its idealism. Initially, the process bestowed the beatific name of Saint Francis on these plains, characterized as they were with so many marvelous birds and animals. Unlike the lifeless desert flats, the plains were wondrously full of noisy animals, all awaiting the word of God. The name *Los Llanos de San Francisco* (The Plains of Saint Francis) was the first expression of an intelligent and self-sacrificing inquiry, one that reopened the Llano to the Spanish mind at the dramatic end of the sixteenth century.

PART TWO

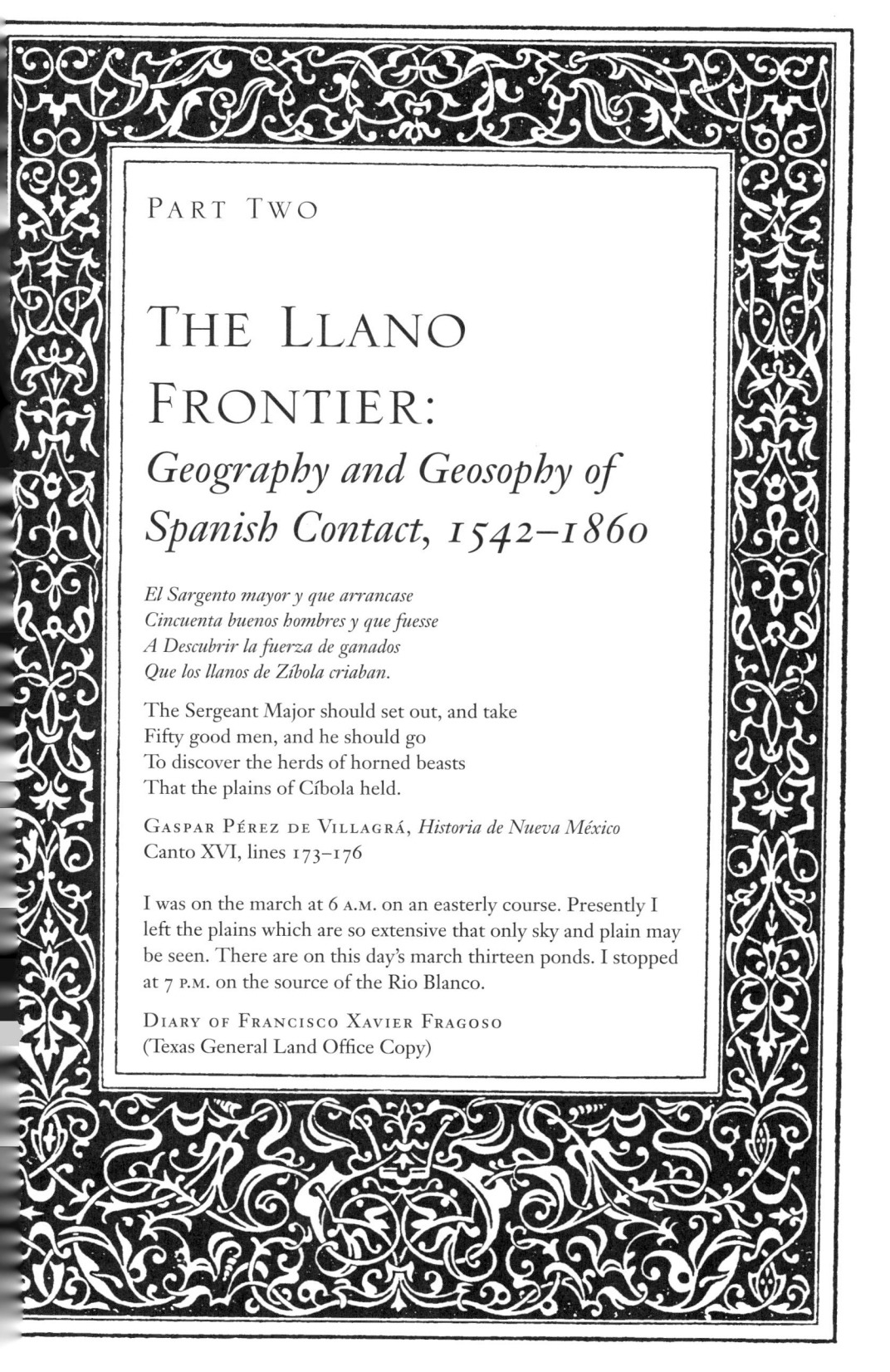

THE LLANO FRONTIER:
Geography and Geosophy of Spanish Contact, 1542–1860

El Sargento mayor y que arrancase
Cincuenta buenos hombres y que fuesse
A Descubrir la fuerza de ganados
Que los llanos de Zíbola criaban.

The Sergeant Major should set out, and take
Fifty good men, and he should go
To discover the herds of horned beasts
That the plains of Cíbola held.

GASPAR PÉREZ DE VILLAGRÁ, *Historia de Nueva México*
Canto XVI, lines 173–176

I was on the march at 6 A.M. on an easterly course. Presently I left the plains which are so extensive that only sky and plain may be seen. There are on this day's march thirteen ponds. I stopped at 7 P.M. on the source of the Rio Blanco.

DIARY OF FRANCISCO XAVIER FRAGOSO
(Texas General Land Office Copy)

· 9 ·

THE PLAINS OF SAINT FRANCIS

Reaching some plains and water-holes, which they gave the name Los Llanos de San Francisco and Aguas Zarcas, they saw many herds of cows that come there to drink.

"Declaration of Pedro de Bustamante, 1582"[1]

The northern frontier of New Spain expanded rapidly in the decades after Coronado's return, fueled by the discovery of great mines. Missionaries and slave raiders, prospectors and miners, soldiers and merchants alike pushed into and settled the lower margin of the greater Southwest by the 1560s. Town founding was a practical expression of this penetration and control. Don Rodrigo del Río de Losa founded Santa Bárbara in 1563 at the site of a routine silver strike in southern Chihuahua. From this new mining town, as at San Bartolomé and elsewhere, Spanish raiding parties ranged north along the Concho River and its junction with the Rio Grande. Despite new laws against the conquest of Indians and new lands, they rode to capture and sell men, or so-called "thieving Indians." These unfortunates were worked to death in the slave pits and mercury mills of Santa Bárbara. The raiders also acted as informal reconnaissances, gathering useful information on the geography ahead. In 1579 Hernán Gallegos helped capture a talkative slave, who reported the presence of the Rio Grande pueblos deep in the interior.

Intrigued by this report of populous towns and cotton cultivation, Gallegos teamed up with another soldier named Chamuscado and a devout Franciscan priest in Santa Bárbara, Fray Augustin Rodríguez. It was likely Fray Rodríguez who drew the scholarly connection between the slave's report and the account of pueblos in Alvar Núñez Cabeza de Vaca's *Relación*. Their reading of the *Relación* would certainly have brought the Cow Nation of the buffalo plains to their attention as well. After two years of speculation and activity, the three men organized a small entrada in 1581 consisting of three Franciscans, nine soldiers, and sixteen servants. The priests were indispensable to avoid charges of illegal conquest of new tribes. They set out to discover, to make *descubrimientos*, in this new land written about by Cabeza de Vaca and spoken of by an informed captive. The entrada is known as the Rodríguez-Chamuscado expedition and is noteworthy for its role in re-opening Spanish awareness of New Mexico.[2]

This clerical reconnaissance also launched the first Spanish rediscovery of the Llano environment, for Fray Augustin Rodríguez and Fray Francisco López traveled in the fall of 1581 to see the buffalo plains for themselves. Like their intrepid predecessor Fray Juan de Padilla, the Franciscan explorers liked what they saw. The great numbers of "humpbacked cattle" on the huge pastures were marvelous. Indeed, for the next half-century the most wide-ranging and persistent group in the Llano rediscovery process was the humble Order of St. Francis. Various profane elements, Juan Pérez de Oñate in particular, pondered the Llano. But clearly the Franciscan delight in *descubrimientos* and zeal in saving lost souls ignited a stronger exploration theography. As religious explorers, they also brought the word of the Christian God to this mesa wilderness. They brought a religious rhetoric that cloaked the wild, profane environment with the old, sacred word of God.

As a reflection of their spiritual and personal optimism, the Franciscan vision of the grassland immensity was not a fearful one. If anything the pious newcomers enjoyed the curious wilderness. The Llano was not a landscape of fear or dread, but a temperate plain of wonders. This response was both linguistic and spiritual. The Franciscans routinely attached ecclesiastical place-names to the important features of a landscape. Many of these toponyms failed to withstand more popular expressions or the tides of time. But the process of taming a region with the tongue—attaching the names of saints, martyrs, and all kinds of biblical references to land—would endure as a process on the plain for two centuries. It suggests that the Llano environment needed the civilizing, reassuring, and sanitizing influence of ritual nomenclature; the conversion of a pagan wilderness into a Christian landscape.

Toponyms were often chosen to honor routine Saint's Days or Feast Days, but others were keyed specially to environmental perceptions of water, land, animals, and features.[3] As a discourse, Southwestern theography drew on the apparent universality of the Catholic Church. Reports from the early period of this theography, from 1581 to 1684, suggest that the Spanish rediscovery of the Llano lent itself to spiritual expression. The Llano was, to be sure, a pagan wilderness of peoples and creatures. But against this backdrop the Franciscans perceived an opportunity for the expansion of the Christian faith.

Fray Rodríguez and Fray López, and most of the others rode east on September 28, 1581, from the Rio Grande Pueblo de Malpartida near Bernalillo, New Mexico. They left "to go to find the cows which they had been informed existed in large numbers some thirty leagues distant, more or less."[4] Their puebloan guides took the group well east of the Manzano Mountains along a nameless aboriginal trail. Around October 9 they had crossed the Pecos River and reached the upper Canadian River. Soon thereafter, in and near the broad canyon valley, the Franciscan explorers encountered the flatland and the shaggy bison. Although there were no permanent settlements, what they encountered pleased them. The Franciscans lent the name of their great mystic to these sunny plains full of animals: *Los Llanos de San Francisco*, or "The Plains of St. Francis." The Canadian Valley thus became the *Valle de San Francisco*.[5] The Andalucian Fray López may have favorably compared the extensive herds of buffalo to the Iberian cattle of his homeland. There were clearly good pastures for cattle in the region. A group of nearby waterholes for the bison was named *Aguas Zarcas* (Pure Waters), presumably after the freshness and clarity of their appearance.[6] They were probably in the Plaza Larga portion of the Llano.

As the 1582 declaration of one of the members, Pedro de Bustamante, noted, they saw "many herds of cows" and "a rancheria of naked Indians of a different nation" on the Plains of St. Francis.[7] These Apaches (or "Querechos" in Coronado's expression) followed the numerous buffalo herds for their living. Bustamante mentioned in particular their curious use of dog travois to lug provisions around the flatland. In another declaration, Felipe de Escalante thought these cows were found "over a continuous space of two hundred leagues in length; the width we do not know,"[8] perhaps a hint that these plains were part of a gigantic entity. While on the Plains of St. Francis, Bustamante and the other soldiers used their harquebuses to bring down at least forty buffalo over a week-long period. A few of the more intrepid may have tested mounted bullfighting techniques on enraged buffalo.

Freshly replenished with jerked beef, on October 19, 1581, the Spanish set out on the return journey to the Rio Grande pueblos. They most likely followed up the Valle de San Francisco or the Canadian Valley, until crossing the watershed divide to the Pecos River and the aboriginal trail westward. Rodríguez and López later stayed behind at Puaray Pueblo to preach the gospel, while the others returned to Santa Bárbara, Chihuahua. Fray Juan de Santa María had already been murdered. The two remaining priests were quickly killed as well.

The next year a Franciscan-inspired rescue mission, concerned about the fate of the two friars, set out from Santa Bárbara under Fray Bernaldino Beltrán and the wealthy Antonio de Espejo. Beltrán and Espejo confirmed the martyrdom of the two Franciscan missionaries, explored the pueblo country, and then traversed the Pecos River frontier of the western Llano on their return. The appearance of so many buffalo east of Cicúye led them to call the Pecos the *Rio de las Vacas* (River of the Cows), a place-name that lasted for many years.⁹ As they continued south they eventually encountered the important Apache "Jumana nation" on the lower Pecos River. Three Jumano hunters were able to advise Espejo on a southwest course across West Texas from the Pecos River to La Junta, and thence their return up the Rio Conchas.

The Spanish probes of the Llano continued, but were now unauthorized. In 1590 Gaspar Castaño de Sosa turned a rowdy mining camp into a militant and completely unofficial colony, and then led about 170 people northward on a trek along the Pecos River for weeks. This armed mob of Europeans attacked Pecos Pueblo and wreaked further havoc before viceregal orders arrived to arrest Sosa and recall the others. Four years later, sometime in 1594, the unauthorized Bonilla-Humaña entrada penetrated the Valle de San Francisco area. Little is known of this expedition since Humaña killed Bonilla farther out on the plains and then died himself in an Indian attack. But one lowly member of the expedition, an Indian native of Culhaucán named Jusephe Gutiérrez, survived, returned after a year of captivity, and gave a report five years later that pointed directly to the Canadian River portion of the great mesa. Jusephe noted that along their route, "they saw many marshes, springs, and arroyos with abundant water," an important reference to a wetlands trail along the springlands of the northern Llano.¹⁰ These waters are likely the Aguas Zarcas seen by the Franciscans in 1581. Jusephe Gutiérrez related they also found "after they left the pueblo of Pecos" great herds of bison, many plum trees in five or six places, and the deserted rancherías of Apaches or "Vaquero Indians." These 1590s *vaqueros* or "cowboys" of the plains were Coronado's Querechos of the 1540s.

Jusephe's 1599 report was made for the imposing new colonizer of New Mexico, Don Juan Pérez de Oñate. With his interest piqued, Oñate dispatched his *sargento mayor*, Vincente de Zaldivar, to locate the buffalo and to investigate the region. Zaldivar, Jusephe, and some fifty-eight other men set out east in mid-September of 1599. On the Gallinas River they met a band of Vaquero Indians or Querechos who greeted them by raising their palms to the sun and then touching the Spanish. These friendly Apache-Vaqueros lent Zaldivar a guide to the region ahead. Following the ancient trade route along the Canadian breaks, both buffalo and natives became more numerous. Zaldivar observed that one Apache group—fresh from trading meat, salt, hides, tallow, and suet for puebloan cotton blankets, maize, pottery, and turquoise—had stampeded the bison away while crossing the Canadian River.¹¹

Vincente de Zaldivar visited one of the rancherías of the Canadian River valley that fall. He found fifty red-and-white, bell-shaped tents of marvelously tanned hides. The natives used "great trains" of dogs for transporting supplies, a frenetic activity that greatly amused the Spanish. Not far from the present-day Texas–New Mexico border, Sergeant-Major Zaldivar and his men established a camp on one of the Llano tributaries to the Canadian River. For three days the men labored to build a large corral from driftwood and cottonwood trees. The next day the Spanish rode onto the adjacent plains, "where on the previous afternoon about a hundred thousand cattle had been seen."[12] At first the buffalo started nicely for the corral, but they soon stampeded and fled after their fashion. For several days the Spanish saw their horses gored and they tried "a thousand ways" to corral the wild animals, but all without much success. Riders roped calves but the young beasts struggled so desperately that they died. Although they killed enough buffalo to render a ton of tallow, they clearly could not corral a herd and take them back to Oñate. The domestication process was going to be more complicated than first thought.

Zaldivar's report on the buffalo plains also dwelled on the marvelous appearance of these cattle. He liked their laughable and frightful appearance. No one could be so melancholy, he declared, "that if he were to see it a hundred times a day he could keep from laughing heartily as many times."[13] The Sergeant-Major's report to Oñate also provided an important description of the Llano environment at the time of renewed European contact:

> These cattle have their haunts on some very level mesas which extended over many leagues, for, after reaching the top of them by a slight grade, or of low hills, thirty leagues were travelled, continuously covered with an infinite number of cattle, and the end of them was not reached. The mesas have neither mountain, nor tree, nor shrub, and when on them they were guided solely by the sun.[14]

Zaldivar's comments indicate that the Spaniards were little troubled by the caprock escarpment—"a slight grade . . . low hills"—before reaching the "very level mesas" on top. Apparently his reconnaissance and hunting party traveled into the interior for some seventy-five miles, reporting more enormous herds of the humpbacked cows, no end to the plains stretching before them, and a landscape so featureless that they resorted to solar reckoning. He thought the Canadian River was a marvel, a river flowing upward. It appeared clearly to him that he was much higher downstream than at its source. From the cedar-clad slopes of the Llano mesas "an infinite number of springs" burst forth, watering small valleys lined further down with lush cottonwood groves.

Zaldivar's further comments pointed to the Apache-Vaquero bond with the environment. The natives fished, caught crustaceans, gathered wood from the tributaries, and set up brush ambuscades at the infinite Llano springs. They also roamed on the plains among the great herds. After a month and a half of discovery, excitement, merriment, and experiment, Vincente de Zaldivar and his party returned to Oñate's headquarters at San Juan Bautista in November of 1599. They had enjoyed the first fall bison hunt of what eventually became an annual Hispano tradition.

Zaldivar's sojourn along the northern Llano received modest literary attention in a 1610 epic poem published in Spain. A former captain with Oñate, Gaspar Pérez de Villagrá, launched a spirited but typically long-winded verse

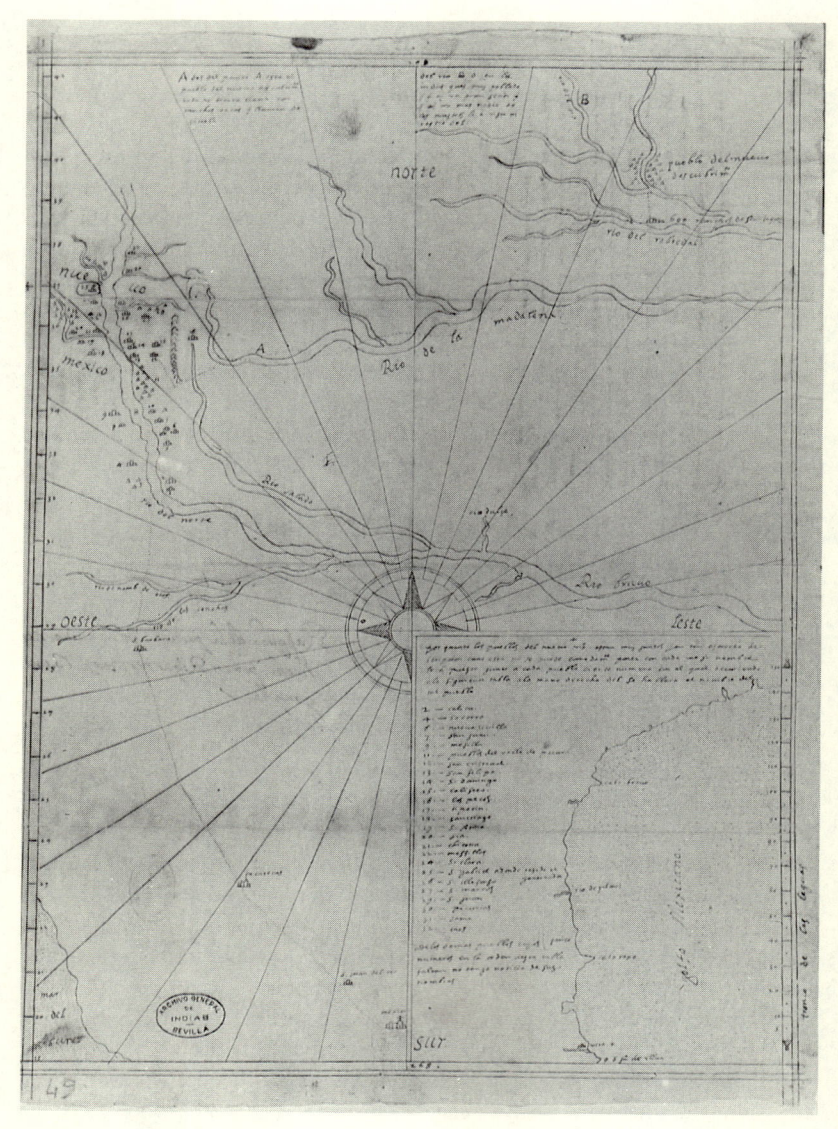

Mapa del Nuevo México por el cosmográfo Enrico Martínez, by Enrico Martínez, ca. 1602. Unpublished manuscript map, 7¹¹⁄₁₆ × 5¹⁵⁄₁₆ inches. This map is believed to be the earliest extant map of the trans-Mississippi West based on personal observations. Cosmographer Enrico Martínez situated the blankness of the Llano above the compass rose. The Canadian River flows across the upper center of the map, with the Rio Grande and Pecos River accurately located. *Courtesy Archivo General de Indias, Seville, Spain, and Archives Division, Texas State Library, Austin.*

epic on the reconquest of New Mexico entitled *Historia de Nueva México*. Cantos XVI and XVII of this historical poem narrated Sergeant-Major Zaldivar's eastward journey into "*los llanos de Zíbola*"—the Plains of Cibola. There was much versifying on difficulties in obtaining guides, amusing incidents, vast herds of bison on *grandes llanos* or great plains, futile Spanish efforts to corral the buffalo of the High Plains, and sightings of nomadic Querechos. There was also one of the first conscious literary efforts to lay bare the poetic soul of the region:

> Y gozan de vnos llanos tan tendidos
> *And they [bison] enjoy such widespread plains*
> Que por seyscientas y ochocientas leguas
> *That for six and eight hundred leagues*
> Vn sossegado mar parece todo,
> *All seems to be a peaceful sea*
> Sin género de cerro ni vallado
> *With no sort of valley or hill*
> Donde en manera Alguna pueda el hombre
> *where a man can in any way*
> Topar la vista acaso o detenerla
> *Limit his vision or rest it*
> En tanto quanto ocupa vna naranja,
> *Upon as much height as a orange occupies,*
> Si assí puede dezirse tal exceso
> *If such excess may so be said.*
> Y es aquesto, señor, en tanto extremo
> *And it is true, lord, to such an extent*
> Que si por triste suerte se perdiesse
> *That if by evil chance a man were lost*
> Alguno en estos llanos, no seria
> *Upon these plains 'twould be the same*
> Más que si se perdiesse y se hallase
> *As though he were lost and did find himself*
> Enmedio de la mar sin esperanza
> *In the midst of the sea, beyond all hope*
> De verse jamás libre de aquel trago.
> *Of ever seeing himself freed from the strait.*[15]

Within two years of Zaldivar's travels, Don Juan de Oñate himself visited these plains: *Los Llanos de Cíbola*. In the summer of 1601 he set off on a search for Coronado's Quivira. Oñate's entrada of eight carts, two Franciscans, seventy men, and hundreds of horses and mules crossed Galisteo Pass to reach the plentiful catfish of the Gallinas River. Three days later they were on the *Rio de la Magdalena*, a theographic reference to the Canadian River. Traveling east along the south side of the river, Oñate took delight in the broad valley. Daily it seemed the climate was growing more temperate and the vegetation becoming more verdant. Oñate claimed that the Rio de la Magdalena "was one of the best rivers which we had seen in all the Indies."[16] Indians "of the nation called Apachi" offered them tasty plums, perhaps from the valley groves visited by Jusephe in 1594.

Upon entering "the plains which they call Cibola or Cebolo," they encountered rocky, outlier formations, "which the mountains of this land give off," a sensitive perception of the basic geomorphology of the Llano.[17] After maneuvering their carts past these obstacles, they traveled rapidly on the level valley plains ahead. As noted on the Enrico Martínez 1602 manuscript map, Oñate's route forded the Canadian River several times (see map, page 140). Especially in the Texas Panhandle the Spanish followed several long stretches along the southside Canadian River tributaries. Oñate's report spoke of "springs of good water and groves of trees" in this pleasant area.[18] With its excellent wood and water, the Canadian Valley was a logical corridor of travel.

The 1602 Martínez map is of special interest for students of Texas cartography. Apparently this cosmographic work was based on firsthand information provided by a Portuguese mariner, Juan Rodríguez. As a soldier Rodríguez accompanied the conqueror of New Mexico on his trip to the plains. The historical cartographer Carl Wheat argued that the 1602 Enrico Martínez drawing is the earliest extant map, "portraying actual on-the-spot observation of any part of the American Transmississippi West."[19] An important orientation to the map occurs at Point "A": *"des del punto a asta el pueblo del nuevo descubrimiento toda es tierra llana con muchas vacas q llaman de civola"* (From point A to the town of new discovery [i.e., Quivira] all the land is flat with many cattle they call [the cattle] of Cibola). Point A then indicates the approximate northwestern corner of the Llano, with its level plains and herds of buffalo ahead. The Llano is at the center of the map, bounded on the west by the *Rio Salado* or Pecos River. In contrast to the settled and detailed Rio del Norte country of New Mexico, it is featureless and plain.

Oñate's report indicates a certain affinity for the Canadian River margin of the *tierra llana*. "Each day the land through which we were travelling became better," he wrote.[20] The weather grew warmer he thought, and innumerable springs gushed from the escarpment bluffs at convenient intervals.[21] Great, delicious quantities of plums and grapes nourished his men, and daily they saw more of "those most monstrous cattle called cibola."[22] *Cíbola* was originally and probably the Spanish corruption of the Zuni self-designation "Ashiwi" or "Shiwi." By 1601 the word had transferred curiously eastward to indicate not men, not a province, but the bison and their plains habitat. Juan de Oñate thought these *cibolas* were a wondrous mixture of different animals, all promiscuously blended together from interspecies reproduction. He also noted droves of several hundred elk, or as he called them, "deer as large as horses." At a time when the great savannahs of Africa were inaccessible and uncharted, Europeans could see for themselves the noisy herds, the predators, the roving tribesmen, and the midlatitude grassland glory of the Plains of Cíbola.

Somewhere before the Canadian sand hills along the 100th meridian of longitude Juan de Oñate and his entrada turned north. Here the northeast curve of the Canadian River launches a course toward Quivira. Although now traveling on the High Plains north of the Llano, many of his comments are applicable to the Southern High Plains. He noted "great plains with innumerable cattle." Although Spanish carts rolled easily on the smooth surface, "the land was so level that daily men became lost in it."[23] Flowers of "a thousand different kinds" even choked out the pasturage for Spanish horses, causing them to send scouts ahead looking for settlements and better grassy pastures. Periodically they crossed a drainage river, the North Canadian and the Cimarron.

Never truly frightened, Oñate was nevertheless pleased to reach the big Arkansas River. Along this river valley he found several major settlements of the Wichita Indians. Their simple grass lodges and fields unfortunately constituted all there was to the luring word of "Quivira." After diverse adventures and disappointments in the summer of 1601, the Oñate entrada retraced their steps homeward. There was no gold in Quivira, although the place clearly existed. Once again they trekked along the Rio de la Magdalena or Canadian River Valley springland trail to the Rio Grande pueblos.

For Oñate the most important environmental discovery of the entrada was the "cattle," the vast herds of *cibolas* as the bison were now called. There was neither gold nor rich mines in the valleys and plains of the east, but there was a plenitude of buffalo. Somehow the superabundance of the Seven Cities of Cibola was now tied to the superabundance of the bison herds, whose numbers, the Spanish thought, were vaster than all of the livestock of New Spain's biggest ranches.[24] Oñate's perception of the Llano was a vision of immense pastures, level ranges already stocked with the finest New World livestock.

For several decades after Oñate's return the Spanish troubled themselves but little with the buffalo plains. Indeed, the exploration impulse passed from the secular to the mystical by 1620. In that year a dark-eyed, pretty, teenaged Spanish nun claimed to have begun a series of ecstatic transports from her convent in Agreda, Spain, to the Jumano Indian camps of the southern Llano. María de Jesús de Agreda was known as the miraculous "Lady in Blue" by the time of Father Massanet in 1692. This modest and intelligent nun later became an influential abbess. She claimed that on occasions of miraculous bilocation she had preached to the tribes east of the Pecos River. And for years in church circles native reports circulated of a saintly lady in a blue cloak who walked into distant Jumano camps to proselytize.

"Who was the *Woman in Blue*," historian Carlos E. Castañeda asked, "who miraculously appeared to the simple children of the great plains and the Teyas to teach them with love and kindness to seek the Truth?"[25] According to the respectful accounts of Catholic scholarship, from 1620 to 1631 a saintly Franciscan abbess, Sister María de Jesús de Agreda, personally explored the spiritual nature of the buffalo plains. Through a process of ecstatic religious contemplation (similar perhaps to yogic astral projection), she found herself *bilocated* on some 500 occasions. From her convent bed in Agreda, Spain, once a week or so this gentle abbess explored the Llano as a Franciscan missionary. Her prayers to God transported her to "a different place and clime."[26] The Catholic scholar and historian Carlos Castañeda designated the Middle Concho River country as the site of her first visit, although there is only supposition for such a claim. Fray Alonso de Benavides, who personally visited her at Agreda in April 1631, claimed her messages were directed to "Quivira." During her ecstatic trances she clearly felt the environmental differences between the Jumano plains of the Llano and her convent cell in Agreda, Spain.[27]

Understanding the plains tribes in an abstract fashion, Sister María de Jesús preached and exhorted one tribe she called *Titlas* (a possible referent to Techas or Teyas) to seek priests and further instruction from the new missions appearing in nearby New Mexico. She was an outstanding Franciscan mystic by most accounts.[28] At a time when Spanish nuns had few chances to explore the terrae incognitae of the New World, Sister María found a way to bring the word of her god to the plains. She also met and corresponded sensibly with King Phillip IV about national affairs. She authored the intense, posthumously published *La Mística Ciudad de Dios*, an interpretive biography of Mary which enraged many male clerics. The Holy Church finally condemned the book in a routine power struggle, and confined it to Spain and Portugal for years to come.[29]

By a "significant coincidence," as Carlos Castañeda noted, Sister María's revelations appeared in Spain at the same time her fellow New Mexican Franciscans sought to expand their conversion activities eastward from New Mexico. The souls of the buffalo plains were real enough to Father Custodian Fray Alonso de Benavides. Shortly after receiving thirty priests for various missionary activities, some fifty "Xumanas" returned again to his Isleta Mission church near Albuquerque, New Mexico, on July 20, 1629. This time the astute emissaries related in sign language that a beautiful woman wearing a blue cloak had instructed them to appeal for religious instruction. Benavides made the connection to María de Agreda's claims of miraculous bilocation back in Spain. Thus, the legend of her miraculous "Conversion of the Jumanos" took shape in the skillful hands of Franciscan publicists.

A more skeptical line of thought regards the "Lady in Blue" as a Franciscan deception, a spiritual mirage instead of a miracle. Hard pressed by other tribes, the Jumanos of the southern Llano sought a Spanish presence in their camps that would entangle the Spanish as allies in their tumultuous wars. Once the

Jumanos intuited how they could help Fray Benavides's expansionist plans, the legend of the "Lady in Blue" grew naturally. Author William Brandon notes, for example, that the Jesuits later fell out bitterly with the Franciscans over María de Agreda's so-called miracles. The Jesuits accused their rivals of having drawn undue promotional attention to Franciscan activities there, mostly in the cynical hope of making New Mexico a more powerful bishopric and Franciscan power base.[30]

Whether lured by miracle or mirage, the Franciscan missionary impulse nevertheless turned toward the southern Llano. The Jumano representatives convinced Fray Benavides to dispatch a patrol to their distant homeland, including priests to instruct them in Christianity. By a happy coincidence the warriors' news of the Lady in Blue meshed with official instructions from Spain to be on the lookout for the tribes reported by Sister María to her confessor. Fray Benavides accordingly dispatched two faithful priests for the long and delicate mission. Fray Juan de Salas and Fray Diego León[31] thus left Santa Fé in late July as theographic scouts on a 600-mile trip to the Jumano nation of the southern Llano.

Led by their Jumano guides, the two friars and a small escort of soldiers crossed Glorieta Mesa through the famous pass, then began the long descent of the Pecos River. Eventually they set off from the river margins for a southeastern advance across the hot southern plains. Considering it was summer, they likely used an aboriginal trail among the waterholes in the vicinity of Seminole Draw. After many days of travel they reached the Middle Concho River of the Colorado River country.[32] For 100 to 112 leagues of their journey they had been on the flat buffalo plains of the Vaquero-Apache nation.[33] Although their terse reports add little insight into the plains environment, Fray Juan de Salas and Fray Diego León were pleased by the discharge springs, wild game, and well-wooded tributaries of the southern-plains canyonlands.

These bountiful waters were lined with tall trees bearing delicious nuts that fall: the famous Texas pecan trees. They also discovered that some of the mussels scooped from the muddy river bottoms yielded large freshwater pearls. This was important news indeed. Fray Juan de Salas's talks with the Jumanos convinced him that in fact Sister María de Agreda had visited with them only a few years before. The "Woman in Blue" had walked into their camps on the Llano many times from 1625 onward. It was said she had converted them. Salas reported that other tribes to the east sought religious instruction as well. During a return proselytizing trip in 1632, Fray Juan de Salas and Fray Juan de Ortega again crossed the buffalo plains of the Llano. Fray Ortega even stayed behind for six peaceful months, getting to know the Jumano lifeway quite well.[34]

After returning to New Mexico the Franciscan reports of pearls on a *Rio de las Nueces*—River of Nuts (the Middle Concho River or equally the upper Colorado River)—brought the later commercial pearling forays of Martin and

Castillo and of Diego de Guadalajara to the southern Llano. Captains Hernán Martin and Diego del Castillo left Santa Fé in 1650 with a force of soldiers and allies. Traveling down the Pecos River for some distance, they eventually veered away to cross the Llano. Somewhere below Roswell, New Mexico, they turned southeast to ascend the Mescalero Escarpment, then continued southeast across the Querecho Plains, probably through the current Texas counties of Gaines, Andrews, Midland, Reagan, and Irion. On the Concho River in Tom Green County they found their *Rio de las Perlas* (The River of Pearls).[35]

The chronicles are vague as to exact course and direction, and the lack of landmarks on the plains obscures their trail to the Rio de las Perlas. They stopped at an important Jumano ranchería, most likely in the upper Concho River country. For almost half a year they hunted, fraternized, and dredged the best spots of the river for freshwater pearls. These pearls were to cover expenses and ensure a profit. Martin and Castillo also journeyed deeper into the new land, well over a hundred miles eastward until they met natives from a reputed "Kingdom of the Teyas." Their successful return to Santa Fé ensured that others would seek to exploit and open trade relations with the Jumanos for pearls, bison hides, and pecans. Reports of a newly discovered Kingdom of the Teyas and the old rumors of a Gran Quivira encouraged thoughts of treasure.

Four years later Viceroy Count de Alba de Liste ordered Captain Diego de Guadalajara to command a second pearling expedition to the southern Llano. There were fears that French or English adventurers might find wealth in the region and lay claims, fears encouraged by Franciscans still seeking to expand their ecclesiastical influence. Departing Santa Fé in 1654, Guadalajara, his thirty soldiers, and some two hundred native allies descended the Pecos River, then turned southeast for the great crossing of the Querecho Plains. As mapped by Gunnar Brune, the Guadalajara route crossed Gaines, Martin, Howard, Mitchel, and Coke Counties in Texas to reach the freshwater pearls of the upper Colorado River in the vicinity of Runnels County.[36]

Like Martin and Castillo, Diego de Guadalajara camped and rested on the southern tributaries and springs of the Llano. The Spanish soon set their allies to work harvesting the pearls. The local and friendly Jumanos were at war with Teyas tribes to the east, one of which attacked a Spanish scouting party seeking contact with the Kingdom of the Teyas. Under the leadership of Andrés López, the Spanish handily defeated these *Cuitao* Teyas, and plundered their camp violently before returning to report to Diego de Guadalajara. Satisfied with his mission, his stock of pearls, and his discoveries, Guadalajara recrossed the lower Llano again, ascended the Pecos River, and returned to Santa Fé. Thereafter, the Spanish-Jumano trade across the Llano would be mostly private in nature. Small but skillful groups of New Mexican traders set out on annual trading expeditions from Albuquerque and elsewhere to profit from relations with the Jumanos of the plains. Probably the Jumanos obtained supplies of lead and powder, and even some highly desireable guns from the informal trade network that now sprang up.

It is not easy to say which had more influence over the buffalo plains of the 1600s, European Christianity or European weapons. The Franciscan vision was powerful, peaceful, and purposeful, even as it rocked and caused upheaval in the traditional native culture. But there were few lasting conversions of the plains peoples, despite the optimistic reports by the missionary-explorers. The natives of the southern Llano were taught the signs of Christianity, but thrown against the reality of a desperate arms race. European weapons were powerful, violent, and disintegrative. As guns and horses transformed plains hunting and warfare, tribe after tribe became aware that access to the new weapons and regular supplies of powder and lead was a strategic necessity for survival. Spanish stinginess in supplying weapons and powder gave an advantage to tribes maintaining regular contacts with less-scrupulous French and English traders. The irony of missionaries offering peace at a time of intensifyingly violent intertribal warfare was a challenging dialectic for the Llano peoples.

By the mid-seventeenth century, the Franciscan impetus to explore the Llano was waning. There were other distractions, problems, rivals, and opportunities. But whereas the follow-up was weak, their initial attention to the region was notable. Many of their environmental toponyms endured for generations. The expression *Rio Salado* captured the sometimes brackish taste of the Pecos River, while the *Rio Concho*—named for the abundant *conchas* or clam shells found in river sediments—denoted a very important riverine ecosystem on certain branches of the upper Colorado River of Texas. Their *Rio de las Nueses*, named for the superabundance of pecan trees, identified another important environmental resource.

Juan Dominguez de Mendoza was the last sixteenth-century official to mount a significant expedition into the southern Llano. His well-organized 1684 entrada, together with Fray López and Fray Sabaleta, started from the new mission at La Junta on the Rio Grande. From the Pecos River they journeyed eastward in late winter, ascending a "little mesa which commands a wide prospect."[37] "All the district is a plain," Mendoza wrote of their subsequent travels in his declaration. Between the Pecos River and the Middle Concho, the Spanish encountered vast stretches of the Llano that had been burned off, a significant report on the native custom of firing the plains before the spring growth. Various camps were named following the theographic practices of the day: *San Ignacio de Loyola, La Conversion de San Pablo, San Honofre, Nuestra Señora de la Candelaria*, and *El Arcanjel San Miguel*.[38]

A Jumano tribe on the eastern Llano called the Jediondos ("The Stinking Ones") emerged from their humble ranchería "at the foot of a great rock" to greet the priest and soldiers with shouts, a banner emblazoned with two blue taffeta crosses, and many rejoicings. The Jumano chiefs requested "that for the love of God" Mendoza and the soldiers should make war on their Apache enemies. At *San Honofre* they met the Arcos Tuertos or "Twisted Bows" natives. But here they could not erect a cross for "the lack of suitable timber," a clue to the treeless nature of the plains.[39] At *El Arcanjel San Miguel* they discovered a mystery surrounding a vast Ogallala aquifer discharge spring:

> There is in the said place a river bearing much water, the source of which is not known because it comes from beneath the earth and issues through some rocks. A holy cross was erected above the orifice from which the river emerges. This place is very aptly named [by the Jumanos] Where-the-Dogs-Live, because there come out from the water many dogs of all colors, of the same size as the other dogs, and of the same species, although bred in the water. They say they are more savage. They tear the people in pieces, and do the same with the buffalo bulls and cows that come to drink at the orifice. We saw the skeletons of the cows and the bulls, and likewise the excrement and tracks of the dogs.[40]

This Llano discharge spring flowed eastward to join the Rio de las Perlas or Middle Concho River. On the latter they found pearls, excellent varieties of fish, huge trees, and "wild hens which make noise at dawn." Mendoza greatly appreciated the buffalo, grapevines, springs, timber, and game of the fertile river bottoms ahead. He even noted the presence of "a variety of very agreeable song-birds." The Mendoza-López expedition soon passed farther to the south, as far as Menard County, killing vast numbers of bison. Returning to the Pecos River via another southern trail, they left the Llano and its "rainwater" camps behind.

From Fray Rodríguez's "Plains of Saint Francis" to Fray Juan de Salas's confirmation of the miraculous conversion of the Jumanos by the Franciscan mystic, María de Jesús de Agreda, the theographic scouts of New Spain had helped open the Llano to both natural and supernatural rediscovery. Furthermore, the pearling forays of Martin-Castillo and of Guadalajara confirmed a commercial possibility. "Some resources in Jumano ranges warranted secular interest," Elizabeth A. H. John has noted, namely, "freshwater pearls in the western tributaries of the Colorado River and countless buffalo."[41] Indeed, over the period of a quarter-century small trading parties annually left New Mexican settlements, crossed the southern Llano, and traded with the friendly Jumanos in the south.[42] These unknown traders of the mid-sixteenth century knew that the southern flanks of the plains held vast stocks of bison, pecans, and even pearls. Their unknown voyages to gather this wealth stir the geographic imagination.

·10·

Land and Logos

Unknown country between the R. Puerco and the sources of the Colorado.

ALEXANDER VON HUMBOLDT (1810)

In conjunction with various military expeditions, local New Mexican hunters, traders, and soldiers had acquired a thorough knowledge of the Llano geography by the early eighteenth century.[1] This was not the case, however, for the imperial Europeans. With little official knowledge of the plains geography, French, English, and Spanish printed maps portrayed the region poorly if imperiously in the seventeenth and eighteenth centuries. The cartographic and imperialistic imagination still depended heavily on a few old place-names as logos for the unknown land. Words were therefore pawns in games of power and circumstance. The effort was on control and position rather than landscape revelation. Ironically, the land between Tiguex and Quivira could be found early on the world's first and most progressive atlases. But after this initial and erroneous burst across the North American continent, the Plains of Cíbola shrank drastically, as layer upon layer of fresh new detail of other regions crowded and filled the maps of the Southwest. Information seemed to flow from everywhere but those first plains. As late as 1810 Alexander von Humboldt could only note "Unknown Country" between the Pecos River of New Mexico and the Colorado River of Texas. Here indeed was a *terra incognita* in the well-traveled Southwest. Humboldt's recourse was a textual substitute for the blankness. One of the first discoveries became one of the last unknowns.

Early European depictions of the country between Cicúye and Quivira appeared within a few decades of Coronado's entrada. In the 1560s Italian cartographers begin to create a fantastic version of Southwestern geography, one destined to endure and spread throughout Europe as standard geosophy for the region. Genoese cartographers like Jacobus Maiolo and Batista Agnese were likely aquainted with the earliest published accounts of the expedition. Ramusio's *Terzo volume delle navigationi et viaggi* appeared in Venice in 1556, for example, with its timely translations of some Coronado documents. About a year later a rare map from a Portolan Atlas—now attributed to the talented Batista Agnese (who had relocated from Genoa to Venice)—directly reflected the assimilation of Coronado's travels.

Agnese's circa 1557 portolan map located new *scorpetas* or discoveries such as "Civola," "Tigues," "Axa," and "Quivira" in the southwestern portion of North America. Unfortunately, these names from the Coronado expedition were applied to the interior above Ulloa's newly discovered Gulf of California. The Venetians confabulated Ulloa's western and Coronado's eastern discoveries, mixing the two together. The cartographer preserved the linear sequence of Coronado's road from the Zuni Pueblos to Quivira's villages with an outward sequence of Cibola/Tiguex/Axa[?]/Quivira. The Italians, however, inadvertently *reversed* the directionality of the expedition, thus taking the discoverers from northeast to northwest. Perhaps this westerly shift seemed logical as it makes the expedition appear to go farther away from the center of gravity in New Spain.

Together these two Venetian assumptions had the effect of locating Quivira several thousand miles to the west of Kansas and Texas. By extension the buffalo plains followed and came to rest inland from the modern California coast of North America. Giving credence to these new places, the cartographer Agnese noted in the region above Quivira: "Fin qui scorperse Franc° Vasquez de Coronado" (The end here [of new land] discovered by Francisco Vazquez de Coronado). The appearance of the place-name "Axa" is unusual as the only toponym between Tiguex and Quivira. Was this an Italian reference to El Turco's supposed settlement of "Haxa," the mythic city destination of the expedition while on the Llano? If so (and Axa reappears on other and later maps), it is a very early reference to an interior place in Texas at a time when almost nothing else was identifiable in the region.[2]

The famous Dutch cartographer Abraham Ortelius included both Axa and Quivira as identifiable place-names on his famous copperplate map of 1564, *Orbis Terrarum*, later reprinted in the world's first atlas.[3] But the countryside between the two toponyms was California coastline above Baja, Mexico. Ortelius did make one important addition with the place-name of "Cicuic," a reference to Pecos Pueblo or Cicúye just west of the Llano. In effect the great Dutch cosmographers elaborated on the Venetian errors, rumors, and misdirection. With the Spanish often concealing their better information, European mapmakers "relied on rumor and suggestion" in their depiction of the area.[4] Paulo Forlani's 1565 "Mappamondo" used "Le Sete Cita" (The Seven Cities) for Cíbola, and continued with Axa and Cicuic place-names. Juan de Martínez's 1578 map even charmingly illustrated the Seven Cities of Cíbola.[5] In the 1570s Gerard Mercator and other leading Dutch cartographers continued and promoted this grievous shift of interior plains discovery to the distant Pacific Coast.

The Spanish certainly knew more about the interior than they were disclosing to the Italians, Dutch, or English. The Royal Cosmographer Alonso de Santa Cruz had access to important expedition documents, particularly for the De Soto expedition but likely for Coronado as well. Alonso de Santa Cruz's 1572 map was also the first to site Quivira reasonably in Texas instead of California. This early map located the celebrated province in the vicinity of the Llano in present western Texas.[6] Compared to the Dutch and Italian depictions, the positioning is sophisticated. Interestingly, he also provides the important environmental context. His map noted in this region that "*desde quevira hasta aqui grandisimas manadas de vacas*" (From Quivira up to here [there are] very large herds of cows). The death of Santa Cruz and his replacement by Geronimo Chaves led to some sharing of information in 1584 between the Spanish and the Dutch. Ortelius's 1584 edition of *Theatrum Orbis Terrarum* included better information on the interior, but still persisted in shifting Axa, Cicuic, and Quivira to the Pacific Coast. Ortelius's work was so influential that his errors continued in European mapmaking for many decades.

After a long period of neglect, cartographers began to recharacterize the Plains of Cíbola in the mid-seventeenth century by using key words for the native tribes. Names of peoples increasingly resistant to European conquest began to dot their maps, perhaps as signs of stiffening native resistance. The influential 1650 map of Nicolas Sanson d'Abbeville noted "Vaquero Apaches" for the approximate area of the Llano, while Quivira is tugged to the east-southeast, or nearer to the French imperial territory. Whatever wealth the word "Quivira" signified, the French preferred that it lay closer to their imperial influence. D'Abbeville's 1656 map sensibly interposed a large and mythic mountain range to separate the conflicting French and Spanish claims. By 1689, the Jumano tribe emerges from official obscurity to mark the southeastern portion of these plains (but still within the context of "Apaches Vaqueros") on V. M. Coronelli's map.[7]

French mapmakers of the early eighteenth century launched a series of deceptive claims on Spanish territory precisely through the spatial appropriation of the area's geosophical words. Their maps became perceptual weapons for the control of the buffalo plains without the bother and expense of sending armies; indeed, "maps anticipated empire" and were "part of the intellectual apparatus of power."[8] Consequently, many of this period's maps, like those of G. Deslisle (1718) or Popple (1733) or H. Moll (1736)[9] say more about French imperial fantasies toward the plains than they do of possession. Although French cartography on the Texas Gulf Coast was active and informative, it paid much less attention to the remote plains interior of Texas.[10] One small exception was the De La Harpe expedition, which ascended the Red River and drew near the Llano before turning back. Beaurain's map of western Louisiana around 1725 noted La Harpe's voyage, and the nomadic presence of a "Nation of Wanderers" (*Nation Errants*) in the plains vicinity, enemies to other tribes.

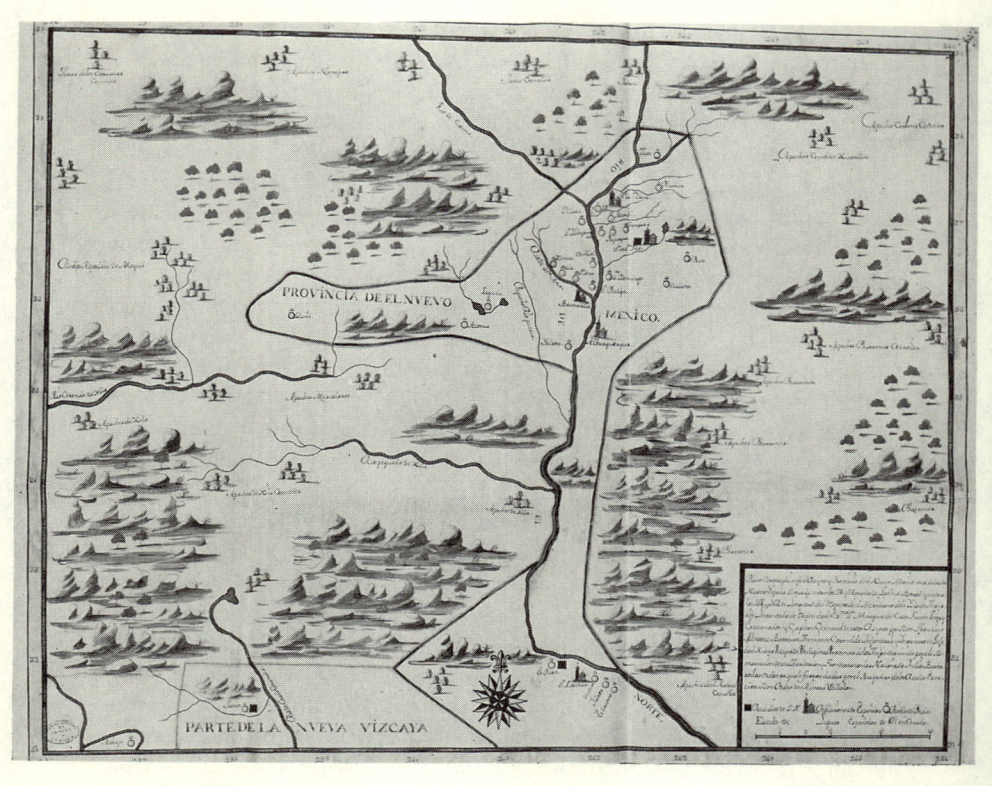

Plano Corographico de el Reyno y Provincia de el Nuevo Mexico, by Francisco Álvarez Barreiro, 1727. Colored manuscript map, 7 × 8¹¹⁄₁₆ inches. The eastern portion of Barreiro's map covers West Texas and the featureless Llano country. *Courtesy Archivo General de Indias, Seville, Spain, and Archives Division, Texas State Library.*

Beauvillier's 1720 map reported on La Harpe's travels and created a magnificent illusion by extending the Red River to the immediate locale of Spanish Santa Fé.[11] By this cartographic sleight-of-hand, the French advanced their claims on the Red River headwaters region all the way to Santa Fé, claims that the Americans preferred to inherit later to the disgust and bitterness of Mexico.

The Spanish cartographic discourse, on the other hand, like Barriero's charming 1727 map, was often less ideologically deceiving. Barriero's map gave the province of New Mexico realistically contracted boundaries and left the western border of the plains entirely to the Jicarillas and the Faraones, an Apache tribe named for their biblical resemblance to the "Pharoah's hordes." Barreiro even left a large blankness east of Pecos and Galisteo, with Apachean Faraones tribes and rancherías spaced around its rough margins. Some of the quaintly illustrated topography suggests the table-hills, breaks and outliers of the Llano borderlands.

Jose Alzate y Ramirez's 1768 map, one of the few published Spanish maps of this area in the entire eighteenth century, is of particular interest. Although it shows erroneous drainages and a mythic interior lake in the shape of a cross, it also makes no pretensions to spatial control of the Apache plains. Furthermore, Alzate y Ramirez created a textual logo for the blank plains area with his paragraph on the presence of "Plains of 300 leagues in extension" with buffalo ("*Bacas de Sibola*") and nomadic Apache bands.[12] With no names for the blankness, an explanatory paragraph provided the important environmental context (just as it had for Alonso de Santa Cruz in 1572 and just as it would for Alexander von Humboldt in 1810). The appearance of a large lake in the Great Plains, apparently as the upper source of the Trinity River, suggested a supply of water or rumors of a great lost lake in the plains interior. Was there a secret lake in the interior?

After two and a half centuries of probes and entradas, official Spanish maps of the 1800 period nevertheless continued to grapple with a *terra incognita* when it came to the Llano. A Californian Quivira, to be sure, was largely purged by 1800 with an equally fantastic but better positioned "Gran Quivira." Cicúye, Axa, and other luring place-names disappeared as well, replaced by the linguistically realistic names of war-like peoples. But while the cartographic depiction of Mexico's province of New Mexico steadily improved, there was little official reflection of new knowledge on the Southern High Plains.

Even Mexico's great guest, the geographer Baron Alexander von Humboldt, was reduced in his excellent 1810 map of New Spain to speak of the uncertainties of the southern plains: "Unknown country," he noted, "between the R. Puerco [Pecos] and the sources of the Colorado." A further paragraph incorrectly ventured that "It is believed" the source of the Red River lies near Mora and Santa Fé.[13] The assumption that the source of the Red River was near Santa Fé constituted a significant environmental deception, one that engaged the geopolitical attention of the Anglo-Americans on the eastern seaboard who saw the Red River as the boundary between the United States and Mexico. If, as Humboldt's map suggested, the upper Pecos River was the source of the Red River (*Rio Rojo de Natchitoches ou Rio de Pecos*), then the rival American imperialists had a strategic interest in the southern plains with President Thomas Jefferson's purchase of French claims in 1803.

It would be a mistake, however, to think that Humboldt's official compilation of geography on the region—"Unknown country"—was the sum total of knowledge of the Plains of Cibola. On the contrary, by 1800 there was a wealth of geographic information on the buffalo plains in the minds of native New Mexicans and various *genizaros*. In fact, the New Mexican hunters, traders, and explorers had keyed dozens of names to specific environmental locales and features of this immense remnant plateau. In particular, generations of New

Mexican buffalo hunters, the colorful *cazadores* who called themselves *ciboleros*, had traversed the area thoroughly.[14]

The historical cartography of the great mesa is ironic. Despite its early discovery and context, it continued to be a featureless feature on official maps. Spanish and French royal cartographers were covetous but could offer few or misleading details. Rather, it was anonymous local personalities who first created a revelatory, textual reading of the mesa landscape during this time. Considering the immense and flat context of these plains, their new Spanish landscape discourse and its nomenclatural identities made a lot of perceptual sense as well. One group in particular, the late-eighteenth-century bison hunters or *ciboleros* had probably forged the basic identity of the region itself—creating the name and legend of *El Llano Estacado*. To understand the connection between land and language, the role of the cibolero at the end of the eighteenth century merits investigation. While European cartographic discourse in the 1700s reflected mostly ignorance, greed, and power struggles, the ciboleros perceived the landscape with geographic interest, close environmental observation, and even some deep affection.

· 11 ·

Cibolero Caravans of the Llano Estacado

> The usual explanation about driving down stakes to avoid getting lost, is an engaging folk tale.
>
> Herbert E. Bolton, *Coronado*

Juan de Oñate's colonists and the later settlers had introduced domesticated horses, cattle, pack animals, crops, fruits, goats, and sheep into New Mexico, beginning a significant transculturation process for regional food supplies and transportation. The natives of the bison plains, for example, quickly exchanged information with the frontier Hispanos about the sport of buffalo hunting. This process developed one of the most symbolic of the eighteenth- and nineteenth-century frontiersmen in the Southwest: the thrilling, sportive, distinctive *cibolero* of the eastern bison plains. The Llano served as the chief acculturation point for many ciboleros, a point where ideas, words, goods, and practices flowed between east and west. The cibolero also facilitated the survival of whole populations, augmenting the ancient flow of bison meat from plain to valley, gradually supplanting and transforming the many hundreds of former native traders.

These bison hunters took their name from their quarry, the *vacas* or "monstrous cattle" now routinely styled *cibolos*.[1] Sometimes the hunters properly were called *cazadores*. These dashing and skilled buffalo hunters rode into the

Llano's herds on a regular basis, often as part of a commercial enterprise after 1800. They used superbly trained horses to race alongside a moving herd of bison, and then shot arrows or plunged a six- to eight-foot-long lance—tipped with a twelve- to sixteen-inch polished iron blade—into the selected animal. A minor error in judgment could therefore be fatal to the cibolero. The relationship between a cibolero and his horse was naturally based on mutual trust.

Ciboleros were already seasoned specialists by the 1820s. They organized or accompanied caravans leaving northern Chihuahua, El Paso del Norte, Albuquerque, Santa Fé, Taos, and many other villages and pueblos. They were too irregular for officials to control really, although the business was booming. Antonio Barreiro estimated the annual harvest at 10,000 to 12,000 buffalo by the 1830s, but these were low figures.[2] On the way to the bison plains of the Llano, they often stopped in frontier villages and pueblos where it was possible to recruit new members, if needed, for the hunting party. After laying up the fall harvests of corn, beans, chilies, and fruits, many poorer villagers indeed were prepared for a final push to lay in a store of *carne* or meat for the cold months ahead. They celebrated a farewell fandango, then rose the next morning to join either a locally organized or a traveling caravan. Often they joined as an *agregado* or lowly helper, or perhaps as a *carrero* or cart driver. Not unlike sharecroppers, these helpers labored hard as skinners, butchers, assistants, drivers, and jerky cutters in return for some routine camp expenses and a share of the harvested meat. The *agregados* packed and transported their share of meat on burros or mules back to a home village. This earned supply of *carne* was important in getting a large family through a long winter. Although there was safety in numbers, sometimes small parties set out eastward as well. Rumors of Comanche perfidy and occasional parties that failed to return made these small ventures riskier.

Eventually, dozens of caravans and parties—with carretas and pack saddles, many men, some women and children, horses, mules, burros, and teams of draft oxen, Taos loaves of coarse bread, other trade items, and various supplies and cibolero equipment—were journeying hundreds of miles eastward into the plains. By the mid-nineteenth century the annual caravans from the settlements to the mesaland were sizable. Josiah Gregg reported that "large parties of New Mexicans . . . drive out into these prairies to procure a supply of buffalo beef for their families."[3] W. W. H. Davis encountered one such caravan on a branch of the upper Canadian River in 1853. "Soon after we encamped the advance of a large party of Mexican buffalo-hunters came in, and stopped just above us upon the stream [Rock Creek]," he reported in his book *El Gringo*. "All told, they numbered a hundred and fifty men, near five hundred animals, and some fifty carts. They were on their annual buffalo-hunt, which they make each fall, when they remain upon the plains six weeks or two months."[4] Their "mottled and uncivilized" looks clearly showed a transculturation process, and many of the ciboleros, agregados, carreros, and others may have shared mixed Hispano and

Indian blood. Davis remarked on their transhumant behavior as well, observing they were not unlike "a party of gipsies migrating to some new field of action."[5] They were gregarious and friendly, offering flasks of the potent local alcohol, *aguardiente*, to Davis and company.

Usually each party was under the iron rule of a *mayordomo* or camp master who enforced discipline and organization. Knowing the way, ciboleros led these assembled parties onto the Southern High Plains at several natural *puertas* or "doors" into the plains. Once on top the caravans drifted along drainages and among playas until they found the right concentrations of late-summer and fall herds. Experience had taught them where to look; indeed, the geography of the herds was very much in their minds. Ciboleros tried to find herds large enough that the caravan could camp in one vicinity for as long as possible. It increased the processing efficiency to stay up to two weeks or more, before a mayordomo was obliged to order a camp relocation to maintain contact with large herds. They might remain on the Llano for one and a half to two months until at last they had accumulated a large quantity of dried meat, skins, tallow, and other products. A few remained late into the season and braved the sudden onset of winter to get the thicker and more valuable bison robes. Some were likely caught in blizzards and froze to death.

These caravans represented a Spanish and later Mexican intensification of the ancient meat and robe trade between the plains and the pueblos. The Spanish allowed the ancient trade to continue with the Puebloans, but added new market demands for their own populous and booming settlements in northern Mexico. Faraon Apaches could only pack so much meat into New Mexican settlements by human and dog muscle. But organized outfits, using *muladas* (trains of pack animals) or draft oxen and carretas, and later wagon trains, revolutionized the transport and facilitated the flow of meat westward. While *las carretas*, the giant two-wheeled carts of local usage, appeared primitive and clumsy to later Anglo-Americans, these durable, jolting, inexpensive carts substantially increased the flow of protein from the frontier of northeast Mexico into the interior. By the late eighteenth century, cibolero caravans delivered countless tons of buffalo meat into northern Mexico as well as into the Hispano and Puebloan settlements of New Mexico. These supplies of jerky were significant sources of protein over long winters for ordinary folk. The severance of these flows would cause economic hardship. One wonders how many of their descendants work in the modern meat-processing plants of the Texas Panhandle.

The bison plains of the Llano attracted ciboleros and caravans from as far away as Chihuahua, Mexico.[6] Hunters could spend six months on the trail before finally reaching the great herds of the High Plains. From Santa Eulalis they passed through El Paso, gathered salt at Big Salt Lake, then crossed to the Pecos River via the Guadalupe Mountains. Once on the Pecos they ascended the river to the traditional Llano jumping-off point near Bosque Redondo.

Many of these caravans were annual commercial ventures. Salted, dried buffalo tongues sold well as delicacies in Mexico City, before the near extermination of the species destroyed the trade. Hides sold for a peso and the dried meat, *carne seco*, sold for up to thirty centavos per kilo.[7]

Tons of meat from the Llano also nourished the slave labor mining the rich silver veins in Chihuahua.[8] Feeding these unfortunates required a steady supply of cheap protein for their rations. Dried and pulverized buffalo meat was called *tesajo*, a frontier staple jerky. It could be eaten either raw or cooked with chilies, eggs, and beans in various recipes. Perhaps a thousand cartloads or more of this meat annually supplied the frontier towns of New Spain. In the process of supplying the market demand for many tons of *tesajo*, hides, tallow, tongues, and humps, the ciboleros mastered the plains environment to a remarkable degree. Some of these dashing hunters were likely the genizaro descendants of the great Tlaxcalan pioneers of New Mexico's frontier. Whatever their origin, as a livelihood their camps, trails, toponyms, trading activities, and folklore began to blanket the region. East of the Pecos River, south of the Canadian River, and north of the Concho River they plied their trade and came to know the land quite well.

They brought a sense of insight into the environment, a perceptual sense of place that seems beautifully Latin. The seasonal extremes of the climate were not especially disturbing to them. They saw the landscape with great passion, and where possible tried to mark the landscape with place-names of great clarity. Their insight into the regional soil, water, sky, and canyon was undoubtedly influenced in some measure by the Comanche presence. Together the transculturation process dissolved the predisposition of the flatland to remain nameless and featureless. There were even aspects of hunting on the Llano that stirred the soul.

A typical cibolero party of the nineteenth century might include over a hundred men, and half as many women and children. Once on top of the Llano, groups drifted southeast along the few drainage draws until they encountered compact herds around places bearing names like Palo Duro, Blanco, Agua Corriente, Tahoka, and Quitaque. There may have been informal territorial arrangements in which New Mexican village caravans went to customary areas to avoid the suggestion of encroaching on another village's happy hunting ground. The Santa Fé trader Josiah Gregg described the exotic but characteristic appearance of a typical plains cibolero in the 1840s:

> As we were proceeding on our march, we observed a horseman approaching, who excited at first considerable curiosity. His picturesque costume, and peculiarity of deportment, however, soon showed him to be a Mexican *Cibolero* or buffalo-hunter. These hardy devotees of the chase usually wear leather trousers and jackets, and flat straw hats; while swung upon the shoulder of each hangs his *carcage* or quiver of bow and arrows. The long handle of their lance

being set in a case, and suspended by the side with a strap from the pommel of the saddle, leaves the point waving high over the head, with a tassel of gay parti-colored stuffs dangling at the tip of the scabbard. Their fusil, if they happen to have one, is suspended in like manner at the other side, with a stopper in the muzzle fantastically tasselled.[9]

This anonymous cibolero was open and friendly, greeting the Gregg party with "demonstrations of joy" (still characteristic behavior on the plains). His unusual attire marked his occupation and suggested some assimilation to native ornamentation, with his tasseled, iron-bladed lance set into a tasseled case attached to the saddle. The old-fashioned gun or fusil carried on the other side of the saddle was most likely for human deterrence. As long as a cibolero held his fire, the gun was a convenient deterrent to occasional threatening parties, no one of whom would decide to die charging the loaded fusil for the benefit of his companions. With stout bow, arrows, knife, tasseled lance, and gun, the cibolero was a professional plainsman.

The spatial logic of the cibolero hunt was exceptional. Chasing one solitary buffalo was frustrating, as the later Anglo-Americans discovered for themselves. But by compacting cíbolas into a *corrida* or moving herd, all the jostling and crowding slowed the animals down, allowing the greater speed of a trained horseman to work the *corrida*. When the buffalo were compacted, in regular motion, and in the desired position, a cibolero dashed up against the rumbling flank and lanced or shot a particular animal. This was exhilarating work. A wounded bison was still a very dangerous animal. And one prairie-dog hole could suddenly throw a rider to the ground with thundering hooves all around.

In her classic work *We Fed Them Cactus*, Fabiola Cabeza de Baca narrated cibolero stories she remembered from "El Cuate," a longtime cook on her father's ranch near Las Vegas, New Mexico.[10] El Cuate was a former cibolero in his youth, and he loved to entertain his employer's daughter with descriptions of exciting buffalo-hunting days. Knowing the migratory habits of the animals, El Cuate and companions arranged for their caravans to intersect the October herds moving southward, great herds prodded by the Arctic fronts blowing stronger. The old cook recalled that various village outfits often consolidated on the trail, forming large, happy processions as they slowly poured onto the Llano. "As we traveled along, we met other caravans on the way," he said, "and when we reached the bluffs of the Llano Estacado, the Staked Plains, we were many companies. Some were already there and it became a small world, this big land of New Mexico."[11] A favorite rendezvous was the extensive alamo groves at Bosque Redondo on the Pecos River. El Cuate remembered as well large herds of thousands of buffalo swimming the Canadian River for pastures around *Los Barrancos Amarillos*, the yellow-loamed gulches and ravines in the vicinity of present Amarillo, Texas. He also sang a sad local *corrido* or ballad for Manuel

Maes, a cibolero who died nearby in 1863, when a new horse shied and a buffalo jolted the horseman's lance into his body.

The sense of danger was persistent. Ciboleros therefore invoked communal rituals in the chase. They located a suitable herd, camped nearby, and readied their equipment and nerves the rest of the day. At dawn the following morning, ciboleros from the various outfits often gathered and planned the first *corrida*. They rode near the herd, then dismounted and gathered to pray in unison. "The hunters formed a group before dashing into the herd," El Cuate told Fabiola Cabeza de Baca, "bowed their heads in prayer and invoked Santiago, the patron saint of Spain, to help them and guide them in the hunt. After making the sign of the cross, into the herd they rode."[12]

They were superb horsemen, often riding bareback to avoid entanglement with gear, and guiding horses by knee pressure alone. Villages trained and pampered cibolero horses, not allowing them to be abused in regular work. Evidently the hunters preferred cows and younger animals.[13] A one-ton buffalo bull was difficult, even dangerous, and the meat apparently less appreciated. After two or three good corridas or runs, with a day's killing of perhaps twenty or more buffalo, the cibolero retired and his less glorious companions set to work. The throats of the dead or dying animals were slit to bleed them properly. There was a strenuous field-butchering, then the meat and hides were packed back to camp on burros or carts if available. There was plenty left behind for the numerous wolves and buzzards of the Llano Estacado, who soon adapted themselves to this regular fall largess.

The cibolero camps of the Llano were busy places in September, October, and November. In addition to cooking and heavy camp chores, the accompanying *agregados* and women helped cure the skins and cut the meat. Indeed, cutting meat properly with the hand-forged butchering knives was an art. Long racks and strings of drying meat festooned the cibolero camps of the Llano. The market preferred thin flat sheets of meat for quick drying and curing in the fall sun. Cloudy or damp days called for smoky bison-dung fires to speed the process. These sheets were then packed tighter by rolling the jerky and trampling it with the bare feet. Besides meat and tongues, the Hispanos also tanned hides, used horns for utensils, kept neck hair for stuffing mattresses, and rendered large amounts of fat into tallow. Although these busy camps might be located wherever the herds were, over time certain favored places of the Llano, usually with access to good water, began to stand out. At these sites casual stakes of cedar or cottonwood were sometimes planted as poles to tie up horses and to set up lines of bison-hide strips to cure meat in the remarkably purifying atmosphere.

These favored places and their adjacent bison herds were admittedly the haunts of the Comanche and Kiowa, the fierce, conquering mounted tribesmen who began pushing the Apache Vaqueros toward the southwestern margins of the Llano after 1715.[14] Only after peaceful relations with these new lords were established could the bison hunters of New Mexican pueblos and towns return to the Llano and keep their scalps. The increasing presence of New Mexican ciboleros on the Llano after 1786 suggests the durability of the trade and diplomatic relations they eventually forged together. By the mid-nineteenth century, the intensification of the annual slaughter may have prompted complaints, retaliations, and incidents in this portion of the *Comanchería*, but in general there seemed to be the opinion that there was enough buffalo for all, using restraint. El Cuate mentioned one wasteful occasion when a cibolero corrida inadvertently led a large, moving herd to plunge madly over the edge of the caprock. The scene of carnage in the canyon below appalled and sickened the hunters. Only the thriving packs of wolves really benefited from the wastefulness.

In no small measure the extent and success of the Llano ciboleros depended upon the continuing goodwill and mutualistic relations they found in the *Comanchería*, such as with the later 1840s Kwahadi bands that favored the flatland immensity.[15] To avoid bloodshed and preserve goodwill it is likely that the early ciboleros of the late eighteenth century also began carrying convenient trade items. Ciboleros were primarily hunters, while comancheros were traders (legal or not), but trade goods helped ensure them both a welcome from the roving lords of these plains. From time to time cibolero maize, trinkets, the ubiquitous coarse bread loaves from village ovens, tobacco, brown sugar, *aguardiente*, and blankets were exchanged for Indian horses, tanned robes, and tolerance. Surely there were also fears that renegade Comanches or other war parties might reclaim barter by waylaying a small or poorly defended band of buffalo-hunters returning to villages in New Mexico. An exhausted Anirecha López arrived at Ft. Bascom on January 13, 1868, with a survivor's sad tale: scores of ciboleros wiped out on the eastern Llano's distant "Agua Azul" by hundreds of hostiles.[16]

The cibolero vision of the Llano involved grand action, calculated risks, and economic necessity. As a transcultural sport it had all the action and danger of today's rodeo events. Autumnal rainfall and cured summer pasturage made the Indian Summer days of late October a special time to experience this singular mesaland. Great quantities of wildfowl flew overhead for the Gulf Coast estuaries. The cooler weather meant the caravans also avoided the debilitating summer heat and high pressure drought spells. In the middle Llano, the hunters encountered the ancient southeast corridor of travel along the lakes, springs, salines, and seasonal draws of the Portales Valley. This natural corridor between the sources of Blackwater Draw and the Brazos also had thousands of playas, long drifts of sand hills, and many campsites. The north Llano provided the hunters with convenient access to New Mexico, and good tributary springs and streams flowing into the *Rio Colorado* (as the Canadian River was then called).

The cibolero vision of the Llano also included an appreciation for the flatland topography. Since a bounding, leaping mass of buffalo in the arroyos or breaks was exceptionally dangerous for their method of hunting, professional hunters chose especially level stretches of the plain—free of prairie-dog towns if possible.[17] They might have to do some maneuvering to get the buffalo on a good stretch of level ground suitable for a run. The amazing flatness of the Llano's vast tracts was in this sense a source of security, a crucial livelihood connection between the cibolero and his perception of the landscape. Whereas the Anglo-American "forest men" found the horizontality disturbing, for the bison hunters it meant an exhilarating chase and less personal risk.

The cibolero cultural ecology exemplified a successful Hispano adaptation to the plains environment. Great historians such as Walter Prescott Webb often underestimated the Spanish adaptation to the plains environment, yet the cibolero was precisely such a notable adaptation and solid economic success. Within two centuries of Zaldivar's vain attempt to corral 4,000 buffalo, Hispano frontiersmen had created an important trade from the annual bison slaughter on the Llano. Great quantities of winter protein, delicacies, and hides for the Santa Fé–Chihuahua trade soon poured from Llano pastures. Finally, cibolero activities probably coined the basic linguistic identity of the great mesa for the century ahead.

The exact origin of the name *El Llano Estacado* remains a mystery. But circumstantial evidence points to a folkloric connection with the Hispano hunters and traders of New Mexico. Particularly after the period of peace inaugurated in 1786 by Governor Anza with the Comanche, the ciboleros and comancheros ranged deep into the bison plains from the Canadian River to the Concho River. Sometime around the turn of the century, in the course of their exploratory travels on the great grassland, both groups began utilizing the singular expression *El Llano Estacado*—The Staked Plain—to signify and unite the vast expanse of level plains on the great mesa.

One correction seems in order. Contemporary accounts suggesting that Coronado used the term "Llano Estacado" are erroneous.[18] There is no trace of this specific toponym in the earliest Spanish entrada accounts. In an otherwise excellent book, A. G. Mojtabai, for example, asserts: "Coronado's men named the land bounded by these cliffs 'Los Llanos Estacados,' the Staked or Palisaded Plains."[19] It is by now a popular myth now that Coronado named the Staked Plains of Texas. But he created no palisades, left no description of stakes, and he complained of the lack of wood. Part of the confusion may stem from historian Herbert E. Bolton's popular 1949 book, *Coronado: Knight of Pueblos and Plains*. In writing of Coronado's approach to the Southern High Plains, Bolton commented:

> they could see the imposing line of rampart-like cliffs which gave the vast level expanse ahead of them the name of Llano Estacado (Stockaded or Palisaded Plain), later mistranslated by Anglo-Americans into "Staked Plains," which completely misses the point of the Spanish designation. They were called Stockaded Plains from the rim-rock which at a distance looks like a strong fortification.[20]

Bolton's translation and vision of the "Stockaded Plains" is quite questionable. The Mescalero ramparts east of the Pecos River are not especially remarkable; instead it was the steep eastern escarpment of the Llano that the Spanish found memorable. Taken out of context Bolton's remarks might further indicate that Coronado and his men used the term "Llano Estacado" in describing the caprock feature, which they simply never did in the preserved records.

A second mystery is not *who* named the great mesa but for *what* they named it. Many theories of the place-name's origin are critically connected to regional environmental perception. A *Llano*, of course, is a large, level plain, with no arguments about its appropriateness. This usage does go back to the Coronado documents. The mystery is with the modifier: *Estacado* has a surprising number of possibilities. Herbert E. Bolton was a strong proponent of the "Stockade" perception. Captivated himself by the appearance of the *eastern* escarpment bluffs, he thought it clear that the first apperceptive image of the mesa was its emergence from the horizon as a natural palisade, but one of stone rather than wooden stakes or *estacas*. The abrupt and steep escarpment slopes acted defensively, making access difficult. Like a fortress, the great plain lay behind an enormous stone stockade: the Stockaded Plains. These stone-palisade images of the Anglos can be traced back to the Texan–Santa Fé Expedition, where Thomas Falconer and George Wilkins Kendall likened the obstacle bluffs and steep caprock formation to a natural palisade or stockade.[21] Later Anglos, like the 1890s geologist W. F. Cummins, keyed on this palisaded plain image as well. Even modern geologists refer to the "Stockaded Plains."[22] But the existing accounts of the early Spanish show surprisingly little notice of the *western* caprock. This inattention may suggest that the bluff margins of the Llano were more perceptually significant to the Anglo-Americans than the Spanish-Hispanos, particularly since observers like Thomas Falconer saw the eastern bluffs first, with their impressive heights and canyons. "Regardless of these words," Panhandle historian H. Bailey Carroll noted, "the eastern escarpment of the Llano does not appear stockaded and no Mexican would ever so call it."[23]

Another theory holds that *estacado* refers to the innumerable stalks of the area yucca plants (*Yucca angustifolia*). Blooming in May and June, large patches of these yuccas on the western range of the Llano still present the appearance of innumerable slender stakes. A linguistic variant of the Stockaded Plain also derived from H. Bailey Carroll's comment on *Destacado*, the informal participle for "upraised, uplifted, embossed." In this mesaland version of land and logos, the "D" of "*Llano Destacado*"—"The Uplifted Plain"—was slurred off by frontier people, and later folk created popular lore on the meaning of *estacado* or staked. *Estacado* itself is the past participle of *estacar*, "to put stakes in the ground, to enclose a spot with stakes" as well as an Iberian expression for a pallisaded spot to fight in, a dueling-ground of terror and death. To leave someone in the *estacado* was to abandon him or her to a cruel fate, to sacrifice a life.[24]

In truth, there is a persistent thread of folkloric meaning associated with the name. "In the question of origins," H. Bailey Carroll wrote, "it has been generally overlooked that the name came from the New Mexican rather than the Texas side."[25] *Llano Estacado* is almost certainly a "folk" as opposed to an "elite" name. The lore of ciboleros and comancheros was that the incredible flatness of the region caused men to go astray. In order to find their way across these plains, the traders and hunters supposedly marked their course from waterhole to waterhole with *estacas* or wooden stakes. Various accounts of this legend exist. W. F. Cummins quotes a letter from Fray Chaves in New Mexico about ancient Spanish gold prospectors departing from Bosque Redondo to reprovision themselves on the plains with buffalo meat. This group of prospectors split into bewildered parties during the return. One party supposedly reached the Pecos River, cut a number of cottonwood stakes, loaded them on mules, and placed them at intervals as they reentered the plains to find their companions.[26]

Like Hansel and Gretel's trail of crumbs, or Theseus's ball of string, the legend of staking one's way through a featureless labyrinth proved popular. By the time of early American exploration, the labyrinth tale was the usual explanation offered by locals for the unusual name. Later on, the "Little Texans" of New Mexico incorporated the Hispano legends of the name into their own lore: "When Pecos Bill lassoed a tornado that threatened his vast herds the tornado bucked, sunfished, and sunned its sides in its efforts to escape; it ranted and tore around until everything was so bare that people had to drive stakes across the country to find their way about."[27] Like the best of lore there is a mythic and narrative quality to the expression. The name was also a warning in its signification. The logos of "*llano estacado*" expresses an eminently practical storyline, a distinct warning that the flat plains ahead required some human ingenuity to master the environment. The folk tale behind the words gives the listener an important message of environmental perception. Whether the sojourner was a prospector, trader, hunter, or wandering Franciscan friar,[28] the story implied caution as to one's location and water supply on the great plain to the east. The name was a *dicho*, or small didactic folk saying. There was also an allegorical quality to the name. One staked a course across the plain as across a difficult stretch of life—with a series of signposts and significations.

These stakes or *estacas* further symbolized the vertical nature of human presence in this labyrinth. A rider felt conspicuous on the open plains precisely as a vertical presence. The stakes therefore could function as a vertical reference system for vertical beings. The name also pointed to the lack of water. An elder Hispano resident of Puerto de Luna, New Mexico, recalled to an interviewer in 1921 that the old *estaca* trail started at the edge of the plain, and ran across by way of the principal waterholes.[29] Organized men drove stakes along the trail to orient themselves and to avoid perishing from the lack of water. This unnamed old-timer also claimed plausibly that once the trails "became distinct by wear the stake system was discontinued, but the name survived."

A final theory is less glamorous but correspondingly more probable. A few historians point to Francisco Amangual's remark in 1808 that, while on "plains so immense that the eye could not see their end," his expedition had found, "where we camped it was necessary to drive stakes for the guard and reserve horses." In this sense, it was the horse, not the human mind, that required staking. As an important part of the ecological exchange between Old World and New World, the horse was by the eighteenth century increasingly common on the plains. But on the Llano campgrounds there were neither trees nor brush to tie up horses. Possibly both Hispano and Comanche *caballadas*, or horse herds, utilized a system of stakes, often at regular, watered camps on important trails across the Llano. H. Bailey Carroll, who thought on the matter more deeply than Bolton, noted that this prosaic explanation for *estacado* had "a certain amount of reasonableness." "In other places stock might be 'tied up,'" he noted, "but not on the Llano."[30] Furthermore, in various interviews with former New Mexican traders and hunters, Carroll recalled, "I have had explained to me that *El Llano Estacado* was the plain where it was necessary to stake the horses."[31] The necessity of staking stock on the Llano was only amplified by the difficulty of finding runaways or scattered horses in the disorienting landscape. Woe to the individual wondering which way to go first in search of a lost mount; there were no heights to climb to get a view.

The origin of the name is useful in speculating on the subjective process of image formation. A very good analyst of perception on the Great Plains, John L. Allen, once proposed a simple process-response model to account for the output of geographical images on the plains.[32] Perhaps it is possible to adapt his systems model for the name and image of the "Llano Estacado" or Southern High Plains:

INPUT	REGULATOR	STORAGE	SUBSYSTEM	OUTPUT
Pre-exploratory Lore	Exploratory Process	Old Lore	Subjective Interpretation	Geographical Image
16th–17th century	18th century	Late 18th–19th centuries	circa 1800	Estab. by 1825
Quivira; Cibola; lo llano;	Comanche, cibolero and comanchero activities	old network of trails and regular camps, many with stakes	"Lost Spanish Prospectors"; folk tales; sound value	"El Llano Estacado" (The Staked Plain)
Quivira	llanos de cibola	estaca trail	Llano Estacado	Llano Estacado

Whether an expression of physical geography or a folktale image of labyrinthine flatness and drought or a routine practice for securing horses, the name El Llano Estacado stuck firmly in the popular imagination. It was already a term widely familiar when American travelers arrived in New Mexico in the

1830s. If the origin remains a mystery, the appropriateness of the name as an environmental metaphor was soon established. In the half-century after 1786 the name took hold in the frontier New Mexican settlements. Whereas official Spanish, French, and American cartographers were mostly "lost," leaving a blank space or creating drainage errors, the borderland Hispanos recognized the region and mentally mapped it. Their Llano Estacado was sprinkled not only with trails and place-names but also with lore and legend.[33]

Many of these locals knew better than anyone that the Llano Estacado could be a land of mirages and illusion. A few of their topographic names even relied upon the region's environmental deceptions: the distant appearance of glittering salt lakes in the middle Llano as sites of false wealth—-"Laguna de Rica" (Rich Lake) and "Laguna de Plata" (Silver Lake)—or the view of barren bluffs as habitations—"Casas de Amarillo" (Yellow Houses). In the end, their informal, insightful, and passionate interpretation of the landscape constituted a rich perceptual heritage for the first Anglo-Americans encountering the great plain. Although they could scarcely have imagined an end to the buffalo, only a few decades after 1860 the vast herds were all destroyed. Suddenly there was no more need for the transcultural ciboleros. In a few shattering years, after an effort at buffalo conservation was aborted by the Texas legislature, a lifeway was lost forever. A noble chase with roots stretching back thousands of years—to the mounted hunting of bulls in the Iberian marshes and plains and to the native stalking of *bison antiquus* around ancient playas and canyons—had ended on the Southern High Plains.

·12·

Trailblazers Across Comanchería

Here we met a Comanche who told us of a lake that is in the middle of the Llano . . .

Diary of Francisco Xavier Fragoso from San Antonio to Santa Fé, June 25 to August 20, 1789

By the mid-eighteenth century, enterprising Frenchmen thought not of Quivira but of Santa Fé. They had already developed significant trading activities with the natives to the west, including the Arkansas River tribes that now controlled the Quivira of legend. What the French lacked, however, were active economic relations with Spanish New Mexico itself. Spanish officials, at times brusquely, shrugged off French economic embraces, complained of border incidents, and competed ineffectually for the Indian trade.[1] All this changed in 1763 when the French ceded their Louisiana possessions to Spain in order to spite the English. After a long period of indecision, the Spanish bureaucracy recognized the advantages of linking their frontier outposts with new trails, new lines of communication, and new mercantile prospects.[2] Although a projected and legal Louisiana–New Mexico commerce never really materialized, a small number of daring explorers blazed trails across or skirting the Llano in anticipation of these ties.

Pierre and Paul Mallet exemplified early French expansionism. Born in Montreal, these adventurous brothers in 1739 led the first overland group of

French traders across the supposedly uncrossable wilderness of modern Nebraska, Kansas, and Colorado. The South Fork of the Solomon River swept most of their goods away, and by June 23 they were again on "the barren prairies, where the only means to light a fire consisted of buffalo chips."[3] A week later the Mallets found "stones with Spanish inscriptions" on the Arkansas River. By mid-July they had ascended the Arkansas and Purgatory Rivers to reach the Jicarilla trail at Raton Pass. Not far from Santa Fé on July 20, 1739, they reached Picuris Pueblo, where church bells rang to honor the brave Frenchmen for their overland crossing of the immense plains. Spanish officials received them kindly at Santa Fé as well, an act of lenience they regretted later.

After wintering in Santa Fé, the Mallets and four or five of their companion traders left the city on May 1, 1740, seeking to discover a new route to New Orleans. They stayed for two days at the "Pequos" mission and then followed the Pecos Valley eastward for several days. It is likely that they received some local advice and guidance at Pecos Pueblo, as their own geographic sensibilities were understandably confused. Margry's abstract noted, for example, that the Mallets thought the Pecos River "could be a branch of the Red River or the Arkansas River," instead of a branch of the Rio Grande.[4] They sensibly left the Pecos River when it turned to the south near modern Santa Rosa, New Mexico, crossed a tributary and a prairie to the east, and discovered "a third river":

> which they supposed runs into the Red River or into the Arkansas
> and believed it to be the same branch beside which they had found
> the Spanish inscriptions on their way to Santa Fe.[5]

They were *not* on the Arkansas, of course, but on the "Riviére Rouge" or "Rio Colorado," now called the Canadian River.[6] They were deceived in part because this river flowed in the same direction as the Arkansas. Thinking they were on another river, the Mallets made an important conjecture. If they could descend this "third river" and reach New Orleans, then, in return, they could ascend the river from Louisiana to within "35 or 40 leagues" of Santa Fé, "to perfect their discoveries."

The Mallet party rode along the south side of the Canadian River Valley, soon beneath the bluffs of the Llano. They apparently paid little attention to the "barren prairies" above them, preferring the riverine corridor with its known wood and water. After three days of trailing the group split in two. Somewhere in or near present-day Oldham County, Texas, three fellow companions crossed over the river "to take the route of the Pani Indians" back to Illinois. Paul and Pierre Mallet and their two remaining companions continued down the Canadian Valley. On May 15, 1740, the party coolly rode into a Comanche village that had many horses.

The Comanches were friendly, organized a feast that night, and the Frenchmen swapped "a few knives and other bagatelles" for additional horses. They continued their eastward course in the days ahead, now rounding the great northeastern curve of the Canadian, a feature that also mimics the Arkansas. On the night of the 22nd they lost six horses (possibly back to the very Comanches who had traded them away for "bagatelles"). For a week thereafter they hugged the flanks of the Llano more closely, watering on the spring-fed tributaries, and concealing themselves in the rougher topography.

As the Mallets left the Llano behind and advanced farther downstream, they found the baseflow of water increasing. They abandoned their horses on June 20 and set out downstream in rapid elm bark canoes. Two days later they saw "two beautiful river mouths" which they incredibly supposed were the Pecos and Gallinas Rivers! The brothers had crossed these two rivers shortly after leaving Santa Fé; they apparently thought these watercourses now flowed into the "Arkansas." Only after further days of canoe travel did they emerge—to their utter surprise—on the real Arkansas River. From there they knew the way back to New Orleans via the Acadian hunting camps and the "Arkansaw Post."

Without really knowing which river they had been on, Paul and Pierre Mallet had nevertheless discovered a highly strategic travel and trade corridor between French Louisiana and Spanish New Mexico.[7] This one particular riverine corridor nicely penetrated the "barren prairies" of the plains, unlike the troublesome Red River itself. French trailblazers had thus found the logical route of trade (or conquest) from New Orleans to Santa Fé. Distant French officials were likely confused, like the Mallets initially, by indiscriminate use of the term "Red River." The Spanish had at least two rivers in north Texas noted for ruddy sediments and red rises: the *Rio Rojo* (Red River) and the *Rio Colorado* (Canadian River). Blending the upper branches of each together into a common "Riviére Rouge" or "Red River" gave interesting geographic results.

But the Mallets now knew that the "third river" branch—the modern Canadian River—led directly from the Arkansas River to within some forty leagues of Santa Fé. With great luck they had succeeded where La Harpe and others had failed. With their penchant for river travel, the "four Canadians" had found the most significant route "to the Spanish territories" in the considered opinion of Governor Bienville of French Louisiana.[8] He duly authorized and financed a major return expedition. With high hopes the Mallet brothers set out a year later as guides to retrace and confirm their great discovery with the official Bruyére Expedition.

André Fabry de la Bruyére was an uninspired leader. Like the French explorer Jean-Baptiste Bénard, sieur de La Harpe, who penetrated Oklahoma in 1719, Bruyére was wedded to the notion that one traveled in the West much as one traveled on the Mississippi: by boat. When shallow waters grounded his dugouts or pirogues on Canadian River sandbars in Oklahoma, the expedition disintegrated. Disgusted by Bruyére, the Mallet brothers and several others took their merchandise and kept going westward, possibly on foot until they procured horses. In either case they encountered and skirted the Llano via the Canadian Valley to reach Santa Fé once more.

The Mallets again had proved the logical route from New Orleans to Santa Fé by ascending a particular branch of the Arkansas River, one that led directly through the plains to the Spanish in New Mexico. Still, the "barren prairies" and shallow river flows constituted an important environmental barrier for the other, boat-bound French. Furthermore, within a decade the Spanish simply resisted all intrusion. When Pierre Mallet and three other traders returned to Santa Fé from the Missouri River in 1751, anxious officials in New Mexico arrested all four and sent them off to Mexico City for disposal. Although the Mallets knew a way to penetrate the "barren prairies" of the Llano and High Plains—the one branch of the Arkansas River that led directly to the settlements in New Mexico—they could not overcome the mercantilist zeal and fears of Spanish officials.

For some four decades there was little official attempt by either Spanish or French to follow up on the Mallets' discovery. Instead, the impetus of discovery largely passed to the illegal traders, the *contrabandistas* mostly French or of French extraction, who traveled and traded extensively with the intervening tribes. Contrabandista outposts along the Arkansas and Red Rivers were soon supplying French merchandise (and horrific smallpox) to the *Comanche Orientals* of the eastern Llano Estacado. It is possible that a few other French traders and gun-runners drew near or encountered the Llano but left no published reports.

After suddenly acquiring the Louisiana possessions in 1763, the Spanish dallied. They badly needed a diplomatic breakthrough with the Comanches to connect their New Mexican and new Louisiana outposts. Finally in 1785 they were ready to advance the old dream of linking their outposts with new lines of communication and commerce. They chose for this delicate task of peacemaking a mysterious Frenchman and former *contrabandista* named Pierre Vial. Don "Pedro" Vial came to be one of the great trailblazers of the Llano. Moreover, his journals and papers provide critical insights into the region.

Born in Lyons, France, around 1746, Pierre Vial came to epitomize the contrabandista practical mastery of Southwestern geography.[9] In the New World Vial became an illegal French trader and turned his blacksmithing skills to good use. Diffusing or slipping into Spanish Texas, probably in the 1770s with a party of French contrabandistas from the historic Arkansas Post, he eventually settled at the Taovaya Villages on the bend of the Red River in present Montague County, Texas, and Jefferson County, Oklahoma. As an honored gunsmith, he forged lance-heads and repaired French weapons. He also learned to speak some Comanche, Wichita, and Spanish as well. As a measure of his strong personality and seemingly supernatural spirit, some called him *Manitou* or "Monsieur Manitou." In 1784 he maintained a blacksmith forge near a spring of one of the twin Taovaya and Wichita villages on the Red River. There a Spanish emissary found him and convinced him to return to San Antonio that fall for a full pardon, and for possible employment as a peacemaker to the Comanches.

Despite his shady past, "Pedro" Vial greatly impressed Governor Cabello in Béxar. Even better the passably literate Vial volunteered his life to penetrate the Comanchería on a mission of peace. Joining him was an equally remarkable (but illiterate) New Mexican companion, a former assimilated Comanche captive and current adventurer named Francisco Xavier Chaves. The astounding diary of the Vial-Chaves peace mission of 1785 is at last available from the Archivo General de Simancas in Spain.[10] This exciting diary describes one of the great diplomatic exploits of the time: how an outlaw Frenchman and a former Indian captive journeyed among the Llano's northeastern drainages to make peace between the Spanish and the Comanche nations.

Vial, Chaves, and fellow native emissaries rode out from the Taovaya Villages in August 1785, heading west along the Red River drainages. After due Comanche precautions and delays, Vial and Chaves were allowed to ride into a great rancheria of the *Cumanches Orientales*, or Cuchanecs, as the Spanish called them. They were now on the *Rio de Vermellón*, often thought to be the Little Wichita River that flows into the upper Red River from the south. There were pointed Comanche inquiries about infectious disease, since prior French traders from "La Zarca" or the Arkansas Post had horribly infected their rancherias with smallpox, perhaps killing two-thirds of the natives.[11] A dramatic council on September 10, 1785, further major peace talks by Vial and the famous "Camisa de Hierro" or Chief Ironshirt, and good words sealed by valuable trade gifts hastened the important peace process.[12]

Returning to San Antonio with Comanche peace emissaries and flush with success, Vial was well suited for Governor Cabello's next step: blazing a trail from San Antonio all the way through the Comanchería itself to Santa Fé.[13] Vial could talk his way past most of the intervening tribes. As for the feared Comanche, the incredible results of his 1785 mission on the Little Wichita River gave him the expectation that friendly Comanche guides would conduct him across that further unknown territory, the mysterious land beyond the Rio de Vermellón. Leaving San Antonio for Santa Fé on October 4, 1786, Vial and a single companion, Cristóbal de los Santos, suffered early mishaps and lengthy delays. Eventually they reached the Taovaya Villages, the familiar but rough trading emporium on the Red River. Here French factory merchandise, Apache slaves of the Comanche, guns, and stolen horses traded briskly as usual.[14] During most of January and February in 1787 Pedro Vial wintered as an honored guest in a Comanche camp located away from the Taovaya Villages toward the Llano. He parlayed further peace there with the legendary chieftain, "Camisa de Hierro" or Ironshirt (also called "Cota de Malla" or "Ecueracapa"). On March 4, 1787, Vial, his brave companion, and a protective Comanche escort under Chief Zoquiné rode out from the camp for Santa Fé.

As part of a general peace with the Spanish, Zoquiné was prepared to show Vial a Comanche trail from the upper Red River to the upper Rio Grande settlements. Unfortunately, Vial's meager diary entries hardly indicate their route at all. He was simply not a reliable or descriptive diarist in this regard. Zoquiné and Vial rode westward that spring, crossed the Rio de Vermellón, and leisurely followed and crossed the arroyos and springs of the upper Red River. In April, somewhere west of the 100th meridian, the party reached the Llano canyons and began to cross the divide between the Red and Canadian Rivers. Vial's diary entry from April 13, 1787, recorded: "We went north from this place until we reached the Colorado River, where we remained six days."[15] *This* Colorado River could well be the Canadian River, as the historians Loomis and Nasatir note.

By a northwest route, perhaps a similar course to the later railroad and highway looking for an easy ascent, Chief Zoquiné possibly avoided the steepest escarpment country of the Caprock. Vial recorded no barrier of note, although later American explorers chose the Prairie Dog Town branch of the Red River and soon perceived the precipitous caprock as an enormous barrier. Once near the "Colorado" or Canadian River, Vial's diary recorded a succession of camps that May in spring-fed canyons or arroyos as he called them. These camps are an important environmental clue, as they establish his route along the springlands of the northern Llano Estacado. Vial and Zoquiné used the curving arc of bluff springs pouring from the Llano to avoid the rigors of the drier plains above. It is, however, quite possible that the group crossed an inconvenient spur of the great mesa. On May 11, 1787, they "entered a large plain, and stopped for the night without water."[16] They continued over this large plain the next day until reaching another canyon spring.

Along the way the Vial party encountered several villages of Yamparika Comanches on the northern Llano frontier. These bands also traveled from east to west, likely using variations of the same bluff spring arc of the northern Llano as a well-watered route. Like their "Cumanches Orientales" allies, these Yamparikas or "Root-Eaters" had developed active trading relations with the Spanish.[17] Following on the heels of the 1786 peace treaty between New Mexico and the *Comanchería*, Vial and his companion were received cordially by the Yamparikas. Continuing their course west past mesa landmarks, trailing between the Llano mesa and the Canadian River, the Vial group crossed the low divide and reached a Pecos River tributary on May 24, 1787. Shortly thereafter they arrived at the welcome town of Santa Fé.

Again a Frenchman had crossed the plains wilderness from east to west. But Vial's route was singular in its overland penetration of *Comanchería* from the southeast. For one of the major obstacles to trade and communication between San Antonio and Santa Fé was the Comanche grip on the Southern Plains. "The great, high, barren Llano Estacado," historian T. R. Fehrenbach notes, "walled off *Comanchería* from the south and west."[18] South of the Canadian

River Yamparikas were the later emergent Kwahadi of the 1840s, the *Kwah-hee-her Kehnuh* or "Sun Shades on Their Backs" from their custom of fashioning bison-hide parasols to protect themselves from the burning intensity of the Llano sun.[19] Their ancestors had helped drive the Apache bands before them in the crucial decades after 1700. Also known as the *Kwerhar-rehnuh* or "Antelopes," both of the band's names reflected the plains environment. They were fond of shade, characteristically standing in the shadows of their horses after dismounting on the Llano Estacado. Perhaps several thousand of these Comanches roamed the immense mesa and its environs. They were later considered, as Fehrenbach notes, "the most remote, aloof, and fierce of all the bands."[20] Vial's route not only penetrated *Comanchería* but also largely avoided these more remote bands.

New Mexico's governor was very pleased to greet Pedro Vial, but he correctly concluded that the Frenchman had not taken the shortest route. Accordingly, he dispatched a retired corporal named José Mares to find a direct and better trail. Mares left Santa Fé on July 31, 1787, with two companions, the intrepid Cristóbal de los Santos and Alejandro Martín. Passing Pecos Pueblo and the Gallinas River, Mares's more detailed diary begins to record the increasing significance of the Llano. By August 5, 1787, he was near the outliers of Tucumcari, New Mexico, following "the mesas all the way, a famous landmark."[21] During the 6th he continued east, "continually skirting the chain of mesas" of the Llano. That night, he slept at a convenient puerta watering place called *Mi Señora del Tránsito*, "because there I crossed the mesa."[22]

On August 7, Mares and his companions ascended the western caprock and struck out into the featureless plain, perhaps the first assigned explorers to do so since the pearling expeditions of the 1650s. "I travelled very rapidly this day across a very wide plain which contains no landmarks," he wrote, "other than an arroyo which runs to the east and which has two clumps of chinaberry trees."[23] The white cliffs of the caprock observed by Mares in this arroyo identify it as upper Tierra Blanca Creek. Mares followed Tierra Blanca Draw eastward, taking his regular August siestas at pleasant stops along the creek, which soon ran with permanent water near modern Friona and Hereford. He then left Tierra Blanca and struck out southeast "across a very large plain." Again there were few landmarks that day: "only one pond" or playa. Eventually the small party of trailblazers reached a well-watered draw, perhaps Frio Draw, which he appropriately named *Arroyo de Cíbolo*.

Moving southward on a Comanche trail the next morning at sunrise, José Mares and his companions crossed "some very broad plains" until reaching the banks of the *Río del Tule* in early afternoon. Here, near present-day Tulia, Texas, Mares took his regular siesta at a spot on Tule Creek. "It is permanent," he observed of the water, despite the August heat, "and has cottonwood trees and many reeds [*tules*]."[24] Mares's comment indicates that the mesaland was not as barren of either wood or water as could be supposed. At three o'clock he rose from his siesta and continued east "across the same plain," camping that evening at a lonely spot he named *San Geronimo*. The next day he arrived suddenly "at the edge of a precipitous mesa." This edge can only be the eastern escarpment of the Llano. The historian Dan Flores has pinpointed Mares's descent by unraveling an important environmental clue.[25] In his journal entry for August 8, Mares observed from his escarpment perch "two rivers" below; "I named one Señor San José and the other Sangre de Cristo." These two watercourses correspond nicely to the North Prong and South Prong of the Little Red River as it drains the spectacular country of the present-day Caprock Canyons State Park. For Flores, Mares's Sangre de Cristo or "Blood of Christ" tributary can only refer to the marvelous sanguine canyonlands of the South Prong, a stretch of escarpment with the "reddest sandstone canyons anywhere along the caprock."

As a dedicated modern explorer and interpreter of the region, Flores's personal intimacy with the canyonlands enabled him to visualize the analogous perception behind Mares's sanguine canyon toponym. Indeed, five of Mares's various rests and camps across the Llano—*Mi Señora del Tránsito* (My Lady of the Passage, that is, the passageway up the caprock and into the mesa), *Río Blanco* (River of the White [cliff], or today's Tierra Blanca Creek), *Arroyo de Cíbolo* (a reference to the presence or trails of the mesa's cíbolas or bison), *Río del Tule* (a routine toponymic reference to the distinctive marshland stretches of *tules* or reeds in the drainage), and *Sangre de Cristo* (the blood-red canyon of the South Prong Fork of Little Red River, just west of the "Redbeds" badlands)— take their names from a key environmental reflection upon the landscape. Perhaps even the hagiographic names of his camps and rests (*Señor San Miguel*, *San Geronimo*, and *Señor San Jose*) are keyed to the surroundings. His lonely camp in the dried-up playa stretch between Tule Creek and the Caprock Canyonlands was named after St. Jerome, the scholar and hermit who endured the solitude of the remote wilderness of Chalcis.

On August 9, 1787, José Mares descended the steep cliffs of the Sangre de Cristo branch by a noticeable path. He found the escarpment slopes cloaked with "much timber" of juniper. In the scenic breaks below, the Mares party soon encountered friendly Comanches who guided them eastward for days across the confusing drainages before reaching the Taovayas Villages on the Red River. From there they turned due south, crossed the Trinity, Brazos, and Colorado Rivers, and were soon in the beautiful but rough Hill Country. Scattering elegant Spanish place-names along the way, José Mares reached San Antonio on October 8, 1787. He rested for three months, then set out to improve further on his route by avoiding the Taovayas Villages detour to the east.

After wintering on the Double Mountain Fork of the Brazos, José Mares and his Comanche guides reencountered the Llano in late March 1788. By April 7 he had ascended "the rough mesas mentioned in the other diary, and made camp for the night at El Tules."[26] Once on top of the mesa he retraced his steps rather carefully across this "plain without landmarks." "All this region is a plain," he noted on April 9. Mares's return across the Llano was more leisurely than before. Journeying up Tierra Blanca Creek on the 13th he found "many trees." By the 18th he was again marching across "a plain that had no landmarks other than a very large pond."[27] But that day he descended the great mesa to reach his old camp at *Mi Señora del Tránsito*. Once more he stayed "close to the mesas" of the northern Llano, as he wound his way westward toward Santa Fé.[28]

Mares's return route of 325 leagues, or 845 miles, was considerably shorter than Vial's grueling 1,157-mile journey. With little fanfare he had blazed a perfectly acceptable trail across the Llano. He also found water, a little timber, and good camps in the middle of the great mesa. Although he spoke frequently of the lack of landmarks, the plains environment did not unnerve him. It was entirely possible, he now knew, to cross the immense mesa almost in a beeline by arcing across the subtle network of watercourses that flowed eastward.

Less than a month after the return of Mares, New Mexico's energetic governor dispatched Don Pedro Vial, this time to find a direct route between Santa Fé and Natchitoches in Louisiana. Vial, the diarists Francisco Fragoso and Santiago Fernandez, and four companions left Santa Fé on June 24, 1788. By Monday, June 30, they had passed "a dark-colored mesa on the right" (Tucumcari Mesa), a harbinger of the immense mesa ahead. Fragoso and Fernandez were more patient diarists than Vial, and their remarks are more keyed to the environment. Hispano toponyms of the Llano frontier by now had begun to appear in the official reports. Fragoso referred to places like Pajarito, Santa Rosa, and San Pedro before they reached the edge of the Llano.[29] On July 2 the New Mexicans were camped at a bluff spring called *El Puerto*. This camp was likely the same "door" onto and into the Llano environment later called "*Puerto de Rivajeños*"[30] or Arroyo del Puerto. A good spring near a natural doorway up the caprock was important to Comanche and New Mexican alike.

The next day Vial's party ascended the mesa and found themselves on plains "so extensive that one sees only sky and plain."[31] The travelers also found "thirteen ponds" (playas) with considerable water that day. The trailblazers soon reached Palo Duro or Tierra Blanca Creek, which they called *Rio Blanco* (providing a later source of confusion with another Rio Blanco farther south in Blanco Canyon). The party descended this stream for several days. By July 4, 1788, they were likely in scenic Palo Duro Canyon, although none of the surviving accounts suggest the sense of sublime awe found in later explorer accounts. But on July 4th they did note their arrival "at the headwaters [*cabeza*] of the Rio Blanco,"[32] and thereafter they found "water, good land, plains, wood, and much pasturage," a resource tribute to the sixty-mile-long Palo Duro Canyon system. Riding along the next day they encountered "unattached Comanches everywhere" and noted the junction of Mares's Tule River with the Prairie Dog Town Fork of the Red River, which they logically persisted in

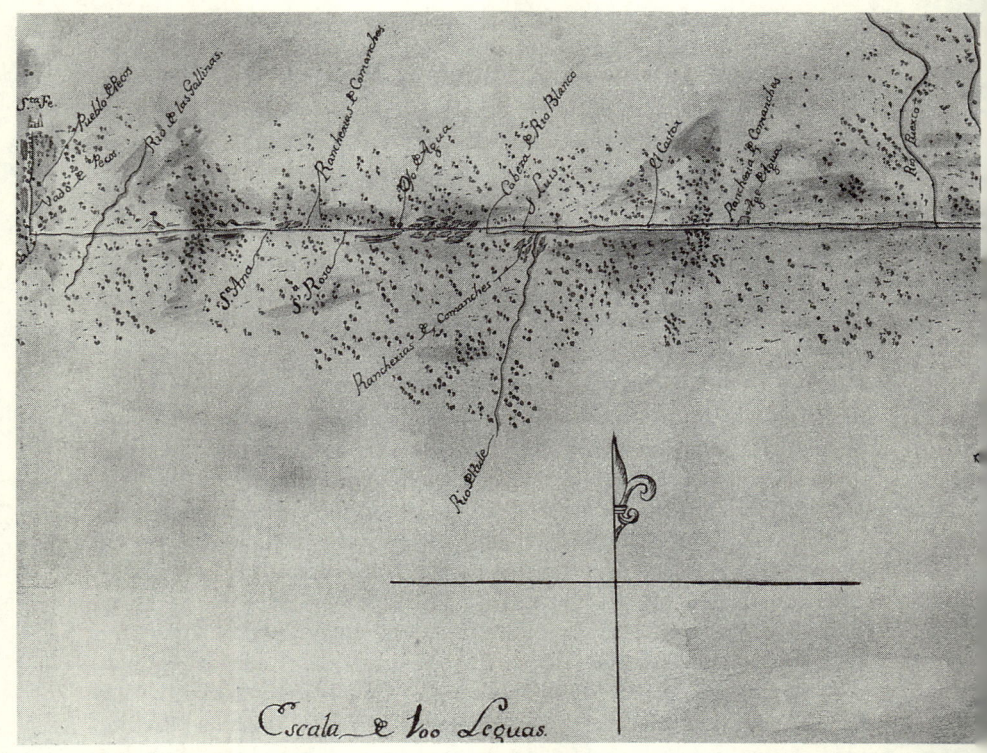

Mapa del territorio comprendido entre la Provincia de Nuevo Mexico y el Fuerte de Natchitoches y Texas, by unknown artist, 1788. Colored manuscript map (detail). Watercolor-and-ink copy. A milestone map on the Llano, its playas, the sources of the Red River, and an improved trail from Santa Fé to Natchitoches, based on the account or *derrotero* of Pierre (Pedro) Vial's second journey across the Llano. Original in the Archivo General de Indias, Seville, Spain. *CN 01347.* Copy courtesy J. P. Bryan Map Collection, Center for American History, University of Texas at Austin.

calling Rio Blanco. Following this tributary Vial, Fragoso, and the others eventually reached the Red River Taovaya Villages, and Natchitoches beyond.

Fortunately, a copy exists of a rare, anonymous 1788 watercolor map of Vial's route from Santa Fé to Natchitoches.[33] This pretty map is not entirely accurate, but it is still a remarkable portrayal of their travels near and on the Llano Estacado. As the detail of this map notes, after crossing the Gallinas River the trailblazers had encountered Comanche rancherias near the Santa Rosa area of the northwest Llano. The black pen-mark hachures east of Santa Rosa may refer to the bluff sides of the great mesa, with their dark, cloaking forests of "savin" (junipers). At the right-hand curve of these markings there is an *Ojo del Agua*, that is, the spring they called El Puerto at the natural doorway to the plains above.

To the right of this spring, they are traveling on the Llano itself. It is perhaps no coincidence that the thirteen ponds they spoke of on July 3 are reproduced on the map as thirteen variably sized lakes. These thirteen elongated bodies of water are undoubtedly the first iconographic representations of the characteristic playas of the Llano. In this manner, the anonymous cartographer used a peculiar environmental feature to characterize the flat plains of the Llano. To the right of the playas, the map notes another feature: the *Cabeza del Rio Blanco*, which is likely the confluence of Palo Duro and Tierra Blanca Creeks as they flow down into Palo Duro Canyon. Rather than recognizing the scenic canyon, the 1788 map chooses to see the magnitude increase of the watercourse and its canyon tributaries. Downstream on the Prairie Dog Town Fork the map shows more Comanche rancherias. It especially notes native villages near the confluence of the *Rio Blanco* with the *Rio del Tule*.[34] It was near here that a friendly Comanche met the explorers and graciously invited them to visit his snug camp for the night.[35]

This map deserves more recognition for its portrayal of the Llano Estacado. In a small space, it managed to capture the northern mesa bluffs, the springs, the peculiar playas, the canyon *cabeza* of Palo Duro, the Comanche camps in the canyonlands, and the confluent presence of other tributaries, like Tule Creek, pouring from the mesa. In one respect Vial's trail was an improvement over that of Mares. Mares had taken some time to cross the mesa, whereas Vial's route minimized the plains by accessing the east-west cañada of the Palo Duro. Vial went on successfully to Natchitoches, thence to San Antonio. By the summer of 1789 he was heading again to Santa Fé along a new trail that encountered the Llano.

Fragoso's diary for the return trip indicates they traveled north with Comanche guides, turning west-northwest at the Brazos River. Possibly they traveled up the Salt Fork, then entered the freshwater flow of White River emerging from Blanco Canyon.[36] On August 2, 1789, they stopped "at the foot of a mesa." Fragoso recorded that,

> Here we met a Comanche who told us of a lake that is in the middle of the Llano, and that in that place there was one lodge of Comanches—toward which we directed our course.

Although "*llano*" was not capitalized in Francisco Fragoso's text, the historians Loomis and Nasatir found its usage compelling, as Fragoso "used a number of different words for 'plain,' though not this before."[37] If so, it is probably a significant recorded instance of the singular word "Llano" to describe the Southern High Plains ahead.

The next day they advanced up "a white canyon containing water that descends from the south." As noted this trail was most likely up Blanco Canyon, whose White River descends *to* the south (see map, page 180). On August 4 they crossed "flat plains"—the celebrated flatness—until they reached the promised lake and Comanche lodge located "in the middle of the Llano." From here they rode northwest, crossed "another white canyon" (Frio Draw), and reached the familiar Rio Blanco (Tierra Blanca Draw) of the previous year.[38] From here the way to Santa Fé was known and they made good progress.

Thus, in the course of a few years, Pierre Vial and José Mares each crossed the Llano twice. Vial even returned again in 1792 on his most dangerous mission: a trail to St. Louis via the Canadian Valley. In the words of historian Frederick W. Rathjen, "the Llano Estacado held no mysteries for the Spaniards." Although they respected its dangers, he noted, "the Spaniards were not terrified of the Llano Estacado as Anglo Americans later appeared to be."[39] Moreover, their scouts were not confused about the sources of the Red River. Indeed, the anonymous 1788 map notation of "Cabeza del Rio Blanco" could be construed as the primary source region of the Red River of Louisiana.

Almost two decades later Vial was certainly careful to distinguish the Canadian River from the Red River. He stayed in the Rio del Norte country after his diplomatic and trailblazing services and grew old peacefully. Periodically he returned to the Llano. Once, while hunting buffalo with ciboleros from New Mexico, Vial encountered a military force under Don Francisco Amangual in the Canadian Valley. On June 1, 1808, he informed this officer that they were then on the Rio Colorado, "but that it does not flow by Natchitoches"; instead, this Rio Colorado joined the *Napestle* or Arkansas River. Vial referred Amangual to a river the Spaniards had passed earlier, on May 22, which "was the Natchitoches [Red] River, and that we had reached its source."[40] As Vial's comments suggest, the frontiersmen of New Mexico knew well the true sources of the Red River in the Llano canyons for over half a century before their Anglo counterparts. Vial stayed in New Mexico and made his home there until his death in 1814.

Although the Spanish officials had laid out a network of trails linking New Mexico, Texas, and Louisiana, the expected rich trade caravans simply failed to materialize. When France reacquired Louisiana and sold it to the Americans in 1803, the Spanish found themselves rethinking the strategic frontier. Concerned now with possible Anglo penetration, frontier officials dispatched two major expeditions to reconnoiter the Llano and beyond. Don Facundo Melgares left Santa Fé in June 1806 on a diplomatic mission to the plains tribes. Melgares's large entourage of 600 soldiers entered the *Comanchería* by following the Canadian River Valley east for some 233 leagues, much as Vial had in 1792 on his adventurous overland trip to St. Louis. With Melgares's show of force accomplished after a Pawnee treaty on the Republican River, he returned to Santa Fé via the upper Arkansas River. His return camps served a little later as unintentional signposts to Lt. Zebulon Pike, the American spy.

American pressure was also encountered in March 1808 when Captain

Francisco Amangual left San Antonio. His 200 men were to make a show of force in finding a northern route to Santa Fé. The men, their carts, and some 800 animals labored through the Texas forests and breaks. On May 8 they encountered the Yamparika Comanches who frequented the breaks east of the mesa.[41] With Yamparika guides they first sighted the Llano on May 12. That day, Amangual had seen "an extensive plain" in the distance. His Comanche guides warned that they should turn north to skirt the mesa for some distance, because to the east "there was nothing [but plains] ahead, and that it was impossible for us to go across during the day without exposing our men and animals to die of thirst."[42] Amangual followed this advice, and for the next ten days his 200 men and carts trudged north along the rough flank of the eastern Llano.

On the way they faced a fierce sandstorm that blew up in the eroded country beneath the mesa. This geomorphic storm terrified many soldiers with its gale-force winds, blocked sun, and massive transport of dust, "which made it look like the end of the world."[43] Later farm removal and ranch disturbance of the Llano's native grassland cover likely modified its aeolian processes, bringing the more hellish sandstorms of the eroded breaks country to the once cleaner plains above.[44] The soldiers also discovered a marvel in one of the bluffs of the mesa, a large cave ornamented with fantastic pictographs. This cultural sighting is an early report of an archeological site on the Southern High Plains.

By the May 21 the Amangual expedition was traveling up an unknown canyon, possibly in the vicinity of Quitaque Canyon. They were now entering "the mesa to the west." The next day, the diary recorded that they ascended the caprock:

> Leaving behind the rims that form the canyon we began to travel over plains so immense that the eye could not see their end. There was nothing but grass and a few small pools of rain water, with very little water, and some dry holes [buffalo wallows], on these plains.[45]

Pedro Vial later informed them that they had been in the drainage of the Red River of Louisiana on that day, but in crossing the intervening plains they had entered a new drainage, that of the Arkansas River. Amangual's diary recorded an interesting detail for May 22: on the immense plains "where we camped, it was necessary to drive stakes for the horses of the guard and for protection."[46] Amangual's staking of his horses may have owed something to the Comanche practice of staking horses on the plains. He not unwisely sought Yamparika guidance on his trip across the flatland. Perhaps in this general manner, the word *estaca* was gradually and casually linked to the word *llano* — the staked plain. The possibility exists, therefore, that the name *Llano Estacado* owes as much to Comanche practice as Hispano.

The men and carts of the expedition rolled across the Llano Estacado for days. For the first time an expedition recorded the fierce winds that could sweep this plain. "Note on the twenty-third," the diary noted, "The wind was so

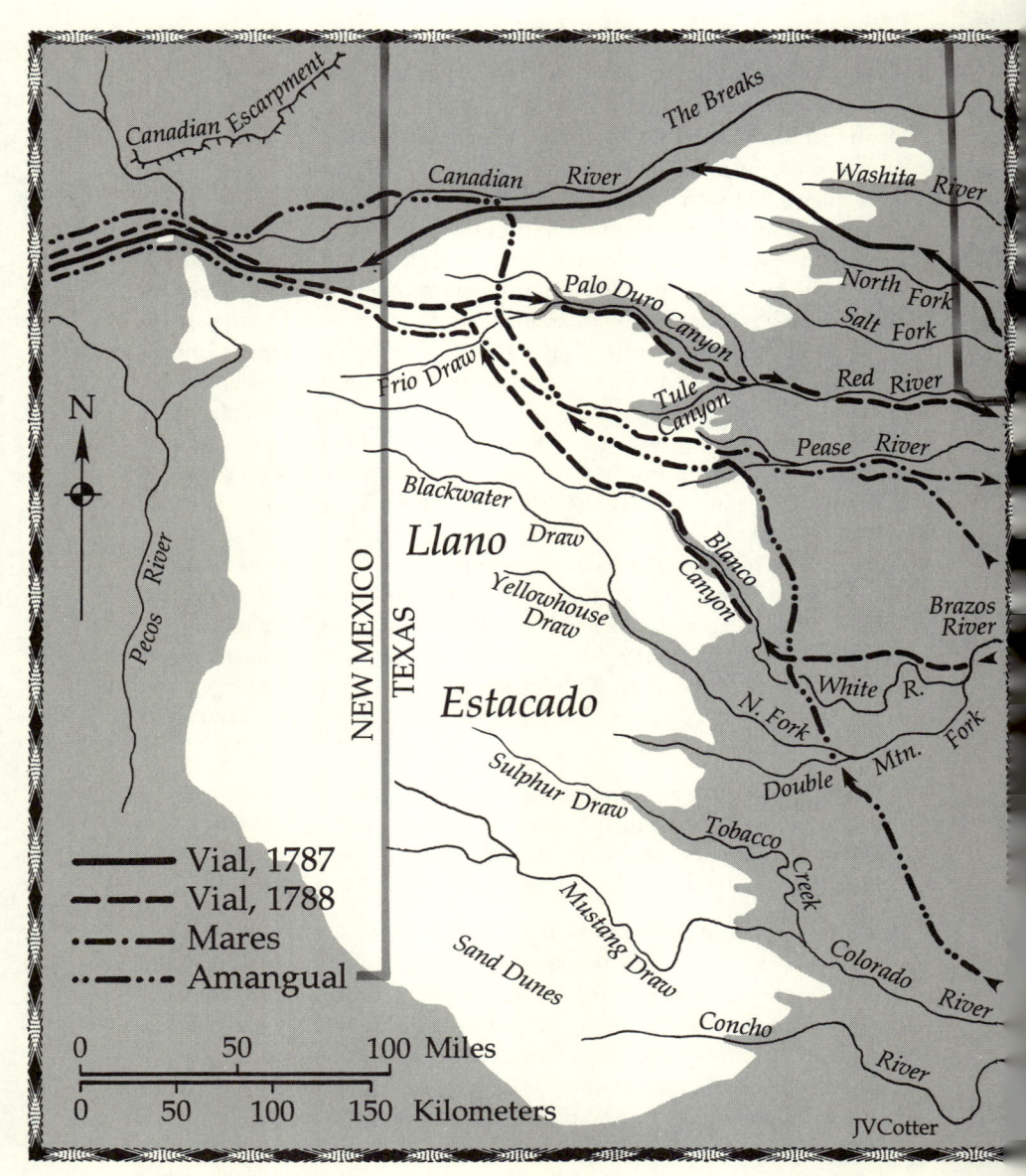

Conjectural Routes of Mares, Vial, and Amangual across the Llano. *Map by John V. Cotter.*

strong that it almost blew the men off the horses."[47] Spanish hats blew off and quickly disappeared in the distance. Although the Llano spring winds of 1808 were fierce, they were not as laden with huge loads of aeolian sediments as the violent sandstorms that swept the degraded Llano in the twentieth-century "dirty thirties" and "filthy fifties." Crossing Tierra Blanca Creek, they traveled ever northward on May 25, "over plains so extensive that the horizon was tiring to the eye." Amangual observed this landscape with an eye to its peculiar waters. There were dry lakes, he wrote, "that showed signs of accumulating much water in time of rain."[48] Some of these playas had little beach-like dunefields shaped by the strong regional winds. A condition so noticeable as to cause "great astonishment" was the droughty aspect of these current plains. The grass was trampled or "so burned up and clean" that they wondered. At the end of the day they pitched camp at a place where "there were buffaloes as far as the eye could see." They had found one of the great herds.

Fatigued and with many of his men badly sunburned by the scorching rays, the expedition rested on May 26 in the heart of the Llano. That night three hunters failed to return, "either they had gone to sleep or they were lost." The next day Francisco Amangual set out north after leaving a small group behind to make smoke signals for orienting the lost hunters. Finally the expedition emerged from the level plains into some grassy hills, with spring-fed pools that nourished a clump of cottonwood trees. This site was likely on an upper tributary of present-day Amarillo Creek.[49] When Captains Agabo and Quintero saw a rim of trees far to the north, their Yamparika guide assured them it was the *Rio Colorado* or Canadian River.[50]

Delayed now by rain for two days, Amangual's scouts explored the nearby area. A tell-tale botanical clue as to their location on a Canadian tributary was the notice of wild grapes and "wild Castilian rose bushes." They reached the banks of the Canadian River on May 30 after some extremely laborious efforts to get their carts down off the Llano and through the maze of cañadas, bluffs, and cliffs. Now traveling west up the river, they soon found the Llano breaks closing in on them once more. Crowbars and pickaxes again tried to smooth the way for the carts. But the going was rough that day and the next. Indeed, it was not until Amangual encountered—of all people—Pedro Vial and a party of ciboleros on June 1, 1808, that he learned of an alternative trail westward. One of the ciboleros out hunting was Manuel Martínez, a veteran of the 1806 Melgares expedition down the Canadian. Martínez carefully informed Amangual about the river's geography, noting "that it was not the one that flows to Natchitoches," and that it was impassable ahead on his present course.

Instead, Martínez recommended that he guide the expedition across the Canadian to the north side to "find a road over which we could travel."[51] This cibolero trail led the Amangual expedition more easily up the valley and through the tiring dunes. On June 3 the military force met the leader of another and larger group of ciboleros heading east. The cibolero trail now recrossed the Canadian to the south bank. Martínez eventually led the expedition, after much toil for their carts, across the divide between the Canadian and Pecos Rivers. From the Pecos they reached Santa Fé on June 19.

Although overlooked or misinterpreted, the eighteenth-and early-nineteenth-century trailblazers of the Spanish northeast frontier were heroic figures. Mares, Vial, and Fragoso covered vast distances, crossed and recrossed the Llano, left accounts of their travels, supplied and recorded toponyms, and operated with no violence in the *Comanchería*. They were also important intermediaries in establishing peaceful relations between Comanche bands and the Spanish. Although many of the expeditions were small, frugal affairs, leaders like Amangual were also capable of getting hundreds of soldiers across the great mesa, the plain where it was necessary to stake horses. Within two decades these men discovered three separate routes across the Llano Estacado (see map, page 180), mapped two of the routes, and provided graphic descriptions of the plains environment. For their time, these trailblazers were among the most accomplished explorers of the Old Southwest.

· 13 ·

LA CEJA Y EL LLANO: THE HISPANO FRONTIER

Q. Your business was as a comanchiere to go down and trade for cattle that the Comanche Indians had was it?
A. Yes sir.
Q. Where did you go?
A. I went to what is called Yellow House, Mucha qua, Quitaque, Punta de Agua, Hardwood, Canon Blanco, Tuly, Le Cej, Palo grande, to the lakes on the plains.

1893 COURT DEPOSITION OF JULIAN BACA[1]

Spanish colonization eastward toward the Llano took its first tentative step in 1794. That year fifty-two restless Tlaxcalan *genizaros* and a few Hispanos petitioned for a land grant to found a settlement called San Miguel del Vado at a popular ford on the Pecos River.[2] By 1806 the brave colonists were able to build a church there. San Miguel prospered, partly due to its strategic geographic position as a new portal to the plains country, and partly because Governor de Anza's resounding 1779 defeat of the Comanches lessened the old terror. San Miguel's growth was part of a general demographic and economic expansion. By the 1820s New Mexican sheep herds totaled some two million animals, and the rich open *vegas* or pastures in the east clearly beckoned.[3]

Between 1834 and 1835 three small settlements appeared on the grassland margins of the Sangre de Cristo Mountains. The new colonies of Mora, Las Vegas, and Anton Chico[4] marked the initial push of Mexican colonization toward the eastern grasslands. Populated by *genizaro* descendants and Hispano pioneers, these frontier communities practiced transhumant sheep-herding using traditions stretching back to the famous Castilian Mesta.[5] Over the following four decades, these pioneers and their sons and daughters probed farther and deeper into the Llano environment.

Roving sheep outfits were soon making great grazing circuits into the outland Llano country. Under the general control of a *mayordomo*, flocks entrusted to pastores slowly trailed from the mountain valleys of New Mexico in January or later, heading slowly and daily toward spring lushness in the warmer eastern grasslands. After May lambing, the pastores moved the flocks to even more distant good pastures and water for the long days of summer. Then, as the days shortened and the first weather fronts arrived, the herders turned them back in time to reach or get close to the new colonies by late fall.

The immense region of mesas, arroyos, canyons, and plains to their southeast had already been explored by the dashing comancheros and ciboleros. But the aggressive expansion of the New Mexican livestock industry in the 1840s and 1850s brought hundreds of new people into an intimate acquaintance with the Llano Estacado. The travels, pursuits, and occupations of these pioneers caused them to spill from the eastern flanks of the Sangre de Cristo past the scrub-timbered *Montoso* lands into the colorful country between the Pecos and Canadian Rivers. Over decades their names and folk observations were linked to the grand topography of the northwestern Llano Estacado: Palomas Mesa, Cuervo Peak, Pintada Mesa, Zanjon, Agua Negra, Ojo del Llano, Mesa Rica, Las Salinas, Luciano Mesa, Cabra Spring, Arroyo de Trujillo, Cherisco Mesa, and so on.

By the 1830s these Hispano frontiersmen and their families had already personified this brilliant eastern frontier of canyons, mesas, springs, and arroyos with the diminutive name *La Ceja*: the Eyebrow.[6] This affectionate, anonymous designation arose from the fanciful, almost illusive resemblance of the juniper-timbered caprock of the Llano and its outliers to a majestic *ceja*, or "brow of the plains." The distant sight of dark, cedared canyon slopes resembled a human brow on the face of the land, with extensive *ojos de agua* or springs below. Once on top of *La Ceja* they could see and experience the great Llano Estacado itself, "so extensive," wrote historian Fabiola Cabeza de Baca, "that one must see it to realize its vastness."[7] There, the ciboleros and comancheros had seen and reported vast grasslands to their pastoral brethren. The land was quite suitable for the flocks now overgrazing the mountain valleys in the west.[8]

For a people accustomed to the forested mountains or "sierras" of north-central New Mexico, the semiarid region to the south and east—despite its rough topography—was perceived as one vast open range; thus the use of the

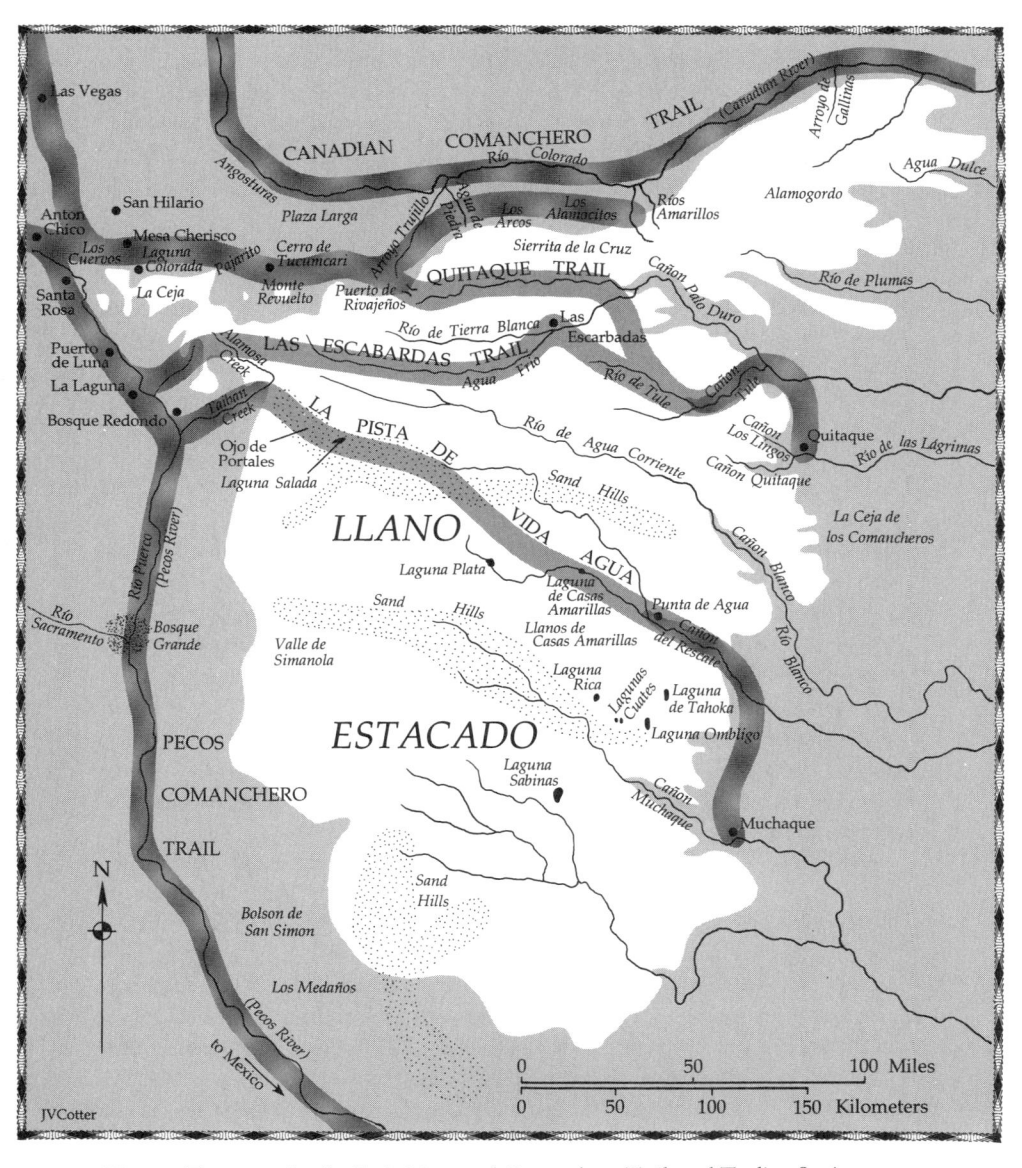

Hispano Toponyms for the Early Llano and Comanchero Trails and Trading Stations.
Map by John V. Cotter.

expression "El Llano" to describe a huge region embracing not only the plateau proper but also its adjacent breaks, flats, mesas, and plains. A hundred years later Anglos already accustomed to the flatness of the Great Plains questioned the perceptual validity of the term "Llano" to characterize this region, embracing as it did so much rough terrain.[9] But New Mexican perspectives had been swaddled by the mountains for so long that they perceived the eastward outwash of the Rockies as El Llano, the soul of the wide, the open, and the immense plains experience.

From the standpoint of historical geography the Hispano pioneers after 1800 were leaving overcrowded mountain valley settlements to penetrate the plains grassland environment. In a situation that the historian Walter Prescott Webb simply failed to address,[10] the Hispano colonization of the southern plains environment was dynamic and preceded its Anglo counterpart. Ironically, at the same time that rebellious, querulous Anglos were displaying territorial ambitions in the Mexican province of Texas, the New Mexicans were engaged in a steady, quieter expansion of their own.

One measure of their success was the introduction of Hispano toponyms for the Llano. Well before its Anglo-American discovery, the Llano Estacado had been linguistically appropriated by the common folk of New Mexico. A key to this 1780–1880 "century of Hispano expansion"[11] was the rapidly growing livestock economy. The raising of sheep for meat and the export of skins and wool for the burgeoning Chihuahua Trail market provided strong mercantilist incentives to enter the eastern grasslands. The perception of the Llano as desirable pastureland began in earnest around 1840. Fabiola Cabeza de Baca stated that in that year, "the sheep owners started sending herders with their flocks into the Ceja and the Llano, and the Hispanos continued to prosper in the sheep industry for more than half a century."[12]

Typically, a flock of about a thousand sheep was entrusted to the care of a lowly pastor. Two or more *pastores* were supervised by a *vaquero*. *Vaqueros* worked under a *caporal*, who in turn reported to the *mayordomo*. The flocks left the mountains in late January, drifted down the Canadian River, and then ventured onto the plains for lambing and summer grazing.[13] Gradually stone corrals and other practical traces of the Hispano stock-raising frontier began to mark the cultural landscape of *La Ceja* and the Llano. An 1842 sheep camp at Laguna Colorado, near the mouth of Bull Canyon, was "just over the Ceja of the Llano."[14] New daughter colonies, such as Chaperito, popped up on the Pecos River and the Canadian River drainages. Certainly by the 1860s drifting sheep men from Mora and booming Las Vegas were entering the Llano Estacado along the Canadian.[15] Founded in 1862, the small Pecos River frontier community of Puerto de Luna was only fifty miles, a few days, due west of the caprock.

It should surprise no one, therefore, that it was the ambitious New Mexicans who first opened the Llano country both to livestock and to settlement.[16] Given their initial geographic control of the upper Pecos and Canadian Rivers, and given an expanding frontier sheep economy keyed to mercantilist forces, it was only a matter of time. In part the process was transformational. Ecological pressure from overgrazed old pastures encouraged kin-based daughter colonies with access to new grasslands. Moreover, the U.S. territorial government increasingly cloistered the nomadic Indians, requiring the purchase of livestock to replace the former spoils of the raid or hunt.[17] This spatial cloistering made it possible to move herds into areas formerly threatened and regulated by Indian depredations. These feedback loops amplified rapid expansion eastward. Supposedly sometime in the late 1860s at least one small *placita* colony was established briefly between the Llano and the Canadian River in present-day Oldham County, Texas.[18]

The period from the 1820s to the 1860s was the golden age of the comanchero trade. Indeed, the Spanish trading in the Llano Estacado was well advanced by the time the first Anglo explorers arrived. No one can say exactly when the initial comanchero trade began. Ancient exchange networks between the plains and the pueblos were well established by the time Coronado arrived in 1541. Comanchero origins likely go back to the mid-seventeenth-century trade in peltries.[19] The records suggest that around 1660 Spanish traders sometimes escorted Christianized puebloans to the plains, where both groups engaged busily in barter. Captain Diego Romero may have traveled to the Llano in 1659 to trade for bison robes and pronghorn antelope skins. In particular the old buffalo robe and the horrible slave trafficking between the plains and the pueblos seems to have continued after the arrival of the Spanish.[20]

This early trade was small, informal in nature, and probably a diplomatic extension of cibolero activities. With the arrival of warlike Comanches around 1705 on the Llano, there were major economic disruptions for long spells, as the newcomers randomly traded with or plundered the Spanish for decades.[21] The Comanches also traded heavily with the French *contrabandistas* out of Louisiana, eventually acquiring better guns than the embarrassed New Mexicans.[22] Nevertheless, by the mid-eighteenth century a haphazard commerce of sorts had developed between the *Comanchería* and New Mexico.[23] Both the *Nuevo Mexicanos* and the Comanches gradually recognized that steady trade relations were better than the alternative: vicious slave-raiding and ceaseless warfare. After Govenor de Anza's fortuitous establishment of a peace treaty with Ecueracapa and the Comanches in 1786, comanchero traders began to visit the Kiowa and Comanche bands frequently. Over several decades pack trails gave way to ox cart roads as the spatial and transport links expanded. The Canadian River Valley, in particular, was an early contact point between Kotsoteka and Yamparika bands of Comanches and the New Mexicans.[24] The later Kwahadi bands who specialized in living on the Llano Estacado also cultivated contacts with the traders and their allies.

This early trade was rather innocuous. Trinkets, cloth, flour, a type of tobacco (*Nicotina attenuata*) called *punche*, and two varieties of bread—*panocha* and *cemita*[25]—were traded to Comanches, Kiowas, and Mescalero Apaches for buffalo robes, deerskins, and horses. A potent home-brewed liquor called "Taos Lightning" entered the trade as well. Although there was at first a certain randomness in trading encounters, gradually in the early 1800s these wayfaring capitalists and the Indians began to organize their haphazard meetings. August and September were the busiest trade months. Three principal Hispano trails then penetrated the Llano Estacado and led to private rendezvous campgrounds (see map, page 185).

The southern trail descended the Pecos River below San Miguel del Vado, curving southeast along the Mescalero Escarpment border to the familiar Bosque Redondo. The cottonwood groves of Bosque Redondo were the scene of many comanchero rendezvous and caravan activities. In 1829 Juan José Arrocha and 125 soldiers parlayed, traded, and negotiated with hundreds of Comanches at this favored site.[26] South of the old campground at Bosque Redondo, the Comanchero Road struck out eastward and ascended Taiban Creek to *La Ceja*. The trail advanced from the caprock to Portales Spring, then past the deflated pluvial lakes in the ancient Portales Valley. Following this corridor of the Llano eventually brought traders to the *Laguna de Casas Amarillas* on Yellow House Draw. From here the trail continued downstream to the *Cañon del Rescate*—the cruel Canyon of Ransom, where grieving captives and slaves were bartered away as easily as horses and cattle.[27] This "Valley of Traffic" was frequented by Yamparika, Kotsoteka, and around the 1840s by Kwahadi bands from July through September. In the 1820s the *Cañon del Rescate* was well known as a convenient place to acquire contraband on the cheap.

This old cibolero trail was sometimes called *La Pista de Vida Agua*, or "Trail of Living Water," because it was almost the only watered, year-round route across the middle girth of the semiarid Llano.[28] Moreover, *La Pista de Vida Agua* gave convenient access to the salt lakes in the Portales Valley, beside whose shores Coronado's main army had wandered on their return crossing. From *Cañon del Rescate* the comancheros often turned south to the Muchaque Peak area for business, especially in the 1860s. This "Trail of Living Water"—virtually lost to later memory—was an important corridor in its day.

Its significance as a Hispano entry into the Llano environment can be gleaned partially from the early U.S. explorers and cartographers, who noted its presence in the 1850s and 1860s. Capt. Randolph Marcy's 1850 map outlined a vague "Comanche Trail. Said to be a good route for wagons with water daily." His 1853 map traced a "Comanche Trail to Bosque-Redondo" across the breadth of the Llano. More interesting was Capt. Allen Anderson's 1864 "Map of the Military Department of New Mexico." Anderson's map not only traced this "Overland route to the Texas Settlements" but also detailed a number of Spanish toponyms along the way.

According to Anderson, this old trail branched off another north-south trail crossing the westernmost Llano mesa to a campsite at *Las Cañaditas*. From there the trail paralleled Alamosa Creek to the southeast to *Cañada del Tule*, probably located at the headwaters of Taiban Creek, thence a day's waterless journey to *Tierra Blanca*. Another day's journey brought the New Mexicans to *Las Portales*, the pretty campsite where refreshing spring waters flowed beneath overhangs resembling portals. As the trail continued to the southeast, below the great curve of the Sand Hills region, more regional toponyms emerge: *La Salada*, *El Coyote*, *La Lomita*, and *Los Tulanes*.

Quite possibly this "Trail of Living Water" was a regular Comanche trail as the Anglo cartographers noted. Indeed, it may have been an even older trail, perhaps a popular Querecho route from the eastern canyons to the western pueblos that the Comanches inherited. In any case, the New Mexican traders not only penetrated the Llano in the early nineteenth century, they appropriated the area linguistically to a larger extent than commonly appreciated. Moreover, as the southern trail toponyms indicate, their perceptions of the region were based on key environmental distinctions.

Other trails intersected and branched off from *La Pista de Vida Agua* as variant routes. Turning eastward from the Pecos River at La Laguna before reaching Bosque Redondo, the comancheros and ciboleros ascended *La Ceja* near Alamosa Canyon. It was not far from here to Laguna Salada, then, branching east, a trail led to Agua Frio, an arid upper tributary of Tierra Blanca. This draw had a fine Ojo Frio spring in it, but the watercourse was often dry. Near the confluence of Agua Frio Draw with Tierra Blanca Creek, the much-used cart road needed an artificial oasis. The Spanish adapted to the local practice of digging for water in the creekbed near the confluence. They called this special place *Las Escarbadas*: the Scrapings.[29] Caravans of cibolero carretas often used this site as a processing station, with women and children helping to cut and dry the meat. A day's journey from *Las Escarbadas* would bring traders to the headwaters of *Río del Tule*. From here a trail joined a northern branch of another comanchero trail to painstakingly descend the Llano at a natural *puerta*.

This "door" in the eastern caprock, or *ceja de los comancheros* from the traders' regular presence on the flank, took the traveler down to the foot of the escarpment, then turned southward to the woeful *Valle de las Lagrimas*, the infamous Valley of Tears where captives were also separated and sold indiscriminately. A little farther to the south lay the comanchero trading station at Quitaque. These hills near Quitaque Canyon in southeast Briscoe County had the advantages of good water, fine grazing, and topographic concealment.[30]

The third trail branched out from Las Vegas and Anton Chico to skirt the northern border of the Llano Estacado, passing *Los Cuervos*, Pajarito Creek, and Tucumcari Mesa before ascending the caprock at *Puerto de Rivajeños*, another natural doorway onto the immense plains above. *Rivajeños* is a contraction of *rio bajeños*, referring to the downstream neighbors of Albuquerque, who apparently used this portal in their hunting and trading forays. This trail, like all the others, probably was a newly titled ancient corridor. The early Comanche custom of accompanying the comancheros on their return (sometimes apparently to rob them) perhaps allowed the Spanish to acquire new environmental lore, like digging for water at *Las Escarbadas*. It was also common for Pueblo Indian traders and hunters to guide Spanish parties along the hazardous journey. These puebloans shared the risks and undoubtedly aided the Spanish in adaptations to a novel geography.

As the trade intensified, New Mexican traders resorted to ox carts for the approaches, often caching their carretas near *Puerto de Rivajeños*, then reloading goods onto pack animals for the stretch across the plains and canyons ahead. Here also the trail forked. The north branch paralleled the Canadian River to reach a fine campground and spring on *Las Tecovas* Creek, northeast of present Amarillo, Texas. The south branch followed a smooth trail across the Llano to a headwater camp on Palo Duro Creek. This branch then turned southward for the head of Tule Canyon, intersecting the *Las Escarbadas* trail to Quitaque.

As sportsmen, market hunters, risk takers, and licensed frontier capitalists, the New Mexican ciboleros and comancheros rapidly signified the Llano environment, even advancing far north on the Great Plains and east to the Wichita Mountains of Oklahoma. Of interest in the scores of geographic names they created for the Llano Estacado region was the strong environmental bias of their nomenclature. Names were nature-centered and keyed to a sensual perception of the natural world. Some like Tucumcari and Taiban were likely borrowings from the Comanche. Consider the following list of early toponyms, many of which are still in use or Anglicized:[31]

Plant and animal
Los Alamocitos—named after the young cottonwood trees in the creek
Arroyo de Gallinas—an abundance of prairie chickens on this Canadian tributary
Laguna Sabinas—a six mile long lake with scrub cedar on nearby hills
Montaño de Camelon—a chameleon mountain at Mesa Redonda, named for the colorful lizard
Palo Duro—the presence of hackberry and wild plum "woods" [*prunus* species]
Río del Tule—abundant rushes or tules in the creek and canyon

Earth
Los Angosturas—"the narrows" on the upper Canadian River near New Mexico Highway 104
Arroyo Piedra—rough rock formations on a Llano tributary to the Canadian
Cañon Blanco—white caprock strata characterized this canyon
Cañoncito Blanco—the small canyon with white stone outcroppings

Casas Amarillas—yellowish bluffs that resembled houses when seen from a distance or through a mirage
Laguna Colorada—a small lake with reddish sediments
Las Escarbadas—water obtained by digging into the sandy creekbed
Los Portales—overhanging mineralized formations at this recessed spring resembled a portico
Mesa Redonda—a round mesa some fifteen miles southeast of Tucumcari
Rios Amarillos—yellowish loam soils exposed in the area creekbanks
Tierra Blanca—the reular exposure of white or caliche caprock soils

WATER
Agua Corriente—a formerly brisk stream that eventually flows into Blanco Canyon
Agua Dulce—a sweetwater creek west of the gypsum badlands
Atascosa—the marshy, boggy area at the confluence of a spring-fed tributary to the Canadian River
Rio Colorado—the presence of sudden, red-sediment rises on the Canadian River
Laguna Plata—a saline lake whose brine precipitates glinted in the sunlight like silver
Laguna Rica—a saline lake rich in salt deposits
Rio de Frio—small drainage named for its cold-water springs

This list points to a strong perceptual orientation in the Hispano lifeway, a folkloric environmental patterning or an ability to characterize a difficult topography succinctly and efficiently. This system of cognitive mapping was useful for most who could not read or write. It could also be a practical means of orientation. With respect to *Alamogordo* or "Fat Cottonwood" Creek, Charles Goodnight once wrote J. Evetts Haley that, "if you were unfamiliar with the country and were at a considerable distance from the stream, they would tell you of an immense cottonwood tree growing upon its banks."[32]

The literate culture of later Anglo settlement enjoyed greater abstraction, or removal from nature, in naming features after events, heroes, themselves, or whatever. But there was an *experiential* dimension in the Spanish local language of landscape, one that seems to endure even though scores of other toponyms were likely lost to history. These place-names reflected the opportunity for anyone to make crucial geographic discriminations based on soils, sediments, and vegetation within a troublesome landscape. The difference between an "Alamogordo" and a "McClellan" Creek is that you can see and compare a cottonwood without reference to a piece of paper, whereas it is hard to see and look for a "McClellan."

By the late 1850s, and especially after the Civil War, the comanchero trade acquired an unsavory reputation.[33] Captivity narratives certainly inflamed the imagination of those living on the east coast.[34] In part the very growth of the trade was to blame. More traders with more goods inflated prices, stimulating the Indians to commit further depredations on a distracted Texas frontier. Furthermore, the U.S. Army round-up and confinement of 8,000 Navajos at Bosque Redondo led to sharp market demands for beef in New Mexico. Stolen cattle from frontier Texas were conveniently assembled in the concealed Llano canyons. From these refuges they were driven across the Llano along the old comanchero trails on their way to Ft. Sumner or Colorado. Ironically, well before Texans Oliver Loving and Charles Goodnight crossed the southern tip of the great plateau to bring cattle up the Pecos River, the eastern frontier New Mexicans and their Comanche allies had established an important network of livestock trails across the northern Llano Estacado.[35] These livestock crossings were possibly less stressful to animals than the one made famous by Goodnight and Loving.

To some degree the very success of the comancheros was their undoing. "They started as small peddlers," wrote Jack Rittenhouse, "and ended as cattle rustlers on a grand scale."[36] By the 1860s traders like José Piedad Tafoya, Julian Baca, José G. Medina, and Manuel Gonzalez piloted caravans of carretas filled with goods to Quitaque. There they purchased thousands of cattle for sale in New Mexico. Everyone knew that the cattle were stolen, but New Mexicans easily rationalized the historic trade. Even the U.S. Army—at Ft. Bascom, an 1863 outpost some fifteen miles from the western caprock,[37] and at Ft. Sumner—colluded with the trade initially. By 1867, however, the get-rich-quick comancheros had to dodge U.S. soldiers from Ft. Bascom who were out to intercept them. The trade was officially restricted, then outlawed, but tens of thousands of stolen cattle and horses continued to pour across the trails, fueling further Hispano homeland expansion. As many as 700 New Mexican traders moved annually onto the Llano. Only by defeating and removing Comanche and Kiowa warriors could the U.S. Army effectively destroy the century-old trade. Even to accomplish this the Army found it useful to employ ex-comancheros as guides or to torture the traders they captured for information.

After the Civil War hundreds of unlicensed, illegal comancheros thus dodged lackluster army patrols to carry on a brisk trade. Whiskey, brandy, guns, pistols, ammunition, and lead replaced the former quaint commodities.[38] What had once begun as an honorable, profitable, regulated, and certainly courageous venture was now increasingly a dangerous criminal enterprise. What gave the trade one final flourish was the twilight Llano glory of Comanches and Kiowas, and the superb environmental knowledge of the comancheros. By the mid-nineteenth century these men, with the conical-crowned sombreros, striped jackets, breeches, and stockings, understood the Llano in minute detail.[39] Their elaborate network of trails and nature-based toponyms made this peculiar landscape very familiar. One could locate and differentiate, for example, *los llanos del Rio de Tule* (the flat plains around Tulia) from *los llanos de las Casas Amarillas* (the flat plains around Lubbock) simply by reference to a cognitive mapping of the environment. Literacy was not required, but environmental perception was needed to match the landscape with the word.

At a time when the great Anglo explorers were first disclosing this plateau to the national imagination, the eastern frontiersmen of the Hispano Homeland in New Mexico had largely mastered its surface geography. They knew its springs, canyons, salt lakes, trails, waterholes, vegetation, and weather. The comanchero stations of the Llano were always rude affairs but scenes of great activity in late summer when trading was heavy. The distinctive traders were capable of crossing the Llano virtually at will, and they came from new settlements reaching for the mesa's western flanks. The cibolero, comanchero, and pastor followed their own cycles of discovery and exploration of the Llano Estacado, but usually well before their Anglo counterparts of ranchers, merchants, and settlers. Their exploits were undoubtedly those of brave and heroic people. There is so little surviving testimony from their oral culture, unfortunately, that the glory often goes to promoters with better-written documentation.

Increasingly the economic relationships between buffalo plains and valley towns were in drastic reorganization. Fabiola Cabeza de Baca's childhood stories included El Cuate's vision of the melancholic ending, as the cibolero lifeway on the Llano slipped into an old-timer's memory:

> With wagons and pack animals loaded, we were a happy bunch of *ciboleros*, saying *adios, hasta el año venidero*. We headed west to our homes along the rivers and to our mountain habitations to spend a good winter well supplied with meat. We said *hasta luego*—but there came a day when we did not return because the wonderful sport had vanished. We have only the tales to remind us of when the Llano belonged to the Indian and to the New Mexicans of Spanish descent. Ballads are still sung in the villages about the *cíbolos* and *ciboleros*, but never again will the colorful processions be seen.[40]

Where Anglo-Americans would soon create a whole melodramatic literature about the perils and starkness of the Llano Estacado, an annual wave of New Mexicans would—under rude circumstances—cross the Ceja and the Llano for their share of the bison herds and trade. At a time when a well-equipped white man could encounter the Llano and become a heroic explorer, a score or more of colorful cibolero caravans would bring hundreds of men, many women and older children, and herds of domestic animals into the heart of the shining mesa to help with the annual seasonal work. Indeed, the intuitive but close perceptual mastery of the Llano environment by ordinary New Mexicans would prove invaluable to the approaching and sometimes fairly nervous Anglo-Americans. Many in this latter group came not expecting to find treasure, but terror itself in the land they thought was new and undiscovered by so-called white men.

Part Three

The Illimitable Prairie:

Anglo-American Imagineers and the Romantic Discovery of the Llano Estacado, 1803–1844

We had already had two alarms of Indians, which although unfounded still tended to dispirit the cowardly pelayos; and added to this, the name of the Llano Estacado, on whose borders we then were encamped, and which lay before us like a boundless ocean, was mentioned with a sort of terror, which showed that it was by them regarded as a place from which we could not escape alive.

Albert Pike

·14·

Terra Incognita

> ... a height, the top of which presents an open plain, so extensive as to require the Indians four days in crossing it, and so destitute of water, as to oblige them to transport their drink in the preserved entrails of beasts of the Forests ...
>
> Gen. James Wilkinson

Late one Sunday afternoon in December 1968 an amateur archeologist, Mrs. Alyce Hart, picked up what she called an "English Inscription Stone" near a playa lake twelve miles south of Lamesa, Texas.[1] The two-sided, sandstone fragment contained an intriguing message: "We are attac by iandian yaer 1771 all may/[over]/kill. I am alone but I know they will kill me here. The...." Taken at its face value this inscription suggested that the Llano Estacado was originally seen by an unknown English speaker in the early 1770s, decades before its official Anglo discovery in the nineteenth century. Without names or additional information, this presence remains as a vague possibility only. But the poignant message carved into the sandstone did reflect two metaphoric aspects of the region, aspects essential in its first signification for the Anglo-Americans: solitude ("I am alone") and death ("they will kill me here").[2]

Predictably, the first information available to the Anglo-Americans simply referred to the region as a *terra incognita*. Consider the 1810 "Map of New Spain" by Baron Alexander von Humboldt. Based in part on the 1776 map by Bernardo de Miera y Pacheco, Humboldt's map showed a large blank void where the Llano Estacado should have been. In the midst of the void, like the "Afric-maps" of yore, was the written confession: "Unknown Country between the R. Puerco [Pecos] and the sources of the E. Colorado."

In the absence of any definitive information this *terra incognita* became the subject of intense speculation. Unwittingly, Humboldt himself furthered confusion by merging the origin of the Red River (Rio Rojo) with that of the Canadian River (Rio Colorado). This error would take half a century to correct

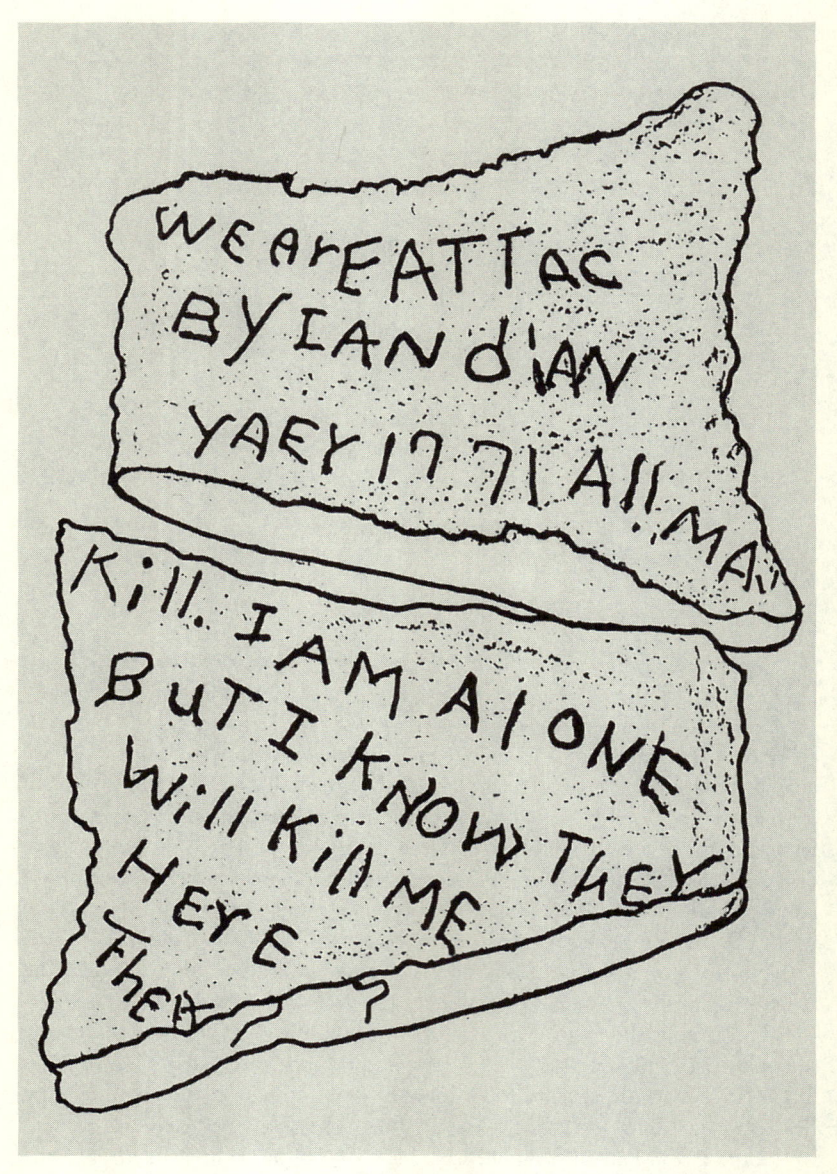

English Inscription Stone, by Alyce Hart. Rubbing. From Alyce Hart, "English Inscription Stone," *Transactions of Seventh Regional Archeological Symposium for Southeastern New Mexico and Western Texas* (Lamesa, Tex.: Dawson County Archeological Society, 1972), 41–45. This inscription stone is said to indicate that English speakers were traveling the Llano Estacado in the late eighteenth century.

fully on the part of U.S. officials. After the American acquisition of Louisiana in 1803, however, suddenly the need to know the western or Red River boundaries of the region assumed geopolitical importance.

President Thomas Jefferson was personally intrigued by speculations about the origins of the Red River, and he took an interest in the southern explorations. Reports by Doctor John Sibley, Phillip Nolan, and William Dunbar indicated a mysterious headwaters, a region with mountains of salt, herds of wild horses, giant water serpents, unicorns, and strange metallic masses that might prove to be platinum.[3] Some of these fabulous stories had been shared among adventurous Red River traders and mustangers for several decades. And there was even some credulous basis for these geosophical accounts. Gypsum deposits could be mistaken for mountains of salt; pronghorn antelope resembled the mythic unicorns; and the heavy, iron-nickel meteorites sometimes found on the southern plains were initially taken for precious lumps of platinum or silver.

There was also the widespread belief at Natchitoches in the early 1800s that the head of the Red River was in the mountains close to Santa Fé. "It was supposed to be navigable for 1,000 miles above Natchitoches," the historian Dan Flores stated, "and was reported to run through a country abounding in rich prairies, where feral cattle and wild horses ranged in innumerable herds."[4] It was a confidential 1804 report, however, prepared by the enigmatic Gen. James Wilkinson that provided the first tentative glimpse of the Llano Estacado for an American president.

Wilkinson's report was apparently based on observations by his late, flamboyant young associate, Phillip Nolan. Nolan's mustanging and contraband operations had taken him deep into Spanish Texas in the 1790s. As a spy for the Americans and an entrepreneur for himself, Nolan's business trips into the Comanchería acquired the status of reconnaissances.[5] General Wilkinson's July 13, 1804, report to Jefferson noted that far upstream the Red River forked. Of interest is his description of its left branch:

> The left branch which is reputed the longest is said to have its source in the East side of a height, the top of which presents an open plain, so extensive as to require the Indians four days in crossing it, and so destitute of water, as to oblige them to transport their drink in the preserved entrails of beasts of the Forests—west of this high plain my informants report certain waters which run to the Southward.[6]

As Flores notes, this "representation of the Llano Estacado, whose existence had not even been imagined by the Americans," was a reasonably accurate sketch of the geographic sources of the Red River.[7] General Wilkinson's account accurately adumbrated the existence of a "height" in the east, a region whose "open plain" top was noted both for its extensiveness and its aridity. Beyond this "high plain" the drainages (of the Pecos River) run southward.

Soon buried in government files this remarkable report sank out of sight. President Jefferson's curiosity eventually led to the Freeman and Custis Red River Expedition in 1806, an expedition designed to chart a waterway route to the fabled city of Santa Fé. Although a Spanish force intercepted and blocked the expedition's ascent up the Red River, fables of the mysterious headwater region persisted. In 1809, trader Anthony Glass saw a fabulous mass of metal on the upper Brazos River. The Schamp and McCall trading expedition returned and acquired this prized 1,635-pound meteorite from the upper Brazos country. Schamp's stories influenced other pioneers to emulate his success. Judge Thomas M. Duke related that in 1819 he and several others projected an expedition "towards the head of the Brazos" to recover another mass of precious metal. The death of their guide terminated the search for another aerolite of the headwaters region.[8]

A second expedition in 1806 also failed to discover the sources of the Red River. The American explorer-spy, Lt. Zebulon Montgomery Pike, set out to trace the river from its origin to its mouth, but he failed to find the river at all. As General Wilkinson's agent, Pike took a keen interest in Santa Fé and the Spanish forces there. Detained by the Spanish in 1807 and escorted south along the Rio Grande, he actually carried on with his reconnaissance work under Spanish supervision. Curiously enough, Pike's 1810 map imaginatively filled in the void of Baron von Humboldt's uncertainty about the plains. Pike's map showed a pair of large—and entirely mythic—lakes as the headwaters of the Brazos and Colorado Rivers in a region of "Immense Herds of Wild Horses." Perhaps the vague report of a sea-serpent or "Uncommon animal" seen by natives, "in a considerable lake in a sequestered situation in New Mexico,"[9] had influenced the creation of these two lakes. Or perhaps he was simply plagiarizing details from earlier Spanish maps, such as that of Alzate in 1768.[10] In any event Pike's map and his narrative furthered two of the most important deceptions of the Llano Estacado for encroaching Anglo-Americans.

First, Zebulon Pike continued to confuse the Red River drainage with that of the Canadian River, ensuring that American boundary and trade hopes would continue to focus on Santa Fé. It seemed there should be a natural riverine corridor to the mythic wealth of Santa Fé, and the Red River must be it. Second, Pike was the early publicist of the North African or desert metaphor for the plains region, an area "incapable of cultivation." "These vast plains of the western hemisphere," he wrote, "may become in time as celebrated as the sandy deserts of Africa."[11] Although he visited neither the Llano Estacado nor the sources of the Red River, Pike did see barren "immense prairies" and oceans of sand in the Rocky Mountain rainshadow. He left the reader with the distinct impression that the area could not be the abode of "civilized" man.

With the conclusion of the Adams-Onís Treaty of 1819, U.S. government interest in the Red River boundary question grew significantly. A second expedition accordingly branched off from the Arkansas River for a reconnaissance of

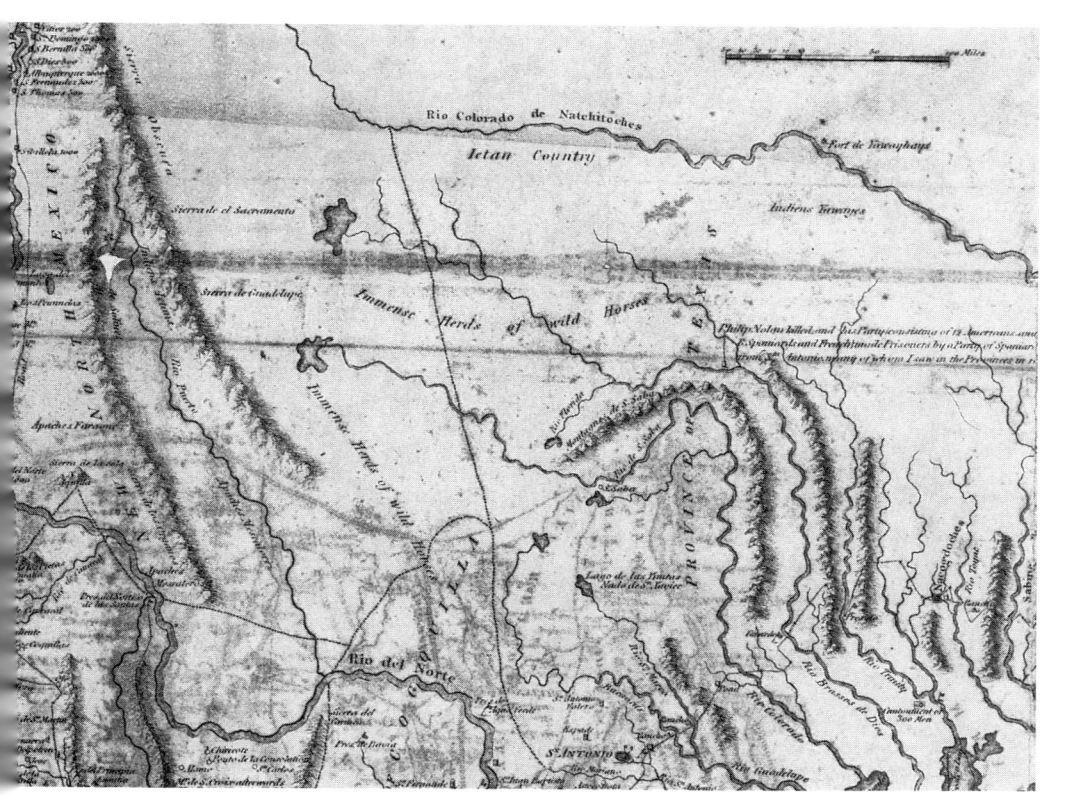

Detail of Zebulon Montgomery Pike's *Map of the Internal Provinces of New Spain*, by Zebulon Montgomery Pike, 1810. Engraved map. From Z. M. Pike, *An Account of Expeditions to the Sources of the Mississippi* . . . (Philadelphia: C. and A. Conrad, 1810). Faced with a void, Pike borrowed heavily for his map from Mexican and other sources, particularly Alexander von Humboldt's earlier map of New Spain. Curiously, the mythic presence of enormous headwater lakes in Pike's Llano country suggests important freshwater resources. Pike may have borrowed these features from late eighteenth-century Mexican maps that depicted a garbled account of saline and freshwater lakes found in the remote plains. *CN 01640. Courtesy Map Collection, Center for American History, University of Texas at Austin.*

the Red River headwaters in the summer of 1820. Commanded by Maj. Stephen H. Long, this expedition also included a botanist, Edwin James. An early member of the U.S. Corps of Topographical Engineers, Major Long belonged to the first generation of scientific explorers of the trans-Mississippi West. His small party faced various hardships before descending Ute Creek to arrive at a large river on August 4, 1820. Here Long's group made a natural mistake. Noticing the large river bore off to the southeast, they were "induced to believe it must be one of the most considerable of the upper tributaries of Red River."[12]

They were in fact in the Canadian River valley near the present Texas–New Mexico border. They toiled eastward for some two weeks down the supposed Red River, experiencing the hot seasonal hardships of August travel. Sand dunes, 105° afternoon temperatures, and a shortage of game made a most unfavorable impression. Once they killed a wild horse for their supper. On August 11, 1820, the Long expedition camped with a band of "Bad Hearts" or Kiowa-Apaches. Dr. Edwin James, the expedition's chronicler, pronounced these inhabitants as some of the "most degraded and miserable of the uncivilized Indians on this side of the Rocky Mountains." In part their "degradation" was determined by the barbaric environment: "Their wandering and precarious manner of life, as well as the inhospitable character of the country they inhabit," he wrote, "precludes the possibility of advancement from the profoundest barbarism."[13] In this deterministic manner early Anglo perception of the local Indians was related to their attitude about the landscape. A barbaric land led to barbarous people.

Winding his way down the Canadian River valley, Edwin James preferred other company, proving to be an assiduous collector of local plants. He later forwarded the specimens to the eminent botanists John Torrey and Asa Gray. A number of these plants were later named after him as they constituted new species. Like the Spanish explorers before him, Edwin James also noted the many grapevines and plum bushes of the Canadian Valley. On August 13 the members of the expedition found a "cheering sight" in the discovery of a grove of trees ahead of them. Like "a discovery of land to the mariner," this grove reminded them of the "comfort and plenty which we had learned to consider inseparable from the forest country."[14]

This comment underscored the woodland bias, the preference toward timber that the Long Expedition carried into plains country. The absence of forests was interpreted as the presence of a desert. Long's experiences on the northern frontier of the Llano Estacado were perhaps instrumental in his labeling the entire plains expanse as the "Great Desert," a characterization that would greatly amuse later residents. But modern dendrochronology points to a period of drought at this time, that is, the climate had swung for a spell to the arid side of its semiarid nature. The sandy stretches of the Canadian River, the cool mornings and the scorching afternoon heat, the occasional lack of water, and the endless, treeless plains off in the distance were also easily transformed by the tree-loving mind-set of eastern explorers into a "desert." A semantic question remains: what if the Long expedition had traveled down the Canadian in the verdant days of a wet-year spring? Would his map have shown then the "Great American *Prairie*"?

The Long expedition stuck closely to the river that August, fearful of not finding any water at all on the vast plains to the south. But as they traveled east game became more visible: black bear, wild turkey, quail, and buffalo were encountered in addition to the area's gray wolves, pronghorn antelope, and Afric "jackals" (coyotes). One afternoon they were also treated to a major West Texas thunderstorm. The men wrapped themselves in blankets, but the one-inch hailstones terrified and pounded their horses as they had Coronado's cavaliers in 1541. James was perhaps the first Anglo-American to complain about the variable local climate when he wrote that "rapid alterations of heat and cold must be supposed to mark a climate little favorable to health."[15]

Tracking along the river eastward eventually brought the Long expedition to the Arkansas River, to their lasting mortification. Major Long then became aware that he had bungled his principal assignment of finding the source of the Red River. Besides this error of geography and other woes, his expedition nevertheless provided the first scientific glimpse of the Llano Estacado's northern border. "For the first time a team of scientists had surveyed the immense plains region in realistic terms," declared historian William H. Goetzmann, "and taken some measure of the possibilities for settlement in that treeless area."[16] The expedition also promoted the environmental image of an area as "almost wholly unfit for civilization and of course uninhabitable by a people depending on agriculture for their subsistence." This was not the first time for such a pronouncement; Zebulon Pike, after all, described "sandy deserts." But the label "Great Desert" was affixed in 1821 by Maj. Stephen Long and Dr. Edwin James to the High Plains region. This geosophical perception took hold in the popular imagination of the press on the East Coast for the next three decades as the "Great American Desert."[17]

Regional boosters and a few historians of the High Plains have been prone to laugh at or to dismiss Major Long's signification of the area as a "Great American Desert," especially since he never described the Llano Estacado *per se*. But as Goetzmann's *Exploration and Empire* reminds us, Long's characterization is not without merit or thought.[18] Given the lack of wood and water, and given the technological and sociological context of 1821, this portion of the Comanchería *was* uninhabitable by a wood-loving Anglo civilization. To promote "headlong expansion" of the region might have been construed as unconscionable. However, even if the Llano was not a fit abode for American settlement, it could still be an important corridor for people going elsewhere.

There was, after all, the fabulous lure of Santa Fé. The very name beckoned to adventurous Americans. Rumors held that there was a great deal of silver and gold in the vicinity, although the exact mines were rarely specified. When a tumultuous Mexico gained its independence in 1821, New Mexican frontier officials suddenly proved receptive to bold trading parties of Americans. As the Santa Fé trade blossomed in the 1820s, it inevitably drew travelers and merchant caravans closer and closer to the Llano Estacado. By 1827 there was already a report and map notation of escarpment "mountains" and outlier mesas ("a few detached mounts") in the Canadian River valley east of San Miguel, New Mexico.[19] Some of the earliest Anglo-American accounts of the Llano were thus from a new generation of fortune seekers, adventurers on the road to wealth.

· 15 ·

THE STAKE PRAIRIE

> This Stake Prairie is to the Comanche what the desert of Sahara is to the Bedouin.
>
> ALBERT PIKE

Aaron B. Lewis was one of these new-generation fortune seekers. Lewis's east-to-west journey along the northern Llano in the fall of 1831 had all the characteristics of an epic adventure. Fortunately, his amazing story was so arresting that it attracted an amanuensis in the person of Albert Pike, a young eastern poet and American *wandervögel*. In 1834 Pike published his own and Lewis's accounts of travels in a remarkable literary work, *Prose Sketches and Poems, Written in the Western Country*.[1] Pike's thoughtful book would become one of the Llano Estacado's most important and romantic interpretations.

Pike's book began with an account of Lewis's trek from Fort Towson to Santa Fé. But clearly this "Narrative of a Journey in the Prairie" is very much concerned with the environmental "world of prairie," a realm rarely, "and parts of it never, trodden by the foot or beheld by the eye of an Anglo-American."[2] Pike seeks to impart a grand vision of regional geography, one in step with the Romantic mood of Victorian America:

> Rivers rise there in the broad level waste, of which, mighty though they become in their course, the source is unexplored. Deserts are there, too barren of grass to support even the hardy buffalo; and in which water, except here and there a hole, is never found. Ranged over by the Comanches, the Pawnees, the Caiwas, and other equally wandering, savage and hostile tribes, its very name is a mystery and a terror.[3]

Into "this great American desert" in September 1831 rode Aaron B. Lewis and two companions. The three men had left the crude frontier outpost of Fort

Towson "allured by the supposed immense riches" of Santa Fé.[4] Pike's comments suggest that Santa Fé had become a new Quivira for Americans. Lewis's "delusion" was that he thought Santa Fé was a utopia where "gold and silver were abundant and easily obtained." As they advanced westward the prairie grew grander and assumed "that look of stern silence" which forcibly impressed the mind. Losing his horse in the Washita country, Lewis struggled on foot across the northeast Llano prairies to the Canadian River country. From there he staggered westward through winter storms and incredibly harsh conditions to reach Santa Fé. He was lucky to be alive.

Pike's subsequent description of the prairie world of the Llano assigned the environment the role of Romantic protagonist. "No man can form an idea of the prairie," he wrote, "from anything he sees to the east of the Cross Timbers."[5] The prairie of the "immense desert" Lewis had entered was "too grand and too sublime to be imaged by the narrow-contracted undulating plains" found in the civilized east. The eastern reader, therefore, can only imagine this strange new world:

> Imagine yourself, kind reader, standing in a plain to which your eye can see no bounds. Not a tree, not a bush, not a shrub, not a tall weed lifts its head above the barren grandeur of the desert; not a stone is to be seen on its hard beaten surface; no undulation, no abruptness, no break to relieve the monotony . . . Imagine then countless herds of buffalo...or a herd of wild horses . . . Imagine here and there a solitary antelope, or, perhaps, a whole herd, fleeting off in the distance, like the scattering of white clouds. Imagine bands of white, snow-like wolves prowling about.[6]

Albert Pike's imagining took lessons from more than routine travel books. He brought to the American spell of the prairie an English sense of the sublime. As a popular aesthetic term in the late eighteenth and early nineteenth centuries, sublimity expressed a new mood and relationship to the works of nature. Landscapes of sufficient grandeur, height, and vastness now inspired the viewer with feelings of awe and exaltation. There was an analogous perceptual linkage between lofty vistas and lofty emotions for example.[7]

For Albert Pike the lofty, vast plains of the American West were natural abodes of the sublime. The most notable of these plains in his opinion was "the illimitable Stake Prairie." It was lofty or elevated, it was vastness incarnate, and it exercised a strong, exalting pull upon a Romantic sensibility. Pike's linkage of the Stake Prairie to the English Sublime reflected a key conception of the early Anglo explorers. He believed that the environment influenced (perhaps determined) the mind of man. Pike's "illimitable Stake Prairie," therefore, was an early acknowledgment that the spatial grandeur of the plains *was considered* to affect the mind.

As a peripatetic poet and something of an American Don Juan,[8] this former Bostonian found a curious fascination in traveling on the plains. Pike was in a sense a Byronic connoisseur of the prairie world, having sampled its diverse moods and appearances, including "the illimitable Stake Prairie, which lies from almost under the shadow of the mountains to the heads of the Brazos and of Red River."[9] This prairie environment made a strong psychological mark: an aesthetic commingling of fear with fascination in the human mind.

As recounted by Pike the environmental atmospherics of the illimitable prairie were sensational. Besides the "splendid deceptions" of mirages and the "moonlight and starlight," there was also "the most magnificent, stern, and terribly grand scene on earth—a storm in the prairie." Indeed, he asserted in a remarkable passage that the prairie had a "stronger hold upon the feelings" than the forests, mountains or oceans:

> Its sublimity arises from its unbounded extent, its barren monotony and desolation, its still unmoved, calm, stern, almost self-confident grandeur, its strange power of deception, its want of echo, and, in fine, its power of throwing a man back upon himself and giving him a feeling of lone helplessness, strangely mingled at the same time with a feeling of liberty and freedom from restraint.[10]

Compare, if you will, this description befitting the illimitable prairie of the Llano Estacado to Charles Darwin's perceptive query about the Patagonian landscape, viewed only two years after Pike's published comments:

> In calling up images of the past, I find the plains of Patagonia frequently cross before my eyes; yet these plains are pronounced by all to be the most wretched and useless. They are characterized only by negative possessions; without habitations, without water, without trees, without mountains, they support only a few dwarf plants. Why then—and the case is not peculiar to myself—have these arid wastes taken so firm possession of my mind?[11]

Darwin's question is, perhaps, answered by Albert Pike's belief that the midlatitude grasslands, the rainshadow deserts of the New World, *throw humans back upon themselves*. The spell of the prairie reawakens primordial instincts of suspense and alertness. While some Anglo-American observers actually froze with terror, for others the ambiguities of an irrational, melancholy, and monotonous landscape promote a vision of the sublime: they allow the individual to touch the very soul of solitude.

"In the prairie," Pike wrote in 1835, "we are alone; we have the same desolate, companionless feeling of isolation, so well expressed by Coleridge."[12] Thus, landscapes like the Stake Prairie turn "our mind inward" to private contemplation of joy or misery. The immensity and the solitude constitute a melancholic landscape of Coleridgian introspection, one that induces a deceptive, oneiric state of mind: "we pass over the desert as men pass through a glimmering and lonely dream," he wrote in a beautiful passage.[13]

Albert Pike's vision of the Llano Estacado, however, relied on more than a synthesis of Romantic aesthetics and frontier hearsay. In the summer of 1832 he joined a group of bold men at Taos, New Mexico, who were determined to trap beaver in the eastern headwaters of the Llano. The story of their adventure is contained in Pike's "Narrative of a Second Journey in the Prairie." After hiring Manuel, "an old Comanche," in San Miguel as a guide, the Campbell and Harris parties of Mexican and American trappers journeyed down the Pecos River in September 1832. At the pleasant cottonwood groves of Bosque Redondo on the Pecos, Albert Pike encountered the legendary nature of the region to the east.

Many of the men traveling with Pike in Campbell's group were Mexicans. Near Bosque Redondo these men had met a returning group of comancheros who warned their fellow citizens about Comanche antipathy to Anglo-Americans. Pike's New Mexican companions grew alarmed, therefore, with their American sojourners and the obvious potential for trouble with the unpredictable Comanches. These Mexicans made it clear to Pike at Bosque Redondo that the area before them was a fearful region. There was, after all, merely, "the name of the Llano Estacado."

Lying before them "like a boundless ocean," the Llano was mentioned "with a sort of terror, which showed that it was by them regarded as a place from which we could not escape alive."[14] Not unlike Pedro de Castañeda, Pike analogously perceived that this "Stake Prairie" was "to the Comanche what the desert of Sahara is to the Bedouin." Apparently it extended a twenty-day journey to the east, had little game or water, and was a "hard, barren and dry" place suitable only for the fierce Comanche.[15]

His companions' sense of dread, the North African desert analogy, the illimitable ocean prairie, and the premonitions of death and solitude were to become classic nineteenth-century characterizations of the Llano Estacado. Fear was sufficient to prompt twenty-three-year-old Albert Pike to switch over to the larger, bolder John Harris party. This group of forty-five men left the Pecos River on September 21, 1832, and followed the southern Comanchero Road past Taiban Spring onto the Llano. Led by a new guide named Antonio, the Harris party was soon traveling on the vast plains toward the southeast.

Their geographical knowledge of the fearful region was clearly a product of the native New Mexican traders. Pike spoke, for example, of two weeks travel to the eastern "*ceja*" or caprock region, from which arose a series of rivers like the Rio Azul, Rio San Saba, Rio Javalines, Rio Mochico, and Rio Las Cruces. These toponyms are confusing to modern researchers, but they do indicate the intrinsic Hispano familiarity with a landscape considered unexplored by the Anglos.

Even with stalwart companions, the dreadful aspects of the "illimitable plain" continued to dominate. There was the blackened, burned-off prairie from fires set by the Comanche, the infrequency of water, people, and game, and the lack of firewood, which required them to cook over smoky blazes of tall weeds. There was also the somber signification of the landscape by human bones: "This day," Pike wrote, "we saw two skulls bleaching in the sun;" and, "found here the remains of a defeated party of Spaniards."[16] There were also the deceptive aspects of the Stake Prairie: its cruel mirages ("we were frequently tantalized by seeing at a distance ponds which appeared to be full of clear rippling water"); its looming ("we thought we saw buffalo . . . but found it to be only weeds looming up in the distance"); and its sudden canyon abysses ("like a well in the desert, the valley cannot be seen until you are close upon it").[17]

Pike and the other men traveled ever southeastward that September along a comanchero road—most likely the "Trail of Living Water" or *La Pista de Vida Agua*—"now broad and plain" past Portales Spring, Salt Lake, and then approximating the course of Blackwater Draw toward Yellow House Canyon.[18] They did not find "the immense quantities of beaver which we had anticipated," but they did encounter plenty of sandburs and other discomforts. Indeed, as J. Evetts Haley noted,[19] Pike's reference to picking sandburs from his feet near Coyote Lake (El Coyote) indicated that some ecological disruption had already begun on the Llano Estacado.[20]

By the early nineteenth century it was likely that one or more invasive weed species—probably associated with wild horses—were being spread over the Llano. Long before farmers arrived with their plows, the Llano environment was being modified by the distant hoofbeats of "ecological imperialism," in the words of Alfred W. Crosby. Opportunistic species such as sandburs could be rapidly spread from one waterhole to another by captured or wild livestock. From a biogeographical standpoint, Pike's brief reference to obnoxious sandburs raises important questions regarding the spread of invasive weeds. Although initially the semiarid plains proved resistant to the cool-weather European plants,[21] the arrival of thousands of wild and Indian horses and later sheep was quite likely the start of ecological modification. Trampling hooves and disturbed ground provided suitable niches for opportunistic species from the Rio Grande Plains, from the Mexican traders and settlers of New Mexico, or even from the incoming settlements of Anglos in lower Texas.

Midway across the Llano Estacado, Albert Pike encountered some isolated hackberry trees in present-day Lamb County. These trees were hailed by the men "as though they had been old friends." Like Major Long and Edwin James, these trappers were decidedly tree-loving. Either trees or mountains constituted companionable landscapes. But "there is nothing adds so much to the loneliness of the prairie," Pike observed, "as the want of timber."[22] Riding through sandhills and shinneries of scrub oak that day had been troublesome, for the wind blew strong and sand stung their eyes. They lost the trail of *La Pista de*

Vida Agua for awhile. Climbing the highest sandhill the men took their bearings, thought they saw buffalo in the distance, and then rode forward to encounter instead a camp of Comanches.

Most of the warriors were away, and those who remained proved relatively friendly to the Harris party. Albert Pike regarded them, however, with distaste. "I imagine that there is no being on earth," Pike wrote, "who would be as valuable to a painter desirous of sketching his satanic majesty as an old Comanche woman."[23] Like Doctor James, Pike viewed these natives as integral components of the barbaric environment. In a state of utter fear one of the trappers, Bill Williams, wanted to shoot down a solitary, defenseless Comanche woman taking firewood to camp, not unlike his casual shooting of antelope now and then on the Llano. Fortunately, Williams's companions restrained him. The Comanche women reminded Pike "strongly of Arab women, whom I have seen painted out in divers veritable books of travels."

Pike's comment indicates that the eastern literary perception of North Africa was an important early analog for describing the Llano Estacado. Growing up in Boston and reading literature and travel books, Pike brought two conflicting viewpoints to the Llano. He was quite comfortable looking at it, first, as a dreadful Arabian desert, and second, as a romantic American prairie. He observed the Comanches with some interest and intelligence, yet little sympathy. He noted, for instance, their habit of carrying "an abundance of stakes for securing their horses," thereby providing an important etymological clue to the origin of the term "Stake Prairie." Although this village only had about twenty lodges, Pike estimated that the natives had a thousand horses and some mules. "Horses are their only riches," he commented. Although he did not explicitly state it, there was the suggestion that the Comanche saw the Llano Estacado as prime horse habitat.

On September 28, 1832, the Harris party rode out from the Comanche village and traveled east down Yellow House Canyon toward the Double Mountain Fork of the Brazos. Within a few days they had descended the eastern caprock and emerged into the broken country of the "Canyon del Rescate."[24] Here Pike found larger Comanche villages, thousands of horses, the first mesquite trees seen so far, and the pangs of hunger. By September 30 the men in the Harris party were reduced to eating prairie dogs, hawks, and the local dry-land terrapins. They also, in the bartering tradition of the comanchero traders who routinely used this "Valley of Traffic" (as Pike called it), swapped tobacco for some dried meat.

There were very few beaver on the Llano headwaters, much to the Americans' disgust. The Harris group soon broke up in dissension; Pike and three companions set out across the gyppy breaks of the Brazos, eventually traveling northeast across the Salt Fork, on through Oklahoma, and finally arriving at Ft. Smith in December. Albert Pike settled down in Arkansas, wrote enough good poetry to earn the critical respect of Edgar Allan Poe, and became an influential lawyer in the years to come. Two years after his 1832 sojourn on the Llano he published his "recital of our adventures in the Western Desert" in Boston.

Albert Pike's *Prose Sketches and Poems, Written in the Western Country* provided the first real introduction of the Llano Estacado to the Anglo-American mind. His romantic sensitivity to the "world of prairie," his informed discussion of the confusing geography, his notice of the comancheros, and his experiential discursions on the psychology of the plains all constituted a powerful testament on its melancholy sense of place. He also experienced the sublimity and brought a Byronic sensibility to the beauty of this wilderness. Finally, Pike's narratives indicated the powerful influence that East Coast literary modes of perception would play in the imagining of the Llano.

·16·

LE GRAND'S
ELEVATED PRAIRIES

This tract of country explored by Le Grand in 1833 is naturally fertile well wooded & with a fair proportion of water.

JOHN ARROWSMITH

The shadows of history suggest that other American explorers were not far behind the 1820 Long expedition in the discovery of the Llano Estacado. In the spring of 1823 a nondescript trader, formerly from Watervliet, New York, apparently set out from the upper Sabine River of the Spanish province of Coahuila y Tejas. With horses and pack mules, John H. Fonda and two contrabandista companions were headed for Santa Fé. They hoped to barter with native tribes along the way. The editor of Wisconsin's Prairie du Chien *Courier* published Fonda's reminiscences in 1858. In these dictated memoirs, John Fonda claimed the three traders traveled "to the source of the Red River, through the Comanche country, north to the forks of the Canadian River where we took the old Santa Fe trail. . . ."[1] The party of three traders arrived in Santa Fé "without any of those thrilling adventures, or Indian fights, that form the burden of many traveler's stories." Fonda gave no details of his route, nor was there much supporting evidence, save for later testimonials to his sterling character. He did refer to the presence of minerals in the "barren country" east of the Canadian River. If he made such a journey he correctly learned that the trail involved leaving "the source of the Red River," going north to the Canadian, and then following up one of the comanchero roads past San Miguel and on to Santa Fé—but this important piece of geography was well known when his memoirs were published.

In contrast to Fonda's belated claims another account of the region was more detailed and influential, but ironically much less coherent. Consider the curious case of Alexander Le Grand. A native of Maryland, Le Grand became a well-known American merchant in the roaring 1820s of Santa Fé. Albert Pike met him in Taos in 1832 and thought him an engaging soul. For many years Texas historians proudly honored Le Grand's claim that he ran a hazardous survey on the Llano Estacado in the summer of 1833, only a year after Pike's adventure. The historian Rupert Norval Richardson, for instance, trumpeted Alexander Le Grand's familiarity with the Llano Estacado and claimed his surveying feat entitled him "to a place among great western explorers."[2] But did he deserve such praise?

Le Grand's 1833 surveying trip was apparently a contractual job between himself and the most aspiring of the "get-rich" Texas impresarios, John Charles Beales. A graduate of the Royal College of Surgeons, Dr. Beales left England for Mexico in 1829 and married the Mexican widow of a late friend, Richard Exter, in 1830. He soon took over the management of his wife's inherited interest in 45,000,000 acres of the distant Llano. With his associate José Manuel Royuela he obtained a renewal of the contract on March 14, 1832. Dr. Beales soon acquired his wiser partner's interest in the incredible enterprise of settling 200 foreign families directly into the southern flank of the Comanchería, an area including a considerable portion of the "Elevated Prairies" or Llano Estacado.[3] Dr. Beales was perhaps the first (but not the last) English capitalist to let Llano land-hunger get the best of him. On paper he soon acquired other grants and assembled a Texas empire of 70,000,000 acres, over fifty times the size of the present-day King Ranch. This empire, much to Beales's inconvenience, was guarded and patrolled by thousands of hostiles. It also needed surveys and settlers to reference and keep the land.

Carl Coke Rister, a careful scholar with a close understanding of the region, believed that Dr. Beales dispatched Major Le Grand in June 1833 from Santa Fé with a properly equipped surveying party. Their dangerous mission was to run boundaries for the Beales and Royuela land grant and divide the huge realm into twelve large blocks. Rister thought the subsequent perilous survey by Le Grand entitled him to the honors of first explorer of the Llano Estacado, as other Texas historians had so concluded before him.[4] Le Grand's field notes and journal of his trip were in fact published in 1841 in William Kennedy's important compendium, *Texas: The Rise, Progress and Prospects of the Republic of Texas*. Their appearance in this respected British source thereby garnered Le Grand wide publicity and disseminated his survey results to distant nations.

I first came to Le Grand's writings on the Llano as an innocent, believing the survey was both possible and reputable. But after studying the account, it appeared so nonsensical and strange as to defy all belief. Indeed, a close examination of the notes and journal raised a most important question of deception—was Le Grand's survey another historical mirage? Ostensibly, from June 27 to October 30, 1833, Le Grand and his men blocked out the huge grant into twelve sections; they faced in the process perils, predatory Indians (who killed three of their number), rattlesnakes, and exhaustion.[5] In sixteen pages of commentary, however, there was no mention of the Llano Estacado itself or even a number of other Spanish toponyms common to the area. This lack of local toponyms is a curious omission. To be sure there were comments on "extensive prairie without water," "ponds of stagnant water," "plums of a large size," and so on, which seemed to be characteristic of the Llano. But many of Le Grand's comments stressed the fertility and fecundity of the region. There were "rich bottoms," a "creek of fine water," "rich and fertile" soils, "timber," and land of "good quality." Moreover, game was quite plentiful for the most part. On two occasions he claimed they killed a large "white bear" or grizzly bear.[6] And "gangs of wild horses," antelope, and herds of buffalo were also observed and common.

Le Grand's account of white bears and black-locust trees is only part of the puzzle. There are only a few occasions where he refers to a familiar topographic feature, such as the "S. Fork of the Canadian." Otherwise, his novel cartographic features are as obscure as the "Sierra Obscura" mountains appearing as a result of his influence on Arrowsmith's 1841 map. What is truly surprising is the general lack of Hispanic nomenclature. Given Le Grand's residence in Santa Fé, he should have absorbed more local geosophy of the eastern plains. Instead, he uses or creates unusual Indian terms for strange branches of the Brazos and Colorado, rivers that reach well into the "Elevated Prairies." And his depiction of the upper "Rio Roxo" in Kennedy's book is surely pure fantasy.

There were many improbable stories told of Alexander Le Grand in the 1830s. Reportedly the half-breed offspring of a French father and Comanche mother, he had apparently educated himself in New York City. He was said—by himself mostly, one suspects—to have been a Comanche chief in later years. What was more likely was that Alexander Le Grand was not only an explorer but also a grand impostor. Moreover, his field notes and journal may have been a good hoax both on his employer and on many other credulous Texans. As explained in the *Handbook of Texas*, evidence uncovered in 1949 pointed to Le Grand's survey as actually being made for the Stephen J. Wilson Grant in the summer of 1827. Moreover, "In spite of the detailed notes of the expedition, there is evidence that Le Grand was not at the places indicated and some reason for suspecting that he may not have run any of the reported survey."[7]

It was over a hundred years later before Alexander Le Grand's "Journal" was exposed to critical scrutiny. Historian Raymond Estep carefully unraveled the Le Grandian deceits in the late 1940s and 1950s. "That he was in the general area is unquestioned," Estep concluded, but "that he made the purported

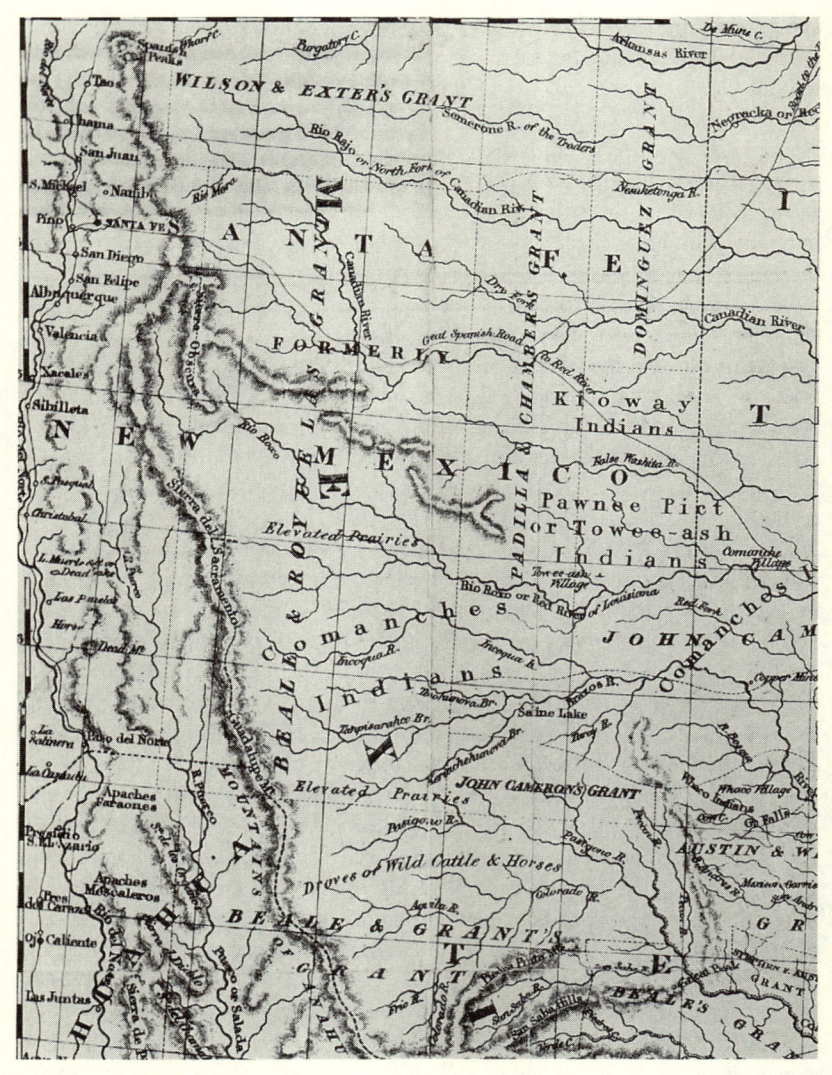

Map of the Republic of Texas and the Adjacent Territories Indicating the Grants of Land . . . , by John Arrowsmith, 1841. Engraving (detail). From William Kennedy, *Texas: The Rise, Progress, and Prospects of the Republic of Texas* (London: Hastings, 1841). John Arrowsmith's map filled the void of the Llano Estacado with strange environmental deceptions extracted from Alexander Le Grand's fictitious survey. *Courtesy Archives Division, Texas State Library, Austin.*

survey is doubtful."[8] Whereas Le Grand's published journal suggested his party left Santa Fé in June 1833, Estep discovered that the actual survey attempt was undertaken on an earlier and mysterious 1827 journey across the Llano—the center of the fabulous Wilson-Exter Grant.

Le Grand had some authentic qualifications for the job. He arrived in Santa Fé as early as July 31, 1824, at the head of a modest trading caravan from the Missouri frontier settlements. From Santa Fé he eventually traveled to Chihuahua and then on to Mexico City. In November 1826 he signed a contract in the capital with the speculator Stephen Julian Wilson. For a goodly sum, perhaps $10,000, he agreed to survey and investigate the impresario's vast domain on the edge of the new state of "Coahuila y Tejas." Le Grand soon left for the coast and caught a boat to New Orleans. Once there he began organizing an ambitious expedition. With the beginning of spring in 1827 Le Grand's party set out, probably taking a steamship and supplies to Natchitoches, thence by horse to the Red River frontier of the raw Arkansas Territory. His force of some fifty to sixty armed men rode into Miller County in the southwest Arkansas Territory in mid-June 1827. The arrival and passage of so large a party occasioned much discussion. William Waldo speculated later in his "Recollections of a Septuagenarian" that Le Grand envisioned a personal alliance with the plains tribes. With native allies and his own armed force he would wrest the enormous region away from the struggling government of a newly independent Mexico. The adventurer would then declare an independent nation with himself as first president. In any event, on June 20, 1827, the entire expedition rode westward from the vicinity of modern Texarkana. They headed for the sources of the Red River.

"From that date until his arrival in Santa Fé on November 15, 1827," wrote Raymond Estep, "Le Grand's movements are shrouded in mystery."[9] I found just enough credible environmental description in his published "Journal" to suggest that he did, in fact, cross the Rolling Plains and Llano Estacado in some manner, although it is now clear that he did not run much of the claimed survey. His published account, for example, claimed an incredible journey from the vicinity of Texarkana to a Midland starting point in only seven days. More likely Le Grand's men truly advanced up the Red River, started some efforts at a survey, encountered the Llano and other difficulties, fought Indians, struggled to explore, grew despondent, and then fought simply to cross the plains. They finally rode into Santa Fé in the fall—cold, exhausted, and grateful to be alive.

The old pioneer William Waldo recalled that Le Grand's survey party actually did ascend the Red River for several hundred miles with little trouble. But then they left the reliable watercourses behind, "and set out over an unknown and unexplored wilderness. Here their difficulties began." Waldo's further comments strongly suggest that the Llano Estacado—a name Le Grand failed to note—broke up their survey schemes, much less any thoughts of an independent republic: "Often, for several days together no water could be found: again no game, their only dependence for food, could be killed: thus they wandered on for months."[10]

If this is all true, Le Grand's mostly fictitious 1827 survey of the Llano Estacado was merely part of shady speculation in general. Dr. Beales's land grant had in fact a troubled past. His Mexican wife received it from her first husband, Richard Exter, who in turn had been in the impresario game with the early English rogue, Stephen Julian Wilson. Wilson's May 1826 contract with Coahuila and Texas called for him to settle 200 families in the Llano Estacado area, an enormously difficult colonization scheme when one remembers the hostile Comanche presence. Wilson organized a stock company, raised funds with his land speculations on the Llano, and was later involved in a serious embezzlement charge. He disappeared in 1831, either dead or gone from the area. What was significant though was the widespread acceptance of Le Grand's promotional view of the Llano Estacado or "Elevated Prairies" environment. Although his notes might have been based on some hearsay acquaintance, they were decidedly deceptive in their environmental optimism. However fantastic Le Grand's descriptions were, they nevertheless formed the basis for cartographic knowledge of the region for almost two decades. Certainly Dr. Beales found the promotional imagery of the "Journal" to be useful when he gained control of the grant.

David H. Burr's 1833 map of Texas offered the first graphic depiction of Le Grand's promotional imaginings for the Llano. This map showed the 1827 "Wilson and Exter's Grant" divided into twelve large blocks. An 1835 updated version of Burr's map noted "Beales & Rayuella" as the new impresarios of record. Both maps displayed an extensive tracery of riverine branches crossing the region. All these good rivers suggested that one was never really far from water in this fertile land. Sometime around 1835 the Colorado & Red River Land Company, a speculative enterprise, published in Brussels and New York the now exceedingly rare *Map of Texas Shewing the Grants in Possession of the Colorado & Red River Land Company*. This attractive colored lithograph included the twelve sections of the Le Grand survey, and it added many of Le Grand's optimistic environmental assessments in small type. "Good prairie," "level rich prairie," "rich bottom," and the like adorned this company's depiction of the "Wilson & Exters Grant." Near the southwest corner of the grant were the chimerical "Gold & Silver Mines" of the Pecos River country. The words gave flesh to the dreams of empire. Here, on the vast holdings of the English capitalists in northern Mexico, was another superabundance of fertile country for the soil-busting, slash-and-burn, westering Anglo-Americans. By appending the desired words to the land, the promotional imagining of these first *fenstermachers* or illusionists fed those desires. The deception loop required mutual trust.

Thus, by 1835 the commercial imagination of the Anglo-Americans had already begun appropriating the Llano Estacado as real estate. Le Grand's opti-

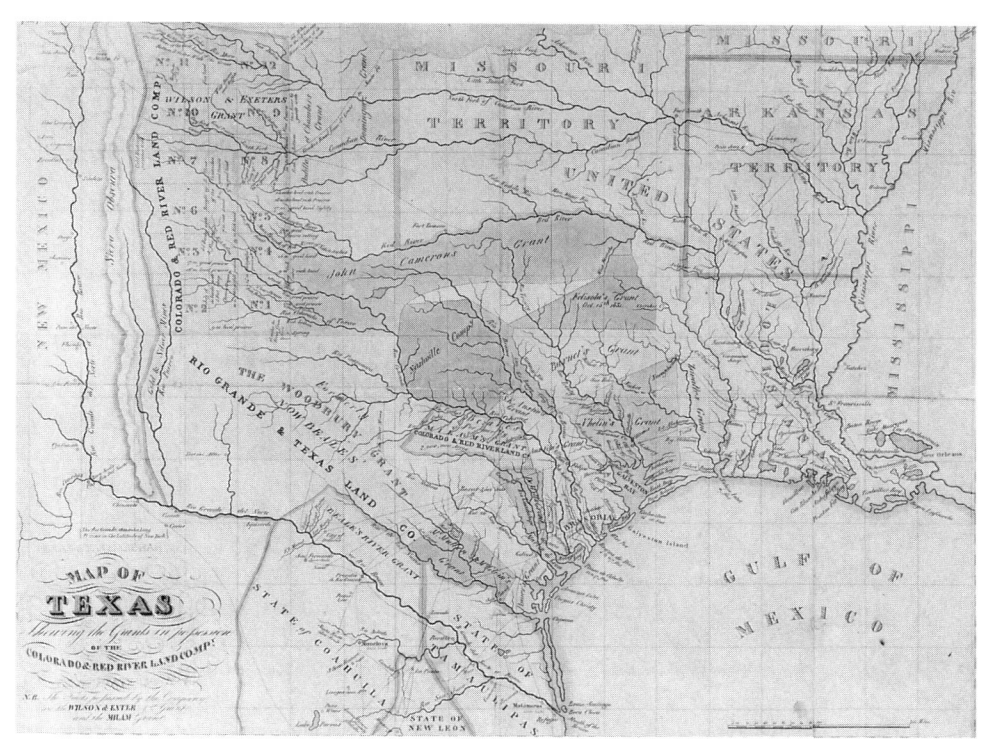

Map of Texas Shewing the Grants in Possession of the Colorado & Red River Land Company, by unknown artist, ca. 1835. Colored lithograph map. A rare and beautiful map that features Dr. John Beale's huge land grant on the Llano Estacado. The legendary Le Grand survey of 1827 is indicated by misleading but promotional remarks in small type. *Courtesy Archives Division, Texas State Library, Austin.*

mistic old field-notes were merely part of the new marketing strategy by the impresarios. What may have surprised even Le Grand, however, was the thorough acceptance of his fertile, well-watered vision of the "Elevated Prairies." Two important 1841 maps, for example, sincerely relied on Le Grand's alleged survey for their glowing depiction of the region. The map in William Kennedy's compendium did so too, as noted earlier. And 1841 also saw the publication of John Arrowsmith's influential *Map of Texas Compiled From Surveys Recorded in the Land Office of Texas.*

Arrowsmith's Llano is a geosophical delight. "This tract of country," he wrote along the 103rd meridian, "explored by Le Grand in 1833 is naturally fertile well wooded & with a fair proportion of water." This comment is clearly more deception than description with reference to the Llano Estacado.[11] Many misleading Le Grandian details are noted as well: "Level Rich Prairie Land," "Good Prairie," "Delightful Prairie," "Cherries, Grapes &c," "Rich Land well timbered," "Game," "River 45 yards wide & 3 ft deep," and "Delightful Country." A network of apparently strong rivers flow across the Llano from their western sources in the "Sierra Obscura," a reputed mountain chain along the 104th meridian. Perhaps these mythic rivers sheltered the elusive beaver that Albert Pike and his trapper companions sought.

John Arrowsmith was an excellent and careful cartographer. Based in London, his reputation as a mapmaker was immense. But his depiction of the Llano Estacado was mostly fantasy. Describing the region from 32° to 35° latitude and 101° to 104° longitude as "well wooded and with a fair proportion of water" was an enormous environmental deception, one more suited to shady land-speculation than cartographic dignity. Perhaps the underlying point of Arrowsmith's depiction was that genuine information on the Llano Estacado was unavailable. "Blank spaces are intolerable to the geographical imagination," John Allen has pointed out, "and people are tempted to fill them with imaginative extrapolation."[12] Despite Albert Pike's sojourn, the region was still virtually a *terra incognita* to the Anglo mind. Thus, competent Englishmen like William Kennedy and John Arrowsmith were tempted in 1841 to fill in the void with the recycled geographic reveries of Alexander Le Grand.

The reveries and derivations continued for years. W. H. Emory's 1844 War Department *Map of Texas and the Countries Adjacent* omitted the misleading minor environmental details. Instead, Emory more correctly showed a large void, an accurate portrayal of official American knowledge of the region. He then added a curving superscript notation that ran: "According to Arrowsmith this tract of Country was explored by Le Grand in 1833, and is naturally fertile, well wooded, and with a fair proportion of water." Thus, Emory helplessly looked to Arrowsmith who looked to Burr and the General Land Office, who all ultimately looked back to an impostor's mysterious trip into the Elevated Prairies in the old summer of 1827. Who was fooling whom?

For almost two decades Le Grand's "Journal" managed to influence images of this huge portion of the Great American Desert. The Llano became something quite different: "a most delightful country" of timber, wild game, and fair water. Its mythical broad rivers, exciting sport, and dangers promised grand adventure. Its pleasant environment was perhaps worth claiming, even though no one had displaced the fierce Comanche who guarded all this good soil. Le Grand's Llano was ultimately an advertising feat worthy of a great illusionist.

Alexander Le Grand's movements from 1827 to 1836 are equally less certain, although it is clear he traveled widely in the Southwest. In early 1836 he left Fort Gibson, Indian Territory, rode for Texas, and actively served the independence movement as a volunteer aide-de-camp. Ambitious and still smooth-talking, Major Le Grand impressed enough Republic of Texas officials in September 1836 to win the role of negotiating peace with the Comanches.

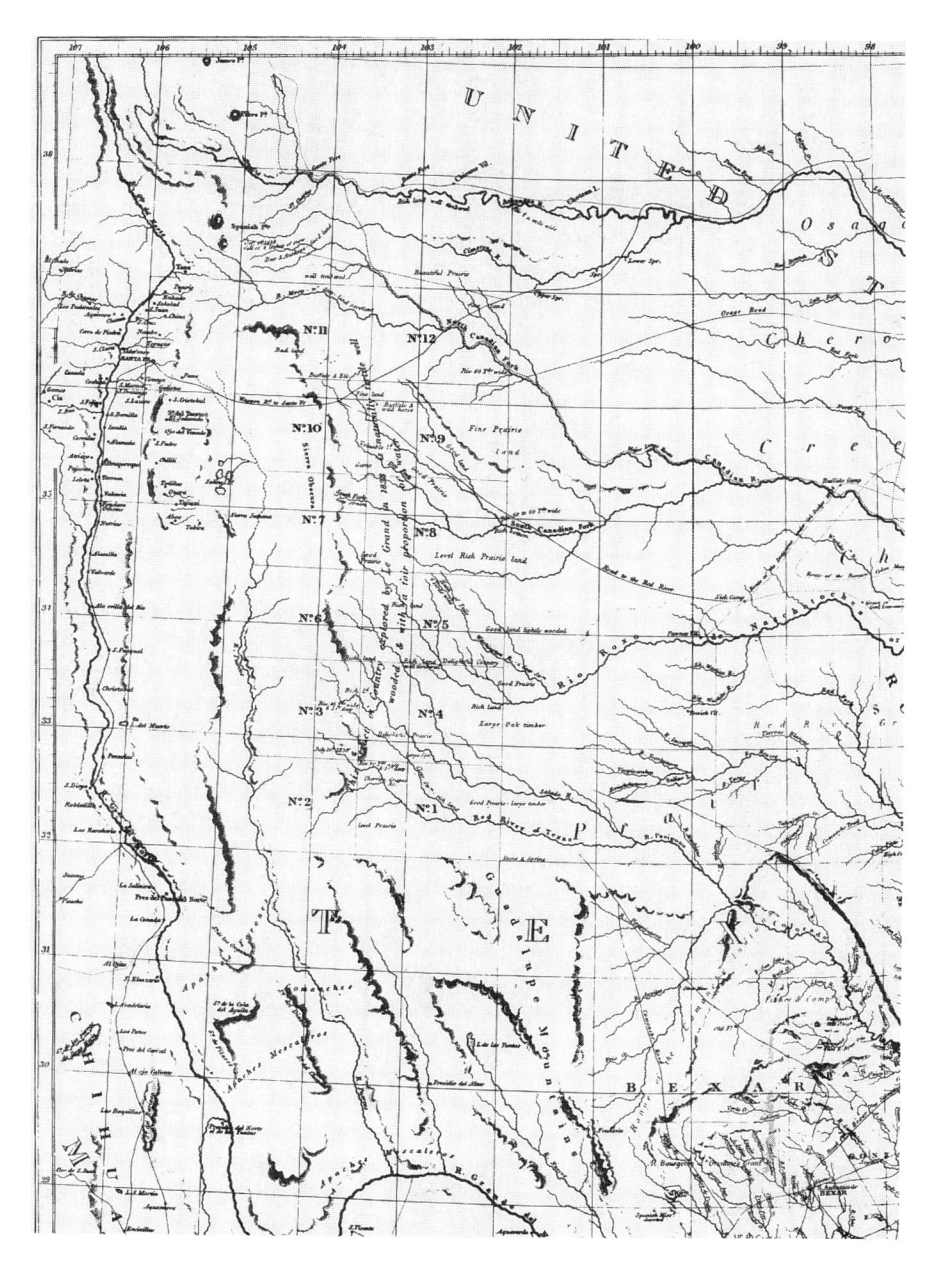

John Arrowsmith Map of Texas, 1843, by John Arrowsmith, 1843. Steel engraving (detail). John Arrowsmith's map popularized and disseminated Le Grand's promotional musings on the Llano environment to a worldwide audience. *Courtesy Archives Division, Texas State Library, Austin.*

Unfortunately his putative diplomacy failed to take effect. President Sam Houston conceived an intense dislike for the major, particularly his incessant efforts over the next few years to collect a significant sum for his services. Worn by travel and financial woes, Le Grand fell ill and died on March 3, 1839, in the city bearing the name of his most bitter foe, Houston, Texas. Only two years later Kennedy's book published his "Journal" to a large and appreciative audience. When the leading London cartographer, John Arrowsmith, enshrined his comments on the Elevated Prairies' region of Texas, Le Grand's greatest illusion spread worldwide.[13]

· 17 ·

GREGG'S TABLE LAND

The most notable of the great plateaux of the prairies is that known to Mexicans as *El Llano Estacado*.

JOSIAH GREGG

Of all the early Anglo-American sojourners on the Llano, the slight figure of Josiah Gregg stands out for his sympathetic studies of prairie phenomena. Gregg's perceptive and conscientious turn of mind would create a strong antidote to the fraud of Le Grand. Even more than Albert Pike, Gregg had a lasting "passion for the prairie," an instinctive liking and psychological affinity for the plains environment that belied his woodland origins. His passion for natural history suffused his great work, the two-volume *Commerce of the Prairies*, which appeared in 1844.[1]

During the 1830s Gregg involved himself with the considerable Anglo-American community in Santa Fé, a class which took advantage of new mercantile relationships between Missouri and Mexico.[2] By 1839 his shrewd commercial instincts and curiosity led him to select a new route from Missouri to Santa Fé, one that swung south, touched the Llano, and then followed the north bank of the Canadian River. Gregg was impressed with the picturesque Canadian River Valley in contrast to the monotonous "open plain or *mesa*" to its north. His party's wagons had only turned from a straight compass point on the mesa to avoid the innumerable playas, "which bespeckled the plain." But after a few days' travel west from Camp Comanche he reached the Canadian breaks again; "one of the most magnificent sights I had ever beheld," Gregg said of the view. It was a majestic landscape of desolation. He wrote:

> A little further on a pillar with crevices and cornices so curiously formed as easily to be mistaken for the work of art; while a thousand other objects grotesquely and fantastically arranged, and all shaded in the sky-bound perspective by the blue ridge-like brow of the mesa

[Llano Estacado] far beyond the Canadian, constituted a kind of chaotic space where nature seemed to have indulged in her wildest caprices.[3]

Gregg's "sky-bound perspective" of the distant Llano was a reflection, perhaps, of the 1840s style of American subversive literature.[4] He described a landscape that subverted norms, one of deceitful form where appearances were often misleading. This sense of "chaotic space" appeared particularly strong, he noted, in the mesa's "bordering *cejas* or brows," the modern breaks of the Canadian River. Gregg was a singular observer of this dissected environment and his "theory" on its geomorphological formation proved intelligent for his day. "The buffalo and other animals have no doubt assisted in these transmutations," he also observed, as their "paths over the brows of the plains, form channels for the descending rains."[5]

Gregg's view of the mesa south of the Canadian River owed much to his conception of "the reputed aridity of the country."[6] Concern now grew within the party that they might be lost, although Gregg remained confident about the route. One of the Mexicans wanted to turn south, but Gregg insisted they continue west, for to go southward would lead them "into the fearful *Llano Estacado*, where we would probably have perished."[7] In spite of the Llano's reputation for aridity, in the spring of 1840 Gregg decided on an alteration of his southern trail for the return journey to Van Buren, Arkansas. This variant trail would take his party directly onto the Llano. Moreover, this lowly wagon route would ultimately grow in significance, turning into a major transportation corridor.[8]

In the company of a Comanche guide,[9] Gregg's return caravan followed the cibolero cart road to the Llano outlier of Tucumcari Mountain. From March 7 to 11 they traveled some fifty miles under the borders of the vast mesa to their south, experiencing a prairie fire and standing off a Pawnee attack. On Thursday morning, March 12, 1840, Gregg's diary recorded their ascent onto "the table land," probably near present-day Adrian, Texas:

> This is the edge of what is called by the Mexicans the Llano Estacado; a very extended table plain, between the waters of the Rio Pecos, the Colorado or Canadian, and Red River. Except at rainy seasons, this plain can only be traversed in a few places, on account of its scarcity of water.[10]

His guide informed Greg that this "table plain" was enshrouded on all sides by rocky cliffs, the so-called *ceja* or brow of the plain.

Once on this "very level *mesa*" Gregg's party made good time, traveling over terrain "as firm and more smooth than a turn-pike."[11] The next evening, however, an arctic front blew in. Their sheep and goats "fled with the wind across the Llano Estacado." This experience proved a severe introduction to the climatic vagaries of the region as they never found the animals again. Gregg was

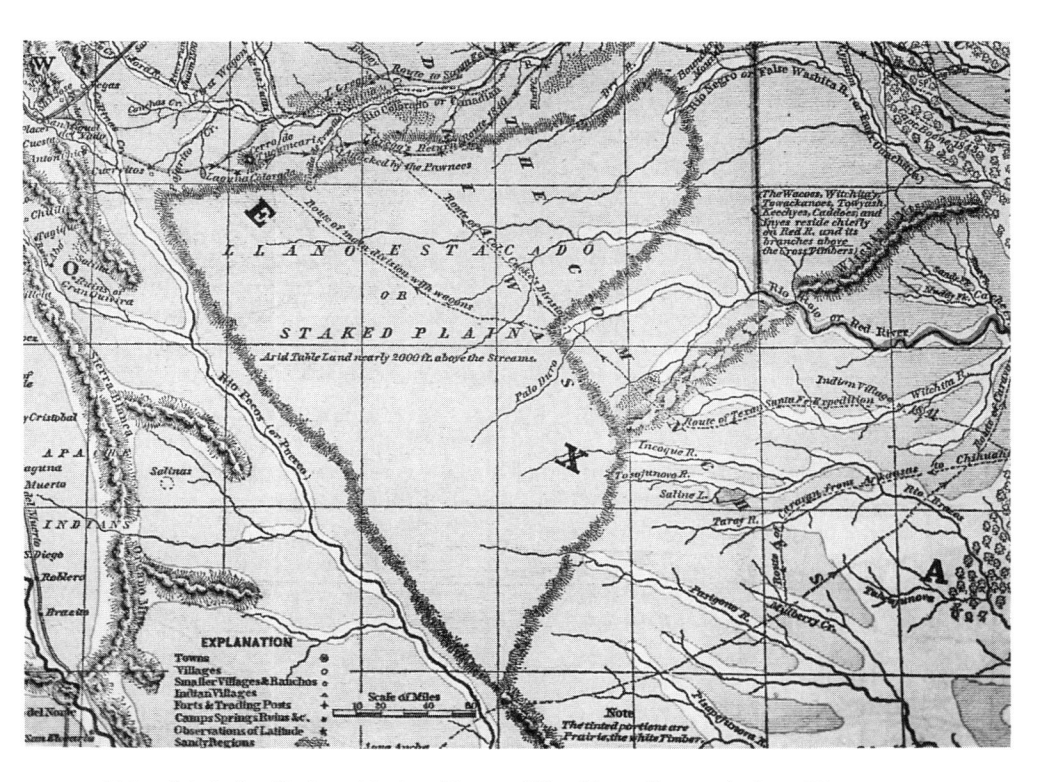

A Map of the Indian Territory, Northern Texas, and New Mexico Showing the Great Western Prairies, by Josiah Gregg, 1844. Engraving (detail). From Josiah Gregg, *Commerce of the Prairies; or, the Journal of a Santa Fé Trader* (New York: Langley, 1844). Josiah Gregg's map shows the bounded and triangular extent of the "Arid Table Land" of the Llano Estacado. The map traces Gregg's Llano route along the Canadian River as well as the two routes of the Texas–Santa Fé pioneers. *Courtesy Archives Division, Texas State Library, Austin.*

deeply interested in water resources on this tableland as several of his diary comments attested. Although he feared the interior of the Llano, he could not help but notice the comforting presence of the playas or "dry ponds" here and there. Indeed on March 14 he camped at Wild Horse Lake in what is now north Amarillo. He astutely concluded that there was a seasonal aspect to the local water supply: "These plains, during the wet season, must be very well watered, for the ponds abound, some of which are quite large."[12] This recognition of seasonality was an important distinction within the general premise of year-round aridity.

Gregg's route nevertheless hugged the tributary creek heads of the Canadian River[13] and within a few days he descended back into the valley itself. He had heard from his guide that there was a *cañada* (apparently Palo Duro Canyon) running from west to east with fair water. But cautious inclinations kept his party close to the known river valley instead. His guide was likely referring to the cibolero and comanchero corridor running southeast along Tierra Blanca Creek. Still, as Gregg and his caravan plodded east below the Llano escarpment he thought further of the water question. He noticed good spring-fed streams often flowing from the Llano bluffs into the Canadian. There was also the peculiar, oxymoronic "Dry River,"[14] a sandy, 200-yard-wide tributary "without a vestige of water." Even the character of the Canadian River changed from a deep narrow channel to a broad, sandbar-choked expanse.

Gregg's journal entries on the Llano Estacado would be amplified in his classic work, *Commerce of the Prairies*. Indeed, Chapter X of Volume II, "Geography of the Prairie," proposed in particular to discuss the natural history of the poorly understood (or appreciated) prairie province. One of the most prominent of the "Great Western Prairies" was clearly the tableland or mesa "known to Mexicans as *El Llano Estacado*."[15] This tableland was an immense triangular region of 30,000 square miles, generally level, with ample buffalo and other wildlife in the *ceja* margins. Gregg maintained that the Llano was "without water for three-fourths of the year," implying that for three months there *was* a wet season.

According to his New Mexican and Indian informants, there was but one year-round route that crossed this plain. This trail, presumably *La Pista de Vida Agua*, had widely placed waterholes, Gregg said, leading traders and ciboleros to mark its course with wooden stakes, "whence it has received the name *El Llano Estacado* or the Staked Plain."[16] Of course, as Albert Pike noted, it was also a Comanche practice to set out numerous stakes for their large herds of horses. Rather than deliberately marking the course with stakes, perhaps the course was simply characterized by its groupings of stakes at convenient places. Gregg was rather ambiguous about the environmental character of this heart of the prairies. He likened this mesa "to the famous steppes of Asia" in Chapter X, an interesting departure from the dreary North African metaphors common then and later. But in the same chapter he also referred to "that immense desert region of the Llano Estacado."[17] Was there a geographical distinction for him between a steppe and a desert? Or was the desert Llano merely an uninhabited steppe? Certainly within the existing Anglo agricultural context Gregg thought that the Llano was at present uninhabitable: "too dry to be cultivated." Yet he was aware of the notable presence of wildlife and good pasturage on these "great steppes."

Gregg also thought that the "genial influences of civilization" could modify the prairie environment to a considerable degree. That is, he posited the view that mankind was an active modifier of the prairie landscape. He correctly believed that fire suppression led to the encroachment of timber. Less correctly, he also thought that cultivation contributed to the "multiplication of showers," and that these pluvial influences could slowly transform the arid soul of the prairie.[18] This *transformational* perspective or theme of human agency was remarkable. Instead of merely writing off the Llano as a romantic desert void (with the mind of man determined by the environment), Gregg envisioned an active ecological component behind the advancing settlers, one that would drive the buffalo toward extinction and beneficially modify the seasons.

To be sure there was a real question of perception/deception dialectics about the prairie regions. "The high plains seem too dry and lifeless to produce timber," Gregg wrote, "yet might not the vicissitudes of nature operate a change likewise upon the seasons?"[19] As the greatest of the high-plains mesas, the Llano may seem like a desert, he was saying, but what could it become under the environmental influences of encroaching civilization? Gregg was an astute and practical man. He knew that beyond the superficial, dreary appearance of the prairie-world there were environmental systems at play: wolves and ravens following the course of wagons; playas and wet seasons; destructive erosion; prairie conflagrations; and the presence of *Homo faber*.

Gregg also appreciated the illusive context of the high plains. The vast dome of sky piqued his interest because of its subversive optical illusions. Indeed, the very act of perception on the "elevated plains" was subject to doubt. "One would almost fancy himself looking through a spy-glass," he wrote, "for objects frequently appear at scarce one-fourth of their real distance—frequently much magnified, and more especially elevated."[20] Whereas the immensity of the land itself distorted one's sense of scale, the sky acted on occasion as a magic-lantern show. Gregg spoke of how commonly vision was deceived: antelope mistaken for elk; buffalo bones transmuted into people; ravens masquerading as buffalo; and buffalo turning into trees. This was a landscape of sensory subversion.

This illusive, perplexing quality was signified for Gregg by the "false ponds," a common occurrence on the Llano Estacado. In addition to atmospheric writhings and loomings that distorted and confused objects, the mirages or "false ponds" symbolized the deceitful soul of the arid tablelands: they promised precious water where there was none. "Even the experienced traveller is often deceived by these upon the arid plains," Gregg observed, "where a disappointment is most severely felt."[21] Conceptually these mirages were troublesome for Gregg. He rejected the refraction argument, hypothesizing instead that the "false ponds" demonstrated the results of *reflection*, "upon a gas emanating perhaps from the sun-scorched earth and vegetable matter." Or perhaps mirages resulted from solar energy acting upon carbonic acid precipitations. Gregg was mistaken, of course, in his perception of the sky reflecting off ponds of accumulating prairie gases. But Gregg correctly noted that the high-plains environment had "singular atmospheric phenomena" piquing the curiosity of natural philosophers.

He also loved the atmospheric purity, the sky-bound perspectives, and the "high excitements which have attached me so strongly to Prairie life."[22] There was a romantic element to this land. He labored to express this emotive connection to the tablelands in *Commerce of the Prairies*. As the prophet of prairie, Gregg's subtle intimation of future settlements and cities has the air of an apologia. "The great American fact of the time," Paul Horgan wrote, "was geographical, the apprehension of a whole new world of creatures and places."[23] Clearly one of these notable places in Gregg's nine years of western sojourning was the Llano Estacado.

Gregg's historic route from Santa Fé to Arkansas through the Llano country was ignored for almost eight years. Mexican officials gave little initial encouragement since this pleasant southern route ran through the hotly disputed territory of Texas. Why encourage trade on this route if trouble followed? Indeed, only a year after Gregg's journey, a large contingent of Texans crossed the Llano on a dubious commercial mission, one that vastly increased Mexican opposition to an Anglo presence on its flat expanses. The issue was ultimately settled by war. Only in 1849 was Gregg's old route resurrected and converted into the significant transportation artery known as the Fort Smith–Santa Fé Trail. Not far from the rutted remnants of this trail, industrial fleets of today's merchant caravans rumble across the Llano on modern Interstate 40.

· 18 ·

The Grand Prairie

September 19—At eight o'clock this morning we commenced the ascent to the grand prairie—the Llano Estacado of the New Mexicans. This was the great plain spoken of at San Antonio.

Thomas Falconer

20th Ascended the mountains about 400 Feet very precipitous, on the "Grand Prairie."

Peter Gallagher Diary

The reader may think I have drawn a fancy sketch—that I have colored the picture too highly; now . . . I would in all sober seriousness say to him, that many of the sensations I have just described I have myself experienced, and so did the ninety-and-eight persons who were with me from the time when we first entered the grand prairie.

George W. Kendall

With the violent birth of the Republic of Texas in 1836, the newly established government inherited the old boundary disputes between Mexico and the United States. The Texan claim of the Rio Grande as the new nation's western boundary implied that both the Llano and the rich trade with Santa Fé were well within its territorial ambitions. Desirous of increasing revenues and commerce and covetous of new territory, the government of Mirabeau Lamar proposed an expedition to Santa Fé in 1839. Two years would pass before such an expedition could be mounted by the precarious new republic.

The so-called Texan–Santa Fé Expedition of 1841 has been the focus of considerable historical discussion for its role in bringing the United States and

Mexico much closer to war. Andrew Jackson dismissed the expedition as a foolish "wild-goose chase," and certainly it did turn into a clumsy border incident between the Republic of Texas and Mexico that further deflated the martial boasts of Texans. Whether it was, as claimed, a simple commercial intrusion from Texas to New Mexico or a sinister Texan army of conquest, it was handled with equal ease by Mexican soldiers and officials. Although the expedition was a total strategic failure by the young republic, it nevertheless accomplished one objective: it opened the mind of Texas, the United States, and eventually Great Britain, France, and other colonial powers to the geography of the Llano Estacado.

The historian Noel M. Loomis noted that the expedition "set out into unknown wilderness and made the first westward crossing of the fearful Llano."[1] H. Bailey Carroll claimed the expedition, "in attempting to tie together the new capital of Texas and the ancient one of New Mexico, revealed a surprising amount of the unsettled, unexplored Southwest."[2] This ill-fated expedition also produced two classic explorer accounts, which appeared in 1844: newspaperman George W. Kendall's *Narrative of an Expedition across the Great South-Western Prairies from Texas to Santa Fé*; and agent Thomas Falconer's "Notes of a Journey through Texas and New Mexico, in the years 1841 and 1842," printed in volume XIII of the *Journal of the Royal Geographical Society*.[3] These two works provided an international audience with a thrilling account of the first large-scale Anglo-American encounter with the Llano Estacado.

As noted in Kendall's *Narrative*, some premonition of the Llano was felt in early discussions about the proper route to take from Austin to Santa Fé. A direct passage was considered problematic because of a supposed "scarcity of water."[4] By going north to the Red River the sojourners thought there would be plenty of game. "But beyond that point," Kendall wrote, "the country was a perfect *terra incognita* . . . and all were eager to partake of the excitement of being among the first to explore it."[5] Thomas Falconer, an accompanying British secret agent, was apparently better informed and less sanguine. "This [Llano Estacado] was the great plain spoken of at San Antonio," he wrote, "as too extensive to travel over, where we would be without timber, without water, and where many of our horses would perish."[6] British officials then took a keen interest in the Texas borderlands as they were eager to prevent the annexation of the region by the United States. The Republic of Texas was their natural bulwark against American imperialism in the Southwest, were it not for the cursed slavery issue.

Geographic errors haunted and dogged the Texan–Santa Fé Expedition from its outset. Among the 321 men who departed from Brushy Creek near Austin on June 19, 1841, there was only one, half-confused, Mexican American guide to the unknown region. The pioneers grossly underestimated the distance needed to travel.[7] Although the merchants and their military escort started out in high spirits, the harsh, dry, summer environment, the plodding slowness of the draft oxen, and the travelers' lack of plains-craft and geographic knowledge proved disastrous. Indeed, as they toiled northward and struggled through the Upper Cross Timbers with the wagons in July, signs of dissension emerged. By the time their guide, Juan Carlos, mistook the red muddy waters of the Wichita River for those of the Red River, the expedition was essentially lost as it entered the *terra incognita* to the west.[8] On August 6 the pioneers toted their figures and reckoned they were only 200 miles from Santa Fé.

In fact they had about 560 miles to go, which included crossing the dreadful Llano Estacado directly ahead. Persistent logistic difficulties continued to demoralize expedition members. As they wandered northwestward through the rough breaks of the Wichita and Pease Rivers east of the Llano, their worried guide deserted, and potable water and game grew scarce. Camp discipline slowly began to fall apart. Seeing their opportunity, Kiowas started a slow guerrilla campaign of murder and harassment. On August 27, 1841, the tattered expedition crossed a mesquite plain and saw ahead the precipitous, mountainous edge of an unusual tableland or "high steppe."

The Texan–Santa Fé pioneers had reached the foot of "the grand prairie," as many were wont to call the Llano Estacado. For Falconer this Grand Prairie appeared as "the most extensive table-land of the N. of Mexico."[9] At first, they thought they saw "mountains" in the distance, as the rough canyons of the Llano loomed in this manner. As another point of confusion, the former guide, Carlos, had instructed the expedition members to watch for three singular mesa formations marking "the Narrows" or "*Angosturas*" of the Canadian River as a sign of their proximity to the settlements of New Mexico. These formations were known to the Hispanos as *Los Cuervos*. George Kendall and others now saw several mesa outliers of the eastern Llano and mistakenly thought they were "The Crows" (which actually arose far to the west near the upper Canadian River).

On the morning of August 28 Kendall reported a tell-tale environmental clue revealing the proximity of the well-watered Llano springlands. He heard "the warbling of innumerable singing-birds," with their familiar songs reminding him of "home and civilization . . . here among the western wilds." But these songs, like so much he was encountering, were only "fallacious promises":

> In our fond imaginings they typified the dove, telling us that the wilderness had been passed; but alas! their song, like the siren's, was uttered but to deceive.[10]

The entire Texan–Santa Fé party, now worn out by the rough breaks, brackish waters, and poor food, were operating under the massive geographic delusion that New Mexican settlements must be quite near. Had they not toiled great distances already? A report of "Mexican cart tracks" that day deepened the illusion. But how could they reach these towns with the apparently impassable "mountains" before them?

Lost, confused, and beset by stealthy Kiowas picking off their horses and men, the pioneers wandered around the Los Lingos Creek area for several days.[11] By now they were reduced to hippophagy, the eating of horses slain by Indians or oxen slaughtered by the pioneers. On August 30 hundreds of men gathered at Camp Resolution. There they reached a desperate decision. They would divide the command, sending a mounted advance party under Captains John S. Sutton and William G. Cooke ahead, while the remainder stayed with the wagons and brooded at the foot of the Llano.[12]

George Kendall traveled with the ninety–eight-man advance party. He was thus to comment on the first perceptions of the pioneers as they moved westward across the Grand Prairie. Although his evocative prose was subject to "journalistic exaggeration," as H. Bailey Carroll has noted,[13] many of his landscape observations were accurate and revealing. On September 1 this advance party followed an Indian trail and ascended the Llano. "Here we were again gratified," Kendall remarked, "by finding spread out before us a perfectly level prairie, extending as far as the eye could reach, and without a tree to break its monotony."[14] Another member of the expedition, George W. Glover, noted they were "agreeably surprised" with the "high prairie," by now hating the toilsome breaks. Behind and below them lay a panoramic and "lovely scene" of the breaks country, a picturesque prospect that reminded Kendall strongly "of one of Salvator Rosa's beautiful landscapes."[15]

This prospect also invited a grand geographic view of the country behind them. Kendall digressed in his *Narrative* at this point to comment on the mysterious sources of the Red River. He concluded correctly that its source "must have been near the base of the high steppe upon which we now stood." Furthermore, he concluded that the Colorado and Brazos Rivers had similar origins. All three of these rivers, he perceived, had similar waters, "being of a dirty, brownish red color, and of a slightly salt and bitter taste, which goes far to prove their common origin."[16] These traits, picked up by the rivers as they drained the ancient, oxidized soils of the Permian formations, could be tasted and observed. That is, a sensitive palate and eye apparently could deduce the vast geographic extent of the eastern escarpments: the origin of three mighty river systems at least. These environmental conjectures also were buttressed, Kendall wrote, by "the testimony of Albert Pike," whose route "across the immense plain called *Llano Estacado*" was known to Kendall by the time he wrote his classic book.

Once on the Llano the Sutton-Cooke party rode northwest in search of civilization. They chased and killed a large black bear that day, while a breakaway mule led them to a "pond-hole" or playa of water. They traveled over the "slightly undulating but smooth surface" when suddenly, with no warning, they arrived at the brink of a "yawning chasm"—the Tule Canyon Narrows, a narrow rent in the earth some 690 feet deep.[17] Camping near the precipitous edge that night, a homesick Kendall was enthralled by a "terrible storm." As lightning played about and thunder reverberated in Tule Canyon, Kendall thought that the Ruler of the elements was displaying "a specimen of his grandest, his sublimest work."[18] This comment reflected again the Romantic impulse engendered by the Llano environment on the mid-nineteenth-century Anglo imagination. The environment was both awful and awfully sublime.

The next day, September 2, the drenched advance guard reconnoitered until it found a rough trail entering Tule Canyon. The descent into the "frightful chasm" was nerve–racking and many of the horses and mules balked. The ascent of the other side was equally troublesome and dangerous. But at last they were back upon "the loan [sic] and dreary prairie."[19] Kendall perceived the tableland landscape now before them in melancholic terms reminiscent of Albert Pike. There was a carpeting of short grass "studded with innumerable strange flowers and plants," with nothing else to break the monotony. This treeless, soulless landscape engendered a strong feeling of loneliness in Kendall.

He strongly missed "the company" of trees on the immense prairie. The sense of solitude was almost overwhelming:

> There is food for thought too, in the ocean wave, not to be found in the unchangeable face of these great Western wastes, and nowhere else does one feel that sickly sensation of loneliness with which he is impressed when nothing but a boundless prairie is around him.
> There he feels as if in the world, but not of it—there he finds no sign or trace to tell him that there is something beyond, that millions of human beings are living and moving upon the very earth on which he stands.[20]

This was an extreme environment for the tree-loving Anglo-Americans, one whose vast, spatial externalities Kendall sought to capture in extreme language: "unchangeable," "nowhere," "nothing," "boundless," "immense." Moreover, Kendall's cultural perceptions were strongly keyed to treed and featureful landscapes:

> Shakespeare was in the woods when he found
> "—tongues in trees, books in the running brooks,
> Sermons in stones, and good in everything."
> Had he been on the immense prairie I am now speaking about, he would have found no such companionship.[21]

The literary allusion was suggestive. Kendall's perceptions were keyed to woodland landscapes, both practically and culturally. Noel Loomis and others have often wondered why the Texan–Santa Fé Expedition toiled for weeks through the delaying Upper Cross Timbers, when they could have skirted them easily via prairies. Perhaps the answer was that these pioneers preferred the emotional companionship of trees to the apparent dreary solitude of grasslands.

When Kendall wrote of that "sickly sensation of loneliness" engendered by this immense open plain, he also was advancing the case for the Grand Prairie as an agoraphobic landscape. For those with a psychological fear of open spaces, few lands were as frightening as this one. For a mind accustomed to the rich, bric-a-brac phenomenology of the Victorian parlor, this minimalist landscape seemed nihilistic. There were no tongues in the trees, no books in the brooks, no sermons in stone in the flatland immensity. The Romantic stance of Pike and Kendall was more than literary pretension; it was also a psychological response to a frightening environmental setting.

The historian H. Bailey Carroll (reflecting the influence of Walter Prescott Webb's *The Great Plains*) has bluntly assessed the expedition: "The traditional woodland army organization proved inadequate in meeting the problems of the Great Plains environment."[22] There is certainly some merit in the hindsight argument that a lighter, more mobile force with wiser scouts and guides could have performed better. However, it is difficult to say exactly how much the woodland perceptions of the expedition contributed to its eventual demise.[23]

There was another problematic aspect of the Llano for Kendall. As a newspaperman in New Orleans, he was used to a richly semiotic environment. But on the Grand Prairie of the Llano he encountered a landscape of little signification. He spoke of the unusual lack of "sign" seen on this prairie on September 2.[24] By "sign" he meant any "evidences seen upon the prairie of the appearance, whether recent or otherwise, of animals or men."[25] This paucity of semiotics or zoosemiotics was significant in so far as it intimated a desert, a region uninhabited by man or beast.

Traveling northwest over "this dreary waste," the advance guard was once more surprised. On September 3 the men suddenly rode upon another "immense rent or chasm in the earth." This abyss was *Cañoncito* or Cita Canyon and it made a lasting impression on Kendall. "No one was aware of its existence," he wrote, "until we were immediately upon its brink, when a spectacle, exceeding in grandeur anything we had previously beheld, came suddenly in view."[26] After the monotony of the prairie, the scenic overlook left the men "lost in amazement." Indeed, after the sky-bound agoraphobia of the plains, they were suddenly confronted with the earth-bound acrophobia of the Palo Duro canyonlands. "A sickly sensation of dizziness was felt by all," Kendall observed, "as we looked down, as it were, into the very depths of the earth."[27]

Kendall, his perceptions suddenly yanked from the extreme horizontal to the extreme vertical, responded by grandiosely signifying this canyon. That is, the mind's eye projected an illusive European architectural presence into the chasm:

> Immense walls, columns, and in some places what appeared to be arches, were seen standing, modelled by the wear of the water, undoubtedly, yet so perfect in form that we could with difficulty be brought to believe that the hand of man had not fashioned them.[28]

While poetic license characterized this description, the point was that the expedition members were eager to find traces of settlements; they wanted to see civilization.[29] Descending into Cita Canyon along a worn, hazardous trail brought Kendall and the other men into closer proximity with its fantastic geomorphology. This proximity only deepened environmental deception.

In a long passage Kendall detailed the phantasmagoric appearances of the "strange and fanciful figures" they encountered. There were walls and columns, forts and castle turrets, and cumbrous stone pillars scattered all about. Alone in the wilderness, their plans in disarray, Kendall saw all around them the abandoned ruins of civilization itself. "Regularity was strangely mixed with chaos," creating a landscape subversive to the bourgeois sense of order. Kendall claimed that Niagara Falls paled in comparison with "the wild grandeur of this awful chasm—this deep, abysmal solitude as Carlyle would call it."[30] His imagination even conjured up the classic cities of Thebes, Palmyra, and ancient Athens: "we could not help thinking that we were now among their ruins." It was a hallucinatory experience. And yet, after laboriously ascending the opposite canyon wall and moving out a hundred yards onto the level prairie, the immense chasm of Cita Canyon simply disappeared from sight, as if it had only been a moment's dream. Acrophobia gave way again to agoraphobia.

For the next five days the Sutton-Cooke advance guard rode northwest and west across the silent plains of the Llano. Kendall was duly impressed with its immensity. "The prairie is undoubtedly the largest in the world," he stated.[31] With their scant rations soon exhausted the men were in a state of "horrible suspense." They thought the settlement of San Miguel was near, but each day dashed their hopes with the same "dreary spectacle, a boundless prairie." As traced by historian Carroll, their route ran southwest across present-day Randall County, and then westward across Deaf Smith County.[32]

Sightings of wildlife assumed great importance for these famished pioneers. Like explorers before them, they sometimes wrote of the land from the perspective of rumbling stomachs. Unfortunately the deer, mustangs, and antelope proved too shy to come into range of gun-toting, crazed strangers. Camping at playa lakes, Kendall reported flocks of curlews, ducks, and large white cranes, perhaps whooping cranes migrating south. At Tierra Blanca Creek, however, they finally encountered a buffalo bull on September 5. Kendall gave a vivid portrait of the consequent wild chase, as desperate men attempted to bring the animal down. In the recitation of this pursuit Kendall commented on the peculiar topography of the plains surface.

Having said previously that the prairie was "smooth," he now disclosed that in fact it had "prairie rolls" and an "uneven surface"—a microtopography of deceitful "holes of the mole and the field-mouse." Horses were troubled by these holes and lost confidence in their footing. Instead of the smooth sportscommon of his boyhood years, Kendall related, the surface of the Llano was inherently a deceptive surface, where a slight prairie roll might hide one's companion from view, or where an animal burrow could tumble a rider and cripple a horse.[33]

Although Kendall and others had peppered the lone bull with shot, the severely wounded animal eluded their buffalo-chip campfires for that night. While staking out his horse that evening a rattlesnake suddenly struck Kendall above the elbow. Incredibly the fangs failed to penetrate his clothing. Nevertheless it was a terrifying contact with the Llano's wildlife, sending "a cold tremor through the system with the suddenness of an electric shock."[34] A severe thunderstorm also blew up, beginning with heavy drops, then a cold, drenching, depressing rain. The wind "howled and moaned" while endless lightning lit up the prairie, thereby amplifying the following darkness into "a wall of gloom."

Kendall's prose reflected his demoralized feelings as the crossing continued. This was no longer the Grand Prairie, but "the gloomy prairie."[35] On September 6 the starving men located the dying buffalo bull and briefly singed his tough flesh for a welcome meal. The howling of wolves that night in western Deaf Smith County was regarded as a favorable "sign" by some, since they believed that "these animals are seldom found far from woods or settlements."[36] The next morning, September 7, the Sutton-Cooke party thought they saw mounted men in the distance. They rode forward with a flag of truce, but then decided they had been deceived by a drove of wild horses. Around noon to everyone's delight they spied a deep-blue range of mountains far in the west.

Finally the pioneers had reached the escarpment edge of the western Llano Estacado. Happily they descended that day from the "dreary waste" of the Llano into the rough breaks of Trujillo Creek below. On September 8 they reached a large river which they followed to the west. Again they argued over whether this was the Red River. (It was the Canadian.) Kendall was convinced now that a "majority of map-makers" would suffer exceedingly from thirst were they to travel along "their imaginary [Red] river."[37] Again he correctly speculated that the Red River headed in the "high steppe" or the "main western steppe" of the Llano Estacado.[38] Pushing along the Canadian and Gallinas Rivers, the advance guard soon disintegrated from hunger and despair. On September 17 they drew their tattered ranks together and surrendered to a superior force of Mexican soldiers. They were marched off to a bitter captivity.

About 200 of the Texan–Santa Fé pioneers still remained at the forlorn foot of the Llano, including the British agent Thomas Falconer and the American merchant Peter Gallagher. Both of them wrote of dismal days in waiting. Unfortunately, their fate was sealed in the good intentions of the advance column. Well before its September 17 mass surrender, the Sutton-Cooke advance party had encountered a New Mexican named Matías and his three fellow comancheros. These frontiersmen agreed to be good samaritans, to find the main group of Texans, and lead them onward to New Mexico, to Santa Fé. The Mexican traders crossed the Llano with ease—a credit to their undeniable plains-craft—and soon found McLeod and the depressing camp of the remaining pioneers. On September 19 Matías and his companions conducted the Texans to the base of the Llano opposite a *"puerta"* or natural doorway onto the plains in southern Briscoe County.[39]

The next morning, as the Gallagher-Hoyle diary states, they ascended "the mountains about 400 Feet very precipitous, onto the 'Grand Prairie.'"[40] Falconer also used the colloquial "grand prairie" expression, but he noted with greater geographic precision that this was in fact "the Llano Estacado of the New Mexicans," whose escarpment looked, "as if staked from the lower ground, and as if boldly lifted up, or else as if the ground about it had at some former time sunk around it."[41] Once on top McLeod's party found themselves entering an extensive tableland, "stretching as far as the eye could reach." Behind them was one last panoramic view. For the next nine days McLeod's men tramped and rode across this singular tableland.

Falconer noted the grass was green and their horses had good pasturage. But there was a serious shortage of provisions among the men. "No game at this season," the Gallagher-Hoyle diary stated, "except Antelopes and they [are] very shy." To Falconer's Victorian horror the famished men soon turned on and ate a pack of Indian dogs following them. They were lucky in their water supply, however, finding "round basins" or playas. But these elusive waterholes or "small lagoons," in Falconer's phrase, were often hidden from view.[42] Fortunately, the recent storms had replenished the playas or else McLeod's men could have suffered horribly from the seasonal torment of thirst.

Marching westward for days through the "prairie solitude" Falconer and the others reached Tierra Blanca Creek on September 23, 1841. Matías and the comanchero guides undoubtedly called this stretch *Las Escarbadas* or "The Scrapings," as Falconer referred to it as "Rio Escaravedra." The name arose from the practice of digging into the dry streambed to allow generous subsurface water to seep in for collection. Here they were all astonished to find a "vast trail" which deceptively resembled "a great highway and important pass" to their minds.[43] Not far away the next day they came upon most welcome signs:

> But the sight that created the greatest pleasure was the remnant of an old Mexican cart. "Thanks be to God!," said Señor Navarro, "behold the signs of a Christian people!"[44]

As the Gallagher-Hoyle diary noted, they had encountered "an old Mexican camp, frames to dry meat, remains of old carts, &c," a silent testimony to the fact that while the land may have been new to them, it was already an outlier of the New Mexican cultural landscape.

They continued to follow Tierra Blanca westward. Hunting for plums and grapes, Dr. Beall and two other starving men wandered away and were presumably killed promptly by Indians. No one really knew their fate or had the energy to investigate. The interesting playas of the Llano contained a seasonal load of wild fowl that September. On the 25th, however, a sense of despair settled upon the company. "We were a mere *tableau vivant* on a most desolate spot," Falconer dramatically explained.[45] The general depression of spirit was in part keyed to the landscape. As the historian Loomis observed: "They were still on the Llano, and it seemed endless."[46]

Although many of the Texans suspected their New Mexican guides of treachery, Matías and the other comancheros were in fact performing admirably. They warned the pioneers of dry camps ahead, and then successfully led the hungry, exhausted men on September 28 to a *puerta* in Apache Canyon. At sunset they "descended from the Grand Prairie," according to the Gallagher-Hoyle journal. From there the demoralized and ragged group wandered below the Llano flanks to the outlier of Tucumcari Peak. On October 5 Mexican forces confronted and compelled the inglorious surrender of the famished expeditioners at Laguna Colorada. After a brief and traumatic respite, all would march off on a grueling trek to prison and years of captivity in Mexico. A few fortunates like the Englishman Falconer were released early at the insistence of the British government.

The Texan–Santa Fé expedition marked an important turning point in the American perception of the Llano. Prior to 1841 the region was so little known as to constitute a *terra incognita*. What reliable information existed came primarily from Americans like Albert Pike and Josiah Gregg, who were in close contact with Hispanos at New Mexican acculturation centers like Santa Fé. There was no lack of unreliable information, however, as the contemporary maps and sanguine editorial comments attested. But the events of August and September in 1841 would within a few years remove the veil of obscurity from the region for the American and English public. In the journals and reports that emerged, the expressions "Llano Estacado," "Staked Plain," and "Grand Prairie" were applied to the unknown country and received wide publicity.[47] Perhaps the first written mention of "Staked Plain" per se can be found in the 1841 Gallagher-Hoyle diary entry for September 7th: "a vast level prairie as far as the eye could reach without a tree or a shrub—Staked Plain." Did they pick up the name from the accompanying comancheros?

A key imagineer in this discovery process was George Wilkins Kendall. This disciple of Horace Greeley and former eastern newspaperman was more than a publicist; he was also a creator of the Llano. Kendall's "Grand Prairie" was never future farm or pasture land. Rather it was a wild, picturesque landscape: a prose version of a Salvator Rosa painting with American Kiowas instead of Italian *banditti*. In his book he explored the sensationalism of the plains environment and celebrated the romantic agony of the Texan–Santa Fé Expedition. The combination of the two was powerful and created a best-seller. The Scottish reviewer of his work in *Chamber's Edinburgh Journal* praised and commended "Mr. Kendall's spirit-stirring pictures of life in the American deserts."[48]

What kind of spirit-stirring steppe was this, Kendall asked, where horizontal and vertical dimensions played—or preyed—upon the imagination so deeply? At one moment his Llano was a dreary waste, at the next it was an architectural Garden of the Gods. It was an illimitable plain whose featureless mask was surrounded and dissected by featureful chasms, abysses like the Cita Canyons of the Palo Duro country with their strange beauty. Its storms were sublime and its aspect that of infinity. In contrast to a laconic Falconer, Kendall's Romantic bent allowed him to perceive the Grand Prairie in a grand and completely sensational manner.

In this regard, Kendall epitomized the dilemma of Anglo-American exploration of West Texas. His Romanticism was in part a withdrawal from outer to inner experience. On the Llano, he wrote, he felt "as if *in* the world, but not *of* it," as if the monotony and the lack of human signification in the landscape turned the mind inward. He was grasping at metaphors from Romanticism to give himself perspective in a landscape usually without one. But this mental journey from the outward to the inward dimension also marked the transition from perception to conception. In essence Kendall was conceiving the geography of the region as strongly as he was perceiving it.

This transition from perception to conception, however, involved an element of environmental deception. At what point did the intrusion of art and inner experience in exploration deceive others? Clearly Kendall's "boundless prairie" was a Romantic cliché, one meant to convey "the thirst for the infinite" that animated poets and writers of the period.[49] In fact the Llano Estacado had boundaries, was not infinite, and Kendall speculated on them in the excellent map accompanying his book. Was the *Stimmung* or nervous apprehension that he felt there the product of the treeless environment or of his active imagination, or both? Were the avian Siren songs of the Llano canyonlands "uttered but to deceive" (conception), or were the birds more simply marking their territorial imperatives (perception)?

"No work of art," Edmund Burke postulated on the sublime, "can be great but as it deceives." From the perspective of Kendall and Pike the Llano environment was artistic precisely in its ability to deceive. The Stake Prairie's sublimity, Pike argued, arose from "its strange power of deception." It had the Romanesque or chimerical qualities of mirages and beautiful canyon formations. It had the picturesque qualities of scenic overlooks that excited one's admiration. And it had the romantic qualities that synthesized the infinite scene and the melancholic emotions into a state of neurotic suspense. It was, then, one of nature's great artworks: a region that Anglos had rarely encountered before and did not have the vocabulary to do it much justice.

The Texan–Santa Fé Expedition pointed to a geopolitical turning point for the region as well as an aesthetic one. The capture of these Anglo "victims of an enveloping geographical environment," in H. Bailey Carroll's phrase, and their subsequent perceived mistreatment in Mexican prisons mightily whipped up

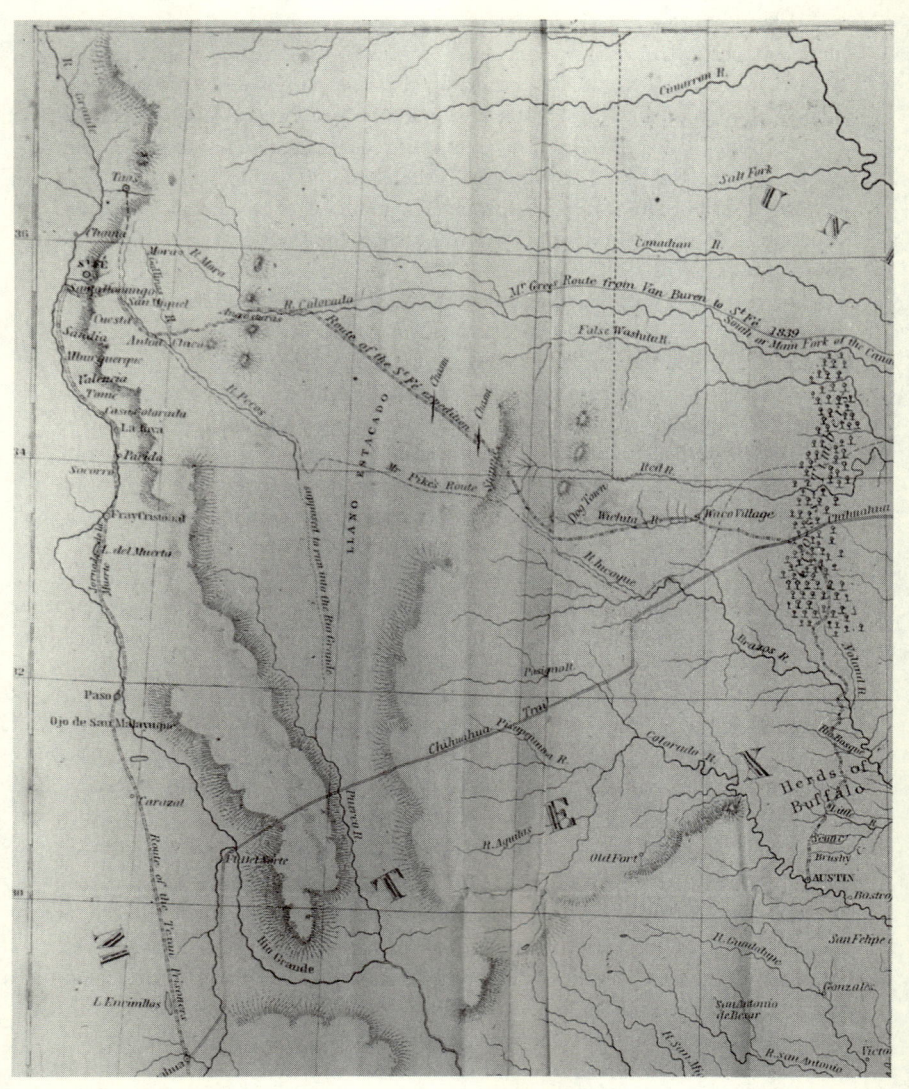

Texas and Part of Mexico & the United States showing the route of the First Santa Fé Expedition (detail), by W. Kemble, 1844. Engraving. From G. W. Kendall, *Narrative of the Texan–Santa Fé Expedition* (New York: Harper & Bros., 1844). Kemble's engraved map reflects limited cartographic knowledge of the Llano Estacado, but significantly includes the western and eastern escarpments and the canyon "chasms." In addition to projecting a crude route for the Texan–Santa Fé expedition, the map also notes the trails of "Mr. Pike" (the romantic poet Albert Pike) and "Mr. Gregg" (Josiah Gregg). *Courtesy the author.*

the indignation of the American public. Angry Texans joined the 1843 Snively Expedition, an ineffectual effort to seek revenge and plunder against Mexican caravans on the Santa Fé Trail. Within a year of publication of Kendall's classic work, the United States and Mexico approached war over the U.S. annexation of the Republic of Texas and the unresolved western boundary issue. The very vagueness of the boundary on the Llano encouraged the arguments. The resulting U.S. intervention and military seizure of the northern part of Mexico swiftly brought the Llano Estacado into the fold of Manifest Destiny. As soon as the power of sword and pen brought the steppeland within United States jurisdiction, the Americans quickly launched an official exploration of its mysteries.

Part Four

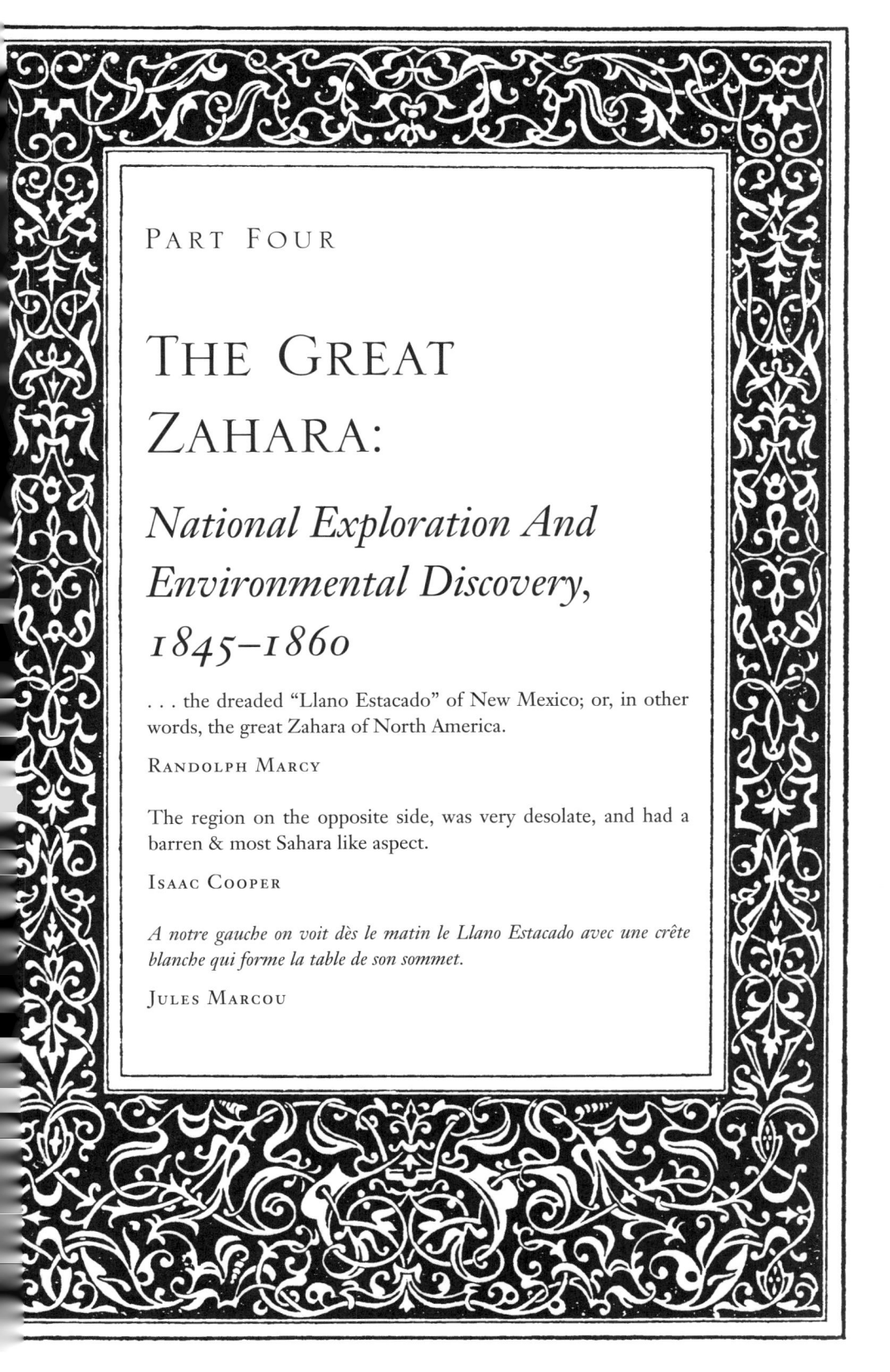

The Great Zahara:

National Exploration And Environmental Discovery, 1845–1860

... the dreaded "Llano Estacado" of New Mexico; or, in other words, the great Zahara of North America.

Randolph Marcy

The region on the opposite side, was very desolate, and had a barren & most Sahara like aspect.

Isaac Cooper

A notre gauche on voit dès le matin le Llano Estacado avec une crête blanche qui forme la table de son sommet.

Jules Marcou

· 19 ·

Prairie Sublime

> The very fact that so little was known about it after centuries of exploration added to its power as a source of sublimity, and it became a challenge not only to man's strength and courage, but also to his imagination.
>
> Chauncey C. Loomis, "The Arctic Sublime"[1]

> They complain that the Plains are flat and bare. Naturally—that is the beauty of them. The scarcity of landmarks, the scale and sweep of the High Plains are what make their sublimity.
>
> Stanley Vestal, *Short Grass Country*[2]

The annexation of Texas by the U.S. Congress on December 29, 1845, closed the first period of discovery on the Llano Estacado for the Americans. Prior to that important date the discovery process was as much a literary one as a scientific and geographic one. It primarily involved peripatetic personages like the poet Albert Pike, the raconteur Alexander Le Grand, the diarist Josiah Gregg, the secret agent Thomas Falconer, and the sensational journalist George Wilkins Kendall. Their written impressions and experiences of the Llano were conditioned in turn by the established socioliterary culture of the age and by their active romantic imaginations. Their initial appropriation of the Llano Estacado was primarily literary or textual rather than physical. It also led to a creation of a profound sense of place, as the remote Llano earned a national reputation as a natural or imagined abode of the Prairie Sublime.

The fact that so little was known about the region only deepened its power and mystery. By 1845 the very name itself conjured up chiaroscuro images of fear and fascination in snug Victorian parlors. Kendall's best-selling book used the mesaland as a vivid tableau for the tragedy of Texan–Santa Fé Expedition, giving the Llano name recognition on both sides of the Atlantic Ocean. As a source of sublimity the region could even be expected to attract exploration. Victorian-era exploration often involved misfits and cultural subversives like Burton and Doughty, drawn to exotic realms of sensation. Indeed, the consequent imagery of the Llano Estacado was often cast in new aesthetic perceptions emerging from the global expansion of "romantic imperialism."[3]

Thus, the Llano's dreadful ordeals, exotic fauna, grotesque canyonland borders, and cosmic sensationalism were all grounded in narrative frameworks which were equally at home in the Arctic ice fields, the Pacific immensities, or the Arabian wastes. In this geography of imagination the Llano Estacado was perceived as a *sublime landscape*, where the notion referred to a refined psychological relationship between the Victorians and Nature.[4] On this vast mesa the very extent of space acquired a haunting presence for Anglo-Americans. The Llano became a symbol of the hot climes, fierce peoples, and bizarre landscapes that thrilled the general public, inviting both fear and awe.

Even if this "Grand Prairie" was alien to the humid American woodland culture, the sensational literature of Victorian discovery had preadapted the public psychologically for this treeless environment. Mary Shelley's *Frankenstein* had thrilled its readers in 1819 with desolate, barren landscapes unknown to civilized society. Shelley's later American lover, Washington Irving, quickly saw the sublimity of the plains when he entered the Far West in 1832. Nineteenth-century literature, art, and poetry all celebrated the new uncovered solitudes. And perhaps the irrational environments being explored in turn affected contemporaneous literature, fostering what the reconstructive critic David Reynolds has called the "American Subversive Style."[5] In contrast to the popular modes—Conventional and Romantic Adventure—the deceitful soul of the Llano Estacado lent itself to a subversive literary style. Would not the phantasmagoric mirages, the frightful solitude, the barren immensity, the refractive loomings, the inquisitorial Indians, the grotesque chasms, and the ever present ravens of this ocean prairie have stimulated the brush of Salvator Rosa or the pen of Edgar Allan Poe? Was not Maj. Alexander Le Grand a consummate confidence man?

Poe liked to insist that beauty must have "some strangeness in its proportion." In late 1846 he was revising an earlier story, "The Landscape Garden." On two rolls of pale blue paper he penned the new story entitled "The Domain of Arnheim."[6] In this classic tale an extraordinarily rich young man, Mr. Ellison, decides to give himself over to landscape gardening in the pursuit of ultimate beauty. But he needs a proper domain to begin. Like other young Americans of his age he toys with the idea of the Pacific South Seas, but this new land is too remote from the company of his fellow man. "I wish the composure but not the depression of solitude," he concludes. After years of travel in North America, and after rejecting a thousand beautiful places, the narrator and Ellison arrive at last at something that entrances even their jaded tastes. It seems like the perfect spot:

> We came at length to an elevated table-land of wonderful fertility and beauty, affording a panoramic prospect very little less in extent than that of Ætna, and, in Ellison's opinion as well as my own, surpassing the far-famed view from that mountain in all the true elements of the picturesque.[7]

Ellison is deeply attracted to this "elevated table-land" with its dizzying panoramas, but ultimately he is forced to reject it because of "the excess of its glory." As an expression of Poe's own aesthetics of the sublime, Ellison's rejection of the perfect tableland is based on its vastness, its spatial "extent":

> The error is obvious. Grandeur in any of its moods, but especially in that of extent, startles, excites—and then fatigues, depresses. For the occasional scene nothing can be better—for the constant view nothing worse. And, in the constant view, the most objectionable phase of grandeur is that of extent; the worse phase of extent, that of distance. It is at war with the sentiment and with the sense of seclusion . . . In looking from the summit of a mountain we cannot help feeling abroad in the world. The heart-sick avoid distant prospects as a pestilence.[8]

In the aesthetical view the grandeur of the Grand Prairie, this extent of the Stake Prairie, first excites the senses, then fatigues and depresses. The constancy of distant views leaves the observer feeling "*abroad*," exposed, vulnerable.

The Anglo-American discovery of the Llano Estacado was quickly placed in a literary context. Reviewers found that its savage experience and novel landscape made good copy for a popular audience. The dashing Irish sportsman-writer "Captain" Mayne Reid used the wild plains to thrill parlor audiences of children, as with his scalp-raising suspense book, *The Boy Hunters; or, Adventures in Search of a White Buffalo*.[9] Reid's 1871 adventure novel, *The Lone Ranche: A Tale of the "Staked Plain,"* was a belated effort that featured a handsome Santa Fé trader from Kentucky and a pretty New Mexican señorita. Against the backdrop of the Llano Estacado, the lovers overcome all obstacles and unite.[10]

But perhaps the most ambitious American writer to avail himself of the invention of the Llano was Charles Wilkins Webber. This impetuous adventurer and novelist employed the Prairie Sublime image to great effect in his fantastic and subversive novel, *Old Hicks, The Guide; or, Adventures in the Camanche Country in Search of a Gold Mine*.[11] Another transplanted Kentuckian, Charles Webber spent some youthful time roaming the Republic of Texas in the late 1830s, soaking up the atmosphere and serving as a Texas Ranger. He eventually became a prolific magazine writer in the teaming barrancas of New York City. Like O. Henry a half-century later, he turned his memories and subversive impressions of Texas into popular stories for a mass audience. Webber was killed in 1856 as a member of the infamous Walker filibuster in Nicaragua, but in 1848 he was a rising young novelist with the publication of *Old Hicks, The Guide*.

Popular in the United States and England, Webber's tale of a Prairie Leatherstocking figure was largely set against a backdrop of 1840s gold fever, misguided love, and scheming lust on the Llano Estacado. The characters are often clichés and the plot meanders as romantic Parisian exiles suffer soap opera woes in the Canadian River Valley and adjacent plains. A cruel and sinister villain, Count Albert, has enlisted an army of local Comanches to help him subject the beautiful heroine, Emilie, to various social indignities and tribulations. With only the peaceable ranger and narrator, Old Hicks, to save the day, there is ample time to devote to regional description.

Indeed, a good deal of volume one is devoted to the guide's ostensible journal entries in search of gold on a trip from the Trinity River of Texas to the upper Canadian River near the New Mexico state line. It was a narrative technique of the time to convert sublime landscape into subversive text, as Poe did so well in his only long work, *The Narrative of Arthur Gordon Pym*. Old Hicks and companions found instead an American precursor to James Hilton's *Shangri La*. They discovered a natural retreat on the Llano, an ecotopia far away from the maddening corruption of all so-called civilization. This retreat was a remote Llano hideaway on the Canadian River that the narrator called "Peaceful Valley." Webber's impressions of the environment were heavily romanticized, even to the point, one critic noted, that his Comanches had become "nature gurus."[12] This worship of nature in *Old Hicks, The Guide* reflected the author's personal fascination with American natural history, an interest nourished by Webber's friendship with John W. Audubon.

The antelope were so tame in Peaceful Valley, this land of natural innocence, that they fearlessly approached armed newcomers, an improbable event for any who have tried to get close to the skittish, alert animals. But Webber's point was not absolute verisimilitude. He used the Llano as a sublime backdrop for a philosophical discussion on the wickedness of man and the goodness of nature. Like the Pacific South Sea islands of Herman Melville, Webber's enchanting, Edenic descriptions of Peaceful Valley on the Canadian River harked back to the persistent pastoral tradition in American and European literature. Webber's Comanches are thus the descendants of Rousseau's Noble Savage and Old Hicks is the heir to Bernardin de Saint-Pierre's Paul and Virginie. Old Hicks's discursive essay, "The Philosophy of Savage Life," partook of a deeply subversive—and deeply American—cult of natural primitivism; indeed, his book was compared favorably by reviewers to *Typee* and *Omoo*. As the critic Henry Nash Smith observed:

> Both Melville and Webber wrote of adventures among primitive peoples in remote parts of the world. Both novelists drew heavily upon their own experiences and cast their narratives in the first person. Both perceived in the simple life of savages values strikingly in con-

trast with the official doctrines of American society, and drew inferences not flattering to refinement, gentility, and civilization.[13]

In this sense the Llano Estacado was a natural realm of innocence, unspoiled by civilization, where the spirit of man could still find the harmonies of a natural life. The wildness of this region could nurture something important—was it freedom?—in the American soul. The Llano was this land of natural innocence in part due to its geographic position between Mexico and the United States; between the demographic press of Mexicans and Americans there were not a lot of "uncivilized" realms left by the late 1840s. It was also a strange environmental realm, a prince of prairies, an ecotopia. Only recently penetrated by the avant garde of civilization—guides, scouts, explorers, fur trappers, and other hardy souls—the upper Canadian was a plausible and attractive locale for the wilder excesses of the Prairie Sublime.

The lower Canadian River already had a literary association with sublimity. A dozen years after the Stephen H. Long Expedition, President Andrew Jackson sent the Stokes Commission to the Indian Territory. This group included three private individuals and writers of distinction: Washington Irving and the Europeans Charles Latrobe and Count Albert-Alexandre de Pourtalès. These writers accompanied the commission on a tour that traversed central Oklahoma, passing through eastern forests until they reached the prairie lands around the North Fork and touched upon the Canadian River itself. Irving thought these plains epitomized the Far West. "An immense extent of grassy, undulating, or as it is termed, rolling country," he wrote, "with here and there a clump of trees, dimly seen in the distance like a ship at sea; the landscape deriving sublimity from its vastness and simplicity."[14] Already the land has claimed a descriptive modifier; to eastern literary tastes the plains are "undulating," but to the locals they are "rolling." Irving also ties the Prairie Sublime to its aesthetic themes of space ("vastness") and innocence ("simplicity"). By 1846 the westward drift of suitable locales for romantic frontiers had moved about 300 miles from Irving's middle Canadian River to Charles Webber's upper Canadian River.[15] The virginity of prairie landscapes was decreasing rapidly.

The heart of *Old Hicks, The Guide* is not its obvious failure as a correspondence between text and landscape. Webber never saw the Peaceful Valley he wrote so lyrically about, while Irving saw his sublime plains on the Canadian River, and he was a better writer as well. Rather, the value of Webber's novel is its suggestion that this new wilderness had the capacity to promote new human thought and feeling. As an environmental or natural history text the book is obviously full of serious shortcomings; as a socioliterary text of the 1840s Prairie Sublime, Webber's subversive novel transcends its signifier.

On this "table-land," "*mesa*," "elevated prairie," "Stake Prairie," "Grand Prairie," one went beyond the limits of the conditioned sensory world of the traditional American woodlands. This vast new realm west of the Mississippi seemed, it was said, to project a form of space-intoxication upon the mind. Sky and ground here conspired to overwhelm the established eastern mind, conditioned as it was to a rich semiotic landscape of constant sign and meaning in established town and field. The alleged aridity of the Llano thrilled readers conditioned to heavy rainfall and snow. As European empires scrambled for exotic colonial landscapes, and doughty explorers fanned out to take their measure, Americans discovered that they also had acquired an empire of romantic inspiration with the newly wrested possessions. The same Victorian exultations of spirit in Algeria, Egypt, Morocco, and South Africa were now available in the Southwest.

On the Llano Estacado there was almost no sign of so-called civilized man, and therefore no conventional meaning. Or there was no meaning that could be readily discerned. Many Americans were content with the Prairie Sublime image of the mesaland, because their own contact with the region—as emigrants, explorers, traders, agents, soldiers, hunters, runaways, surveyors, and scientists—imparted its mystique of place to their self-image as frontiersmen. To cross this great plain was to experience the fear and fascination of the horizontal Prairie Sublime, just as the Rockies or Alps now brought men and women to experience the vertical sublimity of Mountain Glory.[16] Onto the Stake Prairie they projected a psychology of place that linked their dread with their delight, an aesthetic confusion of emotion often expressed and resolved in irony.

Albert Pike thought the monotony of it all turned the mind upon itself, as though the discovery of reality was channeled by the landscape into the process of thought rather than into sensory experience. In this manner the illimitable plain promoted an exultation of the spirit at once terrifying and grand. The landscape was such a perfect blank that one's own thoughts were projected on it. If you feared Indians, the distorted loomings suggested ambush. If you felt tall, the low relief allowed you to feel so. There was a feeling of utter exposure on the Llano Estacado, an existential openness of the Earth's surface. The vastness and simplicity altered the mind. More experienced travelers typically related this feeling of exposure to ocean voyages. On the Stake Prairie or at sea one was exposed to intense sun, fierce storms, optical illusions, and thirst. "All that expands the spirit, yet appalls," explained Byron in *Childe Harold's Pilgrimage* (III, lxii).

The frozen wastes of the Arctic North were a significant realm of the North American sublime for the English. The polar exploits of Capt. James Cook, John Ross, William Edward Parry, George Back, Peter Dease, George Simpson, and others stimulated the Victorian imagination greatly.[17] The sensationalism of the freezing lands and waters was also known to Americans.[18] They too turned out to search for the missing 1845 Franklin Expedition. Matching or imitating the British concern with the Arctic Sublime, however, the Anglo-Americans were now aware of a mimetic realm—the 1840s Prairie Sublime—in the hot elevated plateaus of West Texas.

In both cases the sense of infinite space was profound. Both realms were considered barren expanses, and both would attract explorers looking for ways to cross them, not settle. Consider William Edward Parry's 1821 description of an Arctic landscape, an account that could be substituted easily for the Llano Estacado:

> Not an object was to be seen on which the eye could long rest with pleasure.... The smoke ... and the sound of voices, which ... could be heard at a much greater distance than usual, served now and then to break the silence that reigned round us, a silence far different from that peaceable composure which characterizes the landscape of a cultivated country; it was the deathlike stillness of the most dreary desolation, and the total absence of animated existence.[19]

Like the Arctic immensity the Llano was also an illusive world of novel phenomena. There were similar intense light effects and sound likewise carried over long distances. Both seemed desolate, dreary, devoid of habitation and hearth. Both shared the optical "loomings" of refraction, with the Llano's deceitful soul epitomized by its multiple mirages of lost lakes. In both realms the presence of civilized man seemed intrusive, a direct confrontation with the powers of nature. There was an elemental sensationalism in the experience of each which defied the established life-worlds of those safely back at home. This raw sensationalism of the Llano Estacado appealed to yearning romantic imperialists like Capt. Randolph Marcy, who sought fame in its springs and canyons and who eulogized its seeming desolation.

The feelings of prairie "space-intoxication," to borrow a critical phrase of Marjorie Hope Nicolson,[20] continued well beyond mid-century. But beginning also in 1845 the Anglo-Americans approached the Llano in a qualitatively different manner. In part, the discovery process had ended and the exploration process had begun. This shift of strategy implied a change in perspective and environmental rhetoric. This discursive shift from a romantic to a scientific imagination was part of a larger evaluation and absorption process. Furthermore, after 1846 the Llano was no longer a territorial outland, a borderland "desert" disputed between Texas and Mexico; it was now de facto a part of the United States, and therefore subject to the eventual imperialism of Manifest Destiny. There was certainly a need now for sober inventories of the new possessions. One also needed transport routes across them to accommodate trade, capital, and emigration. Not surprisingly, a new generation of sojourners arrived, explorers connected to the very agency of its appropriation—the U.S. Army. Starting with a rhetoric of Prairie Sublime, they advanced to a scientific imperialism.

Historians call this 1845–1860 period "The Great Reconnaissance."[21] U.S. Army officers and enlisted men, in particular talented men from an invigorated Corps of Topographical Engineers, fanned out across the Southwest to map and explore the new conquests. A number of other specialists, guides, emigrants, boosters, and the like assisted these officials in opening the territories to national attention. A few regions, like California, grew so wildly that businessmen and politicians openly speculated about a transcontinental railroad to link the two coasts. For the Llano Estacado this national exploration impulse meant the arrival of a succession of reconnaissances. Most were connected to the agency of continental exploration, the U.S. Corps of Topographical Engineers. Within a decade talented men like James W. Abert, Randolph Marcy, James Simpson, John Pope, George McClellan, Andrew Belcher Gray, and Amiel Weeks Whipple would penetrate much deeper and more extensively into the Llano's Prairie Sublime.

They also brought to their expeditions an increasingly institutionalized way of looking at the environment, one relying less on the private reminiscences, projected adventures, or thrilling tales of a single author. They relied more on the assembly of specialized government teams, extensive progress reports, reputable scientific analyses of field specimens, heavy infusions of Congressional funding, detailed surveys and studies, up-to-date cartography, and more artistic illustrations copied from life. It was a notable effort to incorporate this portion of the Southwest into accepted science. In particular, the systematic and geographical work of Baron Alexander von Humboldt inspired a new generation of Americans, much as the poetry of Byron had inspired another.

The culmination of this grand new rhetoric of exploration occurred for the Llano Estacado with the expensive 1850s publication of the *Reports of Explorations and Surveys, to Ascertain the Most Practical and Economical Route for a Railroad from the Mississippi River to the Pacific Ocean*, a massive thirteen-volume compendium usually abbreviated as the *Pacific Railroad Surveys*. Of the four reconnaissances in this massive feasibility study, fully half examined or touched upon the Llano Estacado environment. Both the 32nd parallel survey and the 35th parallel survey measured the Llano with an eye to a transcontinental railroad. It was a sensible project to link the United States together at the very time others were concluding the nation was a dangerously divided house. Already the tensions between the industrializing North and the agrarian, slaveholding South had divided the Llano, creating an arbitrary geometric boundary between the slavery of Texas and the hard won tradition of free soil in New Mexico.

·20·

Desert Prairie

By September 2 they had penetrated Comanche territory on the northern edge of the Llano Estacado which stretched from New Mexico into West Texas. From that point on, the Indians were dangerous and unpredictable.

William H. Goetzmann[1]

In the winter of 1845 the dashing, overconfident Capt. John C. Frémont was ordered into the field, among other things to survey the Red River. At Bent's Fort, Frémont divided his group of U.S. Army explorers, sending the young Lt. James W. Abert and a detachment southward to the Canadian River Valley. They would pursue the assigned but mundane tactical reconnaissance, while Frémont took the better scientific instruments and continued westward to California and glorious humiliation. Lieutenant Abert was an inspired choice. A recent West Point graduate with a natural facility for drawing (nourished at West Point by Robert Weir and Seth Eastman), the young Abert was transferred to the Corps of Topographical Engineers, then commanded by his respected father, Col. John J. Abert. As the journal of his 1845 Canadian River Reconnaissance demonstrated, Lt. James W. Abert was a patient explorer with an keen eye for detail.[2] He was also quite brave, since his return route would take the party directly through dreaded Comanche territory.

Abert's party of thirty-three men crossed Raton Pass, followed the river south, and reached the "Grand Canyon" of the upper Canadian gorge at El Vado de Piedras in late August 1845. The deep chasm of this upper drainage made an impressive obstacle, one which Abert's men largely side-stepped by keeping to the plains and straddling the drainage between the "Grand Canyon" and the "*Arroyo de los Utas*" (or Ute Creek) to the east. Earlier accounts apparently greatly exaggerated the depth of this gorge. Expecting to find an immense chasm some 1,500 feet deep, a curious Lieutenant Peck and his escort rode along a spit of plain, dismounted, and scrambled down to a rocky vantage point. From there Peck and his men studied the steep-walled canyon below, only 250 feet deep contrary to "exaggerated accounts"; but, the "Grand Canyon was still sufficiently deep to excite our admiration."[3] Winding its sinuous way along the bottom from bluff to bluff, the Canadian river below watered a "smiling valley."

The panorama called for a romantic Victorian pose and Peck obliged. Eventually "a detached rock started a deer, and . . . broke in upon the dream in which I was indulging on the unbroken solitude of the scene before me."[4] Another member of the expedition, Isaac Cooper, later recorded that the lone silence of this "wild & dreary" region was broken only by the echoing screams of eagles. Whatever the morality of the impending U.S. military conquest of the Southwest, Cooper thought it was eminently a "Mexican landscape, peculiarly appropriate to the hot, barren & dismal desart [sic] which surrounded it."[5] Along the way Lieutenant Abert gathered, recorded, and appropriated the Spanish-American toponyms of the new country. Their descriptive words gave romantic expression to this "Mexican landscape."

Although Abert did not accompany Peck on his side excursion, he did draw a significant conclusion from the latter's description of the canyon gorge. Twice in his journal James W. Abert recorded his on-the-spot understanding for the origin of the mysterious name "Canadian." The name had needed justification ever since the 1820 Stephen H. Long Expedition merely noted the presence of the "Canadian," leaving it to the gentle reader to figure out the etymology. There was even another, older, and traditional name—Rio Colorado—for this picturesque river carving its way down through the sandstone strata. Like the best of the newcomers, Abert was in search of truth. For Abert this "Grand Canyon" country was characterized by its manifest *cañada* features: steep-walled, tributary canyons, natural corridors familiar to the local New Mexican herders and traders. The connection of language to landscape was clear: the river that carved out the "great canyon" was the river "from which is derived the name Canada, or Canadian river."[6]

Off in the distance on September 1, 1845, Abert could see "the beautiful valley of the Canadian spread out, covered with scattering 'buttes.'" A wild bunch of mustangs animated the charming vista. On September 2 the reconnaissance party descended to the junction of Ute Creek with the main river. Abert now noted the distinctive, reddish brown coloration of the river waters, imparted by its erosional work in the cañadas of the rough country upstream:

> Its waters are colored, like its tributaries, and have thereby acquired the name of "Rio Colorado" from the Spaniards, and "Goo-al-pa" from the Indians. The name Canadian, however, is retained as expressive of the nature of the channel through which it flows.[7]

As the editor John Galvin noted in his 1970 edition of the journal, Abert's original manuscript read "Cañada, or Cañadian" with the all-important tilde attached to the toponym. Even the official map of the 1845 Abert-Peck exploration shows the appearance of a tilde in the two instances of "Cañadian River."

In the form of "Canada" though, the printer's missing tilde allowed the revisionist historian Joseph B. Thoburn to construct in 1928 an imaginative theory linking the name "Canadian" to French-Canadian fur trappers on the river in the 1740's, presumably the Mallet brothers. In spite of much evidence to the contrary, this implausible linkage continues, as the historian Beryl Roper recently noted, to be "the most widely accepted idea, so far as encyclopedias, dictionaries of place names, and similar reference works are concerned."[8] Roper's own analysis broadens the connotations to include the nuances of the traditional Spanish "sheepwalk" or *cañada*, and the possible presence of much *caña* or canefields on the lower stretches of the river. Nevertheless, Roper's determined analysis tends to support an inherent geomorphological interpretation: "it would be hard to think of a more superbly appropriate name for the river which divides the northern and southern Great Plains than *Cañada*, or its amplified form, *Cañadon*, meaning the really big or deep *cañada*."[9]

A reasonable Anglicization of *Cañadon* is, of course, Abert's "Cañadian."[10] While a government printer short of a Spanish tilde in the mid-1840s may have contributed to the popular notion of a French-Canadian fur-trapper connection, surely this orthographic and geographic illusion should be put largely to rest.[11] That is, the distinctive environmental awareness by southwestern locals of this river is clearly at home with the nature and character of a *cañada*-esque landscape, whether it refers to *cañada* either as "sheepwalk" or as "box canyon." Both meanings of *cañada* share an underlying and elegant spatial connotation of an *enclosed pathway*. The Meseta *cañadas* of Spain led from the cold mountains to the warm plains. So did the Canadian Valley, an analogous route for roving sheepherders entering present-day San Miguel County.

Historically and perhaps officially this river was still the "Rio Colorado" for bureaucratic purposes. Pablo Montoya's 1824 land grant petition referred to his stretch of it as *El Rio Colorado del Rincón*, an old and very respectable name with the qualifier *rincón* signifying the large basin and its cul-de-sac or corner canyons. Hardly anyone then alive could recall, much less have any reason to commemorate, a few French-Canadian voyageurs like the Mallet brothers who traveled the river in the 1740s. But Lt. James Abert, like Long before him, had an American romantic's penchant for picturesque local expression. His image of "Cañada, or Cañadian" may well reflect a personal acquaintance with a localized Spanish-American metaphor, one drawing a simple and analogous environmental relationship between the land and frontier language.

Edging down from mountain homes into the Canadian Gorge after 1800, the Spanish-American pioneers had brought new colloquial place-names in their transhumant push toward the eastern horizon. The steep-walled, sandstone *cañadas* carved in this eastern watershed possibly suggested the name "Rio Cañadon" for the upper stretch, a colloquialism incidentally adopted by Long in 1820 and widely diffused by later Anglos in the Mexican trade. At least in the form of "Canadian River" the merchant caravans avoided the old mistranslated confusion of Rio Colorado (Vermilion River) with the "Red River" (Rio Rojo) of Natchitoches. With the tilde dropped, converting one letter of the Spanish alphabet into another, and the pronunciation adapted to the English tongue, thus appeared the mysterious Canadian River—with its later legions of French Canadian fur-trappers—and thus disappeared the historic Rio Colorado del Rincón. The 1827 Sibley survey of a wagon road from Arkansas to Taos, New Mexico, for instance, noted on its map the "Cannadian River" while its report carefully described that the river "commonly called the 'Rio Colorado'" was "now well ascertained to be the main branch of The Canadian."[12] As for the international boundary of the Red River of Louisiana, "none of its sources" were to be found "in the great Range of the shining mountains [Rocky Mountains] as has been supposed." They knew that "The Canadian" led to Santa Fé, but the sources of the Red River, like those of the Nile River, were still unknown and in doubt.

At the "Spanish Crossing," near the junction of Ute Creek with the main river, the Abert expedition picked up the regular Comanchero Road heading east down the valley. Their wagons toiled eastward along the Canadian River in late summer in a trek reminiscent of Major Long's two decades before. They encountered the usual difficulties with the fatiguing Canadian sandhills. Near the present Texas–New Mexico border a preparatory campfire spread out of control on September 3, 1845. Fed by strong winds the crackling flames roared off in the night to consume the adjacent plains. These racing flames created for the Americans a fascinating "scene of grand sublimity."[13] Like Long, Lieutenant Abert and his men clung to the river valley floor despite its rough going for their mule-drawn wagons.

Abert's journal recorded an abundance of plant and animal communities along the Canadian River. He clearly had more (if sometimes flawed) botanical knowledge than any previous commander in the region, a reflection perhaps of the better academic training this new generation of explorers could call upon. His detailed account of verdant tributary creeks revealed an autumnal landscape of great beauty. Masses of brilliant cardinal flowers outlined one stream. Beds of tall cane (Spanish *caña*), wild ginger, arrowhead, and "white lotus" wound along other wetland courses of the Llano drainage streams. There were tasty plums and grapes, fragrant buttonwood brush, cottonwoods, hackberry and mesquite groves, cactus and yucca, and such "multitudes of yellow flowering plants" that one was reminded of an "immense flower garden." Cloaked in flowers, scented by fragrant shrubs, and with the sound of innumerable springs and tributaries pouring from the escarpment, the Canadian River Valley was a beautiful wilderness. While in places the valley was quite sandy with drifts and small dune fields, it nevertheless "appeared fertile" to his eye.[14]

There were also the annoying species. Prickly sandburrs irritated everyone on the Comanchero Road. Various spinescent cacti required careful footwork, although the Opuntia fruits from the sampled prickly-pears had a mingled flavor of "the raspberry and water-melon." Abert specifically mentioned the presence of *Melia azedarach* or the chinaberry tree.[15] It would be most surprising to find this tree, native to India, as an "extensive grove" on the Canadian by 1845. Perhaps his Eastern coursework and training misled him into confusing this foreign species with the mature local soapberries or "wild china" (*Sapindus drummondii*), which bear yellow fruit similar to the "Pride of India."[16] Abert tasted the fruit and pronounced it uncommonly disagreeable, no doubt due to the poisonous chemical saponin, used as a folk remedy and to raise a sudsy lather.

There was less to this northern border of the Llano Estacado than romantic cliffs and pretty autumnal flowers, however. Although he appreciated the "extraordinary brightness of a prairie sky," Abert's journal often used conventional expressions of disregard like "desolate desert," "barren waste," "trackless wilds," "great desert," and "sandy waste" to describe stretches of the plains and riverland. "The high and dry table lands," he noted with an eye to botany, "were covered with but a few scattered plants, and were altogether desert-like."[17] Now well within Comanche and Kiowa territory, the expedition began a series of encounters with these potentially lethal bands. But contrary to all "preconceived notions" derived from "popular writers of the day," Abert found the Kiowa unusually fond of frolic, laughing and joking continually to the explorers' astonishment.

By mid-September Abert and his men had followed the great northeast curve of the Canadian. Along the way they paused to admire "Pillar Rock," gathered samples from the gorgeous Alibates flint deposits or "Agate Bluffs,"[18] and noted the glistening gypsum outcroppings of the Llano. Turkeys and other wildlife were more abundant as they proceeded downstream or eastward. On September 15 an Indian friend introduced Abert to several colorful "Comancheeros," as he called the traders. The next day, however, in accordance with instructions, they left the Canadian Valley to proceed overland across the "desolate blackness" of a fire-burned Llano, toward the head of the Washita River. This part of this reconnaissance would take them away from the friendly riverine border and place them upon the vast plain they had preferred to avoid if at all possible.

"September 17.—This is the day," Abert wrote, "which we shall look back upon in our wanderings as the day of anxiety."[19] Leaving the labyrinthine ravines of Red Deer Creek, they struck south and entered upon "the famous table-land known to the Spaniards as 'el Llano Estacado,' the most extensive and continuous of the plains lying in the desert country."[20] Abert's description of their jaunt across this "dry and level tableau" was a classic of environmental perception. The very atmosphere of the Llano Estacado seemed to convey a deceptive, distorting nature:

The sun was pouring down heat as heavy clouds do rain; and, as it rebounds from the surface of the [playa] pools, so did the heat appear to rebound from the extended level of the prairie. These reverberations gave rise to the phenomena commonly termed mirage, so often observed in the desert, where every object appears distorted, and generally in motion. The purity of the atmosphere, the looming, as sailors term it, and the numerous ascending currents of heated air, contribute to produce this effect; so that you often see a tuft of grass dancing on the horizon, a tree, or bush, whilst you are ready to mistake a rabbit bounding across your path for a deer, or perhaps an elk.[21]

Abert's description of their jaunt from Red Deer Creek to the North Fork of the Red River (which he mistakenly thought was the Washita) reflected unusual anxiety. That is, there was a self-conscious, literary quality to his account that makes it seem a bit too dramatic, as if travel on the Llano had been preconceived to be an encounter with dreadfulness. "Our tongues seemed to cleave to the roofs of our mouths, and our throats were parched with dryness," he said.[22] Jokes and laughter died away until they were marching in "dead silence." Campfire tales of "treachery, surprise, and massacre" fed their vivid imaginations. A sense of depression "akin to fear" was evidently contagious. Apparently a mass hallucination of hostile Indians also affected them:

An Indian, mounted, now appeared, and as he swept along the horizon, looked a very giant; another and another burst upon our view, on every side, which led us to believe that we were surrounded.... Could it be possible that the wily savage had laid a plan to decoy us upon this broad desert, rich in the bloody legends of travellers, but to make us an easy prey?[23]

They traveled for hours in this paranoid "state of suspense" until reaching the breaks of the North Fork, where their gloomy despair gave way to exuberant song and laughter. Abert thought it remarkable that their mood could be so easily manipulated by the environment during that day. Isaac Cooper's unpretentious journal confirmed, however, that indeed they were troubled by the illusive nature of the Llano:

The dancing rays of heat reflecting from the plain, frequently deceived us, and the unusual appearance of some[thing] tall seen through them, influenced us with the idea of Indians, and so much so, that our banner, a white mosquito bar, was reared & waved aloft upon a tent pole & borne in advance of the Caravan, in order to inform all strangers around of our pacific intention.[24]

Thus it was that the U.S. Army rode across the empty plain bearing a white flag of mosquito netting, a banner more of paranoia than peace. Cooper's and Abert's accounts suggest that the expeditioners regarded their experience of the Llano Estacado as a formidable "desart" encounter, despite the fact that they were traveling in the fairly well-watered northeast corner. Cooper openly referred to their *mulada* expedition as a "caravan," while the desolate plain now behind them, "had a barren & most Sahara like aspect."[25] Abert of course spoke of "this broad desert" and its unnamed "bloody legends" almost as a French legionnaire might have spoken of Algeria. Both also hated the sand and referred to their transport difficulties through the numerous sandhills of the Canadian Valley and the eastern breaks. "The strong wind heaps the sand upon the banks," Abert observed, "forming constantly changing hillocks, and often advancing inward like the dunes on the seacoast."[26]

Lieutenant Abert, Isaac Cooper, and the others traveled down the North Fork, saw the Antelope Buttes, passed on through Oklahoma, and eventually reached their destination of Fort Gibson. Abert's Canadian River Reconnaissance did not solve the vexing Red River origin problem, but it was a successful venture in many ways. His journal and sketches provided a rare glimpse into the Kiowa lifeway, and his natural history observations constituted a major text on the ecology of the northern Llano. Furthermore, when he and Lieutenant Peck entered on the "famous tableland" on September 17, they became the first U.S. Army command to directly experience this strange desert prairie.

Four years later the Corps of Topographical Engineers authorized a second reconnaissance of the Llano Estacado. After the discovery of gold in California, frontier Arkansas towns quickly advertised their overland links to the Spanish Southwest. Several thousand forty-niners accordingly wanted to take advantage of the Canadian River trails pioneered by Josiah Gregg in 1839–1840.[27] In April of 1849 the largest group of these emigrants, the Fort Smith Company, left Arkansas for California. Accompanying the 479 people, 75 wagons, and 500 mules was a strong military escort under the command of a Capt. Randolph B. Marcy.

Captain Marcy was a seasoned and dutiful officer. At age thirty-seven he had almost two decades of military service behind him, including difficult stints in the Wisconsin wilderness and the recent Mexican War. His 5th Infantry and 1st Dragoon detachment provided necessary firepower for the large emigrant wagon train as far as Santa Fé. Attached to Marcy's command was an equally remarkable officer, Lt. James H. Simpson of the Corps of Topographical Engineers. Simpson and his detachment were to join Marcy's men in surveying a wagon road for a proposed Ft. Smith–Santa Fé Trail. Already both the U.S. War Department and frontier mercantile capitalists were proposing a national road from the East to the new Pacific empire. The 1840 southern route of Josiah Gregg looked like a promising candidate to the residents of the western Arkansas frontier.[28]

Marcy left Ft. Smith in April 1849. On the way west he was fortunate to obtain Black Beaver as a guide. This intrepid Delaware Indian had moved—or been forced—westward into the Canadian River of Oklahoma. Black Beaver knew the plains environment on the upper Canadian River ahead from his own travels. Equally important, he knew how to communicate with the tribes that roamed over the adjacent plains. His services would be invaluable.

By June 1 Marcy and the hundreds of Fort Smith Company emigrants had reached the northeastern breaks of the Llano. They followed the watershed divide between the Washita and Canadian Rivers. But while Gregg's route at this point had hugged the Canadian, Marcy's route crossed Red Deer Creek and then loosely headed the many tributary creeks dissecting the northern Llano.[29] In this manner the caravan avoided the cumbersome Canadian River sandhills, but still had adequate water from the Llano's tributary springs. On June 9 they drew near the river and encountered "Gregg's trace," which they followed for some time.

But Marcy soon chose to ignore the level southward course of Gregg's trail,[30] opting instead for the upper Llano breaks where he felt some wood and spring water would be available. By June 13, 1849, they were traveling directly under the bluffs of the Llano Estacado. With his military perspective, Marcy thought these bluffs near Sierrita de la Cruz presented "the appearance of the walls of fortifications, with glacis revetted with turf."[31] For the past few days they had availed themselves of wild fruits, mesquite timber in the ravines, and good spring water. Marcy was not a botanist like Abert, but he did fancy that day a "beautiful species of cactus" in these breaks, whose numerous pink blossoms made "the desert prairie look like a flower-garden."[32]

He was also fascinated by the enormous "dog-town" they were passing through. A specimen was captured, which he examined trying to figure out why anyone would call it a prairie dog. Marcy thought it a timid animal unless irritated, whereupon it could bite severely, "as one of our young gentlemen can testify." He further satisfied himself that rattlesnakes using the burrows were, in fact, predators:

> At first I was doubtful whether this domestic arrangement [of the rattlesnake] was in accordance with the wishes of the owner of the premises [i.e., the prairie dogs], but, a short time since, I was satisfied no such friendly relations existed between them, for, on killing a rattlesnake at one of the dog-holes, it was found that he had swallowed a young dog.[33]

This observation was classic Marcy nature writing, relying on genteel Victorian personification in explaining the zoology.

The next day, June 14, proved to be most memorable. With progress blocked by a northern spur of the great plain, Marcy led everyone up onto the "summit" of the Llano. For about twenty-eight miles the hundreds of emigrants and their military escort trudged across the flatland immensity near Adrian, Texas, before descending into another of the western drainage creeks. Marcy's comments on this stretch have become immortalized:

> When we were upon the high table land, a view presented itself as boundless as the ocean. Not a tree, shrub, or any other object, either animate or inanimate, relieved the dreary monotony of the prospect; it was a vast, illimitable expanse of desert prairie—the dreaded "Llano Estacado" of New Mexico; or, in other words, the great Zahara of North America. It is a region almost as vast and trackless as the ocean—a land where no man, either savage or civilized, permanently abides; it spreads forth into a treeless, desolate waste of uninhabited solitude, which always has been, and must continue, uninhabited forever; even the savages dare not venture to cross it except at two or three places, where they know water can be found.[34]

This quote became famous precisely because of its bold rendering of the Prairie Sublime. Like William Edward Parry's portrait of the Arctic, Marcy paints us a word picture of exceptional desolation and solitude. His hyperbolic cries of "monotony," "inanimate," "boundless," "illimitable," "dreaded," "savage," "uninhabited solitude," and so on constitute a deliberate, literary act of creating awe. It is also a metonymic description. This is not just *a* desert prairie, it is *the* desert prairie: the Great Zahara of North America itself. Strictly speaking, Marcy's description is also a wild overstatement, but one quite characteristic of his florid style. The Llano was not actually uninhabitable, inanimate, entirely treeless, or necessarily dreary.

By June 28, 1849, Marcy and the gold-fevered migrants reached Santa Fé without mishap. According to one estimate about 3,000 people traveled along their Canadian River route by the end of that year. Some emigrants pronounced it "the worst in the world" and denounced the Arkansas boosters as "a gang of liars."[35] After resting his oxen and mules Marcy boldly decided to journey back by a new route. He engaged "Manuel el Comanche," Josiah Gregg's old guide from San Miguel. Descending the Rio Grande to Doña Ana (where Cooke's California road led westward), Marcy hoped to blaze a new trail eastward from Doña Ana to Fort Smith. By September 16 his eighty-odd men had advanced to the Pecos River. Here, the guide Manuel insisted that they descend the Pecos for some sixty more miles, "as no man (not even an Indian) ever undertakes to cross the 'Llano Estacado' opposite here."[36] Marcy chose to follow this sage advice. On September 21, the expedition forded the Pecos River at "Emigrant Crossing" and headed northeast into unknown country.

Although Randolph Marcy was later acclaimed for his northern and eastern Llano travels, this southern sojourn was actually a more groundbreaking exploration. The Canadian River frontier was generally well known by the fall of 1849 (and known by the Spanish since Zaldivar and Juan de Oñate's journeys over two centuries before), but the Americans knew almost nothing about the southern portion of the Llano Estacado. As Marcy's eighteen-wagon party plodded northeast, on September 25 they encountered an "ocean of sand" that made them pause.

They had in fact reached the line of enormous Pleistocene sands piled against the southern flank of the escarpment. "These hills or mounds, present a most singular and anomalous feature in the geology of the prairies," Marcy noted in his report.[37] He sent Lt. Sackett to explore these tall "white sand hills," now called the Monahans Sandhills. Sackett sought a passage to the south but found none. With little choice Marcy followed his guide's advice about a course directly through the dunes. Fortunately Manuel's suggestions were excellent, and Marcy found—to his great surprise and relief—abundant water at scattered ponds within the dunes.

On September 29 they climbed in cheerless silence onto the Llano by following the plainly marked ribbon of horse trails called the Comanche War Trail. They worried again about finding water, but scouts soon reported a good pond ahead. Marcy was pleased to discover an availability of water in this dune-ridden, desert prairie region; but, some of his formal comments tended to suggest a permanency in the supply that later travelers would not always find. Thus, "judging from present appearance," he wrote, "there will always be water found, except in the dryest season."[38]

What he did not fully acknowledge was that the "driest season" was a variable occurrence on the Llano.[39] What he wanted to realize desperately was a successful new trail from Doña Ana to Fort Smith, including adequate water en route. Marcy contracted dysentery at this point. Some of the Llano waterholes may have been exposed to new pathogens. He now traveled supine in one of the wagons, making periodic stops as nature demanded, while the expedition jolted along just south of present-day Midland, Texas. They finally reached their destination and made camp at a "small lake."

This three-foot deep lake was Mustang Springs, or "Mustang pond," as Randolph Marcy called it. This toponym arose from the numerous wild-horse trails leading to it. He judged that this small lake was a permanent and important waterhole from several environmental considerations. First, the size and presence of rushes (tules) indicated reliability to him. Second, mustangs required water daily and remained only where it was available year round. A second pond was discovered nearby. The explorers signified its location by a stake in the road with written directions to it, as "there is much sameness in the aspect of the prairies upon the Llano Estacado, [so that] persons might pass this place without finding the water," Marcy wrote.[40]

They pushed on northeast to reach the "Laguna" of Salt Lake on present-day Sulphur Springs Creek by the evening of October 1. Marcy discovered a small lake of "slightly sulphurous" water there. Small mesquite brush provided the only available wood for their camp. The next morning his party traveled eight miles, then descended the level plain to reach eventually an enormous spring. Marcy named this large Llano discharge spring the "Big Spring," a name still carried by a proud West Texas community on the spot.[41] The abundant remains of nearby Indian lodges indicated that this Llano springland was a favorite resort for the Comanche. From "Big Spring" Marcy's detachment worked their way across the Colorado and Brazos River tributaries. By the late winter he had returned to his quarters at Fort Smith.

Marcy was not as artistic as Abert, or as astute as Simpson, but he was stalwart, commonsensical, and determined in his explorations. He had made a reconnaissance over an amazing 2,000 miles of new territory in the Southwest, covering both the northern and the (virtually unknown) southern Llano Estacado. Newspapers began to pick up on his exploits, much to his satisfaction. More significant perhaps was his strategic recommendation that the southern route was eminently suited for a transcontinental railroad. Indeed, "the surface of the earth is so perfectly firm and smooth," he wrote, "that it would appear to have been designed by the Great Architect of the Universe for a railroad."[42] That statement proved to be a prophetic discourse on the Southern Pacific Railroad of the later nineteenth century.

Together the travels of Abert, Simpson, and Marcy depict the Llano as a classic "desert prairie." Neither Abert's pedantry nor Marcy's parlor prose attempted to disguise a general antipathy to the dreaded region. Their Llano was a vast expanse of mirages, sand, scarce game, "bloody legends," and "uninhabited solitude." Dominating this blinding vision of a Great Zahara was the unmitigating image of aridity. The sunlit land was simply too barren and dry to accommodate civilized man. In this sense the Llano was the very antithesis of the boundless ocean with which it was often compared. Its overwhelming presence was perceived to be an absence—of rivers, of lakes, of streams, of trees, of wild game, and of course, of people.

· 21 ·

RED RIVER
EXPEDITION

> ... nothing but one vast, dreary, and monotonous waste of barren solitude. It is an ocean of desert prairie, where the voice of man is seldom heard, and where no living being permanently resides.
>
> RANDOLPH MARCY

Legally the Llano Estacado became a part of the United States with the conclusion of the Treaty of Guadalupe Hidalgo early in 1849. President James K. Polk was unhappy with the treaty, however, and soon sacked his personal envoy in Mexico. Congress was even less pleased. Many New England politicians believed that the war had commenced unconstitutionally, seizing territory much as the crudest imperialistic power would have done. They were also afraid of the expansionist plans of the loathsome slavery interests in the South. Equally troublesome was the boundary question between the territory of New Mexico and the impecunious cause of the war—the new state of Texas. On the one hand Texans were agitating to acquire Santa Fé for their state, whereas on the other hand New Mexicans were vociferous about staying out of Texas over the slavery issue. Various eastern schemes to carve up Texas and New Mexico were considered before Sen. James A. Pearce finally conjured in August 1850 a fantastic, gerrymandered, compromise boundary that somehow won the approval of Congress. A notable feature of the compromise-state profile was the linear 103rd meridian of the western Panhandle and South Plains, a straight-line boundary that slashed the western one-fourth of the Llano from the eastern three-fourths. The line still divides the Llano, a reminder of a time when the United States was a house divided.

Marcy's 1849 reconnaissance quickly led to further expeditions to open up trails across West Texas.[1] Lt. Nathaniel Michler of the Topographical Engineers retraced the Marcy Trail in reverse across the southern Llano Estacado in December 1849, noting the objectionable sandhills and lack of wood, but otherwise being favorably impressed with the ease of travel on the route. Michler thought the white sand hills resembled "a perfect miniature Alps ...summit after summit spreading out in every direction...nothing but sand piled upon sand." But his "greatest surprise" was finding large waterholes fringed with willow trees amid the dunes at the base of the Llano.[2] Within a few years hundreds of emigrants would use this trail on their way from Arkansas to El Paso and points west. For several years after 1849, Captain Marcy was preoccupied with minor expeditions and establishing new forts to protect these east and west trails. But in the winter of 1852 he grew restive about a fundamental geographic mystery: the origin of the Red River.

He thought it remarkable that one of the largest and most important rivers was so unknown, "no white man having ever ascended the stream to its sources."[3] The Upper Red River area was still considered by the mid-nineteenth century a *terra incognita*, although solid speculation by Josiah Gregg and George Wilkins Kendall had pointed to its logical origin in the eastern Llano Estacado. On March 5, 1852, Randolph Marcy received approval from Congress to organize an expedition to resolve this vexing question of geography. Like Burton and Speke or Mungo Park, Marcy sought to resolve the unknown source of a great river.

His subsequent 1852 Red River Expedition would be the most thorough scientific study of the Llano Estacado then to date. Marcy was fortunate to have several officers and men of distinction accompany the expedition, including Bvt. Capt. George B. McClellan (who ran for president against Abraham Lincoln a dozen years later), Dr. George G. Shumard, and the adventurous civilian J. R. Suydam. Over the course of almost three months, from May 2 to July 28, 1852, this sixty-six-man expedition reached and ascended the Red River to explore the tributary canyons and plains of the northeastern Llano. In the process they collected a large amount of botanical, zoological, geological, and paleontological data for processing back east. Scientists such as Spencer F. Baird and C. Girard of the Smithsonian Institution then examined the collected specimens and wrote reports. In 1853, these data, two folding maps, and Marcy's lengthy report appeared in a Senate version (with interesting lithographic illustrations by Ackerman of New York) as *Exploration of the Red River of Louisiana, in the Year 1852 . . . With Reports on the Natural History of the Country, and Numerous Illustrations*.

As the expedition wound its way west toward the unknown source of the Red River, Marcy's report reflected a qualitative difference between this and earlier expeditions. Previous sojourners had been prone, for example, to name landscape features according to the environmental attributes of hunting (Panther Creek, Chicken Creek, Antelope Creek), or appearance (Spring

Creek, Bluff Creek, Big Spring), or prior claim (Cerro Tucumcari, Trujillo Creek, Arroyo Amarillo). Although such linguistic appropriation certainly continued, there were also fresh perceptual influences reflecting the expedition's emphasis on natural history. Marcy's report thus reflected a scientific discourse, a rhetoric grounded in the objectifying and empirical systematizing of universal knowledge. In the discourse of discovery in the American Southwest, European Romanticism was giving way to European natural history as epitomized by Alexander von Humboldt.

"Loess creek," for example, was named for the occurrence of shells of *Pupa muscorum*, *succiena elongata*, and *Helix plebeium* in a grayish loam, "similar to the loess found upon the Rhine."[4] A day's march below the Llano bluffs was now noted as passing over "light-colored calcareous sandstone, covered with a drift of quartz and scoria."[5] Picturesque streamside bluffs were now de-romanticized into "friable red sandstone, overlaid with a stratum of coarse gypsum, with a subjacent stratum of bright red clay, interstratified with seams of gypsum."[6]

To be sure Marcy's report continued to reflect the straightforward environmental perceptions of Anglo pioneers. A good freshwater creek in the "salt desert" east of the Llano was named Sweetwater Creek, for instance. Another creek evinced signs of heavy Indian usage and became Kioway Creek. Marcy was also aware that his Delaware guides and scouts perceived the environment in an unusually careful manner. They appeared to see signs of great meaning where he saw almost nothing and vice versa. Marcy marveled at their abilities to read the text of the trail. "These faculties appear to be intuitive," he wrote, "and confined exclusively to the Indian."[7] As an example he mentioned finding a bear-track, which an astute Delaware explained was formed as the result of wind-blown grass creating the deceptive appearance. Because of their "wonderful powers of judging of country," Marcy recommended the use of native auxiliaries in future operations against the prairie tribes. Their regional skills in environmental perception were "almost indispensable."

By mid-June the expedition had entered the Llano to the headwaters of the North Fork of the Red River. Marcy had admired the glistening gypsum bluffs of the country now behind them. New York lithographer H. Lawrence created an illustration for the House of Representatives' version of the report, while the Senate version spread government largess to lithographer James Ackerman. Marcy buried a bottle with a message noting their exploit beneath a large cottonwood tree nearby. On the 17th he and McClellan set out across "the Staked Plain" with their Delaware guide, John Bushman, to reconnoiter. They found the Llano cloaked that summer with good buffalo grass, presenting the appearance of an "interminable meadow."[8] Moving southward on the 20th McClellan discovered a pretty valley dissecting the monotonous and apparently boundless plain; Marcy named it McClellan Creek in ethnocentric honor of "the first white man that ever set eyes upon it."

Despite the reputed aridity of the Llano Estacado, Marcy admitted that

GYPSUM BLUFFS ON NORTH BRANCH RED RIVER

Gypsum Bluffs on North Branch Red River, by Henry Lawrence after unknown artist, 1853. Tinted lithograph. From R. B. Marcy, *Exploration of the Red River of Louisiana, in the Year 1852* . . . (Washington, D.C.: A. O. P. Nicholson, 1854). Vast gypsum deposits along the upper Red River (east of the Llano) suggested mineral wealth and economic potential for the new land. *Courtesy the author.*

rains and dews were plentiful of late. As they traveled the northeast portion of the plain they found good streamflows in the interfingering valleys; indeed, "the whole face of the prairies has been cheered with a rich and verdant vegetation."[9] Many of the playas were full as well.[10] Marcy was also pleased that the upper headwaters of the Salt Fork and North Fork had abundant water "free from salts" as well as timber. Was this the image of the dreaded Llano Estacado cultivated by so many, including Captain Marcy? Had all the publicity over the southern portion characterized the region as a whole?

Marcy had in fact stumbled into the typical wet season. In May and June a succession of thunderstorms often sweep over the plain, filling the playas for slow, cyclic summer evaporation. Contrary to his expectations and contrary to the gypsum badlands to the east (which affected his expectations), Marcy "discovered" that the northeastern Llano Estacado could be a pleasant enough place with fair water and some timber. It was at best, though, a grudging revision that did little to correct his earlier and much starker writings on the Great Zahara.

Fortunately for the Llano's fierce reputation, June 20 warmed rapidly and, "we observed, as usual, upon the 'Llano estacado,' an incessant tremulous motion in the lower strata of the atmosphere, accompanied by a most singular and illusive mirage."[11] Marcy thought that mirages seen elsewhere occurred here "in perfection" owing to the extraordinary refraction of the atmosphere. There was an inherently illusive power about the Staked Plain, a *genius loci* for environmental deception which caused

> Objects in the distance to be distorted into the most wild and fantastic forms, and often exaggerated to many times their true size. A raven, for instance, would present the appearance of a man walking erect; and an antelope often be mistaken for a horse or buffalo.[12]

Almost fourteen years later, Marcy attempted to give visual meaning to this phenomenon of June 20 in an illustration, "The Mirage," in his popular book, *Thirty Years of Army Life on the Border*.[13]

The Mirage, by unknown artist, ca. 1866. Woodcut. From R. B. Marcy, *Thirty Years of Army Life on the Border* (New York: Harper and Bros., 1866). American illustrations of the deceptive mirage—so beloved by Victorian explorers—are scarce. Marcy's eyewitness vision of a Llano mirage portrays a gigantic herd of antelope racing across the sky. *Courtesy the author.*

This hazy image of a sky-bound herd of antelope against a tremulous background apparition of (what may be) an oasis was arguably one of the first iconographic representations of the surface of the Staked Plain, as opposed to its popular canyonland borders. If so, it was an ironic illustration of the area's capacity for deception. Although the Hispanos had undoubtedly seen mirages, it was the Anglo-Americans who raised their appearance to a central metaphor for the region. Thus the atmosphere of the elevated prairies tilted public opinion to the arid side of the semi-arid nature of the land.

Marcy's report of 1852 expanded on the mirage theme with a conventional discussion of "the eye of a stranger...suddenly gladdened by the appearance of a beautiful lake, with green and shady groves directly upon the opposite bank."[14] He does not say that they actually saw such an oasis that day; nor were they so simple as to pursue one. Rather, Marcy's description partook of the stock-in-trade deluded stranger—whose "heart beats with joy"—urging his horse onward and onward toward an ever receding oasis.

"The Mirage" came to be a powerful metaphor for Anglo-Victorian explorers on the High Plains. First, it united them with the European literary tradition of brave colonial encounters with atmospheric phenomena, such as the French Army in Egypt. Second, the metonymic presence of mirages confirmed Marcy's and Abert's environmental characterization of the Llano as a desert realm. Each implied the other. And third, without knowing it Marcy was himself pursuing an epistemological mirage. His thirst was for knowledge, not water; and yet at each advance his understanding of the "real" Llano somehow receded from view. How could he explain the presence of abundant water in June 1852 when the region was known for its "almost total absence of water"?[15]

From June 23 to 26 the expedition traveled south along the eastern border of the Llano Estacado, advancing to the second or "Main South Fork" of the Red River. To their right lay the increasingly towering escarpments of the plain, a remarkably picturesque landscape rendered without its juniper scrub in the Ackerman lithograph as "Border of El-Llano Estacado." Based on Marcy's description and Shumard's rough sketches, this 1852 lithograph would help launch the American public's initial fascination with the eroded canyons of the Southwest. By now Marcy and others realized that the Red River had various tributary sources in the Llano canyons. But their mirage, their geographic impulse, was to find the one true source of the Red River. Marcy decided this true source was to be found at the headwaters of the South Fork.[16]

On June 27 the expedition began to follow the South Fork upstream into Palo Duro Canyon. The abundance of prairie-dog towns along their westward march led Marcy to appropriate the Comanche name "Ke-che-a-qui-ho-no" or "Prairie Dog Town river" for this branch. (The accompanying illustration shows this scene in 1866.) By the 28th they reached the base of the Llano, which rose some 800 feet above them to the "illimitable desert" on top, a region Marcy compared to the Central Asian steppes.[17]

Border of El-Llano Estacado, by Henry Lawrence after unknown artist, 1853. Lithograph. From R. B. Marcy, *Exploration of the Red River of Louisiana, in the Year 1852* . . . (Washington, D.C.: A. O. P. Nicholson, 1854). Like the talented lithographer James Ackerman, Lawrence overly romanticized the eastern escarpment of the Llano, but he also captured its sublime nature as reflected in Marcy's exploration prose. *Courtesy the author.*

Leaving their wagons and other troops behind, the next day Marcy, McClellan, the Delaware John Bushman, and nine other men rode deeper into the canyon to find "the head spring of this the principal branch of Red river."[18] They were exploring in Palo Duro Canyon, riding over the rough terrain, drinking too much gypsum water in the heat, and suffering from stomach cramps or thirst at intervals. By evening on the 30th they reached a fork. Marcy chose the left branch as it "appeared somewhat the largest." As a consequence they left the main Palo Duro and entered into a branch canyon. Historians such as William C. Griggs, Grant Foreman, and Fred Rathjen tend to place Marcy completely in Palo Duro Canyon; Marcy's account, however, said that they took the left, probably meaning the Tule Creek branch of the Ke-che-a-qui-ho-no.[19]

Marcy's account of the next several days and particularly the accompanying illustrations were so fantastic as to call into question the separation between art and science. Consider for example the H. Lawrence lithograph "View Near

PRAIRIE DOG TOWN.

Prairie Dog Town, by unknown artist, 1866. Woodcut. From R. B. Marcy, *Thirty Years of Army Life on the Border* (New York: Harper and Bros., 1866). Prairie dog towns in the flats along the upper Red River attracted Marcy's zoological interest. *Courtesy the author.*

Head of Red River." In the right foreground two tiny neoclassical figures have paused to gaze across the enormous breadth of the Ke-che-a-qui-ho-no River. Before them stretch the enormous, fortress-like, irregular ramparts of the Llano Estacado escarpment and canyonlands. In both the House lithograph by Lawrence and the Senate lithograph by Ackerman the illustrated river was too broad, too full, and lacking the sinuosity characteristic of the Prairie Dog Town Fork. Easterners commonly imagined that many interior Texas rivers spoken of by explorers and pioneers were equivalent to their own big rivers. Thus, Marcy's upper Red River almost resembles the mighty Mississippi River in its breadth and flow. Would steamboats someday ascend this upper Red River, dropping off tourists at Palo Duro Canyon to hike and admire the scenery? It was a common environmental deception to exaggerate the importance of water features like the Ke-che-a-qui-ho-no River.

Furthermore, the depicted Llano bluffs were missing the characteristic flat-top summit of the caprock. Their geomorphological aspects resemble upthrust European crags rather than eroded sandstone canyonlands. The general effect was to present a representative European picturesque vista being admired by casual passersby (one of whom held a pastoral hiking stick), instead of a more realistic picture of a dozen army men toiling across the landscape, suffering from stomach cramps, thirst, and heat in the Llano canyons. Clearly the East Coast Lawrence and Ackerman lithographic perceptions of the great canyonlands would be filtered through the routine, romantic conventions of European lithography.[20]

Marcy's florid prose was equally deceptive about the environment. As they rode forward into Tule Canyon he perceived a landscape analogous to Scottish mountain highlands:

... a very beautiful and quiet little nook, wholly unlike the stern grandeur of the rugged defile [Palo Duro Canyon] through which we

View Near Head of Red River, by Henry Lawrence after unknown artist, 1853. Lithograph. From R. B. Marcy, *Exploration of the Red River of Louisiana, in the Year 1852* ... (Washington, D.C.: A. O. P. Nicholson, 1854). This first lithograph of Palo Duro Canyon captures the romantic and scenic nature of the Llano canyonlands as perceived by the early American explorers. *Courtesy the author.*

had been passing. This glen was covered with a rich carpet of verdure, and embowered with the foliage of the graceful china and aspen, and its rural and witching loveliness gladdened our hearts and refreshed our eyes.[21]

Soapberry and cottonwood we could believe, but "china and aspen" sounds more literary and sensational. That day and night the small group tantalized themselves with thoughts of fancy iced drinks, New York's fresh, cold "Croton water" piped from the mountains, and "huge draughts of ice water."

The next day, July 1, 1852, they continued the difficult ascent. With their passage into the Llano now blocked by huge rocks, they scrambled ahead on foot. Not too far away Marcy finally found the geographic and cultural mirage that he had pursued for so long: the reputed head spring of the Red River! According to him this spring burst out of a cavernous reservoir. During their passage upstream the gigantic, 800-foot-tall sandstone escarpments had gradually closed in, "and finally united overhead, leaving a long narrow corridor beneath, at the base of which the head spring . . . takes its rise."

This was a profound moment for Captain Marcy. "It is impossible for me to describe the sensations that came over me," he wrote in his report, "and the exquisite pleasure I experienced, as I gazed upon these grand and novel pictures."[22] The stupendous escarpments of the canyon enchanted him with their fantastic forms. Indeed, it took, "but little effort of the imagination to convert [them] into works of art," forming one of the "grandest and most picturesque scenes that can be imagined."[23] Reflecting perhaps the contemporary preoccupation with the gothic, Marcy's active imagination transmogrified the Llano escarpments into feudal castles, battlements, watchtowers, and bastions worthy of the architectural "genius of Vauban."[24]

"All here was crude nature," he observed, "as it sprang into existence at the fiat of the Almighty architect of the universe, still preserving its primeval type, its unreclaimed sublimity and wildness."[25] Marcy was quite sincere in his emotionalism; his discovery of the head spring of the Red River was the crowning achievement of his explorations, a discovery that brought him considerable fame. That afternoon his party climbed up to the summit above the spring, where they found themselves facing the ominous level plain of the Llano Estacado. Below them was an oasis; ahead lay "one uninterrupted desert."[26] McClellan computed their position at latitude 34°42' north and longitude 103°7'11" west.

It was a grand moment. It was also an elaborate illusion. To be sure Marcy and his men had ascended a Llano canyon and refreshed themselves at a major headwater spring. But why was this particular spring the true source of the Red River when others—particularly on the other tributaries of the Prairie Dog Town Fork in Palo Duro Canyon—were not? What about the Salt Fork or the North Fork or the lengthy draws of the Llano: Frio, Tierra Blanca, Palo Duro,

View Near the Ke-Che-Ah-Que-Ho-No, by Henry Lawrence after unknown artist, 1853. Tinted lithograph. From R. B. Marcy, *Exploration of the Red River of Louisiana, in the Year 1852* . . . (Washington, D.C.: A. O. P. Nicholson, 1854). Capt. Randolph Marcy considered that he had discovered the true source of the mysterious Red River in this eastern vision of a major escarpment spring in the Llano Estacado. His discovery and exploration prose made him famous. His actual site—due to flawed observations—was not readily identifiable, but it is now believed to be the headwater spring of Tule Canyon. *Courtesy the author.*

HEAD OF KE-CHE-A-QUI-HO-NO.

Head of Ke-Che-Ah-Qui-Ho-No, by unknown artist, 1866. Lithograph. From R. B. Marcy, *Thirty Years of Army Life on the Border* (New York: Harper and Bros., 1866). After two decades, Marcy's memories and illustrations of his Red River discovery grew in grandeur. He delighted in using the exotic Comanche name "Ke-Che-Ah-Que-Ho-No" for the Prairie Dog Town Fork of the Red River. *Courtesy the author.*

and upper Tule Draw? Marcy's choice of *the* source was in fact an arbitrary, cultural one. It was more appropriate to think in terms of sources.

Second, where was this sublime spring? With the exception of historians Eugene Hollon and Dan Flores, later investigators have been largely confused by Marcy's elegiac description. No one positively identified or recognized Marcy's mystic head spring again in the nineteenth century, although the country was well known by 1900. The head spring's stated geographic position was completely inaccurate. McClellan's recorded longitude of 103°7'11" would place it on the Texas–New Mexico border. This locale is some fifty or more miles west of its actual location in the Tule Narrows, as admirably traced by Dan Flores in *Caprock Canyonlands*.[27] As the historian Fred Rathjen pointed out, "it is difficult to reconcile Marcy's text with his map or to reconcile either with modern nomenclature."[28]

Marcy's florid prose was offset partially by the Lawrence and Ackerman lithographs of this headwater area, such as the Lawrence "View Near the Head of the Ke-Che-Ah-Que-Ho-No." This eastern lithograph is an interesting study in environmental depiction, given its reasonable geomorphology and its botany—including the suggestion of a relictual boreal forest at the top of the head spring. The exotic coniferous trees are likely remnant Rocky Mountain junipers, which Flores notes grow to fifty feet, but the aquatic vegetation in the right foreground is still poorly known. Marcy's report continued its iconographic study with a second lithograph that was even more dramatic in the scale and depiction of roaring waters emerging from a dark chasm. It suggests that there was in reality a definite, even a landmark head spring of the Red River. How could such a prominent landmark disappear? As before, the spring summit appears to be heavily timbered with a coniferous species.[29] This lithograph is a further reflection of the clash of aesthetic taste with environmental meaning. There were many springs in many canyons feeding the headwaters, although Marcy persisted in his view that he had discovered the principal one. His stirring 1886 testimony before the U.S. Supreme Court on the matter helped convince the justices to take the disputed county of Greer from Texas and give it to Oklahoma.

These comments should not detract from the point that Marcy did settle the controversy of the Red River origins where others had failed. He also opened the imagination of the American public to the wonders of Palo Duro Canyon. If he indulged on July 1 in a display of Victorian-explorer bravado, he should not be judged too harshly. Where he can be faulted mildly was in his typical compounding of science and art. The New York lithographs of his explorations romanticized the landscape, mixing the European picturesque with Southwestern descriptions. Marcy's oxymoronic conception of the Llano Estacado as an "ocean of desert prairie" would pass largely unchallenged. Indeed, he practically revelled in the derogation of the Llano Estacado:

> The traveller, in passing over it, sees nothing but one vast, dreary, and monotonous waste of barren solitude. It is an ocean of desert prairie, where the voice of man is seldom heard, and where no living being permanently resides. The almost total absence of water causes all animals to shun it.[30]

This was his vision of the Great Zahara in spite of the copious June rains, the canyon springs, the prairie dogs and antelope, the verdant late-spring pastures, the wolves and buffalo, and the ciboleros and prairie Indians.

Ironically, Randolph Marcy rarely ventured into the level plain itself. He preferred to stick to its watered margins if possible, perhaps because he feared that the interior of the Llano Estacado would swallow him in its aridity and monotony. He may have given some credence to fears that the interior was a Sahara with cruel mirages that tempted travelers to their doom. Without really penetrating its heart he was nevertheless prepared to abhor it. He was adamant therefore in his official recommendations that a wagon road or railroad should skirt this "impassable barrier" of a desert.[31]

· 22 ·

WHIPPLE'S OCEAN PRAIRIE

Nature is not dumb, she speaks to us and affords a beautiful noble entertainment to him who understands her language.

DR. J. M. BIGELOW

Here for the first time, we saw what one might call an ocean prairie; so smooth, level, and boundless does it appear.

A. W. WHIPPLE

Border tensions with an aggrieved Mexico gave the U.S. Army a strategic reason to favor a southern transcontinental railroad. Given the long southern border with Mexico, a national railroad in the area could rush troops where needed. Indeed, this impulse was reflected in the Marcy-Simpson mission of 1849. Marcy, of course, demonstrated that year the feasibility of two routes from the east to the west, one along the northern Llano and the other along its southern margin. His 1852 assertion that the main Llano Estacado was an "impassable barrier" to a railroad was predicated on ostensible geographic concerns. The abrupt eastern escarpment was a major topographic problem. The lack of water and wood in the interior would unduly complicate construction and supply costs. Lieutenant Simpson's report duly noted the Canadian Valley possibilities but added the demographic drawback. Since the region was not particularly suitable for settlement, without solid population and economic rationales any railroad might find itself going bankrupt.

Nevertheless, powerful nationalist, mercantile, and industrial interests agitated in 1852 and 1853 for a transcontinental railroad. The 35th parallel was a leading contender, but sectional rivalries between North and South proved intense.[1] As a means of clarifying the location, Congress authorized in the spring of 1853 three major survey-reconnaissances along parallels from the East to the Pacific. Later a fourth was forced on Jefferson Davis by northern interests. Two out of these four great Pacific Railroad Surveys flanked the Llano. The 35th parallel survey (Memphis to Los Angeles) was led by Lt. A. W. Whipple and followed the Canadian River route. The 32nd parallel survey (Vicksburg to San Diego) was commanded by Capt. John Pope and followed a trek across the southern Llano Estacado.[2] Both of these important surveys avoided a head-on confrontation with the "barren mesa." And both reconnaissances also brought new explorers into contact with the Great Zaharan environment.

Lt. Amiel Weeks Whipple was in action by July 1853.[3] Born in Massachusetts in 1818, Whipple was a cool, experienced army explorer and surveyor. As a member of the Corps of Topographical Engineers he already had seen notable arid-land environments while serving for several years with the troubled U.S.-Mexican Boundary Commission. His instructions that summer included not only a feasibility study for a prospective railroad but also a scientific investigation of the surrounding region. Accordingly, he hired a number of specialists to accompany him.

A. H. Campbell, a talented railroad engineer, was employed to lead a team of surveyors and engineers. Dr. John Milton Bigelow, another of Bartlett's men on the U.S.-Mexican Boundary Commission, was hired on as expedition botanist. Bigelow's absent-minded devotion to collecting would occasion several humorous anecdotes. Dr. C. B. R. Kennerly was appointed as physician and naturalist. Whipple also hired two European specialists. The brilliant Swiss scientist Jules Marcou accompanied the expedition as official geologist. And finally, an artistic protégé of the great Alexander von Humboldt, an adventurous German named Heinrich Balduin Möllhausen, was appointed as naturalist, topographer, and draughtsman under a Smithsonian Institution commission.[4] Möllhausen was engaged to the daughter of Humboldt's secretary, and it was the great geographer's personal recommendation that secured his appointment.

The exploring group that Whipple assembled was impressive. There were over a hundred men in the caravan, many heavily armed. Their firepower provided important deterrence for the natives of the plains. A long *mulada* or caravan of some 240 mules provided transport for all the supplies, specimens, and scientific instruments. Whipple's five-man group of scientific specialists thus constituted the most advanced environmental team hitherto assembled to study the Llano. Their reports would mark a major step forward in the American perceptual and linguistic appropriation of the area.

Whipple's Ocean Prairie • 281

CANADIAN RIVER NEAR CAMP 38.

Canadian River Near Camp 38, by T. Sinclair after Heinrich Balduin Möllhausen, 1856. Chromolithograph, 8¾ × 5¾ inches. From A. W. Whipple, *Explorations and Surveys*, volume 3 (Washington, D.C.: Armstrong, 1856). Half-hidden wagons from the Whipple expedition advance against the tableland backdrop of the Canadian River Valley in this lithograph. Driftwood floats down the broad Canadian River. *Courtesy the author.*

The expedition left Fort Smith in July 1853 and by September 4 Whipple and his coterie were in sight of Antelope Hills, the so-called "Boundary Hills" on the 100th meridian border between Texas and the Indian Territory.[5] On September 6 they passed these precursors of the Llano. Within a few days they came in sight of the "celebrated plateau." Back in Washington, D.C., the staff geologist W. P. Blake wrote, "The Antelope hills may be regarded as the commencement of this vast plain, although they are in fact but fragmentary outliers resulting from denudation."[6] They were also entering the known territory of the Comanche and Kiowa.

Jules Marcou also noted the geological presence of the Llano in the isolated "table-hills" or mesa outliers that lay on their route up the Canadian River. He regarded these first mounds as the symbolic avant garde of the huge Llano in the distance. "We have followed the river," he wrote in his fieldbook for September 8, "but at our Camp 38, to the right and left of the Canadian one has the commencement of the Llano, a species of plateau with some flat, isolated mountains as an *avant garde*."[7] Prone to compare New World to Old World geology, Marcou related these features to "the Alb of Wirtemburg [sic] near Hendinger and Balenguen."

Fortunately, the expedition artist Balduin Möllhausen recorded these geological offspring of the Llano in his colored lithograph, "Canadian River Near Camp 38."[8] This interesting lithograph of the Red Deer Creek area of the Panhandle shows some of the perceptual advantages of Möllhausen's on-site sketching, as opposed to the New York City embellishments that accompanied Marcy's 1852 book. Despite a known propensity for artistic license, Möllhausen's hills at least suggest active processes of physical denudation.

Alexander von Humboldt noted his young friend's interest in physical geography (an interest he doubtless inspired) in the preface to Möllhausen's later two-volume account of the Whipple Expedition. Humboldt observed that although Möllhausen's *Diary of a Journey from the Mississippi to the Coasts of the Pacific* was not strictly a scientific work, it nevertheless did "contain much valuable information on the physical geography of the regions investigated."[9] Möllhausen's Canadian River was shown as an active force by the presence of four drift logs floating along, a nice touch of environmental dynamics. Unlike the conventional romantic posturing of Man in the Lawrence and Ackerman lithographs for Marcy's book, Möllhausen subdued the human presence to a glimpse of half-hidden mules, wagons, and a shadowy rider. This symbolic procession emerged from a woodland in the lower right. Ahead of the caravan stretched the Canadian Valley.

Lieutenant Whipple's September 8 report echoed this physiographic perception of the Llano Estacado. "We have passed to-day hills similar in character and form to the Antelope hills," he wrote. These table-hills (in the phrase of geologist William P. Blake), "appear to be the last mesa remnants of a llano, or prairie, which once covered the whole region."[10] Through processes of abrasion and erosion, Whipple suggested, the Llano had been carved into the "undulating prairies, valleys, ravines, and sometimes canyons" of the breaks country. That night the expedition encamped—Camp 38—on good water amid acres of wild grapevines at "Wine Creek," now revealingly called East Dry Creek.[11]

As early as Camp 36, Whipple's "Itinerary" had noted that the Canadian River was "deeper and less muddy than before."[12] The reason for this relative clarity began to emerge as the expedition wound its way across the flowing tributaries in the days to come. For almost 225 miles beyond Camp 38, the Whipple Expedition would find the Canadian River recharged by the Llano springlands. Fed by numerous springs in the bluffs, these oasis tributaries flowed from the High Plains and fed the Canadian River significant amounts of good, clear water, draughts that diluted the muddy sediments below.

Columns of Sandstone, South Bank of the Canadian River, by Heinrich Balduin Möllhausen, 1856. Woodcut. From A. W. Whipple, *Explorations and Surveys*, volume 3 (Washington, D.C.: Armstrong, 1856). Inspired by Alexander von Humboldt, the German artist and naturalist Heinrich Balduin Möllhausen delighted in unusual aspects of geomorphology along the projected 35th Parallel Route for the Pacific Railroad. Despite the caption "South Bank," the sandstone columns are found on the north side of the Canadian River on the present Bivins Ranch. *CN 08930. Courtesy Center for American History, University of Texas at Austin.*

It was these same "springs beneath the Llano cliffs"[13] that also watered the tributary-fringing woods and grapevines, a scene that delighted all. Whipple spoke of the acres of grapevines they encountered as "looking like a cultivated vineyard." Castañeda, of course, had mentioned the Llano's *parrales* or unkempt vineyards. On "Shady Creek" (Bonita Creek), the springs fed "a forest of timber" consisting of cottonwood, white oak, and hickory.[14] Furthermore, a "dense forest of cedars" cloaked the northern bluffs, protecting the watershed and promoting creek recharge. There was an environmental dynamic at work in the Llano springlands that intrigued Whipple and Marcou.

In the days following Camp 38, Whipple's scientists and men wound their way along the river beneath the Llano bluffs. At Indian Creek they encountered a picturesque camp of Kiowas. Möllhausen sketched away while Whipple attempted to barter with the Kiowas for captives. Two harmless "Comancheeros" with the Kiowa camp asked to join the armed expedition. One of these New Mexican traders, José Garcia, would prove helpful as a guide. On September 10 they passed Spring Creek, one of the Llano's many wooded ravines with flowing water and cottonwood trees. Each day they took magnetic inclinations, barometric pressures, and meteorological and astronomical readings. The enthusiastic Dr. Bigelow sometimes strayed from the caravan in search of new plant species. Somewhere along the route at this time Möllhausen made a sketch later turned into an etching, "Columns of Sandstone, South Bank of the Canadian River."[15]

This etching reflected once again his appreciation of the physical geography of the region, a perceptual slant inspired by Humboldt and promoted by Marcou. This faithful but lifeless illustration was included in the *Pacific Railroad Surveys'* "Report on the Geology of the [35th Parallel] Route." Interestingly, Möllhausen soon appropriated these columns for his later surrealistic chromolithograph, "Sandstone Formation in the Prairie Northwest of Texas." This appealing illustration was a zoologically tarted-up version of his geological etching. The image had a prominent place in his book, *Diary of a Journey*, and Möllhausen romanticized the classical-looking columns with flourishes of half-menacing buffalo and distant antelope. This animation of the landscape gave a different impression, however. In comparing the two illustrations, it seems clear that Möllhausen made his etching exotic, compounding science with art in order to animate a landscape and excite the nineteenth-century sensibility.[16] He also located it on the wrong side of the Canadian River. The formation still exists, but it is on the north side of the valley on a modern private ranch.

Near Camp 41 they saw the blown-up and abandoned trading-house of "Bent's Post," the seasonal post from 1843 to 1848 of Bent, St. Vrain & Co. in the Canadian Valley. Later known as Adobe Walls, this small outpost of frontier mercantilism had been essentially a receiving station for stolen horses and mules. Located at an old comanchero campground, a scared Anglo the Kiowas called "Wrinkle Neck" had manned the store for several seasons in an effort to compete with the Mexican traders. Whipple could not resist falling for a local comanchero myth accounting for the ruined appearance "of what the Mexicans call an American fort or trading-house." "There, many years ago," Whipple related the lore on the adobe ruins, "whiskey was sold to the Indians, who, in a fit of intoxication, murdered the occupants and set fire to the establishment."[17]

He may have heard this legend from a competent and otherwise well-informed traveler named José Garcia. Garcia was a "Mexican trader," later a profession considerably darkened by Anglos into the dreadful, leering visage of a drunk comanchero pawing a white woman on the forbidden Llano Estacado.[18]

NO POSTAGE
NECESSARY
IF MAILED
IN THE
UNITED STATES

BUSINESS REPLY MAIL
FIRST CLASS MAIL   PERMIT NO. 7418   AUSTIN, TX

POSTAGE WILL BE PAID BY ADDRESSEE

TEXAS STATE HISTORICAL ASSOCIATION
2.306 Sid Richardson Hall
University of Texas
Austin, TX 78712-9820

Thank you for choosing a Texas State Historical Association book. We hope you enjoy it. Please let us hear from you. Complete this postage-paid card and:

☐ Check here if you would like us to send you a complete catalogue of all TSHA publications.

☐ Check here if you would like information about membership in the Texas State Historical Association. Members receive a 15% discount on all TSHA publications.

Name _____
Address _____
City _____ State _____ Zip _____

Sandstein-Gebilde in der Prairie nordwestl. von Texas, by Hanhart after Heinrich Balduin Möllhausen, 1858. Chromolithograph, 7¼ × 4½ inches. From Möllhausen, *Diary of a Journey from the Mississippi to the Coasts of the Pacific* (London: Longman, Brown, Green, Longmans, & Roberts, 1858). Möllhausen's original and unrefined sketch was deliberately enlivened with representative animals of the Llano Estacado for his European-published memoirs of the 35th parallel survey. *CN 08934. Courtesy Center for American History, University of Texas at Austin.*

Whipple's image of José Garcia is much more relaxed and friendly than current myths on the Mexican traders, as for example in Paul Wellman's best-selling and sensational novel of evil traders, *The Comancheros*.[19] Garcia was also kind enough to straighten out the errors of Humboldt, Pike, Long, and many other high-placed Americans and Europeans on the confusing geography of the Red River source region. The trader related that the Comanches and New Mexicans called the Red River the "Rio Palo Duro," while the Canadian was called the "Rio Colorado." "This confusion of names is doubtless one cause," Whipple explained, "of the mistake of Baron Humboldt and Colonel Long in taking the headwaters of the Canadian for the source of Red river."[20] What is of interest, though, is that the Americans were informed that the source of the Red River could be found in the "Rio Palo Duro," which was absolutely correct but not considered "discovered" until Randolph Marcy's later expedition. On September 12, however, the 35th parallel survey turned south from the river and began to push into the western breaks of the Llano. They encountered that day a traveling group of puebloans from Santo Domingo, hoping to barter bread loaves and flour to the Comanches for buffalo robes and horses. Having approximated Josiah Gregg's 1840 route until then, Whipple was now on the Marcy-Simpson Trail used by the forty-niners.

There was abundant evidence of a native cultural presence around them, especially at their next camp, "Shady Creek," some seven miles northeast of modern Amarillo in Potter County. Amid a canyon woodland was the site of a large and recently abandoned Comanche campground. The explorers estimated that some 300 lodges had formed the main camp, with over a thousand Indian horses, or enough animals to cause overgrazing in the immediate area. Möllhausen got busy with his colors and pencils and sketched a second prominent lithograph recording the curious sight before their eyes. As Whipple related:

> Our predecessors here were Comanches. The Teguas [Puebloans] say that they left twenty days since, either for a buffalo hunt or for war. There appears to be not less than three hundred deserted lodges; indicating a party of six hundred warriors. A thousand horses must have grazed the valley.... The lodges are temporary bowers, made of branches planted in the ground. The form is that of a horse-shoe, and the twigs are twined at the top, affording a space inside to stand or lie screened from the sun. They appear scattered at random; but, without exception, face the north. Beside each wigwam are the remains of a small fire. This camp ground covers several acres upon either side of the stream.

Whipple also recorded in detail the appearance of a ceremonial site with its prominent *estacas* or stakes, firepits, blood smears, and trenches.

Möllhausen's tinted lithograph of this Potter County scene, "Comanche Camp on Shady Creek," appeared in the "Indian Report" of the 35th parallel survey. With inexpensive lithography by New York's Sarony, Major, and Knapp, this little-known lithograph captures a number of significant bioregional features. The focus turns away from the Canadian River and toward the escarpment itself. On the far right canyon slope, the topmost shading suggests a caprock formation. A surprisingly dense forest of dark cedar trees cloaks the lower slopes and flows up distant tributaries into the Llano. A number of round, beehive-shaped lodges lie on the far bank. A gnarled ancient alamo or cottonwood (as seen by a German artist), with one of its heavy branches snapped and trailing on the bank of Shady Creek, dominates a foreground of valley grasses and forbs. In the lower left Möllhausen gives a reasonable portrayal of the Comanche ceremonial site so carefully described by Whipple. The broken

Comanche Camp on Shady Creek, by T. Sinclair after Heinrich Balduin Möllhausen, 1856. Chromolithograph, 8¼ x 5¾ inches. From A. W. Whipple, *Explorations and Surveys*, volume 3 (Washington, D.C.: Armstrong, 1856). Möllhausen's sketch of an abandoned Comanche camp strove for reasonable accuracy in an age still given to romantic excesses in illustration. *CN 08928. Courtesy Center for American History, University of Texas at Austin.*

branch in particular suggests on-the-spot observation, a considerable improvement in the visual depiction of the region. And the four ceremonial stakes remind us that this is, after all, the Staked Plain.

By mid-September the expedition reached "Beautiful View Creek," a present branch of West Amarillo Creek in Potter County. While Jules Marcou was pondering a dolomite with "sulphate of baryta" north of Amarillo, Texas, Whipple paused with his men for a moment to consider the view. According to Möllhausen, Whipple remarked that in New York or Washington, D.C., the view "would attract very little notice; but it is an agreeable surprise here." If Whipple saw the land in terms of wood and water, Möllhausen tended to see the surrounding landscape in terms of art and physical geography. The fantastic formations of the breaks, the bright reddish soils, and the "crippled cedars" heightened "the peculiarity of the landscape." The ravines had a mild chaos of sandstone blocks. To their immediate south lay the brooding edge of the Llano Estacado, "whose grotesque clefts and chasms filled with cedar penetrated far into the plateau, and cut off from it masses like gigantic walls and fortresses."

The next morning Whipple's itinerary began with an unusual atmospheric phenomenon. In the cool, pre-dawn morning of September 16, as camp members scurried with preparations for an early start, the men suddenly observed a vast, glowing, crown of bright light in the eastern sky. Shafts of white light regularly divided the eastern sky. This crown of light above the horizon led A. W. Whipple to record "an extraordinary refraction" seen in the eastern sky. Twenty minutes before sunrise, he wrote, a "crown of light" appeared in the sky "of sufficient brightness to cast a shadow."[21] Shortly thereafter a violent wind sprang up. It blew all day as they commenced the slow, hill-by-hill ascent of the Llano bluffs.

Like other romanticists of the Prairie Sublime, Möllhausen's prose turns purplish as he climbs nearer the Caprock. He recalled majestic scenery that day, with formulations like "frowning fortresses" and "wild dark ravines." He was also enchanted by the teaming wildlife. "Antelope were springing about on the dry hills," he wrote, "deer lurking behind the blue-green cedars, eagles and kites wheeling their flight through the air, and lively little prairie dogs, peeping out and giving tongue from the openings of their dark abodes."[22]

At day's end in this animated landscape they camped beside a high spring at *Rincon de la Cruz*, "a cañon of the Llano Estacado." This Camp 45 was on a pleasant, western branch of Sierrita de la Cruz Creek in Oldham County, about seven miles northeast of Vega, Texas. Around the spring was another "natural vineyard" with an abundance of pleasant-tasting wild grapes. The viticultural possibilities of the Llano springlands were noticed by at least two persons: "Mr. Marcou thinks it would make an excellent wine similar to port," Whipple wrote in his official report, adding himself that the fruit could be improved by cultivation.[23] During their day's journey they had risen some 400 feet in altitude. They were now within a short climb to the level surface of this lofty plateau. Möllhausen noted their Camp 45 altitude with pride—4,278 feet compared to Fort Smith's paltry 460 feet above sea level. On the morrow, Möllhausen mused in his reminiscences, they would find themselves on top of "*el Llano Estacado*,"[24] the "lofty plain" which extended for four degrees of latitude and four degrees of longitude.

Möllhausen explained the distinctive name of the plateau in a rare footnote. He wrote that since this plateau had no features or landmarks, Mexican traders in former times, "planted long poles in the ground, at certain distances, to show the best way across it." The Anglo-Americans, of course, did not want to cross it so much as to avoid it altogether. "A very small part of this vast plain is yet known," he commented, "for travellers shrink from penetrating into regions where they would be liable to perish from want of wood and water, and the

Whipple's Ocean Prairie • 289

BLUFFS OF THE LLANO ESTACADO, (*one hour before sunrise, Sept.* 17.)

Bluffs of the Llano Sunrise, (one hour before sunrise, Sept. 17), by N. Orr after A. W. Whipple, 1856. Woodcut. From A. W. Whipple, *Explorations and Surveys,* volume 3 (Washington, D.C.: Armstrong, 1856). Inspired by the atmospherics of the Llano Estacado, Lt. Amiel Weeks Whipple sketched this magnificent predawn sunrise over the escarpment bluffs. *CN 08931. Courtesy Center for American History, University of Texas at Austin.*

ascent to it is so troublesome, that they are not very willing to cross a corner of it, to avoid a wide and laborious circuit."[25] The men rose before dawn on the 17th for their crossing. There was a full moon, "a pretty effect of light and shade upon the distant peaks," according to Whipple. Möllhausen recalled that it was cold and the Llano's "towers and wall's loomed mysteriously against the sky."

For whatever reason, Möllhausen also transferred September 16th's predawn "crown of light" to his September 17th account on their ascent onto the Llano Estacado. About an hour before sunrise, he claimed, as they were preparing for the final 250-foot ascent, an unusual matutinal phenomenon appeared. Broad shafts of light (similar to the Rising Sun emblem of Japan), "shot upward to the zenith, dividing the whole firmament into regular spaces, so that it was easy to calculate…how far the sun must be still below the horizon."[26]

This pre-dawn moment of ascension was given visual form in an illustration for the *Pacific Railroad Surveys.*[27] This woodcut by Nathaniel Orr was likely based on a Whipple field sketch.[28] Entitled "Bluffs of the Llano Estacado, (one hour before sunrise, Sept. 17)," the etching was meant to capture the strange and aesthetic atmosphere of the new land. Whipple's itinerary clearly stated that they saw the "crown of light" on the morning of September 16th. But Orr's parenthetical dating of "Sept. 17" in his woodcut illustration may have influenced Möllhausen later to mistakenly—if romantically—place their grand ascent onto the mesa against a pre-dawn apotheosis of the prior day. In Möllhausen's more romantic version, great shafts of white light pierced a cloudless eastern sky on September 17 as Whipple's men and wagons advanced to the caprock summit. The denuded Llano bluffs appeared "like a great wall or barrier in the dim light of early morning," a fortress-like impression to the military perspective.[29] Once on top, the moon set to their west while a fiery red sun rose to their east. Whipple was enchanted with this magical aurora, the "characteristic effect of a dry climate and high prairie."

Möllhausen was dazzled as well. As the "darkly glowing" sun rose out of the Llano Estacado on September 17, this German artist rhapsodized on the oceanic quality of it all. This was an aurora from "the boundless ocean" at a time "when the wild waves sleep." With no wind to disturb the glassy surface, millions of dewdrops created a sparkling line of light sketching from the rising sun to observer. This infinitesimal surface film of water deepened the ocean metaphor. But there was a difference in Möllhausen's mind as the Whipple Expedition rode across this spur of the great plain:

> At sea the first thing you do is to look round the horizon for a sail, and to rejoice if you discover one; you feel less forlorn then in the sublime solitude; but in the Llano you would seek in vain for such a consolation; no tree or shrub breaks the monotony of the plain; and while the ocean does but seem to sleep, and its heavings, like the breathings of a leviathan, show it to be still alive, the Llano Estacado is dead, and varied only by the deceitful mirage.[30]

Möllhausen's word-portrait of the Llano was not a flattering one. The "perfect level" of it all was inescapable. With the exception of distant, gamboling antelope herds, it seemed to be a remarkably boring and inanimate landscape. According to Möllhausen's account, Dr. Bigelow rode around for an hour attempting to botanize; he then gave up as there was nothing of floral interest to be seen. Game was equally scarce. The only "fauna" the doctor had seen were some grasshoppers and, in Möllhausen's phrase, "the shadow of an antelope on the distant horizon."

Riding along with Dr. Bigelow, Möllhausen observed that nature seemed to be dead on the Llano.[31] This "lifeless aspect" of the "dreary, monotonous plain"—this lack of animation—correspondingly influenced the mind. Here was a landscape of classic ennui, a huge realm of boredom where weariness and inactivity took its toll on the mind. Whipple's men moved along half asleep, "like so many machines," Möllhausen argued. Dr. Bigelow agreed that "the influence of nature upon the mind of man…is irresistible," but he philosophically counterargued that they could avoid the ennui by understanding more fully the language of nature. Yet, Dr. Bigelow noted:

Even the dry withered grass that crumbles to dust under the feet of our mules, has something to say, but I must own that up here, where not so much as a cactus can take root, I rather prefer conversing with my fellow men.[32]

So the doctor, the artist, and the others passed the time that morning by telling stories. Möllhausen would later turn his considerable anecdotal talents into literary prominence. After returning to Germany he wrote a tremendous number of Western adventure novels, earning the sobriquet "The German Cooper."[33]

Whipple and Marcou's reports likewise showed little of the anxiety and nervousness of earlier reconnaissances. Whipple thought the Llano was "what one might call an ocean prairie; so smooth, level, and boundless does it appear."[34] Whipple's Ocean Prairie had several positive points to mention. First, there was excellent pasturage. Second, the soil seemed to be good and might be quite cultivable with irrigation water. This latter point constituted a fundamental shift in regional environmental perception. All this Great Zahara needed, Whipple was saying, was water. And the geologist Jules Marcou thought he knew where the precious element was.

"Mr. Marcou thinks that here," Whipple wrote of the Llano, "as upon the prairies crossed since leaving the Canadian, artesian wells might easily be made to afford plenty of water."[35] This aqueous thought added a new dimension to Whipple's "ocean prairie" perspective. Although Marcou did not specifically identify the vast Ogallala aquifer beneath the "hard smooth surface" they were traveling over, he clearly saw the probability of groundwater. By observing the Llano springlands, the "numerous springs issuing from the sides of its bluff edges,"[36] Marcou deduced on geological grounds the presence of substantial groundwater below the surface.

For Whipple this combination of decent soil and artesian water opened the mind to the possibility of American rural settlement and regional civilization. Suddenly there was an environmental window of opportunity for conquering the dreaded Llano Estacado. Simpson's demographic argument about the inherent unsuitability of the plain for settlement (and therefore a railroad) might be proven erroneous with artesian water. The availability of good fresh water pouring from the ground could change the desert image suddenly. But was it possible?

Marcou's scientific reasoning fell short in two important respects. Would the groundwater be sufficiently pressurized to flow as artesian water? He apparently thought so, although later pioneers soon learned that strong pumps would be needed. Second, Marcou extended the range of this artesian possibility to encompass the prairie flats beneath the Llano bluffs. Such hydrological generosity implied that artesian water could be found in the valleys beneath the bluffs, that is, below the natural discharge line of Ogallala springs. This confusing point of geology would inadvertently misdirect Capt. John Pope's search for water for years on the southern Llano Estacado.

Untitled, by unknown artist after A. W. Whipple, 1856. Woodcut. From A. W. Whipple, *Explorations and Surveys*, volume 3 (Washington, D.C.: Armstrong, 1856). Less hostile to Native Americans of the Llano than Texas settlers, national explorers like Lt. A. W. Whipple performed important ethnographic work in their studies and sketches of native culture. *CN 08929. Courtesy Center for American History, University of Texas at Austin.*

After eight and a half miles the expedition stopped at a deep ravine on Middle Alamosa Creek near present day Vega, Texas. Marcou was delighted to find this geological window into the celebrated plateau and he carefully recorded the strata.[37] After breakfast and a short rest Whipple's men pushed on. A dry gusty wind sprang up, persisting until sundown. Clouds of dust bothered animals and men. Möllhausen remembered that at the end of the day the wind died down, and they could then hear the faintest sounds from far away. In the manner of narration that later made him famous, Möllhausen described how the small voices of thousands of prairie dogs—"tiny dwellers underground"—mingled eerily together to form a distant ethereal murmur. After a fiery sunset they were still marching across this spur of the great plain.

At night Möllhausen thought the ocean-prairie metaphor even more apt. The men traveled on under the mild light of the Milky Way until moonrise, when they finally reached the "black abyss" of Rocky Dell Creek or Camp 46. Several New Mexican traders had been sent ahead to select a campground, and these men lit fires to guide the expedition down from the plateau. Soon they saw a second moonrise, as the moon rose above the bluffs above them.

After their twenty-eight-mile march across the Llano Estacado, the men and mules were weary. Lt. Whipple ordered a rest for the next day, allowing scientists time to explore the picturesque "Rocky Dell" or Agua de Piedra Creek environs. Here on the northwest flank of the Llano Estacado they found a native "gallery of fine arts," in Whipple's phrase. There were abundant pictographs in this corner of western Oldham County. Intrigued, the lieutenant illustrated a number of them in his published report.[38] Apparently these images were spirit graffiti, mostly made by puebloan traders who frequented this campground. Two of these Indian traders were traveling with Whipple for safety. Möllhausen observed numerous mud garland nests made by cliff swallows under the Agua de Piedra overhangs. Like Whipple he was also intrigued by the pictograph of a fantastic animal, "half dragon, half rattlesnake, with two human feet." The puebloan traders explained that this image was a divine Great Horned Serpent, who had power over all water and punished the wicked. The Indians revered its powers. In truth as Whipple's men rambled about they found (and promptly killed) several enormous diamondback rattlesnakes. These snakes lived in the rock shelters and were said to reach eight or nine feet in length.

Whipple's astronomical readings told him at Agua de Piedra that he was quite near the recently established boundary line between Texas and New Mexico. Although the expedition had come off of the caprock, it would skirt the huge northwestern stub of the Llano and its outliers for two more degrees of longitude. On September 19 the party followed the much-used comanchero road to their west. This old cart road kept the Llano close by to take advantage of the tributary creeks pouring toward the Canadian River. At times the variegated bluffs of the escarpment advanced almost to the road. The nights were

Remnant of a Stratum of Sandstone near Laguna Colorado, by N. Orr after A. W. Whipple, 1856. Woodcut, 5½ × 4 inches. From A. W. Whipple, *Explorations and Surveys*, volume 3 (Washington, D.C.: Armstrong, 1856). American explorers were fascinated by unusual geomorphic features. The fantastic erosional flanks and outliers of *La Ceja*—"The Eyebrow" perceptual region of the Hispanos in the northwest Llano country—readily captured the imagination and interest of Americans influenced by European tastes in exploration literature. *CN 08932. Courtesy Center for American History, University of Texas at Austin.*

growing cold and daily they were more aware that they were entering a New Mexican cultural landscape.

To be sure, the perceptual emphasis on physical geography continued, as shown in the illustration of Laguna Colorada with the Llano bluffs in the background. Whipple observed the dense juniper forest on the northern bluffs and conjectured that the "nakedness of the Staked Plain" was due to the prevalent southwest winds that scoured the region."[39] They named one tributary "Fossil Creek" for the presence of Blancan Age relics. Beyond they could see the famous Llano outlier of *Cerro de Tucumcari*. Marcy and the forty-niners had thought this mountain (so it is called today) resembled the Capitol dome in Washington, D.C. They were now in the scenic Plaza Larga basin country, which Whipple judged "susceptible to cultivation." Should additional irrigation water be needed beyond the Llano springs and runoff, he anticipated that artesian wells could probably provide a "perpetual flow."[40] On the 21st, Dr. Bigelow rode over to the bluffs and ascended the caprock. He collected a number of plants for his herbarium from the forest of juniper and piñons cloaking its slopes. Some were reportedly new species.

The next day they encountered another of the Llano outliers. This obscure 500-foot mound was called "the Pyramid" and it lay west of Tucumcari. Pyramid Mountain would be virtually forgotten by later historians, but in fact this table-rock occasioned a major geological controversy. From his on-site sketches Möllhausen later prepared a colored lithograph of this geomorpholog-

A Conical Hill, 500 Feet High, by Heinrich Balduin Möllhausen after field sketch of Jules Marcou, 1856. Chromolithograph, 8¼ × 5¼ inches. From A. W. Whipple, *Explorations and Surveys*, volume 3 (Washington, D.C.: Armstrong, 1856). Marcou's theories on the Jurassic nature of Llano outliers were controversial and antagonized many American geologists, but he brought worldwide attention to the geological study of this curious region. *CN 08933. Courtesy Center for American History, University of Texas at Austin.*

ical feature against the backdrop of the Llano. Marcou, Dr. Bigelow, and others climbed to the top to explore.

Marcou was quite taken with Pyramid Mountain as one side of it exposed various strata to perfection. In clambering around he also discovered several intriguing fossils—species of *Gryphaea dilatata* and *Ostrea marshii*. These fossils proved critical to Marcou as they enabled him to establish the presence of a new geological period, the Jurassic, in the continental United States. Indeed, he now described the Llano as a Jurassic formation underlain by the Triassic. "The discovery of Jurassic fossils proved to me," Marcou wrote in his 1858 classic, *Geology of North America*, "that I had at last met with the *true Jurassic rocks* in North America."[41]

There was a certain irony in this self-promoting "discovery," as Marcou called the identification. Many American geologists then doubted the existence of the Jurassic Period in the continental United States. But Marcou's exploration of the Llano convinced him that a fundamental similarity existed between this celebrated plateau and "the well known rocks of my native mountains, the Jura."[42] Indeed,

> It will be seen that these rocks of the Llano Estacado occupy, geographically, a large place in the Geology of the Rocky Mountains; but as regards their relative age, they are still more important, for they fill a void until now left in the series of stratified rocks of North America.[43]

Chief evidence for this startling geological discovery consisted of Llano fossils initially identified as "a very large Ostrea" and a new variety, *Gryphaea dilatata var. tucumcarii*, both picked up from a blue "Oxford clay" stratum found on the Llano outliers in the Plaza Larga area. Marcou was fond of these fossils and showed them to the leading geologists of Europe, including Lyell, Agassiz, Murchison, Thurmann, and d'Archiac. His scientific enthusiasm, however, antagonized several important geologists in the United States.

William P. Blake proved particularly adroit in attacking Marcou's study of the Llano. After a misunderstanding with Secretary of War Jefferson Davis, U.S. officials confiscated Marcou's field notebook and related materials and turned them over to his enemy, William P. Blake, for processing. As the staff geologist for the Pacific Railroad Survey office in Washington, D.C., Blake used these items to prepare his "General Report upon the Geological Collections," which cast considerable doubt on Marcou's conclusions. To be fair, however, Blake also translated and published Marcou's original "Resume and Field Notes."[44]

To some degree the resulting "Jurassic Park" controversy that raged in the 1850s reflected professional jealousies between U.S. and European scientists. Blake regarded himself as an apostle of native experience versus a haughty European newcomer. Sitting in his government office years later and sifting through various reports by Whipple, Pope, and others, Blake mistakenly surmised that the Llano Estacado was Upper Cretaceous with no Jurassic at all. (Blancan and Ogallala caliches were thus mistaken for cretaceous deposits, and there was some Jurassic.) He was outraged when Marcou published first a geological map for the American West in 1855, which included the Llano and the Great Plains as Jurassic formations.[45] With James Hall, Blake wrote a devastating review of this map, one urging all scientists to ignore Marcou's glaring errors.

Marcou's map contained significant errors. But even his bad conclusions proved more interesting than Blake and Hall's. As author Walter Keene Ferguson observed, the Americans played skillfully "on a vague national scientific pride" to discredit Marcou's conclusions.[46] An outraged Marcou responded with counterinvective. In the 1858 postscript to his *Geology of North America* he went to great lengths to protest "the use and abuse" of his name in connection with the Whipple Expedition. "Mr. Blake has done his best to nullify and deny all my discoveries on this survey," he wrote ruefully.[47]

The Marcou-Blake controversy over the geological nature of the Llano Estacado soon became a general paleontological debate that lasted for almost four decades.[48] In this *guerre des savantes*, Blake and Hall's stratigraphic mistakes were patriotically accepted over Marcou's. Soon a generation of Texan geologists were infused with some unnecessary deceptions about the complex geology of the immense tableland and its environs.[49]

Two days out from Pyramid Mountain the Whipple Expedition saw the bluffs of the Llano fading to the south. After hundreds of miles of its presence they were finally beyond it. They continued on to Albuquerque, and then farther west to Los Angeles. Several years passed before all the reports were compiled and gathered for publication. When Whipple's report on the 35th parallel route was published in 1856, it provided the best, most comprehensive discussion of the northern Llano. The report even included a recognition of the first European environmental assessment: Francisco López de Gómara's description of "mighty plains and sandy heaths, smooth and wearisome, and bare of wood," on the road to Quivira with the Coronado Expedition. More than sheer data, the Whipple Expedition also perceived the Llano as an intense expression of physical geography. The wholesale introduction of the scientific perspective did not, however, destroy the art or the mystery of the region. The Blake-Marcou controversy quickly revealed that even eminent scientists could perceive the land in quite different ways.

In the background of this marvelous compendium was the new vision of irrigated farming and settlements in the region. Whipple's good soils and Marcou's possible artesian wells placed this "ocean prairie" in direct contrast to Marcy's uninhabitable Great Zahara. Perhaps the very expectations of a transcontinental railroad prepared Whipple to see settlement possibilities where few before him could visualize any form of permanent civilization. Although most of the expedition probably agreed with Möllhausen's characterization of the flatland dimension as a landscape of ennui, the Llano breaks along the Canadian had proved interesting.

Certainly the old sense of landscape terror was largely missing. Storms, mirages, thirst, bloodthirsty Indians, and raw fear were not that much of a problem. What was present was a geomorphological perspective, as Americans and foreign protégés increasingly applied Humboldt's physical geography to the distinctive regional landscape of the Southwest. Indeed, the table-hills, Pyramid Mountain, sandstone columns, and fossils fostered a new way of looking at the environment, an important perceptual shift from the Prairie Sublime school to the pedantic Harvard school of geomorphology. Lt. Amiel Weeks Whipple, later a Major General killed at Chancellorsville in May 1863, was an important part of the process. His surprise at finding that the Hispanos of New Mexico were gradually appropriating the northwestern arm of the mesa west of 103° longitude did not preclude his use of their toponyms. He deduced from the increasing Hispano presence that the Indian tribes to their east were in irreversible decline. With the Indian menace ostensibly fading and the environment considered from a scientific perspective, the Whipple report suggested that the northern Llano was not nearly so dreadful after all.

· 23 ·

WANT OF WATER:
A. B. GRAY ON THE SOUTHERN STAKED PLAIN

It is by no means a desert, or barren waste, for with exceptions of narrow belts less prepossessing, there are vast fields of fine grazing lands.

ANDREW BELCHER GRAY

In the 1850s the Llano Estacado was a much bigger realm in its southern portions than it is today. Also known as the "Staked Plain" or sometimes "Staked Plain*s*," a slight mistranslation gaining momentum, the southern Llano then bulged southward and eastward deep into the Concho River country. Unlike the northern, eastern, or western escarpment borders, there were no major physiographic features in the south that delineated the dry plains of the Llano from the dry plains of the adjacent Edwards Plateau. Certainly the geology of both bioregions was confused.[1]

Modern researchers often draw the line near Johnson Draw, an obscure watershed southeast of Odessa that flows uncommonly northeast.[2] Along the way Johnson Draw merges its identity with the trickles and runoff of Midland Draw, Mustang Draw, and Sulphur Springs Creek, before the runoff all pours past Marcy's "Big Spring" toward the nearby Colorado River. But for the early Anglo-American emigrants, soldiers, and pioneers of West Texas, the Staked Plain ran south of Johnson Draw, far into the Middle Concho River country, and then the land swept westward to the brackish waters of the Pecos River. This large southern extremity of the Llano later constituted portions of Crane, Upton, and Reagan Counties.

Precipitation is low in this area; Crane County averages 12.9 inches annually, much of which falls during a few spring and summer thunderstorms.[3] There is also considerable Dune Land in the western portion, where the wind-blown sands have piled up against the topographic barrier of the Llano Estacado. These eolian areas of mostly barren, often active sand dunes of 20 to 100 feet or more made a strong impression on the early explorers. They are not devoid of vegetation; several years of good rainfall often supports a sparse cover of grasses and oak shinnery.[4] To the wetter east, especially on the headwaters of the Middle Concho, one could find adequate wood and water. But between the western dunes and the eastern springs there was a lonely, flat, cheerless landscape, a desert that in the 1850s belonged to the Great Zahara of the Llano Estacado.

By this expansive reckoning, Captain Marcy was not the first Anglo-American of note to cross the southern Llano. That honor instead went to a Missouri doctor and bold merchant, Dr. Henry Connelly. Connelly obtained fifty dragoons and freighted a reported seven wagons of bullion from Chihuahua, Mexico, to Fort Towson, Oklahoma, in the spring of 1839. "By a course north-of-east," J. Evetts Haley wrote of his trail east of the Pecos, "Connelly passed over the Staked Plains close by the Flat Rock Ponds, to the head of the Middle Concho."[5] Having made his point, the next year Connelly backtracked with another company of merchants to Chihuahua.[6]

A decade later John S. "Rip" Ford and Maj. Robert Neighbors left Austin to open an emigrant wagon road for forty-niners between Austin and El Paso. After obtaining the opportune guidance of a Comanche warrior and two squaws—the reasonable practice of a competent Anglo trailblazer being to find a willing native to show him the way—these seasoned frontiersmen trailed upstream the mellifluous *A-Hope-Ho-Nope* ("Blue River") or Middle Concho. The beautiful *A-Hope-Ho-Nope* was a sinuous line of riverine verdure winding through a grassland ocean. An archipelago of mesas rose in the distance. At the upper watershed they struck out west over seventy miles of the Staked Plain. "Rip" Ford remembered the Llano as a "bare and sterile plain." Their mules stampeded at Mustang Water Holes, and the weather turned bitter cold.[7] Near Flat Rock Pond they crossed Connelly's Chihuahua Trail, but Ford and Neighbors kept heading west, passing through scenic Castle Gap to reach the famous Pecos ford at Horsehead Crossing.[8]

There were, therefore, two wagon roads ascertained across the southern Llano by 1849. Marcy's "Emigrant Trail" via Big Spring tended to service the westering emigrants of Arkansas and Missouri, while the Ford and Neighbors Trail (or "Upper Road") accommodated the agitated California emigrants pouring into Texas cities like Fredericksburg and Austin. Although hundreds of emigrants used these trails,[9] neither route was considered an easy haul. Lt. Francis Bryan traveled on the Upper Road in July 1849 and found the Wild China Ponds bone dry. The lack of water at this camp was a decided disappointment. At Castle Gap there was only a muddy little pool unfit for drinking.

Large emigrant parties under Persifer F. Smith, Captains Tong and Duval, Captain Thomas Smith, Captain John Murchison, and others toiled across the Concho Country portion of the Staked Plain in 1849–1850.[10] Many of the emigrants thought the passing land was utterly destitute. "This portion of Texas is exceedingly poor," observed C. C. Cox, "and so barren that I am of the opinion it will always remain uninhabited [sic]."[11] Despite loud and numerous complaints about the Ford and Neighbors Trail, the 1849 emigrants did demonstrate the practicality of this route in reaching a bustling new town called "Coon's Ranch." This roaring trans-shipment community sprang up on the American side of *El Paso del Norte*, the east-bank antecedent to today's El Paso. "Thus at last the lesson was clear," as J. Evetts Haley summed up. "The best way west from down in Texas was that up the gentle gradient of the Conchos and across the Staked Plains to the Pecos."[12]

A chief concern of the emigrants was the availability of water on the new wagon trails across the southern Llano. Not surprisingly, the early Anglo-American geography of the southern area focused on key waterholes. Marcy's Trail of 1849, as noted, passed from the Big Spring southwest to Emigrant Crossing on the Pecos, with water found mainly at Mustang Springs and in the weird "Sand Hills." Below this trail, Ford and Neighbors' Upper Road crossed the relatively narrow gap between the "Main" or Middle Concho and the Pecos River via four waterholes. The first was "Mustang Water Holes," which lay eight miles west of the Middle Concho head in present-day Reagan County.[13] From a forty-niner standpoint, there was not much to commend this waterhole. Randolph Marcy had probably passed by when the ponds had been freshly recharged. At least some emigrants were absolutely disgusted to find it dry.

About twelve miles farther west were the "Flat Rock Ponds," located just west of contemporary Stiles, Texas. Spring-fed by outcrops of Edwards limestone, these small basins had been a popular layover since ancient times. Mortar holes and pictographs of hands, flowers, and snakes attested to the native presence. The Spanish commander Juan Dominguez de Mendoza probably was describing these springs in his 1684 notice of an *ojo del agua delgado*, or soft-water spring in the general vicinity.[14] Now completely dry and obscure, this waterhole was a welcome stop in its gold-rush heyday.

West from Flat Rock Ponds was a long waterless stretch of almost twenty-seven miles before the traveler reached the remote southern oasis of "Wild China Water Holes" or "Wild China Ponds" in Upton County. Here small springs and ephemeral seeps in China Draw fed shallow basins surrounded by a stand of lonely soapberry trees. Today both the springs and most of the trees are long gone.[15] A little over fourteen miles to the west-southwest was the important landmark and small spring at "Castle Gap." Rising to 3,150 feet in elevation, this small cleft mesa was an important site on the Comanche War Trail. Castle Mountain was also the logical gateway to the famous Horsehead Crossing of the Pecos only twelve miles farther west.[16]

Castle Mountain Pass, Texas, by unknown artist, 1857. Woodcut. From J. R. Bartlett, *Personal Narrative of Exploration and Incidents in Texas* . . . (New York: D. Appleton & Co., 1854). Dr. Henry Connelly's wagons blazed a trail in 1839 along an ancient pass in these limestone mountains between the Llano Estacado and the Pecos River. American travelers, like Boundary Commissioner W. H. Emory, perceived the pleasant illusion of medieval castles in level rimrock formations and quaint stone-debris fields. The natural gateway called "Castle Gap" watered livestock at a spring, and linked weary travelers from the Llano Estacado to the Horsehead Crossing of the Pecos River. *CN 04305B. Courtesy Center for American History, University of Texas at Austin.*

For many years historians considered the location of Horsehead Crossing to be lost to time. It was known that the Comanche trail to Chihuahua left Castle Mountain and crossed harsh alkaline flats down to the steep-banked river. But the actual site of Horsehead Crossing—one of the most violent and legendary sites in West Texas, and the principal crossing of the Pecos River in the mid-nineteenth century—was forgotten and obscured in this century. Bartlett found the crossing marked with numerous horse skulls in 1850, a reflection of the Comanche predilection of driving exhausted stolen stock across the lower plains until the animals finally reached the waters of the Pecos, plunged in, overdrank, and died by the hundreds nearby. Emigrants used the crossing during the 1850s, where it became a stage stop on the Butterfield Overland Mail. Beginning in 1864, a series of westering cattlemen like William Peril, Oliver Loving, and Charles Goodnight used the same crossing, leaving cattle skulls, a few victims, and other debris in the vicinity. Yet by the Texas centennial year of 1936 there was only an approximate idea as to the actual location of the legendary crossing. An educated guess placed a commemorative marker on the Pecos River at the Pecos County–Crane County boundary, about twenty miles northwest of the small oil-town of Girvin and not too far south of Crane, Texas.

Now it is a lonely stretch of river. The newer, more salty taste of the Pecos waters adds a certain bitterness to a land remote from the affairs of most folk. Oil- and gas-field workers and surviving local ranchers work the area and care for its memories. The historic marker near the river goes largely unnoticed by the wider world. Castle Mountain and Old Castle Gap have largely disappeared as well, even their names failing to appear on the otherwise admirable state highway county map of Crane County. A dedicated local historian, however, has recently refocused attention on the actual site of Horsehead Crossing.

Bill Boyd of Crane, Texas, belongs to the new generation of J. Frank Dobie's "Coronado's Children," a modern fraternity of treasure hunters more concerned with finding another's poor past than their own rich future. With the technological boost of arm-held metal detectors, Trail Detectives Bill Boyd and Joe Allen of the Crane County Historical Commission announced the rediscovery of Horsehead Crossing in the spring of 1995. Like Coronado they, too, seek metal, but iron instead of gold. It is the cheap debris of an arriving industrial order that they covet—iron arrowheads, bullets and buckshot, military buttons, insignia, and horseshoe nails. "All the latest stuff that's been written about the crossing—no one ever went down and looked," Boyd remonstrated. "I have. The basic physical evidence supports everything I'm saying."[17] Boyd and Allen's analysis of old maps, written accounts, aerial photos, and especially collected artifact locations take them to a new and important site on the river, but only about a quarter-mile away from the 1936 historic marker, a surprising reflection of past accuracy and historic acuity.

Two principal environmental problems soon emerged with the Upper

Road wagon trail across the southern Llano to Horsehead Crossing. Boundary Commissioner John R. Bartlett had traveled this notorious trail in 1850; in 1852 he heard further loud denunciations of it from travelers. First, a number of emigrants could not find the obscure waterholes amid all the flatness. They felt, as Bartlett noted, that their maps "deceived them as to the watering-places." And second, the water supply was likely to be ephemeral, good for most of the year but drying up seasonally. Bartlett reported in evident disappointment that both Mustang Ponds and Wild China Ponds were dry when he passed. He also recorded the harsh environmental experience facing the emigrants in the southern Llano:

> They expected to find water at the localities designated on the maps and took no precautions in case of meeting with none. On reaching the so-called "Mustang Ponds," they did not recognize them and sought for them in vain for miles around. At the "Flat Rock" and "Wild China ponds," they were equally disappointed. They looked about the desert without success.[18]

Failure to find these waterholes or water in them meant trudging for days without water. Hundreds of mules, oxen, horses, and cows consequently died, to the emigrants' horror. With each passing year the overland trailscape of the southern Llano was further littered with the bleached and mummified remains of livestock. Inadvertently the cultural landscape was becoming even more forbidding.

From the emigrants' standpoint they had been deceived by pernicious cartographers and trail boosters. The latter likely felt that a capricious environment was to blame. In fact both groups were at fault. The early surveys for routes to California along the southern Llano Estacado created expectations of oases with the suggestive power of the word. Despite the increase in formal geographic knowledge of the region following the Mexican War, the Anglo-Americans proved linguistically naïve, perhaps, in their arid-land vocabulary. They borrowed heavily from the Hispano toponyms, of course, and sometimes referred to Indian toponyms, such as the *A-Hope-Ho-Nope*. But Anglo expressions like Mustang *Ponds*, Flat Rock *Ponds*, and Wild China *Ponds* may have lured the thirsty mind into more generous expectations than the reality of spongy soil, shallow basins, and possibly some good water.[19] What the signification of "ponds" did not convey was the stochastic nature of water on the southern Llano, where an oasis might be an environmental probability rather than a cultural certainty. Although road promoters and emigrants disagreed on the presence of oases, both agreed that the surrounding Llano Estacado was a desert realm. As the skeletons of livestock accumulated along the road, the metaphor of Marcy's Great Zahara seemed ever more appropriate.

There were sensitive political reasons, however, why the desert metaphor of the overlanders should not completely dominate the regional geosophy. Many influential Southerners were ardent proponents of a transcontinental railroad along the 32nd parallel.[20] Secretary of War Jefferson Davis also strongly favored this proposed southern route.[21] Logically, of course, this railroad should service a region capable of rapid settlement and rich enterprise. Although the southern crossing of the Llano was only a third as long as the northern or 35th parallel crossing, unfortunately it had by 1853 a significantly nastier reputation. Within a year, two significant imagineers would attempt to mitigate this dreadful perception of the southern route.

The first to get into the field was the adventurous Col. Andrew Belcher Gray. This tough, bright, former midshipman in the Republic of Texas Navy was by 1853 a respected surveyor. Gray was also an ardent Southerner, one who had strongly protested Bartlett's "New England Yankee's" disregard for Southern interests during the bitter boundary dispute with Mexico. Shortly after the Whipple Expedition departed to report on the 35th parallel, Gray left for San Antonio to organize a rival expedition, one whose purpose was to examine the 32nd parallel for a prospective railroad. All his expenses were paid, of course, by a private and very speculative corporation, the "Texas Western Railroad Co." This enterprise was composed of wealthy Southern capitalists desirous of promoting a "Southern Pacific Railroad" and anxious to prevent damned Yankees from ignoring the 32nd's geographic possibilities. On New Year's Day, 1854, Gray and his party of seventeen hired men, almost all Texans, rode out from San Antonio for the newly established federal outpost of Fort Chadbourne.

From this recent army gateway to the Concho and "Staked Plain" country the Gray Reconnaissance moved west on January 17, 1854. By the 22nd they reached Mustang Springs on the Marcy Trail, but at a disconcerting "18 miles from their represented position upon the map in our possession."[22] Emigrant complaints of maps had a foundation indeed. In the space of about a mile Gray found a series of lakes full of wild geese and ducks. The waters tasted bitter but there was plenty. There was also a "perfect golgotha" of horse skeletons, from hippophagous Comanche feasts he thought. All the dismembered skeletons added a new dimension to the name "Mustang Springs."

From Mustang Springs to the Pecos River the expedition had to make a 125-mile transit over the Llano Estacado. Gray thought this "first Steppe east of the Rocky Mountains" was a significant fountain-head region, the origin of the mighty Red River, Brazos River, and Colorado River.[23] In his 1856 book, Gray made light of the desert metaphor. "It is by no means a desert, or barren waste," he wrote appreciatively, since it generally had fine ranching and grazing lands. The whole region was full of wildlife and cloaked with "exuberant grasses."[24]

A charming 1856 lithograph, "American Antelope, of the Llano Estacado," depicted the most prominent game animal seen on these rich southern grasslands. Emulating the practice of government expeditions, Gray had engaged an available European artist to accompany his party as official illustrator. A German emigrant and forty-niner, the geologist Charles Schuchard knew how to draw as a graduate of the Freiberg School of Mines in Germany. He signed on for the money and the adventure. Schuchard and Gray soon argued and did not get along well. Gray wanted to order illustrations tailored to fit his promotional perspectives and visionary tastes. He was, after all, expected to produce results for his moneyed backers. Schuchard's handsome lithograph of a pronghorn antelope also showed an uncommon background of short-grass Llano plains stretching into the distance. Instead of trees, of course, there were framing clumps of huge yuccas.

Up until the Staked Plain, Gray's report had glowed about the climatic and topographical advantages of the 32nd parallel route for a railroad. Out on the dreaded Llano this venture-capital optimist was only a bit more constrained. It would not do to lie, so he admitted the lack of wood, excepting "stunted mezquit."[25] But Gray claimed "inexhaustible quantities of the purest water" could be found in the nearby Sand Hills. Astoundingly, he also claimed, "from close personal observation, I am satisfied that it [water] may be had anywhere not far below the surface."[26] Gray offered no immediate evidence for this startling possibility beyond another expressed confidence that "subterranean streams exist throughout the Llano Estacado, and water will be had by sinking wells anywhere on this line."[27] He had no proof, but he had abundant and prescient faith.

A bitter evening Norther accompanied their arrival at Mustang Springs. Gray and his Texans soon started on across the Llano along Marcy's Emigrant Trail. Gray thought this was the first time an Anglo party had crossed the region in the depths of winter. The ice that now coated their beards was in sharp contrast to the beautiful prairie fires they had seen several days before, when "all was a-blaze, and at night appeared like a vast amphitheater of illuminated cities."[28] Gray thought the lack of timber on the Llano was not due to the soil, which he found was generally good. Rather he blamed the primal forces of fire and ice, the prairie fires and freezing Northers, for scouring this prodigious plain of its timber.[29]

Despite Gray's official gloss on the environment, the men were exhausted and thirsty from their weary tramp across the Llano Estacado before finally reaching the Sand Hills, "heaved together near the lower part of the Staked Plain." They arrived in this peculiar area at night with a good moon. Under the alternating light and shade of moonlight and clouds the Sand Hills were transmogrified into a "granular sea." The hillocks and ridges of white sand strongly resembled a wondrous ocean of frozen, giant waves.[30] They found palatable water fairly quickly at "springs" in this ocean of sand, whereupon men and mules abandoned ceremony in a competition to drink the most.

Gray's official report stated they encamped in the Sand Hills to explore, but the Peter Brady *Reminiscences* were more explicit.[31] They had been so fatigued by the crossing that they simply had to have a few days rest for themselves and their animals. In the midst of this splendid, silent desolation, one of

AMERICAN ANTELOPE,
OF THE LLANO ESTACADO.

American Antelope, of the Llano Estacado, by Middleton, Wallace & Co. after Charles Schuchard, 1856. Chromolithograph, 4 × 6¼ inches. From Andrew Belcher Gray, *Survey of a Route for the Southern Pacific R. R. on the 32nd Parallel* (Cincinnati: Wrightson & Co., 1856). Antelope were abundant on the Llano Estacado when Schuchard saw them with Gray's 32nd parallel survey for a southern transcontinental railway. After railroads were built a generation later, the herds rapidly declined. *CN 08926. Courtesy Center for American History, University of Texas at Austin.*

Pecos River, Texas, by Middleton, Wallace & Co. after Charles Schuchard, 1856. Chromolithograph, 6¼ × 3⅜ inches. From Andrew Belcher Gray, *Survey of a Route for the Southern Pacific R. R. on the 32nd Parallel* (Cincinnati: Wrightson & Co., 1856). More encumbered than Hispano explorers, American expeditions found the active Pecos River to be a further challenge after the rigors of crossing the southern Llano Estacado. CN 08927. Courtesy Center for American History, University of Texas at Austin.

the men heard a distant, unusual cry of distress. Some time elapsed before the source of this cry was discovered—a runaway Arkansas slave, a brave sojourner on his way to Mexico. Apparently this runaway sought to use the new trail through the "desert uninhabited country" to escape detection on his desperate way to freedom across the Rio Grande.[32]

Gray's report for the directors of the Texas Western Railroad Co. minimized the environmental problems of the southern Llano Estacado. Water could be obtained, he suggested, from mysterious subterranean streams, or in a pinch from man-made surface reservoirs. Portions of the Llano were unprepossessing, perhaps, but the gentle, sloping topography and the salubrious climate were certainly fine for a railroad. In short, this ardent Southerner thought the Llano Estacado was not nearly as dreadful as its reputation. Again, personal experience in the Mexican Boundary Survey proved influential. (Indeed, it was

Gray's zealous quarrel with Bartlett over the Mesilla Valley that led to W. H. Emory's appointment as new boundary commissioner and to the Gadsden Purchase of December 1853.) Gray simply felt that he had seen much worse country than the grassy southern Staked Plain. If the want of water could be solved, the area might even be ideal for prosperous ranch country, with adjacent small towns springing up on the former continental steppe.[33]

After resting in the Sand Hills, Gray, Schuchard, and the Texans rode west to the Emigrant Crossing on the Pecos. Schuchard's lithograph of their crossing was a triumph of realism. With the short-grass plains as background, the Pecos appeared as an abrupt, swift, and deep river, a notable contrast to its present strangulated trickle between salt cedar thickets. There were hardly any fringing woods to mark its course. From this crossing they journeyed via the Guadalupe Mountains to El Paso where they paused for a much needed rest.

At a bridge site not far above El Paso, Col. Andrew Belcher Gray met the recently organized government expedition for the 32nd parallel. Bowing to southern demands, Congress had belatedly authorized an official expedition for this lower parallel as well. Command of this fourth important Pacific Railroad survey was given to Capt. John Pope. A bold visionary in the promotional mold of Gray, Captain Pope was even then preparing for his own reconnaissance eastward across the Trans-Pecos and Staked Plain regions. He was delighted to query Gray about the road to the East. He was particular to ask about the supply of water to be expected, for he thought its discovery was crucial.

Untitled [Pope's Wells], by H. S. Sindall, c. 1857. Oil on paper mounted on board, 10 × 14 inches. Only a few extant paintings and watercolors—drawn from life in West Texas by the mysterious but exceptionally talented Sindall—are known to exist. This rare painting shows the 1857–58 "Pope's Wells" encampment and anti-aridity operations on the margin of the southern Llano Estacado. The artist accurately depicts the official bustle, large scale, and industrial activity behind the government-funded search for artesian fountains. Sizable crews were needed simply to freight fuel, work the ferrier wagons, make repairs, and guard the camp and supplies. Other teams worked the primitive cable-tool drilling rig in the middle-ground wooden building with its canvas tent additions for shelter from the elements. John Pope may be one of the foreground figures. A second painting, signed and dated "H. S. Sindall Nov. 1857" depicts a drilling crew caravan crossing a romantic Pecos River. *Courtesy Dan Hynes, Hynes Fine Art, Rockville, VA*

· 2 4 ·

POPE'S WELLS

This miscalled desert . . .

CAPT. JOHN POPE

While lakes that shone in mockery nigh,
Are fading off untouched, untasted . . .

THOMAS MOORE, *Lallah Rookh*

John Pope proved to be one of the great imagineers of the Llano Estacado. Born in Kentucky in 1822, he entered the U.S. Military Academy from Illinois. He did so well at West Point that he was commissioned second lieutenant in the coveted Corps of Topographical Engineers in 1846. His cool professionalism under fire at Buena Vista and Monterrey in the Mexican War advanced him to brevet captain. In late 1853 Secretary of War Jefferson Davis ordered Lieutenant Parke and Captain Pope to conduct the Pacific Railroad Survey for his beloved 32nd parallel. Parke would run the survey west of the Rio Grande and the thirty-year-old Pope, a disagreeable officer to his superior, would run it eastward.[1]

The Pope Expedition left Albuquerque for El Paso, Texas, and then advanced across the Trans-Pecos in the late winter of 1854. By March 8 they reached the pleasant Pecos River Falls at the mouth of Delaware Creek, quite near the Texas–New Mexico border. They set up camp at the adjacent crossing and contemplated the next step. Pope had in mind making a bold improvement on the Marcy Trail across the Llano. Captain Marcy had reached the same point on the Pecos River; but Manuel, his plainsman scout, had dissuaded him from a direct eastward crossing. With discretion being the better part of valor, Marcy had descended the river for sixty miles to his fordable Emigrant Crossing of the Pecos River. Captain Pope, however, wondered if a more direct crossing from Delaware Creek to the Colorado River headwaters was possible after all. J. H. Byrne, who kept the expedition diary, noted on March 9, 1854, that they deemed it best to encounter "that *terra incognita*, the Llano Estacado" quite cautiously.[2] Accordingly, Pope ordered a small party of thirteen men, placed under Capt. Charles L. Taplin, to journey northeastward into this unknown "Jornada"[3] to ascertain a more direct crossing. The advance party was also to examine the environment and pay particular attention to any waterholes.

Captain Taplin's brave men left the Pecos Falls camp at 11 a.m. on March 9. Two wagons carried rations, six kegs of water, and corn; each wagon was drawn by eight mules.[4] Bearing north of east they made eighteen miles the first day. For the next three days Taplin's men rode over the alternately hard and sandy endless flatlands of the Llano Estacado.[5] Small mesquites or "mezquite-brush" were thick in places. A mantle of good grama grass generally covered the plain, but now and then Captain Taplin encountered the cumbersome Dune Lands: linear, colorful stretches of reddish sand hillocks that marbled the grassland immensity. These sandy regions much fatigued the mules with "innumerable mole-holes" (from prairie dogs) and generally poor traction.[6] Taplin noted, however, that even these troublesome stretches were not entirely devoid of vegetation. He described the sparse oak shinnery and distinctive bunch-grasses that characterized and stabilized the dunes.[7] On March 12 he found himself in a "perfect sea of tall, reddish grass, interspersed with hillocks of sand."[8] This "perfect sea" continued the Anglo-Victorian imagery of the plain as a land-ocean.

In this grassland wilderness Captain Taplin and his men saw plenty of wildlife on their journey. "Antelope, deer, rabbits, owls, crows, prairie-hens, and small birds were quite numerous," he wrote in surprise. The abundance of game provided relief from the visual monotony. What they did not see, however, was what they most needed—precious water. At the end of the fourth waterless day Taplin reluctantly ordered the abandonment of the wagons. Fatigued men and animals pushed on the next day, finding a small, muddy playa remnant that the mules alone would touch. Fortunately, early on the next day, March 14, the suffering men and mules arrived at the oasis of Sulphur Springs.

Taplin's men had reached an important landmark. In the broad ravine around them five or so springs flowed; at least one was "tinged with sulphur and saltpetre" while others were fairly fresh and pure. Just below a head spring they found a large pond for watering the animals. The environs showed signs that this special place was a routine Indian campground.[9] Although his situation had never been truly desperate, Captain Taplin was embarrassed to have lost his wagons. His animals also had suffered from the want of water on the approximately 130-mile journey. He dispatched the wagonmaster, Mitchell, and an unidentified Hispano[10] to backtrack across the Llano with his discouraging official report to Pope. "Throughout this whole distance," Taplin wrote to Pope, "there are no permanent watering-places."[11] Yet the gentle topography of the trek indicated that little grading would be needed for a railroad. Taplin also sent word that he was departing from instructions by returning southward along the Marcy Trail.

Taplin's discouraging word reached Pope's camp on the Pecos Falls on March 18, 1854. He prudently gave up the idea of following his assistant into the waterless void. Instead Pope took his wagons down the Pecos to recapitulate Marcy's Emigrant Trail (which in turn retraced a popular branch of the Great Comanche War Trail). A fantastic salt-lake mirage on the way gave evidence of this sky's "power of refraction." They found Marcy's ford at the Pecos River to be an "extremely bad crossing." Once across they advanced on March 25 toward the Llano Sand Hills. Like Lieutenant Michler and Captain Marcy, Pope and Byrne were amazed at the presence of good water in these curious white dune-fields. Stretching fifty by fifteen miles, the conical mounds in the Monahans area appeared to be the worst sort of desert. Marcy had noted this Sand Hills region was the "very last place on earth" where one could expect to find water. Pope's mules sank to their knees in the dry sands. Yet an incredible series of willow-fringed, freshwater ponds (actually the exposed outcrops of the perched watertable) provided plenty of water and a day-at-the-beach atmosphere.

After replenishing their water supplies they continued northeast on March 26, passing a "great quantity of fragments of abandoned wagons" on the way. The origin of these wagon parts led to much speculation by later pioneers. There were stories of Comanche massacres, lost treasure, and spooky sightings. Some thought the winds buried for years and then suddenly uncovered a lost wagon train for a traveler's consternation. These broken parts were likely the remnants of abandoned emigrant wagons, forced, as Taplin had been with his wagons, to forego heavy equipment when water ran too low. Marcy's Emigrant Trail was often and regularly denounced by the argonauts who used it and missed regular water.[12] J. H. Byrne wrote that they were now on a "frightful road." Sand often mired the wagons, the mules were exhausted from their hauls, and there was no water. What would this trail be like on a scorching summer day? Eventually they reached a hard prairie where search parties scattered out to find waterholes; but they all returned unsuccessful and anxiety grew in camp. At least one party had previously grown bewildered on the plain and wandered around for many hours.

Subtle environmental clues in Byrne's entries of the Llano crossing may point to a deteriorating local ecology as early as 1854. After leaving the Sand Hills, for example, Byrne had noted the presence of "tolerably good" grama grasslands on the Llano. Mesquite was also less abundant. But on March 28, "The grass was good until within six miles of our camping place," Byrne wrote, "when it changed becoming poor and full of weeds."[13] Were the great grass-lands of the southern Llano yielding to overgrazing and invasive brush and weeds?

At their nameless, featureless stopover that night the camp entry by Byrne was terse: "No water, the animals evincing signs of fatigue, having been two days and nights without water; grass very poor, mezquite and brush plenty."[14] This description sounds like overgrazed trail conditions, perhaps due to livestock or wild horses crowding around a nearby waterhole. In a conference paper titled "The Virgin Southwest," the noted environmentalist Aldo Leopold claimed that emigrant wagon trains promoted overgrazing and erosion. "This probability is strengthened by the fact," Leopold told a 1933 conference of anthropologists in Santa Fé, "that the erosion is oldest and worst near the water-holes at which the Forty-Niners camped and grazed their thousands of animals."[15] A large Indian traffic in stolen stock may have augmented and maintained the damage. Despite the hard going, Pope thought they were near to Mustang Springs. This thought of water on the morrow kept the men in good spirits that evening. Late that night a pack of wolves stampeded all their sheep, disappearing into the darkness with the moveable feast.

About an hour after breaking camp next morning Pope's men happily encountered Captain Taplin and his party descending the trail toward them. Taplin's group was able to report that Mustang Springs was, thank goodness, quite close by. By 10:30 a.m. the Pope Expedition had reached the large, partly saline lakes at the springs. They also met a shy band of Kiowas—trailing a large herd of stolen horses from Mexico—who were watering their stock there as well. The Kiowas soon moved on to avoid any incidents. Natives had dug various holes around the lake margins in the attempt to obtain a fresher flavor of water. Although there was a considerable amount of mesquite brush for fuel, Byrne reported that grazing was available on nearby hills.

The combined command rode eastward for the Big Spring the next day, finding that, "as we proceed, the grass improves." Fresh green grass covered the plain to their right, a result, they thought, of a recent firing of the prairie by Indians "on the grounds they most frequent." The sandy loam soils impressed diarist Byrne. "This land could, no doubt, be cultivated successfully if there was natural or artificial irrigation," he wrote.[16] This matter-of-fact statement was an acute observation on the underlying fertility of the Llano Estacado soils. Irrigation water could make this desert bloom for farmers. Even without water, Byrne thought livestock "to an incredible extent" could be raised near the scattered waterholes, a remark carried into reality a few decades later. Mesquite was common on the trailscape, becoming "particularly abundant as we approach the 'Springs.'" Shortly after noon they reached the Big Spring of the Colorado. Here wild plum trees in full bloom perfumed the springtime air. Torrents of cool, fresh springwater poured from canyon limestone masses into a long reservoir sixty feet wide and twenty to thirty feet deep. Ancient ledges strewn with petrified oyster-shells were found in the local geology. Much refreshed by the Big Spring, on April 2 the reunited command rode westward.

They rode for Sulphur Springs where five springs—one tinged with sulphur—fed a large pond in Sulphur Springs Draw. Pope's men also found abundant rattlesnakes there, "some of them of a monstrous size."[17] These huge reptiles commanded instant respect but rarely any mercy from armed and phobic men. The rattlesnakes of the southern Llano Estacado were especially dangerous to men on foot. Captain Pope still needed to take survey levels of the Llano Estacado from his old camp at Pecos Falls directly to Sulphur Springs. Accordingly, he dispatched Lieutenant Garrard and four men, well provisioned with kegs of water this time, to cross "the jornada" of the Llano. Pope and the others then sat back to await Garrard's return and results. A sense of ennui gradually affected the camp. "The level plain with which we are surrounded as far as the eye can reach," Byrne wrote in the expedition diary, "without a single brush or tree to break the monotony of the scene, is truly wearisome."[18] Both Taplin and Byrne reported considerable evidence of brush and mesquite along the various trails. At a ravine twenty miles from their camp Taplin had even encountered hackberry trees.

Lieutenant Garrard returned on April 11, having uneventfully run the levels across and back the 125-mile intervening distance. Everyone now made haste to leave the Llano the next day. As the expedition diary grandly noted:

> The surveying of this dreaded Llano Estacado is now accomplished; its reputed horrors, by no means exaggerated, have been overcome; it has been crossed safely by two of our parties without loss or suffering. This jornada is no longer a sealed book; we have now a thorough and practical knowledge of it in every respect.[19]

After rejoining the Marcy Trail, Pope's men made rapid progress, reaching their eastern destination of Fort Washita within two weeks.

Pope's report on his explorations appeared in volume II of the magnificent *Pacific Railroad Surveys*. He had much to say about the Llano Estacado in this report. He had no doubt that this "famous desert" constituted a natural obstacle to wagon roads. Extending from the 35th to the vicinity of the 30th parallel (as noted earlier, the Llano was considered in the 1850s to run far south of the 32nd parallel), there was no "living" or running water on it. Pope was happy to report, however, that mesquite roots provided an abundance of fuel. From Marcy's reports he had gleaned also an impression of sharp escarpment borders. Instead he found an exceedingly level topography from the Pecos to Sulphur Springs on the 32nd parallel, "without the appearance of any of the marked characteristics which had been attributed to it."[20] Topographically, Pope implied, the southern Llano was quite different from and superior to the northern or 35th parallel route. The gradient was so gentle, only their instruments could detect the descent from the Llano summit to the Colorado River headwaters. Calling the Llano Estacado "one of the most marked physical features of the American continent," a staff geologist extolled the flatland as "one of the most perfect examples of an elevated plateau, or mesa, that is found."[21]

The lack of major escarpments, chasms, or the rough terrain celebrated by Marcy's Red River Expedition, all made the 32nd parallel crossing ideal for Captain Pope. Although he thought the Staked Plain presented "no inducements to cultivation under any circumstances," it could become fair pastureland. (His subordinate, Byrne, had thought the soil fit enough for cultivation if only irrigation water could be secured.) Moreover, extensive gypsum deposits on the route promised some degree of mineral wealth. The most important question in John Pope's mind, however, was how to solve the problem of water in this otherwise perfect railroad topography. Steam-powered railroads needed regular water supplies.

At first Pope devoted only a speculative chapter, "Of Boring or Digging for Water on the 'Llano Estacado,'" to this vexing situation. Influenced by new theories on underground water, he began to think this drawback could be solved by drilling for artesian water on the plain. Soon he would devote several years of his life to the search for subterranean fountains. Pope's chapter VI of his report for the *Pacific Railroad Surveys* was immensely visionary. His role in this chapter was to stimulate the regional development of the Llano Estacado by removal of its most serious "natural obstacle": the regular absence of water. Already emigrant traffic was only a fraction of the amount possible because of this problem.

Captain Pope's vision of a remedy began by assuming that there were three sources of water already on the Llano. That is, on and beneath the amazingly level surface (so convenient and cheap for a railroad), Pope sensed a complex hydrography of tremendous size. The first element he called "shallow springs," consisting of ordinary rainwater percolating into the subsurface soils. This rainwater percolated until it hit an impermeable stratum (later identified as the Permian "red beds") and migrated to form nearby springs. Pope nonchalantly suggested that wells "dug at any point of the plain" could tap this shallow groundwater. "The average depth of such wells," he wrote, "would probably not exceed sixty feet, although at some points it might reach one hundred and fifty."[22] This estimation was indeed a close approximation to the vast Ogallala Aquifer, discovered by promoters and settlers some four decades later.

A second element in his remedy was equally farsighted. Captain Pope noted the presence of many "shallow basins" or playa lakes on the gently undulating surface. He proposed a series of reservoirs, built by digging wells or tanks in the beds of the larger playas. These surface reservoirs would retain local runoff well beyond the wet season. This method was later implemented by farmers who hoped to place the playa lands into cultivation. These artificial reservoirs would not provide, however, as abundant or as certain a water supply as Pope's third and grandest idea.

In addition to the "shallow spring" geography of the Staked Plain, Pope also postulated "deep-seated springs"—a vast complex of underground "water-sheets" that lay many hundreds of feet below the monotonous surface of the plain. Pope's remarks were clearly slanted to solicit public funds. With grant funding he envisioned leading an official search for these postulated deep-seated waters, huge subterranean springs which he assured the reader could be tapped to provide magnificent artesian flows. Pope's ideas reflected some of the best available scientific thinking of his day. From his reading and correspondence with the friendly Jules Marcou he had acquired a new vision of the Llano, one based on geological perceptions. That is, Captain Pope was one of the first imagineers to consider—based on the new spatialization of time by Western geology—on the underground environment of the Llano Estacado. What was beneath the superficial monotony?

Pope's "deep-seated springs" corresponded to A. B. Gray's "subterranean streams" and today's "deep aquifers." Their geography was much more complicated, according to Pope, than the shallow groundwater. Pope confidently asserted that, according to Marcou,[23] the Llano Estacado was basically some 700 feet of Jurassic tablelands on top of 3,000 feet of Triassic strata. Quoting Marcou with pleasure, Pope noted:

> The rocks of the Llano Estacado (the Jurassic and Triassic) dip gently to the east-southeast, and as the heads of the strata outcrop at the foot of the Rocky Mountains, called here Sierra Guadalupe, Sierra Sacramento, & c., in boring artesian wells on any point of the Llano, abundant columns of water would be found to gush out over this immense plain; so that the want of water is not an objection to the establishment of a railroad on the Llano Estacado, for it may be obtained anywhere.[24]

Like an Old Testament prophet newly returned from the wilderness, Pope espoused an utter conviction that hidden waters could be made to flow upon the surface at any point. One merely needed to smite the Llano with Moses's Rod—in this case Victorian rods, augurs, chisels, and derrick-irons—for boring through the overlying strata to reach the life-giving waters below.

Pope's vision was a grand one. He believed that by drilling through the "Jurassic" one would encounter vast amounts of Triassic water that underlay the initial impermeable strata. More importantly, the source of this water was distinct from the Staked Plain itself. Pope followed Marcou's grand reasoning that the Llano's Triassic strata was an extension of the "outcrop at the foot of the Rocky Mountains." He also knew that the eastern escarpment had numerous springs. Thus, Pope perceived a hydraulic connection between the "Rocky Mountains" and these "deep-seated springs":

> The deep-seated springs are not nearly so much affected by the rainfall as the land springs, since they not only receive their supply of water at remote points from this source, and from the melting of the mountain-snows, but they are sheltered from the air and sun, and protected from the consequent evaporation.[25]

In this hypnotic view, the snowfalls on the distant Rocky Mountains melted and some flowed into permeable or recharge strata, whence the water descended deep into the earth and migrated southeastward, eventually flowing like an enormous, pressurized, underground river beneath the Llano Estacado. This vision of an underground river was hard to shake. By boring wells into this deeper strata, Captain Pope was confident of tapping enough artesian water to form "the sources of running streams" on the surface.

Pope's optimism and grant-writing skills did not go unnoticed in the capital. Two important Southern politicians, Thomas J. Rusk of Texas and Secretary of War Jefferson Davis, were both anxious to increase the 32nd parallel's competitiveness against other routes. Pope's confident offer to return to the 100,000-square-mile table-lands east of the Rio Grande, and smite the rocks with modern machinery until nature's hidden fountains were released, made good politics for the South and for Texas. The advantage to Col. John J. Abert, Pope's superior as head of the Corps of Topographical Engineers, was the opportunity, as historian William H. Goetzmann notes, to exile "one of his most disagreeable young officers" to a thoroughly disagreeable tour of duty.[26] Accordingly, in the first quarter of 1855 Secretary of War Davis launched a series of geopolitical maneuvers.

First, with the support of Southerners like Texas's Senator Rusk, Davis obtained a major appropriation for Pope to conduct artesian drilling operations on the Llano Estacado. Thus, long before any settlers were present, the government was willing to spend money to promote regional development. Second, Davis announced on February 22 that the 32nd parallel route was the most logical choice for a transcontinental railroad, which it likely was given the technology of the time. If anything, however, the Pacific Railroad surveys had indicated the theoretical feasibility of all four routes. But if only one was to be chosen, Davis felt the evidence supported the southern one, especially with Pope's offer to find abundant artesian water. Certainly the practical 35th parallel route surveyed by Whipple was a smart political compromise. But Davis thought the 32nd parallel route was more sensible.[27]

Third, the secretary of war passed a measure in March for the importation of camels for testing purposes. This colorful experiment in solving transport and supply problems in West Texas received much attention. George Perkins Marsh thought it was a splendid idea.[28] By all accounts the imported camels performed well under the most trying of circumstances. Their use was confined mostly to the Trans-Pecos frontier area, but this decision by Secretary Davis did point to his perception of the Llano and other western regions as "desert" country. In this sense, Pope represented a new perceptual progressivism in the Southwest. Based on his personal experience in the region he saw abundant potential if only federal help could prime the pump, as it were. In contrast, Secretary Davis represented the popular public perception of easterners who "saw the West as a desert—an Algeria to be policed by a camel corps or squadrons of cavalry who would keep the tribes in the hills," as Goetzmann pointed out.[29]

For much of the next three years Pope directed a costly but quixotic search for artesian water on the southern Llano. His vision of artificial streams of distant snowmelt pouring onto the plains was greatly buoyed by reports of artesian water in Algeria. If the African Sahara had prospects of man-made oases, why not the Great Zahara of the American Southwest. With an initial appropriation from Congress he journeyed back to his old camp at Pecos Falls, near the crossing that now bore his name. Here at the mouth of Delaware Creek, he laid in supplies and unloaded his primitive drilling equipment. Three miles below this river crossing he eventually set up a comfortable depot and camp, and constructed several slab stone and adobe residences for himself and principal staff. He was prepared to stay until proven correct. Drilling equipment and supplies were then laboriously transported to a site eight miles east of their camp. With power provided by a new steam boiler laboriously hauled across the plains, Pope began boring into the ground in June 1855.

Boiler fuel was not a problem since Pope discovered that mesquite roots burned well. Although the work must have been tedious, he reported that within one and a half miles of camp his men grubbed and gathered 500 wagonloads of mesquite fuel. Problems with the primitive wooden drilling equipment and shortages in supplies, however, proved to be a constant source of delays and frustrations to everyone. At 360 feet they hit a seam of water which rose in the well for a distance, but nowhere near the surface. Moreover, despite hundreds of feet of slow, additional drilling progress, there was no sign of artesian flow whatsoever at this drilling spot. Where were the deep-seated springs? A third seam of subterranean water was reached that fall, but it caved in the well and the drillers lost their tubing.[30] The well had to be abandoned. He could find water deep below, but he could not make it rise to the surface!

Pope drilled in various other spots between the Pecos River and the Llano from November 1855 to the summer of 1856. Each well was a daily struggle in firing up the boiler and wearing out the hard rock below with their crude bits and drills. In the summer heat the work was merciless. Without the spatializing refinements of theoretical geology, many of the ordinary enlisted men must have wondered if the entire enterprise was one man's insane quest to bring forth sweet water in the middle of a West Texas desert. Moses could do it perhaps. It was less clear if a Yankee could succeed. "At the first Artesian Well, located upon the Llano Estacado, about fourteen miles east of the Pecos River," Dr. George Shumard wrote, "the Marly Clay formation was penetrated to the depth of six hundred and forty-one feet, and at the second one, located a few miles farther south, the borings were carried to the depth of eight hundred and fifty-eight feet, and in neither instance was the base of the formation reached."[31]

The lack of good drilling mud caused so much friction that pipe tubing often heated and warped. Pope drilled each well until his tubing gave out, or the well finally caved in on its own. He found enough casual seams of water that he was encouraged to prod his men and lift their hopes in the otherwise forlorn wilderness camp. In June 1856 he was drilling another deep well and looting his men's ash tent poles to serve as additional boring rods.[32] Although he found no artesian waters, all the abandoned sites now added up to another ironic toponym for the Llano Estacado—"Pope's Wells," later a landmark on the Goodnight-Loving Trail.[33]

For a time Pope had a veteran geological assistant in Dr. George G. Shumard. Shumard not only described the rocks emerging from Pope's Wells but he also collected specimens and recorded observations. During the summer of 1855 Shumard spent several months in camp with Pope and his men. He wrote that the Llano Estacado could be seen easily from Pope's Camp, "stretching for an indefinite distance eastward, in the form of an elevated and gently undulating plateau."[34] Like many visionaries Pope felt free to either take or ignore Shumard's advice on drilling locations, and in truth Shumard was not a great deal of help in finding artesian water where there was none to be had. He eventually packed up and left after doing what he could to help.

After months of hard work, however, there were still no artesian flows pouring onto the plain. Actually, the problem could be traced back partly to the Swiss geologist Marcou. By following Marcou's thinking Pope deduced that he could more efficiently avoid drilling through the Cenozoic strata of the Llano to reach the Mesozoic deep springs by simply starting at the lower strata along the Pecos River. In this manner, he managed to start drilling at one of the worst possible locations. Had he begun drilling much farther east above the caprock, he likely would have encountered the vast Cenozoic deposits of the shallow Ogallala Aquifer. (Elsewhere to the east were reservoirs of oil and gas.) Although these Ogallala waters are not artesian (or flowing under hydrostatic pressure to the surface), their very shallowness and abundance could have suggested the use of primitive steam pumps to make the "artificial streams" flow on the Great Zahara. Instead, by 1856 Pope needed more equipment, men, and money.

Pope was still optimistic. In a May 1, 1856, letter to Pope, Shumard wrote that if "a supply fail to be brought to the surface, such failure will be no evidence that water cannot be obtained upon the Llano Estacado by means of artesian wells."[35] Indeed, his confidence seemed inversely proportional to his lack of success. In December 1856 he published a small but significant promotional pamphlet on the project.[36] This "Letter of Capt. John Pope, U.S. Army, to Hon. T. J. Rusk, in relation to Artesian Wells in Texas and New Mexico" was carefully contrived to support further outlays of federal largess on the project. Pope described the many benefits that would accrue to the 100,000-square-mile region with the discovery of artesian water. Half of this unproductive immense region belonged to the Llano Estacado he claimed. With Jules Marcou having lost the *guerre des savantes* with American geologists, Pope now chose wisely not to mention his theoretical connections to him. In fact, he now claimed that the "Llano" had so few fossils that its formation was a matter of conjecture. Nevertheless,

> To whatever period this formation may be referred, there can be no question that the alternation of strata, pervious and impervious to water, outcropping at high altitudes, eminently adapts it to receive and retain abundant underground reservoirs, and the experiments made by the party under my charge, conclusively exhibit the existence of abundant successive seams of water from three hundred down to eight hundred and sixty feet below the surface, the deepest point to which borings have been carried.[37]

Pope's borings had probably encountered portions of the Dockum or Permian aquifers. Still he found no strong water or artesian flows in "this miscalled desert"[38] of grama. Pope's report and pamphlet proved successful, however, as another appropriation of public funds was forthcoming.[39]

With about a hundred men and more supplies he returned to his old Pecos camp in September 1857 and prepared to renew the tedious boring once again. He now chose for experimentation another well site, this time four miles to the south of his old one. But this location also avoided drilling on top of the Llano, and thus neatly dodged the Ogallala Aquifer. There were the usual breakages in machinery in the fall that slowed drilling. The weather in the winter of 1857–1858 was unusually severe and caused additional anguish. Even the hardness of the local water caused calcification problems with the steam boiler. As one frustration after another bedeviled his crew, the men grew mutinous. The lack of progress was personally frustrating as his monthly reports to Colonel Abert made clear.[40] From time to time in his camp on the Llano's edge, Pope brooded on all he was trying to accomplish.

In his Promethean mind's eye he saw himself unleashing artesian waters. Hidden Rocky Mountain springs would then rise to form streams strong enough to nourish the subsequent advance of Anglo civilization. This civilization would not destroy the Llano environment, but rather recast it. Through farms, pastures, and groves, the very North African nature of the region could be altered, until eventually the Llano Estacado would literally attract moisture all the way from the Pacific Ocean. And with Pacific moisture finally induced by man to water the plains, Pope envisioned a golden age of sustainable harmony between man and nature. He saw the barren desert transformed by men with vision. He saw artesian water pour onto rich cotton fields, nourishing new orchards and bringing life to new settlements.[41] And Pope saw this New Canaan as eventually luring in more rains from the distant Pacific Ocean to sustain it all.

Like Josiah Gregg, Pope very much believed in the "genial influences" of civilization, that human agency modified the land to the land's ultimate climatic benefit. This climatic belief could be one of the more devastating environmental deceptions of the nineteenth century. It made it possible to bless severe ecologic disruption in the name of progressively improving an environment, with the thought that a positive climatic feedback loop would provide the new moisture needed to sustain a New Canaan. But between the vision and Captain Pope lay the much needed reality of finding the artesian waters. The old problems of inadequate equipment (such as wooden drills), Indian incidents, and supply problems continued. He was convinced of the availability of water, in part due to an 1858 excursion to the Monahans sand dunes. A report from him to Abert grandiloquently announces the presence of water amid these forbidding dunes:

> Have also the honor to report for the information of the Bureau that water in great abundance has been discovered on the Staked Plain fifty miles east of the Pecos river along the 32nd parallel.—About two hundred springs have been found bubbling up through beds of fine white sand over a space of nine miles from north to south. . . . In the very midst of these white sandhills which are perfectly bare of vegetation burst up the fresh water springs, some of which are thirty yards in diameter.[42]

Captain Pope seemed to find water everywhere except at his drilling site that spring and summer of 1858. Adding to Pope's disgust the drillers eventually passed the 1,000-foot level without reaching a substantial deep aquifer fountainhead. When they reached 1,080 feet without encountering the hoped-for artesian springs, his funding was low. By the end of summer "Pope's Wells" were a lost cause. In July the noble experiment officially ended with the departure of all the men.

Thus, despite years of relentless effort and $100,000 in federal funds, John Pope had failed to remove the "natural obstacle" of aridity to civilization in the region. "Pope's Wells" and all they stood for were, in practical terms, a mirage, even as they deceptively appeared on new maps as an oasis. His failure was soon overshadowed, however, by the explosive struggle between the North and the South. Political dissension on which route to fund prevented a national consensus from developing any transcontinental railroad. For almost a decade the U.S. Army and its Corps of Topographical Engineers had devoted considerable effort to explore and map the Southwest. By 1858 much of the army's time was devoted to Indian problems, as Robert E. Lee's presence at Big Spring attested.[43] For the record, though, Pope had done more than simply espouse a revisionist perspective; he had actually tried to smite the Great American Desert metaphor. This kind of decisiveness would prove useful in the Civil War ahead.

"Pope's Camp" on the Pecos was soon reoccupied by a risky commercial business. The famous Butterfield Overland Mail Co. established a lonely station there in the fall of 1858 as part of its sprawling system. This pioneering enterprise retraced the old Ford and Neighbors Trail (Upper Road) across the southern Llano, then turned and followed up the army road from Horsehead Crossing to Pope's Crossing of the Pecos River. Several company stations were established on the Llano. Although not in operation for very long, the Butterfield operation did attract media attention to the southern Llano wilderness.

W. L. Ormsby, for example, was a special correspondent for the New York *Herald* on the first through coach. For his eastern readers he described the westward journey across the Llano as a tough passage through a dreadful desert.[44] The Llano was a "well weeded plain" with abundant small mesquite. But Ormsby was swayed to the desert perception by the presence of cacti, bear grass, and Spanish daggers along the route. Curiously, he noted a basic perceptual ambiguity about the region. On one hand Ormsby was delighted by the abundance of wildlife of this plain. "It seemed impossible," he wrote, "that so much life could exist without a constant, never failing supply of water."[45] He saw "droves of antelope" and large numbers of birds.

On the other hand, as the mule-drawn stagecoach lumbered along, the twenty-three-year-old newspaperman was horrified by the Golgotha trailscape. As far as "the eye could reach along the plain" Ormsby saw the depressing, decaying remains of livestock. He claimed that the bones of men also bore witness to a "fearful story of anguish and terrific death from the pangs of thirst,"[46] just the kind of bleak exaggeration to excite the Victorian imagination. Although some of these skeletons perhaps came from Indian raiders driving stolen livestock too hard, Ormsby attributed the losses mostly to the argonauts and emigrants. The sheer abundance of the bones served as a constant reminder and grim signification of death.

By 1860 the overland mail had begun to mitigate the environmental problems posed by the Llano crossing. An outpost called "Centralia Station" was supplied by wagons hauling kegs of water from the nearby Wild China Ponds. In June of that year a roving Englishman named William Tallack left an account of the lonely "Llano Estacado Station," an artificial oasis located thirty-five miles west of the Concho head. Tallack observed numerous prairie flowers and good game in these "clear upland regions." He also related that the major threat to a wagon road across the Llano was not environmental but cultural. Indian depredations were becoming a serious issue. Water haulers were killed, stations attacked, and livestock stolen.[47] By the time of Tallack's visit many people thought the Llano stations were the most dangerous ones on the entire line. The Llano Estacado Station was built therefore as a *posada* fortress with high, slab limestone walls and enclosed premises. There was an accurate expectation of trouble.

By the eve of the Civil War the southern Llano Estacado had several dimensions of death associated with it in the popular media. There was "terrific death from the pangs of thirst" as evinced by the trail bones and mirages; and there was hideous Comanche raiding and scalping at the remote stations. These dark *aperçu* reinforced the eastern predilection to regard the area as a hopeless desert wilderness.[48] Redfield's 1856 map of Texas summed up the prevailing public perception in the note that "El Llano Estacado, or Staked Plain" was "a sterile and desolate plain from 100 to 200 miles in width elevated about 4500 feet above the Gulf of Mexico without water or timber and with a scanty vegetation." This "sterile and desolate plain" is in stark contrast to the "Fertile land with a fair proportion of water" of Le Grand and Arrowsmith only a few years before.

A. B. Gray and John Pope, of course, had opposed the eastern projection of worthless desert and senseless death. Their experience on the border with Mexico revealed that there were much hotter, drier, and more infernal places than the Llano Estacado. Both had a strong, almost compelling intuition that an ocean of water lay beneath the great mesa. Like the ciboleros who admired the levelness for the smooth run it afforded, Gray and Pope admired the gentle grade for the ease of locomotives steaming across the continent. Where others saw a perpetual romantic desert, they projected a great vision for the land: artificial streams nourishing prospering towns and cities amid thousands of farms and ranches. Victorians and their marvelous new machines would even modify the climate beneficially, inducing more moisture from the sky for crops and pastures.

There was one important difference between the two men in 1860. Colonel Gray would die in April 1862 in a boiler explosion after the fighting around Island No. 10. He was serving the Confederate Army as an engineer, convinced that the Llano Estacado should remain an extension of the slave-state Confederacy. Captain Pope became Major General Pope with a rise to fame in the Union Army. Although both men shared a common and somewhat contrary optimism about the Llano, optimism grounded in environmental insight and academic speculation, neither could determine the kind of American society that would soon colonize this worthy land. The looming struggle and subsequent Civil War withdrew other officers like Robert E. Lee and Albert Sidney Johnston from their proximity to the Llano Estacado, marking the temporary cessation of almost all official interest in the region.[49] When next the Civil War survivors returned to the Llano, they came to conquer the land from the Comanche and Kiowa.

The mutual positivism of Gray and Pope derived from a fresh or Western perspective, one that envisioned geographic and commercial potential and that emphasized future growth. This Western perspective was based on first-hand experience and sampling rather than sensational narratives. Environmental constraints were acknowledged, but the hand of man and his ingenious machinery would transform the landscape from a wilderness of solitude to a sky garden of civilized farms, fields, and towns. This optimistic view required the kind of faith demonstrated by the first Europeans in search of Quivira.

·25·

LANGUAGE OF THE LLANO:
A CONCLUSION ON THE JOURNEY OF DISCOVERY

It is a lonely land because of its immensity, but it lacks nothing for those who enjoy Nature in her full grandeur. The colors of the skies, of the hills, the rocks, the birds and the flowers, are soothing to the most troubled heart. It is loneliness without despair. The whole world seems to be there, full of promise and gladness.

FABIOLA CABEZA DE BACA (*We Fed Them Cactus*)

Language is the house of Being. In its home man dwells. Those who think and those who create with words are the guardian of this home.

MARTIN HEIDEGGER (*Being and Time*)

In the beginning the European word was *lo llano*, a linguistic concept traced back thousands of years to the ancient Mediterranean and Near East perception of balance between earth and sky. Among the constellations traveling in the "animal circle" or zodiac was the fortunate seventh sign of Libra. In the Chaldean zodiac of man's fate, Libra was the equal balancing of day and night: the autumnal equinox. Perhaps it was also the accustomed time for Chaldean and Assyrian traders to adjust their scales, beams, and balances for the fall harvest. The sense of symmetry between people and stars, the perception of nature's balance between day and night, registered strongly with the later Greeks and Romans. They adapted the *libra* concept of balance and levelness and applied it to their practical machines and constructions. The Latin diminutive *libella*, a carpenter's level or plumb line, was absorbed and modified in later Romance languages. It emerged eventually as our Level (English through Old French) and our Llano (Spanish), each with their connotations of plain, flat, even, smooth.[1] The Spanish turned the modifier into a descriptive masculine noun, *el llano*, to designate a level field or large even ground, extrapolated into a geographic "plain" common in the New World experience of the Southwest. When considered expansively, level and llano also suggested attributes of openness, simpleness, starkness, and an avoidance of feature.

Finding a balance between attraction and aversion in the perception of the Llano landscape has colored the spectrum of European discovery and exploration of this fascinating realm for four and a half centuries. In the processing or filtering of the new land into narratives a great deal of environmental perception—and inevitably environmental deception—occurred. Is there, however, a common process of discovery between the two cultures of European descent? Indeed, what are the comparisons and contrasts between the Hispano and Anglo-American in observing the same region of objective reality? What cultural similarities and differences characterized their approaches to discovery?

The European exploration of the Llano from 1536 to 1860 was very much an extensional process of knowledge and understanding over time and space, a lengthy and rhetorical process whereby the first discoverers altered the relations between mankind and the environment, sometimes to the disadvantage of later explorers. Exploration was above all a conscious cultural choice, with Spanish and Anglo alike forced to raise funding, engage men, consider logistics, confront obstacles, and reach goals. Similarities and differences emerge strongly from a categorical examination of five exploration qualities: narrative structure, power and ideology, perception, art, and science. These five categories distinguished regional explorers in their appropriation and creation of the various Llanos that emerged from 1541 to 1860. Although considered singly as topics below, there was considerable overlap in their functioning and potential.

Exploration as Narrative

A common structural component uniting the Spanish and American explorers was the significance of the discovery narrative as a means of textualizing the landscape. There was a common storytelling technique to the chroniclers of the 1540s as well as the 1840s. In the basic sense of narrative structure there was little difference between the *relaciónes* of Castañeda and Jaramillo or the *jornadas* of Rodríguez, De Salas, Oñate, Vial, and Amangual from the daily *itineraries* and *reports* of Stephen H. Long, Lieutenant Abert, Captain Marcy, Lieutenant Whipple, Captain Taplin, or the *diaries* of Josiah Gregg, Thomas

Falconer, Peter Gallagher, Isaac Cooper, the Canadian River Forty-Niners, and the others. Like the perceptual similarity of llano and level, there was the shared narrative rhythm of a journey or *jornada*, with both words sharing the meaning of repetitive daily travel or tour (from the Latinate root of "diurnus" or daily, as in "journal" or "day-book").

Both the English- (through Old French) and the Spanish-language explorers thus shared fundamental European linguistic roots and narrative structures in their exploration, despite the intervening three centuries and innumerable political conflicts.[2] The individual narrative, like the early picaresque European novel, thus constitutes a primary text of personal discovery for the reader.[3] Consider that Isaac Cooper's account of the 1845 Abert reconnaissance, *The Plains, Being No Less than a Collection of Veracious Memoranda* . . . , belongs in the seventeenth century as much as the nineteenth with its old-fashioned title and conversion of a scribbler's day-book into serialized narrative. Cooper published his journal under the literary nom de plume of François des Montaignes; selecting a French alias to publish "veracious memoranda" was an ironic affectation.[4]

The traditional journey or *jornada*—a trip or tour with a clear beginning, middle, and end—thus structured the Llano discoveries encountered in the course of geographic exploration. Castañeda's three-part *Relación de la jornada de Cibola*, "The Relation of the Journey to Cibola," was largely as sophisticated in its narrative structure as Whipple's six-part *Report of Explorations for a Railway Route, Near the Thirty-Fifth Parallel of North Latitude*…or Möllhausen's *Tagebuch einer Reise vom Mississippi nach den Küsten Südsee* ("Diary of a Journey from the Mississippi to the Coasts of the Pacific"). The distance between Castañeda and Möllhausen, or Jaramillo and Cooper, varies considerably in content but little in narrative structure. Castañeda, Edwin James, and George Wilkins Kendall were kindred journalists in their counting of days and retellings of vivid journeys across time and space. They came from signifying societies that largely ignored daily camp routine to record sensation, suddenness, plenitude, strange peoples, new customs, geosophy, and commercial possibility; what the modernists might call the "shock of recognition."

Perhaps there is a primal logic to this journey-narrative: the cognitive story of travel to new realms of experience going back to the *Odyssey* or *Gilgamesh*. The *jornada* of Marcy or Oñate is equally a mnemonic device, a memory-aid to tell the story of new land and people. There is also the mimesis of the journey by the reader, who recapitulates the thrilling scenes and wonders at the new discoveries as they progressively reveal themselves. A clear beginning, middle, and end were concordant with the writer's departure, travel and adventures, and a safe return or "happy ending." This narrative progression conforms to the reader's experience as well: the departure from domestic distractions by opening the book, vicarious travel through space and experience, and at the end the reader, too, returns home safely. The journey-narrative or *relación* is therefore a literary simulation for the reader/traveler, a form of representation or mimesis.

In the early and late exploration texts of the Llano, geography and literature synthesize in the journey-narrative, leading to the chronicles of Jaramillo and Vial, the theographics of the millenarian Franciscans, the poetry of Albert Pike, the mournful elegiacs of Randolph Marcy, the georgics of Josiah Gregg, the oral folktales of El Cuate, the *corridas* of Manuel Maes, the surreal literary hoax of Alexander Le Grand, and the agonistic aeneid of the Texan–Santa Fe Expedition by Kendall, or the Coronado Expedition by Castañeda. We should consider carefully then, not only the content but also the socioliterary style of exploration narratives in making the Llano plain. The very name *El Llano Estacado* is a Spanish didactic toponym expressing the featureless character of the region. This landscape requires signposts or *estacas*. In this manner the narrators poured new messages of geography into old bottles of literature. The specific relation of textual form to intended meaning depended heavily upon the context and personal experience of the Llano Estacado. The greater the contact, the closer the fusion. This fusion of geography and rhetorical devices was a common European and American response to new discoveries. Edgar Allan Poe's deliberate use of the personal narrative of exploration likewise provided a crucial verisimilitude for his fantastic fiction.

Like the best of literature, exploration also has its heroes. *Jornada* protagonists of discovery narratives like Cabeza de Vaca, Coronado, Jaramillo, Vial, Oñate, Mares, and De Salas match well with the heroics of Long, Pike, Marcy, McClellan, Whipple, Möllhausen, Gregg, and Kendall. Heroines were not unknown, as in the sad case of the captivity narrative of Sarah Ann Horn.[5] There were even villains of sorts: the sinister, brooding, featureless landscape, a deceitful El Turco, Albert Pike's "cowardly *pelayos*," Kendall's Kiowa "banditti," Falconer's Mexican gaolers, comanchero traffickers, and the fiendish Comanche where appropriate. The reliability of the narrator is equally a concern for all readers. Most of the accounts claim to be fully representational, that is, faithfully mimetic in nature. There is a deliberate and accurate replication of experienced reality.[6] Perhaps Castañeda's and Cabeza de Vaca's narratives are powerful when considered as a break with the illusive literature of chivalry in favor of an early New World realism that culminated in the nineteenth century, the very period of their historicist rediscovery and widespread critical recognition.[7]

The strangeness of the land brought many narrators into ironic and illustrative styles—metaphors, images, word-portraits, aesthetic feelings—that penetrated the discovery narratives with self-consciousness and symbolism. These ironic styles and symbols uncovered or defined recognizable patterns in cultural thought. Hayden White argues that nineteenth-century historiography began and ended in an ironic mode, a suspicious, sophisticated, self-conscious writing that moved from Romance to Tragedy to Comedy.[8] Some narrators were rightfully questionable. Fray Marcos de Niza's *jornada* is still debated, while Le Grand's successful mimesis of a survey on the High Plains of Texas passed into a generation of books and maps. This untruthful realism did not prevent their symbolism from spreading far and wide. Coronado and Castañeda declare their reliability openly and often, while the officers and explorers from the Corps of Topographical Engineers trust to their instruments and sciences. Perhaps the finest antebellum expression of landscape realism was achieved with the publication of the *Pacific Railroad Surveys*.

Both Spanish and Anglo explorers created new metaphors or representations of the great mesa. In the process they often substituted signs of the real for the real. As the Hispano Homeland pushed eastward, its culture bathed the Llano with lore and legend.[9] As the Anglo-American Homeland pushed westward, it brought both its lore and its new techniques of literature and written culture. The American public soon adapted and disseminated symbols from both cultures. A few popular writers like Charles Webber and Mayne Reid suggested fantastic elaborations, but whereas popular literature touched the Llano, it never overshadowed the conventional discovery narrative.

Exploration as Power

Common to Anglo and Hispano exploration was the commercial impulse, captured so eloquently in Josiah Gregg's *Commerce of the Prairies*. The 400-year "boom" that Walter Prescott Webb characterized as the Great Frontier quickly brought the Europeans to the Llano. The Spanish found no mineral wealth and therefore did not settle, choosing an eventual collaboration with the strongest tribe to ride the whirlwind of mounted tribal warfare: the Comanche.[10] Whether as individual enterprise like Albert Pike or Josiah Gregg, or the expensive company expeditions like Coronado or the Texan–Santa Fé Expedition, there were bold motives to realize commerce.[11] Mercantile capitalists directly financed A. B. Gray and Juan De Salas. The dreams of Gran Quivira, Santa Fé, and the glorious plans for a transcontinental railroad all shared the 300-year hope of wealth ferried across the perfect levelness.

The largest promoter of commercial exploration was the government, whether royal or representative. Although their provincial affairs were poorly funded and they failed to follow through, the New Mexican officials nevertheless dispatched Pierre "Pedro" Vial, Fragoso, Amangual, and others to reconnoiter corridors of potential commerce between Louisiana and New Mexico. The comanchero trade was licensed heavily by Spanish, Mexicans, and even the Americans; periodic confiscations of unlicensed trade goods took place. Government interests directly inspired the Texan–Santa Fé Expedition merchants, subsidized for years the fruitless drilling of John Pope, authorized the pearling ventures, and directly financed the expensive Long, Whipple, Pope, and other surveys of conquered territory.

The most pervasive mercantile capitalists were the comancheros of the late eighteenth and nineteenth centuries. Legally, comanchero ventures required government licenses, formal permission to trade upon the plains. Periodic restrictions on the trade helped to regulate relations with the tribes. The licit and illicit trade grew rapidly after De Anza's landmark treaty with the Comanche despite the hazards of Pawnee attack, storms, and possible treachery. Although later demonized as a profession for its role in fueling Comanchería raiding, the trade in captives, and its resistance to white settlement with guns and liquor, by far the bulk of the trade was in comestibles and ordinary trade items. Powder and lead were essential to the hunt as well as the raid. The attempt of Anglo traders at Adobe Walls to horn in on the business was soon over. U.S. military commanders like Carleton simply continued the prior practice of issuing licenses, with little control over the flurry of subleasing that followed. By the eve of the Civil War, the trade in stolen livestock was big business, organized at the community level, and typically illegal.[12] There were few Anglo-Americans on or near the Llano who did not cross paths with the traders or use their trails.[13] Comanchero dugouts at campgrounds around the Llano Estacado established their business locations for the convenience of all concerned. Indeed, the comancheros were indispensable lubricants between the Spanish and Comanche-Kiowa. The extensive trade of these "Prairie Schooner Pirates" only intensified as the newly independent Americans supplanted French ambitions over the Southwest.

Keyed to the seasonal rhythm of New Mexican settlement and the fall migration of the herds, the cibolero caravans in turn harvested the bison of the Llano Estacado. Much like the North Atlantic fishermen harvesting the cod of Georges Bank, bands of processors led by specialists set out onto the level ocean prairie to work the superabundance wherever they encountered it. The sense of plenitude attached to the buffalo was common to the first accounts. This plenitude evidenced the thoughtfulness of God in endowing these fertile new plains with so many *vacas* or cattle.[14]

The Spanish sought early to establish their power over this new nature. The arrival of the horse, first reintroduced to the plains (after some 10,000 years of absence) by Coronado's conquistadors, would of course profoundly and ultimately transform the native tribes of the Southwest.[15] Horses and mounted men were an important part of the early control process, given their proven role in the pacification of rebellious peoples. Unlike the later Anglo explorers, who encountered excellent if not better horsemanship among the natives, the first Spanish explorers enjoyed the enormous extensional power and mobility of the horse. Their guns, armor, and tactics demonstrated their military power most convincingly, although for many years they fought few battles on the plains.

The early Spanish used late-Renaissance instrumentation and technology, but the featurelessness, vastness, and lack of settlements and agriculture on the Llano repulsed them.[16] There were other and better opportunities for colonial settlement. The Franciscan missionaries sought spiritual power or control over the plains tribes. Their alignment with the Jumanos of the South Plains nominally extended the Catholic Church onto the Llano, but to little lasting impact. There was even some later embarrassment over the fantastic spiritual surveys of

María de Jesús de Agreda, "The Lady in Blue." Zaldivar's corrals and domestication efforts on the bison were equally to little avail. Only the transcultural ciboleros established an important relationship to the great herds.

Colonialist power over the Llano was primarily cartographic discourse in the seventeenth and eighteenth centuries. The interests of Spain and France clashed repeatedly over boundaries, trade, and imperial expansion. This colonialist impulse to power and ideology suffused the maps of Le Maire, Delisle, Homann, Seutter, and Beaurain. In this regard, critic José Rabasa is correct that America was "invented" by Eurocentric cultural and commercial interests.[17] These colonialist maps were excellent in areas of expertise and experience such as the Mississippi River or the Gulf of Mexico. But they revealed little of the Llano. The actual means of appropriation involved considerably greater expense and effort, as Marcy's cumbersome 1852 expedition demonstrated. But even Marcy's revelatory maps were full of errors, aesthetic stances, and a lost "head spring." Of necessity each imperial power textualized their arrogant claims to the Indian hinterland with geosophical maps and rhetorical styles in the manner of the day.

Exploration as Art

In the Eurocentric invention of the Llano, art played a successively greater role from the sixteenth to the mid-nineteenth centuries, culminating in the aesthetics of Pike, Kendall, Marcy, Whipple, and Pope. Although narrative structures changed little, the quantum elucidation and elaboration of natural history changed the visual conveyance of information quite noticeably. Contrary to the oral traditions and customs of the New Mexican perception of the Llano, the Anglo-Americans quickly enlisted artists, new printing techniques, and the graphic arts in the regional documentation process. The new technology undoubtedly opened the mind of America to the Southwest and promoted its geographic potential. "From every exotic corner of the globe, artists brought back pictures that they intended as precise illustrations to accompany factual descriptions of what the explorers saw," notes the historian Ron Tyler, "and lithographers and engravers printed and disseminated these images in unprecedented numbers, through newspapers, broadsides and individual prints, and books and portfolios."[18]

There was an unmistakable artistry and visualization that characterized the Anglo explorers of the High Plains. The narrative textual "painting" of George Wilkins Kendall was complemented by a famous early lithograph of buffalo plains in Kendall's work. The artist-naturalist Titian Ramsey Peale of course accompanied the Stephen H. Long Expedition. Lieutenant Abert was noted for his drafting and artistic merits, easing his appointment to the Corps of Topographical Engineers, and Whipple liked to sketch the scenery. This procession of easterners exploring the High Plains of Texas and New Mexico was well-educated in the artistic fashions, skills, and tastes of their day. Many brought preconceptions to the land derived from European models of exploration.

Some explorers were Romantics, the American homespun version of a way of looking and relating to nature. Albert Pike epitomized this early-nineteenth-century perspective applied to the western prairies. There were Byronic styles, poetic arts, and a renewed emphasis on the perception of nature in his depiction. As Webb's Great Frontier progressively rolled westward, the Romantic frontier of poets and artists shifted as well. The new Quivira was Santa Fé, with romantics like Pike, Cooper, Kendall, Falconer, and Gregg fashioning the Llano Estacado along their way. Later romantics like Charles Webber and Mayne Reid adopted the Llano for its very innocence and wilderness, a Lost Eden or garden-world. The American perception of the Llano was therefore deeply colored by aesthetic illusionism. The flatland immensity was thought to exhibit grand sublimity in its immensity, absoluteness, and grandeur. In contrast the escarpment borders evinced the aesthetic qualities of the picturesque: roughness, irregularity, sudden variation. The vertiginous abysses and flat expanses in Caspar David Friedrich's 1818 painting *Chalk Cliffs at Rügen* had an American parallel in Kendall's re-visioning of Tule Canyon, whereas the luminist quality of background light and foreground detail affected Whipple's "Crown of Light" sunrise vision. The landscape of the Llano spoke to the romantics in artistic qualities, and they wrote of regional beauty.

Other explorers were "Humboldt's Children," the heirs of the great German geographer who exercised such a strong influence on the age. Baron Alexander von Humboldt believed each region produced its own form of beauty, and he encouraged explorers to take an aesthetic interest as well as a physical interest in the regionally distinctive landscape. His protégé, the artist-writer Heinrich Balduin Möllhausen, did precisely that in the Llano portion of his narrative. Möllhausen's art was criticized for its lack of fidelity in his own time and later. But his landscape lithographs of the Llano for the 35th Parallel Survey and his subsequent book mark significant and representative environmental imagery. He created illustrations and employed colorful verbal arts (as the "German 'Fenimore Cooper'") to capture and even invent a spirit of place.

Others were appreciative of the Gothic Revival in architecture and the Picturesque in painting. Both Marcy and Kendall saw battlements, glacis, castles, columns, and similar Gothic fantasies in the Red River canyonlands. They recognized the incongruity of their European artistic associations, but the visions of rocky crags, windswept trees, eroded ravines, and wild panoramas seemed straight out of the Apennine canvasses of Salvator Rosa or suitable subjects for the picturesque brushwork of a Claude Lorrain. European landscape aesthetics—prospects, vistas, and panoramas—provided an important cultural lens in the perception of the region. The presence of artists like Schuchard and Möllhausen on expeditions was a further acknowledgment of the promotional power of art in opening the Southwest to the public.

The distinctive American contribution lay with the widespread creation, publicity, and dissemination of new imagery. Rotary steam presses and the rise of tabloid journalism increased the public consumption of new imagery of the Southwest. A rumor that Randolph Marcy's party had been wiped out by hostiles proved a great boon when the explorer and the others returned to an unexpected hero's welcome. The subsequent press attention was reflected in the sheer number and quality of the Ackerman lithographs produced in New York for his Senate *Report*.[19] To be sure the Ackerman and Lawrence lithographs were heavily romanticized, as was Marcy's narrative. "The fanciful and romantic observations of the first observers," noted the art historian Bernard Smith, "were not borne out by closer examination."[20] Marcy's metaphor of the Great Zahara, captured in the later "Mirage" engraving, was a powerful statement of the region's illusionist aspect.

But the detailed text, extensive illustrations, and competent appendices of the 32nd and 35th *Pacific Railroad Surveys* marked a decisive turn to visualization of the environment. Whipple's on-site sketches of pictographs, land forms, and sunrises were processed by Orr into engravings, while Möllhausen's art was converted with new technology into advanced chromolithographs like "Comanche Camp on Shady Creek." There was of course considerable overlap between art, narrative description, and scientific investigation as the Great Reconnaissance also explored the new graphic techniques and technology of representation.

Exploration as Perception

The discovery process within exploration focuses on the novel, the new, the bizarre, the sensational, the extraordinary. Both the Spanish and American explorers claimed the right of "first discovery" through their reportage of the Llano's strange phenomenon. The strangeness of the land often occasioned similar perceptions and remarks. There are, therefore, important correspondences in the Hispano and Anglo perceptions of the Llano Estacado. Pedro de Castañeda and Josiah Gregg both contemplated the interior drainage of playas; Coronado and James W. Abert marveled at the plenitude of buffalo and game; Oñate and Marcy noted their routes along the innumerable escarpment springs; Castañeda and Albert Pike wrote eloquently of the panoply of sky; José Mares and Lt. Whipple named their camps with an eye to local features; and Francisco Amangual and John Pope led similar cavalcades of officers and bored soldiers across the illimitable levelness. They all keenly observed the remarkable native Americans, from Querecho to Teyas to Jumano to Comanche.

The environmental features that emerge from this cross-cultural survey suggest a distinctive *genius loci* for the Llano Estacado based on level plains rich in game, its peculiar topography and hydrography, and the distinctive natives. As a place-setting for discovery, the region of course engendered new sensations and perceptions to the eye, yet also to touch, smell, taste, and hearing. The Lennox copy of Castañeda's manuscript constitutes a particularly impressive discourse on these phenomenological attributes. For Castañeda, taste is one important means of learning. Recognition takes many sensual forms in a new landscape, often symbolized by emblematic objects (*ciruelas*) or metaphors (*el bordo*). Pedro de Castañeda's account suggests that the Llano was a new school for the mind, a discovery or learning process involving contact with all the senses.

Light, sight, and sound were magnified and carried for long distances. New animals—"cibolas," "deer as big as horses," "animals like squirrels," and "unicorns"—stimulated the zoological imagination. Fields of new plants carpeted the ground. Huge storms were plainly seen, but too distant to be heard. The fragrance of spring prairie and the pungent odor of burning bison dung, the pleasing taste of Cona's plums and grapes, the touch and taste of buffalo, the noisy sounds of canyon springs and summer herds, these and a thousand other overlapping sensations created a manifold land. The processing of these new data reached a critical mass such that a qualitative recognition emerged, one that declared this land as a particular kind of place, a distinctive region, a striking realm that lingered in the mind.[21] In such a case one could argue that the great mesa had a presence or spirit. This learning process was keyed to contact, the primal interactive sensations of touch, smell, taste, sight, and hearing between the curious individual and a novel environment.

There were some important differences in the qualitative and aesthetic perceptions of the mesaland.[22] The first explorers interpreted the environment as a wilderness or *despoblado*, but against different environmental and ethnographic contexts. The lack of trees on the plains was more than an inconvenience to woodland-culture easterners; it created a psychological block, keeping their explorations and routes largely confined to the interfingering woodland ecosystems. The climate of the land seemed to trouble the first Spanish explorers less than the first American explorers. Perhaps the climate shifted from Coronado's cooler, wetter time to now, or perhaps the acclimated Spanish traveled at more favorable times, spring and fall. Anglo observers caught in the summer heat (Stephen H. Long) or winter blizzards (Albert Pike) of the Canadian Valley thought the region inhospitable, the so-called Great American Desert, whereas the Spanish explorers traversed the same stretch in early spring (Oñate) and fall (Zaldivar) and found the land fertile and the climate quite pleasant.

There was also a geographic bias in perception between the northern Llano Estacado and its southern margins. The Argonauts of 1849 and after who crossed the southern Llano Estacado in the summer pronounced the region a hopeless and desolate waste. Their stock suffered and died, and skeletal remains accumulated with other flotsam and cast-offs to create the image of death for the trail. The hundreds of horse skulls and skeletal debris at Horsehead Crossing on the Pecos, a gruesome sight for most, arose from the Comanche practice of driving stolen livestock so relentlessly that exhausted horses finally reaching the ford plunged in, overwatered, and died in large numbers. The southern sojourners branded the land as barren and forever uninhabitable; a perception leading Secretary of War Jefferson Davis to experiment with a camel corps modeled on the French conquest of Algeria. At about the same time in the north, Marcy was enjoying early summer rains near McClellan Creek, and appreciative *pastores* began to edge onto the nearby plains in the wake of traders and hunting parties.

There was, however, a common perceptual strangeness to the region that struck observers like Castañeda and Albert Pike alike. Many explorers made reference to the illusive nature of the environment. Mirages, distortions, writhings, and atmospheric loomings gave the land a phantasmagorical character. Images could not be trusted. Marcy wondered at an apparition of antelope bounding across the sky. Fata morgana of lost lakes, mountains, and forests rose from the ground to deceive the viewer. The very atmosphere was a camera obscura. The level plains proved difficult to illustrate because there was no frame, few objects of human interest, and an agoraphobic perspective. The colonial experience with mirages in North Africa suggested the Llano Estacado was analogous to the Sahara Desert. The explorers also noted the potential of the Llano as a landscape of fear—of storms, being lost, hunger, and thirst. There was a foreboding or melancholic quality that marked this environment as a particular challenge. Fire-blackened plains, trail skeletons, lightning, tornadoes, crippling prairie-dog holes, huge rattlesnakes, hunting accidents, hostile natives, dry waterholes, salt lakes, enormous dunefields, and death itself were possibilities. Castañeda feared being lost, Coronado feared there was no gold, Pike feared the blizzards, Kendall feared hunger and rattlesnakes, Marcy feared thirst, Abert feared marauders, and Pope feared there was no artesian water. As a place-setting for fear there seemed to be something for everyone.

The New Mexicans recognized the risks, although it did not deter them from needed travel or group ventures. Like the Argonauts they recognized the safety-in-numbers factor for their caravans. With their excellent system of cognitive mapping, they generally knew where and how to go, avoiding the dissolution that wrecked the Texan–Santa Fé Expedition.[23] Before the chase the ciboleros gathered to say prayers and steady their nerves. Comancheros might find excellent trading with the Comanche only to fall victim to a Pawnee raid on the return home. The nineteenth-century *corrida* of Manuel Maes captured well the sense of danger and dread in a tale of the accidental death of a cibolero:

> *Caballo alazán tostado*
> *Que tu la muerta me dites*
> *En este llano estacado*
> *Vienes a hacer calavera*
> (Ah, my brown-sorrel horse
> That you deliver death to me
> Ah, on this Staked Plain
> You come to make a skull)[24]

There was also a sense that this was a strange land, one that heightened the human senses. There were *cosas señaladas*, in Castañeda's words, "celebrated things."[25] The early Spanish wondered at marvels such as new species, the elk and antelope, asking themselves if these species were the result of promiscuous intercourse among New World species. The American explorers were less innocent perhaps in these matters, but entirely credulous in assertions on the psychology of the region. Pike and Kendall thought the monotony of the Stake Prairie turned the mind inward, upon itself, wherein consciousness appeared as self-consciousness. Their Stake Prairie was a self-referential landscape, a land that made you think about it. The ocular monotony turned travelers to their own inner state, and the journey became a voyage of self-discovery. All observers commented on the exceeding levelness and vastness of the *tierra llana*. There was also a deeper feeling of mystery, that something more was there but unstated or unstateable: the Lady in Blue, white bears, a gigantic bone heap, missing gold, pearls, fata morgana, a massacred wagon train, a celebrated head spring, lost lakes.

This perceptual quality of inexpressibility fed the Romanticism of the best American narrators, although the Spanish also had to find words, give names, and create analogs for the new environment.[26] Grounded in artistic models of exploration and discovery, their texts and illustrations partly sought to ennoble their exploits by reference to the intrinsic bizarreness of the region. Natural history became a fantastic, metaphoric background against the Victorian drama of individual human discovery. Aesthetic models placed the Americans square in the path of epiphanies inspired by the landscape. Thus, the ascent onto the Llano became a veritable feat, while crossing a spur of the mesa constituted a heroic exploit for the Americans, although by 1850 neither was of much note for hundreds of well-informed Hispanos. They approached the Llano with a different cultural ecology, and an environmental perception oriented to the poetic imagination and oral traditions. Their cautiousness was born of experience with its dangers.

Exploration as Science

A significant difference between Spanish and American exploration lay with the increasing empirical perception of the new land after 1800 by the Americans and their European allies. Although both empires were interested in the raw conquest of space and its geographic measure, the Americans were additionally interested in contextualizing the landscape in the systematic sciences of anthropology, biology, geology, meteorology, botany, and zoology. Their claim and acquisition of the Llano coincided with the fundamental scientific revolution shaping the optimistic new nation. They were after diverse kinds of information, especially causality, and not just a tangible mercantile commodity like gold, beaver, bison meat, or horses. Thus, Marcy routed out prairie dogs to examine their relationship to rattlesnakes, Josiah Gregg speculated about special prairie gases causing the mirages of the plains, Isaac Cooper noted the migrating ducks and snipes of the "mirrors of the prairies" or playas, and Jules Marcou climbed Pyramid Mountain to collect fossils that excited his imagination and fueled his theories on the basic geology of North America.

This approach was a qualitatively different kind of perception of the land. Starting from humble speculation and observation in the personal narrative, the scientific gaze eventually required teams of highly trained specialists to assay and assess properly the many new referents. The government expeditions of Whipple, Pope, and Marcy collected hundreds of specimens of rocks, minerals, snakes, mammals, birds, reptiles, and fish for classification. The "shock of recognition" caused by some fossils, species, and rocks led to academic feuds and vitriolic disputes. Marcou never forgave American geologists for debunking his Jurassic theory inspired by the Llano Estacado, while Blake maintained an ideology that U.S. geologists simply knew the empirical landscape much better than many a foreign scientist. In short, the Americans proved diligent classifiers, measurers, quantifiers, and patriots after the initial burst of romantic discovery.

The language of empirical discovery was often arcane and reductionist. Writers and editors relegated these data to appendices of enumerations, measurements, reckonings, and tabular facts. Nevertheless, data of all kinds enormously colored the content of American narratives. The widespread use of instrumentation such as barometers, chronometers, and transits marked another divide between Hispano and Anglo exploration. The momentum of antebellum scientific imperialism crested for the Llano with the Pacific Surveys of the 1850s, as government teams of artists and scientists extensively collected, collated, classified, and published a wealth of empirical data.[27] Collected and pickled specimens of all kinds were sent back to the East Coast by Long, Marcy, Marcou, Shumard, Pope, and others for processing and review by eminent scientists. The degree of sorting and naming of new species, as defined by the European standards of the day, was an important reflection of this subtle way of seeing that separates the Hispano and Anglo discovery, even though Coronado certainly forwarded native crafts, artifacts, and painted bison robes to Viceroy Mendoza.

The presentation of this new documentary data often required new artistic forms of representation, a process described by historian William H. Goetzmann as "scientific art."[28] This process of conveying complex information in visual form was not unknown to the Spanish. Their cartography was generally better informed although less oriented to precise instrumentation. Enrico Martínez's map of 1602 represented superior knowledge of the interior plains and featured a chart.[29] The map of Pierre Vial's journey reflected the positive and negative of Spanish "scientific art": it was based on keen personal perception and astute geographical relationships, but the lack of instrumentation, scale and distance, and the lack of accurate proximate relations made it more artistic than scientific. The local New Mexican knowledge and experience of the Llano

Estacado was indeed superior to the American explorers in most respects, but presumably it appeared in oral forms—corridas, toponyms, and tales—rather than more graphic or visual forms. Gómara's small woodcut of a bison is rightfully a landmark natural history print, but the Spanish did little drawing or illustrative documentation of the Texas plains afterward.

In contrast, after working out their romantic agonies on the Llano the American explorers rapidly applied science to the landscape and realism to its literature. They discovered new realms of meaning that were expressed graphically, as with Marcy and Whipple, in artistic drawings of regional plants, animals, and fossils, in colored lithographs of special scenery and places, in schematics of geology and stratigraphy, and in representative illustrations of land forms and peoples. Engineers and surveyors carefully assessed its potential for a railroad, noting elevations and grades on detailed charts. For empiricists the Llano was very much a place-setting for scientific recognition. Probably the greatest of the shocks was the dawning desire, subsidized by scientists like Marcou and Shumard, that an ocean of water should underlie this "ocean prairie." Captain Pope's restless search for artesian water likewise employed scientific art to buttress its funding.[30]

This paratactic style or "scientific gaze" at the mesa can also be traced, as I have argued throughout this study, back to the Coronado expedition of 1542. Coronado's account of the land, settlements, and geography, and Castañeda's multilinear descriptions of plants, animals, and peoples marked a fresh Renaissance impulse, a spontaneous attitude of curiosity with a new emphasis on ethnography and natural history in the New World. The collision of European newcomers with the Llano people and environment was especially encouraging for inductive inquiry. Consider the account of conquistadors trying to explain—by reference to natural phenomena alone—the enormous boneheap on the south shore of a salt lake. Their inductive reasoning was a new way of seeing. The Spanish tried to read the text of this curious landscape, looking for causal relations behind the marvels. In this new realm the older, crippling, medieval deductivism was of little use to practical minds bent on unraveling the secrets of a landscape. Therefore, the description of new lands and resources was to be based on cosmographic facts if possible, the reliance on fancies producing less than desirable results.

Unfortunately, Castañeda's manuscript suffered from the cloistering of Spanish archival knowledge; that is, no one really knew about his revelatory work until its nineteenth-century archival rediscovery by Ternaux-Compans. This loss of historic visibility impaired the recognition due the great cosmographic results of his travel report, leaving future generations the sensationalistic husks of myth and drama to ponder instead. But Castañeda showed precisely the "spontaneous capacity to observe and describe" that characterized many intellectual encounters of the sixteenth-century Spanish mind with the New World.[31] He was especially interested in the physical and cultural geography of the plains. Castañeda's lack of formal education may have been an advantage, of course, since he had fewer scholastic misconceptions to confuse him on the plains of truth. He rightfully belongs then in the pantheon of Renaissance regional geographers—the missionaries, chroniclers, explorers, and synthesizers active in the hundred years from Columbus to Acosta. The humanistic geographer Edward Relph calls this sense of wonder, "the mark of a pre-scientific attitude—that is, of a compassionate intelligence that seeks to see things in and for themselves."[32] Following other channels this etiological perspective matured and returned to the Llano with the Americans.

American scientists were eager to incorporate the Llano into the general integration of nineteenth-century science. After its qualitative baptism with Romanticism, the land was increasingly quantified, platted, and plotted. The faith in science was strong enough to suffuse realism in the literature. This scientization of the landscape was also a discourse of power, a path to both dominance and affection over the new land, but one that was quite unlike the contemporary loric relationship of the Hispano pioneers. Whipple and Simpson sought to appropriate the past as well as the present of the Llano. Their systematic concern with *origins* reflected an expanded scope of activity for these sons of a second Renaissance. In its new visual power this American scientific gaze attempted to show objective reality, although it still reflected the clinging veils of aesthetic ideology and Victorian culture as Marcy's purple prose made clear. Its mythic discourse was therefore abstractional and national instead of naturalized and local.

This scientific impulse created new perceptions sometimes at odds with the "landscape of fear" conventions of romantic imperialism associated with Abert and Marcy. Marcou's observations of the Canadian River springlands led him to posit a plentiful source of water beneath the plains. A. B. Gray and John Pope struggled against a common public perception of the land as an uninhabitable desert, an infernal Saharan realm unworthy of a railroad. Their rhetorical styles and empiricism together sought to dissociate the Llano from the Great American Desert, and to associate it instead with productive Anglo migration and settlement.[33] The role of science in the promotional conversion of dread to desire was highly significant, as it tended to reverse the earlier romantic excesses that marred Marcy's work, for example, but it also committed excesses of its own in a religious faith in materialism. This scientific gaze saw vast commercial potential, prosperous ranches, irrigated farms, orchards, and towns; indeed, Gray quarreled with the artist Schuchard because of the latter's lack of projection of this commercial potential. "Pope's Wells" was the hopeful metaphor for the very agency of man and machine transforming the land and eventually improving the climate, a grand dream of progress that involved the conquest of nature.

John Pope had a decent idea, as the later artesian wells of the Pecos Valley at Roswell demonstrated, but not much luck. "Pope's Wells" also conveyed the problem of environmental deception, for Pope's etiology or explanation of cause owed more to wishful rhetoric than to reality. Artesian waters stubbornly refused to be where the scientists said they should be found. The Spanish restricted their dreams of conquest to souls, commodities, and tribes, having little thought of altering God's basic creation. The American visual conventions of the Llano reflected this movement from Romanticism to Empiricism in the shift from the picturesque to the documentary, as the casual Claude Lorraine rustics of Lawrence's lithographs of Palo Duro disappeared from view, and schematic cross-sections of dead earth and underground waters replaced them. The new paths of perception lent themselves to new vistas and horizons.

Both the Spanish and Americans resorted to rhetorical devices, narrative structures, metaphors, similes, and other literary conceptions to convey the personal experience of exploring the Llano Estacado. They also used associative or analogous perception to draw similarities between the Llano and the other world regions. The Querechos were like the Moors, said Coronado's chronicler; the bison were like the Moroccan cattle said Cabeza de Vaca; the Comanches were like the Bedouin, said the poet Albert Pike. The Llano was compared to the Sahara by Marcy and the high steppes of Tartary by Gregg. None of them had been to Africa or Central Asia, but they and their readers had read of African deserts, animals, and peoples in diverse books of travel. They contextualized the land with reference to analogous realms found in books and stories.

Both cultures also resorted to distinctive, even whimsically associative toponyms like *"Las Escarbadas"* ("The Scrapings") or "Red Deer Creek" to characterize a region of so little apparent character. For the practical Hispanos of New Mexico, a nature-based system of regional perception served well for cognitive mapping. Environmental features were distinguished by perceptual reference to soils, colors, trees, waters, Indian names, special plants or animals, and sediments. Initially, the Anglo-American linguistic appropriation was similarly nature-based and included many borrowings.[34] But their nomenclature also reflected the new visualization and spatialization of science as with Marcy's geomorphic "Loess Creek" or Whipple's quantifying "Camp 38." The newcomers' environmental confusion was sometimes reflected in oxymoronic expressions like "Dry River," "Ocean Prairie" and "Great American Desert." By the late nineteenth century nature-based toponyms were beginning to give way to increasingly commercial and anthropocentric terms. New names reflected new desires for the land.[35]

The historical geography of the Llano Estacado—a didactic place-name steeped in legend—reflects a gradual shift in environmental perception away from a sacred, idealistic, nature-centered discourse to a more secular, materialistic, human-centered discourse. In many respects it is the movement from storytelling and literature to science and materialism, as oral culture gives way to written culture. There was a numinous quality in much of the Hispano perception, a loric attempt to capture in a few pithy words the local "numen," or spirit of place as in *Laguna Rica, Cañon Blanco, Palo Duro, Punta de Agua, Las Tecovas*, and the richly semiotic *Las Lenguas*. This oral culture, as the critic Walter Benjamin noted, was communal in language, based on shared perceptions, and oriented to the direct exchange of experience.[36]

For Americans this numinous quality was present first as a romantic horizon, a "Prairie Sublime" mirage direct from the Great Zahara. Against a backdrop of heroic exploration, a conscious literary effort created a thrilling scene out of the unfamiliar spirit of place. The journey was mythic: separation from home, dangers, initiation into the landscape, encounters with new peoples, and eventual redemption and return. For an urbanizing age that cultivated the sense of solitude as a geographic aesthetic, the Llano Estacado was a backdrop as suitable for the projection of heroic man as the Arctic wastes or South Pacific expanses. It was the soul of solitude.

With the publication of Marcy's *Exploration of the Red River* and especially with the two pertinent volumes of the *Pacific Railroad Surveys*, the "objective" way of seeing the Llano pioneered by Edwin James and Josiah Gregg made substantial progress. Environmental perception turned from lore to empirical data, classification, visualization, specialization, and reductionism, as the older romantic and chivalrous paradigm shifted to new styles of theoretical discourse and landscape representation. By the time of Pope and Gray, the "objective" optimists began to reconsider the dreadful picture of the romantic Llano Estacado. Or rather scientific imperialism was a new kind of numinalism, one responding to a paradigm shift on the interpretation of Southwestern reality. This abstractional and detailed form of interpretation was beyond the ordinary training of either Hispano or Anglo pioneers, who kept their traditional lore. In the shining new discourse of science there were nevertheless similar questions of environmental deception ("Pope's Wells"), narrator reliability (Marcy's "Head Spring"), ideology (A. B. Gray's Pro-Slavery), and symbolism (Whipple's "Ocean Prairie").

Having paid the Eurocentric vision of the Llano much attention, one notes forlornly that the Amerindian language of the landscape must be equally revealing if largely absent. Some mysteries always remain. By 1800 the Spanish split the powerful Cuchantica, Yamparica, and Jupe divisions of the Comanche into the *Orientales* or "Easterners" and the *Occidentales* or "Westerners."[37] To be sure the true masters of the Llano Estacado in 1860 were still the Nuhmuhnuh or Comanche bands and their close allies. Whipple thought them in serious population decline in the 1850s, a likely possibility after the horrendous smallpox epidemic of 1838. They knew the land exceedingly well, with even the smallest band capable of traveling largely at will. But a detailed consideration of their environmental perception requires methodologies and texts beyond the scope of this study. They were nevertheless active mythologizers of the landscape, known to endow features and places with cultural, historical, personal, and spiritual meanings.[38] The comancheros passed some of these native place-names along to us as with Tecovas, Tucumcari, Toyah, Quitaque, and Muchaque.

Just as questions of boundaries and annexation brought two nations to war over the region, the question of slavery versus free soil turned the victor against itself during the bitter years after 1860. During the Civil War the Llano was largely abandoned to state control, or rather the lack thereof. Ranger A. W. Obenchain penetrated to Casas Amarillas in 1862, but he was the exception. Texas Confederates invaded New Mexico, but were decisively defeated at Glorieta Pass. A major Federal force from New Mexico, including Kit Carson, advanced into the Canadian Valley of Texas in 1864 and fought several battles with the Native Americans. But the Comanche and their allies maintained strategic control and continued to operate an economy based on sensational livestock raiding and trading. Increasingly, their Llano Estacado became a tribal refugium, a final place of retreat far from the U.S. military posts or the pursuing parties from the Anglo-Texan frontier.[39] But these tumultuous years, and the further thrilling and sad narratives of environmental conquest, settlement, and dominion, are so richly detailed and so culturally extensive as to require a separate volume.

The significance of language in the encounter with the Llano was paramount. Both the Spanish and Americans struggled to find the proper words, the appropriate signifiers to reveal the sense of place. A patient and understanding textual analysis allows old, dusty, semiotic systems to shine once more. How we perceive the Llano Estacado environment is not only historical but also geographical, literary, and artistic, requiring interdisciplinary exploration of texts, translations, maps, and iconography. As with the texts themselves the *jornada* or journey is really more important than the conclusion. For along the trail of exploration, discovery becomes essentially identical to the learning process, a form of organized re-seeing and re-thinking, a school for the soul. To this end *El Llano Estacado* illustrates the role of mind and culture in the invention of the Southwest. The land still awakens the senses and the imagination of all people. We continue to mythologize, abstract, scientize, and invent all kinds of knowledge, even while seeking a direct, human understanding through contact, admiration, wonder, and truthful observation. Thankfully we still need, as our ancestors did before us, affective relationships to the great mesa, relations of beauty maintained by the power of words and visions.

THE END OF THE TRAIL

Bibliography

I. Manuscripts, Reports, Catalogues

Abert, James W. "*Gúadal P'A": The Journal of Lt. J. W. Abert from Bent's Fort to St. Louis in 1845*. Edited by H. Bailey Carroll. Canyon, Tex.: Panhandle-Plains Historical Society, 1941.

———. *Through the Country of the Comanche Indians in the Fall of the Year 1845: The Journal of a U.S. Army Expedition Led by Lt. James W. Abert of the Topographical Engineers*. Edited by John Galvin. San Francisco, Calif.: Lawton Kennedy for John Howell, 1970.

———. *Report of an Expedition . . . Upper Arkansas and Through the Country of the Comanche Indians, Made by Lieutenant J. W. Abert, of the Topographic Corps*. Washington, D.C.: 29th Cong., 1st Sess., Senate Executive Document 438, 1846.

Allen, John L. "The Geographical Images of the American Northwest, 1673 to 1806: An Historical Geosophy." Ph.D. diss., Clark University, 1969.

Bandelier, Fanny, trans., and Adolph Bandelier, ed. *The Journey of Alvar Núñez Cabeza de Vaca and His Companions from Florida to the Pacific, 1528–1536*. New York: A. S. Barnes, 1905.

Brown, Lorin W., ed. "Manuel Maes." Manuscript MS CL-1057, New Mexico Historical Museum Library, Santa Fé, New Mexico.

Bryan, Frank. "Coronado Expedition Map," 1962, Coronado Vertical Files, Panhandle-Plains Museum, Canyon, Tex.

Bryan Collection, James [Reproduction]. "Mapa del territorio comprendido entre la Provincia de Nuevo Mexico y el Fuerte de Natchitoches y Texas" (1789), Center for American History, University of Texas at Austin.

Carleton, Gen. James H. "Report . . . " *U.S. Army Series One*, Vol. XLVIII. Washington, D.C.: Government Printing Office, 1864, with Allen Anderson "Map of the Military Department of New Mexico."

Castañeda de Náxera, Pedro de. *Relación de la jornada de Cibola por Pedro de Castañeda de Naçera donde se trata de todos aquellos poblandos y ritos, y costumbres, la qual fue el año de 1540*. Microfilm reel no. 63, Rich Collection, New York Public Library, New York City.

[Coronado Cuarto Centennial Commission]. "The Coronado Magazine," Official Program of the Coronado Cuarto Centennial in New Mexico. n.p., New Mexico: Mrs. Charles E. Butler, 1940.

Corps of Topographical Engineers. "Selected Letters–Received," Microfilmed books from 1840–1860, Old Army Section, Record Group 77, National Archives, Washington, D.C.

Cummins, W. F. "Report on the Geography, Topography, and Geology of the Llano Estacado or Staked Plains," *Third Annual Report of the Geological Survey of Texas 1891*. Austin, Tex.: State Printing Office, 1892.

Emory, W. H. *Report on the United States and Mexican Boundary Survey*. Austin: Texas State Historical Association, 1987.

Gelo, Daniel. "Comanche Belief and Ritual." Ph.D. diss., Rutgers University, New Brunswick, 1986.

Gould, Charles N. *The Geology and Water Resources of the Eastern Portion of the Panhandle of Texas*. Water-Supply and Irrigation Paper No. 154. Washington, D.C.: Government Printing Office,1906.

———. *The Geology and Water Resources of the Western Portion of the Panhandle of Texas*. Water-Supply and Irrigation Paper No. 191. Washington, D.C.: Government Printing Office, 1907.

Gustavson, Thomas C., and Robert J. Finley. *Late Cenozoic Geomorphic Evolution of the Texas Panhandle and Northeastern New Mexico*. Report of Investigations No. 148. Austin, Tex.: Bureau of Economic Geology, University of Texas, 1985.

[Grasses of the Great Plains]. *Report of the Commissioner of Agriculture for the Year 1883*. Washington, D.C.: Government Printing Office, 1883.

[Grasslands]. *Report of an Investigation of the Grasses of the Arid Districts of Texas, New Mexico, Arizona, Nevada, and Utah in 1887*. Washington, D.C.: Government Printing Office, 1888.

Gray, A. B. *Charter of the Texas Western Railroad Company, and Extracts from the Reports of Col. A. B. Gray and Secretary of War, on the Survey of Route, from Eastern Borders of Texas to California*. Cincinnati, Ohio: Porter, Thrall & Chapman, 1855.

Hammond, George and Agapito Rey, eds. *Don Juan de Oñate, Colonizer of New Mexico, 1595–1628* Albuquerque: University of New Mexico Press, 1953.

———. *Narratives of the Coronado Expedition 1540–1542*. Albuquerque, N.Mex.: Coronado Cuarto Centennial Publications, 1940.

———. *New Mexico in 1602: Juan de Montoya's Relation of the Discovery of New Mexico*. Albuquerque, N.Mex.: Quivira Society, 1938.

Hedrick, Basil C. and Carroll L. Riley. *The Journey of the Vaca Party: The Account of the Narváez Expedition, 1528–1536*. . . . University Museum Studies, No. 2. Carbondale, Ill.: Southern Illinois University, 1974.

Herrera, Antonio de. *Historia General de los Hechos de los Castellanos en las Islas y Tierra Firme del Mar Oceano*, Vol. III. Madrid: Barcia, 1728.

Hill, Robert. *On the Occurrence of Artesian and Other Underground Waters in Texas, Eastern New Mexico, and Indian Territory, West of the Ninety-seventh Meridian*. 52nd Cong., 1st Sess., Senate Executive Document 41, IV, pt. 3, 1892, 41–166.

———. *Physical Geography of the Texas Region*, U.S. Geological Survey. Atlas, Folio Three. Washington, D.C.: Government Printing Office, 1900.

Hornaday, W. T. *The Extermination of the American Bison*. Smithsonian Annual Report. Washington, D.C.: Smithsonian Institution, 1887.

Johnson, Eileen [Interview] March 3, 1989, at The Museum, Texas Tech University, Lubbock, Texas.

Johnston, Joseph E. *Reports of the Secretary of War with Reconnaissances of Routes from San Antonio to El Paso . . . and From Fort Smith to Santa Fe . . .* Washington, D.C.: 34th Cong., 1st Sess., Senate Executive Document 64, 1850.

Kavanagh, Thomas W. "Political Power and Political Organization: Comanche Politics, 1786–1875." Ph.D. diss. University of New Mexico, 1986.

[Llano Estacado Experience]. "The Llano Estacado Experience: Utilization of the Arid Lands of Texas," 1986 Sesquicentennial Exhibition Catalog. Lubbock, Tex.: Southwest Collection/International Center for Arid and Semi-Arid Land Studies, 1986.

Mota Padilla, Matias de la. *Historia de la Conquista de la Provincia de la Nueva-Galicia*. Mexico City: Boletin de la Sociedad Mexicana de Geografia y Estadistica, 1870.

Marcy, Randolph B. *Exploration of the Red River of Louisiana, in the Year 1852*. 33rd Cong., 1st Sess. House Executive Document. Washington, D.C.: A.O.P. Nicholson, 1854.

———. "Map of the Country Upon Upper Red River, Explored in 1852." New York: Ackerman Lith., 1853.

———. "Report of Captain R. B. Marcy . . . ," *Reports of the Sec. of War*, 31st Cong., 1st Sess., Senate Executive Document 64, 1850, 169–221.

———. "Topographical Map of the Road from Fort Smith, Arks. to Santa Fe, N.M. . . . " Philadelphia: Duval's Steam Lithograph Press, 1850.

Matthews, William A., III. *The Geologic Story of Palo Duro Canyon*. Austin, Tex.: Bureau of Economic Geology, 1983.

McGookey, Douglas A., Thomas C. Gustavson, and Ann D. Hoadley. "Regional Structural Cross Sections, Mid-Permian to Quaternary Strata, Texas Panhandle and Eastern New Mexico: Distribution of Exaporites and Areas of Evaporite Dissolution and Collapse." Austin, Tex.: University of Texas, Bureau of Economic Geology.

Michler, Lt. Nathaniel H. *Report of . . . Reports of the Sec. of War*, 31st Cong., 1st Sess., Senate Executive Document 64. Washington, D.C.: Government Printing Office, 1850, 35–45.

Mitchell, C. H. "The Role of Water in the Settlement of the Llano Estacado." Master's thesis, University of Texas at Austin, 1960.

Motolinía, Fray Toribio de. *Memoriales*. Mexico City: Pimentel, 1903.

National Park Service. "National Trail Study Environmental Assessment, Coronado Expedition." Denver, Colo.: Public Review Draft, June 1991.

Nativ, Ronit. "Hydrogeology and Hydrochemistry of the Ogallala Aquifer, Southern High Plains, Texas Panhandle and Eastern New Mexico." Austin, Tex.: University of Texas, Bureau of Economic Geology, 1989.

[Ogallala Aquifer]. *Water for Texas, A Comprehensive Plan for the Future*. Volumes I & II. Austin: Texas Dept. of Water Resources, Nov. 1984.

Otero, Miguel, et. al. *Report of the Governor of New Mexico 1892* [through 1903]. Washington, D.C.: Government Printing Office, 1893–1903.

Pacheco, Joaquin F., and Francisco de Cárdenas. *Colección de Documentos Inéditos relativos al descubrimento, conquista, y colonizacion de las posesiones españolas en America y Occeanía*. Volume XV. 42 vols. Madrid: M. G. Hernández, 1870.

[Pacific Railroad Survey]. *Reports of Explorations and Surveys . . . for a Railroad from the Mississippi River to the Pacific Ocean* . . . Washington, D.C.: Government Printing Office, 1855–1860.

[Palo Duro Basin]. *Area Environmental Characterization Report of the Dalhart and Palo Duro Basins in the Texas Panhandle*. Volume II: *Palo Duro Basin*. Office of Nuclear Waste Isolation Technical Report. Gaithersburg, Md.: NUS Corporation, Sept. 1982.

[Pecos Valley]. *The Great Pecos Valley of New Mexico. The Opportunities it Offers*. "Home-Farm" *Irrigated Orchard Facts*. Artesia, N.Mex.: Pecos Valley Immigration & Developing Co., 1909.

[Pecos Valley, Texas]. *Irrigated Farm Homes in the Pecos Valley of Texas* . . . Kansas City, Kan.: Board Land Commission, [1908].

[Playa Lakes]. "Locating and Mapping Playa Lakes on the Texas High Plains." Austin, Tex.: Texas National Resources Information System, Feb., 1980.

[Poe, Edgar Allan]. William H. Koester Collection, Humanities Research Center Library, University of Texas at Austin, Austin, Texas.

Pope, John. "Report on the Exploration of a Route for the Pacific Railroad near the 32nd Parallel of Latitude, from the Red River to the Rio Grande." In *Pacific Railroad Surveys*. 32nd Cong., 2nd Sess., Senate Executive Document 78, 1855, II, pt. 4.

———. "Artesian Well Experiment" in *Report of the Secretary of War*. 35th Cong., 2nd Sess., Senate Executive Document 1, 1858, II, 590–608.

———. "Letter . . . to Hon. T. J. Rusk in Relation to Artesian Wells in Texas and New Mexico." Washington, D.C.: Towers Printers, 1856.

Ragaz, Cheri. "Geography and the Conceptual World: The Significance of Place to Aboriginal Australians with Reference to the Historical Lakes Tribes of South Australia," Inaugural Dissertation, Philosophy Faculty II, University of Zurich. Zurich: Zentralstelle der Studenenschaft, 1988.

Reeves, C. C., Jr., ed. *Playa Lake Symposium*. International Center for Arid and Semi-Arid Land Studies Publication No. 4. Lubbock, Tex.: ICASALS, 1972.

Saarinen, Thomas F. *Perception of the Drought Hazard on the Great Plains*. Geography Research Paper no. 106. Chicago, Ill.: University of Chicago, 1966.

Sauer, Carl Ortwin. *The Road to Cibola*. Ibero-Americana, number 3. Berkeley, Calif.: University of California Press, 1932.

Shumard, George Getz. "Observations on the Geological Formations of the Country between the Rio Pecos and the Rio Grande in New Mexico near the Line of the 32nd Parallel." *Transactions of the Academy of Sciences of St. Louis*, I (1858), 273–289.

———. *A Partial Report on the Geology of Western Texas, Consisting of a General Geological Report and a Journal of Geological Observations along the Routes Travelled by the Expedition between Indianola, Texas and the Valley of the Mimbres, New Mexico during the Years 1855 and 1856* . . . Austin, Tex.: State Printing Office, 1886.

Simpson, James H. *Report from the Secretary of War Communicating . . . the Report and Map of the Route from Ft. Smith, Arkansas to Santa Fe, New Mexico, Made by Lieutenant Simpson*. 31st Cong., 1st Sess., Senate Executive Document 12, 1850, 1–25.

———. "Coronado's March in Search of the 'Seven Cities of Cibolà, and Discussion of their Probable Location." *Smithsonian Report for 1869*. Washington, D.C.: Smithsonian Institution, 1871, 309–340.

Sloan, Dorothy. "The Library of Dr. Paul Burns." *Catalogue Six*. Austin, Tex.: Wind River Press, 1988.

Sloan, Julie and Dorothy Sloan. *Catalogue Three: Women in the Cattle Country*. Austin, Tex.: William Holman, 1986.

Smith, Buckingham. *Coleccion de Varios Documentos para la Historia de la Florida y Tierras Adyacentes*. London: Trubner y Compania, 1857.

Taplin, Charles L. "Letter Report to John Pope on the Exploration of the Llano Estacado." In *Pacific Railroad Surveys*, 1855, vol. II, Appendix A.

Ternaux-Compans, Henri. *Voyages, Relations et Mémoires Originaux Pour Servir à l'Histoire de la Découverte de l'Amérique*. 20 vols. Paris: 1837–1841. Volume IX is devoted to the Coronado expedition.

Ulibarri, Richard O. *American Interest in the Spanish-Mexican Southwest, 1803–1848*. San Francisco, Calif.: R&E Research, 1974.

Vasey, George. *Illustrations of North American Grasses*. Washington, D.C.: Government Publication Office, 1891–1893.

Wendorf, Fred. *Paleoecology of the Llano Estacado*. Santa Fé, N.Mex.: The Museum of New Mexico Press, 1961.

Wendorf, Fred and James J. Hester, eds. *Pleistocene and Recent Environments of the Southern High Plains*. Dallas, Tex.: Southern Methodist University, 1975.

Winship, George Parker. "The Coronado Expedition, 1540–1542."*Fourteenth Annual Report of the Bureau of Ethnology, 1892–1893*, Part I. Washington, D.C.: Government Printing Office, 1896.

II. ARTICLES AND ARTICLES IN BOOKS

Albers, Patricia and Jeanne Kay. "Sharing the Land: A Study in American Indian Territoriality." In Thomas E. Ross and Tyrel G. Moore, eds., *A Cultural Geography of North American Indians*. Boulder, Colo: Westview Press, 1987, 47–92.

Allen, John L. "Exploration and the Creation of Geographical Images of the Great Plains: Comments on the Role of Subjectivity." In Blouet and Lawson, eds., *Images of the Plains; The Role of Human Nature in Settlement*. Lincoln: University of Nebraska Press, 1975.

Archambeau, Ernest R. "The First Federal Census in the Panhandle—1880." *Panhandle-Plains Historical Review*, XXIII (1950), 22–132.

———. "The Fort Smith–Santa Fe Trail along the Canadian River in Texas." *Panhandle-Plains Historical Review*, XXVII (1954), 1–26.

Bandelier, Adolph F. "Quivira." *Nation*, XLIX (Oct. 31, Nov. 7, 1889).

Bender, A. B. "Opening Routes Across West Texas, 1848–50." *Southwestern Historical Quarterly*, XXXVII (1943), 128–138.

Benedict, Ruth. "The Vision in Plains Culture." *American Anthropologist*, XXIV, no. 1 (Jan.–Mar., 1922), 1–24.

Bennett, James. "Oasis Civilization in the Great Plains." *Great Plains Journal*, VII (Fall, 1967), 26–32.

Bolton, Herbert E. "French Intrusions into New Mexico." In H. M. Stephens and H. E. Bolton, eds., *The Pacific Ocean in History*. New York: MacMillan, 1917, 399–400.

Bowden, Martyn J. "The Great American Desert and the American Frontier, 1800–1822: Popular Images of the Plains." In Tamara Hareven, ed., *Anonymous Americans: Explorations in Nineteenth Century Social History*. Englewood Cliffs, N.J.: Prentice-Hall, 1971.

———. "The Perception of the Western Interior of the United States, 1800–1870: A Problem in Historical Geosophy." *Proceedings of the Association of American Geographers*, I (1969), 16–21.

Brown, William R. "Natural History of the Canadian River, 1820–1853." *Panhandle-Plains Historical Review*, LXI (1988), 1–16.

Brune, Gunnar. "Artificial Recharge in Texas." Austin, Tex.: Texas Water Development Board, June, 1970.

Bryan, Frank. "The Llano Estacado: The Geographical Background of the Coronado Expedition." *Panhandle-Plains Historical Review*, XIII (1940), 21–37.

Bryant, Vaughn M., Jr., and Richard G. Holloway. "A Late-Quaternary Paleoenvironmental Record of Texas: An Overview of the Pollen Evidence." In *Pollen Records of Late-Quaternary North American Sediments*. New York: AASP Foundation, 1985, 39–70.

Burroughs, Jean M. "Homesteading the Llano Estacado." *New Mexico Magazine*, LVI (Apr., 1978), 17–23.

Butzer, Karl W. "Cattle and Sheep from Old to New Spain: Historical Antecedents." *Annals of the Association of American Geographers*, LXXVIII (Mar., 1988), 29–56.

———. "An Old World Perspective on Potential Mid-Wisconsin Settlement of the Americas." In Tom Dillehay and David J. Meltzer, eds., *The First Americans: Search and Research*. Boca Raton, Fla.: CRC Press, 1991, 137–156.

Canby, Thomas Y. "The Search for the First Americans." *National Geographic*, CLVI (Sept., 1979), 330–363.

Carlson, Paul H. "Panhandle Pastures: Early Sheepherding in the Texas Panhandle." *Panhandle-Plains Historical Review*, LIII (1980), 1–16.

Carroll, H. Bailey. "Characteristic Similarities of Expeditions into the Great Plains." *Panhandle-Plains Historical Review*, X (1937), 21–35.

———. "George W. Grover's 'Minutes of Adventure From June 1841'." *Panhandle-Plains Historical Review*, IX (1936), 28–42.

———. "Some New Mexico–West Texas Relationships, 1541–1841." *West Texas Historical Association Year Book*, XIV (1938), 92–102.

Chipman, Donald E. "In Search of Cabeza de Vaca's Route across Texas: An Historiographical Survey." *Southwestern Historical Quarterly*, XCI (Oct., 1987), 127–148.

Coleman, Max. "Transformation of the Llano Estacado." *Frontier Times* (July, 1936).

Connor, Seymour V. "Early Ranching Operations in the Panhandle: A Report on the Agricultural Schedules of the 1880 Census." *Panhandle-Plains Historical Review*, XXVII (1954), 47–69.

Conrad, David E. "The Whipple Expedition on the Great Plains." *Great Plains Journal*, II (Spring, 1963), 42–66.

Cox, C. C. "Reminiscences of C. C. Cox." *Southwestern Historical Quarterly*, VI (Oct., 1902; Jan., 1903), 113–138; 204–235.

Culley, John J. and Peter L. Petersen. "Hard Times on the High Plains: FSA Photography During the 1930s." *Panhandle-Plains Historical Review*, LII (1979), 15–38.

Davies, Christopher S. "Life at the Edge: Urban and Industrial Evolution of Texas, Frontier Wilderness—Frontier Space, 1836–1986." *Southwestern Historical Quarterly*, LXXXIX (Apr., 1986), 443–554.

Dellenbaugh, Frank. "The True Route of Coronado's March." *Journal of the American Geographical Society of New York*, XXIX (Dec., 1897), 398–431.

Donoghue, David. "Coronado, Oñate and Quivira." *Preliminary Studies of the Texas Catholic Historical Society*. Vol. III (Apr., 1936), 5–12.

———. "Explorations of Albert Pike in Texas." *Southwestern Historical Quarterly*, XXXIX (Oct., 1935), 135–138.

———. "The Location of Quivira." *Panhandle-Plains Historical Review*, XIII (1940), 38–46.

———. "The Route of the Coronado Expedition in Texas." *Southwestern Historical Quarterly*, XXXII (Jan., 1929), 181–192.

Doughty, Robin. "Settlement and Environmental Change in Texas, 1820–1900." *Southwestern Historical Quarterly*, LXXXIX (Apr., 1986), 423–442.

Enlow, Donald H. and T. N. Campbell. "Some Paleo-Indian Projectile Points from the Southeastern Periphery of the Great Plains." *Panhandle-Plains Historical Review*, XXVIII (1955), 29–37.

Estep, Raymond. "The First Panhandle Land Grant." *Chronicle of Oklahoma*, XXXVI (Winter, 1958–1959), 358–370.

———. "The Le Grand Survey of the High Plains—Fact or Fancy?" *New Mexico Historical Review*, XXIX (Apr., 1954), 81–96.

Falconer, Thomas. "Journey through Texas and New Mexico." *The Journal of the Royal Geographical Society of London. Volume the Thirteenth*. London: Murray, 1843, 199–226.

Fenton, James. "Desert Myth Dies Slowly on the Staked Plain, 1845–1860." *Panhandle-Plains Historical Review*, LXIII (1990), 45–74.

———. "The Lobo Wolf: Beast of Waste and Desolution." *Panhandle-Plains Historical Review*, LIII (1980), 57–70.

Flint, Richard, and Shirley Cushing Flint. "The Coronado Expedition: Cicuye to the Rio de Cicuye Bridge." *New Mexico Historical Review*, LXVII (Apr., 1992), 123–138.

———. "The Location of Coronado's 1541 Bridge: A Critical Appraisal of Albert Schroeder's 1962 Hypothesis." *Plains Anthropologist*, XXXVI (May, 1991), 171–176.

Flores, Dan. "Canyons of the Imagination." *Southwest Art*, XVIII (Mar., 1989), 70–76.

———. "The Plains and the Painters: Two Centuries of Landscape Art from the Llano Estacado." *Journal of American Culture*, XIV (Summer, 1991), 19–28.

Folmer, Henri. "Contraband Trade Between Louisiana and New Mexico in the Eighteenth Century." *New Mexico Historical Review*, XVI (July, 1941), 249–274.

———. "The Mallet Expedition of 1739 Through Nebraska, Kansas and Colorado to Santa Fe." *The Colorado Magazine*, XVI (Sept., 1935), 161–173.

Frison, George C. "Man and Bison Relationships in North America." *Canadian Journal of Anthropology*, I (Spring, 1980), 75–76.

Goodwin, Cardinal. "Fonda's Exploration in the Southwest." *Southwestern Historical Quarterly*, XXIII (July, 1919), 39–46.

Gracy, David B., II. "A Preliminary Survey of Land Colonization in the Panhandle-Plains of Texas." *The Museum Journal*, XI (1969), 53–79.

Gray, A. B. "Fort Chadbourne to the Mustang Springs." In Jacob DeCordova, *Texas: Her Resources and Her Public Men*. Waco, Tex.: Texan Press, 1969.

Guthrie, R. Dale. "Mosaics, Allelochemics and Nutrients: An Ecological Theory of Late Pleistocene

Megafaunal Extinctions." In Paul Martin and Richard Klein, eds., *Quaternary Extinctions: A Prehistoric Revolution*. Tucson: University of Arizona Press, 1984, 259–298.

Haley, J. Evetts. "Charles Goodnight's Indian Recollections." *Panhandle-Plains Historical Review*, I (1928), 3–29.

———. "The Comanchero Trade." *Southwestern Historical Quarterly*, XXXVIII (Jan., 1935), 157–176.

———. "Grass Fires on the Southern Plains." *West Texas Historical Association Year Book*, V (1929), 23–42.

———. "The Great Comanche War Trail." *Panhandle-Plains Historical Review*, XXIII (1950), 11–21.

———. "Lore of the Llano Estacado." In J. Frank Dobie, ed., *Texas and Southwestern Lore*. Austin, Tex.: Texas Folklore Society, VI, 1927, 72–89.

———. "Scouting with Goodnight." *Southwest Review*, XVII (Spring, 1932), 267–289.

Hall, Stephen A. "Quaternary Pollen Analysis and Vegetational History of the Southwest," In *Pollen Records of Late-Quaternary North American Sediments*. New York: AASP Foundation, 1985, 95–123.

Harper, Elizabeth Ann. "The Taovayas Indians in Frontier Trade and Diplomacy."*Panhandle-Plains Historical Review*, XXVI (1953), 41–72.

Harrison, Lowell H., ed. "Three Comancheros and a Trader." *Panhandle-Plains Historical Review*. XXXVIII (1965), 73–94.

Hawkins, Arthur Stuart. "Bird Life in the Texas Panhandle." *Panhandle-Plains Historical Review*, XVIII (1945), 110–150.

Haynes, C. Vance. "Were Clovis Progenitors in Beringia?" In David M. Hopkins et. al., eds., *Paleoecology of Beringia*. New York: Academic Press, 1982, 383–399.

[High Plains of Texas]. "Special High Plains Issue." *Texas Parks and Wildlife*, XLVIII (Oct., 1990).

Hill, Frank "Plains Names." *Panhandle-Plains Historical Review*, X (1937), 36–47.

Holden, W. C. "Coronado's Route Across the Staked Plains." *West Texas Historical Association Year Book*, XX (Oct., 1944), 3–20.

———. "West Texas Drouths." *Southwestern Historical Quarterly*, XXXII (Oct., 1928), 103–123.

Holliday, V. T. and C. Welth. "Lithic Tool Resources of the Eastern Llano Estacado." *Bulletin of the Texas Archeological Society*, LII (1981), 201–214.

Inglehart, Fannie G. "The Peculiarities of the Llano Estacado." *Year Book of Texas*, 1901 (1902), 235–237.

Inglis, G. Douglas. "The Men of Cibola: New Investigations on the Francisco Vazquez de Coronado Expedition." *Panhandle-Plains Historical Review*, LV (1982), 1–24.

Johnson, Eileen and Vance T. Holliday. "Late Paleoindian Activity at the Lubbock Lake Site." *Plains Anthropologist*, XXVI (Aug., 1981), 173–193.

———. "The Archaic Record at Lubbock Lake." *Plains Anthropologist*, XXXI (Nov., 1986), 7–54.

Johnson, Elmer H. "The Texas Region: Its Resources and Opportunities." In Arthur L. Brandon, ed., *The State and Public Education*. University of Texas Publication No. 4020, May 22, 1940, 113–127.

Johnston, C. Stuart. "Prehistory in the Texas Panhandle." *Panhandle Plains Historical Review*, X (1937), 80–86.

Jordan, Terry G. "Perceptual Regions in Texas." *The Geographical Review*, LXVIII (July, 1978), 293–307.

Keleher, William A. "Texans in Early Day New Mexico." *Panhandle-Plains Historical Review*, XXV (1952), 13–28.

Kiser, Edwin L. "The Re-examination of Pedro De Castañeda's Bone Bed by Geological Investigations." *Bulletin of the Texas Archeological Society*, XLIX (1978), 331–340.

Kuykendall, J. H. "Reminiscences of Early Texans I." *Southwestern Historical Quarterly*, VI (Jan., 1903), 236–253.

Leckie, William. "The Red River War of 1874–1875." *Panhandle-Plains Historical Review*, XXIX (1956), 78–100.

LeCompte, Janet. "Coronado and Conquest." *New Mexico Historical Review*, LXIV (July, 1989), 279–304.

Leopold, Aldo. "The Virgin Southwest 1933." *Orion*, X (Winter, 1991), 18–23.

Lovell, W. George. "'Heavy Shadows and Black Night': Disease and Depopulation in Colonial Spanish America." *Annals of the Association of American Geographers*, LXXXII (Sept., 1992), 426–443.

Lowenthal, David. "Geography, Experience and Imagination: Towards a Geographical Epistemology." *Annals of the Association of American Geographers*, LI (Sept., 1961), 241–260.

Marshall, Thomas Maitland. "Commercial Aspects of the Texan Santa Fé Expedition." *Southwestern Historical Quarterly*, XX (Jan., 1917), 242–259.

McCarty, John L. "Literature of the Plains." *Panhandle-Plains Historical Review*, XIII (1940), 80–90.

[McCauley, C. A. H.] "Notes on the Ornithology of the Region About the Source of the Red River of Texas, from Observations Made During the [1876] Exploration Conducted by Lieut. E. H. Ruffner . . . " Eds. Kenneth D. Seyffert and T. Lindsay Baker. *Panhandle-Plains Historical Review*, XLI (1988), 25–88.

Meltzer, David J. and Michael B. Collins. "Prehistoric Water Wells on the Southern High Plains: Clues to Altithermal Climate." *Journal of Field Archaeology*, XIV (Spring, 1987), 9–28.

Morton, Virginia. "Early Settlement of Quay County, New Mexico." *Panhandle-Plains Historical Review*, XIX (1946), 73–85.

Mugerauer, Robert. "Concerning Regional Geography as a Hermeneutical Discipline." *Geographische Zeitschrift*, LXIX (1 Quartel, 1981), 57–67.

Neighbors, Kenneth F. "The Marcy-Neighbors Exploration of the Headwaters of the Brazos and Wichita Rivers in 1854." *Panhandle-Plains Historical Review*, XXVII (1954), 27–46.

Neighbors, Robert S. "The Nauni or Comanches of Texas." In Henry R. Schoolcraft, *Information Respecting the History, Conditions and Prospects of the Indian Tribes of the United States*. Philadelphia, Pa.: U.S. Office of Indian Affairs, 1853.

———. "The Report of the Expedition of Major Robert S. Neighbors to El Paso in 1849." Ed. Kenneth F. Neighbors. *Southwestern Historical Quarterly*, LX (Apr., 1957), 527–532.

Norman, Mary Anne. "Childhood on the Southern Plains Frontier." *The Museum Journal*, XVIII (1979), 49–142.

Nostrand, Richard L. "The Century of Hispano Expansion." *New Mexico Historical Review*, LXII (Oct., 1987), 361–386.

"Panhandle-Plains Prehistory." *Panhandle-Plains Historical Review*. XXVIII (1955).

Popper, Deborah E., and Frank J. Popper. "The Great Plains: From Dust to Dust." *Planning*, LIII (Dec., 1987), 12–18.

Price, B. Byron. "Bolton, Coronado, and the Texas Panhandle." In Diana Everett, ed., *Coronado and the Myth of Quivira*. Canyon, Tex.: Panhandle-Plains Historical Society, 1985.

Rasch, Philip J. "The Pecos War." *Panhandle-Plains Historical Review*, XXIX (1956), 101–111.

Riley, Susan B. "Albert Pike as an American Don Juan." *Arkansas Historical Quarterly*, XIX (Autumn, 1960), 207–224.

Rister, C.C. "Documents Relating to General W. T. Sherman's Southern Plains Indian Policy, 1871–1875." *Panhandle-Plains Historical Review*, pt. I, IX (1936), 7–27; pt. II, X (1937), 48–68.

Romero, José Ynocencio. "Spanish Sheepmen on the Canadian at Old Tascosa." As told to Ernest R. Archambeau. *Panhandle-Plains Historical Review*, XIX (1946), 45–72.

Roper, Beryl. "How Did This River Come to be Called Canadian?" *Panhandle-Plains Historical Review*, LXI (1988), 17–24.

Rowell, Chester M., Jr. "Vascular Plants of the Playa Lakes of the Texas Panhandle and South Plains."*The Southwestern Naturalist*, XV (May 25, 1971), 407–417.

[Ruffner, Lt. E. H., and Carl Julius Adolph Hunnius]. *The Survey of the Headwaters of the Red River, 1875*. Comp. and ed. T. Lindsay Baker. *Panhandle-Plains Historical Review*, LVIII (1985).

Ryland, Isaac. "Untold Tales." *Panhandle-Plains Historical Review*, IX (1936), 61–66.

Schmitt, Edmond J. P. "Ven. Maria Jesus de Agreda: A Correction." *The Quarterly of the Texas State Historical Association*, I (Oct., 1897), 121–124.

Schroeder, Albert H. "A Re-analysis of the Routes of Coronado and Oñate into the Plains in 1541 and 1601." *Plains Anthropologist*, VII (Feb., 1962), 2–23.

Skaggs, Jimmy M. "The National Trail Issue and the Decline of Cattle Trailing." *The Museum Journal*, XI (1969), 3–24.

Sheffy, L. F. "The Arrington Papers." *Panhandle-Plains Historical Review*, I (1928), 30–66.

Slesick, Leonard M. "Fort Bascom: A Military Outpost in Eastern New Mexico." *Panhandle-Plains Historical Review*, LVI (1984), 13–64.

Sokolow, Jayme A. "The Demography of a Ranching Frontier: The Texas Panhandle in 1880." *Panhandle-Plains Historical Review*, LV (1982), 73–126.

Spielmann, Katherine. "Late Prehistoric Exchange between the Southwest and Southern Plains." *Plains Anthropologist*, XXVIII (Nov., 1983), 257–72.

Stanley, F. "Town Series," A collection of 147 city histories. Nazareth, Texas: various dates. Center for American History, Austin, Texas.

Strickland, Rex, ed. "The Recollections of W. S. Glenn, Buffalo Hunter." *Panhandle-Plains Historical Review*, XXII (1949), 21–64.

Studer, Floyd V. "Archeology of the Texas Panhandle." *Panhandle-Plains Historical Review*, XXVIII (1955), 87–95.

Strout, Clevy Lloyd. "The Coronado Expeditions: Following the Geography Described in the Spanish Journals." *Great Plains Journal*, XIV (Fall, 1974), 2–31.

———. "Flora and Fauna Mentioned in the Journals of the Coronado Expedition." *Great Plains Journal*, XI (Fall, 1971), 5–40.

Sublette, James E. and Mary Smith. "The Limnology of Playa Lakes on the Llano Estacado, New Mexico and Texas." *The Southwestern Naturalist*, XII (Dec. 31, 1967), 369–406.

Tyler, Daniel. "Anglo-American Penetration of the Southwest: The View from New Mexico." *Southwestern Historical Quarterly*, LXXV (Jan., 1972), 325–338.

Wedel, Waldo R. "Some Thoughts on Central Plains–Southern Plains Archaeological Relationships." *Great Plains Journal*, VII (Spring, 1968), 53–62.

———. "Coronado's Route to Quivira 1541." *Plains Anthropologist*, XV (Aug., 1970), 161–168.

Wedel, Waldo R. and John Swanton. "In Search of Coronado's Province of Quivira." In *Explorations and Fieldwork of the Smithsonian Institution in 1940*. Washington, D.C.: Smithsonian Institution, 1941.

Wheat, Joe Ben. "Two Archeological Sites Near Lubbock, Texas." *Panhandle-Plains Historical Review*, XXVIII (1955), 71–77.

Wheeler, David L. "The Panhandle Drift Fences." *Panhandle-Plains Historical Review*, LV (1982), 25–36.

[Whipple, Lt. A. W.] *Lieutenant A. W. Whipple's Railroad Reconnaissance Across the Panhandle of Texas in 1853*. Ed. by Ernest R. Archambeau. *Panhandle-Plains Historical Review*, XLIV (1971).

Williams, J. W. "Coronado: From the Rio Grande to the Concho." *Southwestern Historical Quarterly*, XLIII (Oct., 1959), 190–220.

———. "Marcy's Road from Doña Ana." *West Texas Historical Association Year Book*, XIX (1943), 128–138.

Williams, Janis. "Panhandle Grasslands." *Texas Highways*, XXIX (Nov., 1982), 18–29.

Wright, J. K. "*Terrae Incognitae*: The Place of the Imagination in Geography."*Annals of the Association of American Geographers*, XXXVII (Mar., 1947), 1–15.

Zimmerman, James F. "The Coronado Cuarto Centennial." *Hispanic American Historical Review*, XX (Feb., 1940), 158–162.

III. BOOKS

Acuña, Rodolfo. *Occupied America, The Chicano's Struggle Toward Liberation*. San Francisco, Calif.: Canfield Press, 1972.

Adams, Ramon F. *Burs Under the Saddle*. Norman: University of Oklahoma Press, 1979.

Babb, T. A. *In the Bosom of the Comanches*. Amarillo, Tex.: Russell, 1912.

Bailey, L. R. *Indian Slave Trade in the Southwest*. Los Angeles, Calif: Westernlore, 1966.

———. *The A. B. Gray Report, and Including the Reminiscences of Peter R. Brady Who Accompanied the Expedition*. Los Angeles, Calif.: Westernlore Press, 1963.

Bandelier, Adolph F. *The Gilded Man*. New York: Appleton & Co., 1893.

Bannon, John Francis. *Herbert Eugene Bolton: The Historian and the Man, 1870–1953*. Tucson: University of Arizona Press, 1978.

———. *The Spanish Borderlands Frontier, 1513–1821*. Albuquerque: University of New Mexico Press, 1979.

Barba, Preston Albert. *Baldwin Möllhausen, The German Cooper*. Philadelphia: University of Pennsylvania and D. Appleton & Co., 1944.

Barde, Frederick S. *Life and Adventures of "Billy" Dixon of Adobe Walls, Texas Panhandle*. Guthrie, Okla.: Co-operative Publishing, 1914.

Barsness, Larry. *The Bison in Art: A Graphic Chronicle of the American Bison*. Flagstaff, Ariz.: Northland Press, 1977.

Bartlett, John. *Personal Narrative of Explorations and Incidents in Texas, New Mexico, California, Sonora, and Chihuahua, Connected with the United States and Mexican Boundary Commission*. 1854. Reprint, Chicago, Ill.: Rio Grande Press, 1965.

Bechdolt, Fred R. *Tales of the Old-Timers*. New York: Century, 1924.
Berry, Wendell. *The Unsettling of America: Culture and Agriculture*. San Francisco, Calif.: Sierra Club Books, 1986.
Bieber, Ralph. *Exploring Southwestern Trails, 1846–1854*. Glendale, Calif.: Arthur H. Clark, 1938.
———. *Southern Trails to California in 1849*. Glendale, Calif.: Arthur H. Clark, 1937.
Biggers, Don. *From Cattle Range to Cotton Patch*. 1905. Reprint, Bandera, Tex.: *Frontier Times*, 1944.
———. *A Biggers Chronicle, Consisting of a Reprint of the Extremely Rare History That Will Never Be Repeated*. Lubbock, Tex.: Texas Technological College, 1961.
Billington, Ray Allen. *Land of Savagery, Land of Promise: The European Image of the American Frontier in the Nineteenth Century*. New York: W. W. Norton, 1981.
Black, Craig C., ed. *History and Prehistory of the Lubbock Lake Site*. Volume XV of *The Museum Journal*. Lubbock, Tex.: West Texas Museum Association, 1974.
Blakeslee, Donald J. *Along Ancient Trails: The Mallet Expedition of 1739*. Niwot, Colo.: University Press of Colorado, 1995.
Blouet, Brian W. and Merlin P. Lawson, eds. *Images of the Plains: The Role of Human Nature in Settlement*. Lincoln: University of Nebraska Press, 1975.
Bolton, Herbert E. *Coronado: Knight of Pueblos and Plains*. Albuquerque: Whittlesey House, 1949.
———. *Texas in the Middle Eighteenth Century: Studies in Spanish Colonial History and Administration*. New York: Russell & Russell, 1962.
———. *Spanish Exploration in the Southwest, 1542–1706*. New York: Scribner's, 1925.
Bowden, Charles. *Killing the Hidden Waters*. Austin: University of Texas Press, 1977.
Brackenridge, Henry M. *Early Discoveries by Spaniards in New Mexico, Containing an Account of the Castles of Cibola*. Pittsburgh, Pa.: H. Miner & Co., 1857.
Brandon, William. *Quivira: Europeans in the Region of the Santa Fe Trail, 1540–1820*. Athens: Ohio University Press, 1990.
Brooks, Paul. *Speaking for Nature: How Literary Naturalists from Henry Thoreau to Rachel Carson Have Shaped America*. Boston, Mass.: Houghton-Mifflin, 1980.
Browder, Virginia. *Donley County, Land O' Promise*. Burnet, Tex.: Nortex Press, 1975.
Brune, Gunnar. *Springs of Texas*, Vol. I. Fort Worth, Tex.: Branch-Smith, 1981.
Bryan, James. *Texas in Maps*. Austin: University of Texas Press, 1961.
Burroughs, Jean, ed. *Roosevelt County History and Heritage*. Portales, N.Mex.: Bishop Print Co., 1975.
Butzer, Karl W. *Archaeology as Human Ecology: Method and Theory for a Contextual Approach*. New York: Cambridge University Press, 1985.
———. *Dimensions of Human Geography: Essays on Some Familiar and Neglected Themes*. Dept. of Geography Research Paper no. 186. Chicago, Ill.: University of Chicago, Dept. of Geography, 1978.
Calvin, Ross. *Sky Determines*. Albuquerque: University of New Mexico Press, 1948.
Campa, Authur L. *Treasure of the Sangre de Cristos: Tales and Traditions of the Spanish Southwest*. Norman: University of Oklahoma Press, 1963.
Carroll, H. Bailey. *The Texan–Santa Fe Trail*. Volume XXIV of the *Panhandle-Plains Historical Review*. Canyon, Tex.: Panhandle-Plains Historical Society, 1951.
Carter, Hodding. *Doomed Road of Empire: The Spanish Trail of Conquest*. New York: McGraw-Hill, 1963.
Carter, Paul. *The Road to Botany Bay: An Exploration of Landscape and History*. New York: Alfred A. Knopf, 1988.
Carter, Capt. Robert G. *On the Border with MacKenzie, or Winning West Texas from the Comanches*. 1935. Reprint, New York: Antiquarium Press, 1961.
———. *Tragedies of Cañon Blanco. A Story of the Texas Panhandle*. Washington, D.C.: Gibson, 1919.
Castañeda, Carlos E. *Our Catholic Heritage in Texas*. 7 vols. Austin, Tex.: Von Boeckmann-Jones, 1936–1958.
Castañeda de Najera, Pedro de. *The Journey of Coronado, 1540–1542*. Translated by George Parker Winship. New York: Allerton, 1922.
———. *The Journey of Francisco Coronado*. Translated by George Parker Winship. Introduction by Donald Cutter. Aurora, Colo.: Fulcrum Press, 1990.
———. *The Journey of Francisco Vasquez de Coronado*. Translated by George Parker Winship. Edited by Frederick W. Hodge. San Francisco, Calif.: Grabhorn Press, 1933.
Chavez, Fray Angelico. *Coronado's Friars*. Washington, D.C.: Academy of American Franciscan History, 1968.

Chipman, Donald E. *Spanish Texas, 1519–1821*. Austin: University of Texas Press, 1992.
Cobos, Rubén. *A Dictionary of New Mexico and Southern Colorado Spanish*. Santa Fé: Museum of New Mexico Press, 1983.
Cook, Jim "Lane," as told to T. M. Pearce. *Lane of the Llano*. Boston, Mass.: Little, Brown, 1936.
Cook, John R. *The Border and the Buffalo: An Untold Story of the Southwest Plains*. 1907. Reprint, Austin, Tex.: Statehouse Press, 1989.
Cordell, Linda S. *Prehistory of the Southwest*. New York: Academic Press, 1984.
Copeland, Fayette. *Kendall of the Picayune*. Norman: University of Oklahoma Press, 1943.
Corfield, Penelope J. *Language, History and Class*. Cambridge, Mass.: Basil Blackwell, 1991.
Cortes, José. *Views from the Apache Frontier; Report on the Northern Provinces of New Spain, 1799*. Edited by Elizabeth A. H. John. Translated by John Wheat. Norman: University of Oklahoma Press, 1989.
Cosgrove, Denis and Stephen Daniels, eds. *The Iconography of Landscape: Essays on the Symbolic Representation, Design and Use of Past Environments*. New York: Cambridge University Press, 1988.
Cowart, Jack, Juan Hamilton, and Sarah Greenough. *Georgia O'Keefe: Art and Letters*. Boston, Mass.: Bullfinch Press, 1989.
Cox, James. *Historical and Biographical Record of the Cattle Industry and the Cattlemen of Texas and Adjacent Territory*. St. Louis, Mo.: Woodward & Tiernan, 1895.
Cox, Mary L. *History of Hale County, Texas*. Plainview, Tex.: n.p., 1937.
Cronon, William. *Changes in the Land: Indians, Colonists, and the Ecology of New England*. New York: Hill and Wang, 1983.
Crosby, Alfred W., Jr. *The Columbian Exchange: Biological and Cultural Consequences of 1492*. Westport, Conn.: Greenwood Press, 1973.
———. *Ecological Imperialism: The Biological Expansion of Europe, 900–1900*. New York: Cambridge University Press, 1986.
Dary, David. *Cowboy Culture: A Saga of Five Centuries*. New York: Alfred A. Knopf, 1981.
Davis, W. W. H. *El Gringo: New Mexico and Her People*. New York: Harper & Bros., 1857.
Day, A. Grove. *Coronado's Quest: The Discovery of the Southwestern States*. Berkeley: University of California Press, 1940.
Dearen, Patrick. *Castle Gap and the Pecos Frontier*. Fort Worth: Texas Christian University Press, 1988.
De Baca, Fabiola Cabeza. *We Fed Them Cactus*. Albuquerque: University of New Mexico Press, 1954.
DeBuys, William. *Enchantment and Exploitation: The Life and Hard Times of a New Mexico Mountain Range*. Albuquerque: University of New Mexico Press, 1988.
DeCordova, Jacob. *Texas: Her Resources and Her Public Men*. Philadelphia, Pa.: J. B. Lippincott, 1858.
Dick, Evertt. *The Sod-House Frontier, 1854–1890*. Lincoln, Neb.: Johnsen Publishing, 1954.
Dobie, J. Frank. *Coronado's Children: Tales of Lost Mines and Buried Treasures of the Southwest*. New York: Literary Guild, 1931.
———. *Guide to Life and Literature of the Southwest*. Dallas, Tex.: Southern Methodist University Press, 1969.
———. *The Mustangs*. Boston, Mass.: Little, Brown, 1952.
Dobie, J. Frank, ed. *Texas and Southwestern Lore*. Austin: Texas Folk-Lore Society, no. VI, 1927.
Dodge, Col. Richard Irvin. *The Plains of the Great West and Their Inhabitants*. 1877. Reprint, New York: Archer House, 1959.
Domenech, E. *Voyage pittoresque dans les grands deserts du nouveau monde*. Paris: Marizot, 1862.
Dort, Wakefield, Jr., and J. Knox Jones Jr., eds. *Pleistocene and Recent Environments of the Central Great Plains*. Lawrence: University Press of Kansas, 1970.
Doughty, Robin. *At Home in Texas: Early Views of the Land*. College Station: Texas A&M University Press, 1987.
———. *Wildlife and Man in Texas, Environmental Change and Conservation*. College Station: Texas A&M University Press, 1983.
Elliott, Claude, ed. *Theses on Texas History*. Austin: Texas State Historical Association, 1955.
Ellis, Temple. *Road to Destiny: Pioneering the Staked Plains of Texas*. San Antonio, Tex.: Naylor, 1939.
Emmett, Chris. *Texas Camel Tales*. San Antonio, Tex.: Naylor, 1932.
Erickson, John R. *Through Time and the Valley*. Austin, Tex.: Shoal Creek Publishers, 1978.
Everett, Dianna, ed. *Coronado and the Myth of Quivira*. Canyon, Tex.: Panhandle-Plains Historical Society, 1985.
Farah, Cynthia. *Literature and Landscape: Writers of the Southwest*. El Paso: Texas Western Press, 1988.
Fehrenbach, T. R. *Comanches: The Destruction of a People*. New York: Alfred A. Knopf, 1986.

Ferguson, Walter Keene. *Geology and Politics in Frontier Texas*. Austin: University of Texas Press, 1969.
Fifer, Valerie. *American Progress: The Growth of Transport, Tourist, and Information Industries in the Nineteenth-Century West*. Boston, Mass.: Nimrod Press, 1988.
Fischer, John. *From the High Plains*. New York: Harper & Row, 1978.
Flores, Dan L. *Caprock Canyonlands*. Austin: University of Texas Press, 1990.
———. *Jefferson and Southwestern Exploration: The Freeman & Custis Accounts of the Red River Expedition of 1806*. Norman: University of Oklahoma Press, 1984.
———, ed. *Journal of an Indian Trader: Anthony Glass and the Texas Trading Frontier*. College Station: Texas A&M University Press, 1985.
Forbes, Jack D. *Apache, Navaho, and Spaniard*. Norman: University of Oklahoma Press, 1960.
Ford, John Salmon. *Rip Ford's Texas*. Austin: University of Texas Press, 1963.
Foreman, Grant, ed. *Marcy and the Gold Seekers*. Norman: University of Oklahoma Press, 1939.
———. *A Pathfinder in the Southwest*. Norman: University of Oklahoma Press, 1968.
Frison, George C. *Prehistoric Hunters of the High Plains*. New York: Academic Press, 1978.
Garretson, Martin S. *The American Bison*. New York: New York Zoological Society, 1938.
Geiser, Samuel Wood. *Scientific Study and Exploration in Early Texas*. Dallas, Tex.: Southern Methodist University Press, 1939.
Gerhard, Peter. *The North Frontier of New Spain*. 1982. Reprint, Norman: University of Oklahoma Press, 1993.
Giles, Bascom, comp. *Lots of Land*. Austin, Tex.: Steck Co., 1949.
Goeldner, Paul, comp. *Texas Catalog: Historic American Buildings Survey*. Eds. Lucy Pope Wheeler and S. Allen Chambers Jr. San Antonio, Tex.: Trinity University Press, 1974.
Goetzmann, William H. *Army Exploration in the American West*. New Haven, Conn.: Yale University Press, 1959.
———. *Exploration and Empire: The Explorer and the Scientist in the Winning of the American West*. New York: W. W. Norton, 1978.
———. *New Lands, New Men: America and the Second Great Age of Discovery*. New York: Viking, 1986.
Goetzmann, William H., and William N. Goetzmann. *The West of the Imagination*. New York: W. W. Norton, 1986.
Goetzmann, William H., and Glyndwr Williams. *Atlas of North American Exploration, From the Norse Voyages to the Race to the Pole*. New York: Prentice-Hall, 1992.
Gombrich, E. H. *Art and Illusion, A Study in the Psychology of Pictorial Representation*. Princeton, N.J.: Princeton University Press, 1972.
Gonzalez, Nancie L. *The Spanish-Americans of New Mexico: A Heritage of Pride*. Albuquerque: University of New Mexico Press, 1967.
Goodnight, Charles, et al. *Pioneer Days in the Southwest from 1850 to 1879*. Guthrie, Okla.: n.p., 1909.
Graf, Willim L., ed. *Geomorphic Systems of North America*, Centennial Special Volume 2. New York: Geological Society of America, 1987.
Graham, Don. *Texas: A Literary Portrait*. San Antonio, Tex.: Corona Publishing Co., 1985.
Gregg, Josiah. *Commerce of the Prairies; or, the Journal of a Santa Fe Trader during Eight Expeditions across the Great Western Prairies, and a Residence of Nearly Nine Years in Northern Mexico*. 2 vols. New York: Henry G. Langley, 1844.
———. *Diary and Letters of Josiah Gregg, Southwestern Enterprises, 1840–1850*. Edited by Maurice G. Fulton. 2 vols. Norman: University of Oklahoma Press, 1941, 1944.
Green, Donald E. *Land of the Underground Rain: Irrigation on the Texas High Plains, 1910–1970*. Austin: University of Texas Press, 1973.
Greenley, Albert H. *Camels in America*. New York: Bibliographical Society of America, 1952.
Griffin, John Howard. *Land of the High Sky*. Midland, Tex.: First National Bank, 1959.
Graves, Lawrence L., ed. *A History of Lubbock. Part One: Story of a Country Town*. Volume III of *The Museum Journal*. Lubbock, Tex.: West Texas Museum Association, 1959.
Guy, Duane F., ed. *The Story of Palo Duro Canyon*. Canyon, Tex.: Panhandle-Plains Historical Society, 1979.
Guyer, James S. [Buffalo Jim]. *Pioneer Life in West Texas*. Brownwood, Tex.: n.p., 1938.
Haley, J. Evetts. *Charles Goodnight, Cowman & Plainsman*. Austin: University of Texas Press, 1977.
———. *Fort Concho and the Texas Frontier*. San Angelo, Tex.: San Angelo Standard-Times, 1952.
———. *The XIT Ranch of Texas, and the Early Days of the Llano Estacado*. Norman: University of Oklahoma Press, 1953.

Hall, Claude V. *The Early History of Floyd County*. Volume XX of the *Panhandle-Plains Historical Review*. Amarillo, Tex.: Russell Stationery, 1947.

Hallenbeck, Cleve. *Alvar Núñez Cabeza de Vaca: The Journey and Route of the First European to Cross the Continent of North America* . Glendale, Calif.: Arthur Clark, 1939.

Hammock, Robert. *Below the Llano Estacado—and Beyond*. Bonham, Tex.: Hunterdon Press, 1981.

Hamner, Laura V. *Light 'n Hitch: A Collection of Historical Writing Depicting Life on the High Plains*. Dallas, Tex.: American Guild Press, 1958.

———. *The No-Gun Man of Texas: A Century of Achievement, 1835–1929*. n.p. August, 1935.

———. *Short Grass and Longhorns*. Norman: University of Oklahoma Press, 1943.

Hancock, George. *Go-Devils, Flies and Blackeyed Peas*. Corsicana, Tex.: n.p., 1985.

Hastings, Frank S. *A Ranchman's Recollections*. Chicago, Ill.: Donelly, 1921.

Hickerson, Nancy. *The Jumanos*. Austin: University of Texas Press, 1994.

Hodge, Frederick W., and Theodore H. Lewis, eds. *Spanish Explorers in the Southern United States, 1528–1543*. Austin: Texas State Historical Association, 1984.

Holden, W. C. *The Espuela Land and Cattle Company: A Study of a Foreign-Owned Ranch in Texas*. Austin: Texas State Historical Association, 1970.

———. *Rollie Burns, or, an Account of the Ranching Industry on the South Plains*. College Station: Texas A&M University Press, 1986.

Hollon, W. Eugene. *Beyond the Cross Timbers: The Travels of Randolph B. Marcy, 1812–1887*. Norman: University of Oklahoma Press, 1955.

———. *The Great American Desert, Then and Now*. New York: Oxford University Press, 1966.

———. *The Southwest: Old and New*. New York: Alfred A. Knopf, 1967.

Hopkins, D. M., J. V. Matthews, C. E. Schweger, and S. B. Young, eds. *Paleoecology of Beringia*. New York: Academic Press, 1982.

Horgan, Paul. *Josiah Gregg and His Vision of the Early West*. New York: Farrar, Straus and Giroux, 1979.

Hough, Emerson. *The Story of the Cowboy*. New York: Grosset & Dunlap, 1897.

———. *The Story of the Outlaw*. New York: Outing Publishing, 1907.

Hudson, John C. *Plains Country Towns*. Minneapolis: University of Minnesota Press, 1985.

Hughes, David T. and A. Alicia Hughes-Jones. *The Courson Archeological Projects, 1985 and 1986*. Perryton, Tex.: Innovative Publishing, 1987.

Hughes, J. Donald. *American Indian Ecology*. El Paso: Texas Western Press, 1983.

Hunt, George M. *Early Days Upon the Plains of Texas*. Lubbock, Tex.: Avalanche Printing, 1919.

Hunter, J. Marvin. *The Trail Drivers of Texas*. Austin: University of Texas Press, 1985.

Hyde, George E. *Indians of the High Plains: From the Prehistoric Periods to the Coming of Europeans*. Norman: University of Oklahoma Press, 1981.

Hyer, Julian. *The Land of Beginning Again: The Romance of the Brazos*. Atlanta, Ga.: Foote & Davies, 1952.

Inman, Col. Henry. *The Old Santa Fe Trail: The Story of a Great Highway*. New York: MacMillan, 1897.

Irving, Washington. *A Tour on the Prairies*. 1835. Reprint, New York: Pantheon, 1967.

Jackson, A. T. *Picture-Writing of Texas Indians*. Austin: University of Texas Publication no. 3809, 1938.

Jackson, Berenice. *Man and the Oklahoma Panhandle*. North Newton, Kans.: Mennonite Press, 1982.

Jackson, Jack, Robert S. Weddle, and Winston DeVille. *Mapping Texas and the Gulf Coast: The Contributions of Saint-Denis, Olivan, and Le Maire*. College Station: Texas A&M University Press, 1990.

Jackson, William T. *Wagon Roads West: A Survey of Federal Road Surveys in the Trans-Mississippi West, 1846–1869*. Berkeley: University of California Press, 1952.

James, Edwin. *Account of an Expedition from Pittsburgh to the Rocky Mountains*. In *Early Western Travels*, edited by R. G. Thwaites. Cleveland, Ohio: Arthur H. Clark, 1905.

Jameson, Frederic. *The Prison-House of Language*. Princeton, N.J.: Princeton University Press, 1972.

Jochin, Michael A. *Strategies for Survival: Cultural Behavior in an Ecological Context*. New York: Academic Press, 1981.

John, Elizabeth A. H. *Storms Brewed in Other Men's Worlds: The Confrontation of Indians, Spanish, and French in the Southwest, 1540–1795*. Lincoln: University of Nebraska Press, 1981.

Johnson, Eileen. *Lubbock Lake: Late Quaternary Studies on the Southern High Plains*. College Station: Texas A&M University Press, 1987.

Johnson, M. L. *Intensely Interesting Little Volume of True History of the Struggles with Hostile Indians on the Frontier of Texas . . . A Real Cow Boy's Experience with Indians and the Cow Trail*. Dallas, Tex.: n.p., 1923.

Johnson, Vance. *Heaven's Tableland: The Dust Bowl Story*. New York: Alfred A. Knopf, 1947.
Jones, J. H. *A Condensed History of the Apache and Comanche Indian Tribes*. San Antonio, Tex.: Johnson, 1899.
Jordan, Terry G. *North American Cattle-Ranching Frontiers, Origins, Diffusion, and Differentiation* Albuquerque: University of New Mexico Press, 1993.
———. *Trails to Texas, Southern Roots to Western Cattle Ranching*. Lincoln: University of Nebraska Press, 1981.
Kendall, George W. *Narrative of the Texan Santa Fe Expedition*. London: David Bogue, 1845.
Kennedy, William. *Texas: The Rise, Progress, and Prospects of the Republic of Texas*. 1841. Reprint, Fort Worth, Tex.: Molyneaux Craftsmen, 1925.
Kenner, Charles L. *A History of New Mexican Plains Indian Relations*. Norman: University of Oklahoma Press, 1969.
King, C. Richard. *Wagons East: The Great Drought of 1886—An Episode in Natural Disaster, Human Relations, and Press Leadership*. Austin: University of Texas, Journalism Development Program, 1965.
King, Edward and J. Wells Champney. *Texas; 1874*. Edited by Robert S. Gray. Houston, Tex.: Cordovan Press, 1974.
King, Mary Elizabeth and Idris R. Taylor Jr., eds. *Art and Environment in Native America*. Lubbock: Texas Tech University Press, 1974.
Kolodny, Annette. *The Land Before Her: Fantasy and Experience of the American Frontiers, 1630–1860*. Chapell Hill: University of North Carolina Press, 1984.
Knoepflmacher, U. C. and G. B. Tennyson. *Nature and the Victorian Imagination*. Berkeley: University of California Press, 1977.
Kopper, Philip. *The Smithsonian Book of North American Indians, Before the Coming of the Europeans*. Washington, D.C.: Smithsonian Books, 1986.
Kraenzel, Carl Frederick. *The Great Plains in Transition*. Norman: University of Oklahoma Press, 1955.
Kupper, Winifred. *Texas Sheepman: The Reminiscences of Robert Maudslay*. Austin: University of Texas Press, 1951.
———. *The Golden Hoof*. New York: Alfred A. Knopf, 1945.
La Farge, Oliver, ed. *The Changing Indian*. Norman: University of Oklahoma Press, 1942.
Laine, Tanner. *Phantoms of the Prairies*. Hereford, Tex.: Pioneer Book Publishers, 1973.
Lawson-Peebles, Robert. *Landscape and Written Expression in Revolutionary America*. New York: Oxford University Press, 1988.
Leckie, William. *Military Conquest of the Southern Plains*. Norman: University of Oklahoma Press, 1963.
Lee, Nelson. *Three Years Among the Comanches*. Norman: University of Oklahoma Press, 1957.
Lehmann, Herman. *The Last Captive: The Lives of Herman Lehmann*. Edited by A. C. Greene. Austin, Tex.: Encino Press, 1972.
Lehman, Valgene W. *Forgotten Legions: Sheep in the Rio Grande Plain of Texas*. El Paso: Texas Western Press, 1969.
Lewis, Willie Newbury. *Between Sun and Sod*. Clarendon, Tex.: Clarendon Press, 1939.
———. *Tapadero, the Making of a Cowboy*. Austin: University of Texas Press, 1972.
———. *Willie, a Girl from a Town Called Dallas*. College Station: Texas A&M University Press, 1984.
Lisle, Laurie. *Portrait of an Artist: A Biography of Georgia O'Keeffe*. Albuquerque: University of New Mexico Press, 1986.
Loomis, Noel M. *The Texan–Santa Fe Pioneers*. Norman: University of Oklahoma Press, 1958.
Loomis, Noel M., and Abraham Nasatir. *Pedro Vial and the Roads to Santa Fe*. Norman: University of Oklahoma Press, 1967.
Lowenthal, David, and Martin Bowden. *Geographies of the Mind*. New York: Oxford University Press, 1976.
Lowther, Charles C. *Panhandle Parson*. Nashville, Tenn.: Parthenon Press, 1942.
Mails, Thomas E. *Dog Soldiers, Bear Men, and Buffalo Women: A Study of the Societies and Cults of the Plains Indians*. Englewood Cliffs, N.J.: Prentice-Hall, 1973.
Malin, James C. *The Grassland of North America: Prolegomena to Its History with Addenda and Postscript*. Gloucester, Mass.: Peter Smith, 1967.
Malone, Michael P., ed. *Historians and the American West*. Lincoln: University of Nebraska Press, 1983.
Marcou, Jules. *Geology of North America, with Reports on the Prairies of Arkansas and Texas, the Rocky

Mountains of New Mexico and the Sierra Nevada of California. Zurich: Zürcher and Ferrer, 1858.
Marcy, Randolph B. *Adventure on Red River: Report on the Exploration of the Headwaters of the Red River*. Edited by Grant Foreman. Norman: University of Oklahoma Press, 1937.
———. *The Prairie Traveler, A Hand-Book for Overland Expeditions*. New York: Harper & Brothers, 1859.
———. *Thirty Years of Army Life on the Border*. New York: Harper & Brothers, 1866.
Margry, Pierre. *Découvertes et Etablissement des Francais dans l'ouest et dans le sud de Amérique Septentrionale*. 6 vols. Paris: D. Jouaust, 1888.
Marshall, Thomas Maitland. *A History of the Western Boundary of the Louisiana Purchase, 1819–1841*. New York: Da Capo Press, 1970.
Martin, J. C., and R. S. Martin. *Contours of Discovery*. Austin.: Texas State Historical Association, 1982.
———. *Maps of Texas and the Southwest, 1513–1900*. Albuquerque: University of New Mexico Press, 1984.
McHugh, Tom. *The Time of the Buffalo*. Lincoln: University of Nebraska Press, 1979.
McLuhan, T. C. *Dream Tracks: The Railroad and the American Indian, 1890–1930*. New York: Abrams, 1985.
Meinig, D. W. *Imperial Texas: An Interpretive Essay in Cultural Geography*. Austin: University of Texas Press, 1985.
———. *The Great Columbia Plain: A Historical Geography, 1805–1910*. Seattle: University of Washington Press, 1968.
———. *The Interpretation of Ordinary Landscapes: Geographical Essays*. New York: Oxford University Press, 1979.
Miller, Sidney L. *Tomorrow in West Texas: Economic Opportunities along the Texas and Pacific Railway*. Lubbock: Texas Tech Press, 1956.
Miller, Thomas Lloyd. *The Public Lands of Texas, 1519–1970*. Norman: University of Oklahoma Press, 1972.
Mojtabai, A. G. *Blessed Assurance, At Home with the Bomb in Amarillo, Texas*. Albuquerque: University of New Mexico Press, 1986.
Möllhausen, B. *Diary of a Journey from the Mississippi to the Coast of the Pacific . . . with an introduction by Alexander Von Humboldt*. London: Longmans & Roberts, 1858.
———. *Tagebuch einer Reise von Mississippi nach den Küsten der Südsee*. Leipzig: Mendelsohn, 1858.
———. *Vandringer Gjennem det Vestlige Nordamerikas Prairier*. Copenhagen: P. G. Philipsens, 1862.
Moncus, Herman H. *Prairie Schooner Pirates: The Story of the Comancheros*. New York: Carlton Press, 1963
Montaignes, Francois des [Isaac Cooper, pseud.]. *The Plains*. Norman: University of Oklahoma Press, 1972.
Morris, John Miller. *From Coronado to Escalante: The Explorers of the Spanish Southwest*. New York: Chelsea House, 1992.
Munnerlyn, Tom. *Texas Local History: A Source Book for Available Town and County Histories, Local Memoirs and Genealogical Records*. Austin, Tex.: Eakin Press, 1983.
Nasatir, Abraham. *Borderland in Retreat. From Spanish Louisiana to the Far Southwest*. Albuquerque: University of New Mexico Press, 1976.
Newcomb, W. W. *The Indians of Texas: From Prehistoric to Modern Times*. Austin: University of Texas Press, 1978.
Nicolson, Marjorie Hope. *Mountain Gloom and Mountain Glory: The Development of the Aesthetics of the Infinite*. Ithaca, N.Y.: Cornell University Press, 1959.
Norberg-Schulz, Christian. *Genius Loci: Towards a Phenomenology of Architecture*. New York: Rizzoli, 1984.
Nordyke, Lewis. *Cattle Empire—The Fabulous Story of the 3,000,000 Acre XIT*. New York: William Morrow, 1949.
Norwood, Vera, and Janice Monk, eds. *The Desert is No Lady: Southwestern Landscapes in Women's Writing and Art*. New Haven, Conn.: Yale University Press, 1987.
Nostrand, Richard L. *The Hispano Homeland*. Norman: University of Oklahoma Press, 1992.
Noyes, Stanley. *Los Comanches, 1715–1845*. Albuquerque: University of New Mexico Press, 1993.
O'Connor, Robert F., ed. *Texas Myths*. College Station: Texas A&M University Press, 1986.
Oden, Bill. *Early Days on the Texas–New Mexico Plains*. Canyon, Tex.: Hertzog, 1965.
Oliver, Symmes C. *Ecology and Cultural Continuity as Contributing Factors in the Social Organization of the Plains Indians*. Berkeley: University of California Press, 1962.

Parker, W. B. *Notes Taken During the Expedition Commanded by Capt. R. B. Marcy, U.S.A., Through Unexplored Texas, in the Summer and Fall of 1854*. Austin: Texas State Historical Association, 1984.
Pearce, W. M. *Matador Land and Cattle Company*. Norman: University of Oklahoma Press, 1964.
Peterson, John Allen, ed. *"Facts as I Remember Them": The Autobiography of Rufe LeFors*. Austin.: University of Texas Press, 1986.
Peyton, John Rowzee. *A Virginian in New Mexico*. Santa Fé, N.Mex.: Press of the Territorian, 1967.
Phelan, Richard. *Texas Wild: The Land, Plants, and Animals of the Lone Star State*. New York: Excalibur Books, 1978.
Philips, Shine. *Big Spring: The Casual Biography of a Prairie Town*. New York: Prentice-Hall, 1942.
Pichardo, José Antonio. *Pichardo's Treatise on the Limits of Louisiana and Texas*. Volume III. Austin: University of Texas Press, 1941.
Pickles, John. *Phenomenology, Science and Geography*. New York: Cambridge University Press, 1985.
Pike, Albert. *Journeys in the Prairie, 1831–1832*, Vol. XLI of the *Panhandle-Plains Historical Review*. Canyon Tex.: Panhandle-Plains Historical Society, 1968.
———. *Prose Sketches and Poems, Written in the Western Country*. Edited by D. J. Weber. Albuquerque: Calvin Horn Publisher, 1967.
Pike, Zebulon M. *The Expeditions . . . to Headwaters of the Mississippi River, Through Louisiana Territory, and in New Spain, during the years 1805–7*. Edited by Elliott Coués. New York: Harper, 1895.
Porter, Millie Jones. *Memory Cups of Panhandle Pioneers*. Clarendon, Tex.: Clarendon Press, 1945.
Potinaro, Pierluigi, and Franco Knirsch. *The Cartography of North America, 1500–1800*. New York: Crescent Books, 1987.
Poulsen, Richard C. *The Pure Experience of Order: Essays on the Symbolic in the Folk Material Culture of Western America*. Albuquerque: University of New Mexico Press, 1982.
Powell, John Wesley. *Report on the Lands of the Arid Region of the United States*. Edited by Wallace Stegner. Cambridge, Mass.: Belknap Press of Harvard University Press, 1962.
Preston, Douglas. *Cities of Gold: A Journey Across the American Southwest in Pursuit of Coronado*. New York: Simon and Schuster, 1992.
Price, B. Byron, and Frederick W. Rathjen. *The Golden Spread, an Illustrated History of Amarillo and the Texas Panhandle*. Northridge, Calif.: Windsor Publications, 1986.
Prieto, Carlos. *El Sueño de Cíbola*. Mexico City: Regis, 1933.
Quayle, William A. *The Prairie and the Sea*. Cincinnati, Ohio: Jennings and Graham, 1905.
Rabasa, José. *Inventing America: Spanish Historiography and the Formation of Eurocentrism*. Norman: University of Oklahoma Press, 1993.
Rathjen, Frederick W. *The Texas Panhandle Frontier*. Austin: University of Texas Press, 1973.
Reed, St. Clair Griffin. *A History of the Texas Railroads, and of Transportation Conditions under Spain and Mexico and the Republic and the State*. Houston, Tex.: St. Clair Publishing, 1941.
Reid, Capt. Mayne. *The Lone Ranch: A Tale of the "Staked Plain."* London: Chapman & Hall, 1871.
Reinhartz, Dennis, and Charles C. Colley, eds. *The Mapping of the American Southwest*. College Station: Texas A&M University Press, 1987.
Renner, F. G., et. al. *A Selected Bibliography on Management of Western Ranges, Livestock, and Wildlife*. Washington, D.C.: Government Printing Office, 1938.
Reps, John W. *The Forgotten Frontier: Urban Planning in the American West Before 1890*. Columbia: University of Missouri, 1981.
Reynolds, David S. *Beneath the American Renaissance: The Subversive Imagination in the Age of Emerson and Melville*. New York: Alfred A. Knopf, 1988.
Richardson, Rupert Norval. *The Comanche Barrier to South Plains Settlement: A Century and a Half of Savage Resistance to the Advancing White Frontier*. Glendale, Calif.: Arthur H. Clark, 1933.
Riley, Carroll L. *The Frontier People: The Greater Southwest in the Protohistoric Period*. Albuquerque: University of New Mexico Press, 1987.
———. *Rio del Norte: People of the Upper Rio Grande from Earliest Times to the Pueblo Revolt*. Salt Lake City: University of Utah Press, 1995.
Rister, Carl Coke. *Border Captives: The Traffic in Prisoners by Southern Plains Indians, 1835–1875*. Norman: University of Oklahoma Press, 1940.
Rittenhouse, Jack D. *Maverick Tales of the Southwest*. Albuquerque: University of New Mexico Press, 1987.
———. *The Santa Fe Trail*. Albuquerque: University of New Mexico, 1971.
Robertson, Pauline Durrett, and R. L. Robertson. *Panhandle Pilgrimage: Illustrated Tales Tracing History in the Texas Panhandle*. Amarillo, Tex.: Paramount Publishing, 1978.

Robinson, Roxana. *Georgia O'Keeffe, A Life.* New York: Harper & Row, 1989.
Rose, Francis L., and Russell W. Strandtmann. *Wildflowers of the Llano Estacado.* Dallas, Tex.: Taylor Publishing, 1986.
Rosenbaum, Robert J. *Mexicano Resistance in the Southwest: "The Sacred Right of Self-Preservation."* Austin: University of Texas Press, 1986.
Rutherford, Blanche. *One Corner of Heaven.* San Antonio, Tex.: Naylor, 1964.
Salsbury, Stephen, ed. *Essays on the History of the American West.* Hinsdale, Ill.: Dryden Press, 1975.
Sandoz, Mari. *The Buffalo Hunters: The Story of the Hide Men.* New York: Hastings House, 1954.
Sauer, Carl O. *Land and Life.* Edited by John Leighly. Berkeley: University of California Press, 1965.
———. *Sixteenth-Century North America; The Land and People as Seen by the Europeans.* Berkeley: University of California Press, 1971.
Scarborough, A. *Diary of a Member of the First Pack Train to Leave Ft. Smith for California in 1849.* Canyon, Tex.: Panhandle-Plains Historical Society, 1969.
Scarborough, Dorothy. *The Wind.* Austin: University of Texas Press, 1988.
Schofield, Donald F. *Indians, Cattle, Ships and Oil: The Story of W. M. D. Lee.* Austin: University of Texas Press, 1985.
Seamon, David and Robert Mugerauer, eds. *Dwelling, Place and Environment: Towards a Phenomenology of Person and World.* Dordrecht, The Netherlands: Martinus Nijhoff, 1985.
Sellards, E. H. *Early Man in America: A Study in Prehistory.* Austin: University of Texas Press, 1952.
Shafer, Harry J. *Ancient Texans: Rock Art and Lifeways Along the Lower Pecos.* Austin: Texas Monthly Press, 1986.
Sheffy, Lester Fields. *The Francklyn Land & Cattle Company, A Panhandle Enterprise, 1882–1957.* Austin: University of Texas Press, 1963.
———. *The Life and Times of Timothy Dwight Hobart, 1855–1935.* Amarillo, Tex.: Russell Stationery, 1950.
Simmons, Marc, ed. and trans. *Border Comanches: Seven Spanish Colonial Documents 1785–1819.* Santa Fé, N.Mex.: Stagecoach Press, 1967.
Simpson, S. R. *Llano Estacado; or, The Plains of West Texas.* San Antonio, Tex.: Naylor, 1957.
Siringo, Charles A. *A Lone Star Cowboy.* Santa Fé, N.Mex.: n.p., 1919.
Skeat, Walter W. *An Etymological Dictionary of the English Language.* 4th ed. London: Oxford University Press, 1968.
Smith, Henry Nash. *Virgin Land: The American West as Symbol and Myth.* Cambridge, Mass.: Harvard University Press, 1950.
Smythe, William E. *The Conquest of Arid America.* 1899. Reprint, Seattle: University of Washington Press, 1970.
Sonnichsen, C. L. *Cowboys and Cattle Kings: Life on the Range Today.* Norman: University of Oklahoma Press, 1950.
———. *From Hop-a-Long to Hud: Thoughts on Western Fiction.* College Station: Texas A&M University Press, 1978.
———. *The Mescalero Apaches.* Norman: University of Oklahoma Press, 1973.
Spicer, Edward H. *Cycles of Conquest: The Impact of Spain, Mexico and the United States on the Indians of the Southwest, 1533–1960.* Tucson: University of Arizona Press, 1981.
Spikes, Nellie W., and Temple Ann Ellis. *Through the Years: A History of Crosby County, Texas.* San Antonio, Tex.: Naylor, 1952.
Stafford, Barbara Maria. *Voyage into Substance: Art, Science, Nature, and the Illustrated Travel Account, 1760–1840.* Cambridge, Mass.: MIT Press, 1984.
Stanley, F. *Railroads of the Texas Panhandle.* Borger, Tex.: Hess Publishing, 1976.
———. *The Texas Panhandle from Cattlemen to Feed Lots, 1880–1970.* Borger, Tex.: Hess Publishing, 1971.
Starr, Kevin. *Americans and the California Dream, 1850–1915.* New York: Oxford University Press, 1985.
Stegner, Wallace. *The American West as Living Space.* Ann Arbor: University of Michigan Press, 1987.
Stephens, A. Ray, and William M. Holmes. *Historical Atlas of Texas.* Norman: University of Oklahoma Press, 1989.
Thomas, Alfred Barnaby. *After Coronado: Spanish Exploration Northeast of New Mexico, 1696–1727.* Norman: University of Oklahoma Press, 1935.
———. *The Plains Indians and New Mexico, 1751–1778.* Albuquerque: University of New Mexico Press, 1940.

Thomas, Keith. *Man and the Natural World: A History of the Modern Sensibility*. New York: Pantheon Books, 1983.
Thomas, William L., Jr., ed. *Man's Role in Changing the Face of the Earth*. Chicago, Ill.: University of Chicago Press, 1956.
Thompson, Albert W. *They Were Open Range Days: Annals of a Western Frontier*. Denver, Colo.: The World Press, 1946.
Thompson, W. Ernest. *From the Grass Roots: A Land Man's Story*. Austin, Tex.: Steck-Warlich, 1969.
Thorp, N. Howard. *Songs of the Cowboys*. Estancia, N.Mex.: News Print Shop, [1908].
Timmons, William. *Twilight on the Range: Recollections of a Latterday Cowboy*. Austin: University of Texas Press, 1962.
Tolbert, Frank. *Staked Plain*. New York: Doubleday, 1958.
Tomkins, William. *Indian Sign Language*. New York: Dover, 1969.
Towne, Charles Wayland, and Edward N. Wentworth. *Cattle and Men*. Norman: University of Oklahoma Press, 1955.
Townshend, S. Nugent, and J. G. Hyde. *Our Indian Summer in the Far West: An Autumn Tour of Fifteen Thousand Miles in Kansas, Texas, New Mexico, Colorado, and the Indian Territory*. London: Charles Whittingham, 1880.
Tuan, Yi-Fu. *Topophilia: A Study of Environmental Perception, Attitudes, and Values*. Englewood Cliffs, N.J.: Prentice-Hall, 1974.
Turner, Ellen Sue and Thomas R. Hester. *A Field Guide to Stone Artifacts of Texas Indians*. Austin: Texas Monthly Press, 1985.
Turner, Frederick. *Beyond Geography, The Western Spirit Against the Wilderness*. New York: Viking, 1980.
Turner, Mary Honeyman Ten Eyck. *These High Plains*. Amarillo, Tex.: [Russell Stationery], 1941.
Tyler, Ron. *Prints of the West*. Golden, Colo.: Fulcrum Press, 1994.
Tyson, Carl Newton. *The Red River in Southwestern History*. Norman: University of Oklahoma Press, 1981.
Udall, Stewart L. *To the Inland Empire: Coronado and Our Spanish Legacy*. Garden City, N.Y.: Doubleday & Co., 1987.
Velázquez de la Cadena, Mariano, et.al. *New Revised Velázquez Spanish and English Dictionary*. Chicago, Ill.: Follett Publishing, 1967.
Vestal, Stanley [Walter Campbell, pseud.]. *Short Grass Country*. New York: Duell, Sloan & Pearce, 1941.
Viola, Herman J. *Exploring the West*. Washington, D.C.: Smithsonian Books, 1987.
Von Hagen, V. W., ed. *The Green World of the Naturalists*. New York: Greenburg, 1948.
Wagner, Henry R. *The Spanish Southwest*. New York: Alfred A. Knopf, 1967.
Wagner, Henry R., and Charles L. Camp. *The Plains and the Rockies: A Bibliography of Original Narrative of Travel and Adventure, 1800–1865*. Columbus, Ohio: Long's College Book Co., 1953.
Wallace, Edward S. *The Great Reconnaissance. Soldiers, Artists and Scientists on the Frontier, 1848–1861*. Boston, Mass.: Little, Brown, 1955.
Wallace, Ernest. *Ranald S. Mackenzie on the Texas Frontier*. Lubbock: West Texas Museum Association, 1964.
Wallace, Ernest, and E. Adamson Hoebel. *The Comanches, Lords of the South Plains*. Norman: University of Oklahoma Press, 1953.
Wallis, George A. *Cattle Kings of the Staked Plains*. Dallas, Tex.: American Guild Press, 1957.
Ward, David, ed. *Geographic Perspectives on America's Past: Readings on the Historical Geography of the United States*. New York: Oxford University Press, 1979.
Warnock, Barton H. *Wildflowers of the Guadalupe Mountains and the Sand Dune Country, Texas*. Alpine, Tex.: Sul Ross State University, 1974.
Webb, W. E. *Buffalo Land*. Philadelphia, Pa.: Hubbard Brothers, 1872.
Webb, Walter Prescott. *The Great Plains*. Boston, Mass.: Ginn and Company, 1931.
———. *The Texas Rangers*. Boston, Mass.: Ginn and Company, 1935.
Webb, Walter Prescott, H. Bailey Carroll, and Eldon Stephen Branda, eds. *The Handbook of Texas*. 3 vols. Austin: Texas State Historical Association, 1952–1976.
Webber, Charles W. *Old Hicks the Guide; or, Adventures in the Comanche Country in Search of a Gold Mine*. New York: Harper & Bros., 1848.
Weber, David J. *The Mexican Frontier, 1821–1846: The American Southwest Under Mexico*. Albuquerque: University of New Mexico Press, 1982.

———. *Myth and the History of the Spanish Southwest*. Albuquerque: University of New Mexico Press, 1987.
———. *The Spanish Frontier in North America*. New Haven, Conn.: Yale University Press, 1992.
Wedel, Mildred Mott. *The Wichita Indians, 1541–1750: Ethnohistorical Essays*. Lincoln, Neb.: J&L Reprint, 1988.
Wedel, Waldo R. *Central Plains Prehistory: Holocene Environments and Culture Change in the Republican River Basin*. Lincoln: University of Nebraska Press, 1986.
Wellman, Paul I. *The Comancheros*. Garden City, N.Y.: Doubleday, 1952.
———. *Glory, God and Gold, A Narrative History*. Garden City, N.Y.: Doubleday, 1954.
Weniger, Del. *The Explorers' Texas: The Lands and Waters*. Austin, Tex.: Eakin Press, 1984.
Wheat, Carl S. *Mapping the Transmississippi West, 1540–1861*. San Francisco, Calif.: Grabhorn Press, 1957–1963.
White, G. Edward. *The Eastern Establishment and the Western Experience*. Austin: University of Texas Press, 1989.
White, Hayden. *Metahistory: The Historical Imagination in Nineteenth Century Europe*. Baltimore, Md.: Johns Hopkins University Press, 1973.
Whitlock, V. H. [Ol' Waddy]. *Cowboy Life on the Llano Estacado*. Norman: University of Oklahoma Press, 1970.
Wiley, Peter, and Robert Gottlieb. *Empires in the Sun: The Rise of the New American West*. New York: Putnam's, 1982.
Williams, J. W. *Old Texas Trails*. Edited and compiled by Kenneth F. Neighbors. Austin, Tex.: Eakin Press, 1979.
Williams, N. W. *The Big Ranch Country*. 2nd ed. Burnet, Tex.: Nortex Press, 1971.
Wilson, Jane A. *A Thrilling Narrative of the Sufferings of Mrs. Jane Adeline Wilson during her Captivity among the Comanche Indians*. Fairfield, Conn.: Ye Galleon Press, 1971.
Wood, Richard G. *Stephen Harriman Long, 1784–1864: Army Engineer, Explorer, Inventor*. Glendale, Calif.: Arthur H. Clark, 1966.
Woods, Lawrence M. *British Gentlemen in the Wild West: The Era of the Intensely English Cowboy*. New York: Free Press, 1989.
Worster, Donald. *Dust Bowl: The Southern Plains in the 1930s*. New York: Oxford University Press, 1979.
———. *Nature's Economy: A History of Ecological Ideas*. New York: Cambridge University Press, 1985.
Wright, L. H., and J. M. Bynum, eds. *Butterfield Overland Mail*. San Marino, Calif.: Huntington Library, 1942.
Xántus, Janos. *Levelei Éjszakamirikabol*. Budapest, Hungary: Lauffer es Stolp, 1858.
Young, James A., and B. Abott Sparks. *Cattle in the Cold Desert*. Logan: Utah State University Press, 1985.

NOTES

Introduction

1. National Oceanic and Atmospheric Administration, *Climate of Texas* (Asheville, N.C.: National Climatic Data Center, 1982); Walter Prescott Webb, H. Bailey Carroll, and Eldon S. Branda (eds.), *Handbook of Texas* (3 vols.; Austin: Texas State Historical Association, 1952, 1976), II, 69.

2. Connecticut, Delaware, Massachusetts, New Jersey, New Hampshire, Rhode Island, and Vermont.

3. Paul Carter, *The Road to Botany Bay* (New York: Alfred A. Knopf, 1988); William DeBuys, *Enchantment and Exploitation* (Albuquerque: University of New Mexico Press, 1988); Robin Doughty, *At Home in Texas: Early Views of the Land* (College Station: Texas A&M University Press, 1987).

4. An excellent overview of the epistemological problems of historical geography is in Robert Mugerauer, "Concerning Regional Geography as a Hermeneutical Discipline," *Geographische Zeitschrift*, LXIX (First Quarter, 1981), 57–67.

5. José Rabasa, *Inventing America: Spanish Historiography and the Formation of Eurocentrism* (Norman: University of Oklahoma Press, 1993).

6. Donald W. Meinig, *The Great Columbia Plain* (Seattle: University of Washington Press, 1968), xi–xiii.

7. Thomas F. Saarinen, *Perception of Environment* (Washington, D.C.: Commission on College Geography Resource Paper no. 5, 1969); David Lowenthal, "Geography, Experience and Imagination: Towards a Geographical Epistemology," *Annals of the Association of American Geographers*, LI (Sept., 1961), 241–260; Denis Cosgrove and Stephen Daniels (eds.), *The Iconography of Landscape: Essays on the Symbolic Representation, Design and Use of Past Environments* (New York: Cambridge University Press, 1988); D. W. Meinig (ed.), *The Interpretation of Ordinary Landscapes: Geographical Essays* (New York: Oxford University Press, 1979).

8. David Lowenthal (ed.), *Environmental Perception and Behavior* (Chicago: University of Chicago Dept. of Geography Research Paper no. 109, 1967); Thomas F. Saarinen, *Perception of the Drought Hazard on the Great Plains* (Chicago: University of Chicago Dept. of Geography Research Paper no. 106, 1966).

9. David Lowenthal and Martyn Bowden (eds.), *Geographies of the Mind* (New York: Oxford University Press, 1976); Brian W. Blouet and Merlin P. Lawson (eds.), *Images of the Plains: The Role of Human Nature in Settlement* (Lincoln: University of Nebraska Press, 1975).

10. John L. Allen, "Exploration and the Creation of Geographical Images of the Great Plains: Comments on the Role of Subjectivity," in *Images of the Plains*, eds. Blouet and Lawson, 3–12.

11. W. C. Holden, "The Land," in *A History of Lubbock*, ed. Lawrence L. Graves (Lubbock, Tex.: The Museum Journal, 1959), 15–16.

12. George Hancock, *Go-Devils, Flies and Blackeyed Peas* (Corsicana, Tex.: n.p., 1985), 39.

13. Holden, "The Land," 16.

14. J. Evetts Haley, "Lore of the Llano Estacado," in *Texas and Southwestern Lore*, ed. J. Frank Dobie (Austin: Texas Folklore Society, 1927), VI, 72–89.

15. J. K. Wright, "*Terrae Incognitae*: The Place of the Imagination in Geography," *Annals of the Association of American Geographers*, XXXVII (Mar., 1947), 1–15. Reprinted in John Kirtland Wright, *Human Nature in Geography, Fourteen Papers, 1925–1965* (Cambridge, Mass.: Harvard University Press, 1966). See also Martyn J. Bowden, "The Perception of the Western Interior of the United States, 1800–1870: A Problem in Historical Geosophy," *Proceedings of the Association of American Geographers*, I (1969), 16–21.

16. G. Malcolm Lewis, "Rhetoric of the Western Interior: Modes of Environmental Description

in American Promotional Literature of the Nineteenth Century," in *The Iconography of Landscape*, eds. Cosgrove and Daniels, 179–193.

17. Wright, *"Terrae Incognitae,"* 12–15.

18. John L. Kessel, "Foreword," in Herbert E. Bolton, *Coronado: Knight of Pueblos and Plains* (1949; reprint, Albuquerque: University of New Mexico Press, 1990), xv.

19. Marjorie Hope Nicolson, *Mountain Gloom and Mountain Glory: The Development of the Aesthetics of the Infinite* (Ithaca, N.Y.: Cornell University Press, 1959).

20. Robert Mugerauer, "Language and the Emergence of Environment," in *Dwelling, Place and Environment*, eds. R. Mugerauer and D. Seamon (Dordrecht, The Netherlands: Martinus Nijhoff, 1985), 51–70; Tzvetan Todorov, *The Conquest of America: The Question of the Other*, trans. Richard Howard (New York: Harper and Row, 1984).

Chapter One

1. Peter Gerhard, *The North Frontier of New Spain* (rev. ed.; Norman: University of Oklahoma Press, 1993).

2. Frederick W. Hodge and Theodore H. Lewis (eds.), *Spanish Explorers in the Southern United States, 1528–1543* (1907; reprint, Austin: Texas State Historical Association, 1984), 332.

3. A general reference to this intense period of Spanish exploration is chapter 2, "First Encounters," in David J. Weber, *The Spanish Frontier in North America* (New Haven: Yale University Press, 1992), 30–59.

4. George Hammond and Agapito Rey (eds.), *Narratives of the Coronado Expedition, 1540–1542* (4 vols.; Albuquerque, N.Mex.: Coronado Cuarto Centennial Publications, 1940–1966), II.

5. For bibliographic research see Henry R. Wagner, *The Spanish Southwest* (New York: Alfred A. Knopf, 1967), and John Jenkins, *Basic Texas Books* (rev. ed.; Austin: Texas State Historical Association, 1983), 60–64. The important *Joint Report* in Oviedo y Valdés's chapter XXXV is completely translated by Basil C. Hedrick and Carroll L. Riley, *The Journey of the Vaca Party: The Account of the Narváez Expedition, 1528–1536* (Carbondale: Southern Illinois University, University Museum Studies no. 2, 1974).

6. For well-written efforts see Cleve Hallenbeck, *Alvar Núñez Cabeza de Vaca: The Journey and Route of the First European to Cross the Continent of North America* (Glendale, Calif.: Arthur H. Clark, 1940); and Fanny Bandelier (trans.), Adolph Bandelier (ed.), *The Journey of Alvar Núñez Cabeza de Vaca and His Companions from Florida to the Pacific, 1528–1536* (New York: A. S. Barnes, 1905).

7. Donald E. Chipman, "In Search of Cabeza de Vaca's Route across Texas: An Historiographical Survey," *Southwestern Historical Quarterly*, XCI (Oct., 1987), 127–148.

8. Buckingham Smith, translation in Hodge and Lewis (eds.), *Spanish Explorers in the Southern United States, 1528–1543*, 68.

9. Ibid. The geographic sense of "Florida" was an extended one, including the southern Gulf Coast of Texas and Louisiana.

10. Chipman plots a very intelligent and completely different route, one traversing South Texas and northern Mexico. But Chipman's Cabeza de Vaca still nears the vicinity of the Pecos River around Presidio. See Donald E. Chipman, *Spanish Texas, 1519–1821* (Austin: University of Texas Press, 1992), 30–31. Carl Sauer offers a southern variant of Hallenbeck's route in *Sixteenth-Century North America: The Land and the People as Seen by the Europeans* (Berkeley: University of California Press, 1971), 118–119.

11. For the extent of the bison range see David A. Dary, *The Buffalo Book: The Full Saga of the American Animal* (rev. ed.; Athens: Ohio University Press, 1989), 20–43.

12. Hodge and Lewis (eds.), *Spanish Explorers in the Southern United States, 1528–1543*, 100.

13. Ibid., 104.

14. Chipman, *Spanish Texas*, 14.

15. Hodge and Lewis (eds.), *Spanish Explorers in the Southern United States, 1528–1543*, 104.

16. Ibid., 105.

17. Bolton, *Coronado*. This is still the definitive narrative history of the entrada.

18. See chapter two, "The Turquoise Trail," in John Miller Morris, *From Coronado to Escalante: The Explorers of the Spanish Southwest* (New York: Chelsea House, 1992), 21–34.

19. David J. Weber, "Fray Marcos de Niza and the Historians," in *Myth and the History of the Hispanic Southwest* (Albuquerque: University of New Mexico Press, 1987), 19–32.

20. Carroll L. Riley, *The Frontier People* (Albuquerque: University of New Mexico Press, 1987), 182–183.

21. For understanding the context of Coronado's wanderings on the Llano Estacado, see George Parker Winship, "The Coronado Expedition, 1540–1542," *Fourteenth Annual Report of U.S. Bureau of American Ethnology*, 1892–93, Part One (Washington, D.C.: Government Printing Office, 1896); Bolton, *Coronado*; Carl O. Sauer, *The Road to Cibola* (Berkeley: University of California Press, 1932); and Stewart L. Udall, *To the Inland Empire* (Garden City, N.Y.: Doubleday & Co., 1987). For the best source of translated Coronado documents see Hammond and Rey (eds.), *Narratives of the Coronado Expedition, 1540–1542*. See also Dianna Everett (ed.), *Coronado and the Myth of Quivira* (Canyon, Tex.: Panhandle-Plains Historical Society, 1985), and L. F. Sheffy (ed.), "The Coronado Expedition," *Panhandle-Plains Historical Review*, XIII (1940). A recent work of great interest on the trail from the U.S.-Mexico border to Pecos Pueblo is Douglas Preston, *Cities of Gold: A Journey across the American Southwest in Pursuit of Coronado* (New York: Simon and Schuster, 1992).

22. *The Journey of Francisco Vasquez de Coronado*, trans. George Parker Winship, ed. Frederick W. Hodge (San Francisco, Calif.: Grabhorn Press, 1933), 83. Italics added.

23. Ibid., 84.

24. Hammond and Rey (eds.), *Narratives of the Coronado Expedition*, 217.

25. Bolton, *Coronado*, 181.

26. The essential reference on Fray Juan de Padilla's life is Fr. Angelico Chavez, *Coronado's Friars* (Washington, D.C.: Academy of American Franciscan History, 1968). This is a meticulous work correcting many errors in Carlos Castañeda's older historical account in *Our Catholic Heritage*.

27. Ibid., 50 n.3

28. A fragmentary account, believed to be written by Padilla, on the Rio del Norte country at time of contact is in Hammond and Rey (eds.), *Narratives of the Coronado Expedition, 1540–1542*, "Discovery of Tiguex by Alvarado and Padilla," 182–184.

29. Bolton, *Coronado*, 187.

30. The large trade network between Cicúye and the plains is discussed in Carroll L. Riley, *The Frontier People: The Greater Southwest in the Protohistoric Period* (Albuquerque: University of New Mexico Press, 1987), 251–261. The mutual trade relations between pueblos and plains are also discussed in Katherine Spielmann, "Late Prehistoric Exchange between the Southwest and Southern Plains," *Plains Anthropologist*, XXVIII (Nov., 1983), 257–272.

31. Riley, quoting Kidder, *The Frontier People*, 251.

32. Ibid. Riley notes the Santa Rosa area just west of the Llano Estacado was within the territorial domain of Cicúye. Bolton, *Coronado*, 188, takes Alvarado down the Pecos and then over to the Canadian River. Riley amplifies on the deviousness of the guides in chapter 13, "Turk and the Pecos Plot," in *Rio del Norte: People of the Upper Rio Grande from Earliest Times to the Pueblo Revolt* (Salt Lake City: University of Utah Press, 1995).

33. See the evocative article by Frank Bryan, "The Llano Estacado: The Geographical Background of the Coronado Expedition," *Panhandle-Plains Historical Review*, XIII (1940), 21–37.

34. Hammond and Rey (eds.), *Narratives of the Coronado Expedition, 1540–1542*, and Bolton, *Coronado*, 188–189.

35. Paul I. Wellman analyzed these geosophies in *Glory, God, and Gold: A Narrative History* (Garden City, N.Y.: Doubleday & Co., 1954), 37–41.

36. Bolton, *Coronado*, 190.

37. Note the opinions of the chief chronicler of the expedition, Pedro de Castañeda, in Frederick W. Hodge (ed.), "The Narrative of the Expedition of Coronado by Pedro de Castañeda," in *Spanish Explorers in the Southern United States, 1528–1543*, 313.

Chapter Two

1. Bolton, *Coronado*, 198.
2. Hodge and Lewis (eds.), *Spanish Explorers in the Southern United States, 1528–1543*, 314. See also Winship, "The Coronado Expedition, 1540–1542" (1896; reprint, Chicago: Rio Grande Press, 1964; this and subsequent text citations are keyed to this popular reprint), 231.
3. Winship, "The Coronado Expedition, 1540–1542," 130.
4. Ibid., 231.
5. David J. Weber, "Meditations on Coronado and the Myth of Quivira," in Everett (ed.), *Coronado and the Myth of Quivira*, 60.
6. Castañeda said they left on May 5, but this date is in the 1596 Lennox manuscript. The unknown 1596 copyist preparing this copy may have changed Castañeda's original date to conform to the recent Gregorian calendar reforms.
7. Carroll L. Riley's population and livestock estimates are well considered. Riley estimates 1,200 to 1,300 allies with some of the 350 original Spanish remaining at Corazones and a party absent with Captain Tovar. He also points out that the Spanish acquired captives in the Tiguex wars, perhaps hundreds of slaves that they brought with them to the plains. See Riley, *Frontier People*, 262, and *Rio del Norte*, 183. Both higher and lower figures are common.
8. Bolton, *Coronado*, 240.
9. See A. Grove Day, *Coronado's Quest: The Discovery of the Southwestern States* (Berkeley: University of California Press, 1940), chap. 12.
10. This direction is debatable. The chronicler Jaramillo said they turned to the northeast, but both Bolton and Day believe this was an obvious slip for southeast. For Jaramillo's account see Winship, "The Coronado Expedition, 1540–1542," 587–588. Recently William Brandon claimed that Jaramillo's direction was correct. See Brandon, *Quivira: Europeans in the Region of the Santa Fe Trail, 1540–1820* (Athens: Ohio University Press, 1990), 36, and map, 28. Brandon erroneously takes the expedition on the first leg of the Santa Fé Trail, another major aboriginal trade route.
11. Richard Flint and Shirley Cushing Flint, "The Location of Coronado's 1541 Bridge: A Critical Appraisal of Albert Schroeder's 1962 Hypothesis," *Plains Anthropologist*, XXXVI (May, 1991), 171–176; Richard Flint and Shirley Cushing Flint, "The Coronado Expedition: Cicúye to the Rio de Cicúye Bridge," *New Mexico Historical Review*, LXVII (Apr., 1992), 123–138. The Flints have codirected the Coronado's Bridge Project since 1980. I am further indebted to Richard Flint for personal correspondence on the expedition route.
12. Flint and Flint, "The Coronado Expedition," 135–136. Note that Juan Jaramillo wrote that they reached the Rio de Cicúye or Pecos River in *three* days, technically correct if they followed the Cañon Blanco to its confluence with the Pecos.
13. Albert H. Schroeder, "A Re-analysis of the Routes of Coronado and Oñate into the Plains in 1541 and 1601," *Plains Anthropologist*, VII (Feb., 1962), 2–23. The Flints effectively demolish Schroeder's and other claims that the Rio de Cicúye was anything other than the Pecos River in Flint and Flint, "The Location of Coronado's 1541 Bridge," 171–175.
14. Flint and Flint, "The Location of Coronado's 1541 Bridge," 175.
15. Winship, "The Coronado Expedition, 1540–1542," 588, *passim*; Bolton, *Coronado*, 238–248; W. C. Holden, "Coronado's Route Across the Staked Plains," *West Texas Historical Association Year Book*, XX (1944), 3–20; David Donoghue, "The Location of Quivira," *Panhandle-Plains Historical Review*, XIII (1940), 38–46, which locates Quivira on the Canadian River of the Texas Panhandle; J. W. Williams, *Old Texas Trails* (Austin: Eakin Press, 1979).
16. Kessel, "Foreword" to Bolton, *Coronado*, xv.
17. Note the popular forty-niner route on Capt. Randolph B. Marcy's 1850 map; R. B. Marcy, "Topographical Map of the Road from Fort Smith, Arks. to Santa Fe, N.M. . . ." (Philadelphia: Duval's Steam Lithograph Press, 1850).
18. Personal communication from Dr. Donald J. Blakeslee of Wichita State University, August, 1995.

19. Author's translation. For the Spanish see Winship, "The Coronado Expedition, 1540–1542," 142.
20. Hammond and Rey (eds.), *Narratives of the Coronado Expedition 1540–1542*, 186.
21. Hodge and Lewis (eds.), *Spanish Explorers in the Southern United States, 1528–1543*, 381–382.
22. Ibid.
23. Udall, *To the Inland Empire*, 150.
24. Bolton, *Coronado*, 245.
25. Hodge and Lewis (eds.), *Spanish Explorers in the Southern United States, 1528–1543*, 382–383.
26. Ibid., 362. Matias de la Mota Padilla, a later expedition scholar, provides the crucial clue of ground fogs in his *Historia de La Conquista de Nueva-Galicia*.
27. Chipman, *Spanish Texas*, 15.
28. Ibid., 363.
29. See Holden, "Coronado's Route Across the Staked Plains," 3–20.
30. See the prehistorical trade route that Carroll Riley traces across the Llano in Riley, *The Frontier People*, 7. This route ran from Cicúye to the Red River, likely utilizing the Southwest drift of the draws.
31. Hodge and Lewis (eds.), *Spanish Explorers in the Southern United States, 1528–1543*, 330. See Winship, "The Coronado Expedition, 1540–1542," 142, for the Spanish text.
32. See the *Relación Postrera de Sívola* in Winship, "The Coronado Expedition, 1540–1542," and Castañeda's narrative in Hodge and Lewis (eds.), *Spanish Explorers in the Southern United States, 1528–1543*, 332.

CHAPTER THREE

1. New Mexican local researchers such as Fray Angelico Chavez suggest a Puerto de Luna crossing of the Pecos River even farther downstream from Santa Rosa. Such a crossing could only point east, directly to the Mescalero escarpment of the Llano.
2. Quoted in Sauer, *Sixteenth-Century North America*, 149.
3. Research was active on French exploration of the Southwest at the same time. See Thomas Falconer, *On the Discovery of the Mississippi* (London: Samuel Clarke, 1844).
4. Henri Ternaux-Compans, *Voyages, Relations et Mémoires Originaux Pour Servir a l'Histoire de la Découverte de l'Amérique* (20 vols.; Paris: A. Bertrand, 1837–1841), IX. Volume IX is usually called the "Cíbola" volume.
5. Lt. James H. Simpson, "Coronado's March in Search of the 'Seven Cities of Cibolá,' and Discussion of their Probable Location," *Smithsonian Report for 1869* (Washington, D.C.: Smithsonian Institution, 1871), 309–340. Simpson's route east of Cicúye followed a literal northeast bearing to Las Vegas, requiring an improbable bridge across the Gallinas River.
6. Henry M. Brackenridge, *Early Discoveries by Spaniards in New Mexico, containing an Account of the Castles of Cibola* (Pittsburgh, Pa.: H. Miner & Co.,1857).
7. W. W. H. Davis, *El Gringo: New Mexico and Her People* (New York: Harper & Bros., 1857), 112.
8. Ibid., 127.
9. Adolph F. Bandelier, "Quivira," *The Nation*, XLIX (Oct. 31, Nov. 7, 1889), 348–349, 365–366.
10. Adolph F. Bandelier, *The Gilded Man* (New York: Appleton & Co., 1893).
11. See Frank Dellenbaugh, "The True Route of Coronado's March," *Journal of the American Geographical Society of New York*, XXIX (Dec., 1897), 398–431. The Coronado expedition travels the plains on pp. 426–427.
12. The most recent edition of Winship's enduring work contains a good introduction by Donald Cutter, *The Journey of Francisco Coronado* (Aurora, Colo.: Fulcrum Press, 1990).
13. See G. Edward White, *The Eastern Establishment and the Western Experience* (Austin: University of Texas Press, 1989).

14. An excellent study of early corporate imagemakers' use of indigenous culture in the Southwest is in T. C. McLuhan, *Dream Tracks: The Railroad and the American Indian, 1890–1930* (New York: Abrams, 1985), 11–46.

15. James F. Zimmerman, "The Coronado Cuarto Centennial," *Hispanic American Historical Review*, XX (Feb., 1940), 158–162.

16. Thomas Wood Stevens, *The Entrada of Coronado: A Spectacular Historic Drama* (Albuquerque, N.Mex.: Coronado Cuarto Centennial Commission, 1940).

17. New Mexico Coronado Cuarto Centennial Commission, "The Coronado Magazine," Official Program of the Coronado Cuarto Centennial in New Mexico (n.p., N.Mex.: Mrs. Charles E. Butler, 1940). This work contains a reproduction of Peter Hurd's superb painting of Coronado.

18. Ibid.

19. A. Grove Day, *Coronado's Quest: The Discovery of the Southwestern States* (Berkeley: University of California Press, 1949).

20. The publication of Bolton's classic work on Coronado was almost as convoluted as his Llano Trail. The messy details of the Whittlesey House–University of New Mexico Press feud are in John Francis Bannon, *Herbert Eugene Bolton: The Historian and the Man, 1870–1953* (Tucson: University of Arizona Press, 1978).

21. David Donoghue, "The Location of Quivira," *Panhandle-Plains Historical Review*, XIII (1940), 38–46, and his earlier "The Route of the Coronado Expedition in Texas," *Southwestern Historical Quarterly*, XXXII (Jan., 1929), 181–192.

22. W. S. Izzard, "Author's Note" to "The Grandee and the Indian," Amarillo *Globe*, Golden Anniversary Edition (1938).

23. Waldo R. Wedel, "Coronado's Route to Quivira," *Plains Anthropologist*, XV (Aug., 1970), 161–168. See also his early fieldwork on Quivira's archeological location in Kansas, "In Search of Coronado's Province of Quivira," *Explorations and Fieldwork of the Smithsonian Institution in 1940* (Washington, D.C.: Smithsonian Institution, 1941). Wedel and John Swanton explored the way east from Cicúye in 1942. The Kansas booster context of Coronado that Donoghue was reacting against is in Paul A. Jones, *Coronado and Quivira* (Lyons, Kan.: Lyons Publishing Co., 1937). Note the 1970s view, Clevy Lloyd Strout, "The Coronado Expeditions: Following the Geography Described in the Spanish Journals," *Great Plains Journal*, XIV (Fall, 1974), 2–31.

24. New Mexico W.P.A. Writers' Program, *New Mexico: A Guide to the Colorful State* (New York: Hastings House for Coronado Cuarto Centennial Commission, 1940), 62.

25. Brandon, *Quivira: Europeans in the Region of the Santa Fe Trail*; Albert H. Schroeder, "A Reanalysis of the Routes of Coronado and Oñate into the Plains in 1541 and 1601," *Plains Anthropologist*, VII (Feb., 1962), 2–23.

26. Bolton's visit to Palo Duro Canyon is described in B. Byron Price, "Bolton, Coronado, and the Texas Panhandle," in Everett (ed.), *Coronado and the Myth of Quivira*, 5–10.

27. Carl Ortwin Sauer, *The Road to Cibola* (Berkeley: University of California Press, 1932).

28. Sauer, *Sixteenth Century North America*, 145.

29. W. C. Holden, "Coronado's Route Across the Staked Plains," *West Texas Historical Association Year Book*, XX (Oct., 1944), 3–20. Holden lived and taught in Lubbock, Texas, and knew the plains exceptionally well.

30. National Park Service, "National Trail Study Environmental Assessment, Coronado Expedition" (Denver, Colo.: Public Review Draft, June 1991), 31.

Chapter Four

1. See the extensive bibliographic commentary in Winship, "The Coronado Expedition, 1540–1542," 389–403; Bolton, *Coronado*, 423–425; Hammond and Rey (eds.), *Narratives of the Coronado Expedition, 1540–1542*; and Carroll L. Riley, "Appendix—Historical and Documentary Sources," *The Frontier People*, 329–333.

2. Bolton gives a lengthy list of the missing sources in his "Lost Documents" section of the bibliography for *Coronado*, 472–475.

3. The Spanish text is available as Pedro de Castañeda de Náxera, *Relacion de la jornada de Cíbola por Pedro de Castañeda de Nacera donde se trata de todos aquellos poblandos y ritos, y costumbres, la qual fue el año de 1540* (microfilm reel no. 63, Rich Collection, New York Public Library, New York).

4. Winship, "The Coronado Expedition, 1540–1542," 376. Italics added.

5. Ibid., 359.

6. Riley, *Rio del Norte*, 183–198.

7. Fray Toribio de Motolinía, *Memoriales* (Mexico City: Pimentel, 1903), 24; Winship, "The Coronado Expedition, 1540–1542," 342. The *Relación Postrera de Sívola* was found in Motolinía's manuscript by Don Joaquin Garcia Icazbalceta during his bibliographic searches.

8. The Muñoz copy used by Buckingham Smith for his translation has *sueste* or southeast.

9. Winship, "The Coronado Expedition, 1540–1542," 241. Hammond and Rey translated this as the "great deviation toward Florida which they had made." Hammond and Rey (eds.), *Narratives of the Coronado Expedition, 1540–1542*, 241.

10. Hammond and Rey (eds.), *Narratives of the Coronado Expedition, 1540–1542*, 301. Italics added.

11. Ibid., 300. Note that Mota Padilla said El Turco guided the Spanish, "para el oriente, con mucha inclinacion al Norte, y desde entonces los guio via recta al oriente." Mota Padilla, *Historia de la Conquista de la Provincia de la Nueva-Galicia*, 165.

12. *Relación del Suceso.*

13. Winship, "The Coronado Expedition, 1540–1542," 342.

14. For the influence of old romances, see Carlos Prieto, *El Sueño de Cíbola* (Mexico City: Regis, 1933), 30–31.

15. Hammond and Rey (eds.), *Narratives of the Coronado Expedition, 1540–1542*, 289, 310; and Prieto, *El Sueño de Cíbola*, 37.

16. Winship, "The Coronado Expedition, 1540–1542," 235; Hammond and Rey (eds.), *Narratives of the Coronado Expedition, 1540–1542*, 236.

17. Author translation from the Spanish in Winship, "The Coronado Expedition, 1540–1542," 142–143.

18. Note the change by the later Gregorian Calendar, which corrected a ten-day gap.

19. Winship, "The Coronado Expedition, 1540–1542," 143. Walter W. Skeat devotes a lengthy passage to the etymology of *Rumb*, noting Philips' 1706 recognition of "*Rumb* or *Rhumb*, the course of a ship . . . also, one point of the mariner's compass, or 11 ¼ degrees." The spiral nature of Rhumb-lines were drawn on the new Mercator maps as straight lines, but the phrase seems to be an older Portuguese expression for the delineation of motion (that is, a specific course) as determined by instrumentation (any point of the compass) on a chart. Skeat considered "That the word arose among the early Spanish and Portuguese navigators, is in the highest degree probable." Walter W. Skeat, *An Etymological Dictionary of the English Language* (4th ed.; London: Oxford University Press, 1968), 527–528.

20. Ibid.

21. Gunnar Brune, *The Springs of Texas* (Fort Worth, Tex.: Branch-Smith, 1981), 202–204.

22. Winship, "The Coronado Expedition, 1540–1542," 142.

23. Ibid., 143.

24. Brandon argues for Palo Duro; Bolton for Tule Canyon; Day for the upper branch of Brazos; Holden for Blanco or Yellow House; and Williams for the Concho River headwaters.

CHAPTER FIVE

1. See West Texas A&M University Professor David Rindlisbacher's prize-winning painting, "The Meeting of Captains and Ensigns," on the cover of the Amarillo *Observer* (June, 1991), which portrays a beautiful—if improbable—sunrise meeting in Palo Duro Canyon of Coronado and his captains. Ben Carlton Mead's important mural in the Hall of Texas History at the Panhandle-Plains

Museum in Canyon, Texas, presents a Coronado tableau vivant near the *bottom* of the scenic canyon.

2. Weber, *The Spanish Frontier in North America*, 48.

3. David J. Weber, "Reflections on Coronado and the Myth of Quivira," in Weber (ed.), *Myth and the History of the Hispanic Southwest*, 1–18.

4. Winship, "The Coronado Expedition, 1540–1542," 236.

5. Nancy P. Hickerson, *The Jumanos* (Austin: University of Texas Press, 1994); Riley, *Rio del Norte*, 97–101. William Brandon notes an old argument that these Teyas may be in the same Inday family as the Querechos, and should not be confused with the Tayshas of East Texas. Brandon, *Quivira*, 39. Bolton also thought the Teyas were the same people as the historic Jumano. Bolton, *Coronado*, 260.

6. Sauer, *Sixteenth Century North America*, 143.

7. Author translation from the Spanish in Winship (with his "u" for "v"), "The Coronado Expedition, 1540–1542," 161. Winship, quoting a 1555 dictionary, translated the obscure *teules* as "braves." The term was a common one among the early conquistadors, frequently mentioned in the accounts of the Cortés expedition. Compare to Bernal Díaz del Castillo: "When they [natives] witnessed deeds so marvellous and of such importance to themselves they said that no human beings would dare to do such things, and that it was the work of Teules, for so they call the idols which they worship, and for this reason from that time forth, they called us Teules, which, is as much as to say that we were either gods or demons." Bernal Díaz del Castillo, *The Discovery and Conquest of Mexico, 1517–1521*, A. P. Maudslay translation from original manuscript published by Genaro García (New York: Farrar, Straus and Giroux, 1956), 92–93.

Castañeda's use of *teules* indicates that valiantness and elan were crucial meanings behind the word *Teya*. If the semiotics of *Teyas* are linked indeed to *Tejas* (or its former orthographic equivalent, *Texas*), then we must add conspicuous bravery, personal elan, and courageous character to the meaning of the word for the state. Certainly a verifiable usage of *Tejas* occurred some 87 years after Castañeda's narrative. Hernán Martin and Diego de Castillo also crossed the Llano, beyond which they noted in 1650 a further and fierce people, "called Tejas, who were ruled by a king." In 1676 the Bishop of Guadalajara actively urged the missionary penetration of this reputed "Kingdom of the Tejas." Mendoza's expedition crossed the southern Llano plains to the Middle Concho, Nueces, and Colorado Rivers, where in 1684 they likewise noted a *gente del Rio de los Tejas* (people of the River of the Tejas). Contrary to popular assumptions, therefore, the first appearance of the toponym derived from explorations of the Llano headwaters and contact with adjacent tribes.

It was the De León-Massanet expedition to East Texas, however, that enshrined the toponym with the founding of mission *San Francisco de los Tejas* among the Nabedaches of the Caddoan confederation. Fray Damián Massanet especially imprinted history with his interpretive usage of the word "thecas" (also spelled "tayshas," "techas," or "texias") to denote the vast territory of the intertribal "Friends" or "Allies" of the Hasinai confederation. In a 1690 letter to Don Carlos de Sigüenza, Massanet related how natives near modern Goliad County emerged from hiding after peaceful overtures by the Europeans: "Some of them . . . came out and embraced us, saying: 'Thechas! techas!' which means "Friends! Friends!." A clerical companion left at the East Texas mission, Francisco de Jesús María, soon declared that *Tejas* was not a toponym for the general region, but rather meant "friends" and referred only to the Hasinai tribes in league against the Apaches. After a period of obscurity, the Spanish place-name of Texas (pronounced "Tejas") rose to prominence during the 18th century. Whence derived the official state motto of "Friendship" and the subsequent wooing of immigrants and tourists as "The Friendly State." See Carlos Castañeda, *Our Catholic Heritage in Texas*, I, 204–205; H. E. Bolton, "Spanish Occupation of Texas," *Quarterly of the Texas State Historical Association*, XVI (July, 1913), 4–11; *Spanish Exploration in the Southwest*, 359; Tyler et al. (eds.), *New Handbook of Texas*, VI, 273; and W. W. Newcomb, *The Indians of Texas* (Austin: University of Texas Press, 1961), 280.

8. The old man had seen "four others like us many days before, whom he had seen near there and rather more toward New Spain. . . ." Winship, "The Coronado Expedition, 1540–1542," 379.

9. Flores, "Canyons of the Imagination," 52.

10. Mota Padilla, *Historia de la Conquista*, 165; Bolton, *Coronado*, 263.

11. Winship, "The Coronado Expedition, 1540–1542," 236.
12. Ibid., 144. Once more Castañeda uses "lo llano" as a singular signifier for the great mesa as a whole.
13. Bolton, *Coronado*, 261–264; Bobby D. Weaver, "Coronado and the Golden Cities: Spanish Exploration in Texas," in *Coronado and the Myth of Quivira*, ed. Diana Everett (Canyon, Tex.: Panhandle-Plains Historical Society, 1985), 32.
14. Antonio de Herrera, *Historia General* (4 vols.; Madrid: Barcia, 1728), III, 206–207.
15. Winship, "The Coronado Expedition, 1540–1542," 144. Author translation.
16. The expression "barranca de los llanos" is unattributed by Bolton, but a likely phrase.
17. Bolton, *Coronado*, 266.
18. Sauer, *The Road to Cibola*, 145: "The party took its ease for a number of days in the northern barranca (Palo Duro)." See also Weaver (who writes "... what must have been Palo Duro Canyon ..."), "Coronado and the Golden Cities," 32.
19. For the best critique of Bolton's interpretations of the Hispanic Southwest, see David J. Weber, *Myth and History of the Hispanic Southwest* (Albuquerque: University of New Mexico Press, 1988). Bolton's influential visit to Palo Duro Canyon is in B. Byron Price, "Bolton, Coronado, and the Texas Panhandle," in Everett (ed.), *Coronado and the Myth of Quivira*, 5–10.
20. Winship, "The Coronado Expedition, 1540–1542," 359.
21. For research into the fabulous nature of the general expedition, see George P. Hammond, "The Search for the Fabulous in the Settlement of the Southwest," in *New Spain's Far Northern Frontier: Essays on Spain in the American West, 1540–1821*, ed. David J. Weber (Albuquerque: University of New Mexico Press, 1979), 20–22.
22. Modern connections of food, memory, mind, and place are explored in Roger C. Schank, *The Connoisseur's Guide to the Mind* (New York: Summit Books, 1991).
23. An entertaining example of elaborate computations can be found in Dean B. Hiatt's *Ever the Wildebeest: An Autobiography of a Natural Engineer* (Kerrville, Tex.: Kerrville Printing Co., 1978), 191–234. Retiree Hiatt spent days on the plains working out his route for the expedition.
24. J. W. Williams, *Old Texas Trails* (Austin, Tex.: Eakin Press, 1979). See also J. W. Williams, "Coronado: From the Rio Grande to the Concho," *Southwestern Historical Quarterly*, XLIII (Oct., 1959), 190–220, which contains several interesting maps.
25. Williams, "Coronado," 194.
26. Stewart L. Udall, *To the Inland Empire: Coronado and Our Spanish Legacy* (Garden City, N.Y.: Doubleday & Co., 1987), 147–165.
27. Ibid., 162–163.
28. A number of other significant amateur speculations exist, but are not referred to in the table out of a need to be selective. This includes Dean Hiatt, R. M. Wagstaff, and others. Frank Bryan of Groesbeck, Texas, researched the expedition as part of a general study of Spanish exploration, concluding that the First Barranca was Yellow House Canyon and the Second was Blanco Canyon. Bryan however mistakenly locates Quivira in the Canadian River Valley of the Panhandle and Oklahoma. A few weeks before his death in the early 1960s, Mr. Bryan gave a copy of his interesting map of Spanish exploration routes to J. H. Buchanan of the Texas Panhandle. Buchanan's cover letter noted, "Personally, I agree with Mr. Bryan of 'Quivira' being on the Canadian river, but I disagree ... as to the location of the 'first' and 'second' barrancas. Their location evidently was a few miles East of the present city of Canyon, Texas, on the Prairie Dog Town Fork of the Red River, and Possibly Mulberry Creek." Buchanan Letter and Bryan Map, July 20, 1962, Coronado Vertical Files (Panhandle-Plains Museum, Canyon, Tex.).
29. Winship, "The Coronado Expedition, 1540–1542," 237. The spelling of the marginal notation is also in some doubt. Winship gave *alexeres*, but a photocopy of the 1596 text suggests a repeat of *alixares* or possibly *alixeres*.
30. Hammond and Rey (eds.), *Narratives of the Coronado Expedition, 1540–1542*, 239. A missing dot on the *i* of the marginal *alixares* may have misled the translators into spelling it *alexeres*.
31. Richard Flint, personal communication, Sept. 12, 1995.

32. Bolton, *Coronado*, 262–263.
33. Mariano Velázquez de la Cadena et. al., *New Revised Velázquez Spanish and English Dictionary* (Chicago, Ill.: Follett Publishing, 1967), 46.
34. The Lennox text says *prostera* but this is a copyist corruption for *postrera* or "last," "ultimate."
35. Author translation from the Spanish in Winship, "The Coronado Expedition, 1540–1542," 144.

Chapter Six

1. The noted Western artist Frank Reaugh captures this white rim beautifully in his linear oil painting, "Blanco Canyon," in the Southern Methodist University Art Collection of Southern Methodist University, Dallas, Texas.
2. Sauer, *The Road to Cibola*, 145.
3. Clive Ponting, *A Green History of the World* (New York: Penguin Books, 1991), 100–102. Ponting notes that "the real impact of a much worse climate was felt after the middle of the sixteenth century." Bolton noted "long, cold, winter months," high elevations, and that "when cold weather came on, accompanied by snow, his [Coronado's] men from the tropics were in distress. Bolton, "*Coronado*, 193, 231.
4. For a thought-provoking reappraisal of riverine gallery forests on the Great Plains, see William Stolzenburg, "New Views of Ancient Times," *Nature Conservancy*, XLIV (Sept.–Oct .,1994), 12–13.
5. Massive irrigation withdrawals and plunging groundwater levels, particularly in the White River watershed, are graphed in Jaque Emel and Rebecca Roberts, "Institutional Form and Its Effect on Environmental Change: The Case of Groundwater in the Southern High Plains," *Annals of the Association of American Geographers*, LXXXV (Dec., 1995), 671.
6. See also David J. Weber, "Turner, the Boltonians, and the Spanish Borderlands," in Weber, *Myth and the History of the Spanish Southwest*, 35–39.
7. Williams, *Old Texas Trails*, 71.
8. J. Frank Dobie, *A Vaquero of the Brush Country* (Dallas, Tex.: Southwest Press, 1929), 148.
9. Claude V. Hall, "The Panhandle," *The Hesperian* (Floydada, Tex.), X (Dec. 21, 1905).
10. Compare to the attributions in Clevy Lloyd Strout, "Flora and Fauna Mentioned in the Journals of the Coronado Expedition," *Great Plains Journal*, XI (Fall, 1971), 5–40.
11. Donovan S. Correll and Marshall C. Johnston, *Manual of the Vascular Plants of Texas* (Richardson, Tex.: University of Texas at Dallas, 1979), 728.
12. Walter Ebeling, *Handbook of Indian Foods and Fibers of Arid America* (Berkeley: University of California Press, 1986), 452–649.
13. Mrs. Sam Hale, "Tribute to the Pioneers," transcript of radio address by Mattie Hale, published in *The Hesperian* (Floydada, Tex.) in the 1930s. Photocopy provided by Nancy Marble of Floyd County Historical Museum, Floydada, Texas.
14. See Mildred Mott Wedel, *The Wichita Indians, 1541–1750: Ethnohistorical Essay* (Lincoln, Neb.: J&L Reprint, 1988).
15. Riley, *Rio del Norte*, 185.
16. G. Douglas Inglis, "Men of Cibola: New Investigations on the Francisco Vazquez de Coronado Expedition," *Panhandle-Plains Historical Review*, LV (1982), 7.
17. Winship, "The Coronado Expedition, 1540–1542," 144.
18. Hammond and Rey (eds.), *Narratives of the Coronado Expedition, 1540–1542*.
19. Author translation from the Spanish in Winship, "The Coronado Expedition, 1540–1542," 145.
20. Typical of whisking the expedition far to the southeast is the recent A. Ray Stephens and William M. Holmes, *Historical Atlas of Texas* (Norman: University of Oklahoma Press, 1989), 8–9. Stephens and Holmes site Cona at the junction of the Concho River with the Colorado River in distant Coleman County, Texas. This siting is most unlikely even if it does reflect contemporary inflation of the expedition travels.

21. Robert T. Hill, *Physical Geography of the Texas Region*, U.S. Geological Survey Atlas, Folio Three (Washington, D.C.: Government Printing Office, 1900), 6.

22. Stewart L. Udall does an excellent job of debunking this myth in *To The Inland Empire*, 195–210.

23. For the best discussion of Iberian "ecological imperialism," see Alfred W. Crosby, *The Columbian Exchange, Biological and Cultural Consequences of 1492* (Westport, Conn.: Greenwood Press, 1973). Crosby provides a larger context for this concept in *Ecological Imperialism: The Biological Expansion of Europe, 900–1900* (New York: Cambridge University Press, 1986).

24. W. George Lovell, "'Heavy Shadows and Black Night': Disease and Depopulation in Colonial Spanish America," *Annals of Association of American Geographers*, LXXXII (Sept., 1992), 438.

25. Riley, *The Frontier* People, 259.

26. Bill Russell, "Men on Quest for Coronado Clues," *Prairie Dog Gazette* (Summer, 1995), 5.

27. Alice Gilroy, "Historical Finds Prove Presence of Coronado," *Hesperian-Beacon* (Floydada, Tex.), Sept. 7, 1995.

28. Ibid.

Chapter Seven

1. Winship, "The Coronado Expedition, 1540–1542," 367.

2. Ibid., 359.

3. Ibid., 146. Author's translation. For a different interpretation of this passage, see Hammond and Rey (eds.), *Narratives of the Coronado Expedition, 1540–1542*, 242, where "the army was soon on its way back to the Teyas from the barranca. Here they sought guides to take them over a more direct route." It seems unlikely that the army was on its way back to the barranca of the Teyas as that was their starting point.

4. Trail detectives who site Cona much deeper in the Texas interior—on the Concho or Colorado Rivers—must contend with a narrative that immediately puts the Spanish at risk of disorientation shortly after leaving Cona. There is no need for solar reckoning and arrow trajectories if one is leaving Elm Creek of the Concho River. This narrative of plunging into a featureless landscape suggests that Cona is in fact quite near if not within the embrace of the Llano.

5. Ibid. Italics added. See also Hammond and Rey (eds.): "and in this manner they traveled the whole day until they reached some water where they were to stop for the night," *Narratives of the Coronado Expedition, 1540–1542*, 242.

6. Winship, "The Coronado Expedition, 1540–1542," 146.

7. From their juncture with the Pecos River, Arellano's soldiers took four days to reach their bridge over the river. From this crossing it took four days to reach Cicúye, then four more days to arrive back at the Rio Grande.

8. Eileen Johnson (ed.), *Lubbock Lake: Late Quaternary Studies on the Southern High Plains* (College Station: Texas A&M University Press, 1987), 160.

9. W. C. Holden plots an interesting return route via "Running Water Draw," then "Black Water Draw" to "Portales Draw." For a summary see Holden, "A History of Lubbock, Part One: Story of a Country Town," in *The Museum Journal*, III (Lubbock: West Texas Museum Association, 1959), 24–25.

10. *Relación del Suceso* in Winship, "The Coronado Expedition, 1540–1542," 359.

11. Scientists argue over whether Yellow House Draw or Blanco Canyon was the original outlet for the Portales paleodrainage. See Thomas C. Gustavson and Robert J. Finley, *Late Cenozoic Geomorphic Evolution of the Texas Panhandle and Northeastern New Mexico*, Report of Investigations No. 148 (Austin: Bureau of Economic Geology, University of Texas, 1985), 33–34.

12. Author's translation unless noted otherwise; Spanish text from Winship, "The Coronado Expedition, 1540–1542," 146. In a lapse W. C. Holden noted prairie dogs abounded in the late 1800s, but, "The Spaniards who crossed the Plains during the fifteen hundreds made no mention of them." The implication was that prairie dogs had dramatically increased well after the arrival of the Spanish, but before the arrival of Anglo-Americans. Castañeda's statement contradicts this assertion, indicating

that prairie dogs have been part of the regional ecology for a long time. Holden, "A History of Lubbock, Part One," 11.

13. Dan Flores, *Caprock Canyonlands* (Austin: University of Texas Press, 1990), 62. Walter Ebeling lists 447 edible species for the southwestern United States and discusses 150 species at length in the *Handbook of Indian Foods and Fibers of Arid America* (Berkeley: University of California Press, 1986), 461–533. Hackberries, agaritas, wild onions, streamside mints, cucurbits, sunflowers, wild fruits, mesquite pods, and many other plant foods undoubtedly enriched the Teyas diet.

14. Winship translation from the Buckingham Smith *Florida* documents. Winship, "The Coronado Expedition, 1540–1542," 359.

15. These "Lost Lakes" were rumored to exist for some time before U.S. Army explorers and a Texas Ranger named G. W. Arrington revealed their presence to a wider audience. See Walter Prescott Webb, *The Texas Rangers: A Century of Frontier Defense* (Austin: University of Texas Press, 1965), 415. Captain Arrington's account of his 1879 foray claimed the strategic discovery by white men of "lakes of water in the heart of the great desert." L. F. Sheffy, "The Arrington Papers," *Panhandle-Plains Historical Review*, I (1928), 66. Of course it is likely that Capt. Tristán de Arellano and several hundred other so-called "white men" preceded Captain Arrington and his men by 338 years.

16. Fred Wendorf (ed.), *Paleoecology of the Llano Estacado*, no. 1, Fort Burgwin Research Center (Santa Fé: Museum of New Mexico Press, 1961), 12–21; C. C. Reeves Jr., "Drainage Pattern Analysis, Southern High Plains, West Texas, and Eastern New Mexico," in *Ogallala Aquifer Symposium 1*, ICASALS Special Report No. 39, eds. R. B. Mattox and W. D. Miller (Lubbock: Texas Tech University, 1970), 58–71; and Waite R. Osterkamp et al., "Great Plains," in *Geomorphic Systems of North America*, ed. William L. Graf (Boulder, Colo.: Geological Society of America, 1987), 191–194.

17. Winship, "The Coronado Expedition, 1540–1542," 146.

18. Edwin L. Kiser, "The Re-examination of Pedro de Castaneda's Bone Bed by Geological Investigations," *Bulletin of Texas Archeological Society*, XLIX (1978), 331–339.

19. Author's translation from the Spanish in Winship, "The Coronado Expedition, 1540–1542," 178.

20. Ibid., 336.

21. *Relación del Suceso*, in Winship translation, ibid., 359.

22. Wendorf (ed.), *Paleoecology of the Llano Estacado*, 55–56.

23. Winship, "The Coronado Expedition, 1540–1542," 146.

24. Note that New Mexico's Grulla National Wildlife Refuge is in this same area.

25. Carroll L. Riley traces such a general route from the Pecos Pueblo onto the Llano where it branches. One branch goes northeast toward the Quivira province of Kansas, while the other follows the Red River drainage down to the Sabine River and other trade connections. Riley, *The Frontier People*, 7.

26. See Capt. Allen Anderson's 1864 map prepared for Gen. James H. Carleton. "Map of the Military Department of New Mexico," in Carleton's "Report . . . ," *U.S. Army Series One, Vol. XLVIII* (Wasington, D.C.: Government Printing Office, 1864). The infamous creation of the "Reservation of Navajos and Apaches," centered at Bosque Redondo, greatly stimulated the recorded cartography of the proximate area.

27. Winship, "The Coronado Expedition, 1540–1542," 146.

28. Hammond and Rey's translation in their *Narratives of the Coronado Expedition, 1540–1542*, 243. The bushes were *rosales* and the marjoram was *oregano* in the Lennox manuscript. Possibly these bushes were mature stands of bison berries.

29. Riley, *The Frontier People*, 267–277. Riley's excellent study notes that "Cicúye" was possibly from *tshiquite*, the Towa name for their pueblo, with "Pecos" a variant of the Towa name of *pakyoola* or "place where there is water," 253.

30. Bolton identifies most of the members by name. Bolton, *Coronado*, 282–283.

31. Quoted in Bolton, *Coronado*, 268. See also Winship, "The Coronado Expedition, 1540–1542," 367.

32. Winship translation, "The Coronado Expedition, 1540–1542," 367–368.
33. Ibid., 379.
34. Winship translation, ibid., 359. Winship's parentheses are shown as brackets here.
35. "I am convinced by their own statements that the explorers never left the flat Llano Estacado, that they never traversed the rolling plains of Oklahoma, Kansas, or Nebraska." David Donoghue, "The Route of the Coronado Expedition in Texas," *Southwestern Historical Quarterly*, XXXII (Jan., 1929), 181.
36. Riley, *Rio del Norte*, 195.
37. Bolton, *Coronado*, 284.
38. Winship, "The Coronado Expedition, 1540–1542," 152.
39. Ibid., 381.
40. Berenice Jackson, *Man and the Oklahoma Panhandle* (North Newton, Kans.: Mennonite Press, 1982), 133.
41. Ibid., 381.
42. Hodge and Lewis (eds.), *Spanish Explorers in the Southern United States*, 369.
43. Bolton, *Coronado*, 405. Coronado's grave was rediscovered by Paul A. Jones and Joaquin Meade y Sainz Trapaga in the 1930s.

Chapter Eight

1. Winship, "The Coronado Expedition, 1540–1542," 107.
2. Ibid., 167.
3. See Fray Marcos de Niza's account of the two *despoblados* on the road to Cíbola in Hallenbeck, *Alvar Núñez Cabeza de Vaca*.
4. Winship, "The Coronado Expedition, 1540–1542," 167.
5. Ibid., 167–168.
6. Spanish text in Winship, "The Coronado Expedition, 1540–1542," 168.
7. Although Hammond and Rey's version in *Narratives of the Coronado Expedition, 1540–1542*, is a substantial improvement over Winship for the Llano Road to Quivira, the Spanish text should be closely considered with them as well.
8. Winship, "The Coronado Expedition, 1540–1542," 305.
9. Walter Prescott Webb, *The Great Plains* (Boston: Ginn and Co., 1931), 105 n.1.
10. Ibid.
11. From the Spanish in Winship, "The Coronado Expedition, 1540–1542," 183; author's translation.
12. Ibid., 280.
13. W. R. Osterkamp and W. W. Wood, "Playa-Lake Basins on the Southern High Plains of Texas and New Mexico," Parts I and II, *Geological Society of America Bulletin*, XCIX (1987), 215–230.
14. T. C. Gustavson, Vance T. Holliday, and S. D. Hovorka, "Development of Playa Basins, Southern High Plains, Texas and New Mexico," in *Proceedings of the Playa Basin Symposium*, eds. L. V. Urban and A. W. Wyatt (Lubbock: Texas Tech University, Water Resources Center, 1994), 5–14; Ty J. Sabin and Vance T. Holliday, "Playas and Lunettes on the Southern High Plains: Morphometric and Spatial Relationships," *Annals of the Association of American Geographers*, LXXXV (June, 1995), 286–305.
15. See C. M. Woodruff Jr., Thomas C. Gustavson, and R. J. Finley, "Playas and Draws on the Llano Estacado," *Texas Journal of Science*, XXXI (1979), 213–223.
16. See the locational study results on playa roundness and aspect in Sabin and Holliday, "Playas and Lunettes," 298–299. They also note that "the largest and the deepest playas are located in the finest substrate in the north-central region of the Southern High Plains."
17. Osterkamp and Wood, "Playa-Lake Basins on the Southern High Plains of Texas and New Mexico," 224–230. This is sometimes called the Osterkamp-Wood model.

18. See Winship, "The Coronado Expedition, 1540–1542," 279, for his English translation, and 168 for the original Spanish.
19. Based on the new estimates of Sabin and Holliday, "Playas and Lunettes," 299–300.
20. Ibid., 300.
21. *Eleocharis* species.
22. Gustavson, Holliday, and Hovorka, "Development of Playa Basins," 5–14; Sabin and Holliday, "Playas and Lunettes," 286–302.
23. Winship, "The Coronado Expedition, 1540–1542," 168.
24. Weber, *The Spanish Frontier in North America*, 48.
25. Ibid.
26. Winship, "The Coronado Expedition, 1540–1542," 279.
27. Hammond and Rey (eds.), *Narratives of the Coronado Expedition 1540–1542*, 261.
28. Velázquez de la Cadena, *New Revised Velázquez Spanish and English Dictionary*, 384.
29. Hammond and Rey (eds.), *Narratives of the Coronado Expedition 1540–1542*, 278.
30. Ibid., 280.
31. "The illusion of the buffalo and the pine trees was, of course, the mirage." Webb, *The Great Plains*, 105 n.1.
32. Ibid., 278.

Chapter Nine

1. Quotation from the translation by Herbert Eugene Bolton, *Spanish Exploration in the Southwest, 1542–1706* (New York: Scribner's, 1925), 148.
2. See George P. Hammond and Agapito Rey, *The Rediscovery of New Mexico, 1580–1594: The Explorations of Chamuscado, Espejo, Castaño de Sosa, Morlete, and Leyva de Bonilla and Humaña* (Albuquerque: University of New Mexico Press, 1966), 6–15.
3. Cf. the representative place-names for the Mendoza-López Expedition of 1684 in Bolton, *Spanish Exploration in the Southwest, 1542–1706*, 311–344.
4. Ibid., 147.
5. Spanish text from the "Relacion y concudio de el viaje . . . " or the Declaration of Hernan Gallegos, in Joaquin F. Pacheco and Francisco de Cárdenas, *Colección de Documentos Inéditos* . . . (42 vols.; Madrid: M. G. Hernandez, 1870), XV, 92. Note Hammond and Rey's translation: " . . . we reached some lagoons of very brackish water. Here we found many such pools in a valley that extends from these lagoons toward the sunrise. We named this valley and its pools Los Llanos de San Francisco and Aguas Zarcas, because they formed such good plains. In these plains there is a spring, the best to be found in New Spain for people afflicted with dropsy." Hammond and Rey, *The Rediscovery of New Mexico, 1580–1594*, 91.
6. *Aguas Zarcas* in respect to color are "The Skyblue Waters," suggesting the light bluish coloration found in human irises and lakes. But in reference to water *zarca* conventionally suggests clarity and purity (in contrast to muddy stream or river sediments). *Aguas zarcas* could be a reference to the distinctive and intact playas of the western Llano or to the purer Ogallala discharge springs—*ojos de agua*—pouring from the Llano bluffs in to the Valle de San Francisco. The word choice suggests a perception.
7. Bustamante's declaration is also found in Pacheco and Cárdenas, *Colección de Documentos Inéditos*, XV, 80–88, and translated in Bolton, *Spanish Exploration*, 142–150.
8. Bolton, *Spanish Exploration*, 142.
9. Ibid.
10. "Account by an Indian of the Flight of Humaña and Leyba from New Mexico," in *Don Juan de Oñate, Colonizer of New Mexico, 1595–1628*, eds. George P. Hammond and Agapito Rey (Albuquerque: University of New Mexico Press, 1953), 417. See also Bolton, *Spanish Exploration*, 201–202.

11. Note Carroll Riley's comment that "the entire Greater Southwest operated as an interacting entity, with not only trade relationships but also ties of a sociopolitical and religious nature." Riley, *The Frontier People*, 7.

12. Bolton, *Spanish Exploration*, 228. Note the comment by Carlos E. Castañeda: "It is impossible to claim that either Zaldivar or Oñate were ever beyond the confines of the great plains of Llano Estacado." This statement is true for Zaldivar but completely erroneous for Oñate. See Castañeda, *Our Catholic Heritage in Texas* (7 vols.; Austin: Von Boeckmann–Jones, 1936), I, 189.

13. Bolton, *Spanish Exploration*, 228–229.

14. Ibid., 230.

15. Gaspar Pérez de Villagrá, *Historia de Nueva México*, trans. and ed. by Miquel Encinias, Alfred Rodríquez, and J. P. Sanchez (Albuquerque: University of New Mexico Press, 1992), 158 (Canto XVII, lines 95–108). The English translation is a revised and corrected version of the 1920s unpublished translation by Fayette S. Curtis Jr. of Los Alamos, New Mexico. Italics added.

16. Ibid., 252.

17. Ibid., 253. See chapter 22 for details on the later recognition by Jules Marcou, a highly trained geologist of the 1850s, about the outliers given off by the great mesa.

18. Ibid.

19. Carl S. Wheat, *Mapping the Transmississippi West, 1540–1861* (5 vols.; San Francisco, Calif.: Grabhorn Press, 1957–1963), I, 29. See also Marc Simmons, *The Last Conquistador* (Norman: University of Ohlahoma Press, 1991), 161–163.

20. Bolton, *Spanish Exploration*, 253.

21. Contrast to Yi-Fu Tuan's statement, "Spanish conquerors were little concerned with the climate in New Mexico." Tuan, *Topophilia, A Study of Environmental Perception, Attitudes, and Values* (Englewood Cliffs, N.J.: Prentice-Hall, 1974), 66.

22. Ibid.

23. Ibid., 256.

24. Terry Jordan, *North American Cattle-Ranching Frontiers: Origins, Diffusion, and Differentiation* (Albuquerque: University of New Mexico Press, 1993).

25. Castañeda, *Our Catholic Heritage in Texas*, I, 196. Sister María de Jesús is also referred to as the *Lady in Blue*.

26. Juan Mateo Mange, *Luz de Tierra Incognita en la América Septentrional* . . . (Mexico City: Archivo General Publication X, 1926), 192–193.

27. For additional information on her visitations, see also chapter 26 in C. W. Hackett (ed.), *Pichardo's Treatise on the Limits of Louisiana and Texas* (3 vols.; Austin: University of Texas Press, 1931), II.

28. Hodding Carter, *Doomed Road of Empire: The Spanish Trail of Conquest* (New York: McGraw-Hill, 1963), 31–49.

29. Brandon, *Quivira*, 85. See also the appreciation in Edmond J. P. Schmitt, "Ven. María Jesus de Agreda: A Correction," *The Quarterly of the Texas State Historical Association*, I (Oct., 1897), 121–124.

30. Brandon, *Quivira*, 86.

31. Carlos E. Castañeda reported the second priest as "Diego López" in *Our Catholic Heritage in Texas*, I, 201; the *Handbook of Texas* claimed the individual was "Diego León," Webb, Carroll, and Branda (eds.), *Handbook of Texas*, II, 532.

32. Bolton said, "It was clearly a branch of the upper Colorado." Bolton, *Spanish Exploration in the Southwest*, 313.

33. Jack D. Forbes, *Apache, Navaho, and Spaniard* (Norman: University of Oklahoma Press, 1960), 122.

34. Castañeda, *Our Catholic Heritage in Texas*, I, 203–204.

35. Gunnar Brune conjectures that the Martin-Castillo expedition passed Boar Springs (Gaines Co.), Baird Springs (Andrews Co.), and Rock Springs (Midland Co.) on the way to the Concho River in Tom Green County. Brune, *Springs of Texas*, 48, 190, 311, and map supplement. C. E. Castañeda preferred the Concho River country near San Angelo.

36. Brune, *Springs of Texas*, map supplement, "Seventeenth Century Trails and the Major Springs Which Served Them."
37. Bolton translation in *Spanish Exploration in the Southwest*, 330.
38. Ibid., 330–335.
39. Ibid., 333.
40. Ibid., 334.
41. Elizabeth A. H. John, *Storms Brewed in Other Men's Worlds: The Confrontation of Indians, Spanish, and French in the Southwest, 1540–1795* (Lincoln: University of Nebraska Press, 1981), 170. This outstanding history of the period provides a reliable guide to the complex relations of power between the Spanish, Amerindians, French, and Americans.
42. Ibid., 171.

Chapter Ten

1. An example is Hurtado's 1715 expedition against the eastern Apache tribe of "Faraones," a group named for their biblical resemblance to the desert tribes of Egypt. See Alfred Barnaby Thomas, *After Coronado: Spanish Exploration Northeast of New Mexico, 1696–1727* (Norman: University of Oklahoma, 1935), 22–25.
2. Pineda's map of the Gulf Coast was known only to a few. There is little discussion of Axa in the literature of Texas cartography. Castañeda spelled El Turco's city as "Haxa" or "Haya." Possibly the Venetians extracted this place-name to mark an intermediate spot between Tiguex and Quivira.
3. See Pierluigi Potinaro and Franco Knirsch, *The Cartography of North America, 1500–1800* (New York: Crescent Books, 1987), 92–93 and *passim*. This work (pp. 86–87) reproduces Jacobus Maiolo's 1561 inking of the post-Coronado Southwest of North America as part of a *mappamondo* inset map located in North Africa's Sahara Desert.
4. Robert Sidney Martin and James C. Martin, *Contours of Discovery: Printed Maps Delineating the Texas and Southwestern Chapters in the Cartographic History of North America* (Austin: Texas State Historical Association, 1982), 13.
5. Illustrated in William H. Goetzmann and Glyndwr Williams, *Atlas of North American Exploration* (New York: Prentice-Hall, 1992), 38.
6. James P. Bryan and Walter K. Hanak, *Texas in Maps* (Austin: University of Texas Press, 1961), 5.
7. See the excellent portfolio of maps in Martin and Martin, *Contours of Discovery*.
8. J. B. Harley, "Maps, Knowledge, Power," in Cosgrove and Daniels (eds.), *The Iconography of Landscape*, 277–284.
9. Martin and Martin, *Contours of Discovery*; Dorothy Sloan, "The Library of Dr. Paul Burns," *Catalogue Six* (Austin, Tex.: Wind River Press, 1988).
10. Jack Jackson, Robert S. Weddle, and Winston DeVille, *Mapping Texas and the Gulf Coast: The Contributions of Saint-Denis, Olivan, and Le Maire* (College Station, Tex.: Texas A&M University Press, 1990).
11. Both maps are reproduced in Jackson, Weddle, and DeVille, *Mapping Texas and the Gulf Coast*, 66–68. This work discusses the important cartographic contributions made by Le Maire, influencing DeLisle and the other European mapmakers heavily.
12. Martin and Martin, *Contours of Discovery*, 40–41.
13. "It is believed at New Mexico that the River, which rises to the North East of the Village of Taos and receives the R. Mora, is the same which in Louisiana is called Red River." In this manner Humboldt diverted the flow of the Pecos River from the Sangre de Cristos Mountains to the upper Red River watershed, creating a hybrid river called *Rio Rojo de Natchitoches ou Rio de Pecos*.
14. "[The] Llano Estacado held no mysteries for the Spaniards." Little of their knowledge could be found on any official maps however. Rathjen, *The Texas Panhandle Frontier*, 81.

Notes to pages 155–164 • 377

CHAPTER ELEVEN

1. A *cibolo* was a male buffalo bull, a *cibola* a cow.

2. Cited in Charles L. Kenner, *The Comanchero Frontier: A History of New Mexican–Plains Indian Relations* (Norman: University of Oklahoma Press, 1994), 101.

3. Josiah Gregg, *Commerce of the Prairies: or, The Journal of a Santa Fé Trader* . . . (New York: Henry G. Langley, 1844), 96.

4. W. W. H. Davis, *El Gringo: New Mexico and Her People* (New York: Harper, 1857), 43–44. Although Davis was not on the Llano, he was nearby and his remarks are typical for the caravans headed there.

5. Ibid., 44.

6. Frank Collinson, "The Old Mexican Buffalo Hunters," Manuscript, Vertical Files (Panhandle-Plains Historical Museum Research Center, Canyon, Tex.), 5–6. Collinson migrated from England to San Antonio, and then roamed West Texas as an early buffalo hunter, fighter, and cattleman. While hunting buffalo on the Llano he came into contact with ciboleros and studied their methods.

7. Ibid., 6. Other Collinson glimpses can be found in his reminiscences, appearing from 1934 to 1944 in the popular magazine *Ranch Romances*.

8. Ibid., 3.

9. Gregg, *Commerce of the Prairies*, 90.

10. Fabiola Cabeza de Baca, *We Fed Them Cactus* (Albuquerque: University of New Mexico Press, 1954). Details from the stories of El Cuate are on pages 39–45. This is an outstanding work on the Llano sense of place; see also chapter 12 below.

11. Ibid., 41.

12. Ibid., 42.

13. Collinson, "The Old Mexican Buffalo Hunters," 6.

14. John, *Storms Brewed in Other Men's Worlds*; T. R. Fehrenbach, *Comanches: The Destruction of a People* (New York: Alfred A. Knopf, 1986), 104 and *passim*; George E. Hyde, *Indians of the High Plains* (Norman: University of Oklahoma Press, 1981), 63–116. Two important Ph.D. dissertations on the Comanche are Thomas Kavanagh, "Political Power and Political Organization: Comanche Politics 1786–1875" (University of New Mexico, 1986), and my colleague at the University of Texas at San Antonio, Daniel Gelo, "Comanche Belief and Ritual" (Rutgers University, New Brunswick, 1986).

15. Kavanagh, "Political Power and Political Organization: Comanche Politics 1786–1875," finds no documentary evidence for the Kwahadi until the late 1840s.

16. Cited in Kenner, *The Comanchero Frontier*, 112–113.

17. Collinson, "The Old Mexican Buffalo Hunters."

18. Robertson and Robertson, *Panhandle Pilgrimage*, 2–3; Rubén Cobos, *A Dictionary of New Mexico and Southern Colorado Spanish* (Santa Fé: Museum of New Mexico Press, 1983), 100.

19. A. G. Mojtabai, *Blessed Assurance: At Home with the Bomb in Amarillo, Texas* (Albuquerque: University of New Mexico Press, 1986), 15. The very popular Lubbock winery, vinters of the fine "Llano Estacado" wines, also suggests on its labels that the name goes back to the time of Coronado.

20. Bolton, *Coronado*, 243.

21. See W. F. Cummins, "Report on the Geography, Topography and Geology of the Llano Estacado or Staked Plains," *Third Annual Report of the Geological Survey of Texas, 1891* (Austin, Tex.: n.p., 1892), 128–130.

22. Sabin and Holliday, "Playas and Lunettes on the Southern High Plains," 286.

23. H. Bailey Carroll, "The Journal of Lieutenant J. W. Abert from Bent's Fort to St. Louis in 1845," *Panhandle-Plains Historical Review* (1941), 74 n.209. Carroll's long footnote is a closely reasoned mini-treatise on the origin of the name and deserves attention.

24. *New Revised Velázquez Spanish and English Dictionary*, 318.

25. Webb, Carroll, and Branda (eds.), *Handbook of Texas*, II, 70.

26. Cummins, "Report on the Geography, Topography and Geology of the Llano Estacado or Staked Plains," 130.

27. *New Mexico: Guide to the Colorful State* (New York: Hastings House, 1940), 314–315.

28. In a 1965 letter to C. Boone McClure, Fray Angelico Chavez demurs at the "erroneous idea that a friar driving stakes out on the plains gave the name to the Staked Plains." Chavez Letter, McClure File, Vertical Files, Panhandle-Plains Historical Museum Research Center (Canyon, Tex.).

29. Transcribed article from Dallas *News* (Jan. 19, 1921), McClure File.

30. Carroll, "The Journal of Lieutenant J. W. Abert," 74 n.249.

31. Ibid. Note the later-nineteenth-century mustanger practice of planting snubbing-posts on the Llano for breaking wild horses. This echoed a native tradition of erecting posts or stakes on the Llano to tie up camp horses.

32. John L. Allen, "Exploration and the Creation of Geographical Images of the Great Plains: Comments on the Role of Subjectivity," in Blouet and Lawson (eds.), *Images of the Plains*, 3–11.

33. Consider the legend of the fictional Padilla-Fernandez expedition against the Comanche in Rathjen, *The Texas Panhandle Frontier*, 72–73.

Chapter Twelve

1. Herbert E. Bolton, "French Intrusions into New Mexico," in *The Pacific Ocean in History*, eds. H. M. Stephens and H. E. Bolton (New York: MacMillan, 1917), 399–400.

2. John, *Storms Brewed in Other Men's Worlds*, 697–736.

3. From Pierre Margry's *Découvertes et Etablissement des Francais dans l'ouest et dans le sud de Amérique Septentrionale* (6 vols.; Paris: D. Jouaust, 1888), VI, 455–466; Henri Folmer (trans.), "The Mallet Expedition of 1739 Through Nebraska, Kansas and Colorado to Santa Fe," *Colorado Magazine*, XVI (Sept., 1935), 165.

4. Ibid., 169.

5. Ibid.

6. See the informative article by Beryl Roper, "How Did This River Come To Be Called Canadian," *Panhandle-Plains Historical Review*, LXI (1988), 17–24. Donald J. Blakeslee, *Along Ancient Trails: The Mallett Expedition of 1739* (Niwot, Colo.: University Press of Colorado, 1995).

7. See "To Santa Fé from the East: The Explorations of Pierre and Paul Mallet, 1739–40," in Goetzmann and Williams, *The Atlas of North American Exploration*, 98–99. Although I assisted Dr. Goetzmann in the research and mapping of this section, it was an editor in England who added the erroneous impression to the text on page 98 that the Mallets' return trip down the river caused it "from now on to be called the Canadian." This phrase promotes the impression that the river was named Canadian for its exploration by this party of French Canadians, an error that needs to be corrected in general.

8. Brandon, *Quivira*, 202.

9. Two indispensable sources on Pedro Vial are Noel M. Loomis and Abraham P. Nasatir, *Pedro Vial and the Roads to Santa Fé* (Norman: University of Oklahoma Press, 1967); and John, *Storms Brewed in Others Men's Worlds*, 655–691, 718–764.

10. Elizabeth A. H. John (ed.) and Adán Benavides Jr. (trans.), "Inside the Comanchería, 1785: The Diary of Pedro Vial and Francisco Xavier Chaves," *Southwestern Historical Quarterly*, XCVIII (July, 1994), 27–56.

11. As a clue to his origins, Vial's stirring oration to the assembled Comanches on September 10, 1785, noted, "You know me because I have come from the Rio de la Sarca to your rancherías with some goods." John and Benavides (ed. and trans.), "Inside the Comanchería," 39.

12. Ibid., 52–55. The recent appearance of this diary fills the void in explaining Vial's good reception later on with the Comanches of the eastern Llano.

13. John, *Storms Brewed in Other Men's Worlds*, 718–720.

14. Ibid., 317. John's relationship to the Taovaya and Wichita twin villages is discussed in a very

thoughtful article on borderlands research, "A View from the Spanish Borderlands," in *Writing the History of the American West* (Worcester, Mass.: American Antiquarian Society, 1991), 77–87.

15. Loomis and Nasatir, *Pedro Vial and the Roads to Santa Fé*, 283.
16. Ibid., 284.
17. Rupert Norval Richardson, *The Comanche Barrier to South Plains Settlement* (Glendale, Calif.: Arthur H. Clark, 1933), 18–22.
18. Fehrenbach, *Comanches*, 140.
19. Ibid., 144; Kavanagh, "Political Power and Political Organization."
20. Fehrenbach, *Comanches*, 145; see also Gelo, "Comanche Belief and Ritual," 89–120.
21. Loomis and Nasatir, *Pedro Vial and the Roads to Santa Fé*, 290–291.
22. Ibid., 291.
23. Ibid. Possibly the trees were hackberries.
24. Ibid., 293.
25. Flores, *Caprock Canyonlands*, 101–103. I am further indebted to Dr. Flores for bringing this item to my attention in a 1994 communication.
26. Loomis and Nasatir, *Pedro Vial and the Roads to Santa Fé*, 313.
27. Ibid.
28. See map, page 180, for a conjecture on Mares's routes across the Llano.
29. Loomis and Nasatir, *Pedro Vial and the Roads to Santa Fé*, 329–331.
30. See Haley, "The Comanchero Trade," 162.
31. Fragoso's diary says, "a plain so extensive that neither a ridge nor knolls are to be found in any direction." There are four known copies of Fragoso's diary. This version, which explicitly acknowledges the celebrated flatness of the plain, is found in the Archivo General de Mexico, Sección de Historia, vol. 43, no. 17. See Loomis and Nasatir, *Pedro Vial and the Roads to Santa Fé*, 327 n.17, 331 (quotation).
32. Ibid., 332. Loomis and Nasatir provide no reference on this portion of Vial's second trip. Although Carlos Castañeda's guesses are often wrong, see Castañeda, *Our Catholic Heritage in Texas*, V, 158–161.
33. This "Mapa del territorio comprendido entre la Provincia de Nuevo Mexico y el Fuerte de Natchitoches y Texas" is in the Archives of the Indies (Estante 86, Cajon 6, Legajo 9) with the diary and *derrotero* of Fragoso. Carl Wheat thought this remarkable map was drawn in Natchitoches in 1788, "by a hand other than that of the intelligent but obviously untutored Vial." Wheat, *Mapping the Transmississippi West*, II, 239. Both Bolton and Castañeda reproduced this map, but neither scholar analyzed its significant mesa features. An expert watercolor reproduction of the original is in the James Bryan Collection (Center for American History, University of Texas at Austin).
34. Three variants of Fragoso's diary say specifically that the Tule River flowed from the north; the map shows correctly that the Tule flows from the south. See, Loomis and Nasatir, *Pedro Vial and the Roads to Santa Fé*, 332.
35. John, *Storms Brewed in Other Men's Worlds*, 743. John does not mention that this camp was in Palo Duro Canyon. In a telephone interview she cautioned that reconstructions of Vial and Mares's routes necessarily involves some conjecture.
36. Note the July 31 entry, "we stopped on an open plain that is at the foot of a white cliff." Loomis and Nasatir, *Pedro Vial and the Roads to Santa Fé*, 365.
37. Ibid., 365 n.69.
38. Ibid., 366. See also John, *Storms Brewed in Other Men's Worlds*, 748, who notes that "they reached the springs they deemed headwaters of the Red River," once again.
39. Rathjen, *The Texas Panhandle Frontier*, 81–82.
40. Loomis and Nasatir, *Pedro Vial and the Roads to Santa Fé*, 499.
41. Note the assimilation and European accoutrements of these natives: "Upon our arrival, the big chief and the other chiefs of the tribe came out to meet us. They were very well dressed, but they wore very unusual clothes: long red coats with blue collars and cuffs, white buttons, yellow [imitation

gold] galloons; one was dressed in ancient Spanish style: a short red coat, blue trousers, white stockings, English spurs, an ordinary cornered hat worn cocked, a cane with a silver handle shaped like a hyssop." Ibid., 482.

42. Ibid., 485.

43. Ibid., 491.

44. See Jeffrey A. Lee and Vatche Tchakerian, "Magnitude and Frequency of Blowing Dust on the Southern High Plains of the United States, 1947–1989," *Annals of the Association of American Geographers*, LXXXV (Dec., 1995), 684–693.

45. Loomis and Nasatir, *Pedro Vial and the Roads to Santa Fé*, 493. See also Stanley Noyes, *Los Comanches, 1715–1845* (Albuquerque: University of New Mexico Press, 1993), 125

46. Loomis and Nasatir, *Pedro Vial and the Roads to Santa Fé*, 493.

47. Ibid., 494.

48. Ibid., 495.

49. Ibid., 496 n.31. They were possibly under the cottonwoods of upper Bonita Creek nine miles northeast of Amarillo, Texas.

50. See Noyes's brief chapter 11, "Encounters in *Comanchería*, 1808–1845," in *Los Comanches*, 114–126.

51. Loomis and Nasatir, *Pedro Vial and the Roads to Santa Fé*, 499.

CHAPTER THIRTEEN

1. Quoted in Lowell H. Harrison (ed.), "Three Comancheros and a Trader," *Panhandle-Plains Historical Review*, XXXVIII (1965), 88.

2. Richard L. Nostrand, "The Century of Hispano Expansion," *New Mexico Historical Review*, LXII (Oct., 1987), 367.

3. William deBuys, *Enchantment and Exploitation: The Life and Hard Times of a New Mexico Mountain Range* (Albuquerque: University of New Mexico Press, 1985), 80.

4. Anton Chico was an 1834 daughter colony of San Miguel del Vado.

5. See Karl W. Butzer, "Cattle and Sheep from Old to New Spain: Historical Antecedents," *Annals of the Association of American Geographers*, LXXVIII (Mar., 1988), 29–56.

6. Albert Pike mentioned "this ceja, or eye-brow, as they called it" of the Llano Estacado in his book, *Prose Sketches and Poems, Written in the Western Country* (1834; reprint, Albuquerque, N.Mex.: Calvin Horn, 1967), 42.

7. Cabeza de Baca, *We Fed Them Cactus*, 3. This is a classic work that has lost none of its charm.

8. DeBuys, *Enchantment and Exploitation*, 217–222.

9. Ibid.

10. Webb, *The Great Plains*, 130–138. Webb essentially ends the Spanish approach to the Great Plains with the Apache campaigns of 1777–1778.

11. See Nostrand, "The Century of Hispano Expansion," 385, and *The Hispano Homeland* (Norman: University of Oklahoma Press, 1992). Nostrand's research debunks Webb's notion that the Great Plains environment defeated Spanish expansion. Clark Knowlton claims that by the 1850s the Spanish Americans had penetrated the plains significantly. Clark Knowlton, "The Spanish Americans in New Mexico," *Sociology and Social Research*, XLIV (July, 1961), 448–450.

12. Cabeza de Baca, *We Fed Them Cactus*, 5.

13. Erna Ferguson, *Our Southwest* (New York: Alfred A. Knopf, 1940), 330.

14. Cabeza de Baca, *We Fed Them Cactus*, 78, 123.

15. Nostrand, "The Century of Hispano Expansion," 371; Cabeza de Baca, *We Fed Them Cactus*, 5; J. Evetts Haley, *The XIT Ranch of Texas, and the Early Days of the Llano Estacado* (Norman: University of Oklahoma Press, 1953), 33.

16. Note A. J. Taylor's comment that the *pastor* and *padre* "first opened the Texas Panhandle," in "New Mexican *Pastores* and Priests in the Texas Panhandle, 1876–1915," *Panhandle-Plains Historical Review*, LVI (1984), 79.

17. See Nancie L. Gonzalez, *The Spanish-Americans of New Mexico* (Albuquerque: University of New Mexico Press, 1967), 44.

18. John L. McCarty, *Maverick Town: The Story of Old Tascosa* (Norman: University of Oklahoma Press,1946), 8. McCarty does not document his source but claims that this community encountered soil problems in irrigating crops which led to its abandonment.

19. Rathjen, *The Texas Panhandle Frontier*, 69.

20. Herman H. Moncus, *Prairie Schooner Pirates: The Story of the Comancheros* (New York: Carlton Press, 1963); Jack D. Rittenhouse, "Comancheros of the Staked Plains," in *Maverick Tales of the Southwest* (Albuquerque: University of New Mexico Press, 1987), 135–154; H. Bailey Carroll, "Some New Mexico–West Texas Relationships, 1541–1841," *West Texas Historical Association Year Book*, XIV (1938), 92–102; Charles Kenner, *A History of New Mexican–Plains Indian Relations* (1969; reprint, Norman: University of Oklahoma Press, 1995), 17.

21. The Utes introduced the Comanches to raiding the northern Spanish frontier. John, *Storms Brewed in Other Men's Worlds*, 312.

22. Rittenhouse, *Maverick Tales of the Southwest*, 142–143.

23. J. Evetts Haley, "The Comanchero Trade," *Southwestern Historical Quarterly*, XXXVIII (Jan., 1935), 160.

24. Richardson, *The Comanche Barrier to South Plains Settlement*, 19.

25. Haley, *The XIT Ranch of Texas*, 163.

26. Kenner, *A History of New Mexican–Plains Indian Relations*, 71.

27. The canyon southeast of Lubbock on the Double Mountain Fork of the Brazos.

28. See V. H. (Ol' Waddy) Whitlock, *Cowboy Life on the Llano Estacado* (Norman: University of Oklahoma Press, 1970), 10. Whitlock's source for this significant trail-name was an old buffalo hunter and former Indian captive named Jeff Jefferson. The poet and writer Albert Pike used this trail for his crossing in 1832.

29. Haley, "The Comanchero Trade," 162.

30. Kenner, *A History of New Mexico–Plains Indian Relations*, 162–163.

31. All the foregoing citations were consulted; for geosophical accounts see also Frank P. Hill, "Plains Names," *Panhandle-Plains Historical Review*, X (1937), 36–47, and J. Evetts Haley, "Lore of the Llano Estacado," in *Texas and Southwestern Lore*, ed. J. Frank Dobie (Austin: Texas Folk Society Number VI, 1927), 72–89.

32. Haley, "Lore of the Llano Estacado," 75.

33. Rathjen, *The Texas Panhandle Frontier*, 94–95; Rittenhouse, *Maverick Tales of the Southwest*, 150.

34. Carl Coke Rister, *Border Captives: The Traffic in Prisoners by Southern Plains Indians, 1835–1875* (Norman: University of Oklahoma Press, 1940).

35. "This barter had been going on for many decades, but it does not seem that cattle became the chief commodity until about the time of the Civil War." Richardson, *The Comanche Barrier to South Plains Settlement*, 309.

36. Rittenhouse, *Maverick Tales of the Southwest*, 135.

37. Leonard M. Slesick, "Fort Bascom: A Military Outpost in Eastern New Mexico," *Panhandle-Plains Historical Review*, LVI (1984), 13–64.

38. Rittenhouse, *Maverick Tales of the Southwest*, 151; Haley, "The Comanchero Trade," 170–171; Harry Sinclair Drago, *The Great Range Wars* (Lincoln: University of Nebraska Press, 1970), 15.

39. H. Bailey Carroll, *The Journal of Lt. J. W. Abert from Bent's Fort to St. Louis in 1845* (Canyon, Tex.: Panhandle-Plains Historical Society, 1941), 71.

40. Cabeza de Baca, *We Fed Them Cactus*, 43–44.

CHAPTER FOURTEEN

1. Alyce Hart, "English Inscription Stone," *Transactions of the Seventh Regional Archeological Symposium for Southeastern New Mexico and Western Texas* (Midland, Tex.: Lower Plains Archeological Society Press, 1972), 41–45.

2. In 1774 John Rozee Peyton escaped from Santa Fé and made his way to St. Louis, but whether he traveled over the Llano Estacado is not clear. At least one researcher believes he did. See Del Weniger, *The Explorers' Texas* (Austin: Eakin Press, 1984), 22. See also John Rowzee Peyton, *A Virginian in New Mexico*, Series of Western Americana no. 13 (Santa Fé, N.Mex.: Press of the Territorian, 1967).

3. See Dan L. Flores, *Jefferson and Southwestern Exploration* (Norman: University of Oklahoma Press, 1984), 15.

4. Ibid., 14-15.

5. See the interesting discussion of Nolan's activities in chapter 9 of Loomis and Nasatir, *Pedro Vial and the Roads to Santa Fé*, 205-234.

6. Quoted in Flores, *Jefferson and Southwestern Exploration*, 33-34.

7. Ibid., 34

8. See Dan L. Flores, *Journal of an Indian Trader: Anthony Glass and the Texas Trading Frontier* (College Station: Texas A&M University Press, 1985), and *Jefferson and Southwestern Exploration*, 15-17. Duke's reminiscence is in J. H. Kuykendall, "Reminiscences of Early Texans," *Southwestern Historical Quarterly*, VI (Jan., 1903), 249-250.

9. Quoted from William Dunbar's 1801 letter to Jefferson, in Loomis and Nasatir, *Pedro Vial and the Roads to Santa Fé*, 215.

10. Pike's mythic lakes would appear on other maps as his geography was copied widely. What can be considered, however, is whether these lakes were an enlarged acknowledgment of the playas and saline lakes that did characterize the plains landscape.

11. Zebulon Pike, *The Expeditions of Zebulon Montgomery Pike*, ed. Elliott Coues (2 vols., 1895; reprint New York: Dover, 1987), II, 525.

12. Edwin James, *Account of an Expedition from Pittsburgh to the Rocky Mountains, Performed in the Years 1819 and '20 . . . under the Command of Major Stephen H. Long* (2 vols., separate folio atlas, 1822 appendix; Philadelphia, Pa.: 1823); the most accessible version is Edwin James, *Account . . .* in *Early Western Travels*, ed. R. G. Thwaites (Cleveland, Ohio: Arthur H. Clark, 1905), quote from 95.

13. James, *Account of an Expedition from Pittsburgh to the Rocky Mountains*, 90.

14. Ibid. See also Richard G. Wood, *Stephen Harriman Long 1784-1864: Army Engineer, Explorer, Inventor* (Glendale, Calif.: Arthur H. Clark, 1966).

15. Ibid., 130.

16. See William H. Goetzmann, *Exploration and Empire: The Explorer and the Scientist in the Winning of the American West* (New York: W. W. Norton, 1978), 62.

17. See "Creating the Tradition of the 'Great American Desert,'" in *The Great Plains*, Webb, 152-157. See also Martyn J. Bowden, "The Great American Desert and The American Frontier, 1800-1822: Popular Images of the Plains," in *Anonymous Americans: Explorations in Nineteenth Century Social History* (Englewood Cliffs, N.J.: Prentice Hall, 1971).

18. Goetzmann, *Exploration and Empire*, 52.

19. Reprint of 1827 Sibley Commissioners' map in Buford Rowland, "Report of the Commissioners on the Road from Missouri to New Mexico, October 1827," *New Mexico Historical Review*, XIV (July, 1939), 220-221.

CHAPTER FIFTEEN

1. Albert Pike, *Prose Sketches and Poems, Written in the Western Country*, ed. David J. Weber (Albuquerque, N.Mex.: Calvin Horn, 1967). This is a reprint version of the rare 1834 work. A reprint of Pike's two "Narratives" appeared with excellent introduction and notes by J. Evetts Haley, "Albert Pike's Journeys in the Prairie, 1831-1832," *Panhandle-Plains Historical Review*, XLI (1968). All references are to the Weber edition unless noted.

2. Pike, *Prose Sketches*, 3.

3. Ibid.

4. Ibid., 4.

5. Ibid., 9.
6. Ibid.
7. "Those who make fun of the Romantics are mistaken in supposing that there is not intimate connection between the landscape and the poet's emotions. There is no real dualism, says Whitehead, between external lakes and hills, on the one hand, and personal feelings on the other: human feelings and inanimate objects are interdependent and developing together." Edmund Wilson, *Axel's Castle* (New York: Charles Scribner's Sons, 1931), 5.
8. Susan B. Riley, "Albert Pike as an American Don Juan," *Arkansas Historical Quarterly*, XIX (Fall, 1960), 211.
9. Pike, *Prose Sketches*, 10.
10. Ibid., 11. Italics added.
11. Quoted in W. H. Hudson, "The Plains of Patagonia," in *The Green World of the Naturalists*, ed. V. W. von Hagen (New York: Greenburg, 1948), 283–284. Italics added.
12. Pike, *Prose Sketches*, 235.
13. Ibid.
14. Ibid., 40.
15. Ibid.
16. Ibid., 43.
17. Ibid., 43–45, 52.
18. See David Donoghue, "Explorations of Albert Pike in Texas," *Southwestern Historical Quarterly*, XXXIX (Oct., 1935), 136–137.
19. See Haley's footnote to Pike's text, "Albert Pike's Journeys in the Prairie, 1831–1832" 54–55.
20. These sandburs were possibly one of the *Cenchrus* species from the Rio Grande Plains. Coyote Lake is in central Bailey County to the south of Muleshoe, Texas.
21. See Crosby, *Ecological Imperialism*, 291.
22. Pike, *Prose Sketches*, 46.
23. Ibid., 50.
24. Note the route suggested by David Donoghue in "Explorations of Albert Pike in Texas," 135–136. Donoghue's confusing use of toponyms is noted in Weber's edition of Pike, *Prose Sketches*, 41–42.

CHAPTER SIXTEEN

1. Quoted in Cardinal Goodwin, "John H. Fonda's Explorations in the Southwest," *Southwestern Historical Quarterly*, XXIII (July, 1919), 43.
2. R. N. Richardson, *The Comanche Barrier to Southern Plains Settlement* (Glendale, Calif.: Arthur H. Clark, 1933), 93–94.
3. Dr. John Charles Beale attempted a settlement on the southern margin of the grant at La Villa de Dolores on the Rio Grande in the mid-1830s. The Comanche destruction of a caravan of colonists headed for the settlement resulted in the traumatic captivity narrative of Sarah Ann Horn. See the lengthy introduction to an annotated reprinting of the rare *Narrative of Sarah Ann Horn* in Carl Coke Rister, *Comanche Bondage* (Glendale, Calif.: Arthur Clark, 1955), 1–94.
4. Rister, *Comanche Bondage*, 24, quoting from John Henry Brown's *History of Texas from 1685 to 1892*.
5. William Kennedy, *Texas: The Rise, Progress, and Prospects of the Republic of Texas* (Fort Worth: Molyneaux Craftsmen, 1925), 176–191.
6. Dan Flores notes Alexander Le Grand's reportage of "'white bears' along the escarpment of the Llanos," but this report equally could be evidence of Le Grand's general prevarication or his familiarity with grizzly bears near the Santa Fé area. See Flores, *Caprock Canyonlands*, 107.
7. Webb, Carroll, and Branda (eds.), *Handbook of Texas*, II, 47; Raymond Estep, "The Le Grand Survey of the High Plains—Fact or Fancy?" *New Mexico Historical Review*, XXIX (Apr., 1954), 81–96.
8. Estep, "The Le Grand Survey of the High Plains—Fact or Fancy?" 91.

9. Ibid., 87.

10. Ibid. Quoted from William Waldo, "Recollections of a Septuagenarian," *Glimpses of the Past* (10 vols.; St. Louis: Missouri Historical Society), V, 89.

11. See Martin and Martin, *Contours of Discovery*, 54. The Martins call Arrowsmith's High Plains region a "gross mistake."

12. John L. Allen, "Lands of Myth, Waters of Wonder," in Lowenthal and Bowden (eds.), *Geographies of the Mind*, 57.

13. See C. Flemming's 1846 map *Texas*, the German version of Arrowsmith.

Chapter Seventeen

1. Gregg, *Commerce of the Prairies*. This important work first appeared in the Galveston *Gazette and Daily Advertiser*, as noted by Wagner, Camp, and Becker in *The Plains and the Rockies*.

2. This American presence in Santa Fé is analyzed in Richard O. Ulibarri, "American Interest in the Spanish-Mexican Southwest, 1803–1848" (Ph.D. diss., University of Utah, 1963), 102–125.

3. Gregg, *Commerce of the Prairies*, II, 48.

4. David S. Reynolds, *Beneath the American Renaissance* (New York: Alfred A. Knopf, 1988).

5. Gregg, *Commerce of the Prairies*, II, 48–49.

6. Ibid., 10.

7. Ibid., 53.

8. Ernest A. Archambeau, "The Fort Smith–Santa Fé Trail Along the Canadian River in Texas," *Panhandle-Plains Historical Review*, XXVII (1954), 1–26.

9. This guide was possibly a young *Manuel el Comanche*, the cibolero and native of San Miguel, New Mexico, used for some time by Albert Pike as a guide, and whose geographic services would benefit future explorers such as Randolph Marcy.

10. Maurice Garland Fulton (ed.), *Diary and Letters of Josiah Gregg, Southwestern Enterprises, 1840–1847* (Norman: University of Oklahoma Press, 1941), 52.

11. Ibid., 52–53.

12. Ibid.

13. Ernest A. Archambeau traces this route with considerable exactitude. See Archambeau, "The Fort Smith–Santa Fé Trail Along the Canadian River," 5–8.

14. Now called Red Deer Creek.

15. Gregg, *Commerce of the Prairies*, II, 181.

16. Ibid.

17. Ibid., 195.

18. Ibid., 202–203.

19. Ibid.

20. Ibid., I, 98.

21. Ibid., 99. I am unaware of anyone in the historical record following a mirage to their doom on the Llano.

22. Ibid., 156.

23. Paul Horgan, *Josiah Gregg and His Vision of the Early West* (New York: Farrar, Straus and Giroux, 1979), 45.

Chapter Eighteen

1. Noel M. Loomis, *The Texan–Santa Fé Pioneers* (Norman: University of Oklahoma Press, 1958), ix. Loomis later retracted the claim of "the first westward crossing," owing to his research on Pedro Vial, Jose Mares, and Francisco Amangual. See Loomis and Nasatir, *Pedro Vial and the Roads to Santa Fé*, 534, which notes four prior westward crossings by European-descent explorers.

2. H. Bailey Carroll, "The Texan Santa Fe Trail," *Panhandle-Plains Historical Review*, XXIV (1951), xxv–xxxvi.

3. Falconer's writings were later collected and edited by F. W. Hodge in *Letters and Notes on the Texan Santa Fé Expedition 1841–1842* (New York: Dauber & Pine, 1930). Kendall's two-volume *Narrative of the Texan Santa Fe Expedition . . .* (New York: Harper and Brothers, 1844,) went through many editions in the United States and abroad. The rare seventh edition (1856) contains two significant new chapters at the end of volume I. The first new chapter provides a synopsis of Randolph Marcy's recent Red River Expedition. The second chapter reprints Thomas Falconer's account of the expedition. All further references are to the 1845 London edition of Kendall's work printed by David Bogue (hereafter cited as Kendall, *Narrative*), and the 1930 Hodge edition of Falconer.

4. Kendall, *Narrative*, 17.
5. Ibid., 21.
6. Falconer, *Letters and Notes*, 110.
7. Fayette Copeland notes that the editor of the Austin *Sentinel* "guessed that the route would cover four hundred and fifty miles through a 'rich, rolling, well watered country.'" Fayette Copeland, *Kendall of the Picayune* (Norman: University of Oklahoma Press, 1943), 48.
8. This event constituted a classic incident in environmental deception. The tendency of many of the Llano drainage rivers to flow with reddish Permian sediments led to repeated confusion over which one was the real "Red" River.
9. Falconer, *Notes and Letters*, 85.
10. Kendall, *Narrative*, 216.
11. Carroll, "The Texan Santa Fe Trail," 125–133.
12. Loomis, *The Texan–Santa Fé Pioneers*, 64–66.
13. Carroll, "The Texan Santa Fe Trail," 139.
14. Kendall, *Narrative*, 231; H. Bailey Carroll, "George W. Glover's 'Minutes of Adventure From June 1841,'" *Panhandle-Plains Historical Review*, IX (1936), 39.
15. Kendall, *Narrative*, 232. Salvator Rosa was a popular eighteenth-century Italian artist who specialized in exotic and wild landscape studies centered on the Italian Appennini Mountains. He and Claude Lorrain were the leaders of the Picturesque style of landscape painting. Rosa's "wild and gloomy pencil" was a well-known middle-class reference for correspondence between the American West and the exotic picturesque landscape. See Ron Tyler, *Prints of the West* (Golden, Colo.: Fulcrum Press, 1994), for a characterization of the riverboatman Mike Fink as a suitable Salvator Rosa model.
16. Kendall, *Narrative*, 232–233.
17. Dr. Dan Flores has provided me with Kendall's proximate location at this point.
18. Kendall, *Narrative*, 237.
19. "Loan" is a Scottish word for an uncultivated plot of farmland, often pasturage. However, in a later passage (p. 260), Kendall referred to the "lone and dreary appearance" of the Llano; it is likely that loan was a misprint.
20. Kendall, *Narrative*, 241.
21. Ibid.
22. Carroll, "George W. Glover," 32.
23. See H. Bailey Carroll's comparative analysis, "Characteristic Similarities of Expeditions into the Great Plains," *Panhandle-Plains Historical Review*, X (1937), 21–35.
24. Kendall, *Narrative*, 241.
25. Ibid., 62–63.
26. Ibid., 242. Kendall overestimated Tule Canyon's depth, but his hometown of New Orleans was poor preparation for an estimation of heights!
27. Ibid., 243.
28. Ibid.
29. Flores, *Caprock Canyonlands*, 121–122.
30. Kendall, *Narrative*, 245. Niagara Falls is only 167 feet high. This eroded section of Tule Canyon is still distinguished by unusual formations. But where Kendall saw Athens, the modern tourist may see something quite different, an alien world, for instance.
31. Ibid., 245.

32. Carroll, "The Texan Santa Fe Trail," 136. Loomis plots essentially the same route, but takes the Sutton party farther north in Deaf Smith County. Loomis, *The Texan–Santa Fé Pioneers*, 71. Flores projects a route "south of the line of Tierra Blanca Draw across the Llano."
33. Kendall, *Narrative*, 250–255.
34. Ibid., 257.
35. "Grand Prairie" is first mentioned in a footnote on Doctor Beall. Ibid., 62–63. On page 260 both expressions are used.
36. Ibid., 260. This was an incorrect assumption.
37. Ibid., 266.
38. Kendall noted as well Albert Pike's reference to "*Las Cejas*" of the eastern Llano as an origin. See Pike, *Prose Sketches and Poems*, 42.
39. Loomis, *The Texan–Santa Fé Pioneers*, 106.
40. Carroll, "The Texan Santa Fe Trail," 177.
41. Falconer, *Letters and Notes*, 110. Falconer's perception of the word "staked" was contrary to the folklore of the day, which held that Mexican traders had staked their route across the plains from waterhole to waterhole. Nevertheless, his version would give rise to the etymological notion that *Estacado* referred to the "stockaded" or "pallisaded" character of the topography. Of course, part of the attraction of Kendall's account of the plains is its hallucinogenic quality.
42. Falconer also called the playas "lagunas."
43. Falconer, *Letters and Notes*, 112.
44. Ibid.
45. Ibid.
46. Loomis, *The Texan–Santa Fé Pioneers*, 108.
47. Carroll, "The Texan Santa Fe Trail," 175.
48. *Chamber's Edinburgh Journal*, June 1, 1844.
49. Thirst and infinity *are* thematic aspects of the Llano, however.

Chapter Nineteen

1. Chauncey C. Loomis, "The Arctic Sublime," in *Nature and the Victorian Imagination*, eds. U. C. Knoepflmacher and G. B. Tennyson (Berkeley: University of California Press, 1977).
2. Stanley Vestal, *Short Grass Country* (New York: Duell, Sloan & Pearce, 1941), 68. Vestal is a reminder that the Prairie Sublime did not disappear after the nineteenth century.
3. The phrase is borrowed from Goetzmann, *Exploration and Empire*, ix.
4. "The Country of the Mind" in Barry Lopez, *Arctic Dreams, Imagination and Desire in a Northern Landscape* (New York: Charles Scribner's Sons, 1986), 252–301; Knoepflmacher and Tennyson (eds.), *Nature and the Victorian Imagination*.
5. Analyzed by David S. Reynolds, *Beneath the American Renaissance*, 561–567.
6. Manuscript in William H. Koester Collection (Humanities Research Center Library, University of Texas at Austin).
7. Thomas Ollive Mabbott (ed.), *Collected Works of Edgar Allan Poe: Tales and Sketches, 1843–1849* (Cambridge, Mass.: Belknap Press of Harvard University Press, 1978), 1278.
8. Ibid.
9. Mayne Reid, *The Boy Hunters; or, Adventures in Search of a White Buffalo* (Boston: Ticknor, Reed & Fields, 1853). Other Reid titles include *Adventures in Search of a White Buffalo: The Wild Horse Hunters* (1877), *The Scalp Hunters* (1868), and *The War Trail* (1857).
10. Mayne Reid, *The Lone Ranche: A Tale of the "Staked Plain"* (2 vols.; London: Chapman and Hall, 1871).
11. Charles W. Webber, *Old Hicks, The Guide; or, Adventures in the Camanche Country in Search of a Gold Mine* (2 vols.; New York: Harper & Bros., 1848; various editions to 1855; London: 1850). Note the author's spelling of "Comanche."
12. Flores, *Caprock Canyonlands*, 73 (quotation). For the context see chapter 7, "The Innocence

and Wildness of Nature: Charles W. Webber and Others," in Henry Nash Smith, *Virgin Land, The American West as Symbol and Myth* (Cambridge, Mass.: Harvard University Press, 1950), 77–87.

13. Smith, *Virgin Land*, 83. See also Reynolds, *Beneath the American Renaissance*, 561–567.

14. Washington Irving, *A Tour on the Prairie* (1835; reprint, Norman: University of Oklahoma Press, 1956), 106. This work was first published as voume one of the three-volume *The Crayon Miscellany* in 1835.

15. Irving, *A Tour on the Prairie*. Commissioner Ellsworth's version of the tour is found in Henry Ellsworth, *Washington Irving on the Prairie* (New York: American Book Co., 1937).

16. Marjorie Hope Nicolson, *Mountain Gloom and Mountain Glory: The Development of the Aesthetics of the Infinite* (Ithaca, N.Y.: Cornell University Press, 1959). This book is a landmark study of the sublime.

17. An overview of this Arctic exploration is in Goetzmann and Williams, *Atlas of North American Exploration*, 186–187.

18. Ibid., 182–183.

19. W. E. Parry, *Journal of a Voyage for the Discovery of a North-West Passage* (London: McKay, 1821), 125.

20. Nicolson, *Mountain Gloom and Mountain Glory*, 143.

21. Goetzmann, *Exploration and Empire*, and William H. Goetzmann, *Army Exploration in the American West, 1803–1863* (New Haven, Conn.: Yale University Press, 1959). See also Edward S. Wallace, *The Great Reconnaissance* (Boston: Ginn, 1955).

Chapter Twenty

1. Goetzmann, *Army Exploration in the American West*, 125.

2. Originally printed as "Journal of Lieutenant J. W. Abert, from Bent's Fort to St. Louis, in 1845," S. Doc. 23, 29th Cong., 1st Sess., 1848. This journal was reprinted and edited by H. Bailey Carroll as "*Guádal P'a*, "Journal of Lt. J. W. Abert from Bent's Fort to St. Louis in 1845," *Panhandle-Plains Historical Review*, XIV (1941), 9–113. All subsequent references are to this latter work. Abert's pretty watercolor sketches of the Indians are found in John Galvin (ed.), *Through the Country of the Comanche Indians in the Fall of the Year 1845* . . . (San Francisco, Calif.: Lawton Kennedy for John Howell, 1970).

3. Carroll, "*Guádal P'a*," 41.

4. Ibid.

5. Parts of Isaac Cooper's account of the reconnaissance were published in 1853 by the *Western Journal and Civilian* of St. Louis, Missouri. Cooper's journal was later edited by Nancy Mower and Don Russell as François des Montaignes (psuedonym for Isaac Cooper), *The Plains* (Norman: University of Oklahoma Press, 1972), 91.

6. Ibid., 41

7. Ibid., 50. Italics added.

8. Thoburn's pro-(French) Canada revisionist argument was directed against the 1895 orthodox opinion of Elliot Coues, Zebulon Pike's great editor. Coues also argued for a landscape interpretation of "Rio Cañada, or Rio Cañadiano." See Beryl Roper, "How Did This River Come to Be Called Canadian," *Panhandle-Plains Historical Review*, LXI (1988), 17–21. Note also the recent and inadvertant perpetuation of the Mallet travels linked to a (French) Canadian River and spelling in Goetzmann and Williams, *Atlas of North American Exploration*, 98.

9. Roper, "How Did This River Come to Be Called Canadian," 20.

10. Ibid.

11. Goetzmann and Williams, *The Atlas of North American Exploration*, 98.

12. The original plat is in the National Archives. For a reproduction and reprint of the Sibley report, see Buford Rowland (ed.), "Report of the Commissioners on the Road from Missouri to New Mexico, October 1827," *New Mexico Historical Review*, XIV (July, 1939), 213–229.

13. Carroll, "*Guádal P'a*," 52. Note the evidence of the Prairie Sublime aesthetics in Abert's statement.

14. Ibid., 48–55.
15. Carroll, "Guádal P'a," 50; Cooper, *The Plains*, 104.
16. Abert's misidentification is an example of deception. He found a pile of mesquite pods at one point, indicating that the Indians may have spread this food plant along the Llano. Carroll, "Guádal P'a," 61.
17. Carroll, "Guádal P'a," 61.
18. Now called Alibates National Monument, the famous "Paleolithic Pittsburg" or prehistoric flint bluffs of the north Llano. The government explorers overlooked the long-abandoned puebloan ruins in the Canadian Valley.
19. Carroll, "Guádal P'a," 73.
20. Ibid.
21. Ibid., 75.
22. Ibid.
23. Ibid., 76. There were Kiowas in the vicinity, but whether they were hovering around Abert's group was not clear.
24. Cooper, *The Plains*, 135.
25. Ibid., 139.
26. Carroll, "Guádal P'a," 86.
27. William T. Jackson, *Wagon Roads West: A Survey of Federal Road Surveys in the Trans-Mississippi West, 1846–1869* (Berkeley: University of California Press, 1952). Jackson pointed to the capitalist links between exploration, wagon-road surveys, and then railroad construction in the West.
28. Grant Foreman (ed.), *Marcy and the Gold Seekers* (Norman: University of Oklahoma Press, 1939); W. Eugene Hollon, *Beyond the Cross Timbers: The Travels of Randolph B. Marcy, 1812–1887* (Norman: University of Oklahoma Press, 1955), 56–59; Ernest A. Archambeau, "The Fort Smith–Santa Fe Trail Along the Canadian River in Texas," *Panhandle-Plains Historical Review*, XXVII (1954), 10–11.
29. This route is traced with considerable precision on the map by Archambeau, "The Fort Smith–Santa Fe Trail Along the Canadian River in Texas," map following page 26.
30. From March 11 to 15, 1840, Josiah Gregg had headed the Canadian tributaries, delicately following the edge between the breaks and the level plain.
31. Randolph B. Marcy, letter from the Secretary of War George W. Crawford, Feb. 21, 1850, "Route from Fort Smith to Santa Fe," H. Exec. Doc. 45, 31st Cong., 1st Sess., p. 41. Hereafter cited as Marcy's *Route*.
32. Ibid.
33. Ibid., 42.
34. Ibid.
35. W. Eugene Hollon refers to Bieber's estimates in *The Southwest Old and New* (New York: Alfred A. Knopf, 1961), 186. For a firsthand account of the crossing by an Argonaut, see Bessie L. Wright, "Diary of a Member of the First Pack Train to Leave Fort Smith for California in 1849," *Panhandle-Plains Historical Review*, XLII (1969), 61–117.
36. Marcy, *Report*, 60. For a good study of Marcy's return route see J. W. Williams, "Marcy's Road from Dona Ana," *West Texas Historical Association Year Book*, XIX (1943), 128–138.
37. Marcy, *Report*, 62. See also the background commentary in Patrick Dearen, *Castle Gap and the Pecos Frontier* (Fort Worth: Texas Christian University Press, 1988), 111–115.
38. Marcy, *Report*, 63.
39. Marcy seems to have never fully understood that the Llano was a semiarid environment, a stochastic landscape where rainfall was unpredictable. Ponds full and wet one year could be bone-dry the next year, unless regularly recharged by springs.
40. Marcy, *Report*, 64. In this manner Randolph Marcy acted out his etymological understanding of "Staked Plain."
41. Ibid., 64.
42. Quoted in Hollon, *Beyond the Cross Timbers*, 89.

CHAPTER TWENTY-ONE

1. See A. B. Bender, "Opening Routes Across West Texas, 1848–1850," *Southwestern Historical Quarterly*, XXXVII (Oct., 1933), 116–135.

2. Lt. Nathaniel H. Michler, *Reports of the Secretary of War*, S. Exec. Doc. 64, 31st Cong., 1st Sess. (Washington, D.C.: G.P.O., 1850), 37.

3. Randolph Marcy, *Exploration of the Red River of Louisiana, in the Year 1852* . . . , S. Exec. Doc. 54, 32nd Cong., 2nd Sess. (Washington, D.C.: Robert Armstrong, 1853). The House of Representatives version appeared as unnumbered H. Exec. Doc., 33rd Cong., 1st Sess. (Washington, D.C.: A. O. P. Nicholson, 1854). Citations hereafter are to the House version. For quotation see page 2. Marcy could not have known that Pedro (Pierre) Vial knew the source of the Red River.

4. Marcy, *Exploration of the Red River*, 28.

5. Ibid., 37. Text citations are keyed to the widely available House version.

6. Ibid., 45. The discovery of gypsum eventually led to the region's production of sheetrock.

7. Ibid., 32.

8. Ibid., 40.

9. Ibid., 43.

10. "The rains . . . afforded us water in many places where we had no reason to expect it at this season of the year." Ibid., 40.

11. Ibid., 41.

12. Ibid.

13. Randolph Marcy, *Thirty Years of Army Life on the Border* (New York: Harper & Brothers, 1866), 142. Images of mirages are quite uncommon in the exploration of the Great Plains.

14. Marcy, *Exploration of the Red River*, 41.

15. Ibid., 92. Note his June 22 remark: "On the contrary, we have this season been favored with frequent and copious rains, and heavy dews." Ibid., 43.

16. Marcy thought he was the first to discover that the Red River had two principal forks. But as noted earlier the 1804 Wilkinson report to Jefferson mentioned two branches.

17. William Kennedy's 1841 book was the first to characterize West Texas as environmentally similar to the "steppes of Tartary."

18. Marcy, *Exploration of the Red River*, 51.

19. W. Eugene Hollon takes this viewpoint in *Beyond the Cross Timbers*, 143. Gunnar Brune maintains that he branched off into South Cita Canyon farther up the Palo Duro from Tule Canyon. Note, however, the evidence assembled by Dan Flores that Marcy ascended Tule Canyon to the "Narrows." Flores, *Caprock Canyonlands*, 114–124. Flores's photograph on page 114 is compelling in its similarity to the Ackermann lithograph of the Head Spring.

20. See chapter 5, "The Discovery of the West: Government Patronage," in Tyler, *Prints of the West*, 103–107. Tyler admirably conveys the importance of government funding of both exploration and lithography in the discovery of the West. For many Americans, federally subsidized lithography was a critical medium—a visual discourse, so to speak—whereby the U.S. government interpreted and familiarized the novel, conquered landscapes of the American Southwest. Tyler also notes that nonrepresentational or "negative aspects of the reports are equally apparent today." Ibid., 107.

21. Marcy, *Exploration of the Red River*, 54. Aspen and cottonwood are both *Populus* species, while "china" or wild china is *Sapindus drummondii*.

22. Ibid., 55.

23. Ibid., 56.

24. This architectonic "space-intoxication" is quite similar to George Wilkins Kendall's experience of Tule Canyon.

25. Marcy, *Exploration of the Red River*, 56. The scenery of the canyons exemplified the hand of God to Marcy. As the geographer Robin Doughty notes, "Marcy discovered God in the unexplored land." Doughty, *At Home in Texas* (College Station: Texas A&M University Press, 1987), 49.

26. Marcy, *Exploration of the Red River*, 56.

27. Note as well that McClellan's earlier determination of the 100th meridian was off by about fifty miles!

28. Fred Rathjen, *The Texas Panhandle Frontier* (Austin: University of Texas Press, 1973), 138. Carl Newton Tyson confuses the entire sequence of events and geography in *The Red River in Southwestern History* (Norman: University of Oklahoma Press, 1981), 113–116. Gunnar Brune makes a strong case for Marcy's headwater spring location as South Cita Springs, about four kilometers downstream from the Methodist church camp in South Cita Canyon. Here Triassic sandstone cliffs tower above fine springs. See Brune, *The Springs of Texas* (1 vol.; Fort Worth, Tex.: Branch-Smith, 1981), I, 379–380.

29. This illustration is also found in Marcy, *Thirty Years of Army Life on the Border*, 155. Flores correctly maintains that the head spring was not lost, just misidentified.

30. Marcy, *Exploration of the Red River*, 92.

31. Ibid., 110–111.

Chapter Twenty-Two

1. See chapter 7, "In Search of an Iron Trail," in Goetzmann, *Exploration and Empire*, 265–277, and chapter 7, "The Pacific Railroad Surveys" in Goetzmann, *Army Exploration in the American West*, 262–304. See also George L. Albright, *Official Exploration for Pacific Railroads* (Washington, D.C.: Government Printing Office, 1921).

2. *Reports of Explorations and Surveys . . . for a Railroad from the Mississippi River to the Pacific Ocean* (11 vols.; Washington, D.C.: Beverly Tucker Printer, 1855–1856), II, III. Hereafter cited as *Pacific Railroad Surveys*.

3. Grant Foreman provides an edited version of the Whipple itinerary in *A Pathfinder in the Southwest* (Norman: University of Oklahoma Press, 1968).

4. For other details see the listings in Samuel Wood Geiser, *Naturalists of the Frontier* (Dallas, Tex.: Southern Methodist University Press, 1948), appendix B.

5. Whipple's route across the Panhandle was expertly traced by Ernest A. Archambeau (ed.), "Lt. A. W. Whipple's Railroad Reconnaissance Across the Panhandle of Texas in 1853," *Panhandle-Plains Historical Review*, XLIV (1971), 1–128. Archambeau's excellent editorial notes closely tie this reprinting of Whipple's itinerary with the modern landscape.

6. Blake, "General Report . . . ," *Pacific Railroad Surveys*, III, part IV, 23.

7. "Nous avons suivi la rivière, mais à notre Camp 38, à droite et à gauche de la Canadian on a le commencement du Llano, espèce de plateau avec quelques montagnes plates, isolées comme avant garde." Jules Marcou, "Resume and Field Notes," *Pacific Railroad Surveys*, III, part IV, 133.

8. *Pacific Railroad Surveys*, III, part I. David E. Conrad erroneously calls this a lithograph of the Antelope Hills. However, Camp 38 was well west of the Antelope Hills. See Conrad, "The Whipple Expedition on the Great Plains," *Great Plains Journal*, II (Spring, 1963), 50.

9. Balduin Möllhausen, *Diary of a Journey from the Mississippi to the Coasts of the Pacific with a United States Government Expedition*, trans. Percy Sinnett (2 vols.; London: Longman, Brown, Green, Longmans, & Roberts, 1858), I, xii. Möllhausen's lithographs have turned this book into an expensive rare set of volumes. The first German edition is H. B. Möllhausen, *Tagebuch einer Reise vom Mississippi nach den Küsten der Südsee*, with an introduction by Alexander von Humboldt (Leipzig: Mendelsohn, 1858).

10. *Pacific Railroad Surveys*, III, part I, 30.

11. Archambeau, "Whipple's Transcontinental Railroad Survey," 77–78.

12. *Pacific Railroad Surveys*, III, part I, 29.

13. Ibid., III, part II, 16.

14. Ibid., III, part II, 15.

15. Ibid., III, part IV.

16. As noted by Goetzmann, Whipple observed that the only thing Möllhausen drew accurately was a Navajo blanket. Goetzmann, *Army Exploration in the American West*, 332.

17. *Pacific Railroad Surveys*, III, part I, 33.

18. Compare with the dark and sinister comanchero named Blue Duck in Larry McMurtry, *Lonesome Dove* (New York: Simon and Schuster, 1985).

19. Paul I. Wellman, *The Comancheros* (New York: Doubleday and Co., 1952), features a completely sinister "Comanchero Town" in a vastness of the Llano Estacado.

20. *Pacific Railroad Surveys*, III, part I, 33.

21. *Pacific Railroad Surveys*, III, part 1, 35. Whipple's written account of this "extraordinary refraction" shares similarities with the nineteenth-century study of zodiacal lights, a lenticular or cone-shaped field of bright light in the sky before sunrise or after sunset.

22. Möllhausen, *Diary of a Journey*, 238.

23. *Pacific Railroad Surveys*, III, part I, 35.

24. Möllhausen's English translator, Mrs. Percy Sinnett, interestingly translated the German equivalent of the Spanish as "Marked-Off Plain." A footnote explained the Mexican trader custom of planting "long poles in the ground" to show the way.

25. Möllhausen, *Diary of a Journey*, 239.

26. Ibid., 240.

27. *Pacific Railroad Surveys*, III, part IV, 23.

28. David E. Conrad reports that "Whipple was so impressed with the sight that he made a sketch of it and described the event at length in his journal." Conrad, "The Whipple Expedition on the Great Plains," 60.

29. Quote from staff geologist W. P. Blake. See his remarks on this scene in *Pacific Railroad Surveys*, III, part IV, 23.

30. Möllhausen, *Diary of a Journey*, 241.

31. Ibid., 242.

32. Quoted by Möllhausen, ibid., 243.

33. Preston Albert Barba, *Baldwin Möllhausen, The German Cooper* (Philadelphia: University of Pennsylvania Press and D. Appleton and Co., 1914).

34. *Pacific Railroad Surveys*, III, part I, 36.

35. Ibid.

36. Ibid.

37. Ibid.

38. Ibid., III, part III, 37–38. Whipple had encountered little or no evidence of older cultural landscapes up until then. Some of the Rocky Dell pictographs still exist, although vandals have sadly claimed others. The arroyo slumbers in strict privacy now, on private property just north of Interstate 40, after the truck-choked highway descends the western caprock.

39. Ibid., III, part I, 38.

40. Ibid.

41. Jules Marcou, *Geology of North America* (Zurich: Zurcher and Furrer, 1858), 19–20.

42. Ibid.

43. Ibid., 20.

44. Together these reports constitute part IV of *Pacific Railroad Surveys*, III.

45. Ibid., III, part IV, 81. See also Flores, *Caprock Canyonlands*, 7–13, on the geology.

46. Walter Keene Ferguson, *Geology and Politics in Frontier Texas, 1845–1909* (Austin: University of Texas Press, 1969), 56.

47. Marcou, *Geology of North America*, 144.

48. Ferguson, *Geology and Politics in Frontier Texas*, 56.

49. Ibid., 57.

Chapter Twenty-Three

1. Walter Keene Ferguson, *Geology and Politics in Frontier Texas, 1845–1909* (Austin: University of Texas Press, 1969), 56–57. The first Texas state geologist, Benjamin Shumard, was "one of the unwitting victims" of the Blake-Marcou controversy. See also George G. Shumard, *The Geology of*

Western Texas (Austin, Tex.: State Printing Office, 1886), 24–26 and *passim* for George Shumard's arguments with Marcou.

2. Richard Phelan, *Texas Wild* (New York: Excalibur Books, n.d.); Charles Henry Mitchell, "The Role of Water in the Settlement of the Llano Estacado" (M.A. thesis, University of Texas at Austin, 1960).

3. U.S. Dept. of Agriculture, "Soil Survey of Ector and Crane Counties, Texas" (n.p.: National Cooperative Soil Survey, Aug., 1978), 1–2.

4. Ibid., 8.

5. J. Evetts Haley, *Fort Concho and the Texas Frontier* (San Angelo, Tex.: San Angelo Standard-Times, 1952), 15. This is the definitive book by a master stylist and historian on the post and surrounding area. Two recent historians suggest variations. Patrick Dearen takes Connelly's wagons through Castle Gap, while Michael Harter of Amarillo suggests a more southern route.

6. Ibid., 16.

7. John Salmon Ford, *Rip Ford's Texas* (Austin: University of Texas Press, 1963), 122–123.

8. Robert Sidney Martin, "United States Army Mapping in Texas. 1848–50," in *The Mapping of the American Southwest*, eds. Dennis Reinhartz and Charles C. Colley (College Station: Texas A&M University Press, 1987); Robert S. Neighbors (ed.), "The Report of the Expedition of Major Robert S. Neighbors to El Paso in 1849," *Southwestern Historical Quarterly*, LX (Apr., 1957), 527–532.

9. For selected accounts see Ralph P. Bieber (ed.), *Southern Trails to California in 1849* (Glendale, Calif.: Arthur H. Clark, 1937).

10. For specific details see Haley, *Fort Concho and the Texas Frontier*, 45–52.

11. "Reminiscences of C. C. Cox," *Southwestern Historical Quarterly*, VI (Oct., 1902), 131. Cox's perception was a common view.

12. Haley, *Fort Concho and the Texas Frontier*, 52.

13. Williams, *Old Texas Trails*, 375.

14. Gunnar Brune, *Springs of Texas* (Fort Worth: Branch-Smith, 1981), 442.

15. Ibid., 443.

16. Note the 1869 sketch map by Col. Thomas B. Hunt of this area in the late 1850s. Hunt's map shows the "Staked Plains" between "Castle Mts." and "Wild China Ponds." Patrick Dearen, *Castle Gap and the Pecos Frontier* (Fort Worth: Texas Christian University Press, 1988), 45.

17. Boyd quoted in Associated Press article, "Legendary Pecos Crossing Located," *American-Statesman* (Austin), Mar. 20, 1995.

18. John R. Bartlett, *Personal Narrative of Explorations and Incidents in Texas, New Mexico, California, Sonora, and Chihuahua, Connected with the United States and Mexican Boundary Commission, During the Years 1850, '51, '52, and '53* (2 vols.; New York: Appleton, 1854), I, 90–91.

19. Ibid., I, 90.

20. Robert R. Russel, *Improvement of Communication with the Pacific Coast as an Issue in American Politics* (Cedar Rapids, Iowa: Torch Press, 1948).

21. Goetzmann, *Army Exploration in the American West*, 265–273, discusses the southern railroad interests in detail.

22. L. R. Bailey (ed.), *Survey of a Route for the Southern Pacific R.R., on the 32nd Parallel* (1856; reprint, Los Angeles, Calif.: Westernlore Press, 1963), 10.

23. Ibid., 17.

24. Ibid., 18. The 1963 reprint editor of Gray's report, the historian L. R. Bailey, did not make light of the region, heartlessly calling the Llano Estacado "the most god-forsaken wind-swept prairie known to the North American continent."

25. See the accompanying reminiscences of Peter R. Bailey in Bailey (ed.), *Survey of a Route for the Southern Pacific R.R.*, 183. Bailey's memoirs were originally serialized in the 1898 *Arizona Citizen*.

26. Ibid., 18.

27. Ibid., 21.

28. Ibid., 18.

29. The concept of timber apparently did not include small mesquites that could be locally abundant.

30. Bailey (ed.), *Survey of a Route for the Southern Pacific R.R.*, 20–21.

31. Brady's important reminiscences first appeared as a series of newspaper articles in the June 1898 *Daily Citizen* of Tucson, Arizona Territory. They were reprinted in ibid., 169–227.

32. Ibid., 179. Unable to swim the swift Pecos River, the runaway was trapped in the Sand Hills. He was allowed to recover and accompany the Gray party across the Pecos; he then stole a fine horse from Gray and disappeared, presumably onto the free soil of Mexico. How many other African Americans perished or succeeded in crossing the southern Llano Estacado cannot be determined.

33. Jim Fenton, "Desert Myth Dies Slowly on the Staked Plain, 1845–1860" *Panhandle-Plains Historical Review*, LXIII (1990), 45–74.

CHAPTER TWENTY-FOUR

1. Bvt. Capt. John Pope's "Report of Exploration of a Route for the Pacific Railroad Near the Thirty-second Parallel . . ." appeared in the *Pacific Railroad Surveys*, II, part IV.

2. Byrne's important "Diary of the Expedition" constitutes Appendix A of *Pacific Railroad Surveys*, II, part IV. See page 60 for the quotation.

3. This Hispano term for a long waterless crossing was likely acquired during the trek from Albuquerque to El Paso. This term implies an analogous perceptual link between the Llano Estacado and the Jornada del Muerto region of New Mexico.

4. Taplin's initial report is incorporated as Chapter III of Appendix A in *Pacific Railroad Surveys*, II, part IV, 73–75.

5. Ibid.

6. Ibid., 74.

7. Barton H. Warnock provides a floristic account of the Dune Lands in *Wildflowers of the Guadalupe Mountains and the Sand Dune Country, Texas* (Alpine: Sul Ross State University, 1974), xxv–xxvi, 15–16.

8. Taplin in *Pacific Railroad Surveys*, II, part IV, 74. This reddish "sea" was possibly vast stretches of switchgrass.

9. Ibid., 75.

10. This unidentified "Mexican" illustrates once again the army's effective use of Hispanos as perceptual guides to the region.

11. Taplin in *Pacific Railroad Surveys*, II, part IV, 75.

12. Patrick Dearen discusses the many entertaining legends and myths of the "Lost Wagon Train" in *Castle Gap and the Pecos Frontier*, 111–129. In this chapter Dearen discusses the geosophy of these fragments, leading to legends of buried treasure and Indian massacres at "Willow Springs."

13. Byrne in *Pacific Railroad Surveys*, II, part IV, Appendix A, 71.

14. Ibid., 71.

15. Aldo Leopold, "The Virgin Southwest (1933)," *Orion*, X (Winter, 1991), 21. Note that Peter Warshall describes other factors for arroyo-cutting in his article "The Not-So-Virgin Southwest," 24–25, in the same issue of *Orion*.

16. Byrne in *Pacific Railroad Surveys*, II, part IV, Appendix A, 72. See also "Agricultural Capacities of Western Texas," *De Bow's Review*, XVIII (Jan., 1855), 54–55.

17. Ibid.

18. Ibid., 79.

19. Ibid.

20. *Pacific Railroad Surveys*, II, part IV, 8.

21. Ibid., II, part IV, 9

22. Ibid., II, part iv, chapter VI, 36.

23. Since Pope had no geologist on his reconnaissance, he first arranged for Marcou to write a

brief report based on his field notes and Captain Taplin's specimens. Later William Blake assumed the duty.

24. *Pacific Railroad Surveys*, II, part IV, chapter VI, 36.
25. Ibid., 35–36.
26. Goetzmann, *Exploration and Empire*, 274.
27. Ibid., 292–293.
28. George Perkins Marsh both lectured before the Smithsonian in 1854–1855 and wrote an 1856 book on the camel's potential in the West. See Albert H. Greenly, *Camels in America* (New York: Bibliographical Society of America, 1952), 5; and Chris Emmett, *Texas Camel Tales* (San Antonio: Baylor Publishers, 1932).
29. Goetzmann, *Exploration and Empire*, 274.
30. Goetzmann, *Army Exploration*, 366.
31. George G. Shumard, *The Geology of Western Texas* (Austin, Tex.: State Printing Office, 1886), 21.
32. Ibid., 367.
33. Webb, Carroll, and Branda (eds.), *Handbook of Texas*, II, 392.
34. See George G. Shumard, *A Partial Report on the Geology of Western Texas* . . . (Austin, Tex.: State Printing Office, 1886), 88. This work published his 1855–56 journal of geological observations. Actually the caprock was quite distant but Shumard and Pope considered that the Llano extended almost to the banks of the Pecos River.
35. This 1856 letter was republished in George G. Shumard, "Artesian Water on the Llano Estacado," *Geological Survey of Texas, Bulletin no. 1* (Austin, Tex.: State Printing Office, 1892).
36. Capt. John Pope, "Letter . . . to Hon. T. J. Rusk in relation to Artesian Wells in Texas and New Mexico" (Washington, D.C.: Towers Printers, 1856).
37. Ibid., 4–5.
38. Ibid., 5.
39. Goetzmann, *Army Exploration*, 365.
40. Corps of Topographical Engineers, Old Army Section, Record Group 77, United States National Archives, Washington, D.C. Microfilmed copy of "Selected Letters—Received" books from 1840 to 1860.
41. For Pope's cotton fields, see Herman Viola, *Exploring the West* (Washington, D.C.: Smithsonian Institution Press, 1987), 114–115. Viola also reproduces the intriguing colored Pope sketch, "Section of Artesian Well."
42. "Selected Letters—Received," July 2, 1858, "Monthly report and also report of freshwater springs found on the summit of the Llano Estacado . . . ," Corps of Topographical Engineers, Old Army Section, Record Group 77, Microfilm Disk No. 2.
43. Haley, *Fort Concho and the Texas Frontier*, 63–66.
44. Waterman L. Ormsby in *Butterfield Overland Mail*, eds. L. H. Wright and J. M. Bynum (San Marino, Calif.: Huntington Library, 1942), 65–67.
45. Ibid.
46. Ibid., 66. This was likely exaggeration. The Leach Wagon Train of 1857 reported no human bones on this stretch. On September 28 the Leach Train reported: "This portion of country we found extremely sterile and desolate. . . . We continued our course over this stretch of desert, for such it may with propriety be termed." See the journal in J. W. Williams, *Old Texas Trails*, ed. and comp. Kenneth F. Neighbors (Austin, Tex.: Eakin Press, 1979), 352.
47. Haley, *Fort Concho and the Texas Frontier*, 92–96.
48. See chapter 2 in G. Edward White, *The Eastern Establishment and the Western Experience* (Austin: University of Texas Press, 1989). Note that the 1866 map *Johnson's Texas* indicated the Llano Estacado with the daunting annotation that it is "without wood or water."
49. Robert E. Lee's subordinate, Capt. Earl Van Dorn, left Fort Phantom Hill in 1856 to reconnoiter the eastern flank area of the Llano Estacado over the summer. J. Evetts Haley, *Fort Concho and the Texas Frontier* (San Angelo, Tex.: San Angelo *Standard-Times*, 1952), 64–65.

Chapter Twenty-Five

1. Skeat, *An Etymological Dictionary of the English Language*, 337; Mariano Velázquez, *New Revised Velázquez Spanish and English Dictionary* (Chicago: Follett, 1967), 435.

2. José Rabasa, *Inventing America: Spanish Historiography and the Foundation of Eurocentrism* (Norman: University of Oklahoma Press, 1993); David Lowenthal and M. J. Bowden, *Geographies of the Mind: Essays in Historical Geography in Honor of John Kirtland Wright* (New York: Oxford University Press, 1976); Frederick Turner, *Beyond Geography: The Western Spirit Against the Wilderness* (New York: Viking Press, 1980); and Cosgrove and Daniels (eds.), *The Iconography of Landscape*.

3. Wayne Franklin discusses the discovery, exploration, and settlement narrative forms, primarily for the East Coast, in *Discoverers, Explorers, Settlers: The Diligent Writers of Early America* (Chicago: University of Chicago Press, 1989).

4. Cooper, *The Plains*.

5. Carl Coke Rister reprints the rare captivity narrative of Sarah Ann Horn in *Comanche Bondage* (Glendale, Calif.: Arthur H. Clark, 1955). Sarah Ann Horn spent many days on the Llano, but her comments rarely relate to the environment in a recognizable way.

6. Exceptional studies of the problems of representation in Western narrative literature include Erich Auerbach, *Mimesis* (Cambridge, Mass.: Belknap Press of Harvard University Press, 1946); Walker Percy, *The Message in the Bottle* (New York: Farrar, Straus & Giroux, 1975); and Robert Scholes and Robert Kellogg, *The Nature of Narrative* (New York: Oxford University Press, 1975).

7. Castañeda's rediscovery is examined in chapter 3 of the present work; Cabeza de Vaca's *La Relación* first appeared in French in 1837, in German in 1839, and in English in 1851, with Buckingham Smith's translation of the 1555 edition. The Washington, D.C., publisher George Riggs issued only 110 copies of Smith's translation. Jenkins, *Basic Texas Books*, 60–61.

8. Hayden White, *Metahistory: The Historical Imagination in Nineteenth-Century Europe* (Baltimore, Md.: John Hopkins University Press, 1973).

9. J. Evetts Haley, "Lore of the Llano Estacado," in *Texas and Southwestern Lore*, vol. VI, ed. J. Frank Dobie (Austin: Texas Folklore Society, 1927), 72–89

10. John, *Storms Brewed in Other Men's Worlds*.

11. Thomas Maitland Marshall, "Commercial Aspects of the Texan Santa Fé Expedition," *Southwestern Historical Quarterly*, XX (Jan., 1917), 242–259.

12. Kenner, *The Comanchero Frontier*, 78–97; Rupert Norval Richardson, *The Comanche Barrier to South Plains Settlement* (Glendale, Calif.: Arthur H. Clark, 1933), 308–312; Herman H. Moncus, *Prairie Schooner Pirates* (New York: Carlton Press, 1963); Rister, *The Southwestern Frontier*, 85–86.

13. Pike, *Prose Sketches and Poems*, 37, 40–43; Abert, "Report," 53; Gregg, *Commerce of the Prairies*, 147, 257, and *passim*; Kendall, *Narrative*, 88–90; Whipple, *Pacific Railroad Surveys*, III, 31–38; Marcy, "Report," H. Exec. Doc. 45, 31st Cong., 1st Sess., 41–42.

14. Clarence J. Glacken, *Traces on the Rhodian Shore* (Berkeley: University of California Press, 1967).

15. The diffusion of horses to the Comanche is traced in Noyes, *Los Comanches*, xxiii–xxvi.

16. Webb, *The Great Plains*, 85–87. Note Webb's tendency to understate Spanish exploration and adaptability to the plains environment: "The result was that the Spaniards never did more than nibble around the margins of the Great Plains," 87.

17. Rabasa, *Inventing America*.

18. Tyler, *Prints of the West*, 5.

19. Tyler notes that Ackerman sold sets at two cents per lithograph in 1853, followed by a further sale of sets at 1.8 cents each. Ibid., 103.

20. Bernard Smith, *European Visions and the South Pacific* (New Haven, Conn.: Yale University Press, 1988), 181.

21. Hartshorne characterized a region by its distinctiveness of landform, cultural history, climate, and settlements, criteria applicable to the Llano. See R. Hartshorne, *Perspectives on the Nature of Geography* (Chicago, Ill.: Rand McNally, 1969), 130–132.

22. Yi-Fu Tuan discusses the environmental perception of New Mexican "explorers and settlers at the pioneer fringe" in *Topophilia*, 66–70.

23. H. Bailey Carroll, "Characteristic Similarities of Expeditions into the Great Plains," *Panhandle-Plains Historical Review*, X (1937), 21–35.

24. Retranslated from the Spanish quoted in Kenner, *The Comanchero Frontier*, 106. See the English translation by Lorin W. Brown (ed.), "Manuel Maes," Manuscript Collection (CL-1057) (New Mexico Historical Museum Library; Santa Fé, N.Mex.).

25. From the Spanish in Winship, "The Coronado Expedition," 178. A *señal* is a sign, mark, or token, such as a landmark stake that marks a boundary.

26. Bryan Jay Wolf, *Romantic Re-Vision: Culture and Consciousness in Nineteenth-Century American Painting and Literature* (Chicago: University of Chicago Press, 1982). Note that the mystery emerges from the gap between signifier and referrant.

27. Goetzmann, *Exploration and Empire*, 332–348.

28. Ibid., 334. Goetzmann traces the concept back to DaVinci and Vauban.

29. See map by Enrico Martínez (1602), page 140.

30. One of Pope's schematic drawings of an artesian well is reproduced in Viola, *Exploring the West*, 114.

31. Karl W. Butzer, "From Columbus to Acosta: Science, Geography, and the New World," in "The Americas before and after 1492: Current Geographical Research," *Annals of the Association of American Geographers*, LXXXII (Sept., 1992), 543–565, quotation from 543.

32. Edward Relph, "Geographical Experiences and Being-in-the-World: The Phenomenological Origins of Geography," in Seaman and Mugerauer (eds.), *Dwelling, Place, Environment*, 16. Relph notes that Heidegger's term for wonder was "marvelling," reflecting an admiration of the earth.

33. For distinctions between dissociative and associative discourse in the settlement of the West, see Malcolm Lewis, "Rhetoric of the Western Interior," in Cosgrove and Daniels (eds.), *The Iconography of Landscape*, 182–184.

34. Della I. Young identifies this loric process and gives many Anglo-American examples for the Panhandle (Elk Creek, Wolf Creek, Red Deer Creek, Wild Horse Lake, etc.) in "Names in the Old Cheyenne and Arapahoe Territory and the Texas Panhandle," in Dobie (ed.), *Texas and Southwestern Lore*, 90–97. Something particular in the environmental context was often selected as a distinguishing attribute. The properties of water were very important. The wrangler Jim Fulton named Croton Creek for the cathartic nature of the water, while Charles Dietrich made his celebrated sourdough bread from a nearby gyppy creek, leading to the toponym Sour Dough Creek.

35. "Texas toponyms," Jordan notes, "reinforce Anglo mythology." Terry G. Jordan, "The Anglo-Texan Homeland," *Journal of Cultural Geography*, XIII (Spring/Summer, 1993), 77. See also Frank Hill, "Plains Names," *Panhandle-Plains Historical Review*, X (1937), 36–47.

36. Walter Benjamin, *Illuminations*, ed. Hannah Arendt (New York: Schocken, 1968), 84–106. See Robert Mugerauer's views on "authentic meaning" in Seaman and Mugerauer (eds.), "Language and the Emergence of the Environment," in *Dwelling, Place, and Environment*, 51–70. For a critique of the primacy of the linguistic model in Structuralism, see Frederic Jameson, *The Prison-House of Language* (Princeton, N.J.: Princeton University Press, 1972).

37. José Cortes, *Views from the Apache Frontier: Report on the Northern Provinces of New Spain*, ed. Elizabeth A. H. John, trans. John Wheat (Norman: University of Oklahoma Press, 1989), 81–82, 137.

38. "Mesas and bluffs and hills, rivers and springs, the vast plains themselves could be the homes of spirits, each with its power." Noyes, *Los Comanches*, 29.

39. Richardson, *The Comanche Barrier to South Plains Settlement*.

Index

(Illustrations are indicated by boldfaced page numbers)

A

Abert, Lt. James W.: expedition of, 252, 253–259, 263, 270; perceptual approach of, 7, 327, 331, 333, 335, 339
Abert, Col. John J.: 253, 318, 321
Abilene, Texas: Coronado's route near, 68, 98
Ackerman, James: illustrates Marcy's report, 266, 267, **268**, 270, **271**, 272, **273**, **275**, 277, 333
Adams-Oñis Treaty: and Red River explorations, 200
Adobe Walls: comanchero trade at, 330; Whipple at, 284
Adrian, Texas: Gregg at, 224; Marcy at, 261
Agabo, Captain: with Amangual, 181
Agnese, Batista: Llano cartography of, 149–150
Agreda, María de Jesús de: as "Lady in Blue," 143–145, 148, 331, 336
agriculture: at Quivira, 78, 95–96, 111; in Blanco Canyon, 78–79; in the Cow Nation, 15; effect on playas, 123; in Rio Grande Valley, 96; of Teyas, 78, 85
Agua Corriente: buffalo hunters at, 158; drains Blanco Canyon, 76; identification of, 54; naming of, 191
Agua de Piedra Creek: Whipple on, 293
Agua Dulce: naming of, 191
Agua Frio Draw. *See* Frio Draw
Agua Negra: naming of, 184
Aguas Zarcas: Bonilla-Humaña expedition and, 138; Franciscans name, 137
A-Hope-Ho-Nope. See Middle Concho River
Alamagordo Creek: naming of, 191
Alamosa Canyon: comanchero route at, 189; Coronado's route at, 104, 105
Alamosa Creek: comanchero route at, 189; Whipple at, 293
Alba de Liste, Viceroy Count de: and Guadalajara expedition, 146
Albuquerque, New Mexico: Coronado pageant in, 39; Franciscan mission at, 144; trading expeditions from, 146; Whipple at, 297
Alibates flint deposits: 257
Allen, Joe: 303
Allen, John L.: 165, 220
Alvarado, Capt. Hernando: and El Turco, 111; expedition of, 19–21, 23, 25, 32, 44, 54, 71, 112
Alzate y Ramirez, José: Llano map of, 153, 200
Amangual, Francisco: diary of, 6, 333; expedition of, 179–182, **180** (map), 329; and naming of Llano Estacado, 165; Vial encounters, 178
Amarillo, Texas: buffalo near, 159; comanchero route near, 190; Coronado's route at, 42; Gregg at, 225; Whipple at, 286–287

Amarillo Creek: Amangual expedition at, 181; Whipple on, 287
Anaya, Rudolfo: 1
Anderson, Capt. Allen: map of, and Comanche trail, 188–189
Anderson, Clinton: 39
Andrews County (Texas): Martin-Castillo expedition in, 146
Antelope Buttes: Abert at, 259
Antelope Creek: naming of, 266
Antelope Hills: Whipple expedition near, 281
Antillia, Seven Golden Cities of: 17, 21
Anton Chico, New Mexico: Coronado's route at, 26, 31–32; and Spanish penetration of Llano, 184, 189
Apache Canyon: Texan–Santa Fé Expedition in, 238
Apache Indians: as buffalo hunters, 157; and Comanches, 160, 171, 173; Coronado encounters, 29–30; dog travois of, 137, **138**; and early Llano cartography, 151, 152–153; hunting and gathering of, 139; Salas-León expedition and, 145; Spanish expeditions encounter, 138; Spanish trade with, 188; trade of, 138. *See also* Querecho Indians; Vaquero Indians
archeology: of Blanco Canyon, 25, 76, **77** (map), 85; Clovis projectile points, 13, 98; Coronado artifacts, 90–93, 114–115, 337; Garza Complex, 74, 78, 79, 82, 85, 91, 93, 109; and location of Quivira, 108; pictographs, 179, 293, 301; and playas, 124
Archivo General de Simancas (Spain): 171
Arch Lake: Coronado's route at, 103–104, 105
Arctic exploration: 250–251, 261
Arellano, Don Tristán de: at Cona, 85, 86, 89; Castañeda with, 118; return journey to Tiguex, 96–106, **101** (map), 110, 113
Arenal: Indian rebels at, ment., 24
Arizona: Coronado pageant in, 39; Coronado's route in, 36, 119
Arkansas: and gold rush, 259, 261
Arkansas Post: and French trade corridor, 169, 170, 171
Arkansas River: contrabandista trade on, 170; Coronado's route to, 107–112; French trade on, 167; Long expedition on, 203; Mallet expedition on, 168, 169, 170; Melgares expedition on, 178; Oñate on, 143
Armstrong County (Texas): canyons in, 127
Arrington, Capt. G. W.: in Blanco Canyon, 93
Arrocha, Juan José: Comanche trade of, 188
Arrowsmith, John: Le Grand and Llano maps of, 213, 215, **216**, 219–220, **221**, 324
Arroyo Alamogordo: Coronado's route at, 32

Arroyo de Gallinas: naming of, 190
Arroyo del Puerto: Coronado's route at, 27, 47; Vial-Fragoso-Fernandez expedition at, 175
Arroyo de Trujillo: naming of, 184
Arroyo Piedra: naming of, 190
Arroyo San Juan de Dios: Coronado's route at, 32
art: as category of exploration, 326, 332–333, 336, 337–339; Coronado romanticized in, 39–40, 42, 59–60, 61; from Red River expedition, **268, 269, 271, 272, 273, 275, 276**; Indian pictographs, 179, 293, 301; Möllhausen and Whipple expedition, **281, 282, 283, 285, 287, 295**; Schuchard lithograph, **307, 308**; and Spanish cartography, 337; S. Rosa and Llano perception, 232, 238, 246, 332; Whipple's sketches, **289, 292, 294**; woodcut from Bartlett's *Narrative*, **302**
Atascosa: naming of, 191
Audubon, John W.: C. Webber and, 248
Austin, Texas: Coronado's route at, 43; forty-niners route from, 300; route to Santa Fé from, 230
Avavare Indians: Cabeza de Vaca and, 14
Axa: on early maps, 150–151, 153
Aztec Indians: gold of, 16; Parcheesi-like game of, 86

B

Baca, Julian: Llano trade of, 183, 192
Back, George: 250
Bailey County (Texas): salt lakes in, 101, 102
Baird, Spencer F.: and Red River expedition, 266
Bancroft, H. H.: and Coronado's route, 37
Bandelier, Adolph Francis: and Coronado's route, 37
Barbero Canyon: Coronado in, 25
Barranca Creek: Coronado at, 27
Barranca Grande: Blanco Canyon as, 92; Coronado in, 56, 60–74
Barreiro, Antonio: on buffalo harvest, 156
Barreiro, Francisco Alvarez: map by, **152**
Bartlett, John R.: at Horsehead Crossing, 303; and boundary dispute, 305; Gray and, 309; on Upper Road, 304; woodcut from *Narrative*, **302**
Barton, Lucy: 39
Beales, John Charles: and Le Grand survey, 214–215, 217, 218, **219**
Beall, Dr.: with Texan–Santa Fé Expedition, 237
Beaurain: 151; map ment., 331
Beauvillier: 152
Beaver River: Coronado's route at, 110, 112
Beltrán, Fray Bernaldino: rescue mission of, 137–138
Benavides, Fray Alonso de: and "Lady in Blue," 144
Benjamin, Walter: 341
Bent, St. Vrain & Co.: 284
Bent's Fort: Abert expedition leaves, 253
"Bent's Post": Whipple at, 284
Bernalillo, New Mexico: Coronado's route at, 24, 31; Rodríguez expedition near, 137
Bienville, Governor: and French trade route, 169

Bigelow, Dr. John Milton: with Whipple expedition, 279, 280, 284, 290–291, 295–296
Bigotes (Indian guide): 18–21, 24, 46, 54, 106, 111
Big Salt Lake. *See* Great Salt Lake
Big Sandy Creek: primitive area along, 82
Big Spring: R. E. Lee at, 322; Marcy at, 263, 267, 301; naming of, 267; Pope at, 314
Big Spring, Texas: Cabeza de Vaca near, 14; and extent of the Llano, 299
Billy the Kid: on Pecos River, 105
bison. *See* buffalo
Black Beaver (Delaware Indian): 260
Blackwater Draw: A. Pike at, 209; Coronado's route at, 30, 47–48, 105; and playa formation, 122; salt lakes near, 99
Blake, Thomas: 86
Blake, William P.: and the Jurassic controversy, 296–297, 337; and Whipple expedition, 281, 282
Blakeslee, Donald: and Blanco Canyon archeology, 91, 93
Blanco Canyon: agriculture in, 78–79; archeology of, 25, 76, **77** (map), 91, 93; buffalo hunting in, 79–80, 158; Cona in, 74, 75–93, 97–99, 102, 108–109; Coronado in, 25, 56, 70, 106; described, 75–76; ecosystems, modern alterations, 79; naming of, 190, 340; native plant foods of, 80–85; pottery of, 85; Spanish artifacts in, 90–93; Texas Rangers in, 93; Vial in, 177–178
Blaque, Tomas: 86
"Blue River". *See* Middle Concho River
Bluff Creek: naming of, 267
Bolton, Herbert E.: on Cicúye, 19; on Coronado's route, 25, 27, 40, 42, 46, 66, 68, 69, 70, 72, 78, 79, 98, 102, 108, 109; on "Staked Plains," 155, 162–163
Bonilla-Humaña entrada: 138
Bonita Creek: Whipple on, 283
Bosque Redondo: buffalo hunters at, 157, 159; comanchero route at, 188; Coronado's route at, 105; gold prospectors at, 164; Navajos confined at, 192
Boyd, Bill: 303
Boy Hunters; or, Adventures in Search of a White Buffalo, The: 247
Brackenridge, H. M.: and Coronado's route, 36
Brady, Peter: 306
Brandon, William: on Coronado's route, 40, 42; on "Lady in Blue," 145
Brazos River: A. Pike at, 210; Coronado's route at, 40, 68, 70, 87; Kendall on source of, 232; Le Grand on, 215; Marcy on, 263; Mares-Santos-Martín expedition on, 174; meteorite on, 200; northern tributaries of, 76; and Ogallala Aquifer, 129; Vial on, 177; on Z. Pike's map, 200
Brice, Texas: dead soils at, 129
Briscoe County (Texas): canyons in, 127; Coronado's route in, 55, 60, 69, 71, 72–73; Texan–Santa Fé Expedition in, 237

Brushy Creek: Texan–Santa Fé Expedition at, 230
Bruyére, André Fabry de la: expedition of, 169
Bryan, Lt. Francis: on Upper Road, 300
buffalo: Alvarado describes, 20; Amangual encounters, 181; Apaches hunt, 157; bison-hide parasols of Kwahadi, 173; bison robes as wealth, 61; bone graveyard, 102–103, 104; buffalo plains, on early maps, 150, 153–154; Cabeza de Vaca describes, 13–14; Cabeza de Vaca's bison robe, 12, 15, 16, 18; Castañeda describes, 18, 28, 128–129; Coronado encounters, 28, 30, 46, 48; fire used to manage, 13; Jumanos hunt, 62; Llano trails, 52, 56, 88, 129–130, 224; López encounters, 51–52; Maldonado encounters hunters, 55; mirage created by, 120, 130, 227; Oñate encounters, 142, 143; and playa formation, 122; Rodríguez encounters, 137; Spanish hunt, 28–29, 86–89, 98, 103, 137, 139; Spanish reports of, 18–21; Texan–Santa Fé Expedition hunts, 235–236; Teyas hunt, 76, 79; trade products from, 19, 158; woodcut, **34**, 35, 338; Zaldivar and, 139, 331. *See also* ciboleros
Bull Lake: among Coronado's "Lost Lakes," 100
Burke, Edmund: 239
Burr, David H.: map of, 218, 220
Burton, Richard: 246, 266
"Bury Me Not on the Lone Prairie" (song): 2
Bushman, John (Delaware Indian): 267, 271
Bustamante, Pedro de: Declaration of, 135, 137
Butterfield Overland Mail: 303, 322–323
Byrne, J. H.: with Pope expedition, 312, 313–316
Byron, Lord: 250

C

Caballero, Lope de: native wife of, 86
Cabello, Governor: and Vial-Chaves expedition, 171
Cabeza de Baca, Fabiola: on Llano sheep trade, 186; on Llano vastness, 184, 325; recalls cibolero stories, 159–160, 193
Cabeza de Vaca, Alvar Núñez: bison robe of, 12, 15, 16, 18; Cow Nation of, 5, 9–21, 54; and Fr. Rodríguez's expedition, 136; lack of greed of, 61; *La Relación* of, 12–13, 328, 340; and Llano exploration, 12–17; minerals collected by, 12; quoted, 9; "river of nuts" of, 69; route of, 13, 14–16
Cabra Spring: naming of, 184
Cacique (Indian guide): 18–21, 24, 106, 111
Caddoan Indians: Teyas and, 78
California: and early Llano cartography, 150, 151, 153; geographers locate Llano in, 61; gold rush, and Llano exploration, 27, 259–261, 300–304; Llano trade with, 85
camels: imported to W. Texas, 318, 335
Camisa de Hierro. *See* Ironshirt (Comanche chief)
Campbell, A. H.: 208, 280
Camp Comanche: Gregg at, 223
Camp Resolution: Texan–Santa Fé Expedition at, 232
Camp Roberts: Texas Rangers establish, 93

Cañada de Tule: Coronado's route at, 104–105
Canadian, Texas: Coronado's route at, 110
Canadian River: Abert at, 253–259; A. Lewis at, 206; Bonilla-Humaña expedition at, 138; buffalo hunters at, 156, 159, 161, 162, 181–182; Carson at, 342; comanchero route at, 190; Cona on, 68, 70, 83, 87; Coronado at, 25–26, 27, 32, 40, 42, 45, 47, 110, 112; forty-niners trail on, 259–261; Gregg at, 223–226, **225** (map), 259; Mallet expedition at, 168–169; Marcy at, 260; Melgares at, 178; Oñate at, 141–143; origin of name, 254–256; Quivira on, 108; and Red River explorations, 197, 200; Rodríguez at, 137; as romantic literary locale, 248, 249; sand hills on, 143, 256, 259, 260, 266; Spanish sheep-herders on, 186–187; Texan–Santa Fé Expedition and, 231, 236; Vial at, 172, 178; Whipple at, 280, **281**, 282, **283**, 284–286; Zaldivar at, 138–139
Cañon Blanco. *See* Blanco Canyon
Cañoncito Blanco: Coronado's route in, 56; naming of, 190
Cañon del Rescate: comanchero route in, 188
Canyon, Texas: Coronado's route at, 42, 60
Canyon of Ransom. *See* Cañon del Rescate
Caprock: formation of, 127; Spanish name *La Ceya*, 184, 208
Caprock Canyonlands: 100, 277
Caprock Canyons State Park: badlands of, 73; dead soils of, 129; Mares-Santos-Martín expedition at, 174
Caprock Girl Scout Council: at Blanco Canyon, 82
Cárdenas, Capt. Don García Lopéz de: account of, 44, 127–128; at Cona, 86
Cargill, Jerome: 39
Carleton, Major: and Coronado's route, 36–37; and Llano trade, 330
Carroll, H. Bailey: and naming of Llano Estacado, 163–165; and Texan–Santa Fé Expedition, 230, 232, 234, 235, 239
Carson, Kit: 342
cartography: early Llano, 149–154, **152**, 188–189, 197, 200, **201**, 213, 215, **216**, 218–222, **219**, **221**, **225**, **240**, 285, 324, 331, 337
Casas Amarillas ("Yellow Houses"): naming of, 191; Obenchain at, 342
Cassidy, Gerald: romanticizes Coronado, 39–40
Castañeda, Carlos E.: on Coronado's route, 108; and "Lady in Blue," 143–144
Castañeda, Pedro de: 19th-century scholars study, 36–38; account of, and Coronado's route, 45–55, 59; account of, ment., 3, 6, 35, 44, **283**, 334, 338; background of, 118; on buffalo graveyard, 102–103, 104; and Cona, 65–68, 71, 73–74, 78, 80, 84, 86; describes buffalo, 18, 28, 130; on disorientation on Llano, 87–89; on El Turco, 30; on hailstorm, 64–65; handwriting of, **63**; as journalist, 327, 328, 335; Lennox Manuscript of account, 37–38, 46, 50, 71, 81, 333; on Llano sky, 119–121; on name for Texas, 62; on playas, 121–123, 124–126; on prairie

dogs, 100; problems with translating, 50–51, 53, 66, 71–72, 117–120, 129–130; on Querechos, 29; on geography, 9; on Llano Estacado, 23; on route to Quivira, 107; on Spanish greed, 61–62; on Tiguex journey, 96; on trees and canyons of Llano, 125–129
Castaño de Sosa, Gaspar: expedition of, 138
Castilblanco, Fray Antonio de: at Cona, 86; prays following storm, 65
Castillo, Diego del: expedition of, 145–146, 148
Castle Gap: Ford-Neighbors expedition at, 300, 301; trail through, **302**, 303
Castle Mountain. *See* Castle Gap
Castro County (Texas): Coronado's route in, 54
Catholic Church, the: and Llano theography, 136, 330
cattle trade and trails: 192
Central American Flyway: and Llano playas, 124
Centralia Station: Butterfield trail at, 323
Ceya. *See La Ceya*
Chamuscado: with Fr. Rodríguez, 135–137
Channing, Edward: and Coronado's route, 37
Charles V: Coronado's letter to, 45, 55, 95, 107; and New World exploration, 9–12
Chaves, Francisco Xavier: expedition of, 171–172
Chaves, Geronimo: 151
Chavez, Fray Angelico: and Coronado's route, 25; and naming of Llano Estacado, 164
Cherisco Mesa: naming of, 184
Chicken Creek: naming of, 266
Chihuahua, Mexico: Comanche War Trail to, 303; Llano trail to, 186, 300; silver mines in, 135, 158
Childe Harold's Pilgrimage: 250
China Draw: Ford-Neighbors expedition at, 301
Chipman, Donald E.: on Cabeza de Vaca, 14, 15
Cíbola: Coronado expedition on Plains of, 23–30; on early maps, 149–151; food sources at, 71; Fr. Marcos account of, 17; in legend, 17; location of, 36; narratives compiled, 35; Oñate on Plains of, 142–143; origin of word, 142
ciboleros: and the "Agua Corriente," 54; Amangual follows trail of, 181–182; annual harvest of, 156; and Cona, 79–80; El Cuate remembers, 159–160, 161, 193; and geographic perception of the Llano, 154; hunt tactics, 159, 161–162; and linguistic identity of the Llano, 162; Llano trade and trails of, 188, 189, 190, 193, 224, 226, 330; and naming of Llano Estacado, 164; organization and description of Spanish, 155–166; rituals of, 160, 335; Vial with, 178, 181
Cicúye: Alvarado-Padilla expedition at, 19–21; Coronado at, 24–25, 31, 106; and El Turco, 46; and Llano cartography, 153; location of, 36, 43, 60–61; Quivira expedition's return to, 112; Teya trade with, 97, 104; trade route at, 30
Cimarron County (Oklahoma): Coronado's route in, 112
Cimarron River: Coronado's route on, 110, 112; Oñate on, 143

Cita Canyon: Texan–Santa Fé Expedition at, 234–235, 239
Civilian Conservation Corps: and Coronado's route, 61; Silver Falls improvements, 82
Civil War, the: and Llano exploration, 323–324, 342
Clarendon, Texas: Coronado's route at, 110
Clovis, New Mexico: Coronado's route at, 32
Clovis people: artifacts of, 98, 124; and buffalo, 13
Coahuiltecan Indians: Cabeza de Vaca and, 13, 14
Cochran County (Texas): bison site in, 103
Coke County (Texas): Guadalajara expedition in, 146
Coleman County (Texas): Coronado's route in, 70
Colima (Mexico): Llano Estacado compared to, 59
Colonial Dames of America: and Coronado's route, 112
Colonias, New Mexico: Coronado's route at, 26–27, 106
Colorado and Red River Land Company: map by, 218, **219**
Colorado River: Coronado's route on, 43, 44, 70, 87, 89; and extent of the Llano, 299; Kendall on source of, 232; Le Grand on, 215; Marcy on, 263; Mares-Santos-Martín expedition on, 174; and Ogallala Aquifer, 129; pearls of, 146; as River of Nuts, 145; on Z. Pike's map, 200
Columbus: and Quivira, ment., 24
Comanche Indians: Abert and, 253, 257; Apaches and, 160, 171, 173; Arrocha and, 188; at Big Spring, 263; fires set by, 209; Ford-Neighbors expedition and, 300; and French contraband trade, 187; Gregg and, 224, 226; horses of, 165, 210, 226; Le Grand and, 222; Llano trail of, Marcy maps, 188; Mallet expedition and, 168–169; Mares-Santos-Martín expedition and, 174; name for Red River, 270, **276**; as noble savage, 248; and perception of the Llano Estacado, 3, 179, 323, 340, 341; A. Pike and, 208, 210; rancherías of, **176** (map), 177; and Spanish buffalo hunters, 156, 158, 160–161, 162; Spanish peace mission to, 162, 170–172, 183, 187, 330; Vial and, 175–178; War Trail of, 262, 301, 303, 313; Whipple/Möllhausen and, 281, 286, **287**, 333. *See also* comancheros
____, Kotsoteka: and Spanish trade, 187, 188
____, Kwahadi: buffalo hunters and, 161; roam Comanchería, 173; Spanish trade with, 187, 188
____, Yamparika: Amangual and, 179, 181; Spanish trade with, 187, 188; Vial and, 172–173
Comanche Orientals: French trade with, 170; Spanish trade with, 172; Vial and, 171
Comanchería: Beales grant in, 214; buffalo hunting in, 161; effect of comanchero trade on, 330; French and Spanish trails through, 167–182, **176** (map), **180** (map); hostile Comanche tribes on, 173; Melgares in, 178; New Mexican trade with, 187; Nolan in, 199
comancheros: Abert follows trail, 256–257; and the Agua Corriente, 54; Fonda follows trail of, 213,

Index • 401

214; Llano trade of, 161, 162, **185** (map), 186–193, 329–330, 335; and naming of Llano Estacado, 164, **185** (map), 342; A. Pike follows trail, 208, 209; Pueblo Indians and, 190; and Texan–Santa Fé Expedition, 236–238; Whipple and, 284–285, 293

Commerce of the Prairies: 223, 225, 226, 228, 329

Compostela: Coronado at, 26

Cona: breaking camp at, 96; Castañeda on, 65–66; first mention of, 66; food clues to location of, 67–74, 80–85, 80–81 (table), 78; location of, 6, 42, 43, 44, 59–74, 75–93, 97–99, 101–102, 108–109; route to Pecos River from, 105; route to Quivira from, 106–111; Spanish hunt buffalo from, 86–89; Spanish women at, 86

Concho River: buffalo hunters on, 162; Cabeza de Vaca on, 14, 44; Cona on, 68; Coronado's route on, 43, 129; Martin-Castillo expedition in, 146; naming of, 147; Spanish raiding parties on, 135. *See also* Middle Concho River; North Concho River

Connelly, Dr. Henry: Chihuahua trail of, 300, **302**

Coofor Pueblo: Coronado's route at, 24, 31, 106

Cooke, Capt. James: 250, 261

Cooke, William G.: with Texan–Santa Fé Expedition, 232–237

Coons's Ranch: forty-niners at, 301

Cooper, Isaac: with Abert, 243, 254, 258–259, 327, 332, 337

Corazones: native revolt at, 113

Coronado, Francisco Vázquez de: abandons expedition, 113; archeological artifacts of, 90–93, 114–115, 337; Cicúye reconnaissance, 24–25, 31, 106; commemorative stamp, 39; composition of expedition soldiers, 86; death of, 113–114; discoveries of, and Llano cartography, 149–151; exploration narrative of, 328, 333, 335; *fata morgana* of, 5, 130, 335; 400th anniversary of expedition celebrated, 38–39; grave of, 35; in hailstorm, 64–65, 92; historical results of expedition, 114; injured in fall, 113; and J. Wright's categories of imagining, 5; letter to Charles V, 45, 55, 95, 107; location and building of his bridge, 25–26, 32, 40, 42, 46, 105–106; 19th- and 20th-century rediscovery of, 31–44; nutritional distress of expedition, 95–97, 100, 105; publication of expedition documents, 35; Quivira expedition, size, 24; quoted, on Llano Estacado, 23; romanticized in art, 39–40, 42, 59–60, 61; surviving expedition accounts, 44; surviving letters of, 44; and the term "Llano Estacado," 162–163; tried for misconduct, 33, 113; women with, 86. *See also* Castañeda, Pedro de; El Turco (Indian guide)

_____, route of: Arellano's return to Tiguex, 96–106, **101** (map); Bancroft on, 37; Bandelier on, 37; Bolton on, 25, 27, 40, 42, 46, 66, 68, 69, 70, 72, 78, 79, 98, 102, 108, 109; Brackenridge on, 36; Brandon on, 40, 42; C. Castañeda on, 108; contemporary accounts analyzed, 45–57; Davis on, 37; Day on, 40, 43, 70; DeGolyer on, 68, 70; Donoghue on, 40, 59, 68, 70, 108; food resources as clues to, 67–74, 78; four main corridors for, 40, 42–44; Hallenbeck on, 14; Hammond and Rey on, 39, 50, 72, 119, 126, 129; Hodge on, 43, 70, 101; Holden on, 42–43, 70, 102; Kessell on, 6; Kiser on, 102, 103; Llano canyonlands and, 56–57; location of Cona and, 59–74, 75–93; map, **41, 52**; ment., 2, 5–6; popularization of, 38; R. and S. Flint on, 25, 92; Sauer on, 42, 66, 70, 78, 80, 81; Schoolcraft on, 36; Schroeder on, 25, 40, 42, 70; Simpson on, 70; Swanton on, 25, 40; to Quivira, 23–30, 65–68, 85, 106–113; Udall on, 43, 69, 70, 101; Wagstaff on, 68; Wedel on, 25, 40, 70, 102; Williams on, 43, 59, 68–70, 81, 83, 101; Winship on, 31, 37–38, 43, 44, 50, 66, 68, 70, 71–72, 78, 101, 117, 118–120, 125, 129

Coronado, Knight of Pueblos and Plains: 40, 66, 162

Coronado Project: 1995, 92, 93

Coronado's Children: 31

Coronado's Quest: 40, 43

Coronelli, V. M.: Llano map of, 151

Corps of Topographical Engineers: Llano explorations of, 202; 252, 253, 266, 280, 311, 318, 322, 329, 331. *See also* railroads; U.S. Army

Correll, Donovan S.: 84

Cortés, Hernando: Mendoza sees as rival, 17; Mexican conquest, ment., 9; rumors of gold as impetus to, 16

cowboys: on Llano Estacado, song inspired by, 2

Cow Nation: Cabeza de Vaca and, 5, 15; Coronado in, 55; location of, 15–16; Spanish discovery of, 11–21

Cox, C. C.: 301

Coyote Lake: among Coronado's "Lost Lakes," 100; A. Pike at, 209

Crane, Texas: Horsehead Crossing near, 303

Crane County (Texas): and extent of the Llano, 299; Horsehead Crossing in, 303; rainfall in, 300

Crane County Historical Commission: and Horsehead Crossing, 303

Crosby, Alfred W.: 209

Crosby County (Texas): Brazos tributaries in, 76; White River in, 93

Crosbyton, Texas: Coronado's route at, 99

Cross Timbers: Texan–Santa Fé Expedition at, 231, 233

Cuarto Centennial: 38–39

Cuervo Creek: Coronado's route at, 32

Cuervo Mesa: Coronado's route at, 27

Cuervo Peak: naming of, 184

Cummings, W. E.: and naming of Llano Estacado, 163, 164

Curry County (New Mexico): Running Water Draw in, 54

Custis: Red River expedition of, 200

D

d'Abbeville, Nicolas Sanson: and early Llano cartography, 151

Daniel, Burl: 91, 92
Darwin, Charles: 207
Davis, Jefferson: camel experiment of, 318, 335; and the Jurassic controversy, 296; and railroad surveys, 280, 305, 311, 318
Davis, W. W. H.: on buffalo hunters, 156–157; and Coronado's route, 36–37
Day, A. Grove: and Coronado's route, 40, 43, 70
Deaf Smith County (Texas): Texan-Santa Fé Expedition in, 235, 236
De Anza, Governor: treaty with Comanches, 162, 183, 187, 330
Dease, Peter: 250
DeGolyer, Everett Lee: on location of Cona, 68
Delaware Creek: Pope on, 311–312, 319
Delaware Indians: as Marcy guides, 260, 267, 271
Delisle, G.: map ment., 151, 331
De Salas, Fray Juan: expeditions of, 145–146, 328
De Soto expedition: and early Llano cartography, 151
Diary of a Journey from the Mississippi to the Coasts of the Pacific: 282, 284, **285**, 327
Díaz, Capt. Melchior: reconnaissance of, 18
disease: introduced by Spanish, 90, 170, 171, 341
Dobie, J. Frank: Llano work of, ment., 3, 31, 83, 91
Doña Ana, New Mexico: Marcy at, 261, 262
Donoghue, David: on Coronado's route, 40, 59, 68, 70, 108
"Door of the Moon". *See* Puerto de Luna
Dorantes, Andres: with Cabeza de Vaca, 14, 15, 61
Doughty, Charles: 246
"Dry River": Gregg on, 226
Duke, Judge Thomas M.: expedition of, 200
Dunbar, William: Red River exploration of, 199
Dutch, the: and Coronado's route, 61; and early Llano cartography, 150–151
Duval, Captain: emigrant party of, 301

E

Early Discoveries by Spaniards in New Mexico, Containing an Account of the Castles of Cibola: 36
East Coast: perception of the Llano on, 117, 121, 203, 211, 249, 273, 318, 324
East Dry Creek: Whipple on, 282
Eastman, Seth: 253
ecology: modification of Llano, 209, 227, 313–314, 321–322
Edmonson, Texas: Coronado's route in, 54
El Coyote: naming of, 189
El Cuate: 159–160, 161, 193, 328
El Gringo: 156
Elm Creek: Coronado's route at, 70
El Paso, Texas: forty-niners route to, 300–309
El Puerto spring: Vial at, 177
El Turco (Indian guide): 20–21, 23–24, 27, 30, 32, 60, 65, 93, 150, 328; confession and garroting of, 46, 111; Coronado misled by, 45–49, 55, 85, 95, 96; as prisoner of Coronado, 85–86, 106
El Vado de Piedras: Abert at, 253
Emigrant Trail: 300–304, 306
Emory, W. H.: and boundary commission, 309; and Castle Gap, **302**; map of, 220
English, Otis: ranch of, 76, 82
English, the: Llano capitalism of, 214, 218; and Texas annexation, 230
English Inscription Stone: 197, **198**
erosion: and canyon formation, 126–127; forty-niners and Llano, 314
Escalante, Felipe de: on buffalo, 137
Espejo, Antonio de: rescue mission of, 137–138
Estep, Raymond: on Le Grand, 215, 217
Estevanico: with Cabeza de Vaca, 14, 15; in Mendoza's service, 17
Exeter, Richard: land grant of, 215, 217, 218
exploration: Arctic, 250–251, 261; art and, 331–333, 336, 337–339; commercial impulse and, 218–220, 329; gold and impetus to, 16–21; scientific impulse and, 202–203, 251–252, 253–263, 266–267, 280, 284, 294, 297–298, 326, 336–341; Spanish and Anglo approaches to, 326–342; Texas annexation and Mexican-American War sparks, 36; Victorian context for Llano, 250–252. *See also* Romanticism
Exploration and Empire: 203
Exploration of the Red River of Louisiana: 266, **268**, 271
Explorations and Surveys: **281**, **283**, **287**, **292**, **294**, **295**

F

Falconer, Thomas: on naming of Llano Estacado, 163; perceptual approach of, 6, 245, 328, 332; with Texan-Santa Fé Expedition, 229, 230, 236–241
Falcon Reservoir: and Cabeza de Vaca's route, 13
Faraone Indians: as buffalo hunters, 157; and early Llano cartography, 152–153
fata morgana: 5, 130, 335
Fehrenbach, T. R.: on Comanchería, 172–173
Ferguson, Walter Keene: 297
Fernandez, Santiago: expedition of, 175–178, **176** (map)
Flat Rock Ponds: Bartlett at, 304; Connelly at, 300; Ford-Neighbors expedition at, 301
Flint, Richard and Shirley: trace Coronado route, 25, 92
Flores, Dan: on Llano storms, 64; on Marcy's Red River source, 277; on Mares-Santos-Martín route, 174; on Red River, 199; on Yellow House Canyon, 75, 100
Florida: 37
Floydada, Texas: Spanish artifacts near, 91–93
Floyd County (Texas): plums in, 83; Spanish artifacts in, 91–93
Floyd County Historical Museum: Spanish artifacts in, 91
Fonda, John H.: expedition of, 213, 214
Ford, John S. "Rip": wagon road of, 300–301, 323
Foreman, Grant: and Red River expedition, 271
Forlani, Paulo: 150
Fort Bascom: 161; and Llano cattle trade, 192
Fort Chadbourne, Texas: Gray expedition to, 305

Fort Gibson: Abert at, 259; Le Grand at, 220
Fort Smith: A. Pike at, 210; Santa Fé trail from, 228, 259–263; Whipple expedition leaves, 281
Fort Smith Company: 259–261
Fort Sumner, New Mexico: Coronado's route at, 105; and Llano cattle trade, 192
Fort Towson, Oklahoma: and Chihuahua trail, 300; A. Pike expedition leaves, 205–206
Fort Washita: Pope at, 315
forty-niners: and Llano erosion, 314; route of, 27, 259–261, 300–309
Fragoso, Francisco Xavier: expedition of, 133, 167, 175–178, **176** (map), 329
Franciscan missionaries: on Llano Estacado, 6, 17, 19, 27, 57, 65, 86, 130–131, 137–138, 328, 330. *See also* Llano Estacado, Franciscans on
Frankenstein: 246
Franklin Expedition: 250
Freeman: Red River expedition of, 200
Frémont, Capt. John C.: and Abert expedition, 253
French, the: contrabandista trade of, 170; and early Llano cartography, 151–152; Llano diaries of, 6; Llano trade routes of, 167–171. *See also* Llano Estacado, French explorations on
Friedrich, Caspar David: 332
Frio Draw: comanchero route at, 189; and Coronado's route, 29, 47; Mares-Santos-Martín expedition at, 173; and source of Red River, 274; Vial at, 178
Friona, Texas: Coronado's route at, 32; Mares-Santos-Martín expedition at, 173

G

Gadsden Purchase: 309
Gaines County (Texas): Guadalajara expedition in, 146; Martin-Castillo expedition in, 146; salt lakes in, 101
Galisteo Pass: Oñate at, 141
Gallagher, Peter: with Texan–Santa Fé Expedition, 229, 236
Gallagher-Hoyle diary: 236–238
Gallegos, Hernán: captures slave, 135
Gallinas River: Coronado's route at, 26, 32; Mallet expedition and, 169; Mares-Santos-Martín expedition on, 173; Oñate on, 141–143; Texan–Santa Fé Expedition on, 236; Vial on, 176; Zaldivar on, 138
Galvin, John: 254
Garcia, José: 284
Garrard, Lieutenant: 315
Garza Complex: agriculture of, 78; location of Cona in, 74, 78, 79, 82; pottery of, 85; Spanish artifacts at sites, 91, 93; trade routes from, 109
Garza County (Texas): Brazos tributaries in, 76
geography: Dutch geographers and Coronado's route, 61; and early European maps of the Llano, 149–154; and exploration narratives, 328–329, 334, 338–339; historical geosophy and, 5; Horgan on, 228; Whipple expedition and Llano, 283, 284, 287–288, 294
geology: Alibates flint deposits, 257; Caprock formation, 127; the Jurassic controversy, 295–297, 317, 320–321, 337; and Llano water, 291, 295, 297, 306, 308, 316–322, 338, 339; Marcou on Llano, 281–282; Whipple on Llano, 282
Geology of North America: 296, 297
geosophy: defined, 5
Gilded Man, The: 37
Girard, C.: and Red River expedition, 266
Girvin, Texas: Horsehead Crossing near, 303
Glass, Anthony: on Brazos River, 200
Glorieta Mesa: Coronado's route at, 25, 31, 106; Salas-León expedition on, 145
Glorieta Pass: Alvarado-Padilla expedition at, 19; Confederate defeat at, ment., 342
Glover, George W.: 232
Goetzmann, William H.: on Llano exploration, 203, 253, 318–319, 337
gold: at Santa Fé, 204; Bosque Redondo prospectors, 164; route of forty-niners, 27, 259–261, 300–304; rumors of, and Spanish exploration, 16–21, 23–24
Gómara, Francisco Lopéz de: Coronado account by, 33, **34**, 35, 297; woodcut by, ment., 338
Gonzalez, Manuel: Llano trade of, 192
Goodnight, Charles: 191, 192, 303
Goodnight-Loving Trail: 320
Grand Canyon: Cárdenas in, ment., 127–128
Gray, Col. Andrew Belcher: expedition of, 252, 305–306, **307**, **308**, 309, 324; and Llano water, 317; perceptual approach of, 7, 339, 341
Gray, Asa: 202
Great American Desert: as mirage, 5
Great Plains, the: Llano Estacado an extension of, 2
Great Plains, The: 120
Great Salt Lake: among Coronado's "Lost Lakes," 100, 103; buffalo hunters on, 157; Marcy at, 262; A. Pike at, 209
Greeley, Horace: 238
Greer County (Oklahoma): U.S. Supreme Court and, 277
Gregg, Josiah: on buffalo hunters, 156, 158–159; expedition of, 223–228, 238, **240** (map), 286; Indian guide of, 261; and J. Wright's categories of imagining, 5; perceptual approach of, 3, 6, 245, 328, 329, 332, 333, 336–337, 340, 341; and Red River origin, 266
Gregg (Indian wars soldier): grave of, 93
Griggs, William C.: on Red River expedition, 271
Guadalajara, Capt. Diego de: expeditions of, 145, 146, 148
Guadalupe Mountains: Gray in, 309
Gustavson, Thomas: on playa formation, 122
Gutiérrez, Jusephe: report of, 138, 142
Guzman, Nuño de: expedition of, 16

H

Hakluyt, Richard: 35
Hale County (Texas): Coronado's route in, 48, 51, 54, 55
Haley, J. Evetts: 191, 209, 300, 301
Hall, James: 297

Hallenbeck, Cleve: and Cabeza de Vaca's route, 14
Hammond and Rey: translations of Coronado documents by, 39, 50, 72, 119, 126, 129
Hancock, George: on Plains mirages, 4
Harahe settlement. *See* Haxa settlement
Harris, John: expedition of, 208, 209–211
Hart, Mrs. Alyce: and English Inscription Stone, 197, **198**
Hawikuh pueblo: Coronado at, 18–19, 23
Haxa settlement: 49, 54, 65, 150
Heidegger, Martin: 325
Hereford, Texas: Mares-Santos-Martín expedition at, 173
Herrera, Antonio de: on Coronado, 65
Hill, Robert T.: 89
Historia de Nueva México: 135, 141
Historia General de las Indias, La (Gómara): 33, **34**, 35
Historia General de las Indies, La (Oviedo y Valdés): 12
Hockley County (Texas): bison site in, 103; Coronado's route in, 99, 102
Hodge, Frederick W.: and Coronado's route, 43, 70, 101
Holden, William Curry: and Coronado's route, 42–43, 70, 102; on Plains mirages, 4
Holliday, Vance: 122
Hollon, W. Eugene: 277
Hopi Indians: Padilla's reconnaissance to, 19
Horgan, Paul: and Coronado entrada, 39; on geography, 228
Horn, Sarah Ann: 328
horses: and the buffalo hunt, 156, 160; of Comanches, 210, 226; Coronado's, 64, 67, 96; introduced by Spanish, 57, 330; and Llano ecology, 209; and naming of Llano Estacado, 165, 179, 210, 226; Texan–Santa Fé Expedition eats, 232; wild mustangs, 254, 262
Houston, Sam: Le Grand and, 222
Howard County (Texas): Guadalajara expedition in, 146
Hozes, Francisca de: at Cona, 86
Hughes, Jack: 91, 92
Humboldt, Alexander von: inspires scientific exploration, 252, 267, 284, 298; and Llano cartography, 149, 153, 197, 200, 201, 285; and Möllhausen, 280, 282, 332
Hurd, Peter: 39
Hurrah Creek: Coronado's route on, 27

I

Icazbalceta, Joaquín García: Spanish documents collection of, 37, 38, 44
Ice Age: on Llano Estacado, 78, 98, 103
Idalou, Texas: Coronado's route at, 99
Illusion Lake: among Coronado's "Lost Lakes," 100, 102
Inca Indians: gold of, 16
Indian Creek: Whipple on, 284
Indians: pictographs of, 293, 301; as Spanish slaves, 135; Whipple sketches, **292**. *See also* by tribe name
Indian Territory: Gregg map of, **225**; Le Grand in, 220; Stokes Commission to, 249
Irion County (Texas): Martin-Castillo expedition in, 146
Ironshirt (Comanche chief): Spanish peace mission to, 171
Irving, Washington: 246, 249
Isla das Sete Cidades: 17
Italians: and Llano cartography, 149–150

J

Jackson, Andrew: and Stokes Commission, 249; and Texan–Santa Fé Expedition, 230
James, Edwin: as journalist, 327, 341; on Long expedition, 202–203, 210
Jaramillo, Juan de: expedition diary of, 3, 27, 44, 45–49, 85, 95, 107–108, 110, 111, 112, 118, 127, 328
Jediondo Indians: Mendoza encounters, 147–148
Jefferson, Thomas: and Red River explorations, 153, 198–200
Jefferson County (Oklahoma): Vial in, 170
Jicarilla Indians: and early Llano cartography, 152
Jicarilla trail: Mallet expedition on, 168
John, Elizabeth A. H.: 148
John Arrowsmith Map of Texas: **221**
Johnson Draw: and extent of the Llano, 299
Johnston, Albert Sidney: 324
Johnston, Marshall C.: 84
Jones, Paul: 40
Journal of the National Geographic Society: Falconer report in, 230
Journey of Coronado: 38
Jumano Indians: Cabeza de Vaca and, 13–14, 15; and early Llano cartography, 151; Espejo and, 138; Franciscans and, 330; "Lady in Blue" and, 143–145; Martin-Castillo expedition and, 146; Mendoza and, 147–148; origins of, 62; and perception of the Llano, 3; Salas-León expedition and, 145; tattoos of, 62; water dogs of, 148
Junta de los Rios, La: Cabeza de Vaca's route at, 13

K

Kansas: Caddoans of, 78; Cicúye in, 43; El Turco garroted in, 46; Quivira in, 37, 108–111
Kemble, W.: map by, **240**
Kendall, George Wilkins: and J. K. Wright's categories of imagining, 5; and naming of Llano Estacado, 163; perceptual approach of, 6, 233–234, 238–239, 245, 327, 328, 331–332, 335, 336; and Red River origin, 266; and Texan–Santa Fé Expedition, 229–241
Kennedy, William: and Le Grand survey, 214, 219, 220, 222
Kennerly, Dr. C. B. R.: 280
Kessell, John L.: 6
Kiowa Indians: Abert and, 257, 259; Kendall and, 328; and Llano cattle trade, 192; Long and, 202; Pope and, 314; and Spanish buffalo hunters, 160; Spanish trade with, 188, 330;

Index

Texan–Santa Fé Expedition and, 232, 238; Whipple and, 281, 284
Kioway Creek: naming of, 267
Kiser, Edwin L.: on Coronado's route, 102, 103
Knox County (Texas): Brazos tributaries in, 76

L

La Ceya (the eyebrow): origin of name, 184, 208, 226; outliers of, **294**
"Lady in Blue": 143–145, 148, 331, 336
Laguna Colorada: Coronado at, 27; naming of, 191; Spanish sheep-herders on, 186; Whipple at, 294
Laguna Plata: naming of, 191
Laguna Rica: naming of, 191, 340
Laguna Sabinas: naming of, 190
Laguna Salada: Coronado's route at, 103
La Harpe, Jean-Baptiste Bénard, sieur de: expedition of, 169; and Llano cartography, 151–152
La Junta: Coronado's route at, 26; Espejo at, 138; Mendoza at, 147
La Lomita: naming of, 189
Lamar, Mirabeau: and Texan–Santa Fé Expedition, 229
Lamb County (Texas): Coronado's route in, 48, 54; A. Pike in, 209; salt lakes in, 101, 102
Lamesa, Texas: inscription stone found near, 197, **198**
La Mistica Ciudad de Dios: 144
La Pista de Vida Agua: A. Pike follows, 209–210; traders follow, 188, 189, 226
La Salada: naming of, 189
Las Escarbadas: comanchero route at, 189, 190; naming of, 191, 237
Las Lenguas Canyon: Coronado's route in, 56; naming of, 340
Las Salinas: naming of, 184
Las Tecovas Creek: comanchero route at, 190; naming of, 340, 341
Las Vegas, New Mexico: and Spanish penetration of Llano, 184, 186, 189
Latrobe, Charles: 249
Lawrence, H.: illustrates Marcy's report, 267, 271–272, **273**, 277, 333, 340
Lee, Robert E.: 322, 324
Le Grand, Alexander: perceptual approach of, 5, 6; survey of, 214–222, 223, 245, 246, 324, 328; survey of, and Llano maps, 213, **216, 219, 221**
Le Maire: map ment., 331
Lennox Library (New York). *See* Lennox Manuscript
Lennox Manuscript: and Coronado's route, 46, 50, 71, 81, 333; G. Winship studies, 37–38
León, Fray Diego: expedition of, 145–146
Leopold, Aldo: 314
Lewis, Aaron B.: expedition of, 205–206
linguistics: Anglo vs. Spanish place-names, 191; buffalo hunters and Llano identity, 162; and early Llano cartography, 149–154; and environmental perception, 7, 28, 53, 54, 61, 71–74, 80, 87, 95, 109, 128, 130, 136, 184, **185** (map), 186, 189, 190–191, 192–193, 233–234, 254, 255, 266–267, 304; and name "Llano Estacado," 162–166, 210, 226, 238, 288
literature: and exploration narratives, 246–249, 328–329, 341
Little Ice Age. *See* Ice Age
Little Red River: Mares-Santos-Martín expedition on, 174
Little Wichita River. *See* Rio de Vermellón
Llano Estacado: antelope on, **307**; artesian wells of, 291, 295, 297, 306, 308, 316–322, 338, 339; buffalo hunters on, 54, 79–80, 154, 155–166, 178, 181–182, 188, 189, 190, 193, 226, 330, 335; Caprock formation, 127; cartography of, early European/American, **140**, 149–154, **152**, 188–189, 197, 200, **201**, 213, 215, **216**, 218–222, **219, 221, 225, 240**, 324, 330–331, 337; Civil War and, 323–324, 342; commercial imagination appropriates, 218–220, 329; desert metaphor for, 200–203, 205–206, 208, 210, 259, 261, 263, 270, 304, 305, 322, 335, 339; disease on, Spanish-introduced, 90, 170, 171, 341; disorientation on, 28, 30, 33, 44, 46, 48, 86–89, 97, 120, 257–258, 335; drainage patterns of, 47, 53, 76, 79, 98, 99–102, 124, 200, 226; Dutch geographers map, 61; East Coast perception of, 117, 121, 203, 211, 249, 273, 318, 324; ecological modification of, 209, 227, 313–314, 321–322; elevation of, 121; English capitalism on, 214, 218; environmental perception of, concept defined, 3–5; erosion and canyon formation, 126–127; European weapons on, 147; fire on, 13, 125, 147, 209, 224, 306, 314; fortune seekers on, 204, 205; in French and Spanish trade corridor, 167–182, **180** (map); gold as impetus for exploration of, 16–21, 259–261; Ice Age on, 78, 98, 103; Jurassic controversy and, 295–297, 317, 320–321, 337; land grants on, 214–219, 255; linguistic emergence of, 28, 325–326, 328; "Lost Lakes" of, 100–102, 251; lunettes on, 123, 124; Manifest Destiny and, 241, 251; migrating birds on, 124, 161, 235; mirage as exploration metaphor, 270, 274, 333, 335; mirages on, 4–5, 120, 130, 166, 207, 209, 227, 235, 239, 251, 258, **269**, 270, 313, 335, 336; naming of, 155, 162–166, 179, 210, 226, 238, 288; and New Mexico livestock industry, 183–184, 186–187; ocean metaphor for, 48–49, 50–51, 53, 119, 139, 141, 195, 208, 250, 261, 263, 290, 291, 293, 306, 312; pearling expeditions on, 145–146, 148, 329; playas of, 53, 121–125, 129, 161, **176**, 177, 225, 237–238, 258, 316; Pope's theory of water on, 316–318, 321; "Pope's Wells" on, 5, 320, 322, 339, 341; prairie dogs on, 99–100, 103, 161, 260, 270, **272**, 288, 293, 312, 335, 336; railroad surveys on, 252, 263, 279–298, 304–306, **307, 308, 309**, 311–324, 332, 337; rattlesnakes on, 260, 293, 315, 335, 336; romantic interpretations of, 6–7, 205–208, 209–211, 228, 233–234,

238–239, 245–252, 254, 255, 261, 267, **271**, **273**, 274, 277–278, 284, 288, 290, 332–333, 336, 339, 341; salt lakes on, 99, 100, 102, 123, 166, 188, 314, 338; scientific appropriation of, 202–203, 251–252, 253–263, 266–267, 280, 284, 297–298, 326, 336–341; size and extent of, 1, 2, 299; slavery and, 252, 265, 324, 341; slave trade on, 187, 188, 189; soils of, 128; Spanish orientation tactics on, 88–89, 97, 99, 125, 181, 191; Spanish sheep-herders on, 183–184, 186–187; Spanish toponyms for, 184, **185** (map), 186, 189, 190–191, 192–193, 208, 215, 254, 298, 304, 340; Texas/New Mexico boundary and, 265; in Victorian exploration context, 250–252; weather on, 63–65, 92, 121, 179, 181, 202–203, 224–225, 232–233, 236, 268, 306, 334; Whipple's sunrise on, 288, **289**, 290, 332

_____, American explorations on: Abert, 7, 252, 253–259, 263, 270, 327, 331, 333, 335, 339; Bartlett, **302**, 303, 304, 305, 309; Bryan, 300; Campbell, 208, 280; Carson, 342; Connelly, 300; Cox, 301; Duke, 200; Dunbar, 199; Emory, 220, **302**, 309; Falconer, 6; Fonda, 213, 214; Ford-Neighbors, 300–301; Freeman and Custis, 200; Glass, 200; Gray, 7, 252, 305–306, **307**, **308**, 309, 317, 324, 339, 341; Gregg, 3, 5, 6, 223–228, **240** (map), 245, 259, 261, 286, 328, 332, 333, 336, 340, 341; Harris, 208, 209–211; Kendall, 5, 6, 163, 229–241, 245, 266, 327, 328, 331–332, 335, 336; Le Grand, 5, 6, 214–222, **216** (map), **221** (map), 213, 245, 324, 328; Lewis, 205–206; literary context for, 246–249; Long, 202–203, 254, 285, 328, 329, 331, 334, 337; McClellan, 252, 266, 267, 271, 274, 277, 328; Marcy, 3, 5, 7, 243, 251, 252, 259–263, 265–278, 273–274, 279, 285–286, 301, 313, 315, 316, 328, 331–341; Michler, 266, 313; Murchison, 301; Nolan, 199; Obenchain, 342; A. Pike, 6, 195, 205–208, 209–211, 214, 220, 223, 226, 232, 233, 238, 239, **240** (map), 245, 250, 285, 328, 331–336, 340; Z. Pike, 178, 200, 203, **201** (map), 213, 333, 335, 337, 338, 339, 341; Schamp and McCall, 200; Sibley, 199, 256; Simpson, 36, 252, 259–263, 279, 286, 291, 339; P. Smith, 301; T. Smith, 301; Snively, 239, 241; Sutton-Cooke, 232–237; Taplin, 312–313, 314, 315; Texan–Santa Fé Expedition, 6, 163, 229–241, **240** (map); Tong and Duval, 301; U.S. Army, 251–252, 253–263; Whipple, 3, 7, 252, 279–298, 305, 318, 327, 328, 329, 331, 332, 333, 337, 338, 339, 340, 341

_____, Franciscans on, 327, 330; Beltrán, 137–138; Castilblanco, 65, 86; De Salas, 145–146, 328; idealism of, 130–131; "Lady in Blue," 143–145, 148, 331, 336; López, 136, 137, 147–148; Marcos de Niza, 17, 57, 328; mystical explorations of, 143–145; Padilla, 19–21, 23, 25, 65, 85, 106, 108, 111, 112, 118, 136; Rodríquez, 135–137, 148; Sabaleta, 147; Salas-León expedition, 145–146, 148; Salas-Ortega expedition, 145; Santa María, 137

_____, French explorations on: Bruyére, 169; La Harpe, 151–152, 169; Pierre and Paul Mallet, 6, 167–170, 255

_____, Indian tribes on: Apache, 29, 137, 138, 139, 151, 152–153, 157, 160, 171, 173, 188, 202; Avavare, 14; Comanche, 3, 156, 158, 160–161, 162, 165, 168–169, 170–173, 174, 175–179, **176** (map), 187, 188–189, 192, 208, 209, 210, 222, 224, 226, 248, 253, 257, 262, 263, 281, 286, **287**, 300, 301, 303, 313, 329, 330, 340, 342; Faraones, 152–153, 157; Hopi, 19; Jediondo, 147–148; Jicarilla, 152, 168; Jumano, 3, 13–14, 15, 62, 138, 143–145, 146, 147–148, 151, 330; Kiowa, 160, 188, 192, 202, 232, 238, 257, 259, 281, 284, 314, 328, 330; Kotsoteka, 187, 188; Kwahadi, 161, 173, 187, 188; Navajo, 192; Pawnee, 24, 224, 329; Querecho, 29–30, 42, 46, 47, 48, 49, 57, 62, 67, 118, 119, 137, 138, 189, 340; Taovaya, 170–171, 171, 174, 176; Teya, 42, 44, 62–63, 76, 78, 79, 85, 96–112, 146; Tompiro, 62; Towa, 18, 19, 21, 46, 106, 111, 113; Vaquero, 138, 139, 151; Wichita, 110–111, 143, 170; Yamparika, 172–173, 179, 181, 187, 188; Zuni, 16–19, 142, 150

_____, Spanish explorations on: Alvarado, 19–21, 23, 25, 32, 44, 55, 71, 111, 112; Amangual, 6, 179–182, **180** (map), 165, 178, 329, 333; Arellano, 85, 86, 89, 96–106 **101** (map), 110, 113, 118; Bonilla-Humaña, 138; Cabeza de Vaca, 5, 9–21, 55, 61, 69, 136, 328, 340; Castaño de Sosa, 138; Coronado, 2, 3, 5–6, 18–21, 23–74, 75–93, 95–115, 126–130, 328, 333, 335, 337; Cortés, 9, 16; Díaz, 18; Espejo, 137–138; Fragoso, 133, 167, 175–178, **176** (map), 329; Guadalajara, 145, 146, 148; D. López, 49–55, 86, 90; Mares, 6, 328; Mares-Santos-Martín, 173–175, 177, **180** (map); Martin-Castillo, 145–146, 148; Melgares, 178; Mendoza-López, 147–148, 301; Oñate, 6, 136, 138–142, 155, 261, 328, 333, 334; Rodríguez-Chamuscado, 135–137; Vial, 2, 3, 6, **180**, 327, 328, 329, 337; Vial-Chaves, 170–172; Vial-Fragoso-Fernandez, 175-178, **176** (map); Vial-Santos, 171–173; Zaldivar, 138–141, 162, 261, 330, 334

_____, trails: aboriginal, 137, 145; buffalo, 53, 56, 88, 128–129, 224; Butterfield, 303, 322–323; cattle, 192; Chihuahua, 186, 300; cibolero, 188, 189, 190, 193, 224, 226, 330; Comanche, Marcy maps, 188; comanchero trade routes, 187–193, **185** (map), 208, 209, 213, 214, 226, 256–257; Comanche War Trail, 262, 301, 303; Emigrant Trail, 300–304, 306; forty-niners, 27, 259–261, 300–309; prehistoric trade routes, 30, 104, 109, 112, 114, 138; Santa Fé trade routes, 167–172, 200, 203, 204, 213, 214, 217, 223, **225** (map), 228; Upper Road, 300–304, 323; wagon roads, 300–304

Loess Creek: naming of, 267, 340
Lone Ranche: A Tale of the "Staked Plain," The: 247
Long, Maj. Stephen H.: expedition of, 202–203, 254, 256, 285, 329, 331, 334, 337; perceptual approach of, 5, 255, 328
Loomis, Chauncey C.: 245
Loomis, Noel M.: on Fragoso's text, 177; on Texan–Santa Fé Expedition, 230, 238; on Vial-Santos expedition, 172
López, Andrés: with Guadalajara, 146
López, Anirecha: and buffalo hunters, 161
López, Capt. Diego: at Cona, 90; reconnaissance of, 49–55
López, Fray Francisco: on Mendoza expedition, 147–148; on Rodríguez expedition, 136, 137
Lord Tatarrax: 111
Lorraine, Claude: 332, 340
Los Alamocitos: naming of, 190
Los Angeles, California: geographers locate Llano near, 61
Los Angosturas: naming of, 190
Los Cuervos: comanchero route at, 189
Los Lingos Creek: Texan–Santa Fé Expedition on, 232
Los Portales: naming of, 191; on aboriginal trade route, 104
Lost Coronado Trail: as detective story, 5
Los Tulanes: naming of, 189
Louisiana: Spanish acquire, 167, 170
Louisiana Purchase: and Llano exploration, 35, 178, 198
Loving, Oliver: cattle trail of, 192; and Horsehead Crossing, 303
Lubbock, Texas: Coronado's route at, 99; prairie dogs at, 100
Lubbock County (Texas): Coronado's route in, 99
Luciano Mesa: naming of, 184
lunettes: 123, 125

M

McClellan, Capt. George B.: with Red River expedition, 252, 266, 267, 271, 274, 277; romanticism of, 328
McClellan Creek: Marcy at, 335; naming of, 267
Macha, Ray: 92
McLeod: and Texan–Santa Fé Expedition, 237
Maes, Manuel: 159–160, 328, 335
Maiolo, Jacobus: Llano cartography of, 149–150
Maldonado, Alonso de Castillo: with Cabeza de Vaca, 14
Maldonado, María: at Cona, 86
Maldonado, Capt. Rodrigo: reconnaissance of, **52** (map), 55–57
Mallet, Paul: expedition of, 6, 167–170, 255
Mallet, Pierre: arrest of, 170; expedition of, 6, 167–170, 255
Manifest Destiny: 241, 251
Manitou. *See* Vial, Pierre ("Pedro")
Manuel el Comanche (Indian guide): 261, 311
Map of the Indian Territory, Northern Texas, and New Mexico: **225**

Map of the Republic of Texas and the Adjacent Territories: **216**
Map of Texas Compiled From Surveys Recorded in the Land Office of Texas: 219–220
Map of Texas and the Countries Adjacent: 220
Map of Texas Shewing the Grants in Possession of the Colorado & Red River Land Company: 218, **219**
Marble, Nancy: 91
Marcos de Niza, Fray: expedition of, 17, 57, 328
Marcou, Jules: and the Jurassic controversy, 295–297, 320–321, 337; and Llano water, 317, 320; perceptual approach of, 243, 337, 338, 339; sketch by, **295**; with Whipple expedition, 280–283, 288, 290, 293
Marcy, Capt. Randolph: 1849 expedition of, 252, 259–263, 279, 286, 301, 334; Indian guides of, 260, 261, 267; maps of, and Comanche trail, 188; perceptual approach of, 3, 5, 7, 243, 251, 261, 273–274, 277–278, 328, 331–341; Red River expedition of, 265–278, **268**, **271**, **273**, **275**, 286, 316, 331; trail of, and Pope expedition, 311–312, 313, 315
Mares, José: expedition of, 6, 173–175, 177, **180** (map), 328, 333
Marsh, George Perkins: 318
Martín, Alejandro: expedition of, 173–175, 177, **180** (map)
Martin, Hernán: expedition of, 145–146, 148
Martin County (Texas): Guadalajara expedition in, 146
Martínez, Enrico: map of, **140**, 142, 337
Martínez, Juan de: 150
Martínez, Manuel: and Amangual expedition, 181–182
Marzolf, Les: 39
Massanet, Father: and "Lady in Blue," 143
Matador, Texas: springs near, 129
Matías: and Texan–Santa Fé Expedition, 236–238
Medina, José G.: Llano trade of, 192
Melgares, Don Facundo: expedition of, 178, 181
Melrose, New Mexico: Coronado's route at, 104
Melville, Herman: 248–249
Mendoza, Viceroy Antonio de: and Cabeza de Vaca's bison robe, 12; and Coronado, 33, 113, 130, 337; expeditions dispatched by, 16–19
Mendoza, Juan Dominguez de: expedition of, 147–148, 301
Mercator, Gerard: 150
Mesa Redonda: naming of, 191
Mesa Rica: naming of, 184
Mescalero Apache Indians. *See* Apache Indians
Mescalero Escarpment: comanchero route at, 188; Coronado's route at, 101; described, 127; Martin-Castillo expedition on, 146; and naming of Llano Estacado, 163
Mesilla Valley: quarrel over, 309
Mexican-American War: as impetus to exploration, 36
Mexico: boundary dispute with U.S., 229–230, 241, 279, 305; Cabeza de Vaca's route in, 13; Llano buffalo trade to, 157–158. *See also* Chihuahua, Mexico

Mexico City: Coronado buried in, 35, 114; Coronado dies at, 113; Llano buffalo trade at, 158
Michler, Lt. Nathaniel: expedition of, 266, 313
Michoacan province: Guzman sacks, 16
Middle Concho River: Connelly on, 300; and extent of the Llano, 299–300; Ford-Neighbors expedition on, 300, 301; "Lady in Blue" on, 144; pearls on, 145, 148; Salas-León expedition on, 145
Midland, Texas: Marcy at, 262
Midland County (Texas): Martin-Castillo expedition in, 145
Miera y Pacheco, Baron Alexander: map of, 197
Miller, Townshend: 1
Miller County (Texas): Le Grand in, 217
minerals: Alibates flint deposits, 257; collected by Cabeza de Vaca, 12
mines: at Santa Fé, 203–204; buffalo trade and, 158; in Chihuahua, 135, 158; discovered on Llano, 135
mirages: as exploration metaphor, 270, 274, 333, 335; on Llano Estacado, 4–5, 120, 130, 166, 207, 209, 227, 235, 239, 251, 258, **269**, 313, 336
Mississippi River: mound cultures of, Querechos and, 30
Missouri River: P. Mallet on, 170
Mitchel County (Texas): Guadalajara expedition in, 146
Moho: siege of, 24
Mojtabai, A. G.: 162
Moll, H.: 151
Möllhausen, Heinrich Balduin: on naming the Llano, 288; as novelist, 291; perceptual approach of, 288, 290, 327, 328, 332, 333; with Whipple expedition, 280, **281**, 282, **283**, **285**, 286, **287**, 289, 293
Monahans, Texas: sand hills at, Marcy in, 262, 313, 322
Montague County (Texas): Vial in, 170
Montaignes, François des. See Cooper, Isaac
Montaño de Camelon: naming of, 190
Monte Revuelto: Coronado at, 27
Montgomery Ranch: 92
Montova, Pablo: land grant of, 255
Moore, George: 82, 83, 93
Moore, Pam: 82, 93
Moore, Thomas: 311
Moors, the: linguistic borrowings from, 72
Mora, New Mexico: and Spanish penetration of Llano, 184, 186
Mota Padilla, Matías de la: on Llano canyons, 126; on Llano storm, 64; manuscript of, 37, 65
Motolinía, Fray: account of, 44, 55, 87, 96, 107, 109. See also *Relación Postrera de Sívola*
Muchaque Peak: comanchero route at, 188, 342
Mulberry Creek: and Coronado's route, 65
Muleshoe, Texas: Coronado's route near, 103
Muleshoe Lakes: Coronado's route at, 105
Muleshoe National Wildlife Area: Coronado's route in, 103

Murchison, Capt. John: emigrant party of, 301
Mustang Ponds: Bartlett at, 304; Ford-Neighbors expedition on, 300
Mustang Springs: Gray at, 305, 306; Marcy at, 262, 301; Pope at, 314

N

Narrative of an Expedition across the Great Southwestern Prairies from Texas to Santa Fé: 230
Narrative of Arthur Gordon Pym, The: 248
Narváez expedition: Cabeza de Vaca and, 12, 16; Coronado hopes to find survivors, 65
Nasatir, Abraham P.: on Fragoso's text, 177; on Vial-Santos expedition, 172
Natchitoches, Louisiana: Le Grand at, 217; and Red River explorations, 199; trail from Santa Fé to, 175–178, **176** (map)
Navajo Indians: U.S. Army confines, 192
Neighbors, Maj. Robert: wagon road of, 300–301, 323
New Galicia: conquest of, manuscript ment., 37
New Mexico: Barreiro's map, **152**; boundary with Texas, 265; buffalo hunters of, 155–166; Confederate invasion, ment., 342; Coronado pageant in, 39; Coronado's route in, 25–30, 31–32, 36; Cuarto Centennial of, 38–39; early map shows, **176**; as Franciscan base, 144; Gregg map of, **225**; Llano shown on map of, **140**; poem about conquest of, 141; Spanish colonization of, 183–184; and Spanish penetration of the Llano, 6, 183–193. See also Santa Fé, New Mexico; Texan–Santa Fé Expedition
New Orleans, Louisiana: Santa Fé trade corridor to, 167–170
New Spain: and explorations for gold, 16–21; von Humboldt's map of, 153, 197; Z. Pike's map, 201
New York Herald: 323
New York Public Library: Cabeza de Vaca's *Relación* at, 13. See also Lennox Manuscript
Nicolson, Marjorie Hope: 251
Nolan, Phillip: Red River exploration of, 199
North Concho River: Cona on, 68, 69, 70, 87, 89
Nystel: archeological site discovered by, 115

O

Obenchain, A. W.: 342
Odessa, Texas: and extent of the Llano, 299
Ogallala Aquifer: on canyon formation, 127; Marcou intuits, 291; Mendoza at discharge spring of, 148; modern assaults on, 79; playas and, 123, 125, 129; Pope and, 316, 320, 321
Ojo del Llano: naming of, 184
O'Keeffe, Georgia: 119, 122
Oklahoma: Abert in, 259; Coronado's route in, 112; De La Harpe in, 169; and Greer County dispute, 277; Vial in, 170. See also Indian Territory
Oldham County (Texas): Indian pictographs in, 293; Mallet expedition in, 168; Spanish colony in, 187; Whipple in, 288, 293

Old Hicks, The Guide; or, Adventures in the Comanche Country in Search of a Gold Mine: 247–249
Old Texas Trails: 43, 59, 68
Oñate, Juan Pérez de: colonists of, 155; expedition of, 138–143, 261, 334; report of, 6, 136, 328, 333
Oporto, Bishop of: and Cíbola, 17
Ormsby, W. L.: 323
Orr, Nathaniel: woodcut by, **289**, 290, **294**, 333
Ortega, Fray Juan de: expedition of, 145
Ortelius, Abraham: and early Llano cartography, 61, 150–151
Oviedo y Valdés, Capt. Gonzalo Fernandez de: and Cabeza de Vaca's report, 12
Owen, Jimmy: 91–92

P

Pacific Coast: Cabeza de Vaca on, 16; and early Llano cartography, 150–151; Llano trade with, 19. *See also* railroads
Pacific Railroad Surveys: on the Llano, 252, 284, 289, 315, 316, 329, 333, 341. *See also* railroads
Padilla, Fray Juan de: at Cona, 85; expedition of, 19–21, 23, 25, 136; prays following storm, 65; on Quivira expedition, 106, 108, 111, 112, 118
Pajarito Creek: comanchero route at, 189; Coronado's route at, 27, 32
Palo Duro Canyon: buffalo hunters in, 158; Coronado's route in, 42, 44, 47, 56, 65, 66, 68, 69, 70, 79–80, 87, 98, 108–109; first lithograph of, **273**; Gregg and, 226; Lawrence lithographs of, 340; map shows, **176**, 177; naming of, 190, 340; Red River expedition in, 270–273, 277; Texan–Santa Fé Expedition at, 234, 239
Palo Duro Creek: comanchero route at, 190
Palo Duro State Park: Coronado Trail in, 42, 44, 60, 61, 66, 70, 83; soils of, 128
Palomas Mesa: naming of, 184
Panther Creek: naming of, 266
Park, Mungo: 266
Parke, Lieutenant: with Pope, 311
Parmer County (Texas): Coronado's route in, 32
Parry, William Edward: 250–251, 261
Patagonia: 207
Pawnee Indians: Coronado guide from, 24; Gregg and, 224; as Llano threat, 329
Peale, Titian Ramsey: 331
Pearce, Sen. James A.: 265
pearls: Spanish seek on Llano, 145–146, 148, 329
Pease River: Texan–Santa Fé Expedition on, 231
Peck, Lieutenant: with Abert, 253–254, 259
Pecos Bill: and naming of Llano Estacado, 164
Pecos County: Horsehead Crossing in, 303
Pecos Pueblo: Castaño de Sosa attacks, 138; Coronado's route at, 31, 51, 106, 130; on early maps, 150; Mallet expedition at, 168; Mares-Santos-Martín expedition at, 173; Quivira expedition returns to, 112; Spanish-introduced disease at, 90
Pecos River: Alvarado on, 19, 20; Amangual on, 182; Arellano's return journey to, 97–106; brackish taste of, 147; buffalo hunters on, 159; Cabeza de Vaca on, 14, 15; Cabeza de Vaca's Cow Nation on, 15; Castaño de Sosa on, 138; comanchero route at, 188; Coronado on, 24–27, 47; Coronado's bridge on, 26, 46, 105–106; formation, ment., 127; Gray on, 305; Guadalajara on, 146; Harris on, 208; Mallets on, 168; Marcy on, 261; Martin-Castillo on, 146; on Martínez map, **140**, 142; Mendoza-López on, 147, 148; native plant foods on, 105; Quivira expedition returns to, 112–113; as Rio de las Vacas, 137–138; Rodríguez on, 137; route from Cona to, 105; Salas-León on, 145; San Miguel del Vado on, 183; Schuchard lithograph of, **308**; shown on early map, **140**; as source of Red River, 153; Tompiro on, 62; Vial on, 172
_____, Emigrant Crossing: 261, 301, 309, 311, 313
_____, Horsehead Crossing: Butterfield trail at, 323; Castle Gap trail to, **302**; Ford-Neighbors expedition at, 300, 301; location of, 303; skeletal debris at, 334
_____, Pope's Crossing: 319, 322–323
Pecos River Falls: Pope on, 311, 312, 313, 315, 319
Pequeño Río: Coronado at, 52 (map); location of, 53–54
Peril, William: and Horsehead Crossing, 303
Personal Narrative of Exploration and Incidents in Texas: **302**
Peru: Incan gold in, 16
Phillip IV: and "Lady in Blue," 144
Picuris Pueblo: Mallets on, 168
Pike, Albert: expeditions of, 205–208, 209–211, 220, 223, 232, 238, **240** (map), 285, 334; and Le Grand, 214; on naming of Llano, 226; perceptual approach of, 6, 195, 205, 233, 239, 245, 250, 328, 332–336, 340
Pike, Lt. Zebulon M.: Red River exploration of, 178, 200, 203, **201** (map)
Pinco Mesa: Coronado at, 27
Pintada Mesa: naming of, 184
Piro Indians: origins of, 62
Pizarro, Francisco: in Peru, 16
Plains, Being No Less than a Collection of Veracious Memoranda: 327
Plains of Saint Francis: 130, 135–148
Plainview, Texas: Coronado's route near, 54, 55
playas: Abert and, 258; aquifer recharged by, 129; as artificial reservoirs, 316; defined, 53; genesis and description of, 121–125; Gregg notes, 225; map shows, **176**, 177; number and size of Llano, 123; in Portales Valley, 161; and Texan–Santa Fé Expedition, 237–238
Plaza Larga: Coronado's route at, 27, 32, 33, 47; geology of, 294, 297; Rodríguez at, 137
Poe, Edgar Allan: 210, 246–247, 248, 328
Polk, James K.: and Texas/New Mexico boundary, 265
Pope, Capt. John: expedition of, 252, 280, 291, 304, 309, 311–324, 329, 337; his search for artesian water, 316–322, 338; and Jurassic controversy,

320–321; perceptual approach of, 7, 331, 333, 335, 339, 341
"Pope's Wells": 5, **310**, 320, 322, 339, 341
Popple: 151
Portales River: drainage of, 98
Portales Spring: A. Pike at, 209; comanchero route at, 188, 189
Portales Valley: buffalo hunters in, 161; Coronado's route in, 30, 44, 47, 98–105
Portugal: Cíbola romances of, 17
Post, Texas: dead soils at, 128
Potter County (Texas): Whipple in, 286–287
pottery: of Garza Complex, 85; and location of Cona, 92, 114–115
Pourtalès, Count Albert-Alexandre: 249
prairie dogs: and the buffalo hunt, 161; on Llano Estacado, 100, 103, 260, 270, **272**, 288, 293, 312, 335, 336
Prairie Sublime: discovery rhetoric provided by, 6–7
Prose Sketches and Poems, Written in the Western Country: 211
Proust, Marcel: 67
Puaray Pueblo: Fr. López at, 137
Pueblo Indians: and comanchero trade, 190; Whipple and, 286, 293
Puerto de Luna: Coronado route at, 25; Coronado's bridge at, 105–106, 407; and Spanish sheepherders, 186
Puerto de Rivajeños: comanchero route at, 189, 190
Punta de Agua: naming of, 340
Purgatory River: Mallets on, 168
Pyramid Mountain: Whipple at, **295**, 297, 298, 337

Q

Querecho Indians: Arabs compared to, 119, 340; Coronado encounters, 29–30, 42, 46, 47, 48, 49, 57, 62, 67, 118; dog travois of, 137; Llano trail of, 189. *See also* Apache Indians; Vaquero Indians
Querecho Plains: Martin-Castillo expedition on, 146
Quintero, Captain: with Amangual, 181
Quitaque, Texas: Coronado's route near, 56
Quitaque Canyon: Amangual in, 179; buffalo hunters in, 158; cattle trade in, 192; comanchero route at, 189, 190, 342; Coronado's route in, 56, 69, 70, 92; dead soils of, 128; formation of, 129
Quivira: 19th-century scholarship on, 36–37; agriculture of, 78, 95–96, 111; Alvarado reports on, 23–24; Coronado's reconnaissance to, 23–30, 65–68, 85, 106–113, 130; Coronado's route to, contemporary accounts analyzed, 45–57; on early maps, 150–151, 153; effect of rumors on Coronado, 20–21; as *fata morgana*, 5; French trade with, 167; "Lady in Blue" and, 144; location of, 37, 40, 60–61, 108–111; narratives compiled, 35; Oñate's search for, 141–143

R

Rabasa, José: 95, 331
Ragland, New Mexico: Coronado's route at, 28, 32
railroads: transcontinental and Llano exploration, 252, 263, 279–298, 304–306, **307**, **308**, 309, 311–324, 329, 332, 333, 337, 341
Ramusio, Giovanni Battista: Coronado translations of, 35, 150
Randall County (Texas): Texan–Santa Fé Expedition in, 235
Rathjen, Frederick W.: 3, 178, 271, 277
Raton Pass: Abert at, 253; Mallets at, 168
rattlesnakes: 260, 293, 315, 335, 336
Reagan County (Texas): and extent of the Llano, 299; Ford-Neighbors expedition in, 301; Martin-Castillo expedition in, 146
Red Deer Creek: Abert on, 257–258; Marcy at, 260; Whipple on, 282
Redonda Mesa: Coronada on, 27
Red River: Abert expedition and, 253, 256, 258–259; Comanche name for, 270, **276**; Comanche trail on, 172; contrabandista trade on, 170; and Coronado's route, 55–57, 65, 73, 110, 168; and early Llano cartography, 153, 197, 199; Fonda on, 213; French claims to, 151–152; Gypsum Bluffs on, **268**; illegal trade on, 171; indiscriminate use of term, 169; Le Grand on, 215, 217; Llano border from, **271**; Marcy on, 265–278; Marcy's source for, 274, **275**, **276**, 277–278, 285–186; Mares-Santos-Martín expedition on, 174; and Ogallala Aquifer, 129; prairie dogs on, 270, **272**; search for source of, 178, 199–204, 232, 236, 256, 259, 265–278, **273**, **275**, **276**, 285–286; and Texan–Santa Fé Expedition, 230, 231, 236; trade route at, 30; Vial on, 170, 171, 175–176
Reid, Mayne: 247, 329, 332
Relación de la Jornada de Cibola: 327
Relación del Suceso: 44, 45–47, 49, 66, 87, 95, 100
Relación Postrera de Sívola: 44, 45–46, 48–49, 87, 107, 109
Relación Que Dio Alvar Núñez Cabeça de Vaca, La: Zamora edition of, 13
Relation du Voyage de Cibola: 35
Relph, Edward: 339
Remembrance of Things Past: 67
Report of Explorations for a Railway Route, Near the Thirty-fifth Parallel: 327
Republic of Texas: Arrowsmith map, **216**; Le Grand and, 220, 222; and Texan–Santa Fé Expedition, 229, 241
Rey. *See* Hammond and Rey
Reynolds, David: 246
Richardson, Rupert Norval: 214
Rich Lake: naming of, 166
Riley, Carrol L.: 30, 85, 109
Rincon de la Cruz: Whipple at, 288
Rio Abajo: Tompiro of, 62
Rio Blanco: Fragoso on, 133
Rio Blanco Girl Scout Camp: ecology of, 82, 83

Rio Colorado: naming of, 191. *See also* Canadian River
Rio Conchas: Espejo on, 138
Rio de Cicúye. *See* Pecos River
Rio de Frio: naming of, 191
Rio de la Magdalena. *See* Canadian River
Rio de las Nueces. *See* Middle Concho River
Rio de las Palmas: location of, 60–61
Rio de las Perlas: Martin-Castillo expedition on, 146; Ogalalla spring joins, 148
Rio de las Vacas. *See* Pecos River
Río de Losa, Don Rodrigo del: mine founded by, 135
Río del Tule: comanchero route at, 189; Mares-Santos-Martín expedition on, 173, 174; naming of, 190
Rio de Tiguex: on European maps, 60–61. *See also* Rio Grande
Rio de Vermellón: Red River confused with, 256; Vial on, 171, 172
Rio Grande: Alvarado on, 19; Cabeza de Vaca on, 13; Cabeza de Vaca's Cow Nation on, 15; Comanche trail at, 172; Coronado camp on, 21, 23–24; Marcy on, 261; Pecos River joins, 105; Z. Pike on, 200; shown on early map, **140**; Spanish raiding parties on, 135; Tompiro on, 62; as U.S./Mexico boundary, 229. *See also* La Junta
Rio Grande Pueblos: agriculture at, 96; captives from, 67; Coronado base at, 65, 90, 106; Oñate at, 143; Rodríguez at, 137; Spanish conquest of, 21, 24, 113
Rio Salado. *See* Pecos River
Rios Amarillos: naming of, 191
Rister, Carl Coke: 214
Rittenhouse, Jack: 192
River of Nuts: 69, 145. *See also* Middle Concho River
River of Pearls. *See* Rio de las Perlas
Riviére Rouge. *See* Canadian River
Road to Cíbola, The: 42
Roaring Springs: and Ogallala Aquifer, 129
Rocky Dell Creek: Whipple on, 293
Rocky Mountains: and Llano water, 317–318, 321
Rodríguez, Fray Augustin: expedition of, 135–137, 148
Rodríguez, Juan: and Martínez map, 142
Rolling Plains East: Coronado's route at, 70, 87, 128
Romanticism: and Llano exploration, 6–7, 205–208, 209–211, 228, 233–234, 238–239, 245–252, 254, 255, 261, 267, **271**, **273**, 274, 277–278, 284, 288, 290, 332–333, 336, 339, 341
Romero, Capt. Diego: Llano trade of, 187
Roosevelt, Franklin: Good Neighbor policy, ment., 39
Roosevelt County (New Mexico): Coronado's route in, 103
Roper, Beryl: 255
Rosa, Salvator: Llano compared with landscapes of, 232, 238, 246, 332

Roscoe, Texas: dead soils at, 128
Ross, John: 250
Roswell, New Mexico: artesian wells at, 339; and Cuarto Centennial, 39; Martin-Castillo expedition near, 146
Rowe, New Mexico: Coronado's route near, 25
Rowe Rincon: Coronado's route at, 25
Royuela, José Manuel: land grant of, 214–215
Runnels County (Texas): Guadalajara in, 146
Running Water Draw: Coronado's route at, 47–48, 55; drains Blanco Canyon, 76; and Pequeño Rio, 54
Rusk, Thomas J.: and transcontinental railroad, 318, 320

S

Sabaleta, Fray: on Mendoza expedition, 147
Saint-Pierre, Bernardin de: 248
Salinas Pueblos: agriculture of, 78; Tompiro of, 62
Salt Lake. *See* Great Salt Lake
San Angelo, Texas: Coronado's route near, 68, 98
San Antonio, Texas: Gray expedition at, 305. *See also* Santa Fé-San Antonio trail
San Bartolomé, Chihuahua: mine at, 135
sand hills: at Monahans, 262, 313, 322; on Canadian River, 143, 256, 259, 260, 266; Gray in, 306, 309; Marcy in, 262, 301; playas and, 123, 124; in Portales Valley, 161, 189; runaway slave in, 308; vegetation on, 300, 312; water in, 306, 313, 322
sandstorms: Amangual in, 179
Sangre de Cristo Mountains: from Coronado's route, 32; Spanish colonies at, 184
San Jon, New Mexico: Coronado's route at, 28
San Jon Creek: Coronado at, 27
San Miguel County (New Mexico): Coronado's route in, 25; sheepherders in, 255
San Miguel de Culiacán: Cabeza de Vaca near, 16
San Miguel del Vado: comanchero route near, 188, 214; founded, 183; Texan–Santa Fé Expedition and, 235
Santa Bárbara, Chihuahua: mine at, 135; Rodríguez at, 137
Santa Cruz, Alonso de: map of, 151, 153
Santa Fé, New Mexico: Coronado romanticized in, 40; French claims to, 152; Guadalajara at, 146; Martin-Castillo expedition at, 146; Melgares at, 178; Natchitoches trail from, 175–178, **176** (map); and Red River explorations, 199; Romanticism and, 332; Salas-León expedition at, 145; and Texas/New Mexico boundary, 265; trade corridor from, 167–172; trade routes at, 167-172, 200, 203, 204, 213, 214, 217, 223, **225** (map), 228, 229. *See also* Santa Fé-San Antonio Trail; Santa Fé Trail; Texan–Santa Fé Expedition
Santa Fé National Forest: Coronado's route in, 32
Santa Fé-San Antonio trail: of Amangual, 179; of Mares-Santos-Martín, 173–175; of Vial-Santos, 171–173

Santa Fé Trail: and Coronado's route, 42, 44, 112; Marcy surveys, 259–261
Santa María, Fray Juan de: martyrdom of, 137
Santa Rosa, New Mexico: Alvarado near, 20; Coronado's route at, 25, 26, 32, 106; Vial near, 176
Santa Rosa Lake State Park: Coronado's route at, 32
Santa Rosa Mountains: and Coronado's route, 33
Santos, Cristóbal de los: expeditions of, 171–173, 173–175
Sauer, Carl Ortwin: and Coronado's route, 42, 66, 78, 80, 81
Schamp and McCall expedition: 200
Schoolcraft, Henry Rowe: and Coronado's route, 36
Schroeder, Albert: and Coronado's route, 25, 40, 42
Schuchard, Charles: with Gray expedition, 305–306, **307**, **308**, 309, 332, 339
science. *See* exploration
Seminole Creek: and Coronado's route, 47
Seminole Draw: Salas-León expedition at, 145
Seven Cities of Cíbola. *See* Cíbola
Shady Creek: Comanche camp on, 286, **287**
sheep industry: penetrates Llano, 183–184, 186–187
Shelley, Mary: 246
Shumard, Dr. George C.: work of, 266, 270, 319, 319–320, 337, 338
Sibley, Dr. John: Red River exploration of, 199, 256
Sierrita de la Cruz Creek: Marcy at, 260; Whipple at, 288
silver: at Santa Fé, 203–204; Chihuahua mines, 158
Silver Falls, Texas: and location of Cona, 76, 82
Silver Lake: among Coronado's "Lost Lakes," 100, 102; Coronado's route at, 103, 105; naming of, 166
Silver Lake Bison Site: Coronado's route at, 102–103
Silverton, Texas. *See* Quitaque, Texas
Simanola Valley: Coronado's route in, 102
Simpson, George: 250
Simpson, Lt. James H.: expedition of, 36, 252, 259–263, 279, 286, 291, 339
Sindall, H. S.: painting by, **310**
slavery: Llano and, 252, 265, 324, 342
Smith, Bernard: 333
Smith, Buckingham: and Coronado's route, 37
Smith, Henry Nash: 248–249
Smith, Persifer F.: emigrant party of, 301
Smith, Capt. Thomas: emigrant party of, 301
Smithsonian Institution: and Red River expedition, 266; and Whipple expedition, 280
Snively expedition: 241
Sonora Valley: Coronado in, 119
Sotomayor, Pedro de: 46
South, the. *See* slavery
Southern High Plains. *See* Llano Estacado
Southern Pacific Railroad: 263
Spanish, the: acquire Louisiana, 167, 170; approach to exploration, 326–342; as buffalo hunters, 155–166; diseases introduced by, 90, 170, 171, 341; and early Llano cartography, 151–154; gold motivates exploration, 16–21, 23–24; greed of, 61–62; horses introduced by, 56–57, 330; Indian guides of, 18–21, 24, 46–49, 55, 60, 65, 73, 85–86, 96–112, 106, 111, 145, 171–172, 174, 177, 179, 181; Llano orientation strategies of, 88–89, 97, 99, 125, 181; Llano trade and settlements of, 183–193, **185** (map); peace mission to Comanches, 162, 170–172, 183, 187
Speke, John: 266
Spring Creek: naming of, 266
Sterling County (Texas): Coronado's route in, 69, 70
Stevens, Thomas Ward: 39
Stiles, Texas: Ford-Neighbors expedition at, 301
Stinking Springs: Coronado's route at, 104, 105
Stokes Commission: 249
Sulphur Springs Creek: and Coronado's route, 47; and extent of the Llano, 299; Marcy at, 262; Pope at, 314–315; Taplin at, 312
Sunday Canyon: Coronado's route in, 61
Survey of a Route for the Southern Pacific R.R. on the 32nd Parallel: **307**, **308**
Sutton, John S.: with Texan–Santa Fé Expedition, 232–237
Suydam, J. R.: with Red River expedition, 266
Swanton, John: and Coronado's route, 25, 40
Sweetwater Creek: naming of, 267
Swisher County (Texas): Coronado's route in, 54, 55

T

Tafoya, José Piedad: Llano trade of, 192
Tagebuch einer Reise vom Mississippi nach den Küsten Südsee: 327
Tahoka: buffalo hunters at, 158
Taiban Creek: comanchero route at, 188, 189, 208; Coronado's route at, 104
Tallack, William: 323
Taovaya Indians: Mares-Santos-Martín expedition and, 174; Vial and, 170–171, 176
Taplin, Capt. Charles L.: reconnaissance of, 312–313, 314, 315
Tecolotito, New Mexico: Coronado's route at, 26
Tejo (captive): N. de Guzman and, 16
Ternaux-Compans, Henri: Spanish texts translated by, 35, 72, 117, 338
Terzo volume delle navigationi et viaggi: 35, 150
Texan–Santa Fé Expedition: 229–241, **240** (map), 335; captured, 236, 238; commercial impulse and, 329; Mexican guide for, 230–231; and naming of Llano Estacado, 163; Republic of Texas and, 229; romanticism and, 6
Texarkana, Texas: Le Grand at, 217
Texas: annexation of, as impetus to exploration, 36, 230, 245; Arrowsmith maps of, **216**, 219–220, **221**; boundary with New Mexico, 265; Burr map of, 218; Cicúye in, 43; Coronado pageant in, 39; Emory map of, 220; first appearance of name, 62; Gregg map of, **225**; Kemble map of, **240**. *See also* Republic of Texas
———, East: Caddoans of, 78; trade route to, 104

_____, Gulf Coast: French cartography on, 151
_____, Hill Country: Mares-Santos-Martín expedition in, 174
_____, Panhandle: weather in, 63–65
_____, West: Cabeza de Vaca in, 14–15; camels in, 318; shown on early map, **152**
Texas: The Rise, Progress and Prospects of the Republic of Texas: 214
Texas legislature: and buffalo conservation, 166
Texas Panhandle Frontier, The: 3
Texas Rangers: in Blanco Canyon, 93; C. Webber and, 247
Texas Western Railroad Co.: and Gray survey, 305, 308
Teya Indians: agriculture of, 78, 85; Cabeza de Vaca and, 62–63; Castañeda on name, 62; Coronado and, 42, 44, 62–63, 73, 96–112; hunt buffalo, 76, 79; and original name for Texas, 62; rancherias described, 85; Spanish plunder camp, 145; trade of, 97, 104, 109
Teyas, Kingdom of: rumors of, 146
Theatrum Orbis Terrarum: 150, 151
Thirty Years of Army Life on the Border: **269**, **272**, **276**
Thoburn, Joseph B.: 255
Tierra Blanca Creek: Amangual at, 181; comanchero route at, 189, 226; Coronado at, 29, 47; on map, **176**, 177; Mares-Santos-Martín expedition on, 173, 174; naming of, 191; Texan–Santa Fé Expedition at, 235, 237; Vial at, 175, 178
Tierra Blanca Draw: and source of Red River, 274
Tiguex pueblos: Arellano's return to, 96–106, **101** (map), 110, 113; Coronado camp at, 21, 23–24; on early maps, 150–151; food at, 71; location of, 60–61; Quivira expedition returns to, 111–113; sacking of, ment., 46, 90, 106
Timbercreek Canyon: Coronado's route in, 61
Tlaxcalans: and Spanish colonization of New Mexico, 183–184
To the Inland Empire: Coronado and Our Spanish Legacy: 43, 69
Tom Green County (Texas): Martin-Castillo expedition in, 146
Tompiro Indians: origins of, 62; Teyas and, 78
Tong, Captain: emigrant party of, 301
Torrey, John: 202
Tovar, Captain: at Cona, 86; papers of, 33
Towa Indians: at Cicúye, 19, 46; Coronado and, 18, 21, 106, 111, 113; and El Turco's treachery, 111. *See also* Bigotes; Cacique
Toyah: naming of, 342
trade: Apache, 138; Apache/Spanish, 188; buffalo trade, 19, 157–158, 161, 162, 188, 189; Cañon Blanco route for, 25; cattle trade, 192; comanchero, effect on trade, 329–330; comanchero, history, 183, 187–193; Comanche/Spanish, 172, **185** (map), 187, 188; Comanche/Spanish buffalo hunters, 161; contrabandista, 170, 171, 187, 213; French and Spanish trade corridor, 167–182, **180** (map);

from Albuquerque, 146; Garza Complex, 85; Llano/Pacific Coast, 19; Llano slave trade, 187, 188, 189; New Mexico sheep industry, 186; New Orleans–Santa Fé corridor, 167–171; prehistoric routes across Llano, 30, 104, 109, 112, 114, 138; Querecho, 29; Santa Fé, 200, 203, 204, 213, 214, 217, 223, **225** (map), 228, 229; Spanish/Indian arms trade, 147; Spanish/Jumano, 146, 148; Teya, with Cicúye, 104. *See also* comancheros
Trail of Living Water. *See* La Pista de Vida Agua
trans-Mississippi: shown on early map, **140**, 142
trappers: on Llano, 208, 209–211, 220, 255, 256
Traslado de la Nuevas: 44, 45
Treaty of Guadalupe Hidalgo: 265
Trinity River: Mares-Santos-Martín expedition on, 174
Trujillo Creek: Texan–Santa Fé Expedition at, 236
Tucumcari, New Mexico: Mares-Santos-Martín expedition at, 173
Tucumcari Creek: Coronado's route at, 27, 47
Tucumcari Mesa: comanchero route at, 189, 342; Vial at, 175
Tucumcari Mountain: Coronado's route at, 27, 32; Gregg at, 224; Texan–Santa Fé Expedition at, 238; Whipple at, 294–295
Tule Canyon: comanchero route at, 190; Coronado's route in, 42, 47, 56, 60, 66, 69, 70; formation of, 129; Kendall and, 332; Red River expedition in, 273–277, **275**; Texan–Santa Fé Expedition in, 232–233
Tule Creek: map shows, **176**, 177; Mares-Santos-Martín expedition at, 173, 174; Red River expedition on, 271; Vial at, 175
Tule Draws: and Pequeño Rio, 54
Tulia, Texas: Mares-Santos-Martín expedition at, 173
Turquoise Trail: and Coronado's route, 42; Zuni pueblos on, 16
Tyler, Ron: 331

U

Udall, Stewart: and Coronado's route, 43, 69, 101
Ulloa: and early Llano cartography, 150
United States: boundary dispute with Mexico, 229–230, 241, 279, 305; Jurassic controversy in, 295–297; and Texas annexation, 245. *See also* railroads
United States Coronado Exposition Commission: 39
University of New Mexico: Coronado documents published by, 39
Upper Road: 300–304, 323
Upton County (Texas): and extent of the Llano, 299; Ford-Neighbors expedition in, 301
U.S. Army: and Llano cattle trade, 192; roundup of Navajos by, 192. *See also* Corps of Topographical Engineers; railroads
U.S. Bureau of Ethnology: and Coronado's route, 37, 38
U.S. Congress: and Coronado's route, 39, 43

U.S.-Mexican Boundary Commission: Bartlett of, 304; and Castle Gap, 302; Emory and, 309; Gray and, 308–309; Whipple and Bigelow with, 280
U.S. National Park Service: and Coronado's route, 43
U.S. Post Office: Coronado stamp of, 39
U.S. Supreme Court: and Greer County, 277
Ute Creek: Abert on, 254, 256
Uto-Aztecan Indians. *See* Jumano Indians

V

Valle Chimal: Coronado in, 25
Van Buren, Arkansas: Gregg's return to, 224
Vaquero Indians: Oñate encounters, 138. *See also* Apache Indians; Querecho Indians
Vega, Texas: Whipple at, 288, 293
Vermilion River: *See* Rio de Vermellón
Vestal, Stanley: 245
Vial, Pierre ("Pedro"): and Amangual expedition, 179, 181; diary of, 6; hunts with ciboleros, 178; as journalist, 328; and J. Wright's categories of imagining, 5; and Llano trade, 329; manuscript of, ment., 3; map of expedition, ment., 337; peace mission to Comanches, 170–172; route of, 2, **180** (map) and Santa Fé–Natchitoches trail, 175–178, **176** (map); and Santa Fé–San Antonio trail, 171–173
Villagrá, Gaspar Pérez de: poem by, 133, 139–141
Villanueva, New Mexico: "Far Cry Plantation" near, 25

W

Wagstaff, R. M.: 68
Waldo, William: 217–218
Walker filibuster: 247
Washita Indians: Coronado encounters, 110–111
Washita River: Abert and, 257, 258; Coronado's route at, 110; Lewis on, 206
Wayside, Texas: dead soils at, 128
Webb, Walter Prescott: 3; on "boom" of Great Frontier, 329; on Llano flatness, 120; on Spanish colonization of Llano, 162, 186; on Texan–Santa Fé Expedition, 234
Webber, Charles Wilkins: 247–249, 329, 332
Weber, David: 24
Wedel, Waldo R.: on Coronado's route, 25, 40, 91, 102
We Fed Them Cactus: 159, 325
Weir, Robert: 253
Wellman, Paul: 285
Wheat, Carl: 142
Whipple, Lt. Amiel Weeks: describes Comanche camp, 286; expedition of, 252, 279–298, 305, 318, 329, 337; perceptual approach of, 3, 7, 327, 328, 331, 333, 338, 339, 340, 341; sunrise described by, 288, **289**, 290, 332;

woodcuts after, **289**, **292**, **294**
White, Hayden: 328
White River: and Blanco Canyon ecosystem, 76, 79, 81–85; buffalo hunting on, 76, 86; Spanish artifacts found on, 91; Vial on, 177–178
Wichita Indians: Oñate and, 143; Vial and, 170. *See also* Ysopete (Indian guide)
Wichita River: Texan–Santa Fé Expedition on, 231
Wild China Ponds: Bartlett at, 304; Bryan at, 300; and Butterfield trail, 323; Ford-Neighbors expedition at, 301
Wild Horse Lake: Gregg on, 225
Wilkinson, Gen. James: report of, 197, 199; Z. Pike and, 200
Williams, Bill: 210
Williams, J. W.: and Coronado's route, 43, 59, 101; on location of Cona, 68–70, 81
Williams Ranch, Q. D.: 92
Wilson, Stephen Julian: land grant of, 215, 217, 218
Wilson-Exeter Grant: 215, 217, 218
Winship, George Parker: and Coronado's route, 31, 37–38, 43, 44, 50, 66, 68, 70, 71–72, 78, 101, 117, 118–120, 125, 129
Wolf Creek: Coronado's route at, 110
women: in buffalo-hunting camps, 160; Indian, and Blanco Canyon agriculture, 78; Spanish, at Cona, 86
Woodruff, C. M., Jr.: on playa formation, 122
Word, Jim: 91, 92
WPA: and Coronado, 39, 40
Wright, John K.: 5

X

XIT Ranch: lunettes on, 124

Y

Yellow House Canyon: archeology of, 76; Coronado's route in, 56, 69, 70, 79; D. Flores on, 75, 100; A. Pike at, 209, 210
Yellow House Draw: comanchero route in, 188; Coronado's route at, 47, 99, 105; and location of Cona, 68
Yellow Lake: among Coronado's "Lost Lakes," 100, 102; Coronado's route at, 105
Young, John Duncan: 83
Ysopete (Indian guide): 20–21, 25, 48, 55, 85, 109, 110–111

Z

Zabe (Indian guide): 24
Zaldivar, Vincente de: and buffalo, 162; expedition of, 138–141, 261, 331, 334
Zanjon: naming of, 184
Zoquiné (Comanche chief): Vial and, 171–172
Zuni Indians: and Cíbola, 17–19, 142; pueblos, on early maps, 150; tales of gold of, 16

MARICOPA COUNTY COMMUNITY COLLEGES
CHANDLER/GILBERT COMMUNITY
COLLEGE
LEARNING RESOURCE CENTER
2626 EAST PECOS ROAD
CHANDLER, AZ 85225

Chandler-Gilbert
Community College

JUN 0 4 2003

Learning Resource Center